Sherard

Second Edition

Assessment in Special Education

An Applied Approach

Terry Overton
Longwood College

Merrill,
an imprint of Prentice Hall
Englewood Cliffs, New Jersey • Columbus, Ohio

For my parents. Thanks for everything.

Library of Congress Cataloging-in-Publication Data

Overton, Terry.

Assessment in special education : an applied approach / Terry Overton.—2nd ed.

p. cm.

Includes bibliographical references and index.

ISBN 0-02-390007-5 (p)

1. Educational tests and measurements.
2. Special education.
3. Behavioral assessment of children. I. Title.

LB3051.094 1996

371.9—dc20 95-17903

CIP

Cover art: Jason Barbour, Summer Bethel, Brandy Blankenship, Steven Brown, Wade Eberhard, Julie Edmonds, Brett Forney, Kyla Francis, Lisa Kunovich, Jeremy Stalling, Derek Strong, and Steven Swank: Franklin County Board of MR/DD, Southeast School, Columbus, Ohio

Editor: Ann Castel Davis

Developmental Editor: Carol S. Sykes

Production Editor: Patricia A. Skidmore

Photo Editor: Anne Vega

Text Designer: Rebecca M. Bobb

Cover Designer: Proof Positive/Farrowlyne Assoc., Inc.

Design Coordinator: Jill E. Bonar

Production Manager: Patricia A. Tonneman

This book was set in Clearface and Helvetica by The Clarinda Company and was printed and bound by Quebecor Printing/Book Press. The cover was printed by Phoenix Color Corp.

A Simon & Schuster Company
Englewood Cliffs, New Jersey
07632

Photo credits: pp. 2, 66, 146, 190, 222, 292, 372 by Anne Vega, Merrill/Prentice Hall; pp. 11, 42, 92, 412 by Scott Cunningham; p. 26 by Bruce Johnson, Merrill/Prentice Hall; pp. 122 and 258 by Barb Schwartz, Merrill/Prentice Hall; and pp. 129 and 344 by Mark Madden, KS Studios, Merrill/ Prentice Hall.

Printed in the United States of America

10 9 8 7 6 5 4 3 2 1

ISBN: 0-02-390007-5

Prentice-Hall International (UK) Limited, *London*
Prentice-Hall of Australia Pty. Limited, *Sydney*
Prentice-Hall of Canada, Inc., *Toronto*
Prentice-Hall Hispanoamericana, S. A., *Mexico*
Prentice-Hall of India Private Limited, *New Delhi*
Prentice-Hall of Japan, Inc., *Tokyo*
Simon & Schuster Asia Pte. Ltd., *Singapore*
Editora Prentice-Hall do Brasil, Ltda., *Rio de Janeiro*

Preface

The preface of the first edition of *Assessment in Special Education: An Applied Approach* emphasized the need for special education professionals to use extreme caution in the assessment process. Assessment and testing should rely on consistent and accurate methods of collecting data for making educational decisions. Accuracy in testing and assessment continue to be important in the decision-making process.

In addition to accuracy in assessment and testing, special education literature continues to emphasize the need for functional and meaningful assessment practices (Artiles & Trent, 1994). Functional assessment serves as a preventative measure, stressing interventions that prevent placement in special education whenever possible. An important consideration in functional assessment is the context of which the student is a part. The environment influences the student's learning and achievement and may play a role in errors of bias made in the decision-making process (Huebner, 1991). Special education professionals should strive to promote fair and accurate assessment and educational decisions.

There continues to be a need to understand the consequences of labeling and segregating individual students. Minority students are still more highly represented than other students in every category of disability (U.S. Department of Education, 1992). The classic debate between nature versus nurture and the development of cognitive ability and educational achievement is as heated today as ever (Herrnstein & Murray, 1994). The second edition of this text underscores the social responsibility of assessment professionals to exercise fairness and accuracy in the decision-making process. This is possible when accurate standardized assessment procedures are used as one part of the total assessment process.

Format of This Text: A Note to Students

This text combines content and practical activities, called "Check Your Understanding," that provide a hands-on, applied approach to preparing for the actual assessment of students. You will benefit from completing all of the activities as you proceed through each chapter. The exercises at the end of each chapter will help you review chapter content and will provide a foundation for understanding the concepts presented in subsequent chapters. The answers for "Check Your Understanding" activities and the exercises are provided in the Instructor's Manual. Key terms are listed at the beginning of each chapter; each is defined in a marginal note at the appropriate point in the text. Many of the key terms are reintroduced throughout the text as they are used in the context of individual chapters.

Organization and Content

The 14 chapters in this book are divided into four major parts. The first part, "An Introduction to Assessment," introduces the assessment process, describes a comprehensive evaluation, and discusses the mandatory assessment regulations set forth in the Individuals with Disabilities Education Act.

The second part, "Technical Prerequisites of Understanding Assessment," addresses the topics of descriptive statistics, reliability and validity, and norm-referenced assessment.

The third part, "Assessing Students," discusses various types of assessment and reviews specific instruments. Chapter 6 describes tests of educational achievement: the Woodcock-Johnson Psycho-Educational Battery–Revised Tests of Achievement, Peabody Individual Achievement Test–Revised, Kaufman Test of Educational Achievement, Wechsler Individual Achievement Test, and Wide Range Achievement Test–Revision 3. Chapter 7 details standardized educational diagnostic tests, including the KeyMath–Revised and the Woodcock Reading Mastery Tests–Revised. Various informal assessment techniques are described in chapter 8, including criterion-referenced tests, curriculum-based assessment, and informal assessments in various academic areas. Chapter 9 presents methods of assessing behavior. Chapter 10 describes various measures of intelligence and adaptive behavior, including the Wechsler Intelligence Scale for Children–Third Edition, Woodcock-Johnson–Revised Tests of Cognitive Ability, Stanford-Binet IV Intelligence Scale–Fourth Edition, Kaufman Adolescent and Adult Intelligence Test, and the System of Multicultural Pluralistic Assessment. Chapter 11 presents diagnostic instruments that measure language, sensory-motor ability, perceptual development, visual perception, and auditory ability. Chapter 12 presents methods of assessing the abilities of infants, toddlers, and preschool children.

The fourth part, "Interpreting Assessment for Educational Intervention," discusses interpreting test results for interventions and eligibility decisions, writing test results, and using test results to write educational objectives. A case study is also included. The last chapter contains six partially completed case studies; you are asked to use the information you have gained from the text and the activities to complete each case study.

In an effort to encourage professional test administration procedures, some of the *Standards for Educational and Psychological Testing* (American Psychological Association, 1985), particularly those which concern testing in special education, are presented at specific points throughout this text. Yoshida and Friedman (1986) believe that it is imperative that institutions training professionals in assessment require expertise of those professionals in the skills contained in the *Standards* for best practice in testing students with disabilities.

The Joint Committee on Testing Practices (1988) developed a *Code of Fair Testing Practices in Education.* This code presents standards for educational test users and developers in four areas: (a) developing and selecting tests, (b) interpreting scores, (c) striving for fairness, and (d) informing test takers. The *Code of Fair Testing Practices* is included in its entirety in the appendix.

Acknowledgments

I thank the following reviewers for their helpful comments: Paul Beare, Moorhead State University; Blanche Glimps, Marygrove College; and Roberta Strosnider, Hood College.

References

American Psychological Association. (1985). *Standards for educational and psychological testing.* Washington, DC: Author.

Artiles, A. J., & Trent, S. C. (1994). Overrepresentation of minority students in special education: A continuing debate. *The Journal of Special Education, 27,* 4:410–437.

Herrnstein, R. J., & Murray, C. (1994). *The bell curve: Intelligence and class structure in American life.* New York: The Free Press.

Huebner, E. S. (1991). Bias in special education decisions: The contributions of analogue research. *School Psychology Quarterly, 6,* 1, 50–65.

Joint Committee on Testing Practices. (1988). *Code of fair testing practices in education.* Washington, DC: Author.

U.S. Department of Education. (1992). *Fourteenth annual report to Congress on the implementation of the Individuals with Disabilities Education Act.* Washington, DC: Author.

Yoshida, R., & Friedman, D. (1986). Standards for educational and psychological testing: More than a symbolic exercise. *Special Services in the Schools,* 187–193.

Contents

Part One
An Introduction to Assessment

Chapter One
An Introduction 2

Assessment: A Necessary Part of Teaching 3

Assessment: A Continuous Process 3

Preferral 5

Designing An Assessment Plan 14

A Continuous Model of Assessment 17

The Comprehensive Evaluation 20

Chapter Two
Law and Issues 26

The Law: Public Law 94–142 27

IDEA and Assessment 28

Preplacement Evaluation 28

Informed Consent 28

Nondiscriminatory Assessment 30

Evaluating Children with Specific Learning Disabilities 37

Meeting the Needs of Persons with Attention Disorders 37

Multidisciplinary Team Evaluation 38

Parent Participation 41

Determining Eligibility 43

Least Restrictive Environment 44

Developing the IEP 44

Due Process 45

Third-Party Hearing 46

Research and Issues Concerning IDEA 47

Part Two
Technical Prerequisites of Understanding Assessment

Chapter Three
Descriptive Statistics 66

Why Is Measurement Important? 67

Getting Meaning from Numbers 68

Review of Numerical Scales 69

Descriptive Statistics 70

Measures of Central Tendency 71

Average Performance 71

Measures of Dispersion 78

Mean Differences 84

Skewed Distribution 85

Percentiles and z Scores 86

Chapter Four
Reliability and Validity 92

Reliability and Validity on Assessment 93

Reliability 93

Correlation 94

Methods of Measuring Reliability 100

Which Type of Reliability Is the Best? 103

Standard Error of Measurement 106

Estimated True Scores 112

Test Validity 114

Reliability versus Validity 118

Chapter Five
An Introduction to Norm-Referenced Assessment 122

How Norm-Referenced Tests Are Constructed 123

Basic Steps in Test Administration 127

Part Three Assessing Students

Chapter Six
Tests of Education Achievement 146

Achievement Tests 147

The Review of Achievement Tests 149

Research Findings 181

Selecting Academic Achievement Tests 183

Chapter Seven
Standardized Diagnostic Testing 190

When to Use Diagnostic Testing 191

The Review of Diagnostic Tests 192

Other Diagnostic Tests 210

Research and Issues 215

Selecting Diagnostic Instruments 215

Chapter Eight
Informal Assessment Techniques 222

Problems of Norm-Referenced Assessment 223

Criterion-Related Assessment 224

Curriculum-Based Assessment and Direct Measurement 231

Task Analysis and Error Analysis 235

Other Informal Methods of Academic Assessment 237

Issues of Academic Informal Assessment 253

Chapter Nine
Assessment of Behavior 258

Informal Assessment of Behavior 259

Behavioral Observations 260

Structured Classroom Observations 267

Other Techniques for Assessing Behavior 269

Projective Assessment Techniques 278

Computerized Assessment of Attention Disorders 283

Research and Issues 284

Chapter Ten
Measures of Intelligence and Adaptive Behavior 292

The Meaning of Intelligence Testing 293
Litigation and Intelligence Testing 296
Use of Intelligence Tests 297
The Review of Intelligence Tests 298
Research on Intelligence Measures 317
Assessing Adaptive Behavior 318
The Review of Adaptive Behavior Scales 321
Intelligence and Adaptive Behavior: Concluding Remarks 334

Chapter Eleven
Other Diagnostic Instruments 344

Assessing Language 345
Testing Sensory-Motor and Perceptual Abilities 354
Tests of Visual Perception 355
Tests of Auditory Ability 362
Assessing Developmental Levels with Drawing Tests 364
Using Results from Diagnostic Tests 365

Chapter Twelve
Early Childhood Assessment 372

Public Law 99–457 and Assessment 373
Methods of Early Childhood Assessment 378
Assessment of Infants 378
Assessment of Toddlers and Young Children 380
Techniques and Trends in Infant and Early Childhood Assessment 385
Other Considerations in Assessing Very Young Children 388

Part Four
Interpreting Assessment for Educational Intervention

Chapter Thirteen
Interpreting Test Results 394

Interpreting Test Results for Eligibility Decisions 396
The Art of Interpreting Test Results 398
Writing Test Results 401
Writing Educational Objectives 407

Chapter Fourteen
Case Studies 412

Appendix
Code of Fair Testing Practices in Education 436

Name Index 441

Subject Index 445

Part One

Introduction to Assessment

Chapter One
An Introduction

Chapter Two
Law and Issues

Chapter One

An Introduction

Key Terms

testing
assessment
continuous assessment
curriculum-based assessment
criterion-related assessment
criterion-referenced tests
error analysis
checklists
informal assessment
multidisciplinary team
prereferral intervention strategies
overidentification
individualized education program (IEP)
ecological assessment
screening
multiple gating
individual assessment plan
Standards for Educational and Psychological Testing (APA *Standards*)
norm-referenced tests
standardized tests
eligibility meeting
alternative planning
Individual Family Service Plan (IFSP)

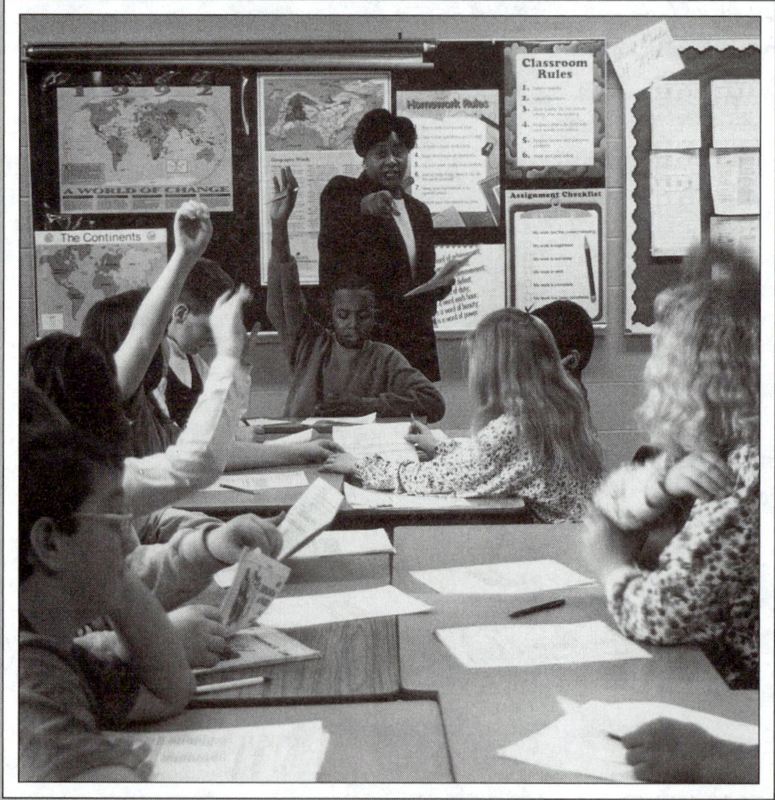

Assessment: A Necessary Part of Teaching

Teachers must test. **Testing** is one method of evaluating progress and determining individual student needs. Testing, however, is only one form of assessment. **Assessment** has been defined as the collection of information in order to identify problems and make educational decisions (Salvia & Ysseldyke, 1988).

testing A method to determine a student's ability to complete certain tasks or demonstrate mastery of a skill or knowledge of content.

assessment The process of gathering information to monitor progress and and make educational decisions if necessary.

Assessment happens every day in every classroom. A teacher observes the behaviors of a student solving math problems. The teacher then checks the student's answers and determines the student's ability to solve that particular type of math problem. If the student made mistakes, the teacher determines the types of errors and decides what steps must be taken to correct the miscalculations. This is one type of assessment. The teacher observes behavior, gathers information about the student, and makes program or instructional changes according to the information obtained.

Assessment in special education is based on the same principles as assessment in the general education classroom. In many cases, the assessment is the same. Behavior is observed, progress is evaluated, and a program is planned. The very best assessment practices, however, must adhere to legal mandates and basic principles of measurement. The special educator has a professional responsibility to be accountable for each assessment decision. Therefore, a knowledge of various types of assessment and when to use each type is necessary.

Assessment: A Continuous Process

Assessment begins in the classroom. The effective teacher monitors students' progress continuously, or in other words, the teacher uses **continuous assessment.** When a student fails to progress as expected, the teacher may use several methods in an attempt to discover why progress has not been made as expected. The teacher may develop assessment measures directly from curriculum mate-

continuous assessment The continuous monitoring of student progress.

curriculum-based assessment Using the content from the currently used curriculum to assess student progress.

criterion-related assessment When items of an assessment instrument are related to meeting objectives or passing skill mastery objectives.

criterion-referenced tests Tests designed to accompany and measure a set of criteria or skill-mastery criteria.

error analysis Using a student's errors to analyze specific learning problems.

checklists Lists of skills developmentally sequenced and used to monitor student progress.

rials. This type of assessment is **curriculum-based assessment.** Curriculum-based assessment is common and also may measure the student's performance against a skill or objective within the curriculum. When students are tested for mastery of a skill or an objective, the assessment is called **criterion-related assessment;** tests of this type may be labeled **criterion-referenced tests.**

Learning how the student performs tasks may also provide insight into the nature of the difficulty. Observing the steps a student takes to solve a problem or complete a task can benefit the teacher, too. The teacher may ask the student to verbalize the steps he takes while reading a paragraph for content or while solving a math equation. The teacher can then note the types or patterns of errors the student made during the process. This type of analysis is known as **error analysis** (e.g., $7 \times 3 = 10$: The student added, rather than multiplied, the numbers).

Teachers also develop **checklists** to identify students who have mastered skills, tasks, or developmental expectations appropriate to their grade level. Checklists may be found in some commercial materials or school curriculum guides. Placement in the specific curriculum within the general education classroom may be based on a student's performance on skills listed on these commercial checklists or on other curriculum-based assessment results.

☐ CHECK YOUR UNDERSTANDING

Complete Activity 1.1.

Activity 1.1

Review the testing terms introduced in the previous paragraphs. Use the following terms to designate the type of assessment described in each statement.

Terms

assessment	criterion-related assessment
error analysis	checklist
curriculum-based assessment	criterion-referenced tests

1. A teacher wants to determine why a student who can multiply single-digit numbers cannot multiply two-digit numbers. The teacher asks the student to verbally describe the steps he is using in the process. This is

   ____

2. The spelling series used in one classroom contains tests that are directly tied to the spelling curriculum. When the teacher uses these tests, ______________________________ is being used.
3. A student is not progressing as the teacher believes he should for his age expectancy. The teacher uses teacher-made tests, observation, and criterion-referenced tests to gather information about the student. This teacher is using different methods of ______________________________ to discover why the student is not making progress.

4. To determine if a student has mastered a specific skill or objective, the teacher uses ______________________.
5. A first-grade student has difficulty with fine motor skills. The teacher is concerned that the student may not have the developmental ability to learn manuscript handwriting. The handwriting series lists skills a student must master before writing letters. Using this device, the teacher has employed a ______________________.
6. Assessment devices in a school's language series provide skills and objectives for each level of English, creative writing, and literature. These are ______________________.

Informal assessment is used every day without students' awareness of the monitoring of progress by this technique. Informal assessment includes worksheets, written samples of students' work, teacher-made tests and quizzes, oral reading assignments, oral responses, group projects, and class assignments. Informal assessment allows teachers to continually screen all students, including those who are academically at risk and those with special needs. (Informal assessment is discussed further in chapter 8.)

informal assessment Nonstandardized methods of evaluating progress such as interviews, observations, and teacher-made tests.

It is usually through informal assessment that a teacher first becomes aware that a student has not progressed as expected. More in-depth classroom assessment and observation techniques can then be used to pinpoint the specific area of difficulty.

When the in-depth assessment provides little help for the classroom teacher, that teacher may seek help from a special education teacher, school psychologist, or educational diagnostician, professionals who commonly make up the **multidisciplinary team** that evaluates students and determines eligibility for special education services. A member of the multidisciplinary team may suggest using educational intervention strategies to gain a clear view of the student's difficulty and possible solutions.

multidisciplinary team A team of professionals from various fields who participate in comprehensive student evaluations and make decisions about special education eligibility and placement.

Prereferral

Before referring a student for a comprehensive evaluation, teachers must clearly target the student's learning or behavioral problem. One method of pinpointing the exact nature of the problem and thus determining if further evaluation is necessary is through the use of **prereferral intervention strategies.** Prereferral intervention strategies are measures taken by the classroom teacher and members of the multidisciplinary team before referring the student for assessment. Ysseldyke and Thurlow (1983) recommended that educators clarify the problem as the initial step of the assessment process. This step specifies the problem exactly and attempts to document its severity. Once the classroom teacher has documented the area of difficulty, she can systematically implement strategies for correction. Ideally, the prereferral strategies will decrease

prereferral intervention strategies Methods used by teachers and other team members to observe and modify student behaviors, learning environment, and/or teaching methods before a formal referral.

referrals by resolving some students' learning or behavioral problems within the general education classroom (Nelson, Smith, Taylor, Dodd, & Reavis, 1992).

Prereferral strategies include observation by objective persons, informal assessment techniques, curriculum modifications, environmental (classroom) modifications, and consultation with the parents and other members of the multidisciplinary team. In one statewide study, successful prereferral interventions also included teacher assistance teams, mainstream assistance teams, and collaborative peer problem solving (Nelson et al., 1992). Increasingly, state education agencies are recommending or requiring that educators implement prereferral interventions before referring a student for a comprehensive evaluation (Carter & Sugai, 1989; Nelson et al., 1992).

The importance of prereferral interventions has become apparent through research studies that identify faulty referral practices and recommend reform in the special education referral process. Students are generally referred because they are difficult to teach or because they are considered behavioral problems (Salvia & Ysseldyke, 1988; Shinn, Tindal, & Spira, 1987). Referral practices have been inconsistent at best. For example, male students were referred more often than female students (Shinn et al., 1987); female teachers referred students with behavioral problems more frequently than did male teachers (McIntyre, 1988); teachers referred students with learning and behavioral problems more often than those with behavioral problems alone (Soodak & Podell, 1993); and the teacher referrals were global in nature and contained subjective rather than objective information in more than half of the cases (Reschly, 1986; Ysseldyke, Christenson, Pianta, & Algozzine, 1983). According to the research, a teacher's decision to refer may be influenced by the student's having a sibling who has had school problems as well as by the referring teacher's tolerance for certain student behaviors; the teacher with a low tolerance for particular behaviors may more readily refer students exhibiting those behaviors (Thurlow, Christenson, & Ysseldyke, 1983). These practices clearly violate the intent and spirit of the laws governing special education.

In another study, it was found that the characteristics of referred students may vary with student age (Harvey, 1991). Males were referred more frequently than female students at all grade levels. In the primary-grade levels, younger students (for grade level) were referred more frequently than students who had birthdates farther from the school admission cut-off date (October 31). Students who were referred in the third grade or later had birthdates distributed evenly throughout the year, which suggests that students in the primary grades exhibited developmental differences rather than true learning or behavioral problems.

Regardless of these and other faulty referral practices, nationwide, more than 90% of the students referred for evaluation were tested. Of those tested, 73% were subsequently found eligible for services in special education (Algozzine, Christenson, & Ysseldyke, 1982). Students who are referred are highly likely to complete the evaluation process.

This research illustrates the problems encountered in the referral process and has influenced a move toward more comprehensive and detailed prereferral intervention strategies. The more frequent use of better prereferral intervention is a step forward in the prevention of unnecessary evaluation and the possibility of misdiagnosis and **overidentification** of special education students. Halgren and Clarizio (1993) found that 38% of the students in special education were either reclassified or terminated from special education. This indicates a need for more specific identification of the learning or behavioral problems through referral and initial assessment. Ysseldyke and Thurlow (1983) advocated changing the focus of the referral process from " . . . referral-to-placement to referral-to-intervention" (p. 14). Providing consulting services to regular education teachers could help resolve student problems before referral (Zins, Graden, and Ponti, 1989). This type of prereferral intervention would place multidisciplinary team members in a consulting role for a large part of their service time and decrease the time they spent testing.

overidentification Describes the phenomenon of identifying students who seem to be eligible for special education services but who are actually not disabled.

Fuchs (1991) found that several features need to exist in the practice of prereferral interventions. The following list is adapted from this study:

1. Prereferral intervention should be included within the job descriptions of those persons responsible for implementation. This includes both professional and paraprofessional staff.
2. A consultant or team should serve to guide the prereferral effort.
3. All staff involved should receive adequate training in the prereferral strategies.
4. The consultation effort should be efficient and exhibit desired outcomes.
5. Consultants should define the problem behavior, set goals for students and/or teachers, collect data, and evaluate effectiveness.
6. Interventions should be agreeable to both consultants and teachers.
7. Strategies should be implemented as designed.
8. Data should be collected at multiple intervals. (Fuchs, 1991, p. 263)

☐ **CHECK YOUR UNDERSTANDING**

Complete Activity 1.2.

Activity 1.2

Refer to the faulty referral practices cited in the research in the previous paragraphs to determine what types of errors have been made in the following cases.

1. Mr. Jones has Billy for fourth and fifth periods each day at Randolph Middle School. Ms. Jarrod stopped by Mr. Jones' room after school one day to tell Mr. Jones that she was going to refer Billy for evaluation for behavioral problems. She said that she cannot tolerate Billy's behavior another day. Mr. Jones remarked that Billy seems to get along fine in his class as long as Mr. Jones provides structure and guidance within the class—including telling Billy when his work is completed nicely. According to research, Ms. Jarrod's feelings might be an example of ____.

2. Mr. Bonderan has just received his class roll for the new school year. His heart sinks when he sees the name Jeffery Dews. Mr. Bonderan knows that he will have to refer Jeffery for special education evaluation just as he had to refer Jeffery's older brother, Jonathan, last year. Mr. Bonderan may be referring Jeffery only because ____
____.

3. A referral turned in last Monday by Ms. Greene contained the following information:
"Susie is just not acting as she should. I think she has a real problem. I have been teaching school for 15 years, and I have never had such a stubborn little girl in my class. I don't know what her problem is, but I can't keep her in my class any longer. I think she should be tested and placed right away. I don't want to try any more interventions. I tried moving her closer to the blackboard. She just doesn't want to learn."
What problems do you see with Ms. Greene's referral? ____________________
____
____
____
____

individualized education program (IEP) A written plan of educational interventions designed for each student who receives special education.

ecological assessment Method of assessing a student's total environment to determine what factors are contributing to learning or behavioral problems.

Traditionally, a student was referred for testing, evaluated by team members, and after being determined eligible for special education services, was given an **individualized education program (IEP)** and placed in a special education setting. Although these steps were reported nationally as those most commonly followed in the evaluation process (Ysseldyke & Thurlow, 1983), they do not include the step of prereferral intervention.

The model proposed by Graden, Casey, and Christenson (1985), however, includes "identifying, defining, and clarifying the problem, analyzing the components of the classroom ecology that affect the problem, designing and implementing interventions, and evaluating intervention effectiveness" (p. 383). As Graden and colleagues have written, this type of prereferral intervention looks at many variables surrounding the student's educational performance rather than assuming first that the difficulty is within the student. This type of assessment, called **ecological assessment,** reflects a major trend toward considering the environment and assessing students in their natural environment (Reschly, 1986).

Messick (1984) proposed a two-phase assessment strategy that emphasizes prereferral assessment of the student's learning environment. The information needed during Messick's first phase includes:

1. evidence that the school is using programs and curricula shown to be effective not just for students in general but for the various ethnic, linguistic, and socioeconomic groups actually served by the school in question.
2. evidence that the students in question have been adequately exposed to the curriculum by virtue of not having missed too many lessons due to absence or disci-

Prereferral Checklist

Name of Student ____

Concerned Teacher ____

Briefly describe area of difficulty:

1. Curriculum evaluation:

_________ Material is appropriate for age and/or grade level.

_________ Instructions are presented clearly.

_________ Expected method of response is within the student's capability.

_________ Readability of material is appropriate.

_________ Prerequisite skills have been mastered.

_________ Format of materials is easily understood by students of same age and/or grade level.

_________ Frequent and various methods of evaluation are employed.

_________ Tasks are appropriate in length.

_________ Pace of material is appropriate for age and/or grade level.

2. Learning environment:

_________ Methods of presentation are appropriate for age and/or grade levels.

_________ Tasks are presented in appropriate sequence.

_________ Expected level of response is appropriate for age and/or grade level.

_________ Physical facilities are conducive to learning.

3. Social environment:

_________ Student does not experience noticeable conflicts with peers.

_________ Student appears to have adequate relationships with peers.

_________ Parent conference reveals no current conflicts or concerns within the home.

_________ Social development appears average for age expectancy.

4. Student's physical condition:

_________ Student's height and weight appear to be within average range of expectancy for age and/or grade level.

_________ Student has no signs of visual or hearing difficulties (asks teacher to repeat instructions, squints, holds papers close to face to read).

Figure 1.1

A prereferral checklist to determine whether all necessary interventions have been attempted.

_________ Student has had vision and hearing checked by school nurse or other health official.

_________ Student has not experienced long-term illness or serious injury.

_________ School attendance is average or better.

_________ Student appears attentive and alert during instruction.

_________ Student appears to have adequate motor skills.

_________ Student appears to have adequate communication skills.

5. Intervention procedures (changes in teaching strategies that have been attempted):

_________ Consultant has observed student:

	Setting	***Date***	***Comments***
1.			
2.			
3.			

_________ Educational and curriculum changes were made:

	Change	***Date***	***Comments***
1.			
2.			
3.			

_________ Behavioral and social changes were made:

	Change	***Date***	***Comments***
1.			
2.			
3.			

_________ Parent conferences were held:

	Date	***Comments***
1.		
2.		
3.		

_________ Additional documentation is attached.

Figure 1.1, *continued*

plinary exclusion from class and that the teacher has implemented the curriculum effectively.

3. objective evidence that the child has not learned what was taught.
4. evidence that systematic efforts were, or are, being made to identify the learning difficulty and to take corrective instructional action, such as introducing remedial approaches, changing the curriculum materials, or trying a new teacher.

Note. From "Assessment in Context: Appraising Student Performance in Relation to Instructional Quality" by S. Messick, 1984, Educational Researcher, 13, p. 5. Copyright 1984 by American Educational Research Association. Reprinted by permission of the publisher.

The referring teacher may use a checklist such as the one in Figure 1.1 to determine if all necessary interventions have been attempted. Using a prereferral checklist clarifies areas of concern and helps the referral-screening committee decide if the evaluation is necessary and, if so, what types of assessment instruments will be administered. It is no longer considered acceptable to refer students who have difficulty in the regular classroom without prereferral interventions unless they appear to be experiencing severe learning and/or behavioral problems or are in danger of harming themselves or others.

Prereferral intervention strategies have had positives effects. In schools where a prereferral intervention model was implemented, consultation services increased within the general education classroom, and both testing and educational placements decreased significantly (Graden, Casey, & Bonstrom, 1985).

Prereferral intervention

In a study by Chalfant and Psyh (1989), the inappropriate referral rate decreased to 63%, and interventions were successful in approximately 88% of the cases. Many special education administrators support the use of prereferral intervention models, although some confusion remains about whether special education or general education should control the process (Nelson et al., 1992). Wide use of prereferral intervention would help increase the numbers of students who would experience academic success within the very least restrictive environment, the general education class setting.

☐ **CHECK YOUR UNDERSTANDING**

Complete Activity 1.3.

Activity 1.3

Look at the partially completed prereferral checklist that follows. Read the interventions carefully. Before completing a referral form, what suggestions might be included as prereferral interventions? Write your suggestions for intervention strategies in section 5 (ignore "Date" and "Comment" columns) of this form. Answer the questions following the form.

Prereferral Checklist

Name of Student Mary Ellen Pollard
Concerned Teacher Ms. J. M. Anderson

Briefly describe area of difficulty:

Mary Ellen has been in my class for 3 months and has not progressed in math. Although she is performing well in reading and spelling, she does not seem to be a happy student. She does not have many friends, and the other children make fun of her during math class.

1. Curriculum evaluation:

- __yes__ Material is appropriate for age and/or grade level.
- __yes__ Instructions are presented clearly.
- __yes__ Expected method of response is within the student's capability.
- __yes__ Readability of material is appropriate.
- _not sure_ Prerequisite skills have been mastered.
- __yes__ Format of materials is easily understood by students of same age and/or grade level.
- _not sure_ Frequent and various methods of evaluation are employed.
- _not sure_ Tasks are appropriate in length.
- __yes__ Pace of material is appropriate for age and/or grade level.

2. Learning environment:

- __yes__ Methods of presentation are appropriate for age and/or grade level.
- __yes__ Tasks are presented in appropriate sequence.
- __yes__ Expected level of response is appropriate for age and/or grade level.
- __yes__ Physical facilities are conducive to learning.

3. Social environment:

- not sure Student does not experience noticeable conflict with peers.
- no Student appears to have adequate relationships with peers.
- yes Parent conference reveals no current conflicts or concerns within the home.
- not sure Social development appears average for age expectancy.

4. Student's physical condition:

- yes Student's height and weight appear to be within average range of expectancy for age and/or grade level.
- yes Student has no signs of visual or hearing difficulties (e.g., asks teacher to repeat instructions, squints, holds papers too close to face to read).
- yes Student has had vision and hearing checked by school nurse or other health official.
- not sure Student has not experienced long-term illness or serious injury.
- no School attendance is average or better.
- not sure Student appears attentive and alert during instruction.
- yes Student appears to have adequate motor skills.
- yes Student appears to have adequate communication skills.

5. ________ Intervention procedures (changes in teaching strategies that have been attempted):

________ Consultant has observed student:

Setting	*Date*	*Comments*
1.		
2.		
3.		

________ Educational and curriculum changes were made:

Change	*Date*	*Comments*
1.		
2.		
3.		

________ Behavioral and social changes were made:

Change	*Date*	*Comments*
1.		
2.		
3		

________ Parent conferences were held:

	Date	*Comments*
1.		
2.		
3.		

Additional documentation is attached.

Questions

1. After reading this checklist, what areas appear to represent problems for Mary Ellen? ______

2. If Mary Ellen were your student, what questions would you seek to answer before requesting a comprehensive evaluation? ______

3. What additional documentation might be beneficial for you to obtain before considering a referral for special education evaluation? ______

Designing an Assessment Plan

screening A process of reviewing a referral to determine if a student needs further evaluation by the multidisciplinary team.

multiple gating Assessment in sequential steps.

Federal law mandates that evaluation measures used during the assessment process are those measures specifically designed to assess areas of concern (*Federal Register,* September 29, 1992). (The specific laws pertaining to the education of individuals with disabilities are discussed in chapter 2.) Through the use of appropriate prereferral intervention strategies, the referring teacher is able to pinpoint specific areas of difficulty, and the assessment team can then design an appropriate assessment plan. At this time, the referring teacher may formally refer the student and begin the **screening** process. A screening committee determines if the referred student should be evaluated further by the multidisciplinary team. If the committee decides that further assessment is warranted, the student is referred to the evaluation team. This multidisciplinary team must then determine which instruments will be administered and which special education professionals are needed to complete the assessment.

Barnett and Macmann (1992) suggested that special educators employ a **multiple gating** system of assessment. In multiple gating assessment, the general education teacher and the team members administer tests sequentially in an effort to determine if a significant problem exists. If a student does not fall within a range of significant difficulty after a screening test, the student does not progress to the next level of more comprehensive individual assessment. Educators would address this student's problems with individual strategies designed to be implemented within the general education environment. If a student scores significantly below peers on the screening instrument, the assessment continues. The multiple gating system may be viewed as an extension of the prereferral strategies designed to resolve difficulties within the general education setting.

Federal law also requires that the instruments selected have been validated for the purpose of intended use. For example, if the student has been referred for problems with reading comprehension, the appropriate assessment instrument would be one of good technical quality that has been designed to measure reading problems, specifically, reading comprehension skills. In addition to requiring selection of the appropriate tests, the law also mandates that persons administering the tests be adequately trained to administer those specific tests and that more than a single instrument be used to determine eligibility for special services.

To meet these mandates, the educator must design an **individual assessment plan** for each student. Maxam, Boyer-Stephens, and Alff (1986) recommended that each evaluation team follow these specific steps in preparing an assessment plan:

individual assessment plan A plan that lists the specific tests and procedures to be used for a student who has been screened and needs further assessment.

1. Review all of the screening information in each of the seven areas (health, vision, hearing, speech and language skills, intellectual, academic/prevocational/vocational).
2. Determine what area(s) need further evaluation.
3. Determine the specific data collection procedures to use (interviews, observation of behavior, informal or formal techniques, standardized tests).
4. Determine persons responsible for administering the selected procedures. These persons must be trained or certified if the assessment instrument calls for specific qualifications.

Note. From Assessment: A Key to Appropriate Program Placement (Report No. CE 045 407, pp. 11–13) by S. Maxam, A. Boyer-Stephens, and M. Alff, 1986, Columbia, MO: University of Missouri—Columbia, Department of Special Education and Department of Practical Arts and Vocational-Technical Education. (ERIC Document Reproduction Service No. ED 275 835.) Copyright 1986 by the authors. Reprinted by permission.

▪ ▪

Activity 1.4

☐ **CHECK YOUR UNDERSTANDING**

Complete Activity 1.4.

Read the following case study. Determine what types of assessment might be used to further evaluate the student. Some suggestions from which to choose are listed after the case study.

REFERRAL

Name of Student George B. Baker, Jr. Grade Placement 5.7
Referring Teacher Ms. C. K. Williamson

Reason for Referral

George has been experiencing difficulties in reading, spelling, writing, and English. Curriculum changes included using a fourth-grade reader and spelling book, allowing George more time to complete assignments, and providing a great deal of individual attention and peer tutoring. George gets along fine with other students and has no academic problems in other subjects as long as he is not responsible for independently reading material above the third-grade level. His fifth-grade science book is read aloud by other students during class time, and he listens intently. George continues to flounder in his fourth-grade reading and spelling curriculum. I think he has the mental capability, but I'm not sure why he struggles so much and experiences no success in language arts.

Methods of Assessment

The following methods are available and are administered by the teacher or special education teacher unless indicated otherwise:

1. Curriculum-based assessment in reading, spelling, English, and math
2. Screening test in all academic areas
3. Individual intelligence test (by school psychologist)
4. Diagnostic reading test and math test
5. Developmental spelling and reading checklists
6. Criterion-referenced test by reading series publisher
7. Vision and hearing screening (by school nurse)
8. General individual academic achievement test
9. Interviews with other teachers
10. Informal assessment of class work
11. Classroom observations during language arts class and other classes
12. Informal reading inventory
13. Parent interview
14. Student interview

Using the referral data provided and the types of assessment available, design an assessment plan for George. In the blanks provided, list the appropriate tests and the team members who will administer them.

ASSESSMENT PLAN

Name George B. Baker, Jr. ______________________

Team Member Name [you] ______________________

Types of Assessment

1. ______________________ by: ______________
2. ______________________ by: ______________
3. ______________________ by: ______________
4. ______________________ by: ______________
5. ______________________ by: ______________
6. ______________________ by: ______________
7. ______________________ by: ______________
8. ______________________ by: ______________

Other suggested measures to use in assessment process:

____

____

In addition to federal mandates and recommendations from professionals in the field of special education, the professional organizations of the American Psychological Association, the American Educational Research Association, and the National Council on Measurement in Education have produced the ***Standards for Educational and Psychological Testing*** (1985), which clearly defines acceptable professional and ethical standards for individuals who test children in schools. Several of these standards are included in later chapters of this text. The APA *Standards* emphasize the importance of using tests for the purpose intended by the test producer and place ethical responsibility for correct use and interpretation on the person administering and scoring tests in the educational setting. The *Code of Fair Testing Practices in Education* is included in the appendix.

Standards for Educational and Psychological Testing (APA Standards) Professional and ethical standards that suggest minimum criteria for assessing students

A student who has been referred for an initial evaluation may be found eligible for services according to the definitions of the various disabling conditions defined in federal law. Figure 1.2 lists the classifications as specified in the Individuals With Disabilities Education Act (IDEA) (discussed further in chapter 2).

A Continuous Model of Assessment

One proposed model of assessment is illustrated in Figure 1.3. This model incorporates informal assessment and prereferral intervention strategies before the formal referral and screening processes. When a student continues to have significant difficulty after numerous prereferral interventions, he usually is referred for a formal evaluation. Once the referral has been received by the special education team, it is screened. During the screening process, the educators may determine that the student needs further assessment. At that time, members of the multidisciplinary team design an individual assessment plan based on the referral information. In reality, screening is nonexistent in some schools, or the screening is performed by the special education teacher and no other members of the multidisciplinary special education team (White & Calhoun, 1987).

Although the professional literature advises careful design of assessment plans, research indicates that problems exist in referral and screening practices. White and Calhoun (1987) found that many special education teachers felt they were "gatekeepers" in the sense of determining which students would be screened and eventually tested for possible special education placement. It also seemed that the formal act of screening affected decisions only when the special education teacher was not certain about the student's eligibility (White & Calhoun, 1987). Ideally, the purpose of the screening process is to determine the need for further testing and what specific types of assessment may be necessary. Ysseldyke, Algozzine, Richey, and Graden (1982) found that much of the information gathered to use in decision making has very little influence in the assessment process. Failure to rely on relevant referral data and to develop an individual assessment plan could lead to unnecessary testing and misdiagnosis.

Autism	A disorder with onset before 30 months of age in which social withdrawal, language deficits, and cognitive deficits are considered extreme.
Deafness	A hearing impairment that is so severe that the child is impaired in processing linguistic information through hearing, with or without amplification, which adversely affects educational performance.
Deaf-blindness	Concomitant hearing and visual impairments, the combination of which causes such severe communication and other developmental and educational problems that the child cannot be accommodated in special education programs solely for deaf or blind children.
Hard of hearing	Hearing impairment, whether permanent or fluctuating, that adversely affects a child's educational performance but is not included under the definition of deaf.
Mental retardation	Significantly subaverage general intellectual functioning existing concurrently with deficits in adaptive behavior manifested during the developmental period, which adversely affects the child's educational performance.
Multiple disabilities	Concomitant impairments (e.g., mental retardation–blindness, mental retardation–orthopedic impairment), the combination of which causes such severe educational problems that the child cannot be accommodated in special education programs solely for one of the impairments; does not include children who are deaf-blind.
Orthopedical impairment	Severe orthopedic impairment that adversely affects a child's educational performance. The term includes impairments caused by congenital anomaly (e.g., clubfoot, absence of some member), impairments caused disease (e.g., poliomyelitis, bone by tuberculosis), and impairments from other causes (e.g., cerebral palsy, amputations, and fractures or burns that cause contractures).

Figure 1.2
Disabilities defined in IDEA for which students are eligible for special education services.

Other health impairment	Limited strength, vitality, or alertness, due to chronic or acute health problems (such as a heart condition, tuberculosis, rheumatic fever, nephritis, asthma, sickle cell anemia, hemophilia, epilepsy, lead poisoning, leukemia, or diabetes) that adversely affect a child's educational performance.
Serious emotional disturbance	A condition exhibiting one or more of the following characteristics over a long period of time and to a marked degree that adversely affects educational performance: **1.** An inability to learn that cannot be explained by intellectual, sensory, or health factors **2.** An inability to build or maintain satisfactory interpersonal relationships with peers and teachers **3.** Inappropriate types of behavior or feelings under normal circumstances **4.** A general pervasive mood of unhappiness or depression **5.** A tendency to develop physical symptoms or fears associated with personal or school problems This term may include those persons with schizophrenia and does not include students who are socially maladjusted unless it is determined that they are also emotionally disturbed.
Specific learning disability	A disorder in one or more of the basic psychological processes involved in understanding or using language, spoken or written, that manifests itself in the imperfect ability to listen, speak, read, write, spell, or do mathematical calculations. The term includes such conditions as perceptual disabilities, brain injury, minimal brain dysfunction, dyslexia, and developmental aphasia. The term does not include learning problems that are primarily the result of visual, hearing, or motor disabilities; mental retardation; or environmental, cultural, or economic disadvantage.

Speech impairment	A communication disorder, such as stuttering, impaired articulation, a language impairment, or a voice impairment, that adversely affects a child's educational performance.
Traumatic brain injury	Injury incurred to the brain that was not present at birth and results in physical or psychosocial disability which affects educational performance; may include cognitive, language, sensory, perceptual, motor, processing, speech, memory, or psychosocial abilities.
Visual impairment	A visual impairment that, even with correction, adversely affects a child's educational performance. The term includes both partially seeing and blind children.

Figure 1.2, *continued*

The federal laws were designed to serve as a safeguard for students and provide structure in the assessment and educational programming process. Research indicates, however, that local education agencies attempting to comply with federal regulations do not necessarily provide beneficial programming for the students referred (Ysseldyke & Thurlow, 1983).

The Comprehensive Evaluation

When a student has had little success in a learning environment after several prereferral strategies have been applied, a formal referral is made. During the screening process, the screening committee makes a decision to recommend a comprehensive evaluation or perhaps an educational alternative, such as a change in classroom teachers. If the committee recommends a comprehensive evaluation, the assessment plan is designed. The appropriate team members are contacted to begin the process.

norm-referenced tests Tests designed to compare individual students with national averages, or norms of expectancy

standardized tests Tests developed with specific standard administration, scoring, and interpretation procedures that must be followed precisely to obtain optimum results

The types of assessment that may be used in a comprehensive evaluation are varied, depending upon the student's needs. Many of the instruments used are **norm-referenced tests** or assessment devices. These instruments have been developed to determine how a student performs on tasks when compared with students of the same age and/or grade level. These tests are also **standardized tests.** This means that the tests were developed with very structured and specific instructions, formats, scoring, and interpretation procedures. These specifics, written in the test manual, must be followed to ensure the tests are used in the manner set forth by the test developers.

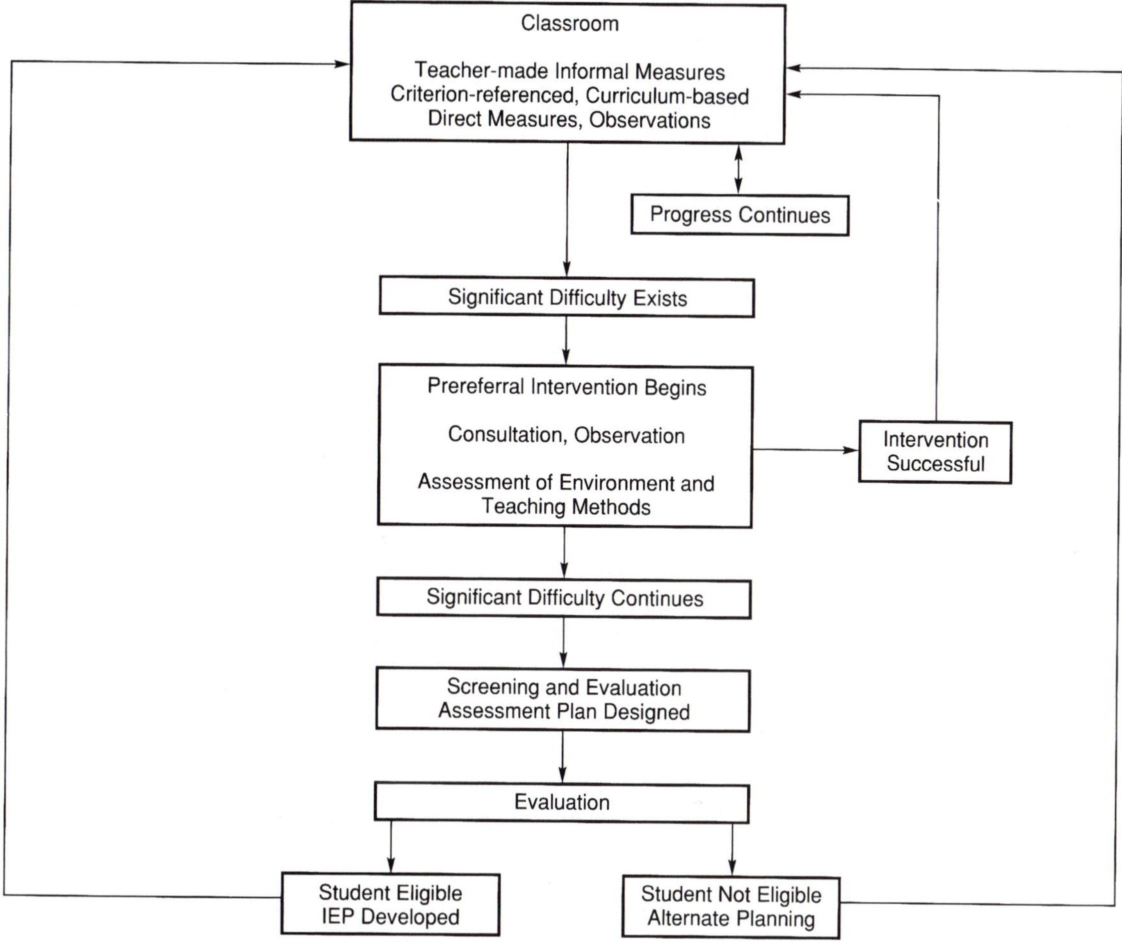

Figure 1.3
Continuous model of assessment.

In addition to standardized norm-referenced tests, team members use informal methods such as classroom observations, interviews with teachers and parents, and criterion-referenced instruments. The team presents the results from these assessment techniques in the **eligibility meeting** held with the parents. This meeting will determine what educational changes are necessary to provide the best instruction for the student.

eligibility meeting A conference held after a preplacement evaluation to determine if a student is eligible for services.

During the eligibility meeting, the team may determine that the student is eligible for services based on the information collected through the evaluation process. If the student is eligible, an IEP must be written for the student. If, however, the student is not eligible for special education services, **alternative planning** should be considered, including educational intervention suggestions for the student.

alternative planning A plan designed for educational intervention when a student has been found not eligible for special education services.

Individual Family Service Plan A plan designed for children ages 3 and younger that addresses the child's strengths and needs as well as the family's needs.

When the referred child is 3 years of age or younger and eligibility for services has been determined, the law requires that an **Individual Family Service Plan (IFSP)** be developed by the team members and parents. The IFSP differs from the IEP because the family's needs are addressed as well as the child's needs. Early childhood assessment is presented in detail in chapter 12.

The steps of the evaluation process are structured by both federal and state laws. The federal mandates are presented in chapter 2.

Exercises

Part I

Match the following terms with the correct definitions.

A. assessment
B. testing
C. curriculum-based assessment
D. error analysis
E. informal assessment
F. prereferral intervention strategies
G. individual assessment plan
H. norm-referenced test
I. multiple gating
J. eligibility meeting
K. checklist
L. continuous assessment
M. overidentification
N. APA *Standards*
O. screening
P. IEP
Q. alternative planning
R. standardized tests
S. IFSP

_______ **1.** Ongoing monitoring of student progress in all classroom settings.
_______ **2.** A developmentally sequenced list of skills.
_______ **3.** A plan designed to address the needs of the child and family when the child is 3 years of age or younger.
_______ **4.** The identification of students who appear to be eligible for services but whose deviations are the result of other variables.
_______ **5.** A plan written for every student receiving special education services; specifies interventions.
_______ **6.** A method of assessment that is sequential over time and involves administering screening instruments before conducting a comprehensive individualized assessment.
_______ **7.** Tests designed to use in comparing an individual with national averages of performance.
_______ **8.** Using student mistakes to analyze learning problems.
_______ **9.** Gathering information to use in educational decision making.
_______ **10.** Using content from classroom curriculum to monitor progress.
_______ **11.** Conference with team and parents following preplacement evaluation; decisions made regarding interventions and/or eligibility.
_______ **12.** Professional ethical criteria to be followed during the assessment of students.

_______ **13.** Method used to determine a student's ability to complete certain tasks or demonstrate mastery of a skill or knowledge of content.

_______ **14.** Methods used, before referral, to modify learning environment or teaching strategies.

_______ **15.** Individual planning for a student who is not determined eligible for special education but who needs educational intervention.

_______ **16.** Nonstandardized methods of assessment that can include observation, teacher-made tests, and so on.

_______ **17.** Process of reviewing referral to determine if student needs further assessment.

_______ **18.** Tests developed with specific administration, scoring, and interpretation techniques, which must be followed to obtain optimum results.

_______ **19.** Plan that designates which types of assessment are necessary for a particular student and who will be responsible for each assessment specified in the plan.

Part II

Answer the following questions:

1. One way to document that many strategies have been attempted before referral is to use a ____.
2. Ysseldyke and Thurlow (1983) recommended that the emphasis of referral practice be changed from referral-to-placement to _______________________
3. Shifting the emphasis of referral to prereferral strategies would decrease the amount of time that multidisciplinary teams spend testing and increase _______________________.
4. Even though referral practices are faulty, research (Algozzine et al., 1982) has shown that more than _______ % of the students referred were tested and that _______ % of those tested were found eligible for services.
5. Messick's (1984) two-phase assessment model stressed the assessment of _______________________.
6. According to the continuous model of assessment, when should assessment be used? _______________________
7. Chalfant and Psyh (1989) reported that inappropriate referral rates _______________________
8. Summarize the best practice procedures from prereferral to the evaluation process. _______________________

References

Algozzine, B., Christenson, S., & Ysseldyke, J. (1982). Probabilities associated with the referral-to-placement process. *Teacher education and special education, 5,* 19–23.

American Psychological Association. (1985). *Standards for educational and psychological testing.* Washington, DC: Author.

Barnett, D. W., & Macmann, G. M. (1992). Decision reliability and validity: Contributions and limitations of alternative assessment strategies. *The Journal of Special Education, 25*(4), 431–452.

Carter, J., & Sugai, G. (1989). Survey on prereferral practices: Responses from state departments of education. *Exceptional Children, 55,* 298–308.

Chalfant, J. C., & Psyh, M. (1989). Teachers assistance teams: Five descriptive studies on 96 teams. *Remedial and Special Education, 10*(6), 49–58.

Federal Register. (1992). Washington, D.C.: U.S. Government Printing Office, September 29, 1992.

Fuchs, D. (1991). Mainstream assistance teams: A prereferral intervention system for difficult to teach students. In Stoner, G., Shinn, M. R., & Walker, H. M. (Eds.), *Interventions for achievement and behavior problems* (pp. 241–267). Silver Spring, MD: National Association of School Psychologists.

Graden, J., Casey, A., & Bonstrom, O. (1985). Implementing a prereferral intervention system: Part II. The data. *Exceptional Children, 51,* 487–496.

Graden, J., Casey, A., & Christenson, S. (1985). Implementing a prereferral intervention system: Part I. The model. *Exceptional Children, 51,* 377–384.

Halgren, D. W., & Clarizio, H. F. (1993). Categorical and programming changes in special education services. *Exceptional Children, 59*(6), 547–555.

Harvey, V. (1991). Characteristics of children referred to school psychologists: A discriminant analysis. *Psychology in the Schools, 28,* 209–218.

McIntyre, L. (1988). Teacher gender: A predictor of special education referral? *Journal of Learning Disabilities, 21,* 382–384.

Maxam, S., Boyer-Stephens, A., & Alff, M. (1986). Assessment: A key to appropriate program placement (Report No. CE 045 407 pp. 11–13). Columbia: University of Missouri—Columbia, Department of Special Education and Department of Practical Arts and Vocational-Technical Education. (ERIC Document Reproduction Service No. ED 275 835).

Messick, S. (1984). Assessment in context: Appraising student performance in relation to instructional quality. *Educational Researcher, 13,* 3–8.

Nelson, J. R., Smith, D. J., Taylor, L., Dodd, J. M., & Reavis, K. (1992). A statewide survey of special education administrators regarding mandated prereferral interventions. *Remedial and Special Education, 13*(4), 34–39.

Reschly, D. (1986). Functional psychoeducational assessment: Trends and issues. *Special Services in the Schools, 2,* 57–69.

Salvia, J., & Ysseldyke, J. (1988). *Assessment in special and remedial education* (4th ed.). Boston: Houghton Mifflin.

Shinn, M., Tindal, G., & Spira, D. (1987). Special education referrals as an index of teacher tolerance: Are teachers imperfect tests? *Exceptional Children, 54,* 32–39.

Soodak, L. C., & Podell, D. M. (1993). Teacher efficacy and student problem as factors in special education referral. *The Journal of Special Education, 27*(1), 66–81.

Thurlow, M., Christenson, S., & Ysseldyke, J. (1983). *Referral research: An integrative summary of findings* (Research Report No. 141). Minneapolis: University of Minnesota, Institute for Research on Learning Disabilities.

White, R., & Calhoun, M. (1987). From referral to placement: Teachers' perceptions of their responsibilities. *Exceptional Children, 5,* 460–468.

Ysseldyke, J., Algozzine, B., Richey, L., & Graden, J. (1982). Declaring students eligible for learning disability services: Why bother with the data? *Learning Disabilities Quarterly, 5,* 37–44.

Ysseldyke, J., Christenson, S., Pianta, B., & Algozzine, B. (1983). An analysis of teachers' reasons and desired outcomes for students referred for psychoeducational assessment. *Journal of Psychoeducational Assessment, 1,* 73–83.

Ysseldyke, J., & Thurlow, M. (1983). *Identification/classification research: An integrative summary of findings* (Research Report No. 142). Minneapolis: University of Minnesota, Institute for Research on Learning Disabilities.

Zins, J., Graden, J., & Ponti, C. (1989). Prereferral intervention to improve special services delivery. *Special Services in the Schools, 4,* 109–130.

Chapter Two

Law and Issues

Key Terms

Public Law 94–142
IDEA
compliance
PL 99–457
due process
preplacement evaluation
comprehensive educational evaluation
informed consent
surrogate parent
consent form
parents' rights booklet
nondiscriminatory assessment
transition services
advocate
special education services
related services
mainstreaming
grade equivalents
standard scores
annual goals
short-term objectives
procedural safeguards
independent educational evaluation
third-party hearing
hearing officer
minority overrepresentation
mediation

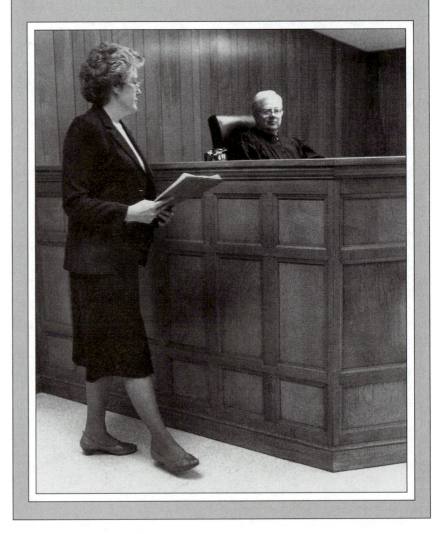

The Law: Public Law 94–142

During the 1970s, substantial legal changes for persons with disabilities occurred. Much of the pressure for these changes came from parents and professionals. Another influential source affecting the language of the law was litigation in the civil court system.

In 1975, the Education for All Handicapped Children Act, referred to as **Public Law 94–142,** was passed. In 1990, under PL 101–476, the act was renamed the Individuals With Disabilities Education Act, or **IDEA.** The regulations were written in 1992 (*Federal Register,* 1992). IDEA contains several major provisions that guarantee the right to education for all persons with disabilities in the United States. The law grants the right to a free appropriate public education in the least restrictive environment. Many of IDEA's provisions concern the process of assessment. The law mandates that state educational agencies (SEAs) ensure that proper assessment procedures are followed (*Federal Register,* 1992). Although the original law has been in effect for two decades, professional educators must continue to monitor **compliance** with the mandates within each local education agency (LEA). Informed teachers and parents are the best safeguards for compliance in each and every school. Even several years after the law was enacted, one study revealed that only 28% of special educators felt they knew special education law (Silver, 1987).

In 1986, the Education of the Handicapped Amendments, **PL 99–457,** were passed. The final regulations, written in 1993 (*Federal Register,* 1993), were developed to promote early intervention for preschool children and infants with special needs and/or developmental delays. Specific issues concerning PL 99–457 and the assessment of preschool children are included in chapter 12.

This chapter contains sections of the law that directly affect the assessment of children and youth of school age. Relevant research and legal issues are included.

Public Law 94–142 The Education for All Handicapped Children Act of 1975; guarantees the right to a free and appropriate education in the least restrictive environment; renamed IDEA.

IDEA Individuals With Disabilities Education Act, passed in 1990 to give new name to PL 94–142.

compliance To be operating within the federal regulations, within the confines of the law.

PL 99–457 IDEA amendments that extend services for special needs children through infancy and preschool years.

IDEA and Assessment

due process The right to a hearing to settle disputes; a protection for children with disabilities and their families.

IDEA is a federal law containing mandates to promote fair, objective assessment practices and **due process** procedures, the foundations for legal recourse when parents and/or schools disagree with evaluation or placement recommendations. Teachers not only should be aware of the law but also should strive to maintain compliance in testing students, recommending placement, and developing IEPs. Teachers can help their local education agencies comply by following guidelines, meeting time lines, and correctly performing educational functions specified in the law. This chapter includes portions of the federal law, taken from the *Federal Register* (1992), that pertain to assessment in special education. Also included are some of the American Psychological Association's *Standards* (APA, 1985). Many of the standards reinforce the basic ethical and professional regulations stated in IDEA.

Preplacement Evaluation

Preplacement evaluation A comprehensive evaluation before receiving special education services.

IDEA

§ 300.531 **Preplacement evaluation**
Before any action is taken with respect to the initial placement of a child with a disability in a program providing special education and related services, a full and individual evaluation of the child's educational needs must be conducted in accordance with the requirements of § 300.532. (*Federal Register*, 1992, p. 44822)

comprehensive educational evaluation A complete assessment in all areas of suspected disability.

Before placing any student in a special education setting or classroom, the members of the multidisciplinary team must complete a comprehensive individual evaluation of the student's needs. This evaluation should reflect consideration of the specific academic, behavioral, communicative, cognitive, motor, and/or sensory areas of concern. This **comprehensive educational evaluation** must be completed before initial placement and once every 3 years for students who receive special education services. The details specified in section 300.532, "Evaluation Procedures," are presented throughout this chapter.

Informed Consent

informed consent Parents are informed of rights in their native language and agree in writing to procedures for the child; may be revoked at any time.

The initial preplacement evaluation cannot take place without parental **informed consent.** The regulation that defines consent follows:

IDEA

§ 300.500 Definitions of "consent" . . .

(a) As used in this part: "Consent" means that—
  (1) The parent has been fully informed of all information relevant to the activity for which consent is sought, in his or her native language, or other mode of communication;

(2) The parent understands and agrees in writing to the carrying out of the activity for which his or her consent is sought, and the consent describes that activity and lists the records (if any) which will be released and to whom; and

(3) The parent understands that the granting of consent is voluntary and may be revoked at any time. *(Federal Register,* 1992, p. 44819)

surrogate parent Person appointed by the court system to be legally responsible for child's education.

According to federal regulations, parental consent means that the parent, guardian, or **surrogate parent** has been fully informed of all educational activities to which he or she is being asked to consent. When a parent gives consent for a preplacement evaluation, for example, this means that the parent has been fully informed of the evaluation procedures and why the school personnel believe these measures are necessary, and that the parent has agreed to the evaluation.

Furthermore, informed consent means that the parent has been informed in his or her native language or mode of communication. If the parent does not speak English, the information must be conveyed verbally or in writing in the parent's native language. In areas where languages other than English are prevalent, educational agencies often employ bilingual personnel to translate assessment and placement information as necessary. Additionally, many state educational agencies provide **consent forms** and **parents' rights booklets** in languages other than English. IDEA's statement regarding mode of communication sends a clear message that parents with visual or hearing impairments must be accommodated. The educational agency must make every effort to provide sign interpreters, for parents with hearing impairments who sign to communicate, and large-print or braille materials, for parents with visual impairments who read in this fashion.

consent form Written permission form that grants permission for evaluation or placement.

parents' rights booklet Used to convey rights to parents in writing.

Parental consent must be obtained before the school releases any student records to a third party. If the school personnel want the records to be mailed to a psychologist in private practice, for example, the parents must consent in writing to the school to release the records and must know exactly which records are to be mailed to whom.

Federal law requires that school personnel inform the parents before assessment and before placement that their consent is considered mandatory and may be revoked at any time. Therefore, if the parents had previously agreed to a placement for their child in a special education resource room for 1 hour per day, and it is later recommended that the student receive services 3 hours per day, the parents may revoke their consent to approve special education services if they believe it to be in the best interest of their child. Should the parents revoke their consent, they are guaranteed the rights of due process. The school personnel are granted the same rights of due process and may decide to file a complaint against the parents. (Due process is discussed further later in this chapter.)

☐ **CHECK YOUR UNDERSTANDING**

Complete Activity 2.1.

Activity 2.1

Use the regulations that concern preplacement evaluation and informed consent to complete this activity. Choose from the phrases listed to answer the questions that follow.

preplacement evaluation	informed of activities
native language	mode of communication
parents' rights booklet	comprehensive evaluation
due process	revoke consent
every 3 years	release of records
voluntary informed consent	

1. The consent given by parents indicates that the parents have been ______________________ that the school personnel feel are necessary and in the child's best interest.
2. In compliance with IDEA, most parents are informed of their legal rights and responsibilities through the use of a ______________________.
3. A teacher would not be allowed to give a student's records to another interested party. Before the ______________________, the parents must consent in writing and receive an explanation of who would receive which records.
4. When parents decide that they no longer agree with a school placement or services for their child, they may ______________________, and if necessary, they may begin ______________________ procedures.
5. For students who are receiving special education services, a ______________ __________ must be completed at least ______________________.
6. It is the responsibility of the school personnel to provide information to parents in their ______________________ or using the parent's ________________ ______ in order to comply with the federal law.

Nondiscriminatory Assessment

nondiscriminatory assessment Fair and objective testing practices for students from all cultural and linguistic backgrounds.

Many of the regulations that guide professionals in the assessment process are concerned with fair testing practice. The first regulation presented on **nondiscriminatory assessment** addresses this issue with a general statement.

IDEA

§ 300.530 General

(b) Testing and evaluation materials and procedures used for the purposes of evaluation and placement of children with disabilities must be selected and administered so as to not be racially or culturally discriminatory. *(Federal Register,* 1992, p. 44822)

Nondiscriminatory assessment is mandated in IDEA to ensure fairness and objectivity in testing. This section requires that the instruments or techniques used in the assessment process are not racially or culturally biased and that the instruments are selected to be used in the evaluation and placement of students in special education.

More specific mandates are included in the "Evaluation Procedures" section of the regulations. This is a lengthy section that will be broken into parts and discussed along with the applicable APA (1985) *Standards*.

IDEA

§ 300.532 Evaluation procedures
State and local education agencies shall insure, at a minimum, that:

(a) Tests and other evaluation materials:
  (1) Are provided and administered in the child's native language or other mode of communication, unless it is clearly not feasible to do so:
  (2) Have been validated for the specific purpose for which they are used; and
  (3) Are administered by trained personnel in conformance with the instructions provided by their producer. (*Federal Register,* 1992, p. 44822)

This section of the law sets forth the minimum criteria for nondiscriminatory assessment practice in special education. The first criterion to ensure fairness in testing is that the tests are presented and administered in the student's language unless it is impossible to do so. This section also requires that the mode of communication used by the student be used in the assessment process. Like the communication standards written for parental consent, this section requires that school personnel find and use appropriate methods, such as sign language or braille, if necessary to assess the individual's ability in the most fair and objective manner.

Section 300.532 (a) 2 states that tests are to be used for the purpose for which they were designed and validated. Therefore, if a student is having difficulty in the areas of spelling and written language, tests designed to measure those areas should be employed to determine the student's educational needs. A test designed to measure reading comprehension skills would not be used to measure spelling and written language. A decision to place an individual in special education or to deny the student services based solely on reading test results when that student was referred for spelling and written language would be out of compliance with this section of the law.

In addition to using tests validated for the purpose for which they will be used, schools must ensure that tests are administered by trained personnel in the manner specified by the test producer. Much information regarding the training of personnel and administration of specific tests can be found in the individual test manuals, which the team member should study thoroughly before administration. Examples of errors made by professionals that do not comply with this section include administering tests or sections of a test to a group of students when the test was designed for individual administration, giving instructions to students in writing when the manual specifies oral presentation, and allowing 2 minutes for a test item when the test manual states that the time allowed is 90 seconds. When an examiner fails to follow directions specified by the developer of a standardized test, the results may lead to inaccurate interpretations and poor recommendations. In this regard, the testing has been unfair to the student.

In addition to the regulations of IDEA, the APA (1985) addressed similar issues with the standards shown in Figure 2.1.

Standard 6.10 (Figure 2.1) clearly indicates to professionals that sensitivity toward children and youth from diverse groups, such as culturally different or disabled children, should be used in the evaluation process. This APA standard emphasizes the need for experienced or trained professionals to administer assessment appropriately in the student's best interest. If the person responsible for test administration is not familiar with the student's characteristic, that professional should seek the advice and support of an experienced examiner.

APA STANDARD 6.10

In educational, clinical, and counseling applications, test administrators and users should not attempt to evaluate test takers whose special characteristics—ages, handicapping conditions, or linguistic, generational, or cultural backgrounds—are outside the range of their academic training or supervised experience. A test user faced with a request to evaluate a test taker whose special characteristics are not within his or her range of professional experience should seek consultation regarding test selection, necessary modifications of testing procedures, and score interpretation from a professional who has had relevant experience. (p. 43)

APA STANDARD 6.12

In school, clinical, and counseling applications, tests developed for screening should be used only for identifying test takers who may need further evaluation. The results of such tests should not be used to characterize a person or to make any decision about a person, other than the decision for referral for further evaluation, unless adequate reliability and validity for these can be demonstrated. (p. 43)

APA STANDARD 8.1

Those responsible for school testing programs should ensure that the individuals who administer tests are properly instructed in the appropriate test administration procedures and that they understand the importance of adhering to the directions for administration that are provided by the test developer. (p. 52)

Figure 2.1
American Psychological Association (APA) standards relevant to nondiscriminatory assessment.

Source: From *Standards for Educational and Psychological Testing* by the American Psychological Association, 1985, Washington, DC: Author. Copyright 1985 by the American Psychological Association. Reprinted by permission.

The requirement of using tests only for their intended purpose is stressed in APA Standard 6.12 (Figure 2.1). This standard warns against the use of screening instruments for diagnosis or any purpose other than screening. It is imperative that teachers and other members of the multidisciplinary team know the purpose of the test and understand the quality of the test and validity of using the test for the purpose stated by the test developers.

Standard 8.1 (Figure 2.1) stresses the knowledge of proper test administration techniques and following specific instructions given by the test developer. These two important components are often taken for granted and not strictly followed. Failure to follow the directions presented in the test manual may result in mistakes in administration and scoring, which constitute unfair testing practice.

IDEA includes additional specific regulations regarding the comprehensive assessment of students. These regulations concern fair assessment practice and sensitivity to students with disabilities that may unjustly lower test scores and influence test results:

IDEA

§ 300.532 Evaluation procedures

(b) Tests and other evaluation materials include those tailored to assess specific areas of educational need and not merely those which are designed to provide a single general intelligence quotient;

(c) Tests are selected and administered so as to best ensure that when a test is administered to an individual with impaired sensory, manual, or speaking skills, the test results accurately reflect the individual's aptitude or achievement level or whatever other factors the test purports to measure, rather than reflecting the individual's impaired sensory, manual, or speaking skills (except where those are the factors which the test purports to measure). *(Federal Register,* 1992, p. 44822)

According to IDEA, the assessment of a student must include measures designed for evaluating specific educational needs rather than using an instrument that yields only a single IQ score. Before the passage of this law, numerous students were unfairly discriminated against due to conclusions based on a single IQ score. Often this resulted in very restrictive placement settings, such as institutions or self-contained classrooms, rather than more appropriate educational interventions. In addition to the federal mandates, court cases, such as *Larry P. v. Riles* (1972), have had a significant impact on discriminatory testing practices. This case, and others, are presented in chapter 10.

Assessment can be discriminatory in other ways. The law mandates that the instruments used to assess one skill or area do not discriminate or unduly penalize a student because of an existing impairment. For example, a student with speech articulation problems who is referred for reading difficulties should not be penalized on a test that requires the student to pronounce nonsense syllables. The student in this case may have incorrectly pronounced sounds, as a result of the speech condition, and the mispronunciations may be counted as reading errors. The reading scores obtained may be substantially lower than the student's actual reading ability because the misarticulations sounded like mispronunciations of the nonsense words.

The APA (1985) provides specific standards for the testing of students with disabilities (Figure 2.2). Enforcement of these standards is imperative for ensuring that a student is not penalized for the impairment.

Standard 14.1 mentions that persons who administer tests to individuals with disabilities should not attempt to change a standardized test unless they have the expertise to make the necessary changes. This standard also states that persons who test individuals with disabilities should know exactly how the disability will affect the results of the particular test being administered. This same philosophy is communicated in the federal regulations by language that advises professionals not to use tests that unjustly penalize a student because of the existing disability.

In Standard 14.2, the APA advises test publishers to include cautionary statements regarding the use of a test with persons with disabilities if the test has not been validated for that use. Although this statement is directed to test developers, special education professionals should study assessment instruments carefully for the inclusion of such cautionary statements or statements of validity for use with persons who are disabled. If a particular test does not address this issue, the examiner should contact the test publisher for further clarification or select an instrument validated for use with students with disabilities.

The final regulations concerning the actual evaluation process stress the need for a thorough evaluation by a group of professionals from various fields.

APA STANDARD 14.1

People who modify tests for handicapped people should have available to them the psychometric expertise for so doing. In addition, they should have available to them knowledge of the effects of various handicapping conditions on test performance, acquired either from their own training or from close consultation with handicapped individuals or those thoroughly familiar with such individuals.

APA STANDARD 14.2

Until tests have been validated for people who have specific handicapping conditions, test publishers should issue cautionary statements in manuals and elsewhere regarding confidence in interpretations based on such test scores. (p. 79)

Figure 2.2

American Psychological Association (APA) standards for testing students with disabilities.

Source: From *Standards for Educational and Psychological Testing* by the American Psychological Association, 1985, Washington, DC: Author. Copyright 1985 by the American Psychological Association. Reprinted by permission.

IDEA

§ 300.532 Evaluation procedures

(d) No single procedure is used as the sole criterion for determining an appropriate educational program for a child; and

(e) The evaluation is made by a multidisciplinary team or group of persons including at least one teacher or specialist with knowledge in the area of suspected disability

(f) The individual is assessed in all areas related to the suspected disability, including, where appropriate, health, vision, hearing, social and emotional status, general intelligence, academic performance, communicative status, and motor abilities. *(Federal Register,* 1992, p. 44822)

The regulations in Section 300.532 (d), (e), and (f) encourage the use of a variety of assessment devices and require the participation of several professionals in the decision-making process. Using many and varied assessment materials helps professionals to establish a more holistic view of the student. The professional expertise provided by a multidisciplinary team aids in promoting fair and objective assessment. It is necessary to involve many different professionals to assess all areas such as vision, emotion, language, and other factors that may need to be evaluated to reach the best educational decision.

These sections include the requirement to assess the student in all areas of suspected disability. In many cases, a referred student is known to have academic difficulty, but the disability might be due to many factors. The best way to determine if the student truly has a disability and, if so, what type of disability, is to assess all of the suspected areas. For example, a referred student who demonstrated immature social skills and inappropriate behavior also demonstrated developmental and learning problems, but when the referral information was submitted, background information was too limited to determine if the student was having emotional problems, specific learning problems, or possibly was subaverage in intellectual ability. In cases such as this, the law mandates that all areas be assessed to determine if a disability exists. In this particular case, the young student was found to have a mild hearing impairment and subsequently had developed some behavioral problems. Appropriate audiological and educational interventions prevented further behavioral problems from developing and helped to remediate academic skills.

APA Standard 6.4. (Figure 2.3) concerns the administration of appropriate tests and their use in the decision-making process. This standard addresses the need for evaluation as a means to determine appropriate decisions. This standard warns the test user against using tests to verify previously made decisions or to justify decisions that were made using other information. For example, a test known through research to yield lower IQ scores than other instruments of better quality cannot be selected and used purposely to obtain the lowest score possible so that a student may be found eligible for services. The tests should be selected and administered in a justifiably fair manner. This emphasizes the need for thorough investigation of tests before their selection and administration.

APA STANDARD 6.4

Test users should accurately portray the relevance of a test to the assessment and decision making process and should not use a test score to justify an evaluation, recommendation, or decision that has been made largely on some other basis. (p. 42)

Figure 2.3
American Psychological Association (APA) standard for administering appropriate tests and using them in the decision-making process.

Source: From *Standards for Educational and Psychological Testing* by the American Psychological Association, 1985, Washington, DC: Author. Copyright 1985 by the American Psychological Association. Reprinted by permission.

Other discriminatory test practices concerned with test bias, examiner bias, and so on are presented in the section "Research and Issues Concerning IDEA," later in this chapter.

☐ **CHECK YOUR UNDERSTANDING**

Complete Activity 2.2.

Activity 2.2

Read the following statements to determine if they represent fair testing practice, and then check the appropriate blank. Write "IDEA" if the statement pertains to the regulations, "APA" if the statement pertain to the *Standards* (APA, 1985), or "both" if the statement represents the federal mandates and the *Standards.*

1. A screening test may be used to make placement decisions about a student who was referred for special education services.
   Fair _________ Unfair _________ Pertains to _________
2. Individuals who administer tests in the Woodlake local education agency are thoroughly trained to use each new instrument through school inservice sessions and graduate courses.
   Fair _________ Unfair _________ Pertains to _________
3. A special education teacher is asked to test a student who speaks only Japanese. The teacher cannot find a test in that language, so he observes the student in the classroom setting and recommends that the student be placed in special education.
   Fair _________ Unfair _________ Pertains to _________
4. A special education teacher is asked to give an educational test to a minority student. The test has been validated and proven to be racially nondiscriminatory.
   Fair _________ Unfair _________ Pertains to _________
5. A student is referred for an evaluation for possible eligibility for special education. The student has cerebral palsy, and the team member has no knowledge of this disorder. The team member asks the physical therapist to give advice

on how to administer the test and requests that the therapist attend and assist during the evaluation.
Fair _________ Unfair _________ Pertains to _________

6. A student is referred for evaluation. The referring teacher feels that the student might have mental retardation. Test results indicate that the student falls within the low average range. The student scored lowest on a test yielding a single IQ score. The teacher feels that this is enough to place the child; however, the team disagrees and does not recommend placement. The team's decision is:
Fair _________ Unfair _________ Pertains to _________

Evaluating Children with Specific Learning Disabilities

Federal regulations include specific criteria that must be used when determining the existence of a possible learning disability. The regulations include an operational definition of specific learning disabilities and also require that observations be a part of the evaluation process.

A student may be diagnosed as having an existing learning disability when the child is not achieving as expected for her age and ability levels and exhibits a severe discrepancy between achievement and intellectual ability in one or more of the following areas: oral expression, listening comprehension, written expression, basic reading skill, reading comprehension, mathematics calculation, or mathematics reasoning. The student may not be found to have a learning disability if the discrepancy between achievement and intellectual ability is the result of a sensory impairment, mental retardation, emotional disturbance, or environmental or cultural disadvantage.

Section 300.542 explains the requirements for observing students suspected of having a learning disability.

IDEA

§ 300.542

(a) At least one team member other than the child's regular teacher shall observe the child's academic performance in the regular classroom setting.
(b) In the case of a child less than school age or out of school, a team member shall observe the child in an environment appropriate for that age. *(Federal Register,* 1992, p. 44823)

Meeting the Needs of Persons with Attention Disorders

When PL 94–142 was revised, attention disorders were studied by the United States Department of Education (U.S. Department of Education, 1991) for possible addition as a new disability category to IDEA. The decision was made that attention disorders (such as Attention Deficit Disorder, or ADD) did not need a separate category because students with these disorders were already served, for the most part, in settings for students with learning or behavioral disabilities. If the student did not meet the criteria for either specific learning disabilities or emotional disturbance, the student could be served in an appropriate setting under the category of other health impaired ". . . in instances where the ADD is a chronic or acute health problem that results in limited alertness, which adversely affects educational performance" (U.S. Department of Education, 1991, p. 3).

In cases where the attention disorder does not significantly impair the student's ability to function in the regular classroom, the student may be served within the regular classroom under the provisions of section 504 of the Rehabilitation Act of 1973. This law requires that students be given reasonable accommodations for their disability in the general education environment.

Students with attention disorders must undergo a comprehensive evaluation by a multidisciplinary team to determine if they are eligible for services and, if so, whether they would be best served by the provisions of IDEA or section 504.

Multidisciplinary Team Evaluation

To decrease the possibility of subjective and discriminatory assessment, IDEA mandates that the comprehensive evaluation be conducted by a multidisciplinary team. As stated in sections 300.532 (e) and (f), each student must be assessed in a variety of areas by a team made up of professionals from various disciplines according to the individual's needs. All areas of suspected disability are assessed. If the team has determined during screening and has specified in the assessment plan that the student needs further evaluation in speech, language, reading, and social/behavioral skills, a speech-language clinician, special education teacher or educational diagnostician, and school psychologist will be members of the assessment team. The team may obtain additional information from the parents, classroom teacher, school nurse, school counselor, principal, and other school personnel. Figure 2.4 illustrates the various members who may be on a multidisciplinary team and their responsibilities.

In compliance with the nondiscriminatory section of the law, team members employ several types of assessment and collect different types of data. Team members select instruments for their validity, technical adequacy, cultural fairness, and objectivity. Because the law requires that a variety of methods be used in assessment, the team should make use of additional classroom observations, informal assessment measures, and parent interviews.

At least one teacher or specialist with knowledge in the suspected area of disability must be included on the multidisciplinary team, according to the regulations. If the screening process reveals that a learning disability is suspected, a learning disability specialist, that is, a resource teacher trained in the area of learning disabilities, is included on the team. If the child is suspected of having a hearing impairment, an audiologist is included on the team.

Team Member	Responsibilities
School nurse	Initial vision and hearing screens, checks medical records, refers health problems to other medical professionals
Special education teacher	Consultant to regular classroom teacher during prereferral process; administers educational tests, observes in other classrooms, helps with screening and recommends IEP goals, writes objectives, and suggests educational interventions
Special education supervisor	May advise all activities of special education teacher, may provide direct services, guides placement decisions, recommends services
Educational diagnostician	Administers norm-referenced and criterion-referenced tests, observes student in educational setting, makes suggestions for IEP goals and objectives
School psychologist	Administers individual intelligence tests, observes student in classroom, administers projective instruments and personality inventories; may be under supervision of a doctoral-level psychologist
Occupational therapist	Evaluates fine motor and self-help skills, recommends therapies, may provide direct services or consultant services, may help obtain equipment for student needs
Physical therapist	Evaluates gross motor functioning and self-help skills, living skills, and job-related skills necessary for optimum achievement of student; may provide direct services or consultant services.
Behavioral consultant	Specialist in behavior management and crisis intervention; may provide direct services or consultant services
School counselor	May serve as objective observer in prereferral stage, may provide direct group or individual counseling, may schedule students and help with planning of student school schedules

Figure 2.4
Multidisciplinary team: Who's who?

Team Member	Responsibilities
Speech-language clinician	Evaluates speech-language development, may refer for hearing problems, may provide direct therapy or consultant services for classroom teachers.
Audiologist	Evaluates hearing for possible impairments, may refer students for medical problems, may help obtain hearing aids
Physician's assistant	Evaluates physical condition of student and may provide physical exams for students of a local education agency, refers medical problems to physicians or appropriate therapists school social worker, or visiting teacher
Home-school coordinator; school social worker, or visiting teacher	Works directly with family; may hold conferences, conduct interviews, and/or administer adaptive behavior scales based on parent interviews; may serve as case manager
Regular education teacher	Works with the special education team, student, and parents to develop an environment that is appropriate and as much like that of general education students as possible; implements prereferral intervention strategies
Parents	Active members of the special education team; provide input for IEP, work with home school academic and behavioral programs

Figure 2.4, *continued*

Each member of the multidisciplinary team must contribute carefully documented information to the decision-making process. This information is presented to the parents during a conference, and a decision regarding eligibility is made.

☐ CHECK YOUR UNDERSTANDING

Complete Activity 2.3.

Activity 2.3

Using the information from Figure 2.4, assign the appropriate team member to solve the following problems.

1. A student in Ms. Whittle's class has been rubbing his eyes frequently and holding books very close to his face. Ms. Whittle should request the help of ____.

2. A young student in your class has a difficult time holding a pencil and using scissors. You have tried several procedures to help the student learn how to use these tools; however, she continues to have difficulty. You decide to refer the student to ______________________.
3. Mr. Powers has a student in his class who seems to be having difficulty staying awake. From time to time, the student seems to be in a daze. He does not know if the child has a physical, emotional, or even drug-related problem. Mr. Powers asks you to help because "You know what to do with these problem children." You advise Mr. Powers to contact ______________________ ______________________.
4. Ms. Stewart has a student who just doesn't seem to be learning. She tells you that she has "tried everything," including changing to an easier textbook. She feels sure that the student has a learning disability and should be tested and "taken out of my room so I can spend more time with the other students." You advise Ms. Stewart to consult ______________________ ______________________.
5. Ms. Henry has a young male student who exhibits aggressive behaviors in class. Ms. Henry is concerned that the student may harm himself or others. Your advice to Ms. Henry is to contact ______________________ or refer to ______________________.

Parent Participation

Every effort should be made to accommodate the parents so that they may attend all conferences pertaining to their child's education. The federal regulations emphasize the importance of parental attendance.

IDEA

§ 300.345 Parent participation

(a) Each public agency shall take steps to insure that one or both of the parents of the child with a disability are present at each meeting or are afforded the opportunity to participate, including:
  (1) Notifying the parents of the meeting early enough to ensure that they will have an opportunity to attend; and
  (2) Scheduling the meeting at a mutually agreed on time and place.

(b) **(1)** The notice under paragraph (a) (1) of this section must indicate the purpose, time, and location of the meeting and who will be in attendance.
  (2) If a purpose of the meeting is the consideration of transition services for a student, the notice must also—
    (i) indicate this purpose
    (ii) indicate that the agency will invite the student; and
    (iii) identify any other agency that will be invited to send a representative.

(c) If neither parent can attend, the public agency shall use other methods to insure parent participation, including individual or conference telephone calls. *(Federal Register,* 1992, p. 44815)

Involve parents through parent-teacher conferences.

The suggestions of arranging the meetings at a mutually agreed on time and place, providing advance notice, and relying on conference telephone calls if necessary are stated in the regulations to encourage parental involvement. If numerous attempts have been made to involve the parents with no results, the law provides for the possibility of reaching an educational decision without parental involvement and then notifying the parents of that decision. All attempts to reach the parents and all contacts with the parents must be carefully documented. It is in the best interest of the child, however, to include the parents whenever possible.

The importance of parent involvement was underscored in the provisions of PL 99–457. These amendments require that the intervention plan, called the Individual Family Service Plan, be designed to include necessary participation of the family members. As mentioned in chapter 1, the IFSP identifies family needs relating to the child's development that, when met, will increase the likelihood of successful intervention. The legislation emphasizes the family and the child with the disability (Turnbull, 1990).

transition services
Services designed to help students make the transition from high school to postsecondary education or work environment.

IDEA stresses the importance of **transition services** to prepare students 16 years or older for a work or postsecondary environment. Where appropriate in educational planning, younger students may also be eligible for such services. The law underscores the importance of early planning and decisions by all members affected, including the student.

Determining Eligibility

The federal regulations include provisions for determining eligibility for special education services. These regulations are included in the "Placement Procedures" section.

IDEA

§ 300.533 Placement procedures

(a) In interpreting evaluation data and making placement decisions, each public agency shall:
  (1) Draw upon information from a variety of sources, including aptitude and achievement tests, teacher recommendations, physical condition, social or cultural background, and adaptive behavior;
  (2) Ensure that information obtained from all of these sources is documented and carefully considered;
  (3) Ensure that the placement decision is made by a group of persons knowledgeable about the individual, the meaning of the evaluation data, and placement options. (*Federal Register,* 1992, p. 44822)

IDEA includes definitions and some fairly global criteria for determining eligibility for services for students with the following disabilities: autism, deaf-blindness, deafness, hearing impairment, mental retardation, multiple disabilities, orthopedic impairment, serious emotional disturbance, specific learning disability, speech or language impairment, traumatic brain injury, and visual impairment including blindness. Most states have more specific criteria for determining eligibility for services, and many have different names for the conditions stated in the law. For example, some states use the term *perceptual disability* rather than *learning disability* or *mental handicap* rather than *mental retardation*. The decision of eligibility is made by the multidisciplinary team members during a conference with the parents.

The school personnel required to attend the eligibility meeting include the child's teacher, a representative of special education, and at least one member of the assessment team who can explain the test results. Other members of the school may attend according to need or at the parent's request. The parents may wish to invite others to attend; for example, if the child has a motor impairment, the parents may request that a physical therapist attend. Parents also may invite an **advocate** who is an expert to attend the meeting. The advocate represents the child's best interest and may be a professional from some specialized area or another interested person. Usually, the local education agency will request that an administrative representative attend to commit resources such as specialized therapies or equipment.

advocate Any person who speaks on the behalf of individuals with disabilities and/or their families.

During the eligibility meeting, all members should contribute data, including informal observations, objectively and professionally. The decision to provide the student with special education services or to continue placement in a regular classroom without special education should be based on data presented

special education services Services not provided by regular education but necessary to enable an individual with disabilities to achieve in school.

related services Those services related to special education but not part of the educational setting, such as transportation, therapies, and so on.

during the eligibility meeting. Parents are to be active participants in the eligibility meeting. School personnel should strive to make parents feel comfortable in the meeting and should welcome and carefully consider all of their comments. If the student has been found eligible for services, the team discusses educational interventions and specific **special education services** and **related services**. The federal regulations recommend that students are educated, in as much as possible, with general education students.

Least Restrictive Environment

The concept of least restrictive environment is promoted through the following general regulations of IDEA.

IDEA

§ 300.550

(b) Each public agency shall insure:

(1) That to the maximum extent appropriate, individuals with disabilities, including individuals in public or private institutions or other care facilities, are educated with individuals who are nondisabled, and

(2) That special classes, separate schooling or other removal of children with disabilities from the regular educational environment occurs only when the nature or severity of the disability is such that education in regular classes with the use of supplementary aids and services cannot be achieved satisfactorily. (*Federal Register,* 1992, p. 44823)

mainstreaming Placement of an individual with disabilities in an environment with nondisabled peers.

grade equivalents Grade score assigned to a mean raw score of a group during norming process.

standard scores Scores calculated during norming process of a test; follow normal distribution theory.

According to the federal mandates, students who have been determined eligible for services are to be placed in the least restrictive environment for appropriate educational intervention. The very least restrictive environment is, of course, the general classroom setting, and the most restrictive is one that is completely removed from the mainstream of society, such as an institutional or hospital setting. Although the term **mainstreaming** is used frequently in education and special education, it never appears in the law. It is left to the members of the multidisciplinary team to determine the exact placement of the student, the amount of time spent in the general education classroom and in special education, and to develop the IEP.

Developing the IEP

annual goals Long-term goals for educational intervention.

short-term objectives Behaviorally stated objectives to plan educational interventions for a short period of time.

Every student receiving special education services must have an IEP. This individualized education program or plan must be written in compliance with the regulations and should include the items stated therein. Current levels of educational achievement are expressed in terms of **grade equivalents,** age equivalents, or a **standard score** of some type. The long-term goals, sometimes called **annual goals,** as well as the **short-term objectives** are included in the IEP. Short-term objectives are the educational steps needed to reach the educational goal. Each specific educational service provided through special education, such as speech therapy, must be stated and the goals specified by the team member responsible for service.

The dates of initiation of services and the expected duration are expressed on the IEP. A team member in each area of service must review the IEP at least annually to determine if progress is being made to achieve the short-term objectives and to determine if the long-term goals continue to be appropriate. The methods of evaluating the short-term objectives are stated as well.

☐ **CHECK YOUR UNDERSTANDING**

Complete Activity 2.4.

Activity 2.4

Read the case study. Using the previous information on parent participation, eligibility, and placement procedures, list the events that are not in compliance with federal regulations.

Case Study

John's teacher, Ms. Nogood, is having problems with John in class. He will not listen and does not appear to be learning anything. Ms. Nogood decided she cannot take John another day, so she refers John for testing to "get him out of my class." The referral is given to Mr. I. Dunno, the special education teacher. Mr. Dunno is a very busy man who does not want to wait to test John. Mr. Dunno calls John's parents but gets no answer. Mr. Dunno told Ms. Nogood that John's parents are not at home and says, "I guess I've tried enough contact, and you can document that for me." Ms. Nogood says, "OK." John is given the Out-of-Date Invalid Screening Test. This test indicates that John is not performing as expected in reading. Mr. Dunno tries to call John's parents that same afternoon—again, no answer. The eligibility meeting is set for the next morning at 7:30 A.M. The school psychologist, Ms. Hurryup, does not attend and neither does the principal, Ms. Toobusy. So the next morning, Mr. Dunno and Ms. Nogood decide that John will be placed in the resource room with Ms. Fixall.

List the events that are not in compliance with IDEA:

____

____

____

____

____

____

____

____

Due Process

IDEA was influenced to a large degree by parent organizations and court cases involving individuals with disabilities and their right to education. Although major structural changes in special education are provided, the law remains a source of guidance, leaving implementation to the individual states and local education agencies. When schools implement the provisions of the law, occasionally differences arise between the schools providing the service and the parents of the student with the disability. Therefore, IDEA contains provisions for parents and schools to resolve their differences. These provisions, or **procedural safeguards,** are called due process provisions.

procedural safeguards Provisions of IDEA designed to protect students and parents in the special education process.

The procedural safeguards are inherent throughout the portions of the law concerned with assessment. For example, parental informed consent is considered a procedural safeguard designed to prevent assessment and placement of students without parents' knowledge. Other provisions promote fairness in the decision-making process. Included in these provisions are the parents' right to examine all educational records and the right to seek an **independent educational evaluation** as well as the right to a hearing to resolve differences.

independent educational evaluation Provided by a qualified independent evaluator; a comprehensive evaluation.

The parents of a student who has been evaluated by school personnel may disagree with the results obtained during the assessment process. Should this occur, the parents have the right to obtain an individual evaluation by an outside examiner. The independent evaluation is provided by a qualified professional not employed with the local education agency. Should the independent evaluation results differ from the evaluation results obtained by school personnel, the school must pay for the evaluation. The exception to this is if the school initiates a **third-party hearing** to resolve the different results and the **hearing officer** finds in favor of the school. In this case, the parents would be responsible for paying for the independent evaluation. If, however, favor is found with the parents as a result of the hearing, the school is responsible for payment.

third-party hearing A hearing by an impartial officer that is held to resolve differences between a school and parents of a student with disabilities.

hearing officer Person qualified to hear disputes between schools and parents; not an employee of school agency.

Third-Party Hearing–

The parents and school are provided with procedures for filing complaints and requesting third-party hearings. In a third-party hearing, the parents, independent evaluators, and the school may each explain their side of the disagreement before an objective hearing officer. The third-party hearing officer is a person qualified to hear the case. In some states, third-party hearing officers are lawyers; in other states, the hearing officers are special education professionals, such as college faculty who teach special education courses to prepare teachers.

Parents should be advised before the hearing that although counsel (an attorney) is not required for the hearing, they do have the right to secure counsel as well as experts to give testimony. After hearing each side of the complaint, the hearing officer reaches a decision. On finding in favor of the parents, the school must comply with the ruling or appeal to a state-level hearing. In turn, if favor is found with the school, the parents must comply. If the parents do not wish to comply, they may be able to request a state-level hearing or file an appeal with a civil court.

While the school and parents are involved with due process and hearing procedures, the student remains in the classroom setting in which she was placed before the complaint was filed.

Research and Issues Concerning IDEA

IDEA states that each school agency shall actively take steps to ensure that parents participate in the IEP process in two major ways. First, the parent must agree by informed consent before the preplacement evaluation and before receiving services in special education. Second, the parents are to participate in the development of the IEP once eligibility has been determined. Legally, parents have the right to participate in the evaluation and IEP processes, and schools are mandated to involve parents; however, research has uncovered several problem areas concerning parental involvement.

The first right, informed consent, is compounded by issues such as parental literacy, parental comprehension of the meaning of legal terminology, and the lack of time professionals spend with parents explaining testing and special education. Roit and Pfohl (1984) studied the readability levels of materials distributed to parents during the assessment and IEP processes and found that the readability ranged from the fifth- to the eighth-grade level with an average readability level of about sixth grade. Parents' rights materials may be made more difficult to understand because of their use of highly specialized vocabulary. According to a study involving observation and analysis of interactions in IEP conferences, parents' rights were merely "glossed over in the majority of conferences" (Goldstein, Strickland, Turnbull, & Curry, 1980, p. 283). This suggests that sufficient time is not allotted to discuss issues of central concern to parents.

The second major provision granted to parents in the IEP process is active participation in the IEP conference by contributing to the formulation of objectives and long-term goals for their children. Evidence clearly indicates that parents remain passive in this process. In the traditional IEP conference, parents were found to be passive and to attend merely to receive information (Barnett, Zins, & Wise, 1984; Brantlinger, 1987; Goldstein et al., 1980; Goldstein & Turnbull, 1982; Vaughn, Bos, Harrell, & Lasky, 1988; Weber & Stoneman, 1986).

Several reasons for the parents' passivity have been hypothesized, including parents' belief that educators are responsible for formulating the IEP, parents feeling out of place during the IEP conference (too many professionals attending made them feel nervous), and parents' contributions having no effect on the formulation of the IEP (Weber & Stoneman, 1986). Other reasons found for lack of participation by parents are that they lacked experience in the IEP process (Barnett et al., 1984) and felt confused about their role during the IEP conference (Goldstein et al., 1980). One study found that parental involvement increased when a school counselor attended the meetings and assumed the role of a parent advocate (Goldstein & Turnbull, 1982), lending support to the notion that parents feel outnumbered and uncomfortable during conferences. In another study, parents involved in conferences concerning their preschool children felt that the information they received about special education services was very important and they valued the opportunity to be involved in the decision-making process (Sontag & Schacht, 1994). It seems that parents gain needed information in eligibility and IEP meetings; however, additional strategies for their involvement would increase parents' contributions.

An area of additional concern involves working with parents of culturally or educationally different backgrounds. Some parents may have difficulty understanding the complex concepts presented due to their reading levels and vocabulary. Parents who do not speak English may have problems with legal terms and specialized concepts even though materials presented to them are in their native language. The parents of students from culturally different backgrounds may lack a basic understanding of the special education process, services available, and their expected role during the IEP process. To compound matters, parents from diverse backgrounds may devalue the importance of their participation or may not be prepared to function as advocates for their child (Barnett et al., 1984). Salend and Taylor (1993) suggested that the parents' level of acculturation be considered, noting that children may become acculturated much more quickly than their parents. In addition, Salend and Taylor have reminded educators to consider the family's history of discrimination and the family structure, since these factors may have an impact on the family's interactions with school personnel.

One method for helping parents understand and work with professionals in special education has been suggested by Clark, Overton, and Williams (1990). In a consulting model they developed for multidisciplinary team members to use with parents, Clark and colleagues advocate using a case manager to work with families during the prereferral stage and throughout the IEP process. Figure 2.5 illustrates the main components of this model. Direct efforts to work with families may eliminate unnecessary assessment and possibly reduce the number of third-party hearings.

Nondiscriminatory Assessment

Perhaps no other area in the field of psychoeducational assessment has received more attention than that of nondiscriminatory assessment. Much of the research and controversial issues center around the overrepresentation of minority students in special education classes. **Minority overrepresentation** is found to occur when the percentage of minority students enrolled in particular special education classes is larger than the percentage of minority students enrolled in the local education agency. In other words, if classes for mildly disabled students were comprised of 28% minority students yet only 12% of the local education agency was comprised of minorities, the local education

minority overrepresentation When the percentage of a culturally different group is greater in special education classes than in the local education agency.

Initial contact

The teacher contacts a multidisciplinary team member (consultant) for the students identified to be "at risk."

Parent, consultant, school

The parent and consultant visit the classroom together to assess environment.

Intervention plan

Parent, teacher, and consultant meet to design intervention plan; parents are trained in strategies.

Evaluation and testing

If intervention strategies prove unsuccessful, the team members complete a psychoeducational evaluation.

Pre-IEP conference training

The consultant prepares the parents for the IEP conference by:
defining terms, both legal and special education terms;
explaining assessment procedures; and
providing advocacy training, role playing, and discussing possible outcomes.

Eligibility and IEP conferences

The consultant helps parents to ask questions, explains terms, and monitors parents' understanding of their rights.

Figure 2.5
Consulting model (Clark et al., 1990).

agency's special education classes would have an overrepresentation of minority students.

Reschly (1988) reported that overrepresentation of minority students appears to occur in classes for students with mild mental retardation. Using data from the Federal Office for Civil Rights (OCR) reports of 1978 and 1980, the Panel on Selection and Placement of Students in Programs for the Mentally Retarded (Heller, Holtzman, & Messick, 1982) reported that in most states disproportionately more minorities than nonminorities are enrolled in classes for students with mild mental retardation; the most disproportionate enrollments occurred in the southern area of the United States. Additionally, the U.S. Department of Education reported in 1992 that minorities, particularly black students, comprise a disproportionate number of the total students receiving special education services.

The number of students classified as learning disabled has increased since the passage of PL 94–142 (Chalfant, 1985). This increase has apparently resulted in disproportionate increases in minority students being labeled as learning disabled as well as mildly mentally retarded. Mick (1985) reported an increase in Hispanic students in classes for students with learning disabilities, and Tucker (1980) reported an overrepresentation of both black and Hispanic students in such classes. A study examining the relationship between state financial resources and special education categories reported that states with higher numbers of children considered living in poverty had lower percentages of students categorized as learning disabled and states with more financial resources had a higher percentage of students with learning disabilities (McLaughlin & Owings, 1992).

Much of the blame for the overrepresentation of minorities in special education has been attributed to referral and evaluation practices. The amount of attention given to the assessment process may be due in part to IDEA's emphasis on nondiscriminatory assessment. The law clearly states that educational agencies should use evaluation procedures that are not racially or culturally discriminatory. This can have many implications when assessing students who have linguistic differences and those who may come from culturally different backgrounds or deprived environments. The following list of problems of bias in assessment is adapted from Reynolds (1982):

1. *Inappropriate content.* Students from minority populations may lack exposure to certain items on the instrument.

2. *Inappropriate standardization samples.* Ethnic minorities were not represented in the normative sample at the time of development of the instrument.

3. *Examiner and language.* White, English-speaking examiners may intimidate minority students and students from different linguistic backgrounds.

4. *Inequitable social consequences.* As a result of discriminatory assessment practices, minority students may be relegated to lower educational placements, which may ultimately result in lower paying jobs.

5. *Measurement of different constructs.* White test developers designed instruments assumed to measure academic or cognitive ability for all students. When used with minority students, however, the instruments may measure only the degree to which the minority students have been able to absorb white middle-class culture.

6. *Different predictive validity.* Instruments designed to predict the educational or academic outcome or potential for white students may not do so for minority students.

Additional problems in biased assessment include overinterpretation of test results. This means that an examiner may report to have assessed a trait, attribute, or characteristic that the instrument is not designed to measure (Flaugher, 1978). For example, an examiner may report a cognitive ability level or a behavioral trait based on the results of a student's academic achievement test. The assessment is inaccurate because the test was designed to measure academic achievement only.

Another problem that may arise in assessment is that of testing students whose dominant language is not English. Although some instruments are published in languages other than English, such as Spanish, the translations may result in different conceptual meanings and influence test performance and test results (Fradd & Hallman, 1983).

A trend in the literature reflects a movement toward complete revision of assessment practice in special education (Artiles & Trent, 1994; Duffy, Salvia, Tucker, & Ysseldyke, 1981; Reschly, 1991; Ysseldyke, 1987). Some studies focus on restructuring the educational system or the educational strategies that occur before the assessment process in order to reduce bias (Artiles & Trent, 1994; Heller et al., 1982; Maheady, Towne, Algozzine, Mercer, & Ysseldyke, 1983; Reschly, 1988; Ysseldyke & Regan, 1980). Additional suggestions for revising the psychoeducational process include improving methods of test selection (Fradd & Hallman, 1983), improving the way test results are used to make important decisions (Reschly, 1981; Taylor, 1991), and earlier educational intervention and general improvements in services for all children (Reschly, 1988).

One proposal to improve the assessment process as well as the special education system in general suggests that students receive academic support through simple 20/20 analysis approach (Reynolds, Zetlin, & Wang, 1993). This approach proposes that students falling below the 20th percentile or placing above the 80th (top 20th percentile) receive interventions that will strengthen or enrich the students' academic achievement. These authors suggest that students would then be served without labels, monies would be distributed to help all in need, and parents would become more actively involved in the planning of interventions.

IDEA mandates that the evaluation of students for possible special education services must involve the use of tests that have been validated for the purpose for which they are used. The APA (1985) *Standards* address this issue as well. Regardless of these legal and professional guidelines, most norm-referenced tests used in schools are not diagnostic in nature but rather measure expected academic achievement or intellectual functioning. The developmental process of many instruments gives little attention to validity studies with disabled populations. Fuchs, Fuchs, Benowitz, and Barringer (1987) called for discontinuing use of tests with no validation data on disabled populations if those tests are used for diagnosis and placement of students with disabilities. The improvements in new instruments and revised instruments with attention given to minority and disabled populations are promising.

The regulations that guide the assessment process call for careful selection of assessment instruments and state that the purpose of the assessment is to determine educational needs. The regulations and the APA (1985) *Standards* emphasize that professionals should select tests that will address all areas of concern. Evidence shows, however, that personnel who administer tests tend to select technically inadequate tests (Davis & Shepard, 1983; LaGrow,

Prochow-LaGrow, 1982; Ysseldyke, Algozzine, Regan, & Potter, 1980) and that educators are seldom concerned with the technical adequacy of those instruments (Ysseldyke & Thurlow, 1983).

Both IDEA and the APA (1985) *Standards* contain language requiring that, at a minimum, professionals be trained in assessment and, more specifically, that training or expertise is available to enable the examiner to evaluate students with disabilities. Many professionals responsible for the evaluation of students with disabilities lack competence in test selection, scoring, and interpretations (Bennett, 1981; Bennett & Shepherd, 1982; McNutt & Mandelbaum, 1980; Ysseldyke & Thurlow, 1983). These findings cast serious doubt that compliance is met by special educators in all cases. McLoughlin (1985) advocated raising the standards for educators who are responsible for using standardized instruments for diagnosis of learning problems.

The prevalence of inadequate skills in test selection, scoring, and interpretation by special educators has resulted in support for simpler measurement methods that are more directly related to actual school curriculum and expected learner outcomes. Alternative assessment techniques, such as informal assessment and curriculum-based assessment, are supported by professionals in the field (Fuchs, Fuchs, & Maxwell, 1988; Reschly, 1991; Shinn, 1988).

Of all of the controversial areas in nondiscriminatory assessment, the most controversial area remains that of IQ testing for the purpose of determining eligibility for services under the diagnostic category of mental retardation. One professional in the field (Jackson, 1975) called for banning the use of IQ tests. Some state and local education agencies, either by litigation or voluntarily, have discontinued the use of IQ tests with minority students. Evidence indicates, however, that IQ scores continue to be the most influential test score variable in the decision-making process (Sapp, Chissom, & Horton, 1984). This practice continues even though regulations state that decisions should not be based on tests that yield a single IQ score. IDEA also requires that other input, such as comments from parents and teachers and adaptive behavior measures, be considered in the decision-making process.

☐ **CHECK YOUR UNDERSTANDING**

Complete Activity 2.5.

Activity 2.5

Use the research presented in the previous section to answer the following questions.

1. Parental literacy, comprehension of terminology, and readability level of IEP materials and parents' rights booklets may all contribute to the overrepresentation of minorities in special education. Explain why, and present suggestions to alleviate these problems.

____

____

____

2. What are the reasons cited in the literature for passive parental participation?

3. Why might the IEP process be discriminatory against parents of students from culturally or linguistically different populations?

4. How would a consulting model aid in eliminating the difficulties faced by parents from culturally or linguistically different backgrounds?

5. How might the assessment process be biased?

6. What do you think about the 20/20 analysis proposal?

The Multidisciplinary Team and the Decision-Making Process

Even though the regulations call for a variety of professionals to be involved in the assessment and IEP processes, the team usually consists of parents, teachers, school psychologist, and administrator (Ysseldyke & Thurlow, 1983). Although parents attend the eligibility and IEP conferences, research has shown that they remain passive participants (Barnett et al., 1984; Goldstein et al., 1980; Vaughn et al., 1988; Weber & Stoneman, 1986; Ysseldyke & Thurlow, 1983). When parents do participate, however, some evidence indicates that their participation does influence decision making (Sontag & Schacht, 1994; Ysseldyke & Thurlow, 1983). The law states that educational decisions are to be made during the conference, but research indicates that very little time is spent discussing educational alternatives; in fact, much of the conference time is used to justify placement recommendations made by the team members (Ysseldyke & Thurlow, 1983). This finding lends support to the notion that many decisions are made before the eligibility meeting and merely supported by input from team members during the conference.

The decision-making process is to include all members of the multidisciplinary team as another method of increasing objectivity. In a review of analogue research, Huebner (1991) determined that often teacher perceptions disproportionately influence the team's decision. This results in inaccurate decision making and may be considered a form of bias in the assessment process. School psychologists, members of the multidisciplinary team, may rely on clinical judgment to make eligibility decisions and fail to consistently consider information across cases; these practices, too, may lead to errors in the decision-making process (Ward, Ward, & Clark, 1991). These errors indicate the need for objectivity and participation by all team members in the decision-making process.

Least Restrictive Environment

IDEA is designed to provide special education support services in the least restrictive environment. In many cases, this means that a student will be served within the general education classroom setting. Macready (1991) proposed that when a decision is made to place a student in an environment other than the general education setting, it should be viewed conceptually as a "foster placement rather than as a placement for adoption" (p. 151).

Decisions of appropriate educational environments should be made carefully. Morsink and Lenk (1992) suggested that each decision be made on an individual basis and that the teacher's training and effectiveness in instruction and all environmental factors, such as the impact on other students or limiting environmental factors, be considered. Morsink and Lenk warned that a proposed placement, seen at first as the least restrictive environment, may indeed be an inappropriate environment when these factors are not considered to be favorable.

The provision of least restrictive environment may be implemented in various ways in different states and LEAs. One study of six states found that finances, parent advocacy, categorically based systems, and varying layers of organizational structure all influenced the way that the least restrictive environment provision was implemented (Hasazi, Johnston, Liggett, & Schattman, 1994). This study found that these variables were complex and interconnected.

The implementation of least restrictive environment has been interpreted through litigation in several state and federal courts (Kubicek, 1994). Several of these court cases recognized the unfair financial burden placed on individual school divisions if all special education students are served in their neighborhood schools. Court decisions have also acknowledged that the impact on students within the general education environment and the time needed by the teacher to serve some individuals with disabilities should be considered in the implementation of least restrictive environment. It seems clear that the concept of least restrictive environment has been narrowly interpreted in some cases heard in the courts.

Due Process

The procedural safeguards provided through due process seek to involve the parents in all stages of the IEP process rather than only during third-party hearings. Due process provisions specify at least 36 grounds for either schools or parents to seek a hearing (Turnbull, Turnbull, & Strickland, 1979). If abused, the process could result in chaos in the operation of school systems. The years since the law was enacted have witnessed a great deal of interpretation of uncertain issues through the judicial system (Turnbull, 1986).

Due process may be discriminatory because its cost may prohibit some families from following this procedure. The cost may involve both financial and human resources. The remaining problems are best summed up by Turnbull (1986):

> Problems remain. The greatest one seems to be the cost of due process. Cost consists of three elements: (1) the actual financial cost of the hearings—preparing for them, hiring attorneys and expert witnesses, paying for the documents required for evidence, and pursuing an appeal; (2) the emotional and psychic cost—the enormous energy and stress involved in a hearing and its appeal; and (3) the cost that consists of time spent and perhaps lost, when the child may (or may not) be receiving an appropriate education. (p. 192)

Because the financial cost may be so burdensome, educators are concerned that due process in IDEA may become yet another vehicle that increases, rather than decreases, discriminatory practices. Budoff and Orenstein (1981) found that due process hearings were overrepresented by upper-middle-class parents and recommended using **mediation** without counsel as an alternative to the expensive hearing process. Increasing parental involvement and communication between parents and schools from the prereferral stage through the decision-making stage may decrease the need for third-party hearings.

mediation Process of settling a dispute between parents and schools without a full third-party hearing.

Should parents or schools exhaust the hearing process without satisfaction, the right remains for either party to take the case through the civil court system. Much of IDEA has yet to be interpreted through the judicial system.

Exercises

Part I

Match the following terms with the correct definitions.

A. PL 94–142
B. short-term objectives
C. grade equivalent
D. preplacement evaluation
E. due process
F. minority overrepresentation
G. procedural safeguards
H. mainstreaming
I. advocate
J. Independent evaluation
K. PL 99-457
L. IDEA

N. compliance
O. informed consent
P. comprehensive educational evaluation
Q. parents' rights booklets
R. hearing officer
S. annual goals
T. case manager
U. nondiscriminatory assessment
V. surrogate parent
W. mediation
X. Individual Family Service Plan

_______ **1.** To be within the regulations or confines of PL 94–142.
_______ **2.** The right guaranteed to citizens receiving special education services to third-party hearings in matters of disagreement.
_______ **3.** Assessment that is fair to persons from diverse cultural and linguistic backgrounds.
_______ **4.** The original act that grants the right to a free appropriate education in the least restrictive environment to all individuals with disabilities.
_______ **5.** A person who speaks on behalf of a student with disabilities and/or the family of that student.
_______ **6.** The term used colloquially to describe the placement of a student with disabilities within the general education classroom.
_______ **7.** The score assigned to a mean raw score for a particular grade of a norming population.
_______ **8.** Long-term plans for educational intervention, usually for the duration of a school year.
_______ **9.** A complete evaluation in all educational areas of suspected disability.
_______ **10.** Evaluation by a qualified professional not employed by the school agency.
_______ **11.** Provisions included in IDEA that are designed to protect disabled individuals and their parents.
_______ **12.** A member of the IEP team who takes charge of a student from the prereferral stage through the evaluation process.
_______ **13.** A qualified independent professional who hears both sides of a dispute involving a special education student and reaches a decision.
_______ **14.** When the percentage of a culturally different group enrolled in special education is greater than the percentage of that group in the local education area.
_______ **15.** Defined by IDEA to mean that parents are aware of the intentions of the school and that they grant permission with the understanding that they may withdraw permission at any time.
_______ **16.** The Education of the Handicapped Act Amendments of 1986.
_______ **17.** Process of settling a dispute before a full third-party hearing.
_______ **18.** Written material that presents to families their rights as provided by IDEA.

________ **19.** A person who has been appointed by the court to legally represent the child when parents are unable to do so.

________ **20.** The intervention plan designed to involve the family in the early education of infants and preschoolers.

________ **21.** The new name for PL 94–142.

________ **22.** Behaviorally stated, these plans are for a short-time period.

________ **23.** This evaluation must be completed before any student can be placed in a special education setting.

Part II

Answer the following questions.

1. What were the sources of pressure that resulted in substantial legal changes in the 1970s? ____

____

2. According to IDEA, what agency is responsible for ensuring that proper assessment procedures are followed? ____

____

3. What are the three major components of the definition of "consent" according to the regulations?

(a) ____

____

(b) ____

____

(c) ____

____

4. In informing parents and assessing students, what does the law require regarding communication? ____

____

____

5. The nondiscriminatory assessment practices must, as a minimum, ensure that evaluation materials are:

(a) ____

____

(b) ____

____

(c) ____

____

(d) ____

____

(e) ____

____

(f) ____

____

(g) ______________________________

(h) ______________________________

6. APA Standard 6.10 states that when a professional is requested to test a student who has a disability with which the examiner is not familiar, that professional should ______________________________

7. APA Standard 6.12, which warns against using screening instruments for purposes other than screening, is like what component of the federal regulations? ______________________________

8. What are the requirements listed by the federal regulations pertaining to parent participation? ______________________________

9. What specific evaluation procedures are included in the regulations for students with learning disabilities? ______________________________

10. How are students with attention problems served in school?
____

11. What statements are used in the regulations that reflect the philosophy of "mainstreaming"?
____

12. How are the federal mandates interpreted over time?
____

Part III

Check each statement that is supported by the research cited in this chapter.

1. Informed consent
   - ________ **a.** Informed consent is compounded by problems of literacy, parental understanding of legal terms, and lack of time professionals spend discussing important issues with parents.
   - ________ **b.** Parents from different cultural or linguistic backgrounds have no more difficulty understanding the IEP process than other parents.

_________ **c.** Parents' rights booklets are written, on the average, at about the sixth-grade reading level.

2. Parental involvement

_________ **a.** Parents seem to remain passively involved in the IEP process.

_________ **b.** Parents may feel out of place, nervous, or outnumbered during conferences.

_________ **c.** Additional strategies to involve parents are not warranted.

_________ **d.** The Clark et al. (1990) consulting model advocates use of a consultant-liaison.

_________ **e.** Parents feel that their input in the decision-making process is valuable.

3. Minority overrepresentation

_________ **a.** This occurs in classes for the mildly mentally retarded.

_________ **b.** Much of the blame for minority overrepresentation is placed on the referral and evaluation practices in the field.

_________ **c.** Students from different linguistic background should have no problem with assessment instruments that have been translated into their native language.

_________ **d.** Minority overrepresentation happens equally across all areas of the United States.

_________ **e.** A recent report from the U.S. Department of Education indicates that minority overrepresentation is no longer a problem in special education.

4. Selection of assessment instruments

_________ **a.** Some experts in the field call for discontinuing the use of tests, with no validation studies on disabled populations, for diagnosis and placement of disabled persons.

_________ **b.** Instruments are to be selected for educational purposes and are always validated for the specific intended use.

_________ **c.** Evidence indicates that professionals always select technically adequate tests.

5. Team decision making

_________ **a.** All team members contribute an equal amount of information and influence in the decision-making process.

_________ **b.** Most of the time spent in meetings is spent explaining the test results and justifying a decision.

6. Least restrictive environment

_________ **a.** The courts have defined least restrictive environment more narrowly than the law's original intent.

_________ **b.** According to some court decisions, the impact on general education students must be considered when determining the least restrictive environment.

________ **c.** Research suggests that financial resources and administrative structure interact and influence how the concept of least restrictive environment is implemented in LEAs.

Part IV

Summarize the research findings.

1. Summarize the research findings on the multidisciplinary team decision-making process. ____
____
____
____
____
____
____
____

2. Summarize the research findings about due process. ________________
____
____
____
____
____

References

American Psychological Association (1985). *Standards for Educational and Psychological Testing.* Washington, DC: Author.

Artiles, A. J., & Trent, S. C. (1994). Overrepresentation of minority students in special education: A continuing debate. *The Journal of Special Education, 27*(4), 410–437.

Barnett, D., Zins, J., & Wise, L. (1984). An analysis of parental participation as a means of reducing bias in the education of handicapped children. *Special Services in the Schools, 1,* 71–84.

Bennett, R. (1981). Professional competence and the assessment of exceptional children. *The Journal of Special Education, 15,* 437–446.

Bennett, R., & Shepherd, M. (1982). Basic measurement proficiency of learning disability specialists. *Learning Disabilities Quarterly, 5,* 177–183.

Brantlinger, E. (1987). Making decisions about special education placement: Do low-income parents have the information they need? *Journal of Learning Disabilities, 20,* 94–101.

Budoff, M., & Orenstein, A. (1981). Special education appeals hearings: Are they fair and are they helping? *Exceptional Education Quarterly, 2,* 37–48.

Chalfant, J. (1985). Identifying learning disabled students: A summary of the national task force report. *Learning Disabilities Focus, 1,* 9–20.

Clark, T., Overton, T., & Williams, V. (1990). Increasing minority parent participation to reduce bias in the referral/assessment process: A consulting model for a multidisciplinary/parental liaison. Unpublished manuscript.

Davis, W., & Shepard, L. (1983). Specialist use of tests and clinical judgement in the diagnosis of learning disabilities. *Learning Disabilities Quarterly, 6,* 128–137.

Duffy, J. B., Salvia, J., Tucker, J., & Ysseldyke, J. (1981). Nonbiased assessment: A need for operationalism. *Exceptional Children, 7,* 427–434.

Federal Register. (1993). Washington, DC: U.S. Government Printing Office, July 30, 1993.

Federal Register. (1992). Washington, DC: U.S. Government Printing Office, September 29, 1992.

Federal Register. (1977). Washington, DC: U.S. Government Printing Office, August 23, 1977.

Flaugher, R. (1978). The many definitions of test bias. *American Psychologist, 33,* 671–679.

Fradd, S., & Hallman, C. (1983). Implications of psychological and educational research for assessment and instruction of culturally and linguistically different students. *Learning Disabilities Quarterly, 6,* 468–477.

Fuchs, D., Fuchs, L., Benowitz, S., & Barringer, K. (1987). Norm-referenced tests: Are they valid for uses with handicapped students? *Exceptional Children, 54,* 263–271.

Fuchs, L., Fuchs, D., & Maxwell, L. (1988). The validity of informal reading comprehension measures. *Remedial and Special Education, 9*(2), 20–28.

Goldstein, S., Strickland, B., Turnbull, A., & Curry, L. (1980). An observational analysis of the IEP conference. *Exceptional Children, 46,* 278–286.

Goldstein, S., & Turnbull, A. (1982). Strategies to increase parent participation in IEP conferences. *Exceptional Children, 48,* 360–361.

Hasazi, S. B., Johnston, A. P., Liggett, A. M., & Schattman, R. A. (1994). A qualitative policy study of the least restrictive environment provision of the Individuals With Disabilities Act. *Exceptional Children, 60*(6), 491–507.

Heller, K., Holtzman, W., & Messick, S. (Eds.). (1982). *Placing children in special education: A strategy for equity,* Washington, DC: National Academy Press.

Huebner, E. S. (1991). Bias in special education decisions: The contribution of analogue research. *School Psychology Quarterly, 6*(1), 50–65.

Jackson, G. D. (1975). Another psychological view from the Association of Black Psychologists. *American Psychologist, 30,* 88–93.

Killalea Associates. (1982). Nationwide special education placements, by sex, and by race or ethnicity. In K. Heller, W. Holtzman, & S. Messick (Eds.), *Children in special education: A strategy for equity* (p. 10). Washington, DC: National Academy Press.

Kubicek, F. C. (1994). Special education reform in light of select state and federal court decisions. *The Journal of Special Education, 28*(1), 27–42.

LaGrow, S., & Prochow-LaGrow, J. (1982). Technical adequacy of the most popular tests selected by responding school psychologists in Illinois. *Psychology in the schools, 19,* 186–189.

Larry P. v. Riles, 343 F. Supp. 1306, aff'd., 502 F.2d 963, further proceedings, 495F. Supp. 926, aff'd., 502 F.2d 693 (9th Cir. 1984).

Macready, T. (1991). Special education: Some thoughts for policy makers. *Educational Psychology in Practice, 7*(3), 148–152.

Maheady, L., Towne, R., Algozzine, B., Mercer, J., & Ysseldyke, J. (1983). Minority overrepresentation: A case for alternative practices prior to referral. *Learning Disabilities Quarterly, 6,* 448–455.

McLaughlin, M. J., & Owings, M. F. (1992). Relationship among states' fiscal and demographic data and the implementation of P.L. 94–142. *Exceptional Children, 59*(3), 247–261.

McLoughlin, J. (1985). Training educational diagnosticians. [Monograph]. *Diagnostique, 10,* 176–196.

McNutt, G., & Mandelbaum, L. (1980). General assessment competencies for special education teachers. *Exceptional Education Quarterly, 1,* 21–29.

Mick, L. (1985). Assessment procedures as related to enrollment patterns of Hispanic students in special education. *Educational Researcher Quarterly, 9,* 27–35.

Morsink, C. V., & Lenk, L. L. (1992). The delivery of special education programs and services. *Remedial and Special Education, 13*(6), 33–43.

Reschly, D. J. (1991). Bias in cognitive assessment: Implications for future litigation and professional practices. *Diagnostique, 17*(1), 86–90.

Reschly, D. J. (1988). Minority mild mental retardation overrepresentation: Legal issues, research findings, and reform trends. In M. C. Wang, M. C. Reynolds, & H. J. Walberg (Eds.), *Handbook of special education: Research and practice: Vol. 2. Mildly handicapped conditions* (pp. 23–41). New York: Pergamon.

Reschly, D. (1981). Psychological testing in educational clarification and placement. *American Psychologist, 36,* 1094–1102.

Reynolds, C. (1982). The problems of bias in psychological assessment. In C. R. Reynolds & T. Gutkin (Eds.), *The handbook of school psychology* (pp. 179–180). New York: Wiley.

Reynolds, M. C., Zetlin, A. G., & Wang, M. C. (1993). 20/20 Analysis: Taking a closer look at the margins. *Exceptional Children, 59*(4), 294–300.

Roit, M., & Pfohl, W. (1984). The readability of P.L. 94–142 parent materials: Are parents truly informed? *Exceptional Children, 50,* 496–505.

Salend, S. J., & Taylor, L. (1993). Working with families: A cross-cultural perspective. *Remedial and Special Education, 14*(5), 25–32, 39.

Sapp, G., Chissom, B., & Horton, W. (1984). An investigation of the ability of selected instruments to discriminate areas of exceptional class designation. *Psychology in the Schools, 5,* 258–262.

Shinn, M. (1988). Development of curriculum-based local norms for use in special education decision-making. *School Psychology Review, 17,* 61–80.

Silver, S. (1987). Compliance with PL 94–142 mandates: Policy implications. (ERIC Document Reproduction Service No. ED 284705)

Sontag, J. C., & Schacht, R. (1994). An ethnic comparison of parent and information needs in early intervention. *Exceptional Children, 60*(5), 422–433.

Taylor, R. L. (1991). Bias in cognitive assessment: Issues, implications, and future directions. *Diagnostique, 17*(1), 3–5.

Tucker, J. (1980). Ethnic proportions in classes for the learning disabled: Issues in nonbiased assessment. *The Journal of Special Education, 14,* 93–105.

Turnbull, H. R. (1986). *Free and appropriate public education: The law and children with disabilities.* Denver, CO: Love Publishing.

Turnbull, H. R. (1990). *Free and appropriate public education: The law and children with disabilities* (3rd ed.). Denver, CO: Love Publishing.

Turnbull, H. R., Turnbull, A. P., & Strickland, B. (1979). Procedural due process: The two-edged sword that the untrained should not unsheath. *Journal of Education, 161,* 40–59.

U.S. Department of Education. (1992). *Fourteenth annual report to Congress on the implementation of the Individuals With Disabilities Education Act.* Washington, DC: Author.

U.S. Department of Education. (1991). *Memorandum to chief state school officers.* Washington, DC: Author.

Vaughn, S., Bos, C., Harrell, J., & Lasky, B. (1988). Parent participation in the initial placement/IEP conference ten years after mandated involvement. *Journal of Learning Disabilities, 21,* 82–89.

Ward, S. B., Ward, T. J., & Clark, H. T. (1991). Classification congruence among school psychologists and its relationship to type of referral question and professional experience. *Journal of School Psychology, 29,* 89–108.

Weber, J., & Stoneman, Z. (1986). Parental nonparticipation as a means of reducing bias in the education of handicapped children. *Special Services in the Schools, 1,* 71–84.

Ysseldyke, J. E. (1987). Clarification of handicapped students. In M. C. Wang, M. C. Reynolds, & H. J. Walberg (Eds.), *Handbook of special education: Research and practice: Vol. 1. Learner characteristics and adaptive education.* New York: Pergamon. Press.

Ysseldyke, J., Algozzine, B., Regan, R., & Potter, M. (1980). Technical adequacy of tests used by professionals in simulated decision making. *Psychology in the Schools, 17,* 202–209.

Ysseldyke, J., & Regan, R. (1980). Nondiscriminatory assessment: A formative model. *Exceptional Children, 46,* 465–466.

Ysseldyke, J., & Thurlow, M. (1983). *Identification/classification research: An integrative summary of findings* (Research Report No. 142). Minneapolis: University of Minnesota, Institute for Research on Learning Disabilities.

Part Two

Technical Prerequisites of Understanding Assessment

Chapter Three
Descriptive Statistics

Chapter Four
Reliability and Validity

Chapter Five
An Introduction to Norm-Referenced Assessment

Chapter Three

Descriptive Statistics

Key Terms

raw score
norm-referenced tests
nominal scale
ordinal scale
interval scale
ratio scale
derived scores
standard scores
descriptive statistics
measures of central tendency
normal distribution
frequency distribution
mode
bimodal distribution
multimodal distribution
frequency polygon
median
mean
standard deviation
variability
measures of dispersion
variance
range
skewed
positively skewed
negatively skewed
percentile ranks
z scores

Why Is Measurement Important?

Psychoeducational assessment using standardized instruments historically has been applied in the educational decision-making process. To properly use standardized instruments, one must understand test-selection criteria, basic principles of measurement, administration techniques, and scoring procedures. Careful interpretation of test results relies on these abilities. Thus, research that questions the assessment competence of special educators and other professionals is frightening because the educational future of so many individuals is at risk.

Of concern are studies indicating typical types of mistakes made by professionals in the field: Professionals identified students as eligible for services when test scores were within the average range and relied instead on referral information to make decisions (Algozzine & Ysseldyke, 1981). Data presented during educational planning conferences played little if any part in the team members' decisions (Ysseldyke, Algozzine, Richey, & Graden, 1982). Professionals continued to select poor-quality instruments when better tests were available (Davis & Shepard, 1983; Ysseldyke, Algozzine, Regan, & Potter, 1980).

Research by Huebner (1988, 1989) indicated that professionals made errors in the diagnosis of learning disabilities more frequently when scores were reported in percentiles. This reflects inadequate understanding of data interpretation.

Eaves (1985) cited common errors made by professionals during the assessment process. Some of the test examiners' most common errors, adapted from Eaves' research, include:

1. Using instruments in the assessment process solely because those instruments are stipulated by school administrators.
2. Regularly using instruments for purposes other than those for which tests have been validated.
3. Taking the recommended use at face value.
4. Using the quickest instruments available even though those instruments may not assess the areas of concern.

5. Using currently popular instruments for assessment.
6. Failing to establish effective rapport with the examinee.
7. Failing to document behaviors of the examinee during assessment that may be of diagnostic value.
8. Failing to adhere to standardized administration rules, which may include:
   a. Failing to follow starting rules.
   b. Failing to follow basal and ceiling rules.
   c. Omitting actual incorrect responses on the protocol, which could aid in error analysis and diagnosis.
   d. Failing to determine actual chronological age or grade placement.
9. Making various scoring errors, such as:
   a. Making simple counting errors.
   b. Making simple subtraction errors.
   c. Counting items above the ceiling as correct and/or items below the basal as incorrect.
   d. Entering the wrong norm table, row, or column to obtain a derived score.
   e. Extensively using developmental scores when inappropriate.
   f. Showing lack of knowledge regarding alternative measures of performance.
10. Ineffectively interpreting assessment results for educational program use. (pp. 26–27)

The occurrence of these types of errors illustrates why educators need a basic understanding of the measurement principles used in assessment. McLoughlin (1985) advocated training special educators to the level of superior practice rather than meeting only minimum competencies of psychoeducational assessment. The *Standards for Educational and Psychological Testing* (APA, 1985) warn that when special educators have little or no training in the basic principles of measurement, assessment instruments could be misused.

Much of the foundation of good practice in psychoeducational assessment lies in a thorough understanding of test reliability and validity as well as basic measurement principles. Borg, Worthen, and Valcarce (1986) found that most teachers believe that understanding basic principles of measurement is an important aspect of classroom teaching and evaluation. Yet research has shown that professionals who were believed to be specialists in working with students with learning problems were able to correctly answer only 50% of the items on a test of measurement principles (Bennett & Shepherd, 1982).

Therefore, this chapter is designed to promote the development of a basic understanding of general principles of measurement and the application of those principles.

Getting Meaning from Numbers

Any teacher who scores a test, either a published test or a teacher-made test, will subtract the number of items a student missed from the number of items presented to by the student. This number, known as the **raw score,** is of little value to the teacher unless a frame of reference exists for that number. The frame of reference might be comparing the number of items the student answered correctly with the number the student answered correctly on the previous day, such as in direct daily measurement (e.g., Monday, 5 out of 10 responses correct; Tuesday, 6 out of 10 responses correct; etc.). The frame of reference might be a national sample of students the same age who attempted the same items in the same manner on a **norm-referenced** standardized test. In all cases, teachers must clearly understand what can and cannot be inferred from numerical data gathered on small samples of behavior known as *tests*.

raw score The first score obtained in testing; usually represents the number of items correct.

norm-referenced tests Tests that are designed to compare an individual student's scores with national averages.

Review of Numerical Scales

Numbers can denote different meanings from different scales. The scale that has the least meaning for educational measurement purposes is the **nominal scale.** The nominal scale consists of numbers used only for identification purposes, such as student ID numbers or the numbers on racecars. These numbers cannot be used in mathematical operations. For example, if racecars were labeled with letters of the alphabet rather than with numerals, it would make no difference in the outcome of the race. Numbers on a nominal scale function like names.

nominal scale Numerical scale that uses numbers for the purpose of identification.

When numbers are used to rank the order of objects or items, those numbers are said to be on the **ordinal scale.** An ordinal scale is used to rank order the winners in a science fair. The winner has the first rank, or number 1, the runner-up has the second rank, or number 2, and so on. In this scale, the numbers have the quality of identification and indicate greater or lesser quality. The ordinal scale, however, does not have the quality of using equidistant units. For example, suppose the winners of a bike race were ranked as they came in, with the winner ranked as first, the runner-up as second, and the third bike rider ranked as third. The distance between the winner and the second-place bike rider might be 9 seconds, and the difference between the second- and third-place bike riders might be 30 seconds. While the numbers do rank the bike riders, they do not represent equidistant units.

ordinal scale Numerical scale in which numbers are used for ranking.

Numbers that are used for identification, which rank greater or lesser quality or amount, and which are also equidistant are numbers used on an **interval scale.** An example is the scale used in measuring temperature. The degrees on the thermometer can be added or subtracted—a reading of 38°F is 10° less than 48°F. The interval scale does not have an absolute zero quality. For example, zero degrees does not indicate that there is no temperature. The numbers used on an interval scale also cannot be used in other mathematical operations, such as multiplication. Is a reading of 100°F really four times as hot as 25°F? An interval scale used in assessment is the IQ scale. IQ numbers are equidistant, but they do not possess additional numerical properties. A person with an IQ of 66 cannot be called two-thirds as smart as a person with an IQ of 99.

interval scale A scale that uses numbers for ranking in which numerical units are equidistant.

When numbers on a scale are equidistant from each other and have a true meaning of absolute zero, they can be used in all mathematical operations. This **ratio scale** allows for direct comparisons and mathematical manipulations.

ratio scale Numerical scale with quality of equidistant units and absolute zero.

When scoring tests and interpreting data, it is important to understand which numerical scale the numbers represent and to realize the properties and limitations of that scale. Understanding what test scores represent may decrease errors such as attributing more meaning to a particular score than should be allowed by the nature of the numerical scale.

☐ **CHECK YOUR UNDERSTANDING**

Complete Activity 3.1.

Activity 3.1

Use the following terms to complete the sentences and answer the questions.

nominal scale ordinal scale
interval scale ratio scale

1. Measuring with a yardstick is an example of using numbers on the ________________ scale.
2. Which scale(s) can be added and subtracted but not multiplied?
____
3. The ribbons awarded in a painting contest illustrate which scale?
____
4. Numbers pinned on the shirts of runners in a marathon are numbers used on the ________________ scale.
5. The ________________ scale has a true meaning of absolute zero.

Descriptive Statistics

When assessing a student's behavior or performance for the purpose of educational intervention, it is often necessary to determine the amount of difference or deviance that the student exhibits in a particular area from the expected level for his age or grade. By looking at how much difference exists in samples of behavior, educational decision makers and parents can appropriately plan interventions. As previously mentioned, obtaining a raw score will not help with educational planning unless the evaluator has a frame of reference for that score. A raw score may have meaning when compared with previous student performance, or a raw score may be used to gain information from another set of scores called **derived scores.** Derived scores may be scores such as percentile ranks, **standard scores,** grade equivalents, age equivalents, or language quotients. Many derived scores obtain meaning from large sets of data or large samples of scores. By observing how a large sample of students the same age or grade level performed on the same tasks, it becomes possible to compare a particular student with the large group to see if that student performed as well as the group, better than the group, or not as well as the group.

derived scores Scores obtained by using a raw score and expectancy tables.

standard scores Derived scores that represent equal units, also known as *linear scores.*

Large sets of data are organized and understood through methods known as **descriptive statistics.** As the name implies, these are statistical operations that help educators understand and describe sets of data. One of the ways to organize and describe data is to see how the data fall together, or cluster. These types of statistics are called **measures of central tendency.**

descriptive statistics Statistics used to organize and describe data.

measures of central tendency Statistical methods for observing how data clusters together around the mean.

Measures of Central Tendency

Measures of central tendency are methods to determine how scores cluster—that is, how they are distributed around a numerical representation of the average score. One common type of distribution used in assessment is called a **normal distribution.**

normal distribution A symmetrical distribution with a single numerical representation for the mean, median, and mode.

A normal distribution has particular qualities that, when understood, help with the interpretation of assessment data. A normal distribution hypothetically represents the way test scores would fall if a particular test was given to every single student of the same age or grade in the population for whom the test was designed. If educators could administer an instrument in this way and obtain a normal distribution, the scores would fall in the shape of a bell curve, as shown in Figure 3.1.

In a graph of a normal distribution of scores, a very large number of the students tested are represented by all of the scores in the middle, or the "hump" part, of the curve. Because fewer students obtain extremely high or low scores, their scores are plotted or represented on the extreme ends of the curve. It is assumed that the same number of students obtained the higher scores as obtained the lower scores. The distribution is symmetric, or equal, on each side of the vertical line. The normal distribution is discussed throughout the text. One method of interpreting norm-referenced tests is to assume the principles of normal distribution theory and employ the measures of central tendency.

Average Performance

Although educators are familiar with the average grade of C on a letter-grading system (interval scale), the numerical ranking of the C grade might be 70 to 79 in one school and 76 to 84 in another. If the educator does not understand the numerical meaning of *average* for a student, the letter grade of C has little value. The educator must know how the other students performed and what

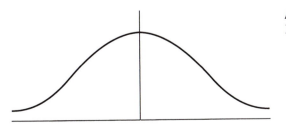

Figure 3.1
Normal distribution of scores, shown by the bell curve.

type of performance or score indicates average, what score is considered excellent, and what score is considered poor. To determine this, the teacher must determine what is considered average for that specific set of data.

frequency distribution Method of determining how many times each score occurs in a set of data.

One way to look at a set of data is to rank the scores from highest to lowest. This helps the teacher see how the group performed. After ranking the data in this fashion, it is helpful to complete a **frequency distribution** by counting how frequently each score occurred. Here is an example of 39 test scores, which the teacher ranked and then counted to record frequency:

Data Set A

Score	*Tally*	*Frequency*
100	|	1
99	|	1
98	||	2
94	||	2
90	~~||||~~	5
89	~~||||~~ ||	7
88	~~||||~~ ~~||||~~	10
82	~~||||~~ |	6
75	||	2
74	|	1
68	|	1
60	|	1

☐ **CHECK YOUR UNDERSTANDING**

Complete Activity 3.2.

Activity 3.2

Place the following set of data in rank order, and complete a frequency count.

Data Set B

92, 98, 100, 98, 92, 83, 73, 96, 90, 61, 70, 89, 87, 70, 85, 70, 66, 85, 62, 82

Score	*Tally*	*Frequency*	*Score*	*Tally*	*Frequency*
________			________		
________			________		
________			________		
________			________		
________			________		
________			________		
________			________		
________			________		

By arranging the data in this order and tallying the frequency of each score, the teacher can determine a trend in the performance of the class.

Another way to look at the data is to determine the most frequently occurring score, or the **mode.** The mode can give the teacher an idea of how the group performed because it indicates the score or performance that occurred the most number of times. The mode for data set A (p. 72) was 88 because it occurred 10 times. In data set B, (Activity 3.2) the mode was 70.

mode The most frequently occurring score in a set of scores.

Activity 3.3

Rank order the following set of data, complete a frequency count, and determine the mode.

Data Set C

62, 63, 51, 42, 78, 81, 81, 63, 75, 92, 94, 77, 63, 75, 96, 88, 60, 50, 49, 74

Score	***Tally***	***Frequency***	***Score***	***Tally***	***Frequency***
________			________		
________			________		
________			________		
________			________		
________			________		
________			________		
________			________		
________			________		

The mode is: ________

☐ **CHECK YOUR UNDERSTANDING**

Complete Activity 3.3.

Some sets of data have two modes or two most frequently occurring scores. This type of distribution of scores is known as a **bimodal distribution.** A distribution with three or more modes is called a **multimodal distribution.**

A clear representation of the distribution of a set of data can be illustrated graphically with a **frequency polygon.** A frequency polygon is a graph with test scores represented on the horizontal axis and the number of occurrences, or frequencies, represented on the vertical axis, as shown for data set A in Figure 3.2.

bimodal distribution A distribution that has two most frequently occurring scores.

multimodal distribution A distribution with three or more modes.

frequency polygon A graphic representation of how often each score occurs in a set of data.

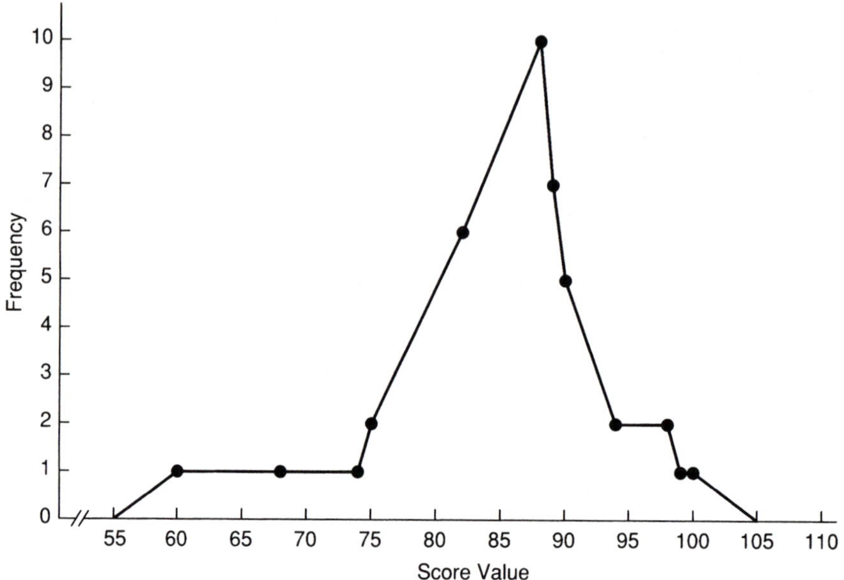

Figure 3.2
Frequency polygon for data set A.

☐ **CHECK YOUR UNDERSTANDING**

Complete Activity 3.4.

Activity 3.4

Rank order the data, complete a frequency count, and make a frequency polygon.

Data Set D

50, 52, 68, 67, 51, 89, 88, 76, 76, 88, 88, 68, 90, 91, 98, 69, 89, 88, 76, 76, 82, 85, 72, 85, 88, 76, 94, 82

Score	*Tally*	*Frequency*	*Score*	*Tally*	*Frequency*
______			______		
______			______		
______			______		
______			______		
______			______		
______			______		
______			______		
______			______		

Draw the frequency polygon here:

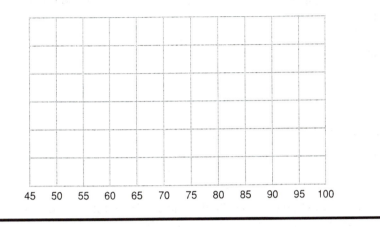

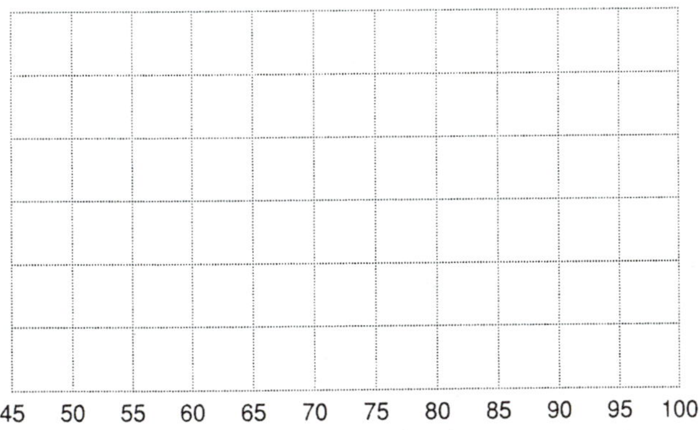

The data that have been rank ordered and for which a mode or modes have been determined give the teacher some idea of how the students performed as a group. Another method of determining how the group performed is to find the middlemost score, or the **median.** After the data have been rank ordered, the teacher can merely count halfway down the list of scores; however, each score must be listed each time it occurs. For example, here is a rank-ordered set of data for which the median has been determined:

median The middlemost score in a set of data.

100
97
89
85
85
78
78 median score
79
79
79
68
62
60

The median score has 50% of the data listed above it and 50% of the data listed below it. In this example, six of the scores are listed above 78 and six are listed below the median. Notice that although 78 is the median, it is not the mode for this set of data. In a normal distribution, which is distributed symmetrically, the median and the mode are represented by the same number.

In a set of data with an even number of scores, the median is the middlemost score even though the score may not actually exist in that set of data. For example,

100
96
95
90
85
83
82
80
78
77

The scores 85 and 83 occur in the middle of this distribution; therefore, the median is 84, even though 84 is not one of the scores.

☐ **CHECK YOUR UNDERSTANDING**

Complete Activity 3.5.

Activity 3.5

Find the median for the following sets of data.

Data Set E	***Data Set F***
100	88
99	88
96	88
88	86
84	80
83	76
82	75
79	74
76	70
75	68
70	
62	
60	
Median: ________	Median: ________

Although the mode and median indicate how a group performed, these measures of central tendency do not accurately describe the average, or typical, performance. One of the best measures of average performance is the arithmetic average, or **mean,** of the group of scores. The mean is calculated as a simple average: Add the scores and divide by the number of scores in the set of data. For example,

mean Arithmetic average of a set of data.

90
80
75
60
70
65
80
100
80
80

$780 \div 10 = 78$

The sum of the scores is 780. There are 10 scores in the set of data. Therefore, the sum, 780, is divided by the number of scores, 10. The average, or typical, score for this set of data is 78, which represents the arithmetic average.

Often teachers choose to use the mean score to represent the average score on a particular test or assignment. If this score seems to represent the typical performance on the specific test, the teacher may assign a letter grade of C to the numerical representation of the mean score. However, as discussed next, extremely high or low scores can render the mean misrepresentative of the average performance of the class.

☐ CHECK YOUR UNDERSTANDING

Complete Activity 3.6.

Activity 3.6

Find the mean, median, and mode for each set of data.

Data Set G

90, 86, 80, 87, 86, 82, 87, 92

Mean: ________ Median: ________ Mode: ________

Data Set H

41, 42, 45, 42, 46, 47, 48, 47, 41, 41

Mean: ________ Median: ________ Mode: ________

Using measures of central tendency is one way teachers can determine which score represents an average performance for a particular group on a particular measure. This aids the teacher in monitoring student progress and knowing when a student is performing well above or well below the norm or average of the group.

The mean can be affected by an extreme score, especially if the group is composed of only a few students. A very high score can raise the mean, whereas a very low score can lower the mean. For this reason, the teacher may wish to omit an extreme score before averaging the data. If scores seem to be widely dispersed, or scattered, using measures of central tendency may not be in the students' best interests. Moreover, such scatter may suggest that the teacher needs to qualitatively evaluate the students' performance and other factors such as teaching methods.

In research and test development, it is necessary to strive for and understand the normal distribution. Because of the symmetrical quality of the normal curve, the mean, median, and mode are all represented by the same number. For example, on tests measuring intelligence, the mean IQ is 100. One hundred is also the middlemost score (median) and the most frequently occurring score (mode). In fact, more than 68% of all of the IQ scores will cluster within one **standard deviation,** or one determined typical unit, above and below the score of 100. The statistic known as standard deviation is very important in special education assessment when the use of tests that compare an individual student with a norm-referenced group is necessary. Finding the standard deviation is one method of calculating difference in scores, or **variability** of scores, known as dispersion.

standard deviation A unit of measurement that represents the typical amount that a score can be expected to vary from the mean in a given set of data.

variability Describes how scores vary.

Measures of Dispersion

Because special educators must determine the degree or amount of difference exhibited by individuals in behaviors, skills, or traits, they must employ methods of calculating difference from the average or expected score. Just as measures of central tendency are used to see how sets of data cluster together around an average score, **measures of dispersion** are used to calculate how scores are spread apart from the mean.

measures of dispersion Statistical methods for observing how data spread from the mean.

The way that scores in a set of data are spread apart is known as the variability of the scores, or how much they vary from each other. When scores fall very close together and are not widely spread apart, the data are described as not having much variability, or **variance.**

variance Describes the total amount that a group of scores varies in a set of data.

Compare the following two sets of data:

Data Set I		***Data Set J***	
100	75	98	75
98	75	96	75
95	75	87	75
91	72	78	75
88	70	75	72
87	69	75	72
82	68	75	72
80	67	75	72
75	51	75	72
75	50	75	72

An easy way to get an idea about the spread is to find the **range** of scores. The range is calculated by subtracting the lowest score from the highest score.

range The distance between the highest and lowest scores in a data set.

Set I	***Set J***
$100 - 50 = 50$	$98 - 72 = 26$

The range for set J is about half that of set I. It appears that set I has more variability than set J. Look at the sets of data again. Both sets have the same median and the same mode, yet they are very different in terms of variability. When the means are calculated, it seems that the data are very similar. Set I has a mean of 77.15, and set J has a mean of 77.05. By using only measures of central tendency, the teacher may think that the students in both of these classes performed in a very similar manner on this test. Yet one set of data has approximately twice the spread, or variability of scores. In educational testing, it is necessary to determine the deviation from the mean in order to have a clearer picture of how students in groups such as these performed. By calculating the variance and the standard deviation, the teacher can find out the typical amount of difference from the mean. By knowing these typical or standard deviations from the mean, the teacher will be able to find out which scores are a significant distance from the average score.

To find the standard deviation of a set of scores, the variance must first be calculated. The variance can be described as the degree or amount of variability or dispersion in a set of scores. Looking at data sets I and J, one could probably assume that set I would have a larger variance than J.

Four steps are involved in calculating the variance:

Step 1 To calculate the amount of distance of each score from the mean, subtract the mean for the set of data from each score.

Step 2 Find the square of each of the difference scores found in step 1 (multiply each difference score by itself).

Step 3 Find the total of all of the squared score differences. This is called the sum of squares.

Step 4 Calculate the average of the sum of squares by dividing the total by the number of scores.

Data Set I

	Step 1: Difference	***Step 2: Multiply by Itself***		***Squared***
100 − 77.15 =	22.85	22.85 × 22.85	=	522.1225
98 − 77.15 =	20.85	20.85 × 20.85	=	434.7225
95 − 77.15 =	17.85	17.85 × 17.85	=	318.6225
91 − 77.15 =	13.85	13.85 × 13.85	=	191.8225
88 − 77.15 =	10.85	10.85 × 10.85	=	117.7225
87 − 77.15 =	9.85	9.85 × 9.85	=	97.0225
82 − 77.15 =	4.85	4.85 × 4.85	=	23.5225
80 − 77.15 =	2.85	2.85 × 2.85	=	8.1225
75 − 77.15 =	−2.15	−2.15 × −2.15	=	4.622
75 − 77.15 =	−2.15	−2.15 × −2.15	=	4.622
75 − 77.15 =	−2.15	−2.15 × −2.15	=	4.622
75 − 77.15 =	−2.15	−2.15 × −2.15	=	4.622
75 − 77.15 =	−2.15	−2.15 × −2.15	=	4.622
72 − 77.15 =	−5.15	−5.15 × −5.15	=	26.5225
70 − 77.15 =	−7.15	−7.15 × −7.15	=	51.1225
69 − 77.15 =	−8.15	−8.15 × −8.15	=	66.4225
68 − 77.15 =	−9.15	−9.15 × −9.15	=	83.7225
67 − 77.15 =	−10.15	−10.15 × −10.15	=	103.0225
51 − 77.15 =	−26.15	−26.15 × −26.15	=	683.8225
50 − 77.15 =	−27.15	−27.15 × −27.15	=	737.1225
		Step 3: Sum of Squares:		3,488.55

Step 4: Divide the Sum of Squares by the Number of Scores

$$3{,}488.55 \div 20 = 174.4275$$

Therefore, the variance for data set I = 174.4275.

☐ **CHECK YOUR UNDERSTANDING**

Complete Activity 3.7.

Activity 3.7

Calculate the variance for data set J, and compare with data set I.

Data Set J

	Step 1: Difference	*Step 2: Multiply by Itself*	*Squared*
98 − 77.05 =			
96 − 77.05 =			
87 − 77.05 =			
78 − 77.05 =			
75 − 77.05 =			
75 − 77.05 =			
75 − 77.05 =			
75 − 77.05 =			
75 − 77.05 =			
75 − 77.05 =			
75 − 77.05 =			
75 − 77.05 =			
75 − 77.05 =			
75 − 77.05 =			
72 − 77.05 =			
72 − 77.05 =			
72 − 77.05 =			
72 − 77.05 =			
72 − 77.05 =			
72 − 77.05 =			

Step 3: Sum of Squares: ________

Step 4: Divide the Sum of Squares by the Number of Scores

The variance is: ________

Which set of data, J or I, has the larger variance? ________

Standard Deviation

Once the variance has been calculated, only one more step is needed to calculate the standard deviation. The standard deviation helps the teacher determine how much distance from the mean is typical and how much is considered significant.

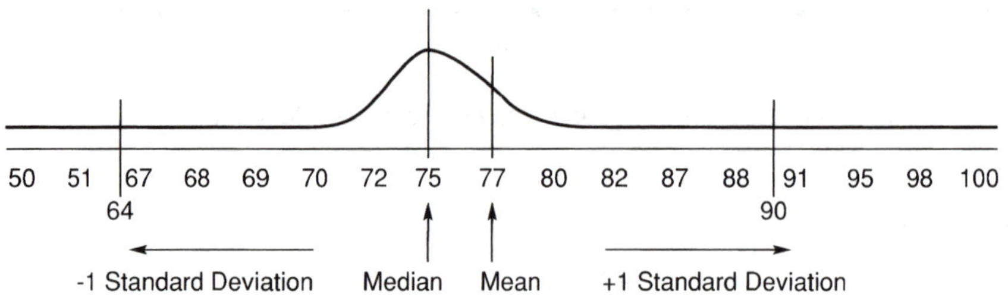

Figure 3.3
Distribution for data set I.

The standard deviation of a set of data is the square root of the variance.

$$\text{Standard Deviation} = \sqrt{\text{Variance}}$$

Because the variance for data sets I and J has already been calculated, merely enter each number on a calculator and hit the square root button. If a calculator is not available, use the square root tables located in most introductory statistics textbooks.

The square root of the variance for data set I is 13.21. Therefore, any test score that is more than 1 standard deviation above or below the mean score, either 13.21 above the mean or 13.21 below the mean, is considered significant. Look at data set I. The test scores that are more than 1 standard deviation above the mean (77.15) are 100, 98, 95, and 91. The scores that are more than 1 standard deviation below the mean are 51 and 50. These scores represent the extremes for this distribution and may well receive the extreme grades for the class: A's and F's. Figure 3.3 illustrates the distribution of scores in data set I.

Look at data set J. To locate significantly different scores, find those that are 1 or more standard deviations away from the mean of 77.05. Which scores are considered to be a significant distance from the mean?

☐ CHECK YOUR UNDERSTANDING

Complete Activity 3.8.

Activity 3.8

Using the following sets of data, complete a frequency count and a frequency polygon; calculate the mean, median, and mode; calculate the range, variance, and standard deviation; and list the scores that are a significant distance from the mean.

Ms. Jones Class Data

95, 82, 76, 75, 62, 100, 32, 15, 100, 98, 99, 86, 70, 26, 21, 26, 82
Frequency count:

Draw the frequency polygon here:

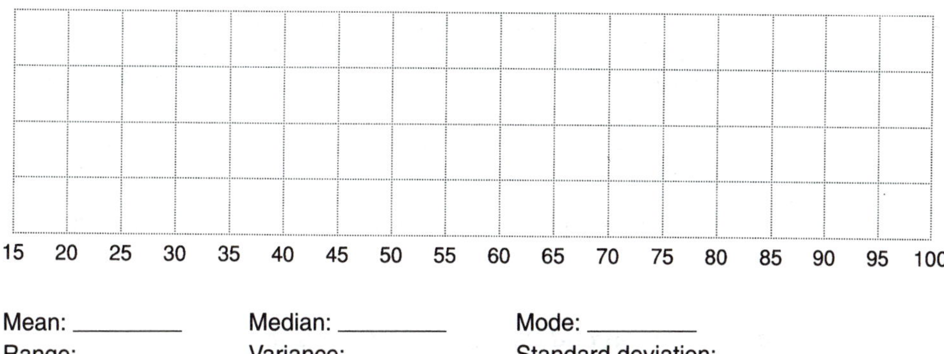

Mean: ________ Median: ________ Mode: ________
Range: ________ Variance: ________ Standard deviation: ________

Test scores that are a significant distance from the mean are:

____

Mrs. Smith's Class Data

76, 75, 83, 92, 85, 69, 88, 87, 88, 88, 88, 88, 77, 78, 78, 95, 98
Frequency count:

Draw the frequency polygon here:

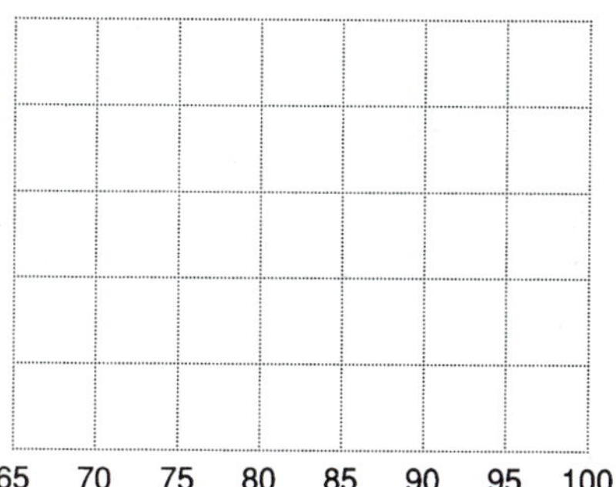

Mean: ________ Median: ________ Mode: ________
Range: ________ Variance: ________ Standard deviation: ________

Test scores that are a significant distance from the mean are:

____

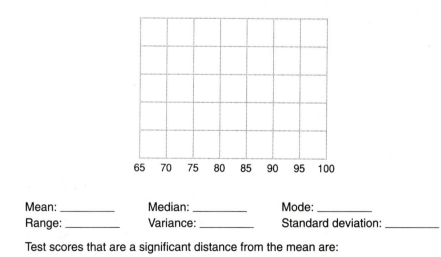

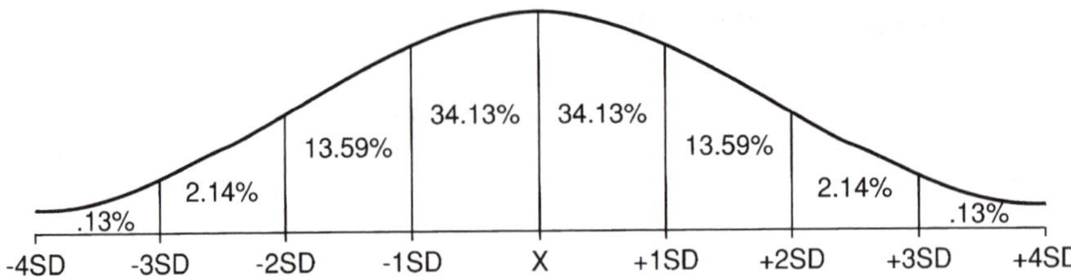

Figure 3.4
Percentages of population that fall within standard deviation units in a normal distribution.

Standard Deviation and the Normal Distribution

In a normal distribution, the standard deviations represent the percentages of scores shown on the bell curve in Figure 3.4. More than 68% of the scores fall within 1 standard deviation above or below the mean. A normal distribution is symmetrical and has the same number representing the mean, median, and mode. Notice that approximately 95% of the scores are found within 2 standard deviations above and below the mean (Figure 3.4). To clarify the significance of standard deviation, it is helpful to remember that one criterion for the diagnosis of mental retardation is an IQ score of more than 2 standard deviations below the mean. The criterion of 2 standard deviations above the mean is often used to determine that a student is within the gifted range. Using a standard deviation of 15 IQ points, an individual with an IQ of 70 or less and a subaverage adaptive behavior scale score might be classified as mentally retarded, whereas an individual with an IQ of 130 or more may be classified as gifted. The American Association on Mental Retardation (AAMR) classification system allows additional flexibility by adding 5 points to the minimum requirement; that is, the student within the 70–75 IQ range may also be found eligible for services under the mental retardation label if there is additional supporting data.

Using this type of criteria, approximately what percentage of the population would be considered to be within the range of giftedness, and what percentage would be considered to fall within the range of mental retardation? (Use Figure 3.4 to determine the answer.)

Mean Differences

Test results such as the ones discussed in the preceding section should be interpreted with caution. Many tests that have been used historically to diagnose disabilities, such as mental retardation, have been shown to exhibit *mean differences.* A specific cultural or linguistic group may have a different mean or average score than that reported for a majority of the population; this is a mean difference. Accordingly, minority students should not be judged by an acceptable average for a different population. This issue is elaborated on in chapter 10, "Intelligence Testing."

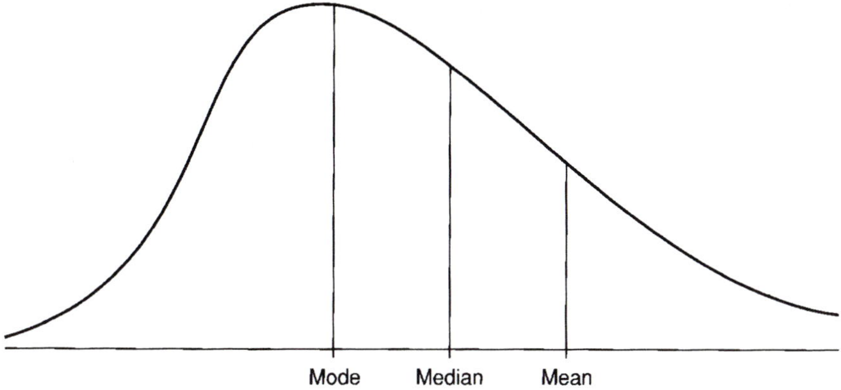

Figure 3.5
Positively skewed distribution.

Skewed Distributions

When small samples of populations are tested or when a fairly restricted population is tested, the results may not be distributed in a normal curve. Distributions can be **skewed** in a positive or negative direction. When many of the scores are below the mean, the distribution is said to be **positively skewed** and will resemble the distribution in Figure 3.5. Notice that the most frequently occurring scores (mode) are located below the mean.

When a large number of the scores occur above the mean, the distribution is said to be **negatively skewed,** as shown in Figure 3.6. Notice that the mode and median scores are located above the mean.

Figures 3.5 and 3.6 illustrate different ways that groups of scores fall, cluster, and are dispersed. As already discussed, extreme scores can change the appearance of a set of scores. Often, when working with scores from teacher-made tests, one or two scores can be so extreme that they influence the way the data

skewed Describes a distribution that has either more positively distributed scores or more negatively distributed scores.

positively skewed Describes a distribution in which more of the scores fall below the mean.

negatively skewed Describes a distribution in which more of the scores fall above the mean.

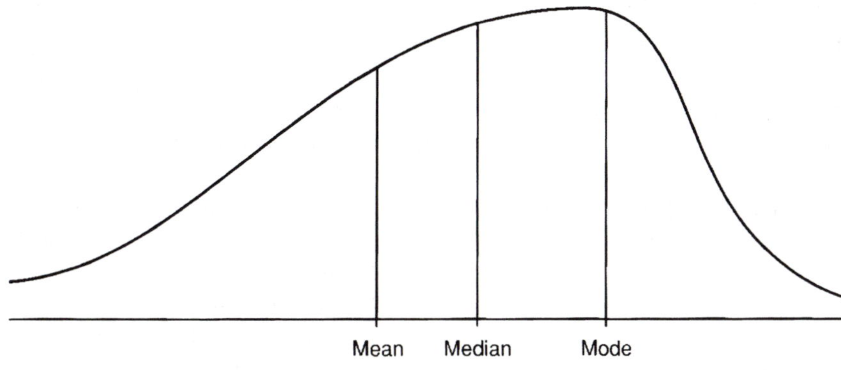

Figure 3.6
Negatively skewed distribution.

are described. That is, the scores may influence or pull the mean in one direction. Consider the following examples:

Ms. Brown	*Ms. Blue*
100	100
92	92
86	86
80	80
78	78
78	78
78	78
75	75
74	72
72	6
813 ÷ 10 = 81.3	745 ÷ 10 = 74.5

The sets of data are very similar except for the one extreme low score. The greater the number of scores in the class, the less influence an extreme score has on the set of data. In small classes like those often found in special education settings, the mean of the class performance is more likely to be influenced by an extreme score. If Ms. Brown and Ms. Blue each had a class objective stating that the class would pass the test with an average score of 80, Ms. Brown's class would have passed the objective, but Ms. Blue's class would have not. When the extreme score is omitted, the average for Ms. Blue's class is 82.1, which meets the class objective.

When selecting norm-referenced tests, special educators must take care to read the test manual and determine the size of the sample used in the norming process. Tests developed using larger samples are thought to result in scores that are more representative of the majority population.

Percentiles and z scores

percentile ranks Scores that express the percentage of students who scored as well as or lower than a given student's score.

z scores Derived scores that are expressed in standard deviation units.

Percentile ranks and ***z*** **scores** provide additional ways of looking at data. Using percentile ranks is a method of ranking each score on the continuum of the normal distribution. The extreme scores are ranked at the top and bottom, and very few people obtain scores at the extreme ends. Percentiles range from the 99.9th percentile to less than the 1st percentile. A person who scores at the extremely high end of a test may be ranked near the 99th percentile. This means that he scored as well as or better than 99% of the students the same age or grade who took the same test. A person who scores around the average, say 100 on an IQ test, would be ranked in the middle, or the 50th percentile. A person who scores in the top fourth would be above the 75th percentile; in other words, the student scored as well as or better than 75% of the students in that particular age group. The various per-

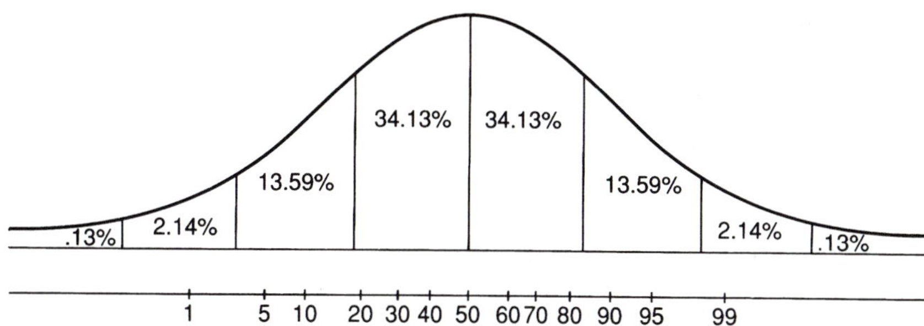

Figure 3.7
Relationship of percentiles and normal distribution.
Source: From *Assessing Special Students* (3rd ed., p. 63) by J. McLoughlin and R. Lewis, 1990, Columbus, OH: Merrill. Copyright 1990 by Macmillan Publishing Company. Adapted with permission.

centile ranks and their location on a normal distribution are illustrated in Figure 3.7.

Another type of score used to describe the data in a normal distribution is called a *z* score. A *z* score indicates where a score is located in terms of standard deviation units. The mean is expressed with 0, 1 standard deviation above the mean is expressed as +1, 2 standard deviations above as +2, and so on, as illustrated in Figure 3.8. Standard deviation units below the mean are expressed as negative numbers. For example, a score that is 1 standard deviation below the mean is expressed using *z* scores as −1, and a score that is 2 standard deviations below is expressed as −2. Conversely, +1 is 1 standard deviation above the mean, and +2 is 2 standard deviations above the mean.

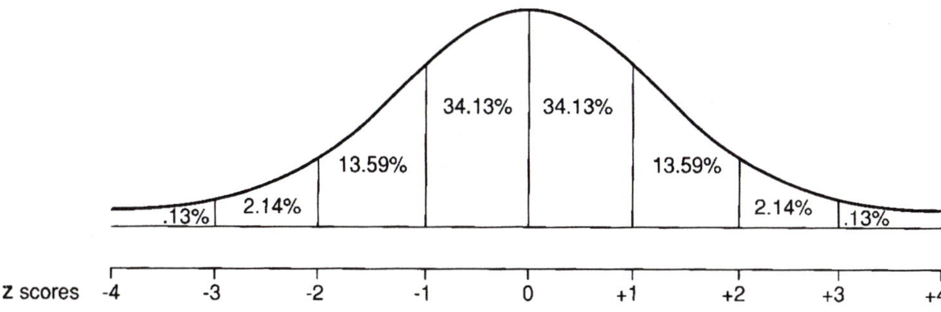

Figure 3.8
Relationship of *z* scores and the normal distribution.
Source: From *Assessing Special Students* (3rd ed., p. 63) by J. McLoughlin and R. Lewis, 1990, Columbus, OH: Merrill. Copyright 1990 by Macmillan Publishing Company. Adapted with permission.

Exercises

Part I

Match the following terms with the correct definitions.

A. nominal scale
B. positively skewed
C. measures of central tendency
D. frequency distribution
E. bimodal distribution
F. ordinal scale
G. multimodal
H. frequency polygon
I. measures of dispersion
J. negatively skewed
K. standard deviation
L. ratio scale
M. interval scale
N. mode
O. range
P. variance
Q. median
R. descriptive statistics
S. mean
T. normal distribution

_________ **1.** A numerical scale that ranks and has equidistant units.
_________ **2.** Statistics used to organize and describe data.
_________ **3.** Statistical methods for observing how data spreads from the mean.
_________ **4.** A numerical scale used for identification purposes only.
_________ **5.** Statistical methods for observing how data clusters together around the mean.
_________ **6.** Numerical scale used for ranking.
_________ **7.** This numerical scale has a true absolute zero value.
_________ **8.** The distance from the highest score observed to the lowest.
_________ **9.** A method of counting how frequently scores occur in a distribution of data.
_________ **10.** The most frequently occurring score in a set of scores.
_________ **11.** When a set of scores has two most frequently occurring scores.
_________ **12.** A graphic representation of how frequently each score occurs in a distribution of data.
_________ **13.** When a distribution has three or more scores which occur most frequently in the set of data.
_________ **14.** The arithmetic average of a set of scores.
_________ **15.** The middlemost score in a distribution of scores.
_________ **16.** When the distribution of scores is symmetric, mean, median, and mode are represented by the same numerical value.
_________ **17.** A unit representing the typical amount that a score may vary from the mean in a set of data.
_________ **18.** When the most frequently occurring scores in a distribution are greater than the mean.
_________ **19.** When the most frequently occurring scores in a distribution are less than the mean of the set of scores.

Part II

Use the following data to rank order data; complete a frequency distribution and a frequency polygon; calculate the mean, median, and mode; and find the range, variance, and standard deviation. Identify scores that are significantly above or below the mean.

Data

85, 85, 99, 63, 60, 97, 96, 95, 58, 70, 72, 92, 89, 87, 74, 74, 74, 85, 84, 78, 84, 78, 84, 78, 86, 82, 79, 81, 80, 86

________	________
________	________
________	________
________	________
________	________
________	________
________	________
________	________
________	________
________	________
________	________
________	________
________	________
________	________
________	________
________	________

Mean: ________ Median: ________ Mode: ________

Range: ________ Variance: ________ Standard deviation: ________

Scores that are a significant distance from the mean are:

____

Draw the frequency polygon here:

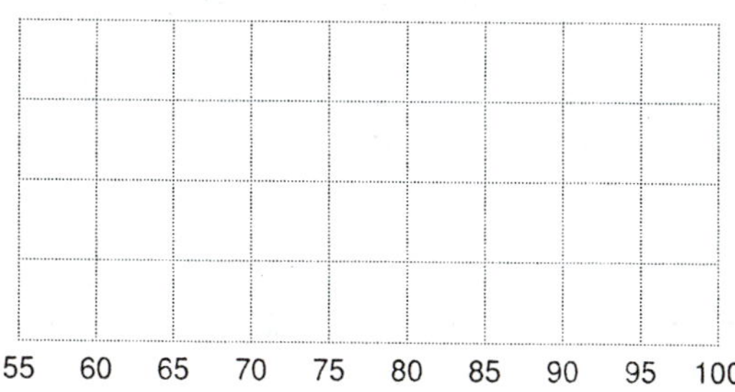

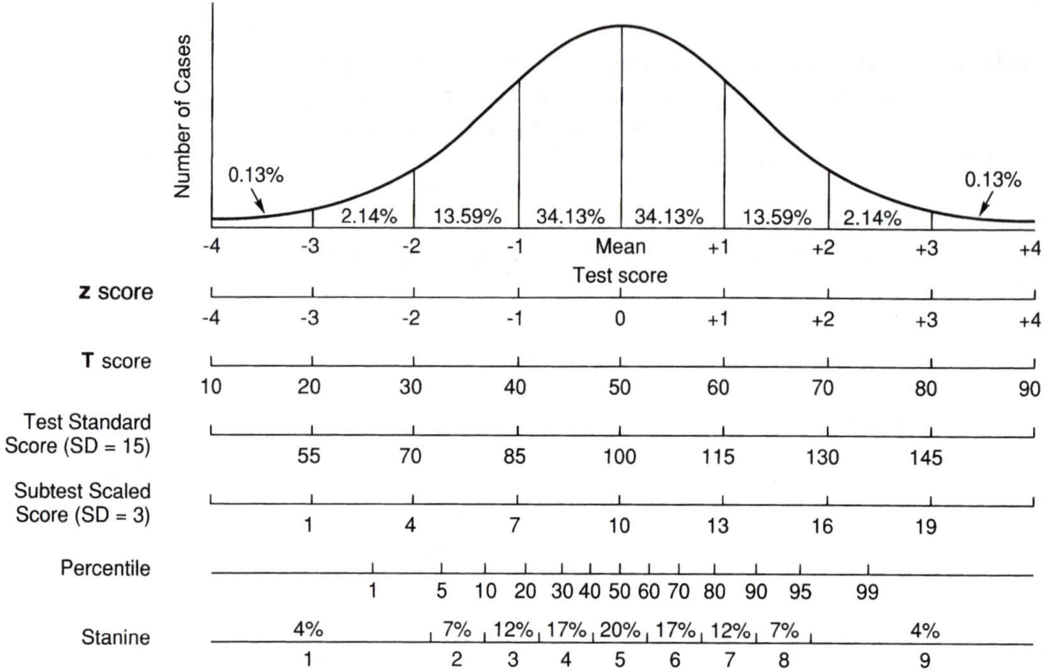

Figure 3.9
Relationships among different types of scores in a normal distribution.
Source: From *Assessing Special Students* (3rd ed., p. 63) by J. McLoughlin and R. Lewis, 1990, Columbus, OH: Merrill. Copyright 1990 by Macmillan Publishing Company. Reprinted with permission.

Use the normal distribution shown in Figure 3.9 to answer the following questions. You may need to use a ruler or straight edge, placed on the figure vertically, to identify the answers.

1. What percentage of the scores would fall between the *z* scores of −2.0 and +2.0? ________
2. What percentile rank would be assigned to the *z* score of 0? ________
3. What percentile rank would represent a person who scored at the *z* score of +3.0? ________
4. Approximately what percentile rank would be assigned for the IQ score of 70? ________
5. Approximately how many people would be expected to fall in the IQ range represented by the *z* scores of +3.0 to +4.0? ________

References

American Psychological Association. (1985). *Standards for educational and psychological testing.* Washington, DC: Author.

Algozzine, B., & Ysseldyke, J. (1981). Special education services for normal children: Better safe than sorry? *Exceptional Children, 48,* 238–243.

Bennett, R., & Shepherd, M. (1982). Basic measurement proficiency of learning disability specialists. *Learning Disabilities Quarterly, 5,* 177–184.

Borg, W., Worthen, B., & Valcarce, R. (1986). Teachers' perceptions of the importance of educational measurement. *Journal of Experimental Education, 5,* 9–14.

Davis, W., & Shepard, L. (1983). Specialists' use of tests and clinical judgments in the diagnosis of learning disabilities. *Learning Disabilities Quarterly, 6,* 128–137.

Eaves, R. (1985). Educational assessment in the United States. [Monograph]. *Diagnostique, 10,* 5–39.

Huebner, E. S. (1988). Bias in teachers' special education decisions as a function of test score reporting format. *Journal of Educational Researcher, 21,* 217–220.

Huebner, E. S. (1989). Errors in decision making: A comparison of school psychologists' interpretations of grade equivalents, percentiles, and deviation IQs. *School Psychology Review, 18,* 51–55.

McLoughlin, J. (1985). Training educational diagnosticians. [Monograph]. *Diagnostique, 10,* 176–196.

McLoughlin, J., & Lewis, R. (1990). *Assessing special students* (3rd ed.). Columbus, OH: Merrill.

Ysseldyke, J., Algozzine, B., Regan, R., & Potter, M. (1980). Technical adequacy of tests used by professionals in simulated decision making. *Psychology in the Schools, 17,* 202–209.

Ysseldyke, J., Algozzine, B., Richey, L., & Graden, J. (1982). Declaring students eligible for learning disability services: Why bother with the data? *Learning Disabilities Quarterly, 5,* 37–44.

Chapter Four

Reliability and Validity

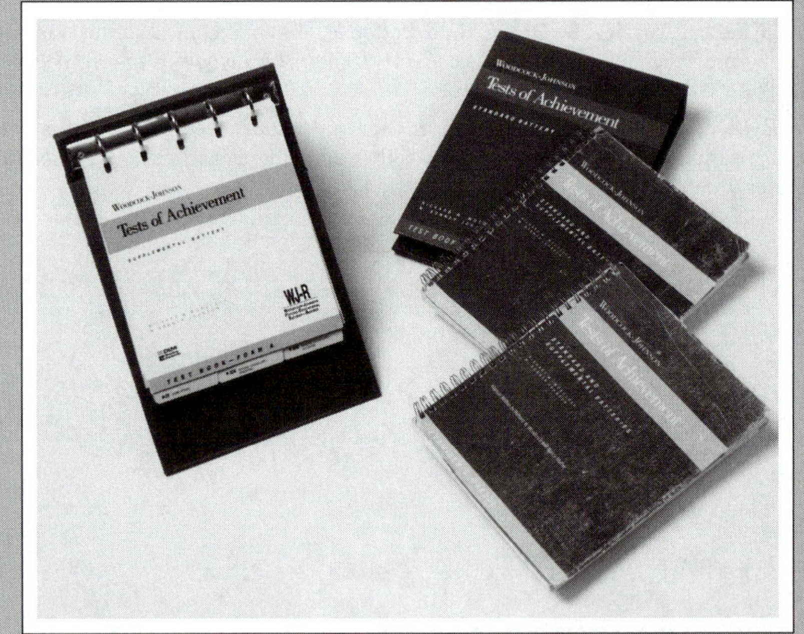

Key Terms

reliability
correlation
correlation coefficient
scattergram
Pearson's *r*
internal consistency
test-retest reliability
equivalent forms reliability
alternate forms reliability
split-half reliability
Kuder-Richardson 20
coefficient alpha
interrater reliability
true score
standard error of measurement
obtained score
confidence interval
estimated true score
validity
criterion-related validity
concurrent validity
predictive validity
content validity
presentation format
response mode
construct validity
validity of test use

Reliability and Validity in Assessment

It is important for educators to feel that the assessment methods used in teaching are providing accurate information. Usually, inferences are made from test data. In each school district, these inferences and subsequent interpretations of test results may change or set the educational future of hundreds of students each school year. An understanding of the concepts of reliability and validity aids the educator in determining test accuracy and dependability as well as how much faith can be placed in the use of instruments in the decision-making process.

Reliability

Reliability in assessment refers to the confidence that can be placed in an instrument to yield the same score for the same student if the test were administered more than once and the degree with which a skill or trait is measured consistently across items of a test. Teachers administering tests of any type, formal or informal, must be aware that error will be present to some degree during test administration. Statistical methods for estimating the probable amount of error and the degree of reliability allow professionals to select instruments with the lowest estimate of error and the greatest degree of reliability. Because educators use assessment as a basis for educational intervention and placement decisions, the most technically adequate instruments are preferred.

reliability The dependability or consistency or an instrument across time or items.

One concept important to the understanding of reliability in assessment is **correlation.** Correlation is a method of determining the degree of relationship between two variables. Reliability is determined by the degree of relationship between the administration of an instrument and some other variable (including a repeated administration of the same instrument). The greater the degree of the relationship, the more reliable the instrument.

correlation A statistical method of observing the degree of a relationship between two sets of data or two variables.

Correlation

Correlation is a statistical procedure calculated to measure the relationship between two variables. The two variables might be two administrations of the same test, administration of equivalent forms of the same test, administration of one test and school achievement, or variables such as amount of time studying and final exam grades. In short, correlation is a method of determining if two variables are associated with each other and, if so, how much.

correlation coefficient The expression of a relationship between two variables.

There are three types of correlations between variables: positive, negative, and no relationship. The degree of relationship between two variables is expressed by a **correlation coefficient** (r). The correlation coefficient will be a number between +1.00 and −1.00. A −1.00 or +1.00 indicates a perfect degree of correlation. In reality, perfect correlations are extremely rare. A correlation coefficient of 0 indicates no relationship.

The closer to ±1.00 the coefficient, the stronger the degree of the relationship. Hence, an r of .78 represents a stronger relationship than .65. When relationships are expressed by coefficients, the positive or negative sign does not indicate the strength of a relationship but the direction of the relationship. Therefore, r values of −.78 and +.78 are of equal strength.

Positive Correlation

Variables that have a positive relationship are those that move in the same direction. For example, this means that when test scores representing one variable in a set are high, scores representing the other variable also are high, and when the scores on one variable are low, scores on the other variable are low. Look at the following list of scores. Students who made high scores on a reading ability test (mean = 100) also had fairly high classroom reading grades at the end of the 6-week reporting period. Therefore, the data appear to show a positive relationship between the ability measured on the reading test (variable Y) and the student's performance in the reading curriculum in the classroom (variable X).

	Scores on the Reading Ability Test (Variable Y)	***Reading Grade at End of 6 Weeks (Variable X)***
John	109	B+
Ralph	120	A+
Sue	88	C−
Mary	95	B+
George	116	A−
Fred	78	D−
Kristy	140	A+

Jake	135	A
Jason	138	A
Betty	95	B−
Jamie	85	C+

To better understand this positive relationship, the scores on these two variables can be plotted on a **scattergram** (Figure 4.1). Each student is represented by a single dot on the graph. The scattergram shows clearly that as the score on one variable increased, so did the score on the other variable.

scattergram Graphic representation of a correlation.

When plotting correlations on a scattergram, the closer the dots approximate a straight line, the nearer to perfect the correlation. Hence, a strong relationship will appear more linear. Figure 4.2 illustrates a perfect positive correlation (straight line) for the small set of data shown here.

	Test 1 (Variable Y)	*Test 2 (Variable X)*
George	100	100
Bill	95	95
Sam	88	88
Larry	76	76

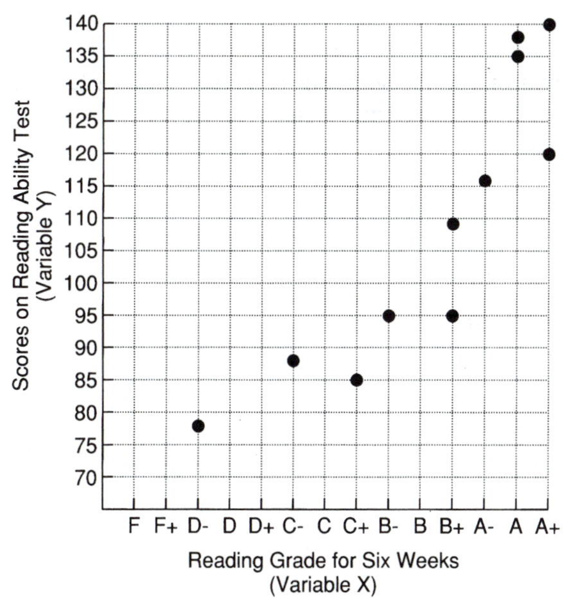

Figure 4.1
Graph showing relationship between scores on reading ability test and reading grade for 6 weeks.

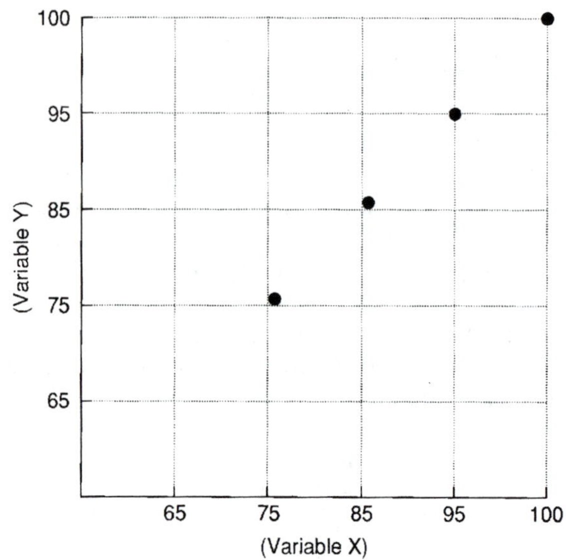

Figure 4.2
Scattergram showing a perfect positive correlation.

☐ **CHECK YOUR UNDERSTANDING**

Complete Activity 4.1.

Activity 4.1

The following sets of data are scores on a mathematics ability test and grade-level achievement in math for fifth graders. Plot the following scores on the scattergram shown here.

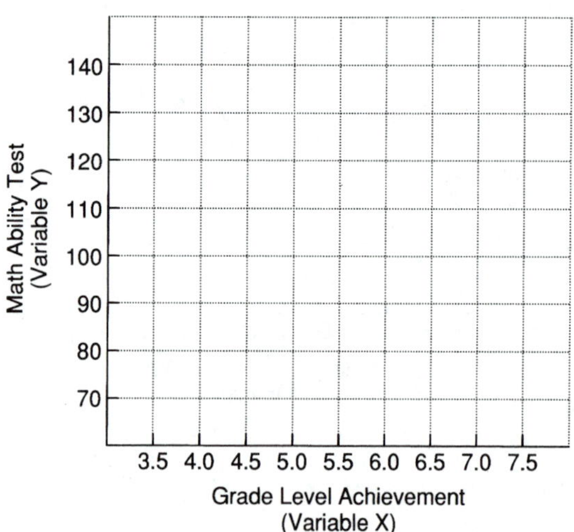

	Mathematics Ability Test Score (Variable Y)	*Grade-Level Achievement (Variable X)*
Wendy	115	6.5
Mary	102	5.5
Brad	141	7.4
Randy	92	4.7
Jamie	106	5.8
George	88	3.9

Examples of other variables that would be expected to have a positive relationship are number of days present in class and semester grade, number of chapters studied and final exam grade, and number of alcoholic drinks consumed and mistakes on a fine-motor test.

Negative Correlation

A negative correlation occurs when high scores on one variable are associated with low scores on the other variable. Examples of probable negative correlations are number of days absent and test grades, number of hours spent at parties and test grades, and number of hours missed from work and amount of hourly paycheck.

☐ **CHECK YOUR UNDERSTANDING**

Complete Activity 4.2

Activity 4.2

Here is an example of a negative correlation between two variables. Plot the scores on the scattergram.

	Test 1 (Variable Y)	*Test 2 (Variable X)*
Heather	116	40
Ryan	118	38
Brent	130	20
William	125	21
Kellie	112	35
Stacy	122	19
Marsha	126	23
Lawrence	110	45
Allen	127	18
Aaron	100	55
Jeff	120	27
Sharon	122	25

Michael	112	43
James	105	50
Thomas	117	33

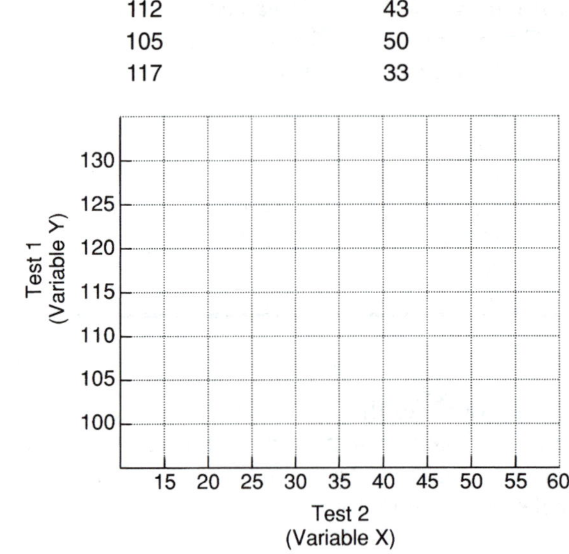

When the strength of a relationship is weak, the scattergram will not appear to have a distinct line. The less linear the scattergram, the weaker the correlation. Figure 4.3 illustrates scattergrams representing weak positive and negative relationships.

No Correlation

When data from two variables are not associated, or have no relationship, the $r = .00$. No correlation will be represented on a scattergram, with no linear

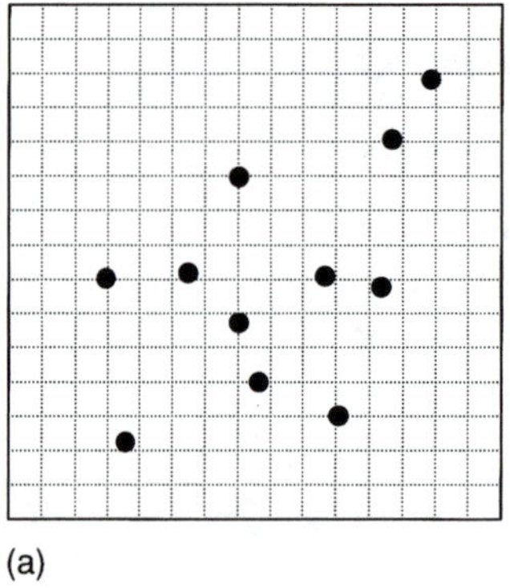

(a)

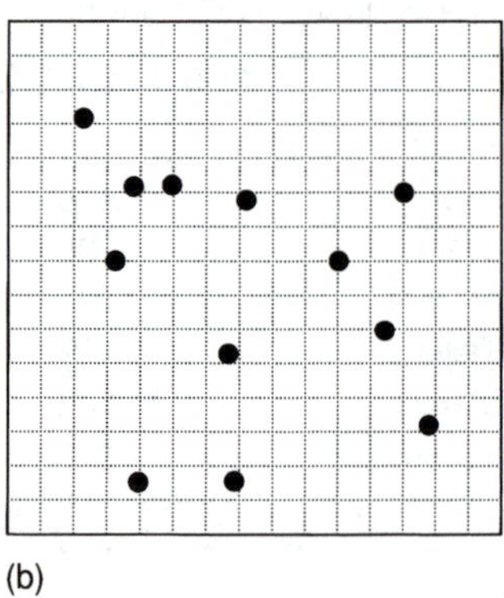

(b)

Figure 4.3
Scattergrams showing (a) weak positive and (b) weak negative relationships.

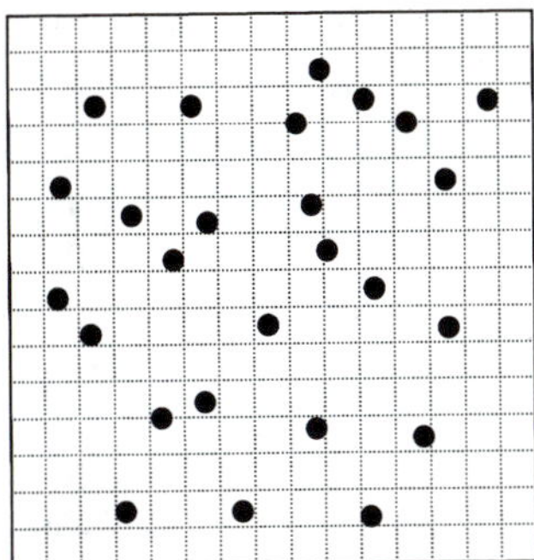

Figure 4.4
Scattergram showing no relationship.

direction either positive or negative. Figure 4.4 illustrates scattergrams of variables with no relationship.

Activity 4.3

☐ **CHECK YOUR UNDERSTANDING**

Complete Activity 4.3

Complete the scattergrams using the following sets of data. Determine if the scattergrams illustrate positive, negative, or no correlation.

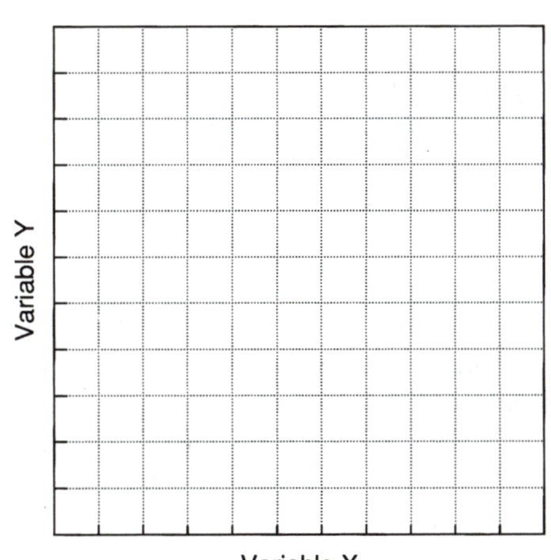

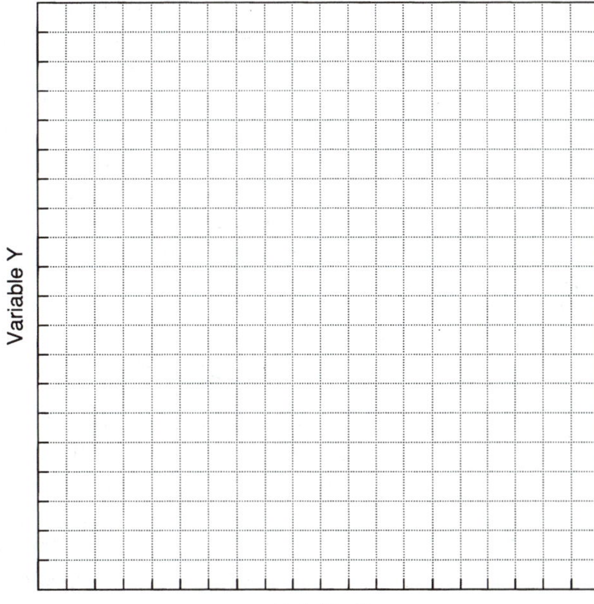

Variable Y	Variable X	Variable Y	Variable X
100	110	6	87
96	94	56	98
86	91	4	80
67	72	10	85
77	85	40	84
		30	20
		20	40
		50	20

Correlation appears to be: ______________ Correlation appears to be: ______________

Methods of Measuring Reliability

A teacher who administers a mathematics ability test to a student on a particular day and obtains a standard score of 110 (mean = 100) might feel quite confident that the student has ability in math above expectancy for her age level. Imagine that a teacher recommended a change in the student's educational placement based on the results of that particular math test and later discovered that the math test was not reliable. Educators must be able to have confidence that instruments used will yield similar results when administered at different times. Professionals must know the degree with which they can rely on a specific instrument.

Different methods can be used to measure the reliability of instruments. The reliability statistics are calculated using correlational methods. One correlational method used is the Pearson's Product Moment correlation, known as **Pearson's *r*.** Pearson's *r* is a commonly used formula for data on an interval or a ratio scale, although other methods are used as well. The correlational studies of the reliability of tests involve checking the reliability of a test over time or the reliability of items within the test, known as **internal consistency.** For these types of studies, the procedures of test-retest, equivalent forms, split-half, and statistical methods called Kuder-Richardson formulas may be used.

***Pearson's* r** A statistical formula for determining strength and direction of correlations.

internal consistency The consistency of the items on an instrument to measure a skill, trait, or domain.

Test-Retest Reliability

One way to determine the reliability of a test is to measure the correlation of test scores obtained during one administration with the scores obtained on a repeated administration. The assumption of **test-retest reliability** is that the trait being measured is one that is stable over time. Therefore, if the trait being measured remained constant, the readministration of the instrument would result in scores very similar to the first scores, and thus the correlation between the two administrations would be positive.

test-retest reliability Study that employs the readministration of a single instrument to check for consistency across time.

Many of the traits measured in psychoeducational assessment are variable and respond to influencing factors or changes over time, such as instruction or student maturity. The readministration of an instrument for reliability studies should therefore be completed within a fairly short time period in an effort to control the influencing variables that occur naturally in the educational environment of children and youth. Typically, the longer the interval between test administrations, the more chance of variation in the obtained scores. Conversely, the shorter the interval between the two test administrations, the less likelihood that students will be influenced by time-related factors (experience, education, etc.). The difficulty with readministering the same instrument within a short period of time is that the student may remember items on the test. This *practice effect* most likely would cause the scores obtained on the second administration to be higher than the original scores, which would influence the correlation. The shorter the interval between administrations, the greater the possibility of practice effect; the longer the interval, the greater the influence of time variables.

The disadvantages of test-retest methods for checking test reliability have led to the use of other methods.

Equivalent Forms Reliability

To control for the influence of time-related and practice-effect variables of test-retest methods, test developers may choose to use **equivalent forms reliability,** also called **alternate forms reliability.** In this method, two forms of the same instrument are used. The items are matched for difficulty on each test. For example, if three items for phonetic attack of consonant blends are included on one version of a reading test, three items of the same nature must be included at the same level on the alternate form of the test. During the reliability study, each student is administered both forms, and the scores obtained on one form of the test are then paired with the scores obtained on the equivalent form. The following are scores obtained on equivalent forms of a hypothetical reading test:

equivalent forms reliability Consistency of a test to measure some domain, trait, or skill using like forms of the same instrument.

alternate forms reliability Synonymous term for equivalent forms reliability.

The Best-Ever Diagnostic Reading Test **(x = *100)****

	Form 1	*Form 2*
John	82	85
Sue	76	78
Bill	89	87
Randy	54	56
Sally	106	112
Sara	115	109

* x = mean of sample.

This positive correlation indicates a fairly high reliability using equivalent forms reliability. In reality, an equivalent forms reliability study would involve a much larger sample of students. If this example had been an equivalent forms study using a large national sample, the educator could assume that both forms of the Best-Ever Reading Diagnostic Test are measuring the tested trait with some consistency.

If the test developer of the Best-Ever Reading Diagnostic Test also wanted the test to measure the stability of the trait over time, the manual would recommend that an interval of time pass between the administration of each form of the test. In using equivalent forms for measuring the stability over time, the reliability coefficient usually will not be as high as in the case of administering the same form of a test a second time. In the case of administering equivalent forms over a period of time, the influence of time-related variables will decrease the reliability coefficient as well as the practice effect that occurs in a test-retest reliability study of the same instrument.

Several published achievement and diagnostic tests that are used in special education consist of two equivalent forms. The advantage of this format is that it provides the educator with two tests of the same difficulty level that can be administered within a short time frame without the influence of practice effect. Often, local educational agencies practice a policy of administering one of the equivalent forms before writing short-term objectives for the year and administering the second form following educational interventions near the end of the school year. Educators administer the second form of the test to determine if the educational objectives were achieved.

Internal Consistency Measures

Several methods allow a test developer to determine the reliability of the items on a single test using one administration of the test. These methods include **split-half reliability, Kuder-Richardson (K-R) 20,** and **coefficient alpha.**

split-half reliability A method of checking the consistency across items by halving a test and administering two half-forms of same test.

Kuder-Richardson (K-R) 20 A formula used to check consistency across items of instrument with right/wrong responses.

coefficient alpha A formula used to check consistency across items of instrument with responses with varying credit.

Split-Half Reliability. Because of its ease of use, test developers rely often on the split-half method of determining reliability. This method uses the items available on the instrument, splits the test in half, and correlates the two halves of the test. Because most tests have the items arranged sequentially, from the easiest items at the beginning of the test to the most difficult items at the end, the tests are typically split by pulling every other item, which in essence results in two equivalent half-forms of the test. Because this type of reliability study can be performed in a single administration of the instrument, split-half reliability studies are often completed even though other types of reliability studies are used in the test development. While this method establishes reliability of one half of the test with the other half, it does not establish the reliability of the entire test. Because reliability tends to increase with the number of items on the test, using split-half reliability may result in a lower reliability coefficient than that calculated by another method for the entire test (Mehrens & Lehmann, 1978). In this case, the reliability may be statistically adjusted to account for the variance in length (Mehrens & Lehmann, 1978).

Coefficient Alpha and Kuder-Richardson 20. As the name implies, internal consistency reliability methods are used to determine how much alike items are to other items on a test. An advantage of this type of reliability study is that a single test administration is required. This reflects the unidimensionality in measuring a trait rather than the multidimensionality (Walsh & Betz, 1985).

Internal consistency is computed statistically by using either the K-R 20 formula for items scored only right or wrong or the coefficient alpha formula for items when more than 1 point is earned for a correct response (Mehrens & Lehmann, 1978).

When a high correlation coefficient is expressed by an internal consistency formula such as coefficient alpha or K-R 20, the educator can be confident that the items on the instrument measure the trait or skill with some consistency. These methods measure the consistency of the items but not the consistency or dependability of the instrument across time like the test-retest method or using equivalent forms in separate test administrations.

Interrater Reliability

Many of the educational and diagnostic tests used in special education are standardized with very specific administration, scoring, and interpretation instructions. Tests with a great deal of structure reduce the amount of influence that individual examiners may have on the results of the test. Some tests, specifically tests that allow the examiner to make judgments about student performance, have a greater possibility of influence by test examiners. In other words, there may be more of a chance that a score would vary from one examiner to another if the same student were tested by different examiners. On tests such as this, it is important to check the **interrater reliability,** or interscorer reliability. This can be accomplished by administering the test and then having an objective scorer also score the test results. The results of the tests scored by the examiner are then correlated with the results obtained by the objective scorer to determine how much variability exists between the test scores. This information is especially important when tests with a great deal of subjectivity are used in making educational decisions.

interrater reliability The consistency of a test to measure a skill, trait, or domain across examiners.

Which Type of Reliability Is the Best?

Different types of reliability studies are used to measure consistency over time, consistency of the items on a test, and consistency of the test scored by different examiners. An educator selects assessment instruments for specific purposes according to the child's educational needs. The reliability studies and information in the test manual concerning reliability of the instrument are important considerations for the educator when determining which test is best for a particular student. An educator should select the instrument that has a high degree of reliability related to the purpose of assessment. An adequate reliability coefficient would be .60 or greater, and a high degree of reliability would be above .80. For example, if the examiner is interested in measuring a trait over time, the examiner should select an instrument in which the reliability or consistency over time had been studied. If the examiner is more concerned with the instrument's ability to determine student behavior using an instrument that allowed for a great degree of examiner judgment, the examiner should check the instrument's interrater reliability.

☐ **CHECK YOUR UNDERSTANDING**

Complete Activity 4.4.

Activity 4.4

Select the appropriate reliability study for the purposes described.

A. split-half reliability
B. equivalent forms, separate administration times
C. K-R 20
D. interrater reliability
E. test-retest
F. coefficient alpha
G. equivalent forms, same administration time

_________ **1.** Educator is concerned with item reliability; items are scored as right or wrong.
_________ **2.** Educator wants to administer same test twice to measure achievement of objectives.
_________ **3.** Examiner is concerned with consistency of trait over time.
_________ **4.** Educator is concerned with item consistency; items are scored with different point values for correct responses.
_________ **5.** Examiner wants to administer a test that allows for examiner judgment.

Reliability for Different Groups

The calculation of the reliability coefficient is a group statistic and can be influenced by the makeup of the group. The best test development and the manuals accompanying those tests will include information regarding the reliability of a test with different age or grade levels and even the reliability of a test with populations who differ on demographic variables such as cultural or linguistic backgrounds. The information in Table 4.1 illustrates how reliability may vary across different age groups.

Table 4.1
Split-half reliability coefficients, by age, for subtest, area, and total-test raw scores from the fall and spring standardization programs.

Subtest/Composite	Program (Fall/Spring)	Age 5	6	7	8	9	10
1. Numeration	F	.73	.82	.85	.90	.81	.85
	S	.51	.82	.89	.88	.89	.81
2. Rational Numbers	F	—	.24	.71	.68	.88	.89
	S	—	.27	.42	.86	.82	.86
3. Geometry	F	.63	.81	.79	.77	.82	.80
	S	.80	.81	.76	.77	.80	.75
4. Addition	F	.63	.65	.79	.84	.78	.40
	S	.58	.78	.84	.82	.84	.66
5. Subtraction	F	.25	.68	.64	.85	.89	.86
	S	.30	.70	.85	.90	.92	.85
6. Multiplication	F	.23	.41	.11	.76	.89	.90
	S	.07	.67	.68	.91	.93	.89
7. Division	F	.55	.49	.52	.51	.82	.86
	S	.18	.34	.53	.77	.80	.84
8. Mental Computation	F	—	.78	.68	.80	.85	.88
	S	—	.65	.67	.78	.78	.90
9. Measurement	F	.77	.89	.57	.77	.76	.77
	S	.92	.84	.85	.87	.84	.70
10. Time and Money	F	.50	.61	.73	.89	.87	.93
	S	.38	.70	.84	.89	.92	.86
11. Estimation	F	.44	.43	.50	.74	.86	.72
	S	.59	.50	.53	.85	.76	.84
12. Interpreting Data	F	.41	.86	.81	.80	.88	.85
	S	.32	.79	.83	.85	.88	.87
13. Problem Solving	F	.36	.60	.73	.71	.82	.86
	S	.55	.60	.77	.76	.87	.92
Basic Concepts Area[a]	F	.78	.87	.89	.91	.92	.93
	S	.82	.88	.87	.92	.92	.92
Operations Area[a]	F	.66	.86	.87	.93	.96	.96
	S	.73	.88	.92	.96	.96	.96
Applications Area[a]	F	.82	.91	.89	.94	.96	.96
	S	.88	.90	.93	.96	.96	.96
TOTAL TEST[a]	F	.90	.95	.95	.97	.98	.98
	S	.92	.95	.97	.98	.98	.98

[a]Reliability coefficients for the areas and the total test were computed by using Guilford's (1954, p. 393) formula for estimating the reliability of composite scores.

Source: From *KeyMath–Revised: A Diagnostic Inventory of Essential Mathematics, Manual. Forms A and B* (p. 67) by A. Connolly, 1988, Circle Pines, MN: American Guidance Service. Copyright 1988 by American Guidance Service. Reprinted by permission.

☐ **CHECK YOUR UNDERSTANDING**

Complete Activity 4.5.

Activity 4.5

Refer to Table 4.1 to answer the questions.

1. What type of reliability is reported in Table 4.1? ________________
2. Look at the reliability reported for age 7. Using fall statistics, compare the reliability coefficient obtained on the Numeration subtest with the reliability coefficient obtained for the Estimation subtest. On which subtest did 7-year-olds perform with more reliability? ________________
3. Compare the reliability coefficient obtained by 9-year-olds on the Estimation subtest with the reliability obtained by 7-year-olds on the same subtest using fall statistics. Which age group performed with more reliability?

   ____

Standard Error of Measurement

In all psychoeducational assessment, there is a basic underlying assumption: Error exists. Errors in testing may result from situational factors such as a poor testing environment or the health or emotions of the student, or errors may occur as a result of the inaccuracies within the test instrument. Error should be considered when tests are administered, scored, and interpreted. Because tests are small samples of behavior observed at a given time, many variables can affect the assessment process and cause variance in test scores. This variance is called error because it influences test results. Professionals need to know that all tests contain error and that a single test score may not accurately reflect the student's **true score.** Salvia and Ysseldyke (1988) stated, "A true score is a hypothetical value that represents a person's score when the entire domain of items is assessed at all possible times, by all appropriate testers" (p. 369). The following basic formula should be remembered when interpreting scores:

true score The student's actual score.

$$\text{Obtained score} = \text{True score} + \text{Error}$$

Conversely,

$$\text{Obtained score} - \text{True score} = \text{Error}$$

standard error of measurement The amount of error determined to exist using a specific instrument, calculated using the instrument's standard deviation and reliability.

True score is never actually known; therefore, a range of possible scores is calculated. The error is called the **standard error of measurement,** and an instrument with a large standard error of measurement would be less desirable than an instrument with a small standard error of measurement.

obtained score The observed score of a student on a particular test on a given day.

To estimate the amount of error present in an individual **obtained score,** the standard error of measurement must be obtained and applied to each score. The standard deviation and the reliability coefficient of the instrument are used to calculate the standard error of measurement. The following formula will enable the educator to determine the standard error of measurement when it has not been provided by the test developer in the test manual.

$$SEM = SD\sqrt{1 - r}$$

where: SEM = the standard error of measurement
SD = the standard deviation of the norm group of scores obtained during the development of the instrument
r = the reliability coefficient

Figure 4.5 uses this formula to calculate the standard error of measurement for an instrument with a given standard deviation of 3 and a reliability coefficient of .78. The manual for this test would probably report the *SEM* as 1.4. Knowing the *SEM* allows the teacher to calculate a range of scores for a particular student, thus providing a better estimate of the student's true ability. Using the SEM of 1.4, the teacher adds and subtracts 1.4 to the obtained score. If the obtained score is 9 (mean = 10), the teacher adds and subtracts the *SEM* to the obtained score of 9:

$$9 + 1.4 = 10.4$$
$$9 - 1.4 = 7.6$$

The range of possible true scores for this student is 7.6 to 10.4.

Thought to represent a range of deviations from an individual's obtained score, the standard error of measurement is based on the normal distribution theory. In other words, by using the standard error of measurement, one can determine the typical deviation for an individual's obtained score as if that person had been administered the same test an infinite number of times. When plotted, the scores form a bell curve, or a normal distribution, with the obtained score representing the mean, median, and mode. As with normal distributions, the range of ± 1 standard error of measurement of the obtained score will occur approximately 68% of the times that the student took the test. This is known as a **confidence interval** because the score obtained within that range can be thought to represent the true score with 68% accuracy. In the previous example, for instance, the student would score between 7.6 and 10.4 about 68% of the time.

confidence interval The range of scores for an obtained score determined by adding and subtracting standard error of measurement units.

$$SEM = 3\sqrt{1 - .78}$$
$$SEM = 3\sqrt{.22}$$
$$SEM = 3 \times .4690415$$
$$SEM = 1.4071245$$

Figure 4.5
Calculating the standard error of measurement (*SEM*) for an instrument with a standard deviation of 3.

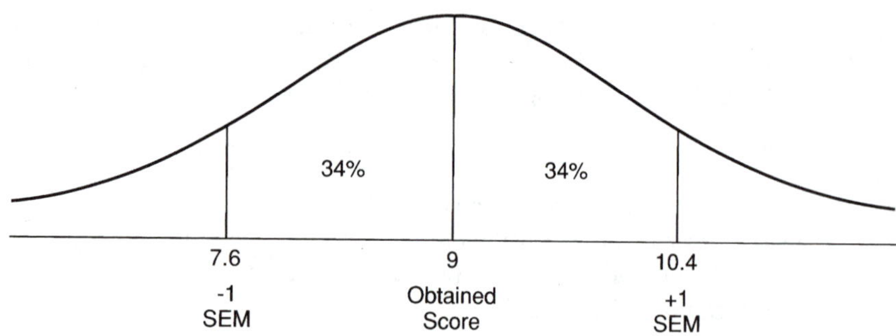

If the teacher wanted 95% confidence that the true score was contained within a range, the band would be extended to ±2 standard errors of measurement of the obtained score. For the example, the extended range would be 6.2 to 11.8. The teacher can assume, with 95% confidence, that the student's true score is within this range.

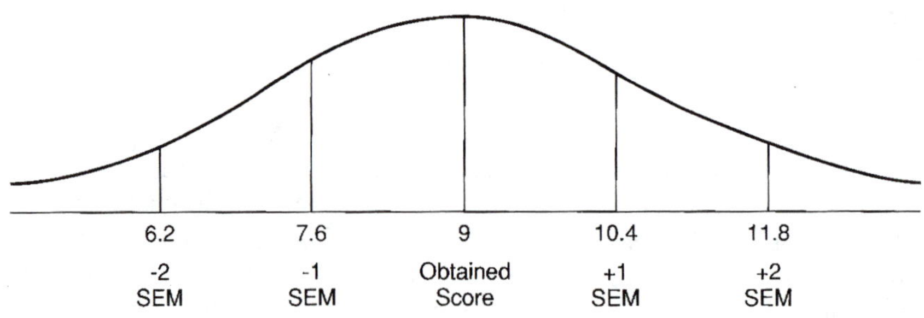

☐ **CHECK YOUR UNDERSTANDING**

Complete Activity 4.6.

Activity 4.6

Use the formula to determine the standard error of measurement with the given standard deviations and reliability coefficients.

$$SEM = SD\sqrt{1 - r}$$

1. $SD = 5$ $r = .67$ SEM: ________
2. $SD = 15$ $r = .82$ SEM: ________
3. $SD = 7$ $r = .73$ SEM: ________
4. $SD = 7$ $r = .98$ SEM: ________
5. $SD = 15$ $r = .98$ SEM: ________

Notice the influence of the standard deviation and the reliability coefficient on the standard error of measurement. Compare the SEMs in problems 3 and 4, which have the same standard deviation but different reliability coefficients. Now compare the SEMs in problems 4 and 5, which have the same reliability coefficient but different standard deviations.

6. What happens to the standard error of measurement as the reliability increases? ____________________

____

7. What happens to the standard error of measurement as the standard deviation increases? ____________________

____

As seen in Activity 4.6, a test with better reliability will have less error. The best tests for educational use are those with high reliability and a smaller standard error of measurement.

Activity 4.7

☐ **CHECK YOUR UNDERSTANDING**

Complete Activity 4.7.

All other factors being equal, which test would you select?

1. Test A: $SD = 4$, $r = .89$ Test B: $SD = 7$, $r = .88$
   Select test: ________
2. Test C: $SEM = 3.20$, $r = .76$ Test D: $SEM = 5.6$, $r = .62$
   Select test: ________

In each of the following problems, calculate the standard error of measurement. Use the calculated SEM to determine the range of scores for the obtained student score. Include the ranges for both the 68% confidence level and the 95% confidence level. Plot the range of scores on the distribution curves provided.

3. $SD = 8$, $r = .74$ Student's score = 85 ($x = 100$)
   $SEM =$ ________ Range for 68% confidence = ________
   Range for 95% confidence = ________

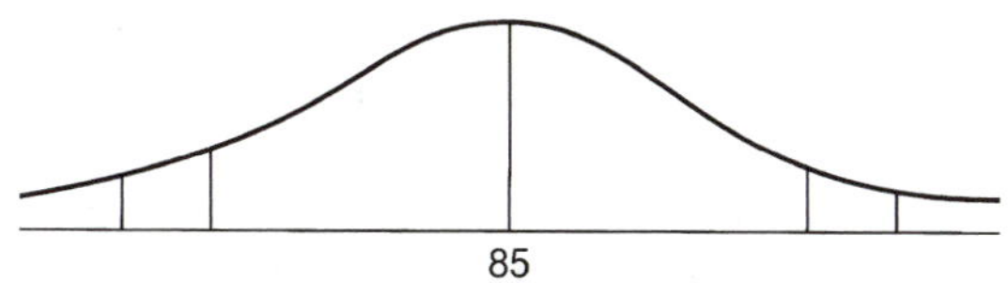

4. $SD = 7$, $r = .82$ Student's score = 82 ($x = 100$)
   $SEM =$ ________ Range for 68% confidence = ________
   Range for 95% confidence = ________

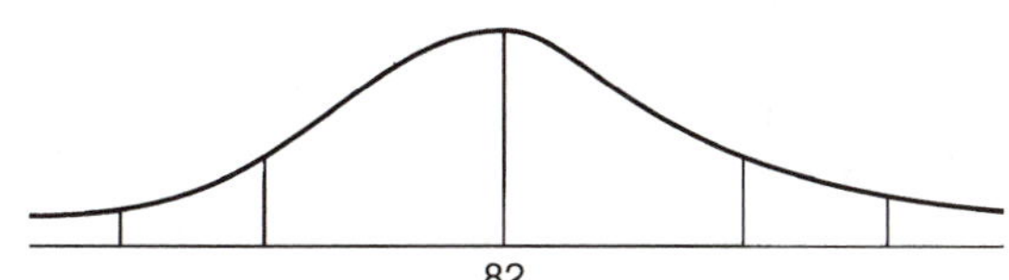

5. Of these two obtained scores, which one would be more representative of a student's true score? Why? ____
____

Applying Standard Error of Measurement

Williams and Zimmerman (1984) stated that whereas test validity remains the most important consideration in test selection, using the standard error of measurement to judge the test's quality is more important than reliability. Williams and Zimmerman pointed out that reliability is a group statistic easily influenced by the variability of the group on whom it was calculated.

Sabers, Feldt, and Reschly (1988) observed that some, perhaps many, testing practitioners fail to consider possible test error when interpreting test results of a student being evaluated for special education services. The range of error and the range of a student's score may vary substantially, which may change the interpretation of the score for placement purposes.

In addition to knowing the standard error of measurement for an assessment instrument, it is also important to know that the standard error of measurement will actually vary by age or grade levels and by subtests. A test may contain less error for certain age or grade groupings than for other groupings. This information will be provided in the technical section of a good test manual.

Table 4.2 is from the KeyMath–Revised (Connolly, 1988) technical data section of the examiner's manual. The standard errors of measurement for the individual subtests are low and fairly consistent. There are some differences, however, in the standard errors of measurement on some subtests at different levels.

Consider the standard error of measurement for the Division subtest at ages 7 and 12 in the spring (S) row. The standard error of measurement for age 7 is 2.0, but for age 12 it is 1.0. The larger standard error of measurement reported for age 7 is probably due to variation in the performance of students who may or may not have been introduced to division as part of the school curriculum. Most 12-year-olds, on the other hand, have probably practiced division in class for several years, and the sample of students tested may have performed with more consistency during the test development.

Given the two standard errors of measurement for the Division subtest at these ages, if a 7-year-old obtained a scaled score (a type of standard score) of 9 on this test ($x = 10$), the examiner could determine with 68% confidence that the true score lies between 7 and 11 and with 95% confidence that the true score lies between 5 and 13. The same scaled score obtained by a 12-year-old would range between 8 and 10 for a 68% confidence interval and between 7 and 11 for 95% confidence. This smaller range of scores is due to less error at this age on this particular subtest.

Table 4.2
Standard errors of measurement, by age, for scaled scores and standard scores from the fall and spring standardization programs.

Subtest/Composite	Program (Fall/Spring)	Age							
		5	6	7	8	9	10	11	12
1. Numeration	F	1.3	1.2	1.0	1.0	1.1	1.1	1.2	1.1
	S	1.7	1.1	1.0	1.0	1.0	1.2	1.1	1.0
2. Rational Numbers	F	—	—	—	—	1.2	1.0	1.0	1.0
	S	—	—	—	1.1	1.3	1.1	1.0	0.8
3. Geometry	F	1.5	1.3	1.4	1.4	1.2	1.2	1.3	1.1
	S	1.2	1.2	1.3	1.3	1.4	1.3	1.3	1.1
4. Addition	F	1.6	1.4	1.4	1.3	1.4	1.7	1.5	1.3
	S	1.8	1.4	1.3	1.4	1.4	1.5	1.3	1.3
5. Subtraction	F	—	1.6	1.5	1.3	1.1	1.1	1.5	1.3
	S	—	1.5	1.3	1.3	1.0	1.1	1.0	1.1
6. Multiplication	F	—	—	—	1.4	1.2	0.9	1.2	1.4
	S	—	—	—	1.0	1.1	1.2	1.1	1.1
7. Division	F	—	—	1.8	1.9	1.6	1.1	1.2	1.0
	S	—	—	2.0	1.6	1.4	1.2	1.1	1.0
8. Mental Computation	F	—	—	—	1.4	1.2	1.1	1.2	1.0
	S	—	—	1.7	1.3	1.2	1.1	1.1	0.9
9. Measurement	F	1.3	1.1	1.5	1.3	1.3	1.2	1.1	1.1
	S	1.2	1.1	1.2	1.1	1.1	1.3	1.1	0.9
10. Time and Money	F	—	1.6	1.3	1.1	1.0	1.0	1.0	1.0
	S	—	1.5	1.2	1.0	0.9	1.0	0.9	0.9
11. Estimation	F	—	1.7	1.8	1.4	1.3	1.3	1.2	1.0
	S	—	1.7	1.7	1.3	1.3	1.2	1.2	1.0
12. Interpreting Data	F	—	—	1.4	1.3	1.1	1.1	1.1	1.1
	S	—	—	1.3	1.2	1.1	1.1	1.1	1.0
13. Problem Solving	F	—	—	1.8	1.6	1.3	1.1	1.2	0.9
	S	—	—	1.6	1.4	1.2	1.1	1.1	0.9
Basic Concepts Area	F	5.8	5.3	4.8	4.7	4.0	3.7	3.9	3.3
	S	5.5	4.8	4.8	4.0	4.2	3.9	3.7	3.0
Operations Area	F	7.7	5.0	4.8	4.0	3.5	3.0	3.7	3.1
	S	7.1	5.0	4.3	3.5	3.2	3.3	2.9	2.7
Applications Area	F	5.8	4.1	4.3	3.6	3.1	2.8	3.0	2.6
	S	5.3	4.4	3.9	3.0	2.9	2.9	2.7	2.3
TOTAL TEST	F	4.1	3.0	2.9	2.5	2.2	1.9	2.2	1.8
	S	3.8	3.0	2.7	2.1	2.1	2.0	1.8	1.6

Source: From *KeyMath–Revised: A Diagnostic Inventory of Essential Mathematics, Manual. Forms A and B* (p. 72) by A. Connolly, 1988, Circle Pines, MN: American Guidance Service. Copyright 1988 by American Guidance Service. Reprinted by permission.

□ **CHECK YOUR UNDERSTANDING**

Complete Activity 4.8.

Activity 4.8

Use Table 4.2 to locate the standard error of measurement for the following situations.

1. The standard error of measurement for a 7-year-old who was administered the Problem Solving subtest in the fall: ________
2. A 12-year-old's standard error of measurement for Problem Solving if the test were administered in the fall: ________
3. Using the standard errors of measurement found in problems 1 and 2, calculate the ranges for each age level if the obtained scores were both 7. Calculate the ranges for 68% and 95% confidence intervals.
   Range for 7-year-old for 68% confidence: ________
   Range for 7-year-old for 95% confidence: ________
   Range for 12-year-old for 68% confidence: ________
   Range for 12-year-old for 95% confidence: ________

Estimated True Scores

estimated true score A method of calculating the amount of error correlated with the distance of the score from the mean of the group.

Another method for approximating a student's true score is called the **estimated true score.** This calculation is founded in theory and research that the farther from a test mean a particular student's score is, the greater the chance for error within the obtained score. Chance errors are correlated with obtained scores (Salvia & Ysseldyke, 1988a). This means that as the score increases away from the mean, the chance error increases. As scores regress toward the mean, the chance error decreases. Therefore, if all of the obtained scores are plotted on a distribution and all of the values of error are plotted on a distribution, the comparison would appear like that in Figure 4.6. Note that the true scores are located closer to the mean with less spread, or variability. The formula for estimated true score (Nunnally, 1967, p. 220) is:

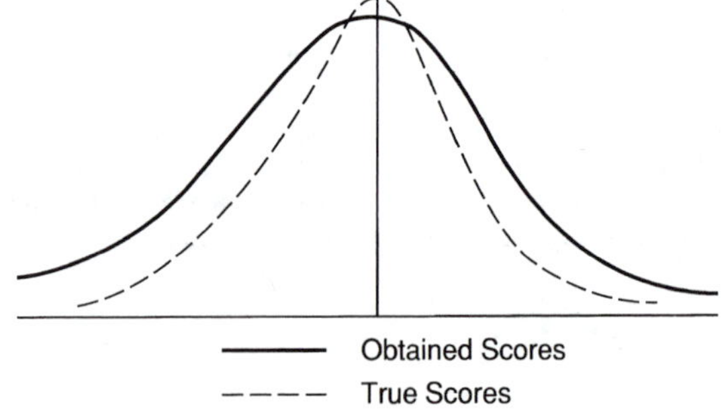

Figure 4.6
Comparison of obtained and true scores.

$$\text{Estimated true score} = M + r(X - M)$$

where: M = mean of group of which person is a member
r = reliability coefficient
X = obtained score

This formula enables the examiner to estimate a possible true score. Because of the correlation of error with obtained scores, the true score is always assumed to be nearer to the mean than the obtained score. Therefore, if the obtained score is 120 (mean = 100), the estimated true score will be lessthan 120. Conversely, if the obtained score is 65, the true score will be greater than 65.

Using the formula for estimated true score, the calculation for an obtained score of 115 with an r of .78 and a mean of 100 would be as follows:

$$\begin{aligned}\text{Estimated true score} &= 100 + .78\,(115 - 100)\\ &= 100 + .78(15)\\ &= 100 + 11.7\\ &= 111.7\end{aligned}$$

In this example, 111.7 is closer to the mean of 100 than 115.

Following is an example where the obtained score is less than the estimated true score:

Obtained score = 64, mean = 100, r = .74

$$\begin{aligned}\text{Estimated true score} &= 100 + .74(64 - 100)\\ &= 100 + .74(-36)\\ &= 100 - 26.64\\ &= 73.36\end{aligned}$$

The estimated true score can then be used to establish a range of scores by using the standard error of measurement for the estimated true score. Assume that the standard error of measurement for the estimated true score of 111.7 is 4.5. The range of scores ± 1 standard error of measurement for 111.7 would be 107.2 to 116.2 for 68% confidence and 102.7 to 120.7 for 95% confidence.

The use of estimated true scores to calculate bands of confidence using standard error of measurement rather than using obtained scores has received some attention in the literature (Cahan, 1989; Feldt, Sabers, & Reschly, 1988; Sabers et al., 1988; Salvia & Ysseldyke, 1988a; Salvia & Ysseldyke, 1988b). Whether using estimated true scores to calculate the range of possible scores or obtained scores to calculate the range of scores, several important points must be remembered. All test scores contain error. Error must be considered when interpreting test scores. The best practice, whether using estimated true scores or obtained scores, will employ the use of age- or grade-appropriate reliability coefficients and standard errors of measurement for the tests or subtests in question. When the norming process provides comparisons based on demographic variables, it is best to use the appropriate normative comparison.

Test Validity

To review, reliability refers to the dependability of the assessment instrument. The questions of concern for reliability are: (a) Will students obtain similar scores if given the test a second time? (b) If the test is halved, will the administration of each half result in similar scores for the same student? (c) If different forms are available, will the administration of each form yield similar scores for the same student? (d) Will the administration of each item reliably measure the same trait or skill for the same student?

validity The quality of a test; the degree to which an instrument measures what it was designed to measure.

Validity is not concerned with repeated dependable results but rather with the degree of good results for the purpose the test is designed. In other words, does the test actually measure what it is supposed to measure? If the educator wants to assess multiplication skills, will the test provide the educator with a valid indication of the student's math ability? Several methods can be used to determine the degree to which the instrument measures what the test developers intended the test to measure. Some methods are better than others, and some of the methods are more easily understood. When selecting assessment instruments, the educator should carefully consider the validity information.

Criterion-Related Validity

criterion-related validity Statistical method of comparing an instrument's ability to measure a skill, trait, or domain with an existing instrument or other criterion.

Criterion-related validity is a method for determining the validity of an instrument by comparing its scores with other criteria known to be indicators of the same trait or skill that the test developer wishes to measure. The test is compared with another criterion. There are two main types of criterion-related validity, which are differentiated by time factors.

concurrent validity A comparison of one instrument with another within a short period of time.

Concurrent Validity. **Concurrent validity** studies are conducted within a small time frame. The instrument in question is administered, and shortly thereafter an additional device in used, typically a similar test. Because the data are collected within a short time period, often the same day, this type of validity study is called concurrent validity. The data from both devices are correlated to see if the instrument in question has significant concurrent criterion-related validity. The correlation coefficient obtained is called the *validity coefficient.* As with reliability coefficients, the nearer the coefficient is to ± 1.00, the greater the strength of the relationship. Therefore, when the students in the sample obtain similar scores on both instruments, the instrument in question is said to be measuring the same trait or a degree or component of the same trait with some accuracy.

Suppose the newly developed Best in the World Math Test was administered to a sample of students, and shortly thereafter the Good Old Terrific Math Test was administered to the same sample. The validity coefficient obtained was .83. The educator selecting the Best in the World Math Test would have some confidence that it would measure, to some degree, the same traits or skills measured by the Good Old Terrific Math Test. These types of studies are helpful in determining if new tests and revised tests are measuring with some degree of accuracy the same skills as those measured by older, more researched instruments. Studies may compare other criteria as well, such as teacher ratings or motor performance of a like task. As expected, when comparing unlike instruments or criteria, these would probably not correlate highly. A test measuring creativity would probably not have a high validity coefficient with an advanced algebra test, but the algebra test would probably correlate better with a test measuring advanced trigonometry.

Predictive Validity. **Predictive validity** is a measure of a specific instrument's ability to predict performance on some other measure or criterion at a later date.

predictive validity A measure of how well an instrument can predict future on some other variable.

Common examples of tests that predict future ability are a screening test to predict success in first grade, a Scholastic Aptitude Test (SAT) to predict success in college, a Graduate Record Exam (GRE) to predict success in graduate school, and an academic potential or academic aptitude test to predict success in school. Much of psychoeducational assessment conducted in schools concerns using test results to predict future success or failure in a particular educational setting. Therefore, when this type of testing is carried out, it is important that the educator selects an instrument with good predictive validity research. Using a test to predict which students should enroll in basic math and which should enroll in advanced algebra will not be in the students' best interests if the predictive validity of the instrument is poor.

Content Validity

Professionals may assume that instruments that reflect a particular content within the name of the test or subtest have **content validity.** In many cases, this is not true. For example, on the Wide Range Achievement Test–Revision 3 (Wilkinson, 1993), the subtest Reading does not actually measure reading ability. It measures only one aspect of reading: word recognition. A teacher might use the score obtained on the subtest to place a student, believing that the student will be able to comprehend reading material at a particular level. In fact, the student may be able to recognize only a few words from that reading level. This subtest has inadequate content validity for measuring overall reading ability.

content validity Occurs when the items contained within the test are representative of the content purported to be measured.

For a test to have good content validity, it must contain the content in a representative fashion. For example, a math achievement test that only has 10 addition and subtraction problems but no other math operations has not represented the content of the domain of math adequately. A good representation of content will include several items from each domain, level, and skill being measured.

Some of the variables of content validity may influence the manner in which results are obtained and can contribute to bias in testing. These variables may conflict with the nondiscriminatory test practice regulations of IDEA and the APA (1985) *Standards*. These variables include **presentation format** and **response mode**:

presentation format The method in which items of an instrument are presented to a student.

response mode The method required for the examinee to answer items of an instrument.

1. *Presentation format.* Are the items presented in the best manner to assess the skill or trait? Requiring a student to silently read math problems and supply a verbal response could result in test bias if the student is unable to read at the level presented. The content being assessed may be math applications or reasoning, but the reading required to complete the task has reduced the instrument's ability to assess math skills for this particular student. Therefore, the content validity has been threatened, and the results obtained may unduly discriminate against the student.
2. *Response mode.* Like presentation format, the response mode may interfere with the test's ability to assess skills that are unrelated to the response mode. If the test was designed to assess reading ability but required the student to respond in writing, the test would discriminate against a student who had a motor impairment that made writing difficult or impossible. Unless the response mode is adapted, the targeted skill—reading ability—will not be fairly or adequately measured.

Content validity is a primary concern in the development of new instruments. The test developers may adjust, omit, or add items during the field-testing stage. These changes are incorporated into a developmental version of the test that is administered to samples of students.

Construct Validity

construct validity The ability of an instrument to measure psychological constructs.

Establishing **construct validity** for a new instrument may be more difficult than establishing content validity. *Construct,* in psychoeducational assessment, is a term used to describe a psychological trait, personality trait, psychological concept, attribute, or theoretical characteristic. To establish construct validity, the construct must be clearly defined. Constructs are usually abstract concepts, such as intelligence and creativity, that can be observed and measured by some type of instrument. Construct validity may be more difficult to measure than content because constructs are hypothetical and even seem invisible. Creativity is not seen, but the products of that trait may be observed, such as in writing or painting.

In establishing the construct validity of an instrument, the validity study may involve another measure that has been researched previously and has been shown to be a good indicator of the construct or of some degree or component of the construct. This is, of course, comparing the instrument to some other criterion, which is criterion-related validity. (Don't get confused!) Often in test development, the validity studies may involve several types of criterion-related validity to establish different types of validity. Anastasi (1988) listed the following types of studies that are considered when establishing a test's construct validity:

1. *Developmental changes.* Instruments that measure traits that are expected to change with development should have these changes reflected in the scores if the changeable trait is being measured (such as academic achievement).
2. *Correlations with other tests.* New tests are compared with existing instruments that have been found valid for construct being measured.
3. *Factor analysis.* This statistical method determines how much particular test items cluster together, which illustrates measurement of like constructs.
4. *Internal consistency.* The degree with which individual items appear to be measuring the same constructs in the same manner or direction.
5. *Convergent and discriminant validation.* Tests should correlate highly with other instruments measuring the same construct but should not correlate with instruments measuring very different constructs.
6. *Experimental interventions.* Tests that are designed to measure traits, skills, or constructs that can be influenced by interventions (such as teaching) should have the intervention reflected by changes in pretest and posttest scores. (pp. 153–159)

Validity of Tests versus Validity of Test Use

Professionals in special education and in the judicial system have understood for quite some time that test validity and **validity of test use** for a particular instrument are two separate issues (Cole, 1981). Tests may be used inappropriately even though they are valid instruments (Cole, 1981). The results obtained in testing may also be used in an invalid manner by placing children inappropriately or predicting educational futures inaccurately (Heller, Holtzman, & Messick, 1982).

validity of test use The appropriate use of a specific instrument.

Some validity-related issues contribute to bias in the assessment process and subsequently to the invalid use of the test instruments. Content, even though it may validly represent the domain of skills or traits being assessed, may discriminate against different groups. *Item bias,* a term used when an item is answered incorrectly a disproportionate number of times by one group compared to another group, may exist even though the test appears to represent the content domain. An examiner who continues to use an instrument found to contain bias may be practicing discriminatory assessment, which is failure to comply with IDEA.

Predictive validity may contribute to test bias by predicting accurately for one group and not another. Educators should select and administer instruments only after careful study of the reliability and validity research contained in test manuals.

Reliability versus Validity

A test may be reliable; that is, it may measure a trait with about the same degree of accuracy time after time. The reliability does not guarantee that the trait is measured in a valid or accurate manner. A test may be consistent and reliable, but not valid. It is important that a test has had thorough research studies in both reliability and validity.

Exercises

Part I

Match the following terms with the correct definitions.

A. reliability
B. validity
C. internal consistency
D. correlation
E. coefficient alpha
F. scattergram
G. estimated true score
H. Pearson's *r*
I. interrater reliability
J. test-retest reliability
K. equivalent forms reliability
L. true score
M. predictive validity
N. criterion-related validity
O. positive correlation
P. K-R 20
Q. validity of test use
R. negative correlation
S. confidence interval
T. split-half reliability
U. standard error of measurement

_______ **1.** The dependability of a test across time or items.
_______ **2.** Consistency of a test across examiners.
_______ **3.** A statistical formula for calculating the degree of a relationship between two sets of variables
_______ **4.** Graphic representation of a correlation.
_______ **5.** Relationships between two variables.
_______ **6.** Degree to which a test measures what it was designed to measure.
_______ **7.** A study that repeats the administration of a single instrument to study consistency across time.
_______ **8.** The consistency with which a trait or skill is measured across items on a single instrument.
_______ **9.** Measuring the consistency of two halves of a test.
_______ **10.** Measuring the consistency of two like forms with items matched for difficulty levels.
_______ **11.** Stands for Kuder-Richardson formula to measure internal consistency.
_______ **12.** Like K-R 20, checks for internal consistency of an instrument.
_______ **13.** A typical amount of error contained in an obtained score on a specific instrument.

_________ **14.** A method of calculating a true score that is based on the correlation of chance error with distance from the mean.

_________ **15.** Procedure of checking an instrument's validity against another criterion.

_________ **16.** Determining if a test is appropriate to use with a particular student.

_________ **17.** Measure of how well an instrument predicts future performance on a different criterion.

_________ **18.** Describes the relationship between variables that seem to move in the same direction; high scores on one variable are associated with high scores on the other variable.

_________ **19.** The range of scores calculated using the standard error of measurement for the obtained score.

_________ **20.** Describes relationship between variables that move in different directions; high scores on one variable are associated with low scores on the other variable.

Part II

Complete the following sentences and solve the problem.

1. The score obtained during the assessment of a student may not be the _________________ score, because all testing situations are subject to chance _________________ .
2. A closer estimation of the student's best performance can be calculated by using the _________________ _________________ score.
3. A range of possible scores can then be determined by using the _________________ for the specific test.
4. When calculating the range of possible scores, it is best to use the appropriate standard error of measurement for _________________ or _________________ if this is provided in the test manual.
5. The confidence with which the examiner wants to interpret the obtained score can be based upon ±1 standard error of measurement for _________________ % confidence or ±2 standard error of measurement for _________________ % confidence.
6. The larger the standard error of measurement, the less _________________ the test, and the smaller the standard error of measurement, the more _________________ the test.
7. Use the following set of data to determine the mean, median, mode, range, variance, standard deviation, standard error of measurement, and possible range for each score assuming 68% confidence. The reliability coefficient is .85.

   Data: 50, 75, 31, 77, 65, 81, 90, 92, 76, 76, 74, 88

   Mean: _________ Median: _________ Mode: _________

   Range: _________ Variance: _________ Standard deviation: _________

Standard error of measurement: ________

Obtained Score	Range of True Scores	
a. 50	From ________	to ________
b. 75	From ________	to ________
c. 31	From ________	to ________
d. 77	From ________	to ________
e. 65	From ________	to ________
f. 81	From ________	to ________
g. 90	From ________	to ________
h. 92	From ________	to ________
i. 76	From ________	to ________
j. 76	From ________	to ________
k. 74	From ________	to ________
l. 88	From ________	to ________

8. Using a mean of 100 and a reliability coefficient of .79, calculate the estimated true score for the observed score of 118. The formula to use is:

$$\text{Estimated true score} = M + r(X - M)$$

where: M = mean of group of which person is a member
R = reliability coefficient
X = observed score

Estimated true score: ________

Part III

Check the statements that are true concerning reliability and validity.

________ **1.** Criterion-related validity can be either concurrent or predictive depending on the time variable.

________ **2.** A test-retest reliability coefficient can be inflated by practice effect.

________ **3.** The reliability coefficients obtained in an equivalent forms study will be at least as high as those scores obtained in a test-retest study.

________ **4.** Construct validity seeks to establish that measurement of a psychological construct has occurred by use of a particular instrument.

________ **5.** According to Anastasi (1988), one method of documenting construct validity is to show that little or no correlation occurs with instruments that measure unlike constructs.

________ **6.** A test that has good validity can be used appropriately in any situation.

References

American Psychological Association. (1985). *Standards for educational and psychological testing.* Washington, DC: Author.

Anastasi, A. (1988). *Psychological testing* (pp. 153–159). New York: Macmillan.

Cahan, S. (1989). Don't throw the baby out with the bath water: The case for using estimated true scores in normative comparisons. *The Journal of Special Education, 22,* 503–506.

Cole, N. (1981). Bias in testing. *American Psychologist, 36,* 1067–1075.

Connolly, A. (1988). *KeyMath–Revised: A diagnostic inventory of essential mathematics, manual. Forms A and B.* Circle Pines, MN: American Guidance Service.

Feldt, L., Sabers, D., & Reschly, D. (1988). Comments on the reply by Salvia and Ysseldyke. *The Journal of Special Education, 22,* 374–377.

Flaugher, R. (1978). The many definitions of test bias. *American Psychologist, 33,* 671–678.

Heller, K., Holtzman, W., & Messick, S. (Eds.). (1982). *Placing children in special education: A strategy for equity.* Washington, DC: National Academy Press.

Mehrens, W., & Lehmann, I. (1978). *Standardized tests in education.* New York: Holt, Rinehart & Winston.

Nunnally, J. (1967). *Psychometric theory.* New York: McGraw-Hill.

Sabers, D., Feldt, L., & Reschly, D. (1988). Appropriate and inappropriate use of estimated true scores for normative comparisons. *The Journal of Special Education, 22,* 358–366.

Salvia, J., & Ysseldyke, J. (1988a). *Assessment in remedial and special education* (4th ed.). Dallas: Houghton Mifflin.

Salvia, J., & Ysseldyke, J. (1988b). Using estimated true scores for normative comparisons. *The Journal of Special Education, 22,* 367–373.

Walsh, B., & Betz, N. (1985). *Tests and assessment.* Englewood Cliffs, NJ: Prentice-Hall.

Wilkinson, G. S. (1993). *The Wide Range Achievement Test: Administration manual.* Wilmington, DE: Jastak, Wide Range.

Williams, R., & Zimmerman, D. (1984). On the virtues and vices of standard error of measurement. *The Journal of Experimental Education, 52,* 231–233.

Chapter Five

An Introduction to Norm-Referenced Assessment

Key Terms

domain
item pool
developmental version
field test
norm-referenced test
sample
norm group
interpolation
chronological age
test manual
protocol
raw score
basal
ceiling

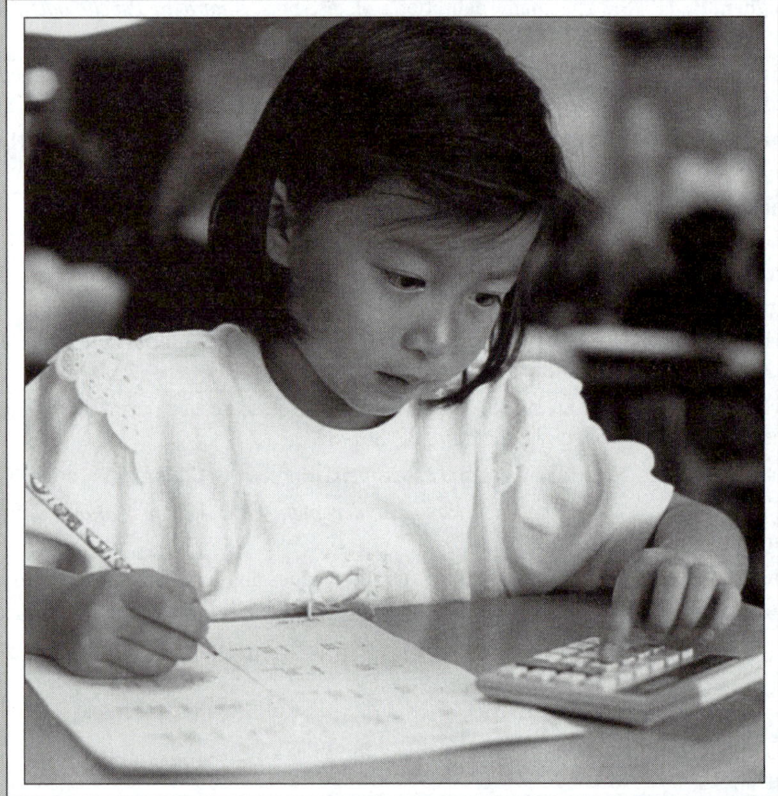

How Norm-Referenced Tests Are Constructed

Test developers who wish to develop an instrument to assess an educational **domain,** behavioral trait, cognitive ability, motor ability, or language ability, to name a few areas, will establish an **item pool** of test items. An item pool is a representation of items believed to thoroughly assess the given area. The items are gathered from several sources. For example, developers may use published educational materials, information from educational experts in the field, published curriculum guides, and information from educational research to collect items for the initial item pool for an educational domain. These items are carefully scrutinized for appropriateness, wording, content, mode of response required, and developmental level. The items are sequentially arranged according to difficulty. The developers consult with professionals with expertise in the test's content area, and after thorough analysis of the items, administer a **developmental version** to a small group as a **field test**. During the field-testing stage, the test is administered by professionals in the appropriate discipline (education, psychology, speech-language, etc.). The professionals involved in the study critique the test items, presentation format, response mode requirements, administration procedures, and the actual test materials. At this time, revisions may be made, and the developmental version is then ready to be administered to a large sample of the population for whom it was designed.

A **norm-referenced test** is designed to provide the teacher with the capability of comparing the performance of one student with the average performance of other students in the country who are of the same age or grade level. It is not practical or possible to test every student of that same age or grade level; therefore, a **sample** of students is selected as the comparison group, or **norm group**. In the norming process, the test is administered to a representative sample of students from across the country. A good representation will include a large number of students, usually a few thousand students, who represent diverse groups. Ideally, samples of students from all cultures and linguistic backgrounds who represent the diverse students for whom the test was developed

domain An area of cognitive development or ability thought to be evidenced by certain behaviors or skills.

item pool A large collection of test items thought to effectively represent a particular domain or content area.

developmental version The experimental edition of a test that is field-tested and revised before publication.

field test The procedure of trying out a test by administering it to a sample population.

norm-referenced test A test designed to yield average performance scores, which may be used for comparing individual student performances.

sample A small group of people thought to represent the population for whom the test was designed.

norm group A large number of people who are administered a test to establish comparative data of average performances.

will be included in the norming process. The norming process should also include students with various disabilities.

The development of a norm-referenced test and the establishment of comparison performances usually occur in the following manner. The items of the test, which are sequentially arranged in the order of difficulty, are administered to the sample population. The performance of each age group and each grade group is analyzed. The average performance of the 6-year-olds, 7-year-olds, 8-year-olds, and so on is determined. The test results are analyzed by grade groups as well, determining the average performance of first graders, second graders, and so on. The analysis of the test results may resemble Table 5.1.

The average number correct in Table 5.1 represents the arithmetic average number of items successfully answered by the age or grade group of students who made up the norming sample. Because these figures will later be used to compare other students' performances on the same instrument, it is imperative that the sample of students be representative of the students who will later be assessed. Comparing a student to a norm sample of students who are very different from the student will not be an objective or fair comparison. Factors such as socioeconomic, cultural, or linguistic background; existing disabilities; and emotional environment are variables that may influence a student's performance. The student should be compared with other students with similar backgrounds and of the same age or grade level.

The data displayed in Table 5.1 illustrate the mean performance of students in a particular age or grade group. Although the data represent an average score for each age or grade group, often test developers analyze the data further. For example, the average performance of typical students at various times throughout the school year may be determined. To provide this information, the most accurate

Table 5.1
Analysis of results from the Absolutely Wonderful Academic Achievement Test.

Grade	Average Number of Items Correct	Age	Average Number of Items Correct
K	11	5	9
1	14	6	13
2	20	7	21
3	28	8	27
4	38	9	40
5	51	10	49
6	65	11	65
7	78	12	79
8	87	13	88
9	98	14	97
10	112	15	111
11	129	16	130
12	135	17	137

norming process would include nine additional administrations of the test, one for each month of the school year. This is usually not practical or possible in most instances of test development. Therefore, to obtain an average expected score for each month of the school year, the test developer usually calculates the scores using data obtained in the original administration through a process known as **interpolation,** or further dividing the existing data (Anastasi, 1988).

interpolation The process of dividing existing data into smaller units for establishing tables of developmental scores.

Suppose that the test developer of the Absolutely Wonderful Academic Achievement Test actually administered the test to the sample group during the middle of the school year. To determine the average performance of students throughout the school year, from the first month of the school year through the last month, the test developer further divides the correct items of each group. In the data in Table 5.1, the average performance of second graders in the sam-

Table 5.2
Interpolated grade equivalents for corresponding raw scores.

Number of Items Correct	Grade
17	2.0
17	2.1
18	2.2
18	2.3
19	2.4
20	2.5
20	2.6
21	2.7
22	2.8
23	2.9
24	3.0
25	3.1
26	3.2
27	3.3
27	3.4
28	3.5
29	3.6
30	3.7
31	3.8
32	3.9
33	4.0
34	4.1
35	4.2
36	4.3
37	4.4
38	4.5
39	4.6
40	4.7
42	4.8
43	4.9

Table 5.3
Interpolated age equivalents for corresponding raw scores.

Average Number of Items Correct	Age Equivalents
57	11-0
58	11-1
60	11-2
61	11-3
62	11-4
63	11-5
65	11-6
66	11-7
68	11-8
69	11-9
70	11-10
71	11-11
72	12-0

ple group is 20, the average performance of third graders is 28, and the average performance of fourth graders is 38. These scores might be further divided and listed in the test manual on a table like Table 5.2.

chronological age The numerical representation of a student's age, expressed in years, months, and days.

The obtained scores also might be further divided by age groups so that each month of a **chronological age** is represented. The scores for age 11 might be displayed in a table like Table 5.3.

It is important to notice that age scores are written with a dash or hyphen, whereas grade scores are expressed with a decimal. The reason for this is that grade scores are based on a 10-month school year and can be expressed by using decimals, whereas age scores are based on a 12-month calendar year and therefore should not be expressed using decimals. For example, 11-4 represents an age of 11 years and 4 months, but 11.4 represents the grade score of the 4th

☐ **CHECK YOUR UNDERSTANDING**

Complete Activity 5.1.

Activity 5.1

Answer the following questions.

1. In Table 5.1, what was the average score of the sample group of students in grade 7? ________
2. According to Table 5.1, what was the average number of correct items of the sample group of students who were 16 years of age? ________
3. What was the average number of correct items of the sample group of students who were 6 years of age? ________
4. Why did students who were in first grade have an average number of 14 correct responses while students in grade 6 had an average of 65 correct responses? ____

____

5. According to the information provided in Table 5.2, what was the average number of correct responses for students in the 3rd month of grade 3?

____

6. Were students in the sample tested during the 3rd month of the third grade? _________ By what means was the average for each month of the school year determined? _________

7. According to the information provided in Table 5.3, what was the average number of correct responses for students of the chronological age 11-2?

____

8. Write the meaning of these expressions:
   4.1 means _________
   4-1 means _________
   3.3 means _________
   6-7 means _________
   10.8 means _________

---

month of the 11th grade. If the scores are expressed incorrectly, a difference of about 6 grades or 5 years could be incorrectly interpreted.

Basic Steps in Test Administration

When administering a norm-referenced standardized test, it is important to remember that the test developer specified the instructions for the examiner and the examinee. The **test manual** contains much information, and the examiner must read it thoroughly and understand it before administering the test. The examiner should practice administering all sections of the test many times before using the test with a student. The first few attempts of practice administration should be supervised by someone who has had experience with the instrument. Legally, any individual test administration should be completed in the manner set forth by the test developer and should be administered by trained personnel, according to IDEA. The *Standards* of the American Psychological Association (1985) hold educators responsible for the administration of any test that may be used in making educational decisions (see chapter 2).

test manual A manual that accompanies a test instrument and contains instructions for administration and norm tables.

The examiner should carefully carry out the mechanics of test administration. The first few steps are simple; however, careless errors can occur and may make a difference in the decisions made regarding a student's educational future. The **protocol** of a standardized test is the form used during the test administration and for scoring and interpreting test results. The first page of the protocol provides space for writing basic information about the student. Figure 5.1 shows the first page of the protocol of the *Kaufman Test of Educational Achievement* (Kaufman & Kaufman, 1985). The examiner must complete the top portion of the protocol before administering the test. The remainder of the protocol is completed during and after the administration of the test.

protocol The response sheet or record form used by the examiner to record the student's answers.

Comprehensive Form

K-TEA

KAUFMAN TEST of EDUCATIONAL ACHIEVEMENT

by Alan S. Kaufman & Nadeen L. Kaufman

INDIVIDUAL TEST RECORD

Student's Name ____ Sex ____

Parent's Name ____

Home Address ____ Home Phone ____

Grade ____ Teacher ____

School ____ Examiner ____

	Year	Month	Day
Test Date			
Birth Date			
Chronological Age			

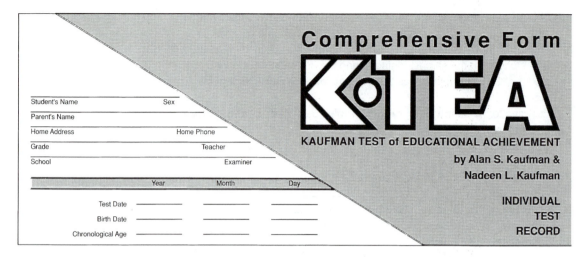

Figure 5.1

Kaufman Test of Educational Achievement, Comprehensive Form protocol.

Source: From *Kaufman Test of Educational Achievement,* K-TEA Comprehensive Form protocol, by A. Kaufman and N. Kaufman, 1985. Circle Pines, MN: American Guidance Service. Copyright 1985 by American Guidance Service. Reprinted by permission.

Beginning Testing

The following suggestions will help the examiner establish a positive testing environment and increase the probability that the student will feel comfortable and therefore perform better in the testing situation.

1. Establish familiarity with the student before the first day of testing. Several meetings in different situations with relaxed verbal exchange are recommended. The examiner may wish to participate in an activity with the student and observe behavior and language skills informally.

2. When the student meets with the examiner on test day, spend several minutes in friendly conversation before beginning the test. Do not begin testing until the student seems to feel at ease with the examiner.

3. Explain why the testing has been suggested at the level of understanding that is appropriate for the student's age and developmental level. It is important that the student understand that the testing session is important; however, the child should not feel threatened by the test. Examples of explanations include the following:

- To see how you work (solve) math problems
- To see how we can help you achieve in school
- To help you make better progress in school
- [Or if the student has revealed specific weaknesses] To see how we can help you with your spelling [or English, or science, etc.] skills.

Proper testing posture allows the examiner to observe the students' performance and easily record responses.

4. Give a brief introduction about the test. The introduction might be: "This test is about school work. It has some math problems and reading passages like you have in class." Or, "This test will help us learn how you think in school," or "This test will show us the best ways for you to learn."

5. Begin testing in a calm manner. Be certain that all instructions are followed carefully.

During test administration, the student may ask questions or give answers that are very close to the correct response. On many tests, clear instructions are given that tell the examiner when to prompt for an answer or when to query for a response. Some items on certain tests may not be repeated. Some items are timed. The best guarantee for accurate assessment techniques is for the examiner to become very familiar with the test manual. General guidelines for test administration, suggested by McLoughlin and Lewis (1990), are presented in Figure 5.2.

Calculating Chronological Age

Many tests have protocols that provide space for calculating the student's chronological age on the day that the test is administered. It is imperative that

Test administration is a skill, and testers must learn how to react to typical student comments and questions. The following general guidelines apply to the majority of standardized tests.

STUDENT REQUESTS FOR REPETITION OF TEST ITEMS

Students often ask the tester to repeat a question. This is usually permissible as long as the item is repeated verbatim and in its entirety. However, repetition of memory items measuring the student's ability to recall information is not allowed.

ASKING STUDENTS TO REPEAT RESPONSES

Sometimes the tester must ask the student to repeat a response. Perhaps the tester did not hear what the student said, or the student's speech is difficult to understand. However, the tester should make every effort to see or hear the student's first answer. The student may refuse to repeat a response or, thinking that the request for repetition means the first response was unsatisfactory, answer differently.

STUDENT MODIFICATION OF RESPONSES

When students give one response, then change their minds and give a different one, the tester should accept the last response, even if the modification comes after the tester has moved to another item. However, some tests specify that only the first response may be accepted for scoring.

CONFIRMING AND CORRECTING STUDENT RESPONSES

The tester may not in any way—verbal or nonverbal—inform a student whether a response is correct. Correct responses may not be confirmed; wrong responses may not be corrected. This rule is critical for professionals who both teach and test, because their first inclination is to reinforce correct answers.

Figure 5.2
General guidelines for test administration.
Source: From *Assessing Special Students* (3rd ed., p. 77) by J. McLoughlin and R. Lewis, 1990, Columbus, OH: Merrill. Copyright 1990 by Macmillan Publishing Company. Reprinted by permission.

this calculation is correct because the chronological age may be used to determine the correct norm tables used to interpret the test results.

The chronological age is calculated by writing the test date first and then subtracting the date of birth. The dates are written in the order of year, month, and day. In performing the calculation, remember that each of the columns represents a different numerical system, and if the number that is subtracted is larger than the number from which the difference is to be found, the numbers must be converted appropriately. This means that the years are based on 12 months, and the months are based on 30 days. An example is shown in Figure 5.3.

REINFORCING STUDENT WORK BEHAVIOR

Although testers cannot praise students for their performance on specific test items, good work behavior can and should be rewarded. Appropriate comments are "You're working hard" and "I like the way you're trying to answer every question." Students should be praised between test items or subtests to ensure that reinforcement is not linked to specific responses.

ENCOURAGING STUDENTS TO RESPOND

When students fail to respond to a test item, the tester can encourage them to give an answer. Students sometimes say nothing when presented with a difficult item, or they may comment, "I don't know" or "I can't do that one." The tester should repeat the item and say, "Give it a try" or "You can take a guess." The aim is to encourage the student to attempt all test items.

QUESTIONING STUDENTS

Questioning is permitted on many tests. If in the judgment of the tester the response given by the student is neither correct nor incorrect, the tester repeats the student's answer in a questioning tone and says, "Tell me more about that." This prompts the student to explain so that the response can be scored. However, clearly wrong answers should not be questioned.

COACHING

Coaching differs from encouragement and questioning in that it helps a student arrive at an answer. The tester must *never* coach the student. Coaching invalidates the student's response; test norms are based on the assumption that students will respond without examiner assistance. Testers must be very careful to avoid coaching.

ADMINISTRATION OF TIMED ITEMS

Some tests include timed items; the student must reply within a certain period to receive credit. In general, the time period begins when the tester finishes presentation of the item. A watch or clock should be used to time student performance.

	Year	Month	Day
	89	12 → 3 →	30
Test date	~~90~~	~~4~~	2
Birth date	−81	−10	−8
Chronological age	8	5	24

Figure 5.3
Calculation of chronological age for a student who is 8 years and 6 months old.

Notice (in Figure 5.3) that when subtracting the days, the number 30 is added to 2 to find the difference. When subtraction of days requires borrowing, a whole month, or 30 days, must be used. When borrowing to subtract months, the number 12 is added, because a whole year must be borrowed.

When determining the chronological age for testing, the days are rounded to the nearest month. Days are rounded up if there are 15 or more days by adding a month. The days are rounded down by dropping the days and using the month found through the subtraction process. Here are some examples:

	Years	*Months*	*Days*	
Chronological age:	7-	4-	17	rounded up to 7-5
Chronological age:	9-	10-	6	rounded down to 9-10
Chronological age:	11-	11-	15	rounded up to 12-0

☐ **CHECK YOUR UNDERSTANDING**

Complete Activity 5.2.

Activity 5.2.

Calculate the chronological ages using the following birth dates and test dates.

			Year	Month	Day
1. Birth date:	5-4-84	Date of test:	________	________	________
Test date:	3-2-94	Date of birth:	________	________	________
		Chronological age:	________	________	________
2. Birth date:	7-5-85	Date of test:	________	________	________
Test date:	11-22-93	Date of birth:	________	________	________
		Chronological age:	________	________	________
3. Birth date:	10-31-87	Date of test:	________	________	________
Test date:	6-20-90	Date of birth:	________	________	________
		Chronological age:	________	________	________

4. Round the following chronological ages to years and months.

Years	Months	Days	Rounded to:
7-	10-	23	**4.** ________
11-	7-	14	**5.** ________
14-	11-	29	**6.** ________

Calculating Raw Scores

raw score The first obtained score in test administration; usually the number of items counted as correct.

The first score obtained in the administration of a test is the **raw score.** On most educational instruments, the raw score is simply the number of items the student answers correctly. Figure 5.4 shows the calculation of a raw score for one student. The student's correct responses are marked with a 1, incorrect responses with a 0.

The number of items answered correctly on this test was 8, which is expressed as a raw score. The raw score will be entered into a table in the test manual to determine the derived scores, which are norm-referenced scores ex-

1.	1	11.	0
2.	1	12.	1
3.	1	13.	0
4.	1	14.	0
5.	0	15.	0
6.	0	16.	
7.	1	17.	
8.	1	18.	
9.	0	19.	
10.	1	20.	

Raw Score: 8

Figure 5.4
Calculation for student who began with item 1 and correctly answered 8 of 15 attempted items.

pressed in different ways. The administration of this test was stopped when the student missed 3 consecutive items, because the test manual stated to stop testing when this occurred.

Determining Basals and Ceilings

The student whose scores are shown in Figure 5.4 began with item 1 and ended when 3 consecutive errors were made. The starting and stopping points of a test must be determined so that unnecessary items are not administered. Some tests contain hundreds of items, many of which may not be developmentally appropriate for all students.

Most educational tests contain starting rules in the manual, protocol, or actual test instrument. These rules are guides that can help the examiner begin testing with an item at the appropriate level. These guides may be given as age recommendations—for example, 6-year-olds begin with item 10—or as grade-level recommendations—for example, fourth-grade students begin with item 25. These starting points are meant to represent a level at which the student could answer all previous items correctly and are most accurate for students who are functioning close to age or grade expectancy.

Often, students referred for special education testing function below grade- and age-level expectancies. Therefore, the guides or starting points suggested by the test developers may be inappropriate. It is necessary to determine the **basal** level for the student, or the level at which all easier items, those items located at lower levels, could be answered correctly. Once the basal has been established, the examiner can proceed with testing the student. If the student fails to obtain a basal level, the test may be considered too difficult, and another instrument should be selected.

basal Thought to represent the level of skills below which all test items would be answered correctly.

The rules for establishing a basal level are given in the test manuals, and many tests contain the information on the protocol. The basal rule may be the same as a ceiling rule, such as 3 consecutively correct responses or 5 consecutively correct responses. The basal rule may also be expressed as completing an entire level correctly. No matter what the rule, the objective is the same: to establish a level that is thought to represent a foundation and at which all easier items would be assumed correct.

The examples shown in Figure 5.5 illustrate a basal rule of 3 consecutive correct responses on Test I and a basal of all items answered correctly on an entire level of the test on Test II.

It may be difficult to select the correct item to begin with when testing a special education student. The student's social ability may seem to be age appropriate but his academic ability may be significantly below expectancy for his age and grade placement. The examiner may begin with an item that is too easy or too difficult. Although it is not desirable to administer too many items that are beneath the student's academic level, it is better to begin the testing session with the positive reinforcement of answering items correctly than with the negative reinforcement of answering several items incorrectly, and experiencing a sense of failure or frustration. The examiner should obtain a basal by selecting an item believed to be a little below the student's academic level.

Even when the examiner chooses a starting item believed to be easy for a student, sometimes the student will miss items before the basal is established. In this case, most test manuals contain instructions for determining the basal. Some manuals instruct the examiner to test backward in the same sequence, until a basal can be established. After the basal is determined, the examiner proceeds from the point where the backward sequence was begun. Other test manuals instruct the examiner to drop back an entire grade level or to drop back the number of items required to establish a basal. For example, if 5

Figure 5.5
Basal level established for test I for 3 consecutive correct responses; basal level for test II established when all items in one level (grade 1) are answered correctly.

TEST I		***TEST II***		
1.	______	**Level K**	**1.**	______
2.	______		**2.**	______
3.	______		**3.**	______
4.	______		**4.**	______
5.	______	**Grade 1**	**5.**	1
6.	1		**6.**	1
7.	1		**7.**	1
8.	1		**8.**	1
9.	0	**Grade 2**	**9.**	0
10.	1		**10.**	1
			11.	0
			12.	1

consecutive correct responses are required for a basal, the examiner is instructed to drop back 5 items and begin administration. If the examiner is not familiar with the student's ability in a certain area, the basal may be even more difficult to establish. The examiner in this case may have to drop back several times. For this reason, the examiner should circle the number of the first item administered. This information can be used later in the test interpretation.

Students may establish two or more basals; that is, using the 5-consecutive-correct rule, a student may answer 5 correct, miss an item, then answer 5 consecutive correct again. The test manual may address this specifically, or it may not be mentioned. Unless the test manual states that the examiner may use the second or highest basal, it is best to use the first basal established.

☐ **CHECK YOUR UNDERSTANDING**

Complete Activity 5.3.

Activity 5.3

Using the following basal rules, identify basals for these students.

Test I (Basal: 5 consecutive correct)			Test II (Basal: 7 consecutive correct)	
1.	______	Grade 4	25.	______
2.	______		26.	______
3.	______		27.	______
4.	______		28.	______
5.	______		29.	______
6.	1		30.	______
7.	1	Grade 5	31.	1
8.	1		32.	1
9.	1		33.	1
10.	1		34.	1
11.	0		35.	1
12.	1	Grade 6	36.	1
13.	0		37.	1
14.	1		38.	0
			39.	1
			40.	0

Basal items are: ________ Basal items are: ________

The instructions given in the test manual state that if a student fails to establish a basal with 5 consecutive correct items, the examiner must drop back 5 items from the first attempted item and begin testing. Which item would the examiner begin with in the following examples?

Example 1		Example 2	
22.		116.	
23.		117.	
24.		118.	
25.		119.	
26.		(120.)	1
27.		121.	1
28.		122.	1
(29.)	1	123.	0
30.	0	124.	
31.		125.	
32.		126.	
Drop to item:		Drop to item:	

When calculating the raw score, all items that appear before the established basal are counted as correct. This is because the basal is thought to represent the level at which all easier items would be passed. Therefore, when counting correct responses, count items below the basal as correct even though they were not administered.

ceiling Thought to represent the level of skills above which all test items would be answered incorrectly; the examiner discontinues testing at this level.

Just as the basal is thought to represent the level at which all easier items would be passed, the **ceiling** is thought to represent the level at which more difficult items would not be passed. The ceiling rule may be 3 consecutive incorrect or even 5 items out of 7 items answered incorrectly. Occasionally, an item is administered above the ceiling level by mistake, and the student may answer correctly. Because the ceiling level is thought to represent the level at which more difficult items would not be passed, these items usually are not counted. Unless the test manual states that the examiner is to count items above the ceiling, it is best not to do so.

Using Information on Protocols

The protocol, or response form, for each test contains valuable information that can aid in test administration. Detailed instructions regarding the basal and ceiling rules for individual subtests of an educational test may be found on most protocols for educational tests.

Many tests have ceiling rules that are the same as the basal rules; for example, 5 consecutive incorrect responses are counted as the ceiling, and 5 consecutive correct responses establish the basal. Some tests, however, have different basal and ceiling rules, so it is necessary to read instructions carefully. If the protocol does not provide the basal and ceiling rules, the examiner is wise to write this information at the top of the pages of the protocol for the sections to be administered.

☐ CHECK YOUR UNDERSTANDING

Complete Activity 5.4.

Activity 5.4

Calculate the raw scores for the following protocol sections. Follow the given basal and ceiling rules.

Protocol 1 (Basal: 5 consecutive correct; Ceiling: 5 consecutive incorrect)		Protocol 2 (Basal: 3 consecutive correct; Ceiling: 3 consecutive incorrect)	
223.	______	**10.**	______
224.	______	**11.**	1
225.	______	**12.**	1
226.	______	**13.**	1
227.	1	**14.**	0
228.	1	**15.**	1
229.	1	**16.**	1
230.	1	**17.**	1
231.	1	**18.**	1
232.	0	**19.**	0
233.	1	**20.**	1
234.	1	**21.**	1
235.	0	**22.**	1
236.	0	**23.**	0
237.	0	**24.**	0
238.	0	**25.**	0
239.	0	**26.**	______
Raw score:	________	Raw score:	________

1. Which protocol had more than one basal? ________
2. What were the basal items on protocol 1? ________
3. What were the ceiling items on protocol 1? ________
4. What were the basal items on protocol 2? ________
5. What were the ceiling items on protocol 2? ________

The protocols for each test are arranged specifically for that test. Some forms contain several subtests that may be arranged in more than one order. On very lengthy tests, the manual may provide information about selecting only certain subtests rather than administering the entire test. Other tests have age- or grade-appropriate subtests, which must be selected according to the student's level. Some instruments use the raw score on the first subtest to determine the starting point on all other subtests. And finally, some subtests require the examiner to begin with item 1 regardless of the age or grade level of the student. Specific instructions for individual subtests may be provided on the protocol as well as in the test manual.

Educational tests often provide training exercises at the beginning of subtests. These training exercises help the examiner explain the task to the student and better ensure that the student understands the task before answering the first scored item. The student may be allowed to attempt the training tasks more than once, or the examiner may be instructed to correct wrong answers and explain the correct responses. These items are not scored, however, and a subtest may be skipped if the student does not understand the task. The use of training exercises varies.

Administering Tests: For Best Results

Students tend to respond more and perform better in testing situations with examiners who are familiar with them (Fuchs, Zern, & Fuchs, 1983). As suggested previously, the examiner should spend some time with the student before the actual evaluation. The student's regular classroom setting is a good place to begin. The examiner should talk with the student in a warm manner and repeat visits to the classroom before the evaluation. It may also be helpful for the student to visit the testing site to become familiar with the environment. The examiner may want to tell the student that they will work together later in the week or month. The testing session should not be the first time the examiner and student meet. Classroom observations and visits may aid the examiner in determining which tests to administer. Chances for successful testing sessions will increase if the student is not overtested. Although it is imperative that all areas of suspected disability be assessed, multiple tests that measure the same skill or ability are not necessary.

☐ CHECK YOUR UNDERSTANDING

Complete Activity 5.5.

Activity 5.5

Using the protocol and the responses in Figure 5.6, calculate the raw score for this subtest of the Peabody Individual Achievement Test–Revised (Markwardt, 1989). Determine the basal and ceiling items for this student.

1. How many trials are allowed for the training exercises on this subtest?
   ____
2. According to the responses shown, what items are included in the student's basal level? ________
3. What instructions are provided about establishing the basal? ________
   ____
4. According to the responses shown, what items are included in the student's ceiling level? ________

After the examiner and student are in the testing room, the examiner should attempt to make the student feel at ease. The examiner should convey the importance of the testing situation without making the student feel anxious. As

SUBTEST 2
Reading Recognition

Training Exercises

	Trial 1	Trial 2	Trial 3
Exercise A.	(1) ______	(1) ______	(1) ______
Exercise B.	(3) ______	(3) ______	(3) ______
Exercise C.	(2) ______	(2) ______	(2) ______

Basal and Ceiling Rules
Basal: *highest* 5 consecutive correct responses
Ceiling: *lowest* 7 consecutive responses containing 5 errors

Starting Point
The item number that corresponds to the subject's raw score on General Information.

43. ledge ____1____
44. escape ____1____
45. northern ____1____
46. towel ____1____
47. kneel ____1____
48. height ____0____
49. exercise ____1____
50. observe ____1____
51. ruin ____0____
52. license ____1____
53. uniforms ____0____
54. pigeon ____1____
55. moisture ____0____
56. artificial ____1____
57. issues ____0____
58. quench ____0____
59. hustle ____0____
60. thigh ____0____

READING RECOGNITION
Ceiling Item ______
minus Errors ______
equals RAW SCORE ______

Figure 5.6
Basal and ceiling rules and response items for a subtest from the Peabody Individual Achievement Test–Revised.

Source: From *Peabody Individual Achievement Test–Revised,* subtest 2, Reading Recognition, by F. C. Markwardt, 1989, Circle Pines, MN: American Guidance Service. Copyright 1989 by American Guidance Service. Reprinted by permission.

suggested by McLoughlin and Lewis (1990), the examiner should encourage the student to work hard and should reinforce the student's attempts and efforts, not correct responses. Responses that reinforce the efforts of the student may include statements such as "You are working so hard today," or "You like math work," or "I will be sure to tell your teacher [or mother or father, etc.] how hard you worked." If the student asks about his performance on specific items ("Did I get that one right?"), the examiner should again try to reinforce effort.

Young students may enjoy a tangible reinforcer upon the completion of the testing session. The examiner may tell the student near the end of the session to work just a few more items for a treat or surprise. Reinforcement with tangibles is not recommended during the assessment, because the student may lose interest in the test or no longer pay attention.

During the administration of the test, the examiner must be sure to follow all instructions in the manual. As stated in the APA (1985) *Standards* and IDEA, tests must be given in the manner set forth by the test developer, and adapting tests must be done by professionals with expertise in the specific area being assessed who are cognizant of the psychometric changes that will result.

Cole, D'Alonzo, Gallegos, Giordano, and Stile (1992) suggested that examiners consider several additional factors to decrease bias in the assessment process. The following considerations, adapted from Cole et al. (1992), can help the examiner determine whether the test can be administered in a fair way:

1. Do sensory or communicative impairments make portions of the test inaccessible?
2. Do sensory or communicative impairments limit students from responding to questions?
3. Do test materials or method of responding limit students from responding?
4. Do background experiences limit the student's ability to respond?
5. Does the content of classroom instruction limit students from responding?
6. Is the examiner familiar to the student?
7. Are instructions explained in a familiar fashion?
8. Is the recording technique required of the student on the test familiar? (p. 219)

Obtaining Derived Scores

The raw scores obtained during the test administration are used to locate other derived scores from norm tables included in the examiner's manuals for the specific test. The derived scores may include percentile ranks, grade equivalents, standard scores with a mean of 100 or 50, and other standardized scores, such as z scores.

There are advantages and disadvantages to using the different types of derived scores. Of particular concern is the correct use and interpretation of grade equivalents and percentile ranks. These two types of derived scores are used

	YEAR	MONTH	DAY
Test date	91	10	5
Birth date	84	11	10
Chronological age	____	____	____

General Directions:

Read Chapter 3 in the *Manual* carefully before administering and scoring the test. The correct procedures for establishing the subtest basal and ceiling are detailed in the chapter. Briefly, the criteria are as follows: *The basal is the 3 consecutive correct responses immediately preceding the easiest item missed; the ceiling is 3 consecutive errors.*

Begin administration at the Numeration item designated as the starting item for the student's grade level. Score items by penciling a 1 (correct) or 0 (incorrect) in the box. Continue administration until a basal and a ceiling have been extablished for the Numeration subtest. Use the Numeration basal item (the first item of the Numeration basal) to determine the starting points for the remaining subtests; for example, if the student's Numeration basal item is 18, begin the Rational Numbers subtest at item 2, begin the Geometry subtest at item 13, and so on.

The item-score boxes are positioned in columns indicating which domain each item belongs to. When totaling the scores in a domain column, count as *correct* the *un*administered items in that column that *precede* the easiest item administered. The resulting total for the column is the domain score. The sum of the domain scores is the subtest raw score.

1 NUMERATION

GRADE	Item	Numbers 0-9	Numbers 0-99	Numbers 0-999	Multi-digit numbers
K,1 ▸	1. how many deer	1			
	2. as many fingers	1			
	3. read 5, 2, 7	1			
	4. read in order 5, 2, 7	1			
	5. how many people	0			
2,3 ▸	6. fourth person	1			
	7. ____ 20 ____		0		
	8. read in order 36 15 70 32		1		
	9. how many rods		0		
4 ▸	10. how many dots		0		
	11. order 643 618 305 648			1	
5-7 ▸	12. blue dot		0		
	13. 729 739 749 ____ ____			0	
	14. order 3,649 3,581 3,643				0
	15. how many small cubes				
8,9 ▸	16. round to nearest hundred				
	17. how many pencils				
	18. four-digit number				
	19. read 6,019,304				
	20. number in blue box				
	21. how many small cubes				
	22. three-digit number				
	23. less than positive four				
	24. what does 10^4 represent				
____ CEILING ITEM	DOMAIN SCORES				

SUBTEST RAW SCORE (Sum of domain scores) ____

Figure 5.7
Chronological age portion and Numeration subtest from the KeyMath–Revised protocol.

Source: From *Key Math–Revised,* protocol B, individual test record (pp. 1, 2) by A. J. Connolly, 1988, Circle Pines, MN: American Guidance Service. Copyright 1988 by American Guidance Service. Reprinted by permission.

frequently because the basic theoretical concepts are thought to be understood; however, these two types of scores are misunderstood and misinterpreted by professionals (Huebner, 1988, 1989; Wilson, 1987). The reasons for this misinterpretation are the lack of understanding of the numerical scale used and the method used in establishing grade-level equivalents.

Percentile ranks are used often because they can be easily explained to parents. The concept, for example, of 75% of the peer group scoring at the same level as or below a particular student is one that parents and professionals can understand. The difficulty in interpreting percentile ranks is that they do not represent a numerical scale with equal intervals. For example, the standard scores between the 50th and 60th percentiles are quite different than the standard scores between the 80th and 90th percentile ranks.

The development of grade equivalents needs to be considered when using these derived scores. Grade equivalents represent the average number of items answered correctly by the students in the standardization sample of a particular grade. These equivalents may not represent the actual skill level of particular items or of a particular student's performance on a test. Many of the skills tested on academic achievement tests are taught at various grade levels. The grade level of presentation of these skills depends on the curriculum used. The grade equivalents obtained therefore may not be representative of the skills necessary to pass that grade level in a specific curriculum.

Exercises

Part I

Match the following terms with the correct definitions.

A. domain
B. norm-referenced test
C. item pool
D. test manual
E. sample
F. ceiling
G. raw score
H. developmental version
I. grade equivalent
J. norm group
K. interpolation
L. chronological age
M. protocol
N. basal
O. field test

_______ **1.** A small group of people thought to represent the population for whom the test was designed.

_______ **2.** An area of cognitive development or ability thought to be evidenced by certain behaviors or skills.

_______ **3.** Thought to represent the level of skills below which all test items would be answered correctly.

_______ **4.** The first obtained score in the administration; usually the number of items counted as correct.

_________ **5.** The response sheet or record form used by the examiner to record the student's answers.

_________ **6.** A large collection of test items thought to effectively represent a particular domain or content area.

_________ **7.** The experimental edition of a test that is field-tested and revised before publication.

_________ **8.** The process of dividing existing data into smaller units for establishing tables of developmental scores.

_________ **9.** A large number of people who are administered a test to establish comparative data of average performances.

_________ **10.** The numerical representation of a student's age, expressed in years, months, and days.

_________ **11.** A manual that accompanies a test instrument and contains instructions for administration and norm tables.

_________ **12.** A test designed to yield average performance scores, which may be used for comparing individual student performances.

_________ **13.** Thought to represent the level of skills above which all test items would not be answered correctly; the examiner discontinues testing at this level.

_________ **14.** The procedure of trying out a test by administering it to a sample of the population.

Part II

Using the portions from the KeyMath–Revised (Connolly, 1988) protocol in Figure 5.7, determine the following:

1. Chronological age: _________
2. Domain scores: _________
3. Raw score: _________
4. Basal item: _________
5. Ceiling item: _________

References

American Psychological Association. (1985). *Standards for Educational and Psychological Testing.* Washington, DC: Author.

Anastasi, A. (1988). *Psychological testing* (6th ed.). New York: Macmillan.

Cole, J., D'Alonzo, B., Gallegos, A., Giordano, G., & Stile, S. (1992). Test biases that hamper learners with disabilities. *Diagnostique, 17,* 209–225.

Connolly, A. J. (1988). *KeyMath–Revised.* Circle Pines, MN: American Guidance Service.

Fuchs, D., Zern, D., & Fuchs, L. (1983). A microanalysis of participant behavior in familiar and unfamiliar test conditions. *Exceptional Children, 50,* 75–77.

Huebner, E. (1988). Bias in teachers' special education decisions as a further function of test score reporting format. *Journal of Educational Research, 21,* 217–220.

Huebner, E. (1989). Errors in decision-making: A comparison of school psychologists' interpretations of grade equivalents, percentiles, and deviation IQs. *School Psychology Review, 18,* 51–55.

Kaufman, A. S., & Kaufman, N. L. (1985). *Kaufman Test of Educational Achievement.* Circle Pines, MN: American Guidance Service.

Markwardt, F. C. (1989). *Peabody Individual Achievement Test–Revised.* Circle Pines, MN: American Guidance Service.

McLoughlin, J., & Lewis, R. (1990). *Assessing special students* (3rd ed.). Columbus, OH: Merrill.

Wilson, V. (1987). Percentile scores. In C. R. Reynolds & L. Mann (Eds.), *Encyclopedia of special education: A reference for the education of the handicapped and other exceptional children and adults* (p. 1656). New York: Wiley.

Part Three

Assessing Students

Chapter Six
Tests of Educational Achievement

Chapter Seven
Standardized Diagnostic Testing

Chapter Eight
Informal Assessment Techniques

Chapter Nine
Assessment of Behavior

Chapter Ten
Measures of Intelligence and Adaptive Behavior

Chapter Eleven
Other Diagnostic Instruments

Chapter Six

Tests of Educational Achievement

Key Terms

achievement tests
screening tests
group achievement tests
aptitude tests
diagnostic tests
adaptive behavior scales
individual achievement tests
subtests
norm referenced tests
curriculum-based assessment
W score

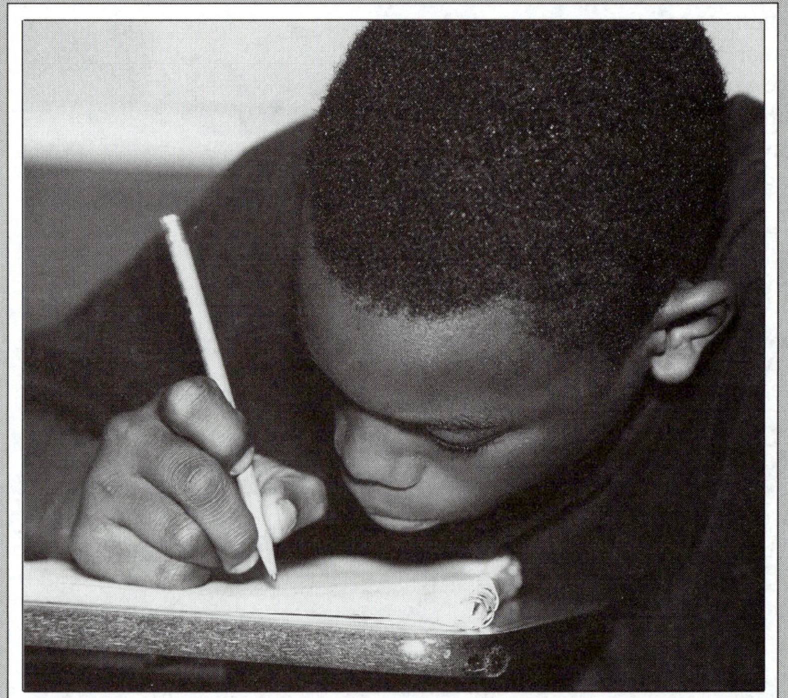

Professionals working with students who need special services or special education are concerned with how those students perform on educational measures. One way to measure educational performance is to use achievement tests. Of all standardized tests, individually administered achievement tests are the most numerous (Anastasi, 1988). Other types of tests, such as group screening tests, diagnostic tests (chapter 7), aptitude tests, and adaptive behavior scales (chapter 10) are used not only to measure educational performance but also to diagnose specific learning weaknesses and identify strengths. This chapter focuses on individually administered achievement tests.

Achievement Tests

Used in virtually every school, **achievement tests** are designed to measure what the student has learned. These tests may be developed to measure a specific area of the educational curriculum, such as written language, or to measure across several areas of the curriculum, such as math, reading, spelling, and science. Achievement tests that assess across many areas are known as **screening tests** and contain items that survey a range of skill levels and content areas. Screening tests assess no one area in depth. These achievement tests provide the educator with a method to determine weak areas rather than specific skill mastery.

achievement tests Tests used to measure academic progress, what student has retained in curriculum.

screening tests Broad-based tests that sample a few items across a curriculum.

Group achievement tests are created to assess in a screening fashion. These achievement tests can be given to a class or several students at a time. Multiple curriculum areas are tested, and test results show general strengths and weaknesses. Although these instruments thoroughly assess the curriculum areas included, the administration of a group achievement test requires little effort or training of the examiner. These tests may be machine scored by a testing company, which sends a printout of the results, sometimes with interpretations, to the school and parents. Because they are computer generated, interpretations of the test results follow a somewhat standard format, providing few implications for educational planning. Group achievement tests are often used to indicate which students may need further diagnostic testing.

group achievement tests Tests administered to a group of students to measure academic gains.

aptitude tests Tests designed to measure strength, talent, or ability in a particular area or domain.

diagnostic tests Individually administered tests designed to determine specific academic problems or deficit areas.

adaptive behavior scales Instruments that assess a student's ability to adapt to the world in different situations.

Aptitude tests contain items that measure what a student has retained but are also designed to indicate how much the student will learn in the future. Aptitude tests are thought to indicate current areas of strength as well as future potential. These tests are used in educational planning and include both group and individually administered tests. **Diagnostic tests** are those used to measure a specific ability, such as fine-motor ability. **Adaptive behavior scales** measure how well students adapt to different environments.

Group versus Individual Achievement Tests

Tests that are constructed to be administered to large groups of students are not appropriate for most special education purposes. When administered a test in a group environment, a student does not have access to the examiner for query or clarification of test items. Many group tests are timed, which may limit the responses of the special education student. Moreover, group testing does not allow the examiner to observe behaviors of the special education student, which may be beneficial in educational intervention planning. Many students receiving special education support services may not perform as well on group achievement tests due to a readability level and a test format that require the student to sustain attention for long periods of time and to work independently. Standardized group achievement tests may be beneficial for screening students in the mainstream who may need prereferral interventions or referral for additional individual assessment.

individual achievement tests Tests administered to individual students to measure academic progress.

subtests Parts of a test that measure skills in specific areas or domains.

In special education, the achievement tests used most often to measure academic gain are **individual achievement tests.** Individual achievement tests may be screening tests or diagnostic tests. Screening tests measure across several curriculum areas, and diagnostic tests measure achievement in one specific area. A diagnostic reading test, for example, might contain the following **subtests**: recognition of letters, word recognition, word comprehension, oral reading, and phonetic skills. Diagnostic tests often include information to help the educator analyze errors and plan educational objectives. Some diagnostic tests have suggestions for specific skill remediation or strategies for learners to master skill deficits. Specific educational diagnostic tests are presented in chapter 7.

Standardized Norm-Referenced Tests versus Curriculum-Based Assessment

norm-referenced tests Tests designed to compare individual students with national averages, or norms of expectancy.

The use of **norm-referenced tests** to measure academic achievement helps educators make both placement and eligibility decisions. When selected and administered carefully, these tests yield fairly reliable and valid information. As discussed in the previous chapter, norm-referenced instruments are researched and constructed in a systematic way and provide educators with a method of comparing a student with a peer group evaluated during the standardization process of the test development. Comparing a student to a norm reference group allows the educator to determine if the student is performing as expected for her age or grade. If the student appears to be significantly behind her peers developmentally, special services may be recommended.

Curriculum-based assessment tests students on the very curriculum used for instruction. In this method of determining mastery of skills or specific curriculum, the student may be compared with her past performance on similar items or tasks. Curriculum-based testing, which is very useful and necessary in special education, is discussed further in chapter 8.

curriculum-based assessment Using content from the currently used curriculum to assess student progress.

The Review of Achievement Tests

This text is designed to involve the student in the learning process and to help the student develop skills in administering and interpreting tests. Rather than including numerous tests, many of which the future teacher may not use, this chapter presents achievement tests selected because of their frequent use in schools and/or because of their technical adequacy. The following are individually administered screening achievement tests used frequently by special educators:

1. *Woodcock-Johnson Psycho-Educational Battery.* Frequent use of this test battery was reported by teachers of students who have learning disabilities and by teachers of students who have been diagnosed as mentally retarded (Connelly, 1985). The newly revised edition of the Tests of Achievement includes two new writing subtests that have shown high to moderate correlation with the Test of Written Language, the Picture Story Language Test, and the MAT6 Writing Test of the Metropolitan Achievement Test (Mather, 1989).

2. *Peabody Individual Achievement Test.* This test was listed as one of the most frequently used by professionals in Child Service Demonstration Centers (Thurlow & Ysseldyke, 1979); by school psychologists (LaGrow & Prochnow-LaGrow, 1982); by special education teachers who listed this as one of the most useful tests (Connelly, 1985); and by teachers who are in both self-contained and resource classrooms for students with learning disabilities (German, Johnson, & Schneider, 1985).

3. *Kaufman Test of Educational Achievement.* This relatively new test has received favorable review (Worthington, 1987) and has had positive correlations with the Wide Range Achievement Test in both spelling and math and moderate correlation with the reading subtests (Webster, Hewett, & Crumbacker, 1989).

4. *Wide Range Achievement Test.* This test was listed as useful by teachers of students with emotional disabilities, learning disabilities, and mental retardation (Connelly, 1985); by teachers in self-contained and resource rooms for students with learning disabilities (German, Johnson, & Schneider, 1985); by school psychologists (LaGrow & Prochnow-LaGrow, 1982; Reschly, 1988); and by teachers in Child Service Demonstration Centers (Thurlow & Ysseldyke, 1979). This text describes the third edition of the Wide Range Achievement Test (Wilkinson, 1993).

These tests, which represent several academic areas, are discussed in the following sections. Their reliability and validity are presented in an effort to encourage future teachers to be wise consumers of assessment devices.

Woodcock-Johnson Psycho-Educational Battery–Revised (WJ–R) Tests of Achievement

This revised version of the Woodcock-Johnson Tests of Achievement (Woodcock & Johnson, 1989), presented in an easel-type format, comprises two parallel achievement batteries, which allow the examiner to retest the same student within a short amount of time with less practice effect. The battery of subtests allows the examiner to select the specific subtests needed for a particular student. This achievement battery has standard subtests and supplemental subtests. The test developers recommend that the beginning examiner learn to administer the Standard Battery before attempting to learn the Supplemental Battery. The developers recommend that examiners conduct practice sessions and use the practice exercises contained in the examiner's manual (Woodcock & Mather, 1989).

Some of the features of the WJ–R Tests of Achievement include the following:

1. Basal and ceiling levels on most of the subtests occur when the student answers 6 consecutive items correctly (basal) and 6 consecutive items incorrectly (ceiling). The examiner is instructed to continue testing by complete pages so that additional items may be administered beyond the ceiling level. When items are administered above the ceiling or below the basal, occasionally items will be answered correctly above the ceiling or incorrectly below the basal. As a general rule, the manual advises the examiner to count any incorrect response as incorrect and any correct response as correct.

2. Derived scores can be obtained for each individual subtest and also for clusters of subtests.

W *scores* Derived scores of the Woodcock-Johnson Psycho-Educational Battery.

3. The protocol gives derived scores for ***W* scores,** age equivalents, grade equivalents, and standard error of measurement, allowing quick scoring during testing.

4. The norm group ranged in age from 2 to 90 years and also included students at the college/university level. Examiners can conduct testing at extreme ages and now have better data for comparative analysis of college-level students.

5. The use of extended age scores provides a more comprehensive analysis of children and adults who are not functioning at a school grade level.

6. Several subtests require paper and pencil responses, which can be used to analyze written expressive language. In addition, the Dictation subtest provides for analysis of grammatical structure, spelling, and punctuation.

Figure 6.1 illustrates the organization of the WJ–R Tests of Achievement. Note that the subtests are grouped into broad clusters to aid in the interpreta-

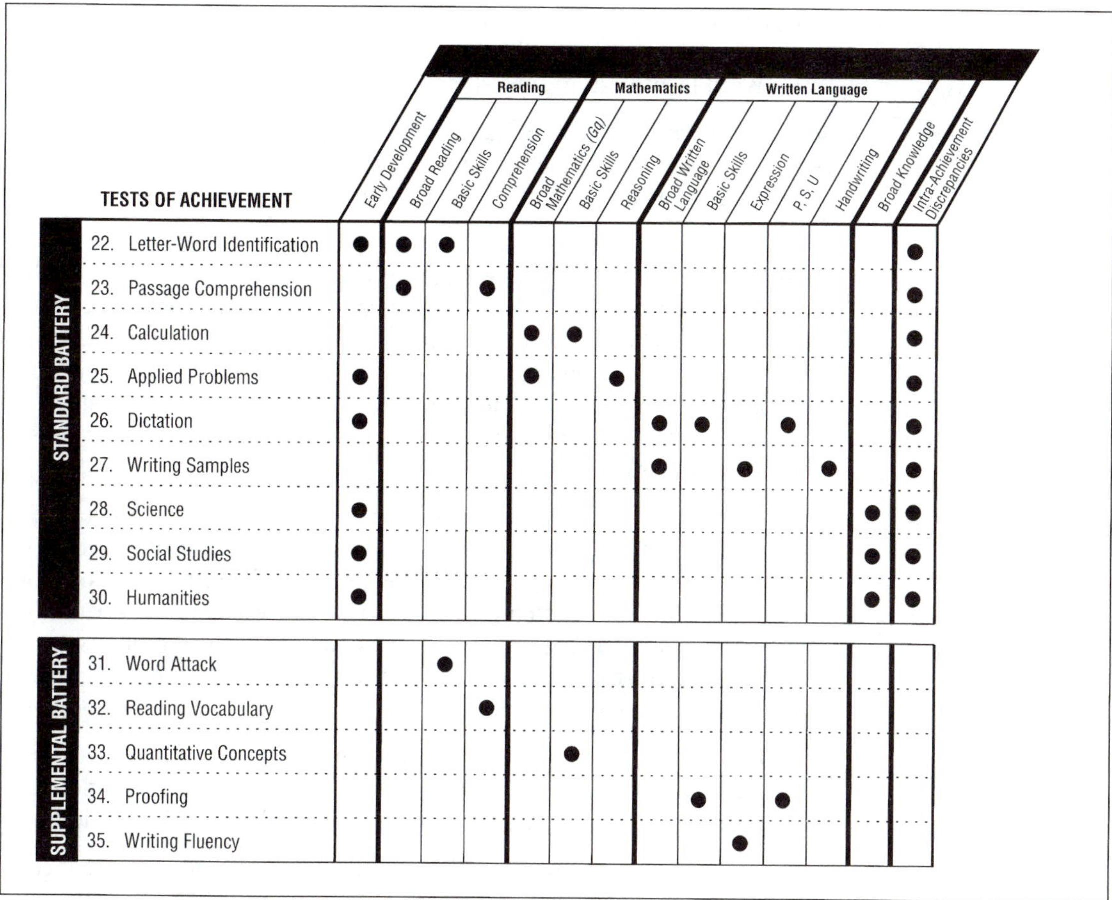

TESTS OF ACHIEVEMENT		Reading			Mathematics			Written Language						
	Early Development	Broad Reading	Basic Skills	Comprehension	Broad Mathematics (Gq)	Basic Skills	Reasoning	Broad Written Language	Basic Skills	Expression	P. S. U	Handwriting	Broad Knowledge	Intra-Achievement Discrepancies
STANDARD BATTERY														
22. Letter-Word Identification	●	●	●											●
23. Passage Comprehension		●		●										●
24. Calculation					●	●								●
25. Applied Problems	●				●		●							●
26. Dictation	●							●	●		●			●
27. Writing Samples								●		●		●		●
28. Science	●												●	●
29. Social Studies	●												●	●
30. Humanities	●												●	●
SUPPLEMENTAL BATTERY														
31. Word Attack			●											
32. Reading Vocabulary				●										
33. Quantitative Concepts						●								
34. Proofing									●		●			
35. Writing Fluency										●				

Figure 6.1

Selective testing table of the WJ–R Tests of Achievement.

Source: From *Woodcock-Johnson Psycho-Educational Battery–Revised Tests of Achievement: Standard and Supplemental Batteries, Examiner's Manual* (p. 12) by R. W. Woodcock and N. Mather, 1989, Allen, TX: DLM Teaching Resources. Copyright 1989 by DLM Teaching Resources. Reprinted by permission.

tion of scores. The examiner may select the specific subtests needed to screen a student's achievement level.

Standard Battery. The subtests in the Standard Battery are described in the following paragraphs.

Letter-Word Identification. The student is presented with a picture, letter, or word and asked to identify it orally. The basal and ceiling levels are 6 consecutive items correct and incorrect, respectively.

Passage Comprehension. The examiner shows the student a passage with a missing word, and the student must orally supply the word. The basal and ceiling levels are 6 consecutive correct and incorrect items, respectively.

Calculation. Math problems are presented in a paper and pencil format. The basal and ceiling levels are the same as for the Passage Comprehension and Letter-Word Identification subtests.

Applied Problems. The examiner reads a "story" math problem, and the student must answer orally. Picture cues are provided at the lower levels. The basal and ceiling levels are determined in the same manner as for the Calculation subtest.

Dictation. This subtest includes spelling, punctuation, and usage items. Using an answer sheet, the student writes responses to items such as "write the word used when there is more than one knife." The examiner's test manual provides specific instructions about when to count errors for misspelled words (only on spelling items) and when misspelled words are allowed (such as on a punctuation item). The basal and ceiling levels are 6 consecutive correct and incorrect items, respectively.

Writing Samples. This subtest requires the student to construct age-appropriate sentences meeting specific criteria (for syntax, content, etc.). The items are scored as 2, 1, or 0 based on the quality of the responses. The examiner's manual provides a comprehensive scoring guide and, for experienced examiners, a brief scoring guide that give examples and qualifications for responses. Although this subtest requires the most time to score, it provides useful information for intervention.

Science. The examiner orally presents open-ended questions that cover scientific content. The basal and ceiling levels are 6 consecutive correct and incorrect items, respectively. Picture cues are given at the lower and upper levels.

Social Studies. The examiner orally presents open-ended questions that cover topics about society and government. The basal and ceiling levels are the same as for the Science subtest. Picture cues are given at the lower levels.

Humanities. The open-ended questions in this subtest cover cultural topics. The basal and ceiling levels are the same as for the Science and Social Studies subtests.

Supplemental Battery. The test authors advise that beginning examiners learn to administer and score the Standard Battery before learning the Supplemental Battery. The supplemental subtests can provide additional information for areas that may need further assessment. Therefore, the beginning examiner would be wise to master the Standard Battery so that the Supplemental Battery may be used in the assessment process. The supplemental subtests are described in the following paragraphs.

Word Attack. The student is asked to read nonsense words aloud. This subtest measures the student's ability to decode and pronounce new words. The basal is established when a student answers 1 item correctly, and the ceiling is 6 consecutive incorrect responses.

Reading Vocabulary. This subtest contains two sections: Part A: Synonyms, and Part B: Antonyms. The student is asked to say a word that means the same as a given word in Part A and to say a word that has the opposite meaning of a word in Part B. Only one-word responses are acceptable. The examiner obtains a raw score by adding the number of items correct in the two subtests. The basal and ceiling levels are 4 consecutive correct and incorrect responses, respectively.

Quantitative Concepts. Items cover math vocabulary and concepts. The examiner's manual states that no mathematical decisions are made in response to these test items. Picture cues are given for some items in the lower levels. The basal and ceiling levels are 6 consecutive correct and incorrect responses, respectively.

Proofing. The student is asked to locate and correct errors in written passages shown on the easel page. The basal and ceiling levels are 6 consecutive correct and incorrect responses, respectively.

Writing Fluency. This paper and pencil subtest consists of pictures paired with three words. The examiner instructs the student to write sentences about each picture using the words. The student is allowed to write for 7 minutes. Correct responses are complete sentences that include the three words presented.

Punctuation and Capitalization, Spelling, and Usage. This subtest does not require an additional administration. To score this subtest, the examiner analyzes responses obtained during the administration of the Dictation and Proofing subtests. The raw scores from spelling items on the Dictation and Proofing subtests are added together, and these raw scores are then used to enter tables on the protocol to obtain *W* scores, age equivalents, and grade equivalents for each of the areas.

☐ CHECK YOUR UNDERSTANDING

Complete Activity 6.1.

Activity 6.1

Answer the following questions.

1. How many parallel forms are included in the revised version of the Woodcock-Johnson Tests of Achievement? ________ What is the advantage of having different forms of the same instrument? ________________________________
____
____
2. In what way do the test authors recommend that the beginning examiner proceed to learn the WJ–R Tests of Achievement? ________________________
____
____
3. What is the age range of the WJ–R Tests of Achievement? ________

4. What populations were included in the norming process of the revised edition?

____

____

____

5. For what new school group have norm tables been provided? ____________

____

____

6. According to the information provided in Figure 6.1, what standard and supplemental subtests would be administered to measure broad mathematics?

____

____

Scoring. The raw scores obtained during the administration of the subtests can be used to determine *W* scores and age and grade equivalents by using the tables provided on the protocol (Figure 6.2). As shown in the circled row in Figure 6.2, a raw score of 45 on the Letter-Word Identification subtest yields a *W* score of 511, an age equivalent of 12–0, and a grade equivalent of 6.7. The figure also provides the standard error of measurement for *W* scores.

The age and grade profiles for subtests can be plotted on the outside pages of the protocol. As shown in Figure 6.3, the *W* score is used to chart a profile of a student's abilities by locating the *W* score on the top line of a number line and shading in the area to the same *W* score on the bottom line. The figure plots a *W* score of 470 obtained on the Dictation subtest.

Figure 6.2
Section of the letter-word identification protocol of the WJ–R Tests of Achievement.
Source: From *Woodcock-Johnson Psycho-Educational Battery–Revised Tests of Achievement: Standard and Supplemental Batteries, Protocol* (Form A, p. 4) by R. W. Woodcock and M. B. Johnson, 1989, Allen, TX: DLM Teaching Resources. Copyright 1989 by DLM Teaching Resources. Reprinted by permission.

Test 22 — Letter-Word Identification
Form A
SCORING TABLE
Encircle entire row for the Raw Score

Raw Score	W	SEM (W)	AE	GE
40	495	5	9-11	4.7
41	498	5	10-4	5.1
42	501	5	10-9	5.4
43	504	5	11-2	5.8
44	507	5	11-7	6.2
45	511	5	12-0	6.7
46	514	5	12-6	7.1
47	517	6	13-0	7.6
48	520	6	13-7	8.2
49	524	6	14-3	8.9
50	528	6	15-1	9.7

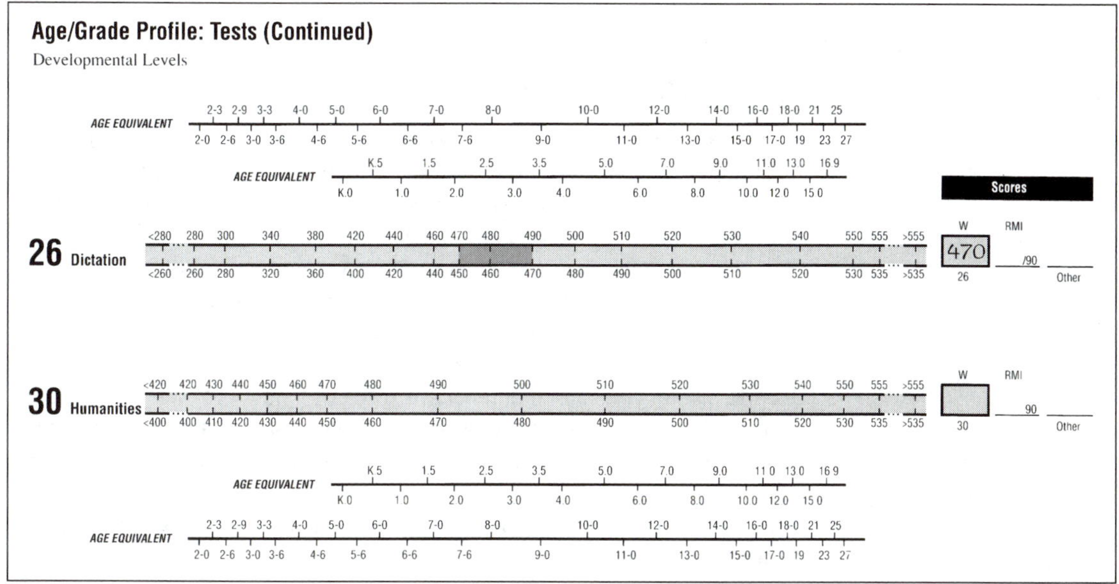

Figure 6.3
Age and grade profiles of the WJ–R Tests of Achievement.
Source: From *Woodcock-Johnson Psycho-Educational Battery–Revised Tests of Achievement: Standard and Supplemental Batteries, Protocol* (Form A, p. 24) by R. W. Woodcock and M. B. Johnson, 1989, Allen, TX: DLM Teaching Resources. Copyright 1989 by DLM Teaching Resources. Reprinted by permission.

Obtaining the additional scores for percentile ranks, standard scores, cluster scores, and differences between expected and actual scores can be determined by using norm tables contained in the Tests of Achievement manual.

The examiner first obtains the *W* score by entering the raw score in the Scoring Table (see Figure 6.2) given for each subtest. Then, referring to Norm Table C, the examiner locates the reference *W* score, standard error of measurement (for standard score), and column number (see Figure 6.7a), which will be used in another section of the protocol (Figure 6.7b). The examiner is given two choices for the column number depending on the difference score. The difference score is the obtained *W* score minus the reference *W* score. If the difference is positive (the student's obtained *W* score is greater than the reference score), the left column number is used. If the difference is negative, (the student's obtained *W* score is less than the reference *W* score) the right column number is used. The difference score is used to enter Norm Table D (Figure 6.8) to locate the relative mastery index, standard score, and percentile rank.

The standard scores can be used to compare the clusters of the achievement battery in the intra-achievement discrepancies section of the protocol. The WJ–R also includes a cognitive battery, Tests of Cognitive Ability (described in chapter 10). If the cognitive battery has been administered to the student, the examiner can compare the two batteries.

☐ **CHECK YOUR UNDERSTANDING**

Complete Activity 6.2.

Activity 6.2

Complete the following problems.

1. The student you are testing obtained the following raw scores on the WJ–R Tests of Achievement: Science, 30; Social Studies, 26; and Humanities, 32. Use the raw scores to determine the *W* scores and the age and grade equivalents on the tables shown in Figures 6.4, 6.5, and 6.6.
2. Use the information provided on Norm Table C (Figure 6.7a) to locate the student's reference *W* score and standard error of measurement for the standard score. Calculate the difference score to locate the column number. Write your answers in the appropriate spaces in Figure 6.6.
3. Use the difference score to enter Norm Table D (Figure 6.8) and locate the appropriate column. Record the student's relative mastery index (RMI), standard score (SS), and percentile rank (PR) in the appropriate spaces in Figure 6.7b. Plot the standard scores by shading in each score ±1 SEM in the appropriate spaces in Figure 6.9. This will also result in the percentile band being plotted.

Test 28 — Science
Form A
SCORING TABLE
Encircle entire row for the Raw Score

Raw Score	W	SEM (W)	AE	GE
25	498	7	9-10	4.5
26	502	6	10-8	5.2
27	506	6	11-6	6.0
28	510	6	12-5	6.9
29	514	6	13-4	8.1
30	518	6	14-4	9.2
31	521	6	15-9	10.4
32	524	5	17-4	11.6
33	527	5	19	13.0
34	530	5	26[50]	14.4

Figure 6.4
Section of the scoring table of the Science subtest protocol of the WJ–R Tests of Achievement.
Source: From *Woodcock-Johnson Psycho-Educational Battery–Revised Tests of Achievement: Standard and Supplemental Batteries, Protocol* (Form A, p. 10) by R. W. Woodcock and M. B. Johnson, 1989, Allen, TX: DLM Teaching Resources.

Test 29 — Social Studies
Form A
SCORING TABLE
Encircle entire row for the Raw Score

Raw Score	W	SEM (W)	AE	GE
25	511	5	12-1	6.6
26	514	5	12-6	7.0
27	517	5	13-0	7.4
28	519	5	13-6	7.9
29	522	5	14-0	8.5
30	525	5	14-6	9.1
31	527	5	15-1	9.7
32	530	5	15-9	10.4
33	532	5	16-6	11.0
34	535	5	17-4	11.7

Figure 6.5
Section of the scoring table of the Social Studies subtest protocol of the WJ–R Tests of Achievement.
Source: From *Woodcock-Johnson Psycho-Educational Battery–Revised Tests of Achievement: Standard and Supplemental Batteries, Protocol* (Form A, p. 11) by R. W. Woodcock and M. B. Johnson, 1989, Allen, TX: DLM Teaching Resources.

Test 30 — Humanities Form A SCORING TABLE Encircle entire row for the Raw Score				
Raw Score	**W**	**SEM (W)**	**AE**	**GE**
25	498	5	9-8	4.2
26	500	5	10-2	4.8
27	503	5	10-8	5.3
28	505	5	11-2	5.8
29	507	5	11-8	6.3
30	510	5	12-3	6.8
31	512	5	12-10	7.5
32	514	5	13-6	8.2
33	517	5	14-2	8.9
34	519	5	15-0	9.7

Figure 6.6
Section of the scoring table of the Humanities subtest protocol of the WJ–R Tests of Achievement.
Source: From *Woodcock-Johnson Psycho-Educational Battery–Revised Tests of Achievement: Standard and Supplemental Batteries, Protocol* (Form A, p. 12) by R. W. Woodcock and M. B. Johnson, 1989, Allen, TX: DLM Teaching Resources. Copyright 1989 by DLM Teaching Resources. Reprinted by permission.

GRADES 11.6 THRU 11.9 ►	11.6			
			COLUMNS	
	REF W	SEM (SS)	+ DIFF	− DIFF
28 Science	524	6	23	83
29 Social Studies	535	5	22	85
30 Humanities	525	6	24	83

(a)

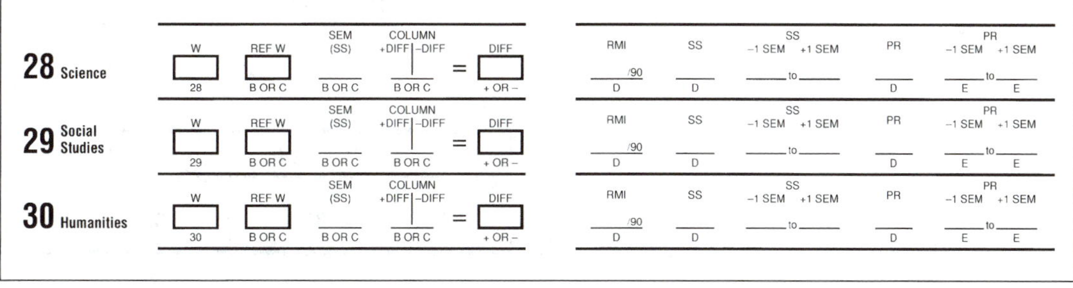

	W	REF W	SEM (SS)	COLUMN +DIFF | −DIFF		DIFF	RMI	SS	SS −1 SEM +1 SEM	PR	PR −1 SEM +1 SEM
28 Science	28	B OR C	B OR C	B OR C	=	+ OR −	/90 D	D	___ to ___	D	___ to ___ E E
29 Social Studies	29	B OR C	B OR C	B OR C	=	+ OR −	/90 D	D	___ to ___	D	___ to ___ E E
30 Humanities	30	B OR C	B OR C	B OR C	=	+ OR −	/90 D	D	___ to ___	D	___ to ___ E E

(b)

Figure 6.7
(a) Section of Norm Table C of the WJ–R Tests of Achievement. (b) Section of the WJ–R protocol.
Source: (a) From *Woodcock-Johnson Psycho-Educational Battery–Revised Tests of Achievement: Standard and Supplemental Batteries,* Norm Tables (p. 144) by R. W. Woodcock and M. B. Johnson, 1989, Allen, TX: DLM Teaching Resources. Copyright 1989 by DLM Teaching Resources. Reprinted by permission. (b) From *Woodcock-Johnson Psycho-Educational Battery–Revised Tests of Achievement: Standard and Supplemental Batteries, Protocol* (p. 2) by R. W. Woodcock and M. B. Johnson, 1989, Allen, TX: DLM Teaching Resources. Copyright 1989 by DLM Teaching Resources. Reprinted by permission.

Figure 6.8
Sections of Norm Table D of the WJ–R Tests of Achievement.

Source: From *Woodcock-Johnson Psycho-Educational Battery–Revised Tests of Achievement: Standard and Supplemental Batteries,* Norm Tables (pp. 189, 192) by R. W. Woodcock and M. B. Johnson, 1989, Allen, TX: DLM Teaching Resources. Copyright 1989 by DLM Teaching Resources. Reprinted by permission.

	Columns ▶	COLUMN 83	
DIFF	**RMI**	**SS**	**PR**
0	**90/90**	100	50
–1	**89/90**	99	48
–2	**88/90**	98	46
–3	**87/90**	98	44
–4	**85/90**	97	42
–5	**84/90**	96	40
–6	**82/90**	95	38
–7	**81/90**	95	36
–8	**79/90**	94	34
–9	**77/90**	93	32
–10	**75/90**	92	30
–11	**73/90**	91	28
–12	**71/90**	91	27
–13	**68/90**	90	25
–14	**66/90**	89	23

	Columns ▶	COLUMN 85	
DIFF	**RMI**	**SS**	**PR**
–15	**63/90**	89	24
–16	**61/90**	89	22
–17	**58/90**	88	21
–18	**55/90**	87	20
–19	**53/90**	86	18

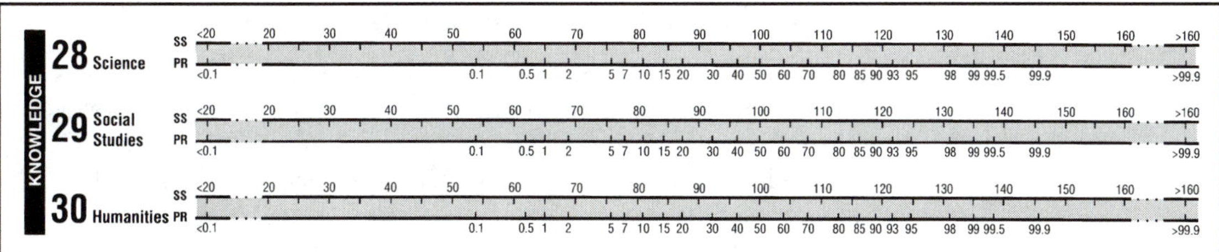

Figure 6.9
Standard score/percentile rank profile of the WJ–R Tests of Achievement.
Source: From *Woodcock-Johnson Psycho-Educational Battery–Revised Tests of Achievement: Standard and Supplemental Batteries, Protocol* (p. 21) by R. W. Woodcock and M. B. Johnson, 1989, Allen, TX: DLM Teaching Resources. Copyright 1989 by DLM Teaching Resources. Reprinted by permission.

Technical Data

Norming Process. For the standardization and norming process of the WJ–R Tests of Achievement, the test developers included a sample of more than 6,000 subjects ranging in age from 2 to 90 years. The subjects represented a geographic variety of communities. Variables that were considered included sex, race, occupational status, level of education (including college level), and household income. The examiner's manual includes information about studies with students from special populations, including students with learning disabilities, mental retardation, and giftedness.

Reliability. Internal consistency reliability information in the manual states that coefficients ranged from .59 to .97 for subtests. Reliability coefficients for clusters ranged from .84 to .98.

Validity. The manual provides concurrent validity information for studies with subtests from the Kaufman Assessment Battery for Children, the Boehm Test of Basic Concepts, the Bracken Basic Concepts Scale, and the Peabody Picture Vocabulary Test–Revised for ages 2–6 to 3–7. The validity coefficients ranged from .29 to .71. School-aged samples were studied by comparing the Woodcock-Johnson Tests of Achievement to commonly used instruments such as the Wide Range Achievement Test–Revised, the Peabody Individual Achievement Test, the Kaufman Assessment Battery for Children, and the Kaufman Test of Educational Achievement, as well as some group achievement tests. These coefficients ranged from a low of .19 comparing the Wide Range Math subtest and the Woodcock-Johnson broad Reading cluster (age 17 sample) to .85 comparing the Peabody reading composite and the Woodcock-Johnson broad Reading cluster (age 9 sample).

Peabody Individual Achievement Test–Revised PIAT–R

The PIAT–R (Markwardt, 1989) is contained in four easels, called Volumes I, II, III, and IV. For this revision, the number of items have been increased on the existing subtests. The subtests are General Information, Reading Recognition, Reading Comprehension, Mathematics, Spelling, and Written Expression.

Subtests

General Information. Questions in this subtest are presented in an open-ended format. The student gives oral responses to questions that range in topic from science to sports. The examiner records all responses. A key for acceptable responses is given throughout the examiner's pages of the subtest and provides suggestions for further questioning.

Reading Recognition. The items at the beginning level of this subtest are visual recognition and discrimination items that require the student to match a picture, letter, or word. The student must select the response from a choice of four items. The more difficult items require the student to pronounce a list of words that range from single-syllable consonant-vowel-consonant words to multisyllable words with unpredictable pronunciations.

Reading Comprehension. This subtest is administered to students who earn a raw score of 19 or better on the Reading Recognition subtest. The items are presented in a two-page format. The examiner asks the student to read a passage silently on the first page of each item. On the second page, the student must select from four choices the one picture that best illustrates the passage. The more difficult-to-read items also have pictures that are more difficult to discriminate.

Mathematics. Math questions are presented in a forced-choice format. The student is orally asked a question and must select the correct response from four choices. Questions range from numeral recognition to trigonometry.

Spelling. This subtest begins with visual discrimination tasks of pictures, symbols, and letters. The spelling items are presented in a forced-choice format. The student is asked to select the correct spelling of the word from four choices.

Written Expression. This subtest allows for written responses by the student; level I is presented to students who are functioning at the kindergarten- or first-grade level, level II to students functioning in the 2nd- to 12th-grade levels. The basal and ceiling levels do not apply.

Scoring. The examiner uses the raw score on the first PIAT–R subtest, General Information to determine a starting point on the following subtest,

Reading Recognition. The raw score from the Reading Recognition subtest then provides a starting point for the Reading Comprehension subtest, and so on throughout the test. The basal and ceiling levels are consistent across subtests. A basal level is established when 5 consecutive items have been answered correctly. The ceiling level is determined when the student answers 5 of 7 items incorrectly. Because the Written Expression subtest requires written responses by the student, the basal and ceiling levels do not apply.

The PIAT–R yields standard scores, grade equivalents, age equivalents, and percentile ranks for individual subtests and for a Total Reading and a Total Test score. The manual provides for standard error of measurement for obtained and derived scores. The raw score from the Written Expression subtest can be used with the raw score from the Spelling subtest to obtain a written language composite. Scoring procedures are detailed in Appendix I of the PIAT–2 examiner's manual.

☐ **CHECK YOUR UNDERSTANDING**

Complete Activity 6.3.

Activity 6.3

Complete the following problems.

1. Using the information provided on the portion of the PIAT–R protocol in Figure 6.10, determine the Total Reading raw score. Add the Reading Recognition and the Reading Comprehension raw scores. To determine the Total Test raw score, add all subtest raw scores. Write the sums in the appropriate boxes in Figure 6.10.
2. Using the raw score data determined in problem 1, locate the standard scores from the section of table provided in Figure 6.11. Write the standard scores in the appropriate places in Figure 6.10.

Technical Data

Norming Process. The PIAT–R sample was selected with consideration for geographic region, socioeconomic status, and race or ethnic group (Markwardt, 1989). The manual gives no indication of the inclusion of students identified with disabilities.

Reliability. Several reliability studies are presented in the examiner's manual, with coefficients ranging from the .80s to the high .90s. The studies included split-half, K-R 20, test-retest, and item response theory.

Validity. The manual reports on content validity and construct validity. The construct validity studies included correlation with other tests and factor analysis.

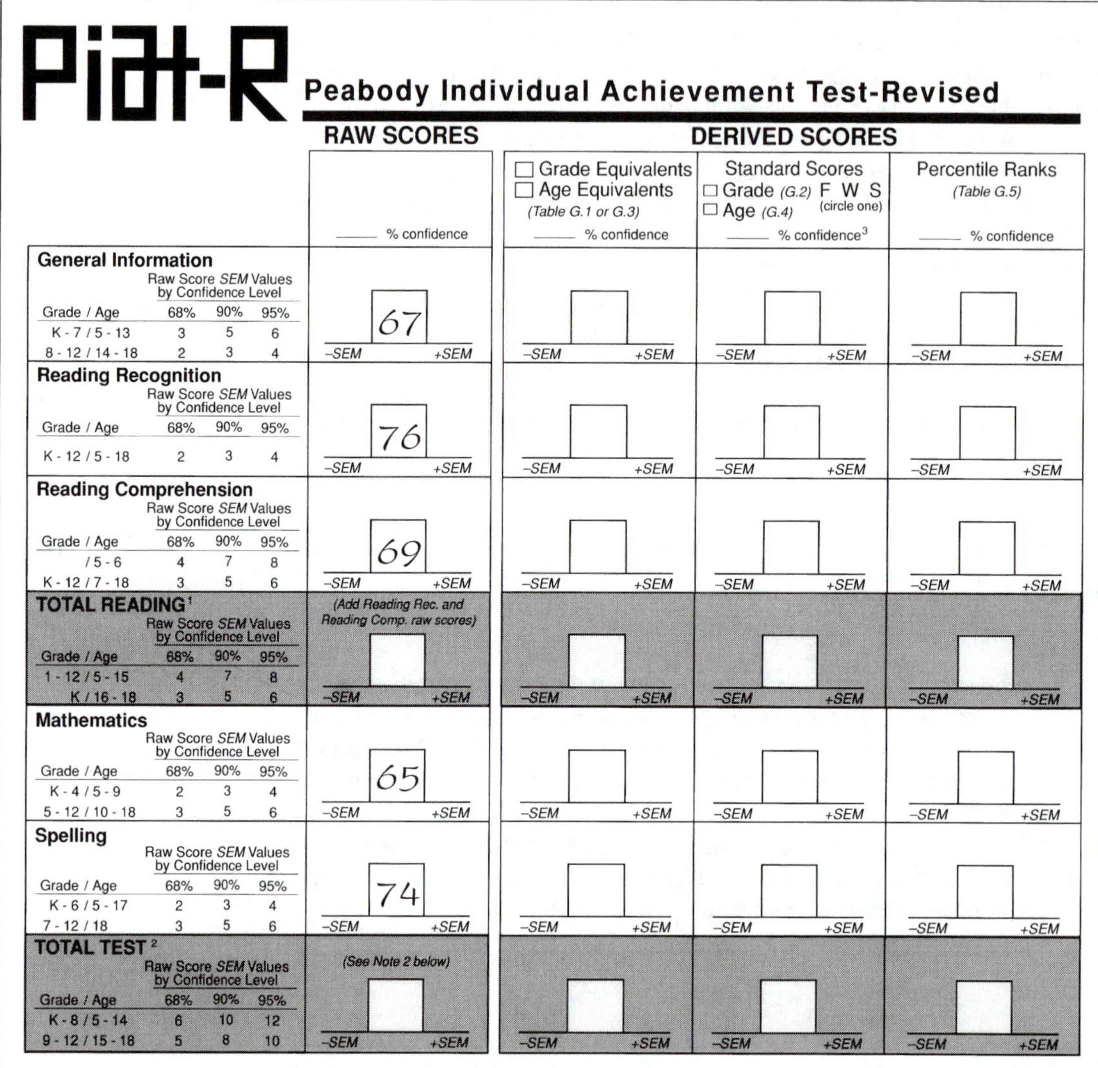

PIAT-R Peabody Individual Achievement Test-Revised

	RAW SCORES	DERIVED SCORES		
		☐ Grade Equivalents ☐ Age Equivalents (Table G.1 or G.3)	Standard Scores ☐ Grade (G.2) F W S (circle one) ☐ Age (G.4)	Percentile Ranks (Table G.5)
	____ % confidence	____ % confidence	____ % confidence[3]	____ % confidence
General Information	67 –SEM +SEM	–SEM +SEM	–SEM +SEM	–SEM +SEM
Reading Recognition	76 –SEM +SEM	–SEM +SEM	–SEM +SEM	–SEM +SEM
Reading Comprehension	69 –SEM +SEM	–SEM +SEM	–SEM +SEM	–SEM +SEM
TOTAL READING[1]	(Add Reading Rec. and Reading Comp. raw scores) –SEM +SEM	–SEM +SEM	–SEM +SEM	–SEM +SEM
Mathematics	65 –SEM +SEM	–SEM +SEM	–SEM +SEM	–SEM +SEM
Spelling	74 –SEM +SEM	–SEM +SEM	–SEM +SEM	–SEM +SEM
TOTAL TEST[2]	(See Note 2 below) –SEM +SEM	–SEM +SEM	–SEM +SEM	–SEM +SEM

Raw Score *SEM* Values by Confidence Level

Subtest	Grade / Age	68%	90%	95%
General Information	K - 7 / 5 - 13	3	5	6
	8 - 12 / 14 - 18	2	3	4
Reading Recognition	K - 12 / 5 - 18	2	3	4
Reading Comprehension	/ 5 - 6	4	7	8
	K - 12 / 7 - 18	3	5	6
TOTAL READING[1]	1 - 12 / 5 - 15	4	7	8
	K / 16 - 18	3	5	6
Mathematics	K - 4 / 5 - 9	2	3	4
	5 - 12 / 10 - 18	3	5	6
Spelling	K - 6 / 5 - 17	2	3	4
	7 - 12 / 18	3	5	6
TOTAL TEST[2]	K - 8 / 5 - 14	6	10	12
	9 - 12 / 15 - 18	5	8	10

Figure 6.10

Portion of the protocol PIAT–R.

Source: From *Peabody Individual Achievement Test–Revised* (p. 10) by F. C. Markwardt, 1989, Circle Pines, MN: American Guidance Service. Copyright 1989 by American Guidance Service. Reprinted by permission.

Kaufman Test of Educational Achievement (K-TEA)

The K-TEA (Kaufman & Kaufman, 1985a, 1985b) is an individually administered achievement test for school-aged students. It consists of two forms: the Comprehensive Form and the Brief Form. Both forms are presented in easel

Standard Score	General Infor-mation	Reading Recog-nition	Reading Compre-hension	TOTAL READING	Mathe-matics	Spelling	TOTAL TEST	Standard Score
	Raw Score							
130	—	—	81	163	—	—	368-369	130
129	—	84	—	161-162	66	81	365-367	129
128	72	83	80	160	—	80	363-364	128
127	—	—	79	159	65	79	360-362	127
126	—	82	—	158	—	—	357-359	126
125	71	81	78	157	64	78	354-356	125
124	70	—	77	155-156	63	—	352-353	124
123	—	80	—	154	—	77	349-351	123
122	69	79	76	153	62	76	347-348	122
121	68	—	75	151-152	—	—	344-346	121
120	—	78	—	150	61	75	341-343	120
119	67	77	74	149	60	74	339-340	119
118	66	76	73	147-148	—	—	336-338	118
117	—	—	72	146	59	73	333-335	117
116	65	75	—	144-145	58	72	331-332	116
115	64	74	71	143	—	—	328-330	115
114	63	—	70	142	57	71	326-327	114
113	—	73	69	140-141	—	—	322-325	113
112	62	72	—	139	56	70	320-321	112
111	61	71	68	137-138	—	69	316-319	111

Figure 6.11
Standard scores corresponding to subtest and composite raw scores from the PIAT–R.
Source: From *Peabody Individual Achievement Test–Revised* (p. 117) by F. C. Markwardt, 1989, Circle Pines, MN: American Guidance Service. Copyright 1989 by American Guidance Service. Reprinted by permission.

fashion with computation and spelling subtests using pencil and paper tasks. Starting points are suggested by grade-level functioning, and the ceiling level on both forms is determined when the student fails every item in one unit or section. The test authors have named this the "discontinue rule" (Kaufman & Kaufman, 1985a, 1985b).

Comprehensive Form. Although the two forms of the K-TEA are similar in format, the Comprehensive Form is much more detailed in scoring and provides better information for planning. The Comprehensive Form includes two more subtests than the Brief Form, and generally, each subtest contains more items.

Comprehensive Form subtests include Mathematics Applications, Reading Decoding, Spelling, Reading Comprehension, and Mathematics Computation. The subtest scores are combined into reading and mathematics composites as well as a total battery composite. The scores can be compared for intra-individual differences.

Mathematics Applications. This subtest presents story-type problems printed on the easel pages. The examiner reads the problems aloud to the student. The student may use pencil and paper to help calculate the answers and may also use finger counting. Picture cues accompany some of the problems. The problems are presented orally and require an oral response.

Reading Decoding. This subtest presents words visually for the student to read aloud to the examiner. These are real words (not nonsense words as on the Woodcock-Johnson Word Attack subtest) and range from single letters and primer-level words to very difficult and unpredictable words.

Spelling. This subtest is presented as a typical spelling test. The examiner states a word, reads the given sentence containing the word, and states the word again. The student writes the word in a student answer booklet, which also contains the math computation problems. The examiner scans the student's protocol after each page to check for errors and to watch for the ceiling level to be reached.

Reading Comprehension. This subtest presents sentences and passages for the student to read and respond to. The lower level items are short sentences that require the student to respond by taking some action, such as "Open your mouth" (Kaufman & Kaufman, 1985b). The examiner prompts the student by saying, "Do what this says" (Kaufman & Kaufman, 1985b). The student may read silently or aloud and then responds by actions. The higher level items are short passages followed by questions. The student reads the passages and questions silently or aloud and then responds orally.

Mathematics Computation. This subtest includes 60 math problems presented in the student's answer booklet. The student may use a pencil and eraser, as well as finger counting, as needed to answer the problems. The examiner scans the answer booklet as the student works to determine when the discontinue rule has been reached and the student must stop working. The examiner then circles in blue the number of the problem that indicates the end of a unit or section. The problems range in difficulty from simple operations to algebra.

Scoring the Comprehensive Form. The examiner determines the raw score by counting the number of responses answered correctly. The advantage of using the K-TEA Comprehensive Form is that the protocol includes skill category information. This information helps the examiner to determine which skills are represented by items answered correctly and which unmastered skills can be identified by items answered incorrectly. The examiner can use the information obtained on the protocol to form IEP objectives. The information regarding the student's errors can be used to compare the number of errors the student made with the number of errors made by the norm group on those same skills. The inclusion of skill categories on this norm-referenced test means that the K-TEA is also considered a criterion-referenced test. These criteria can be used when determining if a student has met specific criteria necessary to progress to a higher skill curriculum. For example, when a student has mastered all skills necessary for introduction to an algebra curriculum, the student will be considered ready to progress to that algebra curriculum. By the same token, if a student has not mastered basic operations, measurement, fractions, or decimals, beginning a curriculum of algebra would not be recommended.

Raw score information and errors made by skill categories are transferred to the error analysis summaries page by skill categories for all five subtests of the Comprehensive Form. This allows the examiner to compare the student with norm tables to determine if the student's skill status is considered weak, average, or strong.

☐ **CHECK YOUR UNDERSTANDING**

Complete Activity 6.4.

Activity 6.4

Complete the following problems.

1. Look at the responses made by the third-grade student on the K-TEA Spelling subtest in Figure 6.12. Use the portion of the protocol to mark the errors and count the number of errors by skill category.
2. Transfer the number of items missed to the error analysis summaries page in Figure 6.13. Use the information from the norm table in Figure 6.14 to determine if the number of spelling errors places the student in the average, weak, or strong category for a third-grade student. If the student made more errors than other third graders, the student is considered weak in the area or skill assessed. If the student made the same number of errors, she is considered average. If she made fewer errors, the student is considered strong in that area or skill. Circle the appropriate skill status in Figure 6.13 for each of the assessed skills.

The second part of scoring the K-TEA Comprehensive Form uses norm tables to determine standard scores, percentile ranks, bands of error, grade equivalents, and descriptive categories for student performance. The examiner transfers the raw scores to the front of the protocol and refers to norm tables to obtain scores. The norm tables are provided by age and grade and are also listed by either fall or spring testing. The most accurate comparison of the student with the norm group will use the appropriate tables, which depend on the semester when the testing is completed. If the testing is completed in the fall, then fall norm tables will be used.

The third step in scoring the K-TEA Comprehensive Form is to compare the student with her own performance. To determine *specific skill comparisons,* the examiner finds the difference between the Reading Decoding and Reading Comprehension standard scores and the difference between the Mathematics Applications and Mathematics Computation standard scores. To determine *global skill comparisons,* the examiner finds the difference between standard scores on the Reading Composite and Mathematics Composite, Reading Composite and Spelling subtest, and Mathematics Composite and Spelling subtest.

Spelling

Item	Stimulus	Score	Prefixes & Word Beginnings	Suffixes & Word Endings	Closed Syllable (Short) Vowels	Open Syllable (Long) & Final e Pattern Vowels	Vowel Digraphs & Diphthongs	r-Controlled Patterns	Consonant Clusters & Digraphs	Single & Double Consonants	Whole Word Error Type
			WORD PARTS								
26	praise	1				_e	ai		pr	s	
27	objection	1	ob	tion	e					j c	
28	education	1		tion	e	u a				d c	
29	celebrate	1		ate	e	e			br	c l	
30	accident	1	ac	ent		i				c d	
31	employed	1	em	ed			oy		pl		
32	loyalty	0		al ty			oy			l	
33	rumor	0		or		u				r m	
34	definition	0	de	tion	i	i				f n	
35	opposite	0	op	ite		o				p s	
36	initial	0		tial	i i					n	
37	schedule	0			e	u_e			ch	s d l	
38	anticipate	0	anti	ate		i				c p	
39	inferior	0	in	ior				er		f	
40	familar	0		iar	i	a				f m l	
			Total Errors by Skill Category								

	Prefixes & Word Beginnings	Suffixes & Word Endings	Closed Syllable (Short) Vowels	Open Syllable (Long) & Final e Pattern Vowels	Vowel Digraphs & Diphthongs	r-Controlled Patterns	Consonant Clusters & Digraphs	Single & Double Consonants	Whole Word Error Type
Ceiling Item ______ minus Errors ______ equals Raw Score ______									

Figure 6.12

Responses on the Spelling subtest protocol of the K-TEA.

Source: From *Kaufman Test of Educational Achievement, Comprehensive Form, Protocol* by A. S. Kaufman and N. L. Kaufman, 1985, Circle Pines, MN: American Guidance Service. Copyright 1985 by American Guidance Service. Reprinted by permission.

Grade ______ Ceiling Item ______	Spelling	Average Number of Errors	Student's Number of Errors	Skill Status		
				Weak	Average	Strong
	WORD PART	Table 20	Page 7			
	Prefixes & Word Beginnings	______	______	W	A	S
	Suffixes & Word Endings	______	______	W	A	S
	Closed Syllable (Short) Vowels	______	______	W	A	S
	Open Syllable (Long) & Final *e* Pattern Vowels	______	______	W	A	S
	Vowel Digraphs & Diphthongs	______	______	W	A	S
	r-Controlled Patterns	______	______	W	A	S
	Consonant Clusters & Digraphs	______	______	W	A	S
	Single & Double Consonants	______	______	W	A	S

Figure 6.13
Error comparison section of the K-TEA Comprehensive Form, Spelling subtest.
Source: From *Kaufman Test of Educational Achievement Comprehensive Form, Protocol* by A. S. Kaufman and N. L. Kaufman, 1985, Circle Pines, MN: American Guidance Service. Copyright 1985 by American Guidance Service. Reprinted by permission.

Grade 3

Word Part	Ceiling Item									
	5	10	15	20	25	30	35	40	45	50
	Average Number of Errors									
Prefixes & Word Beginnings	—	—	—	—	0-1	1	1	1	1	1
Suffixes & Word Endings	—	—	—	—	0	0-1	2	3-5	3-5	4-6
Closed Syllable (Short) Vowels	0	0	0	0	0	0	0-1	1-2	2-3	1-2
Open Syllable (Long) & Final *e* Pattern Vowels	—	—	—	0	0	1-2	3-4	3-4	3-4	4-6
Vowel Digraphs & Diphthongs	—	—	0-1	1-3	1-2	1-2	1-2	0-1	0	1
r-Controlled Patterns	—	—	—	—	—	—	—	—	—	—
Consonant Clusters & Digraphs	—	0	0	0	0	0	0	0	0-1	0-1
Single & Double Consonants	0	0	0	0-1	0-1	1-3	2-4	2-4	3-5	3-5

Figure 6.14
Norm table of the Comprehensive Form of the K-TEA for average number of errors by category.
Source: From *Kaufman Test of Educational Achievement Comprehensive Form, Manual* (p. 536) by A. S. Kaufman and N. L. Kaufman, 1985, Circle Pines, MN: American Guidance Service. Copyright 1985 by American Guidance Service. Reprinted by permission.

The examiner records the standard score differences in the standard score difference box and uses norm tables to determine if the difference is significant. The determination of a significant difference between either specific or global skills may help the educator effectively plan strategies for the student.

☐ **CHECK YOUR UNDERSTANDING**

Complete Activity 6.5.

Activity 6.5

The following K-TEA standard scores are those obtained by a 9-year-old girl.

	Standard Score
Mathematics Applications	136
Reading Decoding	105
Spelling	100
Reading Comprehension	105
Mathematics Computation	141
Reading Composite	106
Mathematics Composite	141
Battery Composite	119

1. Write the scores in the appropriate spaces on the protocol in Figure 6.15a.
2. Using the information provided on the norm table, Figures 6.15b and c, determine if the differences between both global and specific scores are significant. Circle the significance levels in the space provided on the protocol.

Technical Data for the Comprehensive Form

Norming Process. The K-TEA examiner's manual contains information regarding the standardization and norming process. The test developers administered the Comprehensive Form during the fall and spring to establish norms for these two testing times of the school year. The fall sample included 1,067 students in the norm group, and the spring sample included 1,409 students in the norm group. The fall sample did not contain the desired number of at least 100 students per grade, but this number was reached during the spring testing.

The ratio of male to female students was approximately equal for the standardization of this test. Other variables considered were geographic region, educational level of parents, and race or ethnic group.

Reliability. The test developers studied the reliability of the K-TEA Comprehensive Form using the methods of split-half reliability, test-retest, intercorrelations among subtests and composites, and a study comparing the two batteries, Brief and Comprehensive. Split-half reliability coefficients were high, ranging from .83 to .97 on individual subtests and from .93 to .99 on composite

Comprehensive Form

K-TEA

KAUFMAN TEST of EDUCATIONAL ACHIEVEMENT

by Alan S. Kaufman & Nadeen L. Kaufman

INDIVIDUAL TEST RECORD

Student's Name ______ Sex ______

Parent's Name ______

Home Address ______ Home Phone ______

Grade ______ Teacher ______

School ______ Examiner ______

	Year	Month	Day
Test Date			
Birth Date			
Chronological Age			

COMPREHENSIVE FORM SUBTESTS Mean = 100; SD = 15	RAW SCORES Reading Composite	Mathematics Composite	Battery Composite	Standard Score* Table___	Band of Error ___% Confidence Table 5 or 6	%ile Rank Table 7	Other Data	
Mathematics Applications					±			
Reading Decoding					±			
Spelling					±			
Reading Comprehension					±			
Mathematics Computation					±			
Sum of Subtest Raw Scores								

Transfer sums to Composite Scales, *Sum of Subtest Raw Scores* column.

*Standard Scores Derived from (Circle the table used):	AGE	GRADE
Fall Norms (August–January)	Table 1	Table 2
Spring Norms (February–July)	Table 3	Table 4

COMPREHENSIVE FORM COMPOSITE SCALES Mean = 100; SD = 15	Sum of Subtest Raw Scores	Standard Score* Table___	Band of Error ___% Confidence Table 5 or 6	%ile Rank Table 7	Descriptive Category	Other Data
Reading Composite			±			
Mathematics Composite			±			
Battery Composite			±			

		Indicate >, <, or ≈		Standard Score Difference	Circle the Significance Level
GLOBAL SKILL COMPARISONS	Reading Composite		Mathematics Composite		NS .05 .01
	Reading Composite		Spelling Subtest		NS .05 .01
	Mathematics Composite		Spelling Subtest		NS .05 .01
SPECIFIC SKILL COMPARISONS	Reading Decoding		Reading Comprehension		NS .05 .01
	Mathematics Applications		Mathematics Computation		NS .05 .01

AGS®

(a)

Figure 6.15
(a) Portion of protocol from the K-TEA Comprehensive Form.

Age	Significance Level	Reading Composite versus Mathematics Composite	Reading Composite versus Spelling	Mathematics Composite versus Spelling
		Standard Score Difference Required for Significance		
8	.05 .01	11 13	10 12	12 14
9	.05 .01	9 11	9 11	10 13
10	.05 .01	10 12	10 12	11 13

(b)

Age	Significance Level	Reading Decoding versus Reading Comprehension	Mathematics Applications versus Mathematics Computation
		Standard Score Difference Required for Significance	
8	.05 .01	11 13	15 19
9	.05 .01	10 12	12 15
10	.05 .01	12 15	13 17

(c)

***Figure 6.15** continued*

(b) K-TEA Comprehensive Form standard score differences when comparing global skills. (c) K-TEA Comprehensive Form standard score differences when comparing specific reading and mathematics skills.

Source: From *Kaufman Test of Educational Achievement, Comprehensive Form, Protocol* (p. 1) *and Manual* (pp. 500, 502) by A. S. Kaufman and N. L. Kaufman, 1985, Circle Pines MN: American Guidance Service. Copyright 1985 by American Guidance Service. Reprinted by permission.

comparisons. Test-retest reliability coefficients ranged from .90 to .97 across all grade levels (Kaufman & Kaufman, 1985b). Intercorrelations between subtests and composites ranged from .50 to .82. The reliability study (test-retest) on the Comprehensive and Brief forms yielded coefficients ranging from .66 to .97.

Validity. The examiner's manual presents information regarding the content validity of subtests. Concurrent validity studies for the K-TEA and several other tests are presented, including comparisons with the Wide

Range Achievement Test, the PIAT, the Kaufman Assessment Battery for Children, and the Peabody Picture Vocabulary Test–Revised. The manual also gives information regarding concurrent validity between the K-TEA and group achievement tests. The validity coefficients are adequate, ranging from .24 to .92.

Brief Form. The major differences between the Brief and Comprehensive forms of the K-TEA are the test length and the data available from test results. The Brief Form contains fewer items per subtest and has only three subtests, compared with five on the Comprehensive Form. With less detailed scoring and no error analysis, the Brief Form provides the educator with only a screening tool for determining if a student needed further diagnostic evaluation. The results allow for comparison between subtests but not between composites or global skills. The protocol contains the student response booklet, or answer sheet. The subtests are described in the following paragraphs.

Mathematics. This subtest presents some story problems with picture cues and some computation problems. The overall administration of the subtest combines the easel format and the student answer booklet. The first 25 problems are presented within the answer booklet, whereas problems 26 through 52 are presented on the easel. Students in the lower grades may not complete all the computation problems but may continue on to the orally presented story problems. The discontinue rule, which is used on the K-TEA Comprehensive Form, is applied on the Brief Form as well.

Reading. The examiner first presents single letters for the student to name aloud. The next several items are words for the student to read aloud. Items 24 through 52 are items that the student may read aloud or silently but require an oral or action response. Some items require the student to perform a gesture or action, whereas other items require oral responses to questions about short passages that the student has just read.

Spelling. The Spelling subtest is presented like a standard spelling test. The examiner reads a word, reads a sentence containing the word, and repeats the word. The student responds by writing the spelling word on the answer sheet. The discontinue rule is applied, so the examiner should scan the student's work.

Scoring the Brief Form. The raw scores obtained on the individual subtests are transferred to the front page of the protocol. Norm tables are used to determine standard scores, percentile ranks, grade equivalents, and bands of error. The subtest scores can be compared by finding the difference between subtests and using a norm table to determine if the difference is significant. The examiner should be sure to use the appropriate fall or spring norm tables according to the time when testing was completed.

☐ **CHECK YOUR UNDERSTANDING**

Complete Activity 6.6.

Activity 6.6

Complete the following problems and questions.

1. Record the following standard scores on the protocol in Figure 6.16. Using the 90% confidence level, determine the band of error (Figure 6.17) for the three subtests of the K-TEA Brief Form for a 10-year-old girl. Record the band of error information in Figure 6.16.

	Standard Score
Mathematics	110
Reading	85
Spelling	75

2. Write the range of possible standard scores that the student may obtain as true scores using the bands of confidence found in problem 1.

	Obtained Standard Score	*Range of Scores*
Mathematics	110	________
Reading	85	________
Spelling	75	________

3. How might the bands of error be used in test interpretation? Would this influence your confidence in obtained test scores? Would this influence your educational planning? ____
____
____
____

Technical Data for the Brief Form

Norming Process. The standardization of the Brief Form was carried out as part of the fall standardization of the Comprehensive Form. The variables of geographic region, educational level of parents, race or ethnic group, and male to female ratio are reflected. The total sample for the Brief Form was 589 students.

Reliability. The examiner's manual includes information on split-half reliability, test-retest reliability, and the study between the Comprehensive and Brief forms discussed in the technical data section of the Comprehensive Form. The reliability coefficients ranged from .72 to .98 on the split-half reliability study and from .84 to .94 on the test-retest reliability study.

Validity. The examiner's manual provides information regarding concurrent validity studies with other tests. Tests compared with the K-TEA brief were the Wide Range Achievement Test, the Peabody Picture Vocabulary Test, the Kauf-

Brief Form					**Individual Test Record**
BRIEF FORM SUBTESTS Mean = 100 SD = 15	Raw Score	Standard Score*	Band of Error % Confidence Table 5 or 6	%ile Rank Table 7	Other Data
MATHEMATICS			±		
READING			±		
SPELLING			±		
BATTERY COMPOSITE Mean = 100 SD = 15			±		Descriptive Category

Figure 6.16
Portion of protocol of the K-TEA Brief Form.

Source: From *Kaufman Test of Educational Achievement, Brief Form* (p. 1) by A. S. Kaufman and N. L. Kaufman, 1985, Circle Pines, MN: American Guidance Service. Copyright 1985 by American Guidance Service. Reprinted by permission.

Age	Confidence Level	Mathematics	Reading	Spelling	Battery Composite
		Band of Error			
8	99%	± 17	± 12	± 12	± 9
	95%	± 13	± 9	± 9	± 7
	90%	± 11	± 7	± 8	± 6
	85%	± 9	± 6	± 7	± 5
	68%	± 7	± 5	± 5	± 4
9	99%	± 11	± 7	± 8	± 6
	95%	± 9	± 5	± 6	± 5
	90%	± 7	± 4	± 5	± 4
	85%	± 6	± 4	± 4	± 3
	68%	± 4	± 3	± 3	± 2
10	99%	± 15	± 10	± 11	± 9
	95%	± 11	± 8	± 9	± 6
	90%	± 10	± 7	± 7	± 5
	85%	± 8	± 6	± 6	± 4
	68%	± 6	± 4	± 4	± 3
11	99%	± 12	± 11	± 12	± 8
	95%	± 9	± 8	± 9	± 6
	90%	± 8	± 7	± 7	± 5
	85%	± 7	± 6	± 6	± 4
	68%	± 5	± 4	± 5	± 3
12	99%	± 15	± 13	± 15	± 10
	95%	± 11	± 10	± 11	± 7
	90%	± 9	± 8	± 10	± 6
	85%	± 8	± 7	± 8	± 5
	68%	± 6	± 5	± 6	± 4

Figure 6.17
Bands of error (confidence intervals) for age standard scores, ages 8 through 12, from the K-TEA Brief Form.

Source: From *Kaufman Test of Educational Achievement, Brief Form* (p. 275) by A. S. Kaufman and N. L. Kaufman, 1985, Circle Pines, MN: American Guidance Service. Copyright 1985 by American Guidance Service. Reprinted by permission.

man Assessment Battery for Children, and the Peabody Picture Vocabulary Test–Revised. Correlations ranged from .25 to .92. Overall concurrent validity studies appear to be adequate for the K-TEA brief.

Wechsler Individual Achievement Test (WIAT)

The WIAT (Psychological Corporation, 1992) is an individually administered achievement test made up of eight subtests. The examiner may administer all eight subtests for a comprehensive assessment or three of the subtests as a screening instrument. Students ages 5–0 to 19–11 or grades K through 12 may be administered this instrument. Standardized as part of the research effort to revise the Wechsler Intelligence Scale for Children–Third Edition, the WIAT was designed to help educators in determining discrepancies between measured intellectual ability and academic achievement. The test format includes easels and paper and pencil tasks. Starting points and ceiling rules, which vary by subtests, are presented in the manual and on the protocol form. Examiners are also provided rules for testing backward if the student does not establish a basal. These so-called reverse rules are provided in the examiner's manual and on the protocol.

The WIAT includes subtests in the areas of oral expression and listening comprehension. These areas are not typically assessed through academic achievement testing and may offer the educator useful information for intervention. This test provides skill information on the protocol of the math subtests that can easily be adapted to write educational objectives.

Subtests

Basic Reading. This subtest assesses the student's ability to decode and read words. The beginning items require the student to point to words that begin or end with the same sound as the picture presented on the easel. On more difficult items, the student reads words aloud. This subtest is one of the three included for the screening instrument.

Mathematics Reasoning. This subtest requires the student to solve math problems that require reasoning. The student is presented with items on the easel and, in most cases, in the response booklet as well. This subtest is included as part of the screening instrument.

Spelling. The student responds in writing to letters, sounds, or words dictated by the examiner. This is the third subtest of the screening instrument.

Reading Comprehension. In this subtest, the student reads written passages and then responds to questions asked by the examiner. Many of the items include picture cues.

Numerical Operations. The student responds in writing to solve calculation problems or, at the lower levels, writes numbers dictated by the examiner.

Listening Comprehension. Following orally presented items, the student responds to questions asked by the examiner. The items include picture cues, and the lower levels require the student to point to the answer.

Oral Expression. This subtest assesses the student's ability to use words to describe picture cues, give directions, or provide explanations. The student responds orally.

Written Expression. Administered to students in grades 3 through 12 only, this subtest requires the student to respond, in writing, to various prompts. Skills assessed include use of punctuation and capitalization, and organization of ideas. The manual suggests that this subtest not be administered to students who earn a raw score of 15 or below on the Spelling subtest or to students who may not be able to write sentences. The examiner stops students after 15 minutes of writing.

Scoring. Items on the Basic Reading, Mathematics Reasoning, Spelling, Reading Comprehension, Numerical Operations, and Listening Comprehension subtests receive 1 point when answered correctly and 0 when incorrect. Scoring the Oral Expression subtest is slightly more complicated. Correct answers on items 1–10 receive 1 point, but remaining items on the subtest can receive a varying number of points. Instructions are provided in the manual. The Written Expression subtest is scored for ideas, organization, vocabulary, sentence structure, grammar, and punctuation. Students earn up to 4 points in each of the elements. Practice exercises are provided for scoring this writing subtest.

Raw scores are used to obtain derived scores that may be based on either grade or age normative data. Grade norm tables are presented for fall, winter, and spring. The correct table is determined by the date of testing according to the following guidelines: fall for August–November, winter for December–February, and spring for March–July. Standard scores, with a mean of 100, percentile ranks, age equivalents, and grade equivalents are available for both subtests and composites. Tables are provided to determine significance differences between individual subtest scores and composite scores. To assist in decisions regarding significant discrepancies between ability and achievement, tables are provided that display differences between scores on the WIAT and the Wechsler Intelligence Scale for Children–Third Edition, between the WIAT and the Wechsler Adult Intelligence Scale–Revised, and between the WIAT and the Wechsler Preschool and Primary Scale of Intelligence. Tables are provided with levels of statistical significance for differences between predicted and actual subtest scores and composite scores for using the predicted-achievement method. The application of these methods is presented in chapter 13. An example of the protocol illustrating the comparison of ability and achievement is shown in Figure 6.18.

Technical Data

Norming Process. The standardization sample included 4,252 students ranging in age from 5 to 19, in grades K through 12. Most age groups included at

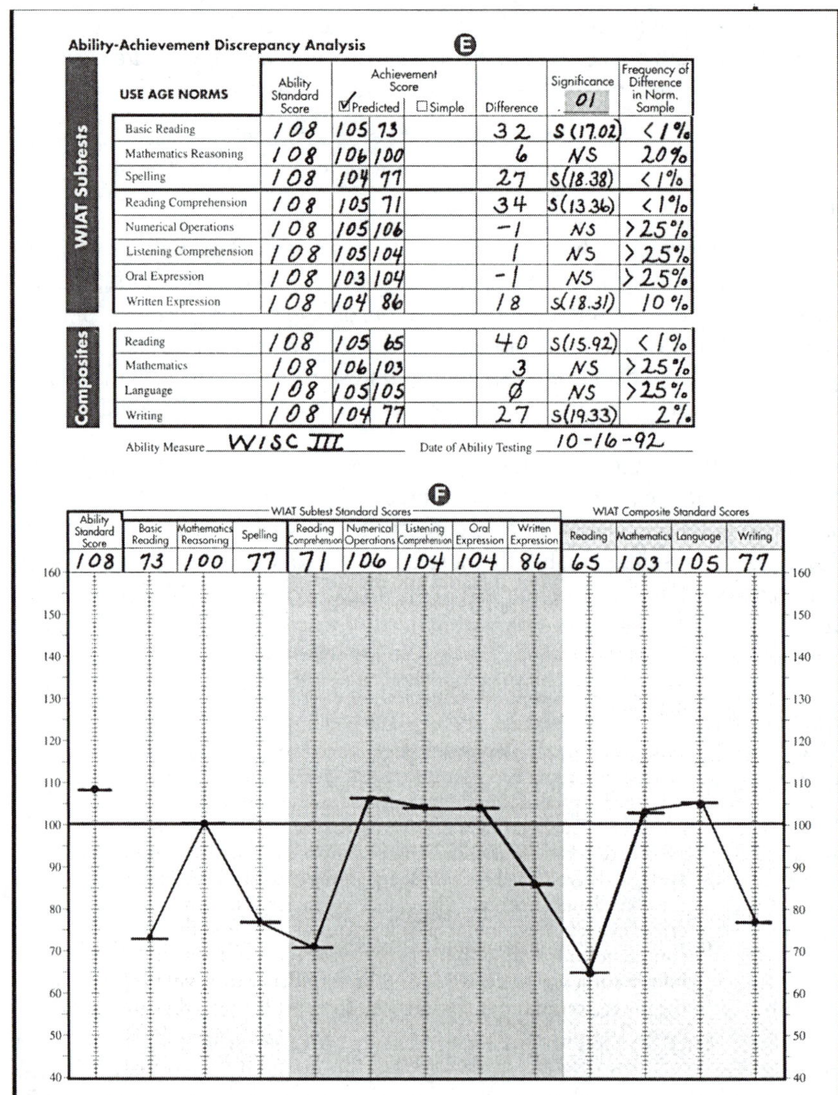

Ability-Achievement Discrepancy Analysis E

USE AGE NORMS	Ability Standard Score	Achievement Score ✓Predicted		☐Simple	Difference	Significance .01	Frequency of Difference in Norm. Sample
WIAT Subtests							
Basic Reading	108	105	73		32	S (17.02)	<1%
Mathematics Reasoning	108	106	100		6	NS	20%
Spelling	108	104	77		27	S(18.38)	<1%
Reading Comprehension	108	105	71		34	S(13.36)	<1%
Numerical Operations	108	105	106		-1	NS	>25%
Listening Comprehension	108	105	104		1	NS	>25%
Oral Expression	108	103	104		-1	NS	>25%
Written Expression	108	104	86		18	S(18.31)	10%
Composites							
Reading	108	105	65		40	S(15.92)	<1%
Mathematics	108	106	103		3	NS	>25%
Language	108	105	105		Ø	NS	>25%
Writing	108	104	77		27	S(19.33)	2%

Ability Measure WISC III Date of Ability Testing 10-16-92

F

Ability Standard Score	WIAT Subtest Standard Scores: Basic Reading	Mathematics Reasoning	Spelling	Reading Comprehension	Numerical Operations	Listening Comprehension	Oral Expression	Written Expression	WIAT Composite Standard Scores: Reading	Mathematics	Language	Writing
108	73	100	77	71	106	104	104	86	65	103	105	77

Figure 6.18

Example of completed section of WIAT summary page.

Source: From *Wechsler Individual Achievement Test Manual* (p. 33) by The Psychological Corporation, 1992, San Antonio, TX: Author.

least 330 students, although the kindergarten level included only 173. Some groups contained 392 students. Genders were nearly equally represented and were approximately equal at all grade levels. Other variables considered in the sample were race/ethnicity, geographic region, and level of parents' education.

The 1988 U.S. Census data provided the criteria for determining the representation of the sample.

Additional studies were completed with special populations and the mean standard scores, and standard deviations are provided in tabular form in the manual. The special groups included students classified as gifted, students with mental retardation, students with emotional disturbance, students with learning disabilities, students with attention deficit disorder, and students with hearing impairments. Information is provided in the examiner's manual to aid the examiner in the assessment of students with physical disabilities.

Reliability. Reliability was studied using a split-half method, and correlations were corrected using the Spearman-Brown formula. Correlations were calculated for both individual subtests and composites. Reliability coefficients are reported by age and grade in the examiner's manual.

Validity. The manual presents information regarding the research studies of content validity, construct validity, and criterion-related validity. Instruments used in the criterion-related validity studies include the Woodcock-Johnson–Revised Tests of Achievement, the Wide Range Achievement Test–Revised, the K-TEA, the Differential Ability Scales, the Basic Achievement Skills Individual Screener, and the Peabody Picture Vocabulary Test–Revised. Correlation coefficients ranged from .42 to .90, with most reported in the .70s and .80s.

Wide Range Achievement Test–Revision 3 (WRAT3)

The WRAT3 is a screening achievement test that was designed to "measure the codes which are needed to learn the basic skills of reading, spelling, and arithmetic" (Wilkinson, 1993, p. 10). This test is composed of three subtests that may be administered in any order and may be given to persons ages 5 through 75. Because it is a screening instrument, the WRAT3 should not be used to diagnose learning problems but rather to determine if additional testing is necessary. This third revision, unlike the WRAT–R, may be given to any person within the age range of 5–75 and is no longer divided by age levels. The test includes alternate forms, the Blue Test and Tan Test, which may be administered alone or together for a combined score. Students who are not administered the items for ages 5–7 are given credit for those items. The Spelling and Reading subtests use a 5/10 rule for the basal and ceiling. This means that individuals age 8 and above must be presented with the beginning items if they do not correctly answer the first 5 items presented and that testing stops when students miss 10 consecutive items. The Arithmetic subtest uses a 5/15 minute criterion: Students age 8 and above must answer at least 5 items correctly or be given the beginning oral items, and testing stops at the 15-minute time limit.

Subtests

Reading. This subtest contains a plastic card with a small sample of letters and words that the student reads aloud to the examiner. The naming of letters is considered a prereading task. The student is allowed 10 seconds to recognize each word. The examiner scores the subtest by crossing out the first letter of incorrect words and by circling the item number for correct responses. Each correct item is worth 1 point. This subtest does not measure word attack or any form of reading comprehension.

Spelling. This subtest begins with name writing and letter writing for students ages 5 through 7. Students are asked to write their name and then to write letters spoken by the examiner. The student is then asked to spell words presented orally: The examiner pronounces a word, gives a sentence that includes the word, and then repeats the word; the student responds in writing on the protocol.

Arithmetic. This subtest contains a few counting items and oral response items, but the remainder of the subtest is a paper and pencil task of computation. Students may first solve a small sample of math problems presented on the protocol. Students ages 5 through 7 begin this subtest with the oral problems and progress to the calculation items. There is 15-minute time limit for this subtest.

Scoring. The raw scores on the WRAT3 may be used to obtain standard scores, grade scores, and absolute scores. Absolute scores have a mean of 500 and were determined by using the Rasch analysis to determine item difficulty. The absolute scores allow for a person to be compared with the entire continuum of the domain or areas without using age or grade comparisons. Item analyses using the absolute scores are provided in the WRAT3 examiner's manual.

☐ **CHECK YOUR UNDERSTANDING**

Complete Activity 6.7.

Activity 6.7

Complete the problems and answer the questions that follow.

1. Figure 6.19 shows the responses of a 15-year-old student on the Spelling subtest of the WRAT3 Tan Test. Use this information to score the subtest. Remember to add the 15 points for the beginning items that were not administered. Write your answer in the "5/10 Rules" box on the protocol (Figure 6.19).
2. What is the raw score for the Spelling subtest? Write your answer in the "Tan Test Scores" area on the protocol (Figure 6.19).
3. Use the raw score to obtain the absolute score, standard score, and grade score from the table in Figure 6.20 for the 15-year-old student. Write the scores in the "Tan Test Scores" area on the protocol (Figure 6.19). Leave the "%ile" column blank.
4. Plot the standard score for the Spelling subtest on the graph in Figure 6.21. In what areas does this student need further assessment? ______________

____

____

WIDE RANGE ACHIEVEMENT TEST □ REVISION 3

NAME Jake GENDER: □M □F

DATE 11-5-94 BIRTH DATE 2-6-86 AGE 8

SCHOOL ______ GRADE 3

REFERRED BY ______ EXAMINER ______

TAN TEST SCORES	Raw Score	Std. Score	%ile	Grade Score	Absolute Score
READING					
SPELLING					
ARITHMETIC					

Use only standard scores for comparisons

SPELLING/A MEASURE OF WRITTEN ENCODING

by Gary S. Wilkinson

NAME ______ (1&2)

(3) (4) (5) (6) (7) (8) (9) (10) (11) (12) (13) (14) (15)

1. go	16. cdct	31.
2. cat	17. purchus	32.
3. boy	18. instit	33.
4. run	19. sugeshion	34.
5. will	20.	35.
6. kut	21.	36.
7. arm	22.	37.
8. dres	23.	38.
9. train	24.	39.
10. showt	25.	40.
11. wuch	26.	
12. gron	27.	
13. kichen	28.	
14. rsult	29.	
15. hevan	30.	

5/10 RULES

Name/Letter Writing	
Word Spelling +	
Total Spelling	

WIDE RANGE

15 Ashley Place, Suite 1A, Wilmington, DE 19804-1314

Figure 6.19

Portion of WRAT3 protocol with student responses for Spelling subtest.

Source: From *The Wide Range Achievement Test, Protocol* by G. S. Wilkinson, 1993, Wilmington, DE: Wide Range, Inc. Copyright 1993 by Jastak Associates. Reprinted by permission.

Figure 6.20
WRAT3 scoring table for Spelling subtest.
Source: From *The Wide Range Achievement Test: Administration Manual* by G. S. Wilkinson, 1993, Wilmington, DE: Wide Range, Inc. Copyright 1993 by Jastak Associates. Reprinted by permission.

SPELLING

Raw Score	Absolute Score	Standard Score	Grade Score
0	407	—	—PRESCHOOL—
1	413	—	
2	424	—	
3	430	—	
4	434	—	
5	437	—	
6	440	—	
7	442	45	
8	444	48	
9	446	51	K
10	448	55	K
11	450	58	K
12	452	61	K
13	454	64	K
14	456	68	K
15	458	70	K
16	460	72	K
17	462	74	K
18	468	77	1
19	470	80	1
20	473	84	1
21	475	87	1
22	480	90	1
23	483	93	2
24	486	97	2
25	487	100	2
26	491	103	3
27	492	107	3
28	495	110	3
29	497	113	4
30	499	116	4

Technical Data

Norming Process. The norming sample for the WRAT3 included 4,433 persons from four geographic regions. Consideration was given for the following variables: male/female subjects; racial division of white, black, Hispanic, or other; and socioeconomic level. The sample included some students receiving special education services; only students who could not physically respond to items were excluded from the study.

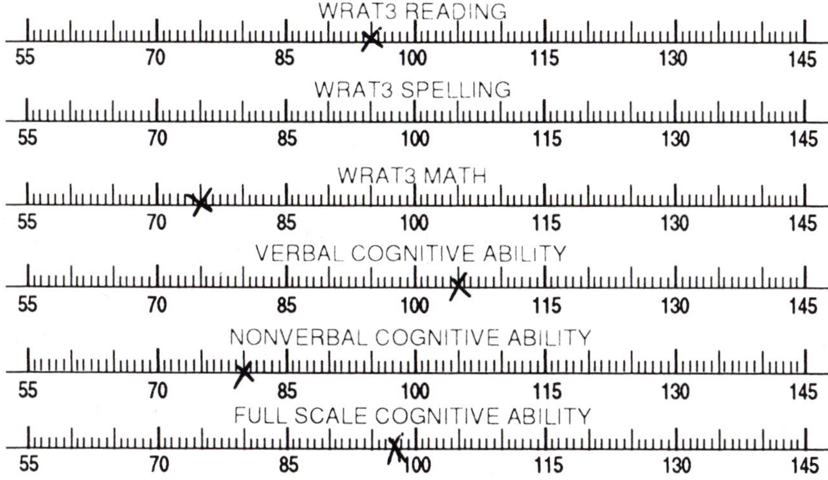

Figure 6.21
Profile of WRAT3 scores for student in Activity 6.7.
Source: From *The Wide Range Achievement Test: Administration Manual* by G. S. Wilkinson, 1993, Wilmington, DE: Wide Range, Inc. Copyright 1993 by Jastak Associates. Reprinted by permission.

Reliability. Test-retest reliability is reported in the examiner's manual for both individual forms and combined scores. Internal consistency measured using coefficient alphas ranged from .85 to .91 (median for all ages). Alternate forms reliability coefficients ranged from .89 to .93 (median for all ages).

Validity. Validity measures discussed include content validity, construct validity, and criterion-related validity. Rationale are provided in the manual to establish a theoretical basis for content and construct validity. Criterion-related validity studies include correlations with the California Test of Basic Skills (CTBS), the California Achievement Test (CAT), and the Stanford Achievement Test (SAT). Coefficients ranged from .58 to .84 on the CTBS, from .41 to .77 on the CAT, and from .52 to .87 on the SAT.

Research Findings

Research is emerging on the newly revised versions of the tests presented in this chapter but is scant on the newly developed instruments, such as the WIAT. Some of the existing research and reviews of the instruments are summarized in this section.

1. One study (Prewett & Giannuli, 1991a) found moderate correlations between scores on the reading subtests of the WJ–R, the K-TEA, and the PIAT–R and the Stanford-Binet IV Composite Score and the Wechsler Intelligence Scale for Children–Revised IQ score. This study used referred students for the sample.

2. The reading subtests of the WJ–R, K-TEA, WRAT–R, and the PIAT–R were highly intercorrelated in one study by Prewett and Giannuli (1991b); however, scores varied when students were tested concurrently using these instruments. The scores obtained on the K-TEA and the WRAT–R reading subtests varied the most (11.1 points), indicating that caution should be applied when using these tests for educational decisions. Prewett, Bardos, and Fowler (1990) pointed out that when tests yield different scores from the same student, diagnosis may be influenced by the test instrument selected for assessment. The scores did not seem to vary as much on the WJ–R and the PIAT–R. Generally, the scores on the WRAT–R and the PIAT–R were lower than those on the WJ–R and the K-TEA reading subtests (Prewett & Giannuli, 1991b).

3. In a study comparing students with learning disabilities with students from the standardization sample without learning disabilities, it was found that the writing subtests of the WJ–R discriminated the students with learning disabilities (Mather, Vogel, Spodak, & McGrew, 1991). The lowest subtest scores for the students with learning disabilities were obtained on the Dictation subtest. This study also found high interrater reliabilities on the Writing Samples subtest.

4. Mather (1989) found that the new writing subtests of the revised Woodcock-Johnson Tests of Achievement had fairly high correlations with the Test of Written Language (r = .80), the Picture Story Language Test (r = .66), and the MAT6 holistic scoring (r = .86).

5. Hultquist and Metzke (1993) found that use of the WJ–R, the PIAT–R, and the K-TEA to measure survival reading words as well as to measure progress of general reading and spelling skills may result in lower scores due to curriculum bias. Use of the tests for these purposes may therefore enable fewer students to exit from special education services.

6. In a study comparing reading word lists of the PIAT, WRAT–R, K-TEA, Woodcock Reading Mastery Tests, and five basal reading series, grade equivalent scores appeared to be more accurate in grades 1 and 2, with the variability of equivalents increasing with grade level (Shapiro & Derr, 1987).

7. Doll (1989) recommended caution in using the K-TEA with first-grade students. There do not appear to be enough lower level or floor items for students at the readiness level. Doll wrote, "For first graders, all subtests of both forms award standard scores higher than two standard deviations below the mean (i.e., within the normal range) to raw scores of 0" (p. 161).

8. Prewett, Bardos, and Fowler (1991) found that the K-TEA Brief seemed to be more accurate as a screening instrument than the WRAT–R. In this study, the K-TEA Comprehensive Form was used to determine which screening instrument yielded scores most like the Comprehensive Form. The K-TEA Brief appeared to be a better predictor of the K-TEA Comprehensive scores, yielding scores with less difference than the WRAT–R, which yielded lower scores overall.

9. In another study, the WRAT–R and the K-TEA were administered to students with learning disabilities and referred students who were not placed (Prewett et al., 1990). The administration of the WRAT–R resulted in lower scores for both groups of students than the K-TEA.

10. Prewett, Lillis, and Bardos (1991) found that administration of the K-TEA Brief and the WRAT–R level 2 to incarcerated youth yielded scores that were similar when the administration was in counterbalance order. This finding is in contrast to other studies cited.

11. Webster et al. (1989) found that scores obtained on the K-TEA were consistently higher than scores obtained on the WRAT–R. When these two measures were compared with actual student performance estimated by classroom teachers, neither instrument was significantly better in predicting actual classroom performance.

12. Students assessed on the K-TEA, WRAT–R, and the PIAT reading subtests obtained scores that seem to vary as a function of their reading curriculum (Webster & Braswell, 1991). Some students scored significantly higher than current reading curriculum placement would suggest, whereas others scored significantly lower. The data obtained for the entire group were significantly higher than teacher estimates based on performance in reading curriculum.

13. A review of the PIAT–R (Allinder & Fuchs, 1992) cautioned that the format of the instrument, including multiple choice on some subtests, may encourage guessing. These reviewers also cautioned that information obtained from multiple choice items is diagnostically different from information obtained when a response must be produced independently by the student. They reminded consumers that this instrument was designed as a wide range screening instrument and should therefore not be used in educational decision-making involving placement, eligibility, or planning.

Selecting Academic Achievement Tests

The tests reviewed in this chapter represent the more commonly used instruments in public school assessment. One instrument may be particularly better to use in one situation but not another. The strengths and weaknesses are presented in Table 6.1 to provide some guidance in selecting instruments.

Table 6.1
Summary of achievement tests

Instrument	Strengths	Weaknesses
Woodcock-Johnson–Revised Tests of Achievement, Standard and Supplemental Batteries	Comprehensive academic achievement test Good technical quality Derived scores available for each subtest Improved writing samples Proofing and Word Attack moved to supplemental battery Improved quick scoring for grade equivalents	Requires fair amount of time to administer (45 min to 1½ hr for both batteries) Requires fair amount of time to score and interpret Addition of column-scoring procedures
Peabody Individual Achievement Test–Revised	Improved items Quick to administer Includes Writing Samples subtest Provides a total reading score and total test score Improved technical quality	Forced-choice Format for most subtests may inflate scores Screening test only
Kaufman Test of Educational Achievement: Comprehensive Form	Comprehensive academic test Provides error analysis and can assist in writing objectives Good technical quality Easy to score	Requires fair amount of time to administer (45 min to 1 hr) May yield some higher scores than Woodcock-Johnson
Kaufman Test of Educational Achievement: Brief Form	Quick to administer and score	Screening only Should not be used to make eligibility decisions No error analysis provided
Wechsler Individual Achievement Test	Designed for use with the Wechsler Intelligence Scales and provides for discrepancy analysis Includes measures in the areas of listening comprehension and oral expression not found on most achievement measures Skill information provided for math domains—can use in writing objectives	More complicated to give and score than some other well-established instruments Does not contain as many items in some areas as other areas, particularly at lower levels
Wide Range Achievement Test–Revision 3	Quick to administer and score	Inadequate information obtained from administration of this test Should be used as rough screening only Should not be used for eligibility decisions

Exercises

Part I

Match the following terms with the correct definitions.

A. *W* scores
B. screening tests
C. group achievement tests
D. diagnostic tests
E. composite scores
F. achievement tests
G. individual achievement tests
H. aptitude tests
I. curriculum-based assessment
J. adaptive behavior scales
K. norm-referenced tests
L. subtests

_______ **1.** Instruments that assess a student's ability to adapt to the world in different situations.
_______ **2.** Tests administered to a group of students to measure academic gains.
_______ **3.** Using the content from the currently used curriculum to assess student progress.
_______ **4.** Tests designed to compare individual students with national averages, or norms of expectancy.
_______ **5.** Parts of a test that measure skills in specific areas or domains.
_______ **6.** Tests used to measure academic progress.
_______ **7.** Broad-based instrument that samples a few items across a curriculum.
_______ **8.** Derived scores of the Woodcock-Johnson Psycho-Educational Battery–Revised.
_______ **9.** Individually administered tests designed to determine specific academic problems or deficit areas.
_______ **10.** An individually administered test that measures academic progress.
_______ **11.** Designed to measure strength, talent, or ability in a particular area or domain.

Part II

Match the following test names with the correct descriptions.

A. Woodcock-Johnson–Revised: Tests of Achievement
B. Kaufman Test of Educational Achievement: Brief Form
C. Kaufman Test of Educational Achievement: Comprehensive Form
D. Peabody Individual Achievement Test–Revised
E. Wide Range Achievement Test–Revision 3
F. Wechsler Individual Achievement Test

_______ **1.** This test provides an error analysis summary that is not provided in the shorter version.
_______ **2.** This test includes a Total Reading and a Total Test score.

_________ **3.** This test has standard and supplemental batteries.

_________ **4.** This test provides cluster scores and individual subtest scores.

_________ **5.** This test may be administered to persons ages 5–75.

_________ **6.** This shorter test version should be used for screening purposes.

_________ **7.** This achievement test includes a Language composite that measures both expressive and listening skills.

_________ **8.** This test includes many multiple-choice items that may encourage guessing.

_________ **9.** This test may be given as a comprehensive achievement test or as a "screener composite."

_________ **10.** This test is the only one presented in this chapter that does not use an easel format.

Part III

Write a *C* next to the statements that are correct according to the research presented in this chapter.

_________ **1.** The WRAT–R always yields higher scores on the reading subtests than the K-TEA.

_________ **2.** Neither the K-TEA nor the WRAT–R were better in predicting classroom performance.

_________ **3.** Students with learning disabilities were distinguishable on the writing subtests of the WJ–R.

_________ **4.** The variability of scores obtained on the PIAT, WRAT–R, K-TEA, and Woodcock Reading Mastery Tests seemed to decrease as the grade level increased.

_________ **5.** The K-TEA does not appear to have an adequate number of items at the pre-academic levels.

_________ **6.** The Writing Samples subtest of the WJ–R seems to have fairly high interrater reliability.

References

Allinder, R. M., & Fuchs, L. S. (1992). Screening academic achievement: Review of the Peabody Individual Achievement Test–Revised. *Learning Disabilities Research & Practice, 7,* 45–47.

Anastasi, A. (1988). *Psychological testing.* New York: Macmillan.

Connelly, J. (1985). Published tests—Which ones do special education teachers perceive as useful? *The Journal of Special Education, 19,* 149–155.

Doll, E. J. (1989). Review of the Kaufman Test of Educational Achievement. In J. C. Conoley, J. J. Kramer, & L. L. Murphey (Eds.), *The tenth mental measurements yearbook.* Lincoln: University of Nebraska Press.

German, D., Johnson, B., & Schneider, M. (1985). Learning disability vs. reading disability: A survey of practitioners' diagnostic populations and test instruments. *Learning Disability Quarterly, 8,* 141–156.

Hultquist, A. M., & Metzke, L. K. (1993). Potential effects of curriculum bias in individual norm-referenced reading and spelling achievement tests. *Journal of Psychoeducational Assessment, 11,* 337–344.

Kaufman, A. S., & Kaufman, N. L. (1985a). *Kaufman Test of Educational Achievement, Brief Form.* Circle Pines: MN: American Guidance Service.

Kaufman, A. S., & Kaufman, N. L. (1985b). *Kaufman Test of Educational Achievement, Comprehensive Form,* Circle Pines, MN: American Guidance Service.

LaGrow, S., & Prochnow-LaGrow, J. (1982). Technical adequacy of the most popular tests selected by responding school psychologists in Illinois. *Psychology in the Schools, 19,* 186–189.

Markwardt, F. C. (1989). *Peabody Individual Achievement Test–Revised.* Circle Pines, MN: American Guidance Service.

Mather, N. (1989). Comparison of the new and existing Woodcock-Johnson writing tests to other writing measures. *Learning Disabilities Focus, 4,* 84–95.

Mather, N., Vogel, S., Spodak, R. B., & McGrew, K. S. (1991). Use of the Woodcock-Johnson–Revised writing tests with students with learning disabilities. *Journal of Psychoeducational Assessment, 9,* 296–307.

Prewett, P., Bardos, A. N., & Fowler, D. B. (1990). Use of the K-TEA and the WRAT–R with learning disabled and referred but not placed students. *Journal of Psychoeducational Assessment, 8,* 51–60.

Prewett, P. N., Bardos, A., & Fowler, D. B. (1991). Relationship between the K-TEA Brief and Comprehensive forms and the WRAT–R level 1 with referred elementary school students. *Educational and Psychological Measurement, 51,* 729–734.

Prewett, P. N., & Giannuli, M. M. (1991a). Correlations of the WISC–R, Stanford-Binet Intelligence Scale, fourth edition, and the reading subtests of three popular achievement tests. *Psychological Reports, 69,* 1232–1234.

Prewett, P. N., & Giannuli, M. M. (1991b). The relationship among reading subtests of the WJ–R, PIAT–R, K-TEA, and WRAT–R. *Journal of Psychoeducational Assessment, 9,* 166–174.

Prewett, P. N., Lillis, W. T., & Bardos, A. N. (1991). Relationship between the Kaufman Test of Educational Achievement Brief Form and the Wide Range Achievement Test–Revised level 2 with incarcerated juvenile delinquents. *Psychological Reports, 68,* 147–150.

Psychological Corporation. (1992). *Wechsler Individual Achievement Test.* San Antonio, TX: Author.

Reschly, D. (1988). Special education reform: School psychology revolution. *School Psychology Review, 17,* 459–475.

Shapiro, E., & Derr, T. (1987). An examination of overlap between curricula and standardized achievement tests. *The Journal of Special Education, 21,* 59–67.

Thurlow, M., & Ysseldyke, J. (1979). Current assessment and decision-making practices in model programs. *Learning Disabilities Quarterly, 2,* 15–24.

Webster, R. E., & Braswell, L. A. (1991). Curriculum bias and reading achievement test performance. *Psychology in the Schools, 28,* 193–198.

Webster, R., Hewett, B., & Crumbacker, M. (1989). Criterion-related validity of the WRAT–R and the K-TEA with teacher estimates of actual classroom academic performance. *Psychology in the Schools, 26,* 243–248.

Wilkinson, G. S. (1993). *The Wide Range Achievement Test: Administration Manual.* Wilmington, DE: Jastak Associates.

Woodcock, R. W., & Johnson, M. B. (1989). *Woodcock-Johnson Psycho-Educational Battery–Revised Tests of Achievement: Standard and Supplemental Batteries.* Dallas: DLM Teaching Resources.

Woodcock, R. W., & Mather, N. (1989). *Woodcock-Johnson Psycho-Educational Battery–Revised Tests of Achievement: Standard and Supplemental Batteries: Examiner's Manual.* Dallas: DLM Teaching Resources.

Worthington, C. (1987). Kaufman Test of Educational Achievement, Comprehensive and Brief. *Journal of Counseling and Development, 65,* 325–327.

Chapter Seven

Standardized Diagnostic Testing

Key Terms

diagnostic tests
instructional level
informal instruments
probes
direct measurement
domains

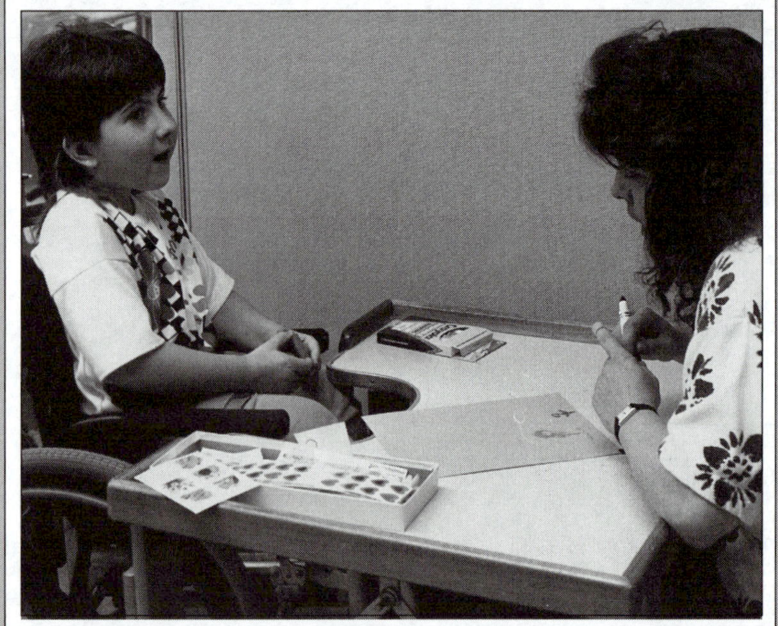

The norm-referenced tests presented in chapter 6 assess achievement across a broad curriculum. Achievement tests are designed to provide the educator with a general view of the student so that he can determine areas of strengths and weaknesses. This information assists the educator in designing an evaluation plan to assess weaknesses diagnostically. The special educator assesses general areas of weakness in greater depth through the use of **diagnostic instruments.** These instruments aid the teacher in educational planning by revealing types of errors the student makes as well as strengths that may be used to determine the proper **instructional level** and possible teaching and learning strategies. The use of diagnostic instruments can also help the teacher in designing **informal instruments** and **probes** to assess student progress using **direct measurement** techniques. Informal assessment and direct measurement are presented in detail in chapter 8.

diagnostic instruments Individually administered tests designed to determine specific academic problems or deficit areas.

instructional level The determined level in the curriculum in which the student should receive instruction.

informal instruments Nonstandardized methods used to collect information about students.

probes Tests used for in-depth assessment of the mastery of a specific skill or subskill.

direct measurement Measuring progress by using the same instructional materials or tasks used in the classroom.

When to Use Diagnostic Testing

Diagnostic tests may be used to measure mastery of specific skills, strengths, and weaknesses whenever the educator wishes to monitor student progress or change the educational program. These tests may be used as a part of the eligibility testing, for reevaluation for annual reviews, or for further diagnostic planning within the classroom. Because these instruments may be used more frequently than general achievement tests, the educator should select the tests or subtests carefully. The educator is encouraged to use equivalent forms of the same test, if available, when testing a student a second time.

The special education teacher should select diagnostic academic tests based on the content area, the method of assessment (oral questions, oral reading, math paper and pencil items, silently read items, timed or untimed tests, etc.), and the method of response (written responses, oral responses, pointing, etc.) required of the student. The format for presentation and response should be considered when interpreting results and making educational intervention plans.

The Review of Diagnostic Tests

The tests presented in this chapter represent those commonly used by teachers and have also been selected because of existing research. For the instruments that have recently been revised, only the revised versions are discussed. The assessment of the basic skill areas of reading, mathematics, spelling, and written language are presented in this chapter. Chapter 11 presents other diagnostic tests, such as instruments to measure receptive language or visual-motor ability.

KeyMath–Revised

The KeyMath–Revised (Connolly, 1988) is presented in an easel format and consists of two equivalent forms, A and B. Many of the items are presented orally by the examiner. The Operations items are presented as paper and pencil tasks. This test includes subtests that are grouped into three areas: Basic Concepts, Operations, and Applications. Table 7.1 presents the areas, **domains,** and strands of the revised KeyMath. Significant strengths and weaknesses may be determined by calculating the differences between standard scores for the various areas. The domain scores may be used to compare abilities and determine if the student's performance is considered to be weak, average, or strong compared to the norm grade-level group.

domains Areas of cognitive development or ability thought to be evidenced by certain behaviors or skills.

Subtests

Numeration. These items sample the student's ability to understand the number system and the functional application of that system. Items include tasks such as counting, identifying numbers, identifying missing numbers in a sequence, understanding concepts of more and less, and reading multidigit numbers.

Rational Numbers. This subtest measures understanding of fractions, decimals, and percents. Lower level items include understanding of the two equal parts of an object, and higher level items include changing fractions into mixed numbers and percents.

Geometry. These items range from understanding spatial concepts and recognizing shapes, to interpreting angles and three-dimensional figures.

Addition. This subtest assesses the student's ability to add objects and perform addition computation problems. Beginning items are orally presented, and later items are paper and pencil computations.

Subtraction. Presented in the same format as the addition subtest, this subtest measures the student's ability to perform subtraction computations. Items begin with simple subtraction of objects and progress to computations involving multidigit numbers, regrouping, and fractions and mixed numbers.

Multiplication. This subtest is presented in the same format as the addition and subtraction subtests and includes simple grouping problems (sets) and more difficult multiplication of mixed numbers and fractions.

Table 7.1
Content specification of KeyMath–R: Areas, strands, and domains.

Areas:	**Basic Concepts**	**Operations**	**Applications**
Strands and domains:	**Numeration** 1. Numbers 0–9 2. Numbers 0–99 3. Numbers 0–999 4. Multidigit numbers and advanced numeration topics **Rational Numbers** 1. Fractions 2. Decimals 3. Percents **Geometry** 1. Spatial and attribute relations 2. Two-dimensional shapes and their relations 3. Coordinate and transformational geometry 4. Three-dimensional shapes and their relations.	**Addition** 1. Models and basic facts 2. Algorithms to add whole numbers 3. Adding rational numbers **Subtraction** 1. Models and basic facts 2. Algorithms to subtract whole numbers 3. Subtracting rational numbers **Multiplication** 1. Models and basic facts 2. Algorithms to multiply whole numbers 3. Multiplying rational numbers **Division** 1. Models and basic facts 2. Algorithms to divide whole numbers 3. Dividing rational numbers **Mental Computation** 1. Computation chains 2. Whole numbers 3. Rational numbers	**Measurement** 1. Comparisons 2. Using nonstandard units 3. Using standard units—length, area 4. Using standard units—weight, capacity **Time and Money** 1. Identifying passage of time 2. Using clocks and clock units 3. Monetary amounts to one dollar 4. Monetary amounts to one hundred dollars and business transactions **Estimation** 1. Whole and rational numbers 2. Measurement 3. Computation **Interpreting Data** 1. Charts and tables 2. Graphs 3. Probability and statistics **Problem Solving** 1. Solving routine problems 2. Understanding nonroutine problems 3. Solving nonroutine problems

Source: From *KeyMath Revised: A Diagnostic Inventory of Essential Mathematics, Manual* (p. 6) by A.J. Connolly, 1988, Circle Pines, MN: American Guidance Service. Copyright 1988 by American Guidance Service. Reprinted by permission.

Division. Like the Addition and other operations subtests, the Division subtest presents lower level items on the easel and more difficult items as paper and pencil computations. The items cover a range of difficulty levels and contain some multistep, or "long" division, computations.

Mental Computation. This orally administered subtest includes math operations problems and more difficult problems that require several steps and operations to complete.

Measurement. Items range from recognition and identification of units of measurement to problems that involve application and changing of the various units of measurement.

Time and Money. These items involve telling time, understanding concepts of time, recognizing times and money, and the understanding and application of money to solve problems of transaction.

Estimation. The student must estimate numbers for sums or amounts, estimate measurements, and estimate the answers in computations.

Interpreting Data. The student interprets charts, graphs, and tables that range from picture charts to tables involving numbers and statistical probabilities.

Problem Solving. These problems range from simple predictable problems to nonroutine problems.

Scoring. The basal and ceiling levels on the KeyMath–R are consistent throughout the test: 3 consecutive correct items constitute the basal, and 3 consecutive incorrect items determine the ceiling. The responses are recorded on the protocol within the appropriate domain boxes. The responses are recorded as 1 for correct and 0 for incorrect.

The examiner lists the domain scores separately and then sums the scores for the subtest raw score. The examiner uses the raw scores to locate scaled scores and percentile ranks for each subtest and then sums the raw scores of the subtests for the area raw score. The area raw scores are used to determine area standard scores, percentile ranks, and age or grade equivalents.

In Activity 7.1, you will score the Basic Concepts area of the KeyMath–R.

☐ CHECK YOUR UNDERSTANDING

Complete Activity 7.1.

Activity 7.1

Complete the following problems.

1. One student's responses in the Geometry subtest are shown on the KeyMath–R protocol in Figure 7.1. Calculate the raw score, and then write your answer on the protocol.

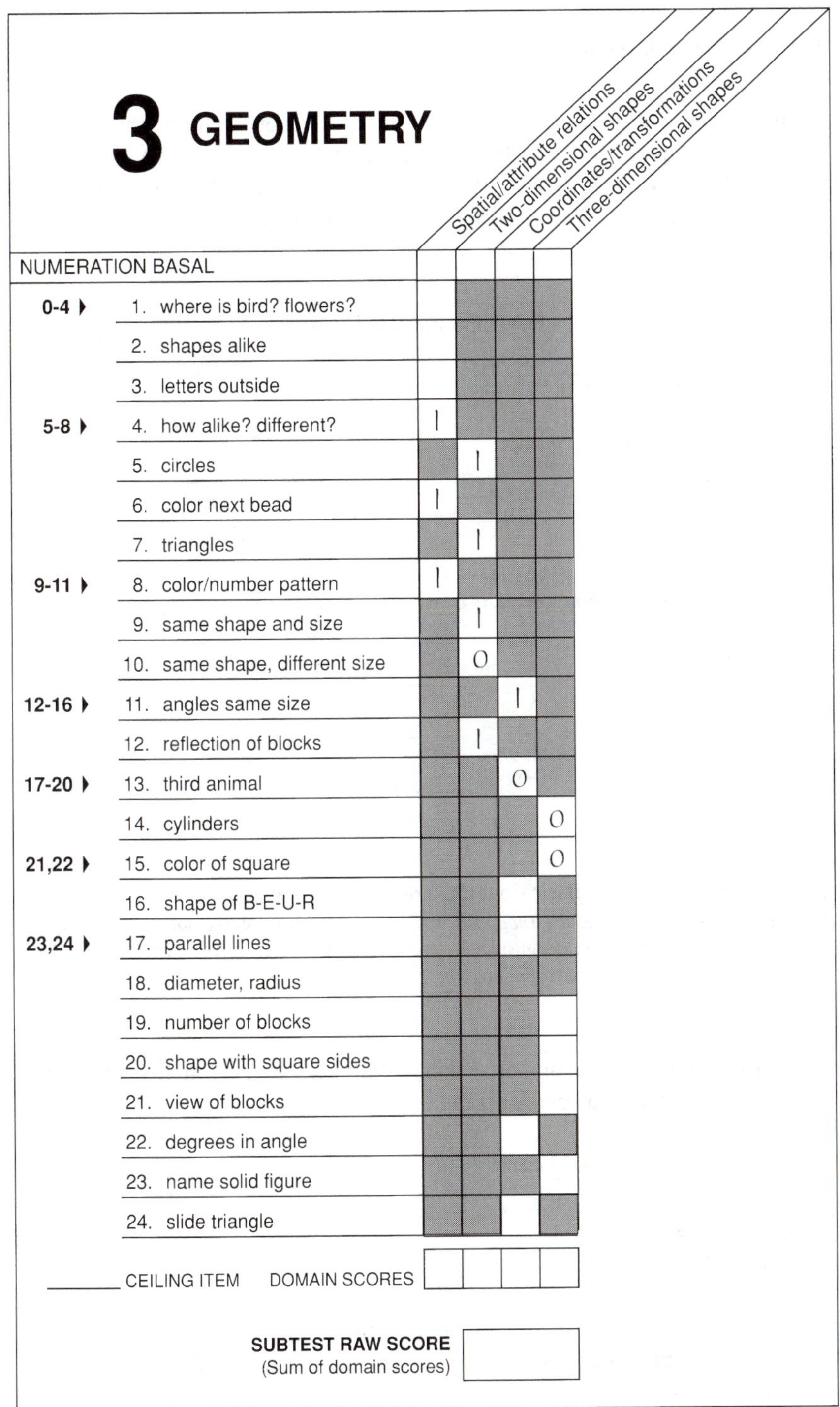

3 GEOMETRY

NUMERATION BASAL	Item	Spatial/attribute relations	Two-dimensional shapes	Coordinates/transformations	Three-dimensional shapes
0-4 ▸	1. where is bird? flowers?				
	2. shapes alike				
	3. letters outside				
5-8 ▸	4. how alike? different?	1			
	5. circles		1		
	6. color next bead	1			
	7. triangles		1		
9-11 ▸	8. color/number pattern	1			
	9. same shape and size		1		
	10. same shape, different size		0		
12-16 ▸	11. angles same size			1	
	12. reflection of blocks		1		
17-20 ▸	13. third animal			0	
	14. cylinders				0
21,22 ▸	15. color of square				0
	16. shape of B-E-U-R				
23,24 ▸	17. parallel lines				
	18. diameter, radius				
	19. number of blocks				
	20. shape with square sides				
	21. view of blocks				
	22. degrees in angle				
	23. name solid figure				
	24. slide triangle				
_______ CEILING ITEM	DOMAIN SCORES				

SUBTEST RAW SCORE
(Sum of domain scores)

Figure 7.1
Geometry section of protocol of the KeyMath–R.

Source: From *KeyMath–Revised: A Diagnostic Inventory of Essential Mathematics, Protocol* (p. 3) by A. J. Connolly, 1988, Circle Pines, MN: American Guidance Service.

2. This student's other raw scores for the Basic Concepts subtests have been entered in Figure 7.2. Write the raw score calculated in problem 1 in the appropriate space in Figure 7.2. Add the subtest raw scores to determine the area raw score, and then write this score on Figure 7.2.

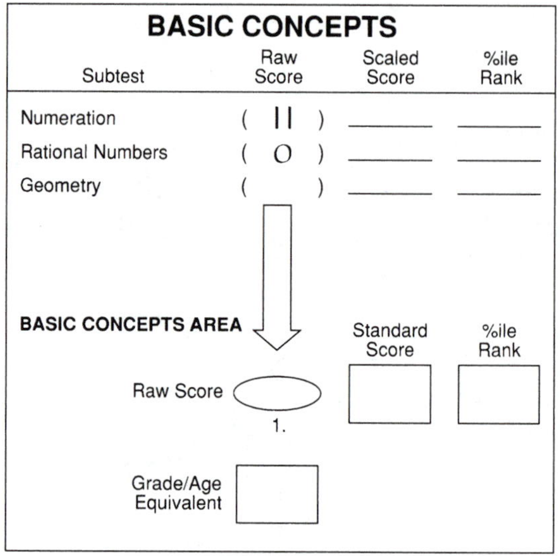
BASIC CONCEPTS

Subtest	Raw Score	Scaled Score	%ile Rank
Numeration	(11)	______	______
Rational Numbers	(0)	______	______
Geometry	( )	______	______

BASIC CONCEPTS AREA

Raw Score ( ) 1.

Standard Score [ ]

%ile Rank [ ]

Grade/Age Equivalent [ ]

Figure 7.2
Summary of scores for the Basic Concepts area of the KeyMath–R.
Source: From *KeyMath–Revised: A Diagnostic Inventory of Essential Mathematics Protocol* (p. 1) by A. J. Connolly, 1988, Circle Pines, MN: American Guidance Service. Copyright 1988 by American Guidance Service. Reprinted by permission.

3. The raw scores for Numeration, Rational Numbers, and Geometry were used to locate the following scaled scores:

	Scaled Scores
Numeration	8
Rational Numbers	1
Geometry	7

Write these scaled scores in the appropriate spaces in Figure 7.2. Use the scaled scores to locate the percentile ranks from the table in Figure 7.3. Complete the "%ile Rank" column in Figure 7.2.

Scaled Score	Standard Score	Percentile Rank	Stanine	Normal Curve Equivalent
9	95	37		43
	94	34		42
	93	32	4	40
	92	30		39
8	91	27		37
	90	25		36
	89	23		35
	88	21		33
	87	19		32
	86	18		30
7	85	16	3	29
	84	14		28
	83	13		26
	82	12		25
	81	10		23
6	80	9		22
	79	8		21
	78	7		19
	77	6	2	18
	76	5		16
5	75	5		15
	74	4		13
	73	4		12
	72	3		11
	71	3		9
4	70	2		8
	69	2		6
	68	2		5
	67	1		4
	66	1	1	2
3	65	1		1
	64	1		Below 1
	63	1		
	62	1		
	61	Below 1		
2	60			
	59			
	58			
	57			
	56			
1	55			

Figure 7.3
Table from the revised KeyMath showing derived normative data for locating percentile ranks, stanines, and normal curve equivalents.

Source: From *KeyMath–Revised: A Diagnostic Inventory of Essential Mathematics, Manual* (p. 309) by A. J. Connolly, 1988, Circle Pines, MN: American Guidance Service. Copyright 1988 by American Guidance Service. Reprinted by permission.

4. The area raw score was used to locate the standard score of 83. Write this in the appropriate space in Figure 7.2. Use the standard score to locate the percentile rank from Figure 7.3. Write this in the "%ile Rank" box in Figure 7.2.
5. Use the area raw score to locate the grade equivalent in Figure 7.4. Write the answer in the appropriate space in Figure 7.2.

Figure 7.4
Grade equivalents corresponding to area and total-test raw scores.

Source: From *KeyMath–Revised: A Diagnostic Inventory of Essential Mathematics, Manual* (p. 310) by A. J. Connolly, 1988, Circle Pines, MN: American Guidance Service. Copyright 1988 by American Guidance Service. Reprinted by permission.

Grade Equivalent	Basic Concepts
	Raw Score
4.9	—
4.8	35
4.7	—
4.6	34
4.5	—
4.4	33
4.3	—
4.2	32
4.1	—
4.0	31
3.9	—
3.8	30
3.7	—
3.6	29
3.5	28
3.4	—
3.3	27
3.2	—
3.1	26
3.0	—
2.9	25
2.8	—
2.7	24
2.6	—
2.5	23
2.4	22
2.3	—
2.2	21
2.1	20
2.0	—

Comparing Area Standard Scores for Significance. The examiner compares the standard scores obtained on the three areas in the section of the protocol titled "Area Comparisons," shown in Figure 7.5. The examiner writes the standard scores in the appropriate spaces and writes >, <, or = on each of the lines between the boxes. The standard score differences are determined by subtracting the scores. To determine significance level, the examiner refers to a table in the manual that lists the differences that are considered significant. If the difference is listed as significant at the .05 level, this means that the chances are 95 out of 100 that a true difference exists and that there are only 5 chances out of 100 that the difference is by error or chance. The level of .01 means that the difference exists with only 1 possibility of 100 that the difference is by error or chance.

In Activity 7.2, you will determine if a significant difference exists between the area standard scores.

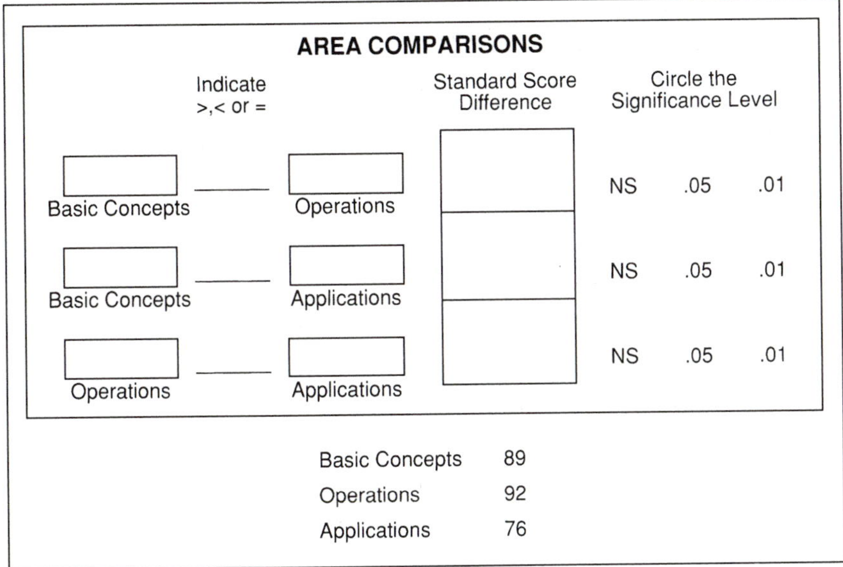

Figure 7.5
Write scores for comparing three areas of KeyMath–R.
Source: From *KeyMath–Revised: A Diagnostic Inventory of Essential Mathematics, Protocol* (p. 12) by A. J. Connolly, 1988, Circle Pines, MN: American Guidance Service. Copyright 1988 by American Guidance Service. Reprinted by permission.

☐ CHECK YOUR UNDERSTANDING

Complete Activity 7.2.

Activity 7.2

Complete the following problems.

1. A third-grade student obtained the KeyMath–R area standard scores shown in at the bottom of Figure 7.5. Write the standard scores in the appropriate spaces. Indicate if the comparisons are >, <, or = and determine the differences.
2. Using the information provided in Figure 7.6 for third-grade comparisons, determine if the differences found in problem 1 are significant. Mark the significance level—NS, .05, or .01—for each of the area comparisons in Figure 7–5.

Determining Domain Strengths and Weaknesses. A student's performance can be analyzed by domains by comparing the obtained domain scores with the average scores listed in the KeyMath–R manual (Figure 7.7). This information aids the educator in determining skill mastery or deficit in the various domains.

Grade	Significance Level	Basic Concepts versus Operations	Basic Concepts versus Applications	Operations versus Applications
		Minimum Standard-Score Difference		
K	.05	23	19	22
	.01	28	23	27
1	.05	19	17	16
	.01	23	21	20
2	.05	19	17	17
	.01	23	21	21
3	.05	17	16	15
	.01	20	19	18
4	.05	14	13	13
	.01	18	16	16
5	.05	13	12	12
	.01	16	14	14
6	.05	14	12	12
	.01	17	15	15
7	.05	11	10	10
	.01	14	13	12
8	.05	11	11	10
	.01	14	13	13
9	.05	11	11	10
	.01	14	13	13

Figure 7.6
KeyMath–R, minimum differences required for statistical significance in comparisons of area standard scores, grades K through 9.
Source: From *KeyMath–Revised: A Diagnostic Inventory of Essential Mathematics, Manual* (p. 312) by A. J. Connolly, 1988, Circle Pines, MN: American Guidance Service. Copyright 1988 by American Guidance Service. Reprinted by permission.

Subtest and Domain	Ceiling Item															
	3	4	5	6	7	8	9	10	11	12	13	14	15	16	17	18
Numeration																
Numbers 0-9	3	4	5	6	6	6	6	6	6	6	6	6	6	6	6	6
Numbers 0-99	—	—	—	—	—	—	3	4	4	4-5	4-5	4-5	4-5	4-5	5-6	5-6
Numbers 0-999	—	—	—	—	—	—	—	—	—	—	—	—	2-3	2-3	2-3	2-3
Multi-digit numbers and advanced numeration topics	—	—	—	—	—	—	—	—	—	—	—	—	—	—	—	—

Figure 7.7
KeyMath–R average domain scores, by ceiling item, grade 3, spring, to grade 4, fall.
Source: From *KeyMath–Revised: A Diagnostic Inventory of Essential Mathematics, Manual* (p. 324) by A. J. Connolly, 1988, Circle Pines, MN: American Guidance Service. Copyright 1988 by American Guidance Service. Reprinted by permission.

In Activity 7.3, you will determine one student's weaknesses and strengths for each domain of the Numeration subtest.

☐ CHECK YOUR UNDERSTANDING

Complete Activity 7.3.

Activity 7.3

Complete the problems and answer the questions that follow.

1. A fourth-grade student obtained the following domain scores on the Numeration subtest. Write the scores in the appropriate spaces on the portion of the protocol in Figure 7.8. The ceiling item reached was 15.

Numeration Domain	*Score*
Numbers 0–9	6
Numbers 0–99	5
Numbers 0–999	0
Multidigit numbers and advanced numeration topics	0

2. Use the information provided in Figure 7.7 to determine if the performance by this fourth-grade student is strong, average, or weak in each of the domains. Circle the correct domain statuses on Figure 7.8. The performance is considered weak if the raw score is less than the expected score, average if the raw score is the same as the expected score, and strong if the performance is better than the expected score.
3. Based on the student's strengths and weaknesses as determined in this activity, which skills should the teacher begin to teach and emphasize in planning the instructional program? ______________________________

____

____

____

BASIC CONCEPTS AREA

Subtest	Domain	Domain Score	Average Score (Table 16)	Domain Status		
Numeration: (24 items)	Numbers 0–9	_____	_____	W	A	S
	Numbers 0–99	_____	_____	W	A	S
Ceiling	Numbers 0–999	_____	_____	W	A	S
Item _____	Multi-digit numbers and advanced numeration topics	_____	_____	W	A	S

Figure 7.8
Basic Concepts scoring area from KeyMath–R protocol.
Source: From *KeyMath–Revised: A Diagnostic Inventory of Essential Mathematics, Protocol* by A. J. Connolly, 1988, Circle Pines, MN: American Guidance Service. Copyright 1988 by American Guidance Service. Reprinted by permission.

Technical Data

Norming Process. The total number of students in the standardization and norming process for the KeyMath–R was 1,978. Test developers considered the variables of geographic region, grade, sex, socioeconomic status, race or ethnic group, and parental educational level. The sample included students from grades K through 9. The variables of parental educational level, geographic region, and race or ethnic group were representative of U.S. population data from the Bureau of Census. The census reports relied on 1985 data and projections through 2080 for the Hispanic population. The KeyMath–R offers both fall and spring testing norms, and the norming procedures are adequately detailed in the examiner's manual.

Reliability. Reliability studies included alternate forms reliability studies presented by age and grade from the fall testing sample and split-half reliability studies for both fall and spring testing. Data also are presented for an item response theory using the Rasch model (cited in Connolly, 1988). Total test reliability coefficients for the alternate forms study ranged from .91 for grade-based standard scores to .92 for total test age-based standard scores.

Validity. The examiner's manual presents information regarding the content validity based on the construction and model of the test, a construct validity study addressing both developmental change and internal consistency, and concurrent validity studies. The data from the concurrent validity studies included comparisons with the original KeyMath, the Comprehensive Test of Basic Skills, and the Iowa Test of Basic Skills. Data presented compare the instruments by subtests, areas, and total tests. Total test comparisons yielded validity coefficients that ranged from .66 comparing the Total Mathematics scores of the Comprehensive Test of Basic Skills to .93 comparing the performance of seventh-grade students on the original and revised versions of the KeyMath.

Test of Mathematical Abilities–2 (TOMA–2)

The TOMA (Brown, Cronin, & McEntire, 1994) was designed to assess some of the areas of math that may not be addressed by other instruments. This test, now in its second edition, was developed to be used with students who range in age from 8-0 to 18-11. The test authors present the following questions, not answered by other instruments, as their rationale for developing the TOMA:

1. What are the student's expressed attitudes toward mathematics?
2. What is the student's general vocabulary level when that vocabulary is used in a mathematical sense?
3. How knowledgeable is the student (or group of students) regarding the functional use of mathematics facts and concepts in our general culture?

4. How do a student's attitudes, vocabulary, and general math information compare with the basic skills shown in the areas of computation and story problems?
5. Do the student's attitudes, vocabulary, and level of general math information differ markedly from those of a group of age peers? (Brown, Cronin, & McEntire, 1994, p. 1)

This instrument was developed to help the teacher find the answers to these questions. The TOMA–2 consists of five subtests, with the fifth subtest, Attitude Toward Math, considered supplemental. The remaining subtests are Vocabulary, Computation, General Information, and Story Problems. The subtests yield standard scores with a mean of 10, a math quotient with a mean of 100, age equivalents, and percentile ranks. The manual gives precautions against misinterpretation of test scores and encourages further diagnostic assessment if a math disability is suspected.

The test authors list three diagnostic questions that the TOMA–2 may help educators answer:

1. Where should the student be placed in a curriculum?
2. What specific skills or content has the student mastered?
3. How does this student's overall performance compare with that of age or grade peers? (Brown, Cronin, & McEntire, 1994, p. 1)

Technical Data

Norming Process. The norming sample of the TOMA–2 consisted of 2,082 students in 26 states geographically spread across the United States. The variables of gender, race (black, white, and other), community (urban-suburban and rural), disability status (no disability, learning disabilities, other handicapping conditions), and region were considered and seemed to reflect the percentages from the 1990 census.

Reliability. Reliability was studied using coefficient alpha for internal consistency, and group coefficients ranged from .73 to .98. Test-retest coefficients appear to be adequate, .66 to .93.

Validity. Concurrent criterion-related validity was studied using the math tests of the PIAT, the KeyMath, WRAT, and the Scientific Research Associates (SRA) Achievement Series. Low to adequate correlations were found, with the Story Problems subtests of the TOMA–2 and the SRA having the highest coefficient of .72. Construct validity was supported in the presentation of developmental data and by comparing the TOMA to cognitive tests (the Wechsler and the Slosson intelligence tests), resulting in modest to adequate correlations.

Woodcock Reading Mastery Tests–Revised (WRMT–R)

The WRMT–R (Woodcock, 1987) consists of two forms that are not exactly equivalent. One form, G, contains two additional reading readiness subtests and a supplementary Letter Checklist. For this reason, Form G is the version that should be used with younger or lower level readers. The other form, H, contains subtests equivalent to the four other subtests contained in Form G. A general screening of reading ability can be obtained by administering the Short Scale, which includes only the Word Identification and the Passage Comprehension subtests.

Subtests. For this revision of the WRMT, the subtests of Word Identification, Word Attack, and Passage Comprehension remained basically unchanged in presentation format. The Word Attack subtest contains an error analysis inventory, but the presentation format remains the same. Substantial changes have been made in some of the subtests, and these changes affect their presentation. A new subtest, Visual-Auditory Learning, has been added.

Visual-Auditory Learning. In this subtest, the examiner visually presents a picture or rebus-type symbol while orally presenting a word. After seeing four symbols and hearing their accompanying words, the student must use the newly learned symbols to "read" sentences presented on the subsequent easel page. The student then sees four new symbols and is asked to "read" sentences that include both the first symbols and the new symbols. This process continues throughout the subtest unless the student reaches a ceiling by making a specific number of errors. If the student reaches a ceiling, the cutoff score based on total errors is used to determine the raw score. If the student does not make the number of errors used to stop the testing but rather completes all of the stories on the subtest, the number of total errors is subtracted from the number 134 to determine the raw score. This subtest is found only on Form G of the WRMT–R.

Letter Identification and Supplementary Letter Checklist. These two subtests are contained only on Form G of the revised WRMT. The Letter Identification subtest does provide norm scores; however, the supplementary Letter Checklist is used for error analysis only. The examiner has the option of presenting the task to measure the student's ability to name the letters or the sounds of the letters.

Word Identification. This subtest measures the student's ability to orally read the visually presented words. The words at the easiest level represent sight words and other words selected from several basal reading series. The more difficult words were selected from various sources. This subtest attempts to measure identification of the word. The student must say the word aloud, and comprehension of the word is not measured.

Word Attack. This subtest visually presents nonsense words, which the student must decode orally. This test measures the student's ability to use phonetic attack and structural analysis in reading new words aloud. An error analysis page included in the protocol assists the examiner in identifying specific phonetic errors that need educational remediation.

Word Comprehension. This subtest samples the student's ability to provide missing words for analogies, synonyms, and antonyms. This subtest actually is comprised of three smaller subtests, which can be analyzed by categories for understanding vocabulary. The examiner calculates three raw scores and locates the *W* score on the protocol rather than from norm tables.

Passage Comprehension. This subtest presents a sentence or passage with a missing word. The student orally provides the missing word after silently reading the passage. The lower level items contain picture cues, and most of the difficult items are fairly content specific. The most difficult items were taken from textbooks, newspaper articles, and the like.

Scoring. On most of the WRMT–R subtests, the student establishes the basal after answering 6 consecutive items correctly and the ceiling after answering 6 consecutive responses incorrectly. The Visual-Auditory Learning subtest, however, contains a cutoff score chart to determine when the student has reached a ceiling level.

In Activity 7.4, you will determine the student's score on the Visual-Auditory Learning subtest.

☐ **CHECK YOUR UNDERSTANDING**

Complete Activity 7.4.

Activity 7.4

Complete the following problems.

1. A student taking the WRMT–2 Visual-Auditory Learning subtest completed stories 1 through 4 and made 46 errors. In Figure 7.9, find the row that contains stories 1–4, because the student completed four stories. Locate the number 46, and then locate the total error estimate beneath in the total errors row (stories 1–7). Write the total error estimate in the appropriate space in Figure 7.9.
2. Subtract the total error estimate from 134 to obtain the raw score for this subtest. Write the score on Figure 7.9.

Scoring the WRMT–R will result in comprehensive information about the student's individual reading ability. In addition to an error analysis for the Word Attack subtest and qualitative scoring of the supplementary Letter Checklist, this battery can provide the examiner with the following information:

1. Standard error of measurement is provided for each *W* score, and confidence bands may be calculated for each subtest.

CUTOFF SCORE TO TOTAL ERRORS

Story 1:	-	9	-	-	-	-	-	-	-	-	-	-	-	-	-	-	-	-	-	-	-	-	-	-	-	-	-	-	-	-	-	-	-	-	-	-	-
Stories 1-2:	22	-	21	-	-	-	20	-	-	19	-	-	-	18	-	-	-	17	-	-	16	-	-	-	15	-	-	-	-	-	-	-	-	-	-	-	-
Stories 1-4:	-	56	-	55	54	-	53	-	52	-	51	-	50	49	-	48	-	47	-	46	-	45	-	44	-	43	-	42	-	41	-	40	-	39	-	38	37
Stories 1-6:	105	104	103	102	-	101	100	99	98	97	96	95	94	-	93	92	91	90	89	88	-	87	86	85	84	83	82	-	81	80	79	78	77	-	76	75	74
TOTAL ERRORS (Stories-1-7):	**133**	**132**	**131**	**130**	**129**	**128**	**127**	**126**	**125**	**124**	**123**	**122**	121	**120**	**119**	**118**	**117**	**116**	**115**	**114**	**113**	**112**	**111**	**110**	**109**	**108**	**107**	**106**	**105**	**104**	**103**	**102**	**101**	**100**	**99**	**98**	**97**

Stories 1-4:	-	36	-	35	-	34	-	33	-	32	-	31	30	-	29	-	28	-	27	-	26	-	-	25	-	-	-	-	-	-	-	-	-	-	-	-	-
Stories 1-6:	73	72	71	70	69	68	67	-	66	65	64	63	62	61	60	59	-	58	57	56	-	55	54	53	52	51	50	49	48	47	46	45	44	43	42	41	40
TOTAL ERRORS (Stories-1-7):	**96**	**94**	**93**	**92**	**91**	**90**	**89**	**88**	**87**	**86**	**85**	**84**	82	**81**	**80**	**79**	**78**	**77**	**76**	**75**	**74**	**73**	**72**	**71**	**70**	**69**	**67**	**66**	**65**	**63**	**62**	**61**	**60**	**59**	**57**	**56**	**55**

134 – _______ = Test 1 Raw Score ◯
Total Errors

Figure 7.9
Table to obtain total errors using cutoff score of the WRMT–R Visual-Auditory Learning subtest.

Source: From *Woodcock Reading Mastery Tests–Revised, Form G, Protocol* (p. 3) by R. W. Woodcock, 1987, Circle Pines, MN: American Guidance Service. Copyright 1976 by American Guidance Service. Reprinted from the *Woodcock-Johnson Psycho-Educational Battery,* copyright 1977, DLM Teaching Resources, Allen, TX 75002. Used under license.

2. Space on the protocol for error responses helps the examiner complete an error analysis of reading ability.
3. Several diagnostic profiles may be plotted according to the student's performance based on percentile ranks, grade equivalents, and relative performance index scores.

Once the examiner has mastered the scoring, he obtains a comprehensive evaluation of reading. The examiner uses raw scores to enter tables to obtain the derived scores of *W* scores, grade and age equivalents, and standard error of measurement for *W* scores. The examiner compares the student's obtained *W* scores with reference scores for age or grade-level comparisons.

The table that contains the reference scores also contains column numbers. The column numbers are used to find percentile ranks and standard scores on another table. Two column numbers are given for each reference score. When the examiner has made the comparison by subtracting the reference score from the obtained *W* score, he selects the correct column number and enters the relative performance index table, a portion of which is shown in Figure 7.10.

The examiner determines the correct column by the following criteria: If the difference between the *W* and the reference score is less than 100, the column number on the left is used to enter the table; if the difference is greater than 100, the column number on the right is used to enter the table. The

Table G. Relative Performance Indexes, Percentile Ranks, and Standard Scores (mean = 100, *SD* = 15)

Column												
25		26		27		28		29		30		
PR/Std		PR/Std		PR/Std		PR/Std		PR/Std		PR/Std		DIFF
98	**132**	98	130	**97**	**129**	96	126	**93**	**122**	90	119	**144**
98	**131**	98	129	**97**	**128**	95	125	**93**	**122**	90	119	**143**
98	**130**	97	129	**97**	**127**	95	125	**92**	**121**	89	119	**142**
98	**129**	97	128	**96**	**127**	95	124	**92**	**121**	89	118	**141**
97	**129**	97	127	**96**	**126**	94	124	**91**	**120**	88	118	**140**
97	**128**	96	127	**96**	**125**	94	123	**91**	**120**	87	117	**139**
97	**127**	96	126	**95**	**125**	93	122	**90**	**119**	87	117	**138**
96	**127**	95	125	**95**	**124**	93	122	**90**	**119**	86	116	**137**
96	**126**	95	125	**94**	**123**	92	121	**89**	**118**	86	116	**136**
95	**125**	95	124	**94**	**123**	92	121	**88**	**118**	85	115	**135**
95	**124**	94	123	**93**	**122**	91	120	**88**	**117**	84	115	**134**
94	**124**	93	123	**92**	**122**	90	119	**87**	**117**	83	115	**133**
94	**123**	93	122	**92**	**121**	90	119	**86**	**116**	83	114	**132**
93	**122**	92	121	**91**	**120**	89	118	**85**	**116**	82	114	**131**
92	**122**	91	121	**90**	**120**	88	118	**85**	**115**	81	113	**130**
92	**121**	91	120	**90**	**119**	87	117	**84**	**115**	80	113	**129**
91	**120**	90	119	**89**	**118**	86	117	**83**	**114**	79	112	**128**
90	**119**	89	118	**88**	**118**	86	116	**82**	**114**	79	112	**127**
89	**119**	88	118	**87**	**117**	85	115	**81**	**113**	78	111	**126**
89	**118**	87	117	**86**	**116**	84	115	**80**	**113**	77	111	**125**
87	**117**	86	116	**85**	**116**	83	114	**79**	**112**	76	111	**124**
86	**117**	85	116	**84**	**115**	82	114	**78**	**112**	75	110	**123**
85	**116**	84	115	**83**	**114**	81	113	**77**	**111**	74	110	**122**
84	**115**	83	114	**82**	**114**	80	112	**76**	**111**	73	109	**121**
83	**114**	82	114	**81**	**113**	78	112	**75**	**110**	72	109	**120**
82	**114**	81	113	**80**	**112**	77	111	**74**	**110**	71	108	**119**
81	**113**	79	112	**78**	**112**	76	111	**73**	**109**	70	108	**118**
79	**112**	78	112	**77**	**111**	75	110	**72**	**109**	69	108	**117**
78	**111**	77	111	**76**	**110**	74	109	**71**	**108**	68	107	**116**
76	**111**	75	110	**74**	**110**	72	109	**70**	**108**	67	107	**115**

Figure 7.10
Table G all forms, columns 25 to 30, difference scores 115 to 144.

Source: From *Woodcock Reading Mastery Tests–Revised Examiner's Manual* (p. 172) by R. W. Woodcock, 1987. Circle Pines, MN: American Guidance Service. Copyright 1987 by American Guidance Service. Reprinted by permission.

column numbers may be different for the scores obtained in the standard error of measurement confidence bands. When the standard error of measurement is added to the difference score, the new score may be greater than 100 when the original difference score was less than 100. This means that the column number on the right would be used to determine the relative performance index and percentile rank for the confidence band scores. When the standard error of measurement is subtracted from the difference score, the new score may be less than 100 when the original score was not. Again, the new score found by using the standard error of measurement would require a different column number for the relative performance index table.

The WRMT–R presents cluster scores for reading as well as individual subtest scores. The clusters are Readiness (Form G only), Basic Skills, and Reading Comprehension. The Readiness cluster includes the Visual-Auditory and Letter Identification subtests. Word identification and Word Attack subtests make up the Basic Skills cluster. The Reading Comprehension cluster is made up of the Word Comprehension and Passage Comprehension subtests. The cluster *W* scores are obtained by finding the average of the two subtest *W* scores in each cluster. A Total Reading cluster score is found by averaging the four subtests contained on both forms of the test: Word Identification, Word Attack, Word Comprehension, and Passage Comprehension.

☐ CHECK YOUR UNDERSTANDING

Complete Activity 7.5.

Activity 7.5

Complete the problems and answer the questions that follow.

1. Use the information in Figure 7.11 to determine the difference between the obtained *W* score and the reference score for the Word Identification subtest. Choose from the figure the column number that will be used to find the relative performance index and the percentile rank for the obtained *W* score.
2. Using the obtained difference score from problem 1, complete the confidence bands (Figure 7.11) by adding and subtracting the standard error of measurement given in the figure. Write the answers in the appropriate spaces on the portion of the protocol in Figure 7.11. Choose from the figure the column number that will be used to find the relative performance index and percentile ranks for the confidence band scores.
3. The relative performance index for this student is 99/90. Write 99 in the appropriate spaces in Figure 7.11. Use Figure 7.10 to find the standard score and percentile rank for the obtained difference score found in problem 1 for the Word Identification subtest. Write your answer in the appropriate spaces in Figure 7.11.

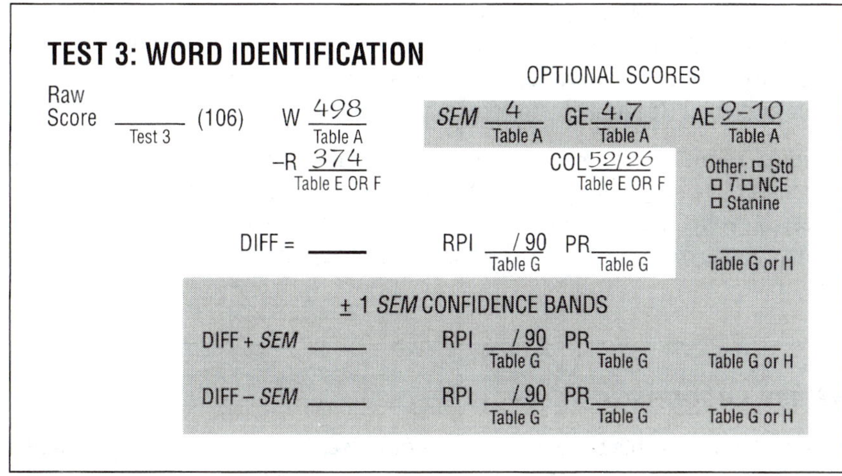

TEST 3: WORD IDENTIFICATION

OPTIONAL SCORES

Raw Score ______ (106) W 498 (Table A) SEM 4 (Table A) GE 4.7 (Table A) AE 9-10 (Table A)
Test 3

–R 374 (Table E OR F) COL 52/26 (Table E OR F) Other: ☐ Std ☐ *T* ☐ NCE ☐ Stanine

DIFF = ______ RPI ___/90 (Table G) PR______ (Table G) ______ (Table G or H)

± 1 *SEM* CONFIDENCE BANDS

DIFF + *SEM* ______ RPI ___/90 (Table G) PR______ (Table G) ______ (Table G or H)

DIFF – *SEM* ______ RPI ___/90 (Table G) PR______ (Table G) ______ (Table G or H)

Figure 7.11
Protocol section for WRMT–R Word Identification subtest.

Source: From *Woodcock Reading Mastery Tests–Revised, Protocol* (p. 12) by R. W. Woodcock, 1987, Circle Pines, MN: American Guidance Service. Copyright 1987 by American Guidance Service. Reprinted by permission.

4. Use Figure 7.10 to obtain the standard scores and percentile ranks for the confidence bands. Write your answer in the appropriate spaces in Figure 7.11.

5. What do the confidence band scores represent? ______________________

____

____

6. Why are the confidence bands necessary for accurate interpretation of the student's ability? ______________________

____

____

Technical Data

Norming Process. The standardization and norming process of the WRMT–R included a sample of 6,089 people, ranging from kindergarten to college/university and adult age levels. The test developers considered the variables of age, sex, community size, race, origin, and geographic regions for all subjects. The variables of occupation, adult occupation, and type of college (private, public, university, 2-year, or 4-year) were considered for the adult and college samples.

Reliability. The examiner's manual includes internal reliability studies. These split-half reliability coefficients for the equivalent forms (G and H) and cluster reliability coefficients were reported. Reliability coefficients for both the Short Scale and Total Reading cluster scores were in the .90s.

Validity. The examiner's manual contains information on both content and concurrent validity. Correlations with the Woodcock-Johnson reading tests for selected groups were included in the manual. Total reading correlation coefficients ranged from .48 on the Short Scale to .91 on the Full Scale Total Reading scores.

Other Diagnostic Tests

The remainder of this chapter briefly summarizes several other tests frequently used in the classroom situation. Some of these tests will not require the lengthy test administration time required by tests presented in the first section of the chapter. Some of these tests may be administered, in part or whole, to groups of students. These tests are included in this chapter because they provide useful information to the educator for diagnosing deficits in specific academic areas and aid in educational planning.

Test of Written Language–2 (TOWL–2)

The revision of the original TOWL includes two alternate forms test booklets (A and B) and is organized into three composites: Overall Written Language, Contrived Writing, and Spontaneous Writing (Hammill & Larsen, 1988). TOWL–2 contains 10 subtests, of which four are calculated from the spontaneously written story. This instrument may be administered in small groups; however, for optimal monitoring of written responses, individual administration appears to be best. The skills measured by each subtest are as follows:

1. Vocabulary measures knowledge of word meanings and classes through the writing of meaningful sentences.
2. Spelling measures the ability to spell dictated words.
3. Style measures the ability to punctuate sentences and capitalize properly.
4. Logical Sentences measures the ability to recognize and correct through rewriting illogicalities existing in stimulus sentences.
5. Sentence Combining measures the ability to incorporate the meaning of several sentences into a comprehensive single sentence containing embedded phrases, introductory clauses, adjective sentences, etc.
6. Thematic Maturity measures the ability to write in a logical, organized fashion, to generate a specific theme, to develop a character's personality, and to incorporate other compositional skills.
7. Contextual Vocabulary measures the ability to use complex sentences com-

prised of introductory and concluding clauses, embedded phrases, adjective sequences, etc.

8. Syntactic Maturity measures the ability to use complex sentences comprised of introductory and concluding clauses, embedded phrases, adjective sequences, etc.
9. Contextual Spelling measures the ability to spell words properly when they appear in a self-generated composition.
10. Contextual Style measures the ability to apply the rules governing punctuation of sentences and capitalization of words when they appear in a written composition. (Hammill & Larsen, 1988)

The examiner may wish to obtain the computer scoring system for the TOWL–2. This system analyzes raw scores and compares information from other tests administered to the student to determine if discrepancies in performance exist.

Technical Data

Norming Process. The test developers standardized and normed the TOWL–2 on a sample of 2,216 students from 19 states. The following demographic variables were considered and appeared to reflect U.S. population information: sex, rural and urban communities, race (white, black, other), geographic area, and ethnicity (American Indian, Hispanic, Asian, everyone else). Approximately 100 students for each age group (7 through 17) for each form (A and B) were tested.

Reliability. The manual provides information for the following reliability studies: interscorer correlation, internal consistency using coefficient alpha and split-half methods, and test-retest using alternate forms. All coefficients appear to be adequate to high on all reliability studies, with many falling in the .90s range.

Validity. The manual presents both concurrent criterion-related validity and construct validity information. Concurrent validity studies employed the SRA Achievement Series, with the Language Arts and Contrived Writing scores yielding the highest coefficient of .70. Construct validity was presented with the supporting data of age differentiation, interrelationships among subtests, group differentiation, grade differentiation, item validity, and relationship to both achievement and intelligence tests. Factor analysis supported the two components of Contrived Writing and Spontaneous Writing.

Test of Written Spelling–3 (TWS–3)

A standardized spelling test, the TWS–3 (Larsen & Hamill, 1994) consists of two subtests that can be administered to individual students or to groups of students ranging in age from 6-0 to 18-11. Instructions for starting points and basal and ceiling levels are presented in the examiner's manual. During administration of this test to an individual student, the basal is established when the student has correctly spelled 5 consecutive words. The ceiling is established when the student misses 5 words consecutively.

The subtests of the TWS–3 are Predictable Words and Unpredictable Words. The Predictable Words subtest contains words that follow the general spelling rules; those in the Unpredictable Words subtest do not conform to general spelling rules. Each correct item receives 1 point. All items below the basal are scored correct. Raw scores are used to enter tables for standard scores with a mean of 100, percentile ranks, age equivalents, and grade equivalents.

This revision of the TWS includes more elaboration for examiners regarding the appropriate use of the instrument, additional research on criterion-related validity, and research designed to support the absence of gender or racial bias of the instrument (Larsen & Hammill, 1994).

Technical Data

Norming Process. The standardization sample included data from 3,805 students in the TWS–2 sample, plus an addition 855 new students from a total of 23 states. The variables of age, race, gender, ethnicity, and geographic region were considered. The sample appears to be representative of the national averages reported in the manual.

Reliability. Reliability studies included internal reliability and test-retest reliability studies. Internal reliability coefficients ranged from .94 to .99 for total test reliability, and the test-retest reliability coefficients ranged from .92 to .97 for total test coefficients. The interscorer reliability coefficient was .99.

Validity. Validity information presented in the manual includes content validity, criterion-related validity, and construct validity. Content validity is presented in terms of item selection. Criterion-related validity studies compared the TWS–3 with basal reading lists and with spelling sections of the WRAT–R, California Achievement Test, Durrell Analysis of Reading, and the SRA Achievement Series. Criterion-related validity coefficients ranged from .72 to .97. A discussion of construct validity focuses on developmental gains based on comparisons of mean scores by ages and the relationship of the TWS–3 to other types of tests.

Formal Reading Inventory

The Formal Reading Inventory (Wiederholt, 1986) contains tasks similar to informal reading inventories (see chapter 8) but with the advantages of norm-referenced data. This standardized reading inventory assesses the student's ability to answer comprehension questions after silently reading passages and provides measurement of miscues of orally read passages. The comprehension questions are answered using a multiple-choice format, and the silent reading subtest can be administered with ease; however, recording miscues for oral reading requires some practice before mastering the technique. The oral miscues, other miscues, and other observations are shown in Figure 7.12.

Technical Data

Norming Process. The Formal Reading Inventory was standardized on 1,737 students in 12 states (Wiederholt, 1986). The demographic data appeared to be representative of the population of the United States, with the following variables considered: sex, urban or rural community, race (white, black, other), geographic region, ethnicity (American Indian, Hispanic, Asian, other). Students ranged in age from 6 to 17.

Reliability. Reliability studies included both internal consistency using the coefficient alpha method and alternate forms reliability. Internal consistency coefficients were high—.90s at six age levels—and the alternate forms reliability coefficient for the silent forms was .75.

Validity. The manual presents content, criterion-related, and construct validity. Criterion-related validity included two concurrent validity studies, one with the Comprehensive Test of Basic Skills and one with the California Achievement Test. Correlations ranged from .21 to .69. Construct validity was pre-

Oral Reading Miscues	***Other Miscues***	***Other Observations***
Meaning similarity	Omissions	Slow reading rate
Function similarity	Additions	Word-by-word reading
Graphic/phonemic similarities	Dialect	Poor phrasing
Multiple sources	Reversals	Lack of expression
Self-correction		Pitch too high or low; voice too soft or strained
		Poor enunciation
		Disregard of punctuation
		Head movement
		Finger pointing
		Loss of place
		Nervousness
		Poor attitude
		Other

Figure 7.12
Miscues and other observations during oral reading tasks of the Formal Reading Inventory.

sented through a discussion of developmental progress and relationship to age, progression of difficulty of tasks, and one study. The study used a sample of 17 adolescent females and correlated the instrument with the Detroit Test of Learning Aptitude–2.

Gray Oral Reading Tests–Third Edition (GORT–3)

The GORT–3 was designed to provide information about "(a) oral reading rate and accuracy, (b) oral reading comprehension, (c) total reading ability, and (d) oral reading miscues" (Wiederholt & Bryant, 1992, p. 4). This test consists of two equivalent forms that contain passages, increasing in difficulty level, to be read aloud by the student. Following each passage are five multiple-choice comprehension questions to be read by the examiner and answered orally by the student. The examiner records miscues for the orally read passages in a fashion similar to that previously presented for the Formal Reading Inventory. Derived scores include standard scores for the comprehension and passage scores (mean of 10), percentile ranks for comprehension and passages, and an Oral Reading Quotient (mean of 100).

Technical Data

Norming Process. The standardization sample of the GORT–R consisted of 1,485 children from 18 states (Wiederholt & Bryant, 1992). The variables considered were gender, urban or rural community, race (white, black, or other), ethnicity (American Indian, Hispanic, Asian, or other), and geographic region. Demographics appeared to represent 1990 census information as presented in the manual.

Reliability. The manual presents information on internal consistency and alternate forms reliability studies. Internal consistency studies yielded coefficients in the .90s for 12 age group intervals. Alternate forms reliability coefficients were in the low .80s for rate, accuracy, passage, and Oral Reading Quotient. The alternate forms reliability coefficient for the comprehension score was .62.

Validity. Information presented in the manual for validity of the GORT–3 includes content validity, criterion-related validity, and construct validity. According to the test authors, careful control of reading difficulty levels and item selection validate the content of the test. The concurrent criterion-related studies included correlations with several reading, achievement, and diagnostic tests. The validity coefficients obtained and presented in the manual exhibit a large degree of variability ranging from NS (not significant) to the upper .80s. A discussion of construct validity covers developmental progression, relationship to age, and relationship to other language and achievement scores.

Test of Reading Comprehension–Revised Edition (TORC–R)

This revised edition of the TORC (Brown, Hammill, & Wiederholt, 1986) contains the same subtests as the earlier edition; however, the vocabulary subtests for mathematics, science, and social studies, as well as the Reading Directions for Schoolwork, are considered supplementary. The technical revisions and updated normative data are noted changes.

Research and Issues

The following summaries represent some of the research and reviews on the diagnostic tests included in this chapter. The newly revised editions of tests may have little research to date.

1. Shriner and Salvia (1988) found little content validity when they compared items on the KeyMath with mathematics curriculum used in schools.

2. Greenstein and Strain (1977) determined that the KeyMath did successfully discriminate adolescent students with learning disabilities.

3. The KeyMath yielded fairly high correlation coefficients in a criterion-related study with the Cognitive Levels Test (Eaves, Darch, Mann, & Vance, 1989). Moderate correlations between the WRMT and the Cognitive Levels Test were also found.

4. In a concurrent validity study, Powell, Moore, and Callaway (1981) found that the Word Comprehension subtest on the WRMT appeared to measure word identification skills rather than a more general verbal factor.

5. In a review of the WRMT–R, Cooter (1989) found the revised edition to be a reliable instrument that should be considered useful for assessing different parts of reading tasks and skills.

6. In a review by Jaeger (1989), cautions were issued to examiners using the revised WRMT because the tests were not believed to be representative of "real" reading tasks. Jaeger stated that diagnosis and planning with the WRMT–R should be considered after more extensive testing or further observations of the students tested.

7. In a review of the revised TWS, Noyce (1989) stated that the TWS–2 seemed to measure the targeted types of spelling skills and pointed out the advantages of easy administration and good test construction.

8. Erickson's (1989) review of the TWS–2 described it an excellent instrument for screening that does not, however, measure the many complex aspects involved in spelling.

Selecting Diagnostic Instruments

The instruments presented in this chapter are among those most used by educators to diagnose academic problems. Some instruments are recommended for specific academic areas. Thus, an examiner may appropriately select one instrument because it contains a subtest that will yield information necessary for academic planning and intervention. Table 7.2 summarizes some of the strengths and weaknesses of the diagnostic tests presented in this chapter.

Table 7.2
Summary of diagnostic tests.

Instrument	Strengths	Weaknesses
KeyMath–Revised	Equivalent forms available Improved scoring Area comparisons for domains provided Objectives given Error analysis available Improved technical quality Comprehensive math instrument Good diagnostic value	More time needed to administer and score
Test of Mathematical Abilities–2	Addresses math attitude, conceptual understanding and computation skills May be given to group of students with appropriate reading ability Adequate technical quality	To be used with additional instrument for eligibility decisions
Woodcock Reading Mastery Tests–Revised	Two versions available with some equivalent subtests Decoding words error analysis provided Reading readiness subtests available on form G Good technical quality Good diagnostic value	Does not provide measure of oral passage reading Addition of column scores confusing time-consuming to score
Test of Written Language–2	Alternate forms booklets Good measures of written language samples May be administered to small groups	Time-consuming to administer and score Somewhat subjective to score
Test of Written Spelling–3	Analysis of student's ability to spell predictable and unpredictable words Can be given to a group	No error analysis provided except for Predictable Words and Unpredictable Words subtests

Instrument	Strengths	Weaknesses
Test of Written Spelling–3	Easy to administer and score Adequate technical quality	
Formal Reading Inventory	Good diagnostic measure of oral passage reading Adequate technical quality	Examiner must practice somewhat difficult administration and scoring of oral passages,
Gray Oral Reading Test–3	Equivalent forms provided Diagnostic value for reading of passages orally	Criterion-related validity coefficients considered fair
Test of Reading Comprehension–Revised	Subtests rearranged Updated normative data May be administered to small groups	No measure of oral passage reading or word attack

Exercises

Part I

Match the following terms with the correct definitions.

A. diagnostic tests
B. screening tests
C. ability tests
D. subtests
E. achievement test
F. probes
G. direct measurement
H. individual achievement test
I. norm-referenced tests
J. aptitude tests
K. curriculum-based assessment
L. group achievement tests
M. adaptive behavior scales
N. instructional level
O. domain
P. informal instruments

_______ **1.** Instruments that assess a student's ability to adapt to the world in different situations.

_______ **2.** Tests that are administered to a group of students to measure academic gains.

_______ **3.** Using content from the currently used curriculum in test items to assess student progress.

_______ **4.** Tests designed to compare individual students with national averages, or norms of expectancy.

_______ **5.** An individually administered test that measures academic progress.

_________ 6. Individually administered tests designed to determine specific academic problems or deficit areas.

_________ 7. A part of a test that contains items to measure specific behaviors, content, or domains.

_________ 8. Broad-based tests that sample a few items across a curriculum.

_________ 9. Designed to measure specific strengths in certain cognitive domains; may also measure some achievement.

_________ 10. General term used for tests that measure what student has retained from school experiences.

_________ 11. Nonstandardized methods used to collect information about student progress.

_________ 12. The determined level of curriculum at which a student should receive instruction.

_________ 13. In-depth assessment of the mastery of a specific skill or subskill.

_________ 14. Measuring academic progress using the same instructional materials or tasks used in classroom instruction.

_________ 15. Area of cognitive development or ability thought to be evidenced by certain behaviors or skills.

Part II

Match the following test names with the correct descriptions.

A. KeyMath–Revised
B. Woodcock Reading Mastery Tests–Revised
C. Test of Written Spelling–3
D. Test of Mathematical Abilities–2
E. Test of Written Language–2
F. Gray Oral Reading Tests–Third Edition
G. Test of Reading Comprehension–Revised Edition
H. Formal Reading Inventory

_________ 1. This math test provides comparison by domains.

_________ 2. This test contains two forms, G and H.

_________ 3. This test measures the ability to spell two types of spelling words.

_________ 4. This test contains a subtest that measures the ability to read directions for schoolwork and supplementary subtests for math, science, and social studies vocabulary.

_________ 5. Form H of this subtest contains only reading subtests for readers above the readiness age.

_________ 6. This test provides an error analysis inventory for decoding nonsense words.

_________ 7. This test measures attitudes and aptitudes of math.

_________ 8. This is an oral reading test only.

_________ 9. This reading test will yield a Silent Reading Quotient and Oral Reading Miscues.

_________ 10. This revised test has three composites: Overall Writing, Contrived Writing, and Spontaneous Writing.

Part III

Answer the following questions.

1. Explain how fall and spring norm tables may provide a more accurate analysis of student performance. ______

2. How does the analysis of individual domains on the KeyMath–R help in the planning for instructional intervention? ______

3. Explain the meaning of levels of significance for standard score differences. How does this analysis benefit the teacher in educational planning? ______

References

Brown, V. L., Cronin, M. E., & McEntire, E. (1994). *Test of Mathematical Abilities, Second Edition.* Austin, TX: Pro-Ed.

Brown, V. L., Hammill, D. D., & Wiederholt, J. L. (1986). *The Test of Reading Comprehension (Rev. Ed.)* Austin, TX: Pro-Ed.

Connolly, A. J. (1988). *KeyMath–Revised: A Diagnostic Inventory of Essential Mathematics.* Circle Pines, MN: American Guidance Service.

Cooter, R. (1989). Review of the Woodcock Reading Mastery Tests–Revised. In J. Conoley & L. Kramer (Eds.), *The tenth mental measurements yearbook* (pp. 910–913), Lincoln: The University of Nebraska Press.

Eaves, R., Darch, C., Mann, L., & Vance, R. (1989). *The Cognitive Levels Test: Its relationship with reading and mathematics achievement.* Paper presented at the 67th Annual Council for Exceptional Children Convention, San Francisco, CA.

Erikson, D. (1989). Review of the Test of Written Spelling–Revised Edition. In J. Conoley & J. Kramer (Eds.), *The tenth mental measurements yearbook* (pp. 858–859). Lincoln: The University of Nebraska Press.

Greenstein, J., & Strain, P. (1977). The utility of the KeyMath Diagnostic Arithmetic Test for adolescent learning disabled students. *Psychology in the Schools, 14,* 275–282.

Hammill, D. D., & Larsen, S. C. (1988). *Test of Written Language–2.* Austin, TX: Pro-Ed.

Jaeger, R. (1989). Review of the Woodcock Reading Mastery Tests–Revised. In J. Conoley & J. Kramer (Eds.), *The tenth mental measurements yearbook* (pp. 913–916). Lincoln: The University of Nebraska Press.

Larsen, S. C., & Hammill, D. D. (1994). *Test of Written Spelling–3.* Austin, TX: Pro-Ed.

Noyce, R. (1989). Review of the Test of Written Spelling–Revised Edition. In J. Conoley & J. Kramer (Eds.), *The tenth mental measurements yearbook* (pp. 860–861). Lincoln: The University of Nebraska Press.

Powell, G., Moore, D., & Callaway, B. (1981). A concurrent validity study of the Woodcock Word Comprehension Test. *Psychology in the Schools, 18,* 24–27.

Shriner, J., & Salvia, J. (1988). Chronic noncorrespondence between elementary math curricula and arithmetic tests. *Exceptional Children, 55,* 240–248.

Wiederholt, J. L. (1986). *Formal Reading Inventory: A method of assessing silent reading comprehension and oral reading miscues,* Austin, TX: Pro-Ed.

Wiederholt, J. L., & Bryant, B. R. (1992). *Gray Oral Reading Tests, Third Edition,* Austin, TX: Pro-Ed.

Woodcock, R. W. (1987). *Woodcock Reading Mastery Tests–Revised.* Circle Pines, MN: American Guidance Service.

Chapter Eight

Informal Assessment Techniques

Key Terms

criterion-related assessment
criterion-referenced tests
probes
subskill
curriculum-based assessment
direct measurement
direct daily measurement
task analysis
subtasks
error analysis
informal assessment
checklists
work samples
permanent products
questionnaires
portfolio assessment

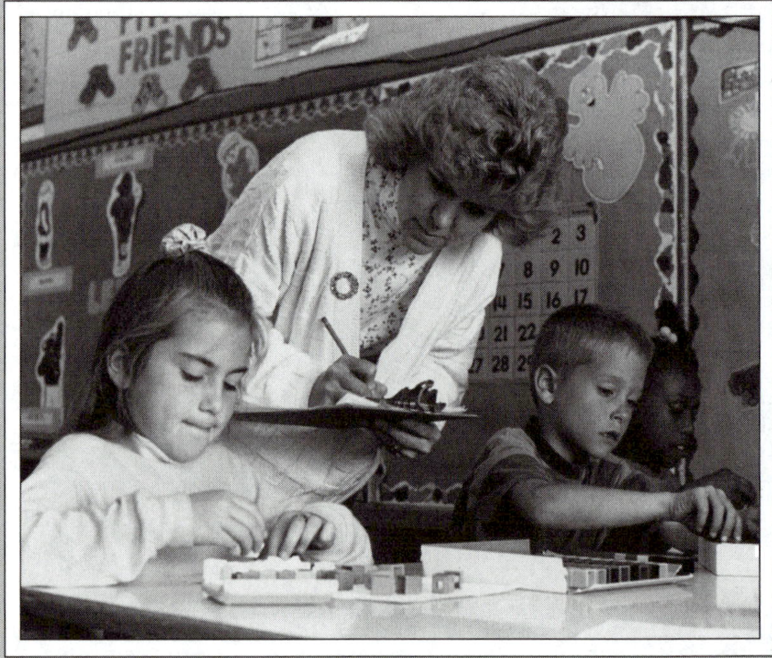

Norm-referenced assessment, the educational measurement method presented in the previous chapters, is the method that compares a student with the age or grade-level expectancies of a norm group. Norm-referenced assessment is the standard method used in placement and classification decisions. The degree or amount of deviance from the expected norm is an important factor in determining whether a student meets the requirements of eligibility necessary to receive special education services (Shapiro, 1989).

Researchers have identified several problems in using norm-referenced assessment in the classroom. These weaknesses have influenced the development of other assessment techniques more suited to use in special education and regular education classrooms. These additional assessment methods are described as informal because they are not norm-referenced and, in most cases, not standardized. These methods assist the teacher and should be used with norm-referenced assessment, in a multimethod approach, to provide a complete assessment of the student's functioning levels (Bennett, 1982). This chapter presents methods other than norm-referenced assessment methods.

Problems of Norm-Referenced Assessment

The weaknesses attributed to norm-referenced assessment include problems specific to the various instruments and problems with test administration and interpretation. Norm-referenced tests may not adequately represent material actually taught in a specific curriculum (Shapiro, 1989). In other words, items on norm-referenced tests may include content or skill areas not included in the student's curriculum. Salvia and Hughes (1990) wrote:

> The fundamental problem with using published tests is the test's content. If the content of the test—even content prepared by experts—does not match the content that is taught, the test is useless for evaluating what the student has learned from school instruction. (p. 8)

Good and Salvia (1988) studied the representation of reading curricula in norm-referenced tests and concluded that a deficient score on a norm-referenced reading test could actually represent the selection of a test with inadequate content validity for the current curriculum. Hultquist and Metzke (1993) determined that curriculum bias existed when using standardized achievement tests to measure the reading of survival words and reading and spelling skills in general. In addition, the frequent use of norm-referenced instruments may result in bias because limited numbers of alternate forms exist, creating the possibility of test wiseness among students (Fuchs, Tindal, & Deno, 1984; Shapiro, 1989). Another study revealed that norm-referenced instruments are not as sensitive to academic growth as other instruments that are linked more directly to the actual classroom curriculum (Marston, Fuchs, & Deno, 1986). This means that norm-referenced tests may not measure small gains made in the classroom from week to week. According to Reynolds (1982), the psychometric assessment of students using traditional norm-referenced methods is fraught with many problems of bias, including cultural bias, which may result in test scores that reflect intimidation or communication problems rather than ability level. These difficulties in using norm-referenced testing for special education planning have led to the emergence of alternative methods of assessment.

Criterion-Related Assessment

criterion-related assessment When items of an assessment instrument are related to meeting objectives or passing skill-mastery objectives.

criterion-referenced tests Tests designed to accompany and measure a set of criteria or skill-mastery criteria.

Criterion-related assessment and **criterion-referenced tests** compare the performance of a student to a given criterion rather than to the performance of students in a norm group. The criterion may be a specific objective written by the teacher, or it may be a skill or sequential task, considered to be a standard, included in a scope and sequence chart of a published curriculum. The student is assessed to ascertain if she can perform the task or complete the objective with accuracy and consistency. Although many criterion-referenced instruments are nonstandardized or perhaps designed by the teacher, a few criterion-referenced instruments are standardized. Some norm-referenced instruments yield criterion-related objectives or the possibility of adding criterion-related objectives with little difficulty. Examples of these instruments are the KeyMath–Revised (Connolly, 1988), K-TEA (Kaufman & Kaufman, 1985), and the WRMT–R (Woodcock, 1987).

probes Tests used for in-depth assessment of the mastery of a specific skill or subskill.

Adapting standardized norm-referenced instruments to represent criterion-referenced testing is accomplished by writing educational objectives for the skills tested. To be certain that the skill or task has been adequately sampled, however, the educator may need to prepare additional academic **probes** to measure those skills. Objectives written for skills tested or items on a norm-referenced instrument may represent long-term learning rather than short-term gains. This determination will be based on the amount of the material or the scope of the task tested by the norm-referenced test. Figure 8.1 illustrates how an item from the WRMT–R might be expanded to represent criterion-referenced testing.

Items missed	On the Word Attack subtest: the long a–e pattern in nonsense words–*gaked, straced;* the long i–e pattern in nonsense word–*quiles*
Deficit-skill	Decoding words with the long vowel-consonant-silent-*e* pattern
Probe	Decoding words orally to teacher: *cake, make, snake, rake, rate, lake, fake, like, bike, kite*
Criterion	Decode 10/10 words for mastery. Decode 8/10 words to 6/10 words for instructional level. Decode 5/10 words or less for failure level; assess prerequisite skill level: discrimination of long/short vowels (vowels: *a,i*).

Figure 8.1
Examples of criterion-referenced testing.

In addition to adapting published norm-referenced instruments for criterion-related assessment, educators may use published criterion-referenced test batteries, such as the Brigance Inventories, that present specific criteria and objectives. Teachers may also create their own criterion-referenced tests.

The Brigance Inventories

The Brigance (Brigance, 1977, 1981, 1991) is a standardized assessment system that provides criterion-related assessment at various skill levels. Each battery contains numerous subtests, and each item is referenced by objectives that may be used in developing IEPs. The Brigance system includes three criterion-referenced instruments for the various age groups served in special education. In each system, the educator should select only the areas and items of interest to identify specific strengths and weaknesses. The Brigance instruments should not be administered in their entirety.

The Brigance Diagnostic Inventory of Early Development–Revised (Brigance, 1991) is an inventory within the system that was designed to assess the skills and development of children from birth to age 7. Many of the subtests concern developmental areas of motor development. This test provides criterion-related measurement for self-help skills, prespeech, and speech development, general knowledge, social and emotional development, reading readiness, manuscript writing, and beginning math.

The Brigance Diagnostic Inventory of Basic Skills (Brigance, 1977) was designed for use with elementary school-aged students. This criterion-referenced inventory includes many areas and subtests within each area. Figure 8.2 lists the various areas and subtests for this level of the Brigance system.

Figure 8.2
Areas tested by the Brigance Diagnostic Inventory of Basic Skills.

- **I.** Readiness
- **II.** Reading
  - **A.** Word Recognition
  - **B.** Reading
  - **C.** Word Analysis
  - **D.** Vocabulary
- **III.** Language Arts
  - **A.** Handwriting
  - **B.** Grammar Mechanics
  - **C.** Spelling
  - **D.** Reference Skills
- **IV.** Math
  - **A.** Grade Level
  - **B.** Numbers
  - **C.** Operations
  - **D.** Measurement

subskill A small part of a skill, used in task analysis.

For each of the areas listed in Figure 8.2, several **subskill** areas are assessed. The subskill areas for Word Analysis are illustrated in Figure 8.3. For each of the items assessed within the subskill areas, objectives are included. When the student fails to show mastery of a particular subskill, the objective for that subskill will be used in educational planning. The objective for C-10, "initial clusters visually," is shown in Figure 8.4.

The Brigance system comprises large, multiple-ring notebook binders that contain both student and examiner pages. The pages may be turned to resemble an easel-like format, or the pages to be administered may be removed from the binder. A warning included in the test cautions the examiner to select the necessary subtests and avoid overtesting.

The Brigance Diagnostic Inventory of Essential Skills (Brigance, 1981) is the part of the system designed for intermediate- and secondary-age students. This test contains subtest areas that allow criterion-referenced testing in the areas of academics, everyday survival skills, and vocational skills. The individual subskill areas for one subtest of the Brigance for secondary students are shown in Figure 8.5.

In Activity 8.1, you will determine if the student responses illustrated indicate mastery of the subskill assessed by the Basic Skills test.

Technical Data. The Brigance tests are not norm referenced, and therefore norming information is not provided. The tests were field tested and appear to have content validity. The manual includes suggested grade levels to provide teachers with an idea of where to place students in classroom curriculum materials. The suggested grade levels are not norm-referenced grade equivalents and should not be used as a basis for eligibility decisions.

II. Reading
  C. Word Analysis
    C-1, Auditory discrimination
    C-2, Initial consonant sounds auditorily
    C-3, Initial consonant sounds visually
    C-4, Substitution of initial consonant sounds
    C-5, Ending sounds auditorily
    C-6, Vowels
    C-7, Short vowel sounds
    C-8, Long vowel sounds
    C-9, Initial clusters auditorily
    C-10, Initial clusters visually
    C-11, Substitution of initial cluster sounds
    C-12, Diagraphs and dipthongs
    C-13, Phonetic irregularities
    C-14, Common endings of rhyming words
    C-15, Suffixes
    C-16, Prefixes
    C-17, Meaning of prefixes
    C-18, Number of syllables auditorily
    C-19, Syllabication concepts

Figure 8.3
Subskill areas for Word Analysis tested by the Brigance Diagnostic Inventory of Basic Skills.

Teacher-Made Criterion-Referenced Tests

Instead of relying on published instruments, the classroom teacher may develop his own criterion-referenced tests. This type of assessment allows the teacher to directly link the assessment to the currently used curriculum. By writing the criterion to be used as the basis for determining when the student has reached or passed the objective, the teacher has created a criterion-referenced test. When the test is linked directly to the curriculum, it also becomes a **curriculum-based assessment** device and may be referred to as **direct measurement.** For example, the teacher may use the scope and sequence chart from the reading series or math text to write the objectives that will be used in the criterion-related assessment.

curriculum-based assessment Using content from the currently used curriculum to assess student progress.

direct measurement Measuring progress by using the same instructional materials or tasks as are used in the classroom.

One difficulty that teachers may have in constructing criterion-referenced tests is arriving at the exact criterion for determining whether the student has passed the objective or criterion. Shapiro (1989) suggested that one quantitative method of determining mastery would be to use a normative comparison of the performance, such as using a specific task that 80% of the peers in the class or grade have mastered. The teacher may wish to use a criterion that is associated

INITIAL CLUSTERS VISUALLY

SKILL: Can articulate correct sound when cluster is presented visually.

DIRECTIONS: Point to the first letters (sh).

Say: *Look at these letters. Tell me the sound they have when they are together at the beginning of a word.*

If the student does not understand, explain the first blend.

Say: *These letters have the sound of sh as in shock or shape.*

See NOTE #2 and the next page for alternate method of administration.

DISCONTINUE: After three consecutive errors.

TIME: 10 seconds per response.

ACCURACY: Give credit for each correct response.

NOTES:

1. You may wish to check the student's understanding of the voiced and unvoiced "th."

   Say: *Can you tell me the other sound "th" makes?, after the student has given one sound.*

2. An alternate method of assessing this skill is to present the initial clusters in combination with a vowel. The results of the alternate method may have more validity if the student has been taught by a method which always presents the clusters in combination with a vowel such as Duggins or *Words in Color.* See next page for alternate administration.

OBJECTIVE: When presented with a list of 33 blends and digraphs (clusters) listed in an order commonly taught, the student will indicate the sound ______ (quantity) the consonants have or make in the initial position.

Source: From *Brigance Diagnostic Inventory of Basic Skills* (p. 56) by A. H. Brigance, 1977, N. Billerica, MA: Curriculum Associates. Copyright by Curriculum Associates. Reprinted by permission.

Figure 8.4
Objective for "initial clusters visually," subskill C-10 of the Brigance Diagnostic Inventory of Basic Skills.

X. Travel and Transportation
- X-1, Traffic signs
- X-2, Traffic symbols
- X-3, Car parts and vocabulary
- X-4, Identifies car parts
- X-5, Application for driver's instruction permit
- X-6, Auto safety rating scale
- X-7, Gas mileage and cost
- X-8, Mileage table
- X-9, Bus schedule and map of route
- X-10, Road maps

Figure 8.5
Subskills of Travel and Transportation of the Brigance Diagnostic Inventory of Essential Skills.

with a standard set by the school grading policy. For example, answering 75% of the items correctly indicates that the student needs improvement; 85% correct may be an average performance; and 95% correct may represent mastery. Or, the teacher may decide to use a criterion that the student can easily understand and chart, such as 5 out of 7 items correct indicating that the student continues with same objective or skill and 7 out of 7 items correct indicating that the student is ready to move up to the next level skill. Often, the teacher sets the criterion using logical reasoning rather than a quantitative measurement (Shapiro, 1989).

Other considerations for establishing criteria for mastery have been suggested by Evans and Evans (1986):

> Does passing the test mean that the student is proficient and will maintain the skills?
>
> Is the student ready to progress to the next level in the curriculum?
>
> Will the student be able to generalize and apply the skills outside the classroom?
>
> Would the student pass the mastery test if it were given at a later date? (p. 10)

The teacher may wish to use the following indications for establishing criterion-referenced tests:

More than 95% = mastery of objective

90% to 95% = instructional level

Less than 76% = failure level

☐ CHECK YOUR UNDERSTANDING

Complete Activity 8.1.

Activity 8.1

Answer the question.

Look at the student responses on the Brigance sample in Figure 8.6. Has the student mastered the objective? ________

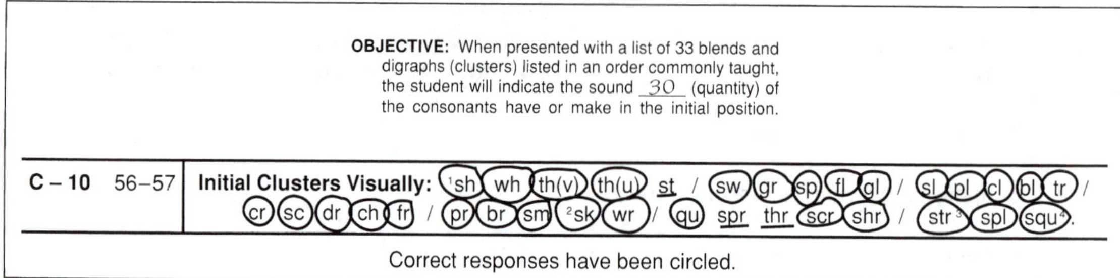

OBJECTIVE: When presented with a list of 33 blends and digraphs (clusters) listed in an order commonly taught, the student will indicate the sound 30 (quantity) of the consonants have or make in the initial position.

C – 10	56–57	**Initial Clusters Visually:** [1]sh wh th(v) th(u) st / sw gr sp fl gl / sl pl cl bl tr / cr sc dr ch fr / pr br sm [2]sk wr / qu spr thr scr shr / str [3] spl squ[4].

Correct responses have been circled.

Figure 8.6
Sample student responses for Brigance subskill C-10.
Source: From *Brigance Diagnostic Inventory of Essential Skills* (p. v) by A. H. Brigance, 1981, N. Billerica, MA: Curriculum Associates. Copyright 1981 by Curriculum Associates. Reprinted by permission.

Similar standards may be set by the individual teacher. The teacher may wish to adjust objectives when the student performs with 76% to 89% accuracy and when the student performs with more than 95% accuracy. It is important to remember that students with learning difficulties should experience a high ratio of success during instruction to increase the possibility of positive reinforcement during the learning process. Therefore, it may be better to design objectives that promote higher success rates.

Figure 8.7 illustrates a criterion-referenced test written by a teacher for addition facts with sums of 10 or less. The objective, or criterion, is included at the top of the test.

OBJECTIVE

John will correctly answer 9 out of 10 addition problems with sums of 10 or less.

5	3	8	9	4	6	7	2	4	1
+2	+2	+2	+1	+5	+2	+3	+4	+3	+6

Performance: ________

Objective passed: ________ Continue on current objective: ________

Figure 8.7
Criterion-referenced test of addition facts.

The skills included in Activity 8.2 resemble those that would be included in a beginning level of a reading series. In this activity, you will select the information from one skill to write an objective and construct a short criterion-referenced test. The test should measure the student's mastery of the objective.

Using criterion-related assessment may provide better information about student achievement levels and mastery of academic objectives; however, the criterion-referenced test may not always adequately represent growth within a given curriculum. To measure student progress within a curriculum more effectively, teachers should rely on measures that use that curriculum, such as curriculum-based assessment and direct measurement.

Curriculum-Based Assessment and Direct Measurement

The previous discussion gave an example of how criterion-related assessment might also employ curriculum-based assessment and direct measurement. But, to review, not all criterion-related assessment is also curriculum-based. For example, the criterion-referenced instrument may be a commercially produced instrument, such as the Brigance, that is separate from the actual curriculum used in everyday instruction. The criterion-referenced test may be an adaptation of a norm-referenced standardized instrument that is not linked directly to achievement in the curriculum.

For the very best measure of how much a student has mastered in a curriculum, assessment items should be composed of material from the curriculum, or the items should be the actual curriculum tasks used daily in the instruction **(direct daily measurements).** The differences between these two types of assessment are minor but may be understood by this example: A second-grade math curriculum-based assessment will contain items from a second-grade math text used in the classroom instruction; a direct daily measurement of progress may be the assigned daily math problems from the text used in class or a sample of problems used in daily work. These daily measures may include teacher-made tests, classwork, independent work, homework, quizzes, and so on.

direct daily measurement The daily measurement of progress using instructional materials.

In designing curriculum-based measurement, the teacher must first determine what skills or concepts are to be developed from the instruction (Rosenfield & Kurait, 1990). The educator also must understand the scope of the cur-

Activity 8.2

Read the following list of skills necessary to complete level P1 of the Best in the Country Reading Series adopted by all school systems in the world. Answer the questions that follow.

☐ CHECK YOUR UNDERSTANDING

Complete Activity 8.2.

P1 Skills

1. Associates pictures with story content.
2. Follows sequence of story by turning pages at appropriate times.
3. Associates the following letters with their sounds: *b, d, c, g, h, j, k, l, m, n, p, q, r, s, t.*
4. Can match letters (from 3) to pictures of objects that begin with the same sounds.
5. Can correctly sequence the following stories:

   "A School Day": Mary gets on the bus, goes to school, George brings a rabbit to class; the rabbit gets out of the cage. Mary helps George catch the rabbit.

   "The Field Trip": Ralph invites the class to visit his farm. Sue, John, Mary, and George go on the trip. The animals are (a) a chicken, (b) a goat, (c) a cow, and (d) a horse. The goat follows the class; the goat tries to eat Ralph's shirt.
6. Can name all characters in preceding stories.
7. Can summarize stories and answer short comprehension questions.

8. Select one P1 skill and write a behaviorally stated objective that includes the criterion acceptable for passing the objective. ________________________
____
____
____
9. Design a short criterion-referenced test to measure the skill objective written in question 1 of this activity.
10. By including the actual curriculum in the criterion-related assessment, what other types of assessment have been used? ________________________
____

---

riculum and set educational goals for the student based on the curriculum. If there is an instructional mismatch, the educator should determine prerequisite competencies needed for the task and assess which competencies the student has mastered and which ones are weaknesses. Progress must be measured frequently throughout the instruction so that effective interventions can be implemented.

According to Shinn, Nolet, and Knutson (1990), most curriculum-based measures should include the following tasks:

1. In reading, students read aloud from basal readers for 1 minute. The number of words read correctly per minute constitutes the basic decision-making metric.
2. In spelling, students write words that are dictated at specific intervals (either 5, 7, or 10 seconds) for 2 minutes. The number of correct letter sequences and words spelled correctly are counted.
3. In written expression, students write a story for 3 minutes after being given a story starter (e.g., "Pretend you are playing on the playground and a spaceship

lands. A little green person comes out and calls your name and . . ."). The number of words written, spelled correctly, and/or correct word sequences are counted.

4. In mathematics, students write answers to computational problems via 2-minute probes. The number of correctly written digits is counted. (p. 290)

Figure 8.8 presents an example of how curriculum-based measurement is used to determine when an instructional change is indicated. The student failed to make the projected progress and therefore needs an educational change to progress within the curriculum.

Curriculum-based assessment and direct daily measurement of progress have been found to noticeably affect academic achievement when the results are used to modify instructional planning. When curriculum-based assessment was used for instructional programming, students were found to have somewhat greater gains than when it was used for testing purposes alone (Fuchs, Fuchs, & Hamlett, 1989). The more effective teachers were sensitive to the results of the assessment and used them to adapt or modify instruction rather

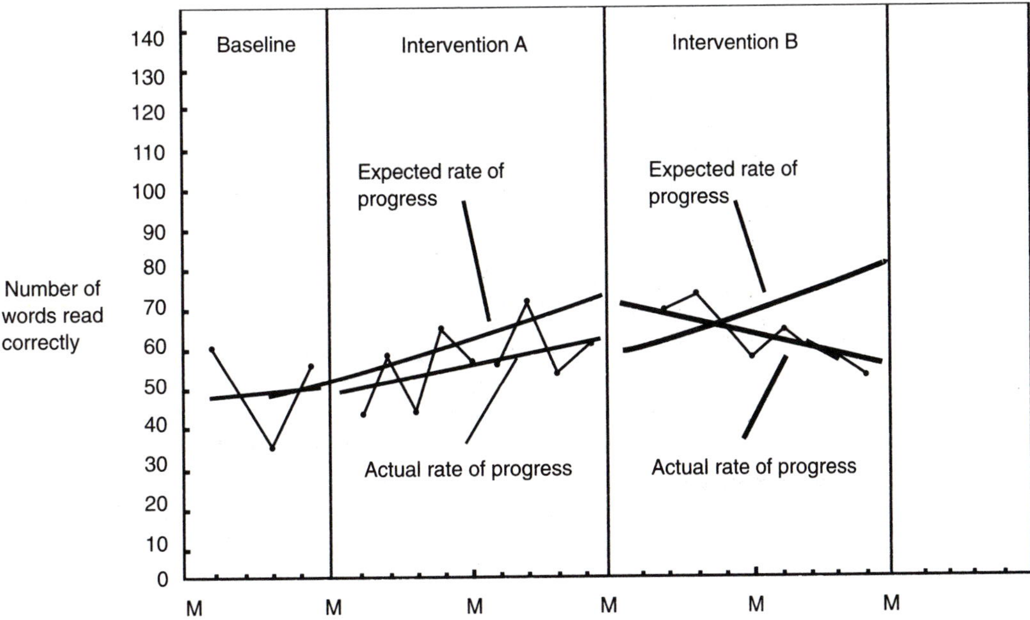

Figure 8.8
Curriculum-based measurement data for two interventions used with one student.
Source: From *Best Practices in School Psychology—II* (p. 301) by A. Thomas and J. Grimes, 1990, Silver Spring, MD: National Association of School Psychologists. Copyright 1990 by the National Association of School Psychologists. Reprinted by permission of the publisher.

than merely using curriculum-based assessment as a measurement device, such as grading or establishing a working level for IEP objectives.

The use of curriculum-based assessment has been linked to better understanding, by students, of expectancies of academic performance (Fuchs, Butterworth, & Fuchs, 1989). Students in this study indicated that they received more feedback than students not receiving curriculum-based assessment. Research has also indicated that teachers using curriculum-based assessment tended to set goals with higher expectations than teachers who were not using these methods (Fuchs et al., 1989). Use of curriculum-based assessment with instructional intervention strategies provided to general education teachers suggested promise in increasing the achievement of low achieving students and students in general education classes with learning disabilities (Fuchs, Fuchs, Hamlett, Phillips, & Bentz, 1994).

Curriculum-based assessment has been studied as one method of determining special education eligibility (Marston, Mirkin, & Deno, 1984). Curriculum-based assessment was found to be an accurate screening measure for referral for special education and was less influenced by teacher variables (Marston et al., 1984). Its use appeared to result in less bias as evidenced by more equity in male/female ratio of referrals (Marston et al., 1984). Shapiro (1989) advised that, because its use in special education screening is new, curriculum-based assessment should supplement norm-referenced assessment but not replace traditional methods of preplacement testing. Canter (1991) supported using curriculum-based assessment to determine eligibility for special education services by comparing the student's progress in the classroom curriculum with the expectations within the average range for the grade level. The student's actual progress may indicate the need for special education intervention.

Curriculum-based measurement has been studied as a possible method to identify students in special education placements who are ready to move back into the general education setting (Shinn, Habedank, Rodden-Nord, & Knutson, 1993). Use of this method may help general education teachers smoothly integrate students from special education environments by providing data to assess progress and use in planning interventions.

It also has been suggested that curriculum-based measures may be beneficial in measuring the effects of treatment by medication of students with attention disorders (Stoner, Carey, Ikeda, & Shinn, 1994). Initial research seems to indicate that curriculum-based measures for math and reading are promising for assessing medication effects when academic performance is of concern. This research (Stoner et al., 1994) points out concerns in this emerging area, such as the need for additional studies of the sensitivity of curriculum-based assessment for this purpose.

Teachers can easily adapt curriculum-based assessment methods to include direct daily measurement. Although several methods of developing precise direct daily measurement have been described (Howell & Morehead, 1987; Shapiro, 1989), teachers may construct their own direct measurements from curriculum materials used in the classroom.

Task Analysis and Error Analysis

Teachers often use task and error analyses without realizing that an analysis of student progress has been completed. **Task analysis** involves breaking down a task into the smallest steps necessary to complete the task. The steps actually reflect subskills or **subtasks,** which the student must complete before finishing a task. In academic work, many of these subskills and tasks form a hierarchy of skills that builds throughout the school years. As students master skills and tasks, they face new, more advanced curriculur tasks that depend on the earlier skills. In mathematics, for example, understanding of numerals and one-to-one correspondence must precede understanding of basic addition facts. A student must conquer addition and subtraction before tackling multiplication and division. Therefore, a thorough task analysis of skill deficits, followed by an informal assessment, may provide the teacher with information about what the student has or has not mastered.

task analysis Analyzing a task by breaking it down into the smallest steps or skills.

subtasks Small units of a task used to complete a task analysis.

Activity 8.3

Answer the following questions.

1. Look at the following task analysis. Can you identify other smaller steps, or subskills, which should be included? Write the additional steps on the spaces provided.

   Skill: Adding numbers greater than 10

   Adds numbers 0–10 with sums greater than 10

   Adds number facts 1–9 with sums greater than 10

   Adds number facts 1–9 with sums less than 10

   Adds number facts 1–8 with sums less than 10

   Identifies numbers 1–10

   Can count objects 1–10

   Additional subskills:

   ____

   ____

   ____

   ____

   ____

   ____

2. Write a task analysis for the following skills:

   Skill: Recognizes initial consonant sounds and their association with the consonant letters of the alphabet.

   Necessary subskills:

   ____

   ____

☐ **CHECK YOUR UNDERSTANDING**

Complete Activity 8.3.

error analysis Analyzing a student's learning problems by determining error patterns.

Error analysis is an assessment method that a teacher can use with formal, informal, and direct measures, such as classwork. This is a method of discovering patterns of errors. A teacher may notice that a student who understands difficult multiplication facts, such as those of 11s, 12s, and 13s, continues to miss computation problems of those facts. With a careful error analysis of responses on a teacher-made test, the teacher determines that the student has incorrectly lined up the multiplicands. The student understands the math fact but has made a mistake in the mechanics of the operation.

☐ **CHECK YOUR UNDERSTANDING**

Complete Activities 8.4 and 8.5.

Activity 8.4

Look carefully at the student's responses in the following work sample from a language class. Analyze the errors the student made. Write your analysis in the space provided.

NAME Ralph

1. i went to zoo.
2. him an me will go
3. do you want Come to ?

Errors: ______________________________

Write a behavioral objective for one of the errors analyzed. ______________________________

Activity 8.5

Use the terms discussed in the chapter to complete the following sentences.

1. Using material from the curriculum content in test items is called ________ ________ .
2. Using informal assessment composed of actual curriculum materials is called ________________ .
3. A teacher who adds behavioral objectives following the analysis of test items on a standardized norm-referenced test has adapted the instrument to reflect ________________ testing.
4. When a student has not mastered a specific skill, the teacher may wish to test the student more thoroughly on the one skill by developing a ____________ ____ .
5. When a teacher assesses daily from the curriculum content, the assessment is called ________________ .
6. Assessing the subskills, or substeps, within a task is referred to as ________ ________ .
7. Analyzing the types of errors made on a test or on student work samples is called ________________ .
8. Teacher-made quizzes, curriculum-based assessment, criterion-related assessment, class assignments, and tests are all types of ________________ assessment.

Other Informal Methods of Academic Assessment

Teachers employ many other **informal assessment** methods to monitor the academic progress of students. Some of these methods combine the techniques of error analysis, task analysis, direct measurement, curriculum-based assessment, probes, and criterion-related assessment. These methods include making **checklists** and **questionnaires** and evaluating student **work samples** and **permanent products.**

Teacher-made checklists may be constructed following an error analysis, identifying the problem area, and completing a task analysis. For each subskill that is problematic for the student, the teacher may construct a probe, or more in-depth assessment instrument. Probes may appear to be short quizzes and may be timed to determine content mastery. For example, a teacher may give 10 subtraction facts for students to complete in 2 minutes. If the teacher uses items from the curriculum to develop the probe, it will be curriculum-based. The teacher may also establish a criterion for mastery of each probe or in-depth teacher-made test. This added dimension creates a criterion-related assessment device. The criterion may be 9 out of 10 problems added correctly. To monitor

informal assessment Nonstandardized methods of measuring student progress.

checklists Lists of academic or behavioral skills that must be mastered by the student.

questionnaires Questions about a student's behavior or academic concerns, which may be answered by the student or by the parent or teacher.

work samples Samples of a student's work; one type of permanent product.

permanent products Products made by the student that may be analyzed for academic or behavioral interventions.

the growth of the student effectively, the teacher may set criteria for mastery each day as direct measurement techniques are employed. As the student meets the mastery criterion established for an objective, the teacher checks the subskill off of the checklist and progresses to the next more difficult item on the list of subskills.

Another informal method designed by teachers is an interview or questionnaire method. Figures 8.9 and 8.10 represent a teacher-constructed interview form and a checklist that includes behavioral observations of the student (Wiener, 1986).

Teachers can also gather helpful information by informally reviewing students' work samples—actual samples of work completed by the student. These may include daily work, homework, tests, and quizzes. Work samples are one kind of permanent product. Other permanent products evaluated by the teacher include projects, posters, art, and so on.

Informal Assessment of Reading

Comprehension, decoding, and fluency are the broad areas of reading that teachers assess using informal methods. Comprehension is the ability to derive meaning from written language, whereas decoding is the ability to associate sounds and symbols. Fluency is the rate and ease with which a student reads orally.

Howell and Morehead (1987) presented several methods to informally assess comprehension. These techniques include the following:

1. *Answering questions.* After reading a passage, the student answers questions about the passage. These questions may focus on details, sequence of events in the story, or the main idea of the story. This method provides a general screening of which students are able to comprehend written material and which students are not. It may be difficult to obtain diagnostic information unless the questions are carefully constructed by the teacher.

2. *Paraphrasing.* The student restates the story in her own words.

3. *Story Retelling.* This technique requires that the student read the story and then retell it using the same words that were used in the story.

4. *Cloze.* The student does not read the story in advance. The teacher selects a passage and rewrites it with selected words left out. The first and last sentences in the passage have all original words. The student must read the passage and supply the missing words.

5. *Maze.* As in the cloze method, sentences are written with missing words. In this method, however, the student selects the correct response from words provided beneath each blank. The level of difficulty may be increased by making the choices of words more similar; thus, the student must discriminate between words with like meanings.

Student Name: _______ Date: _______ Examiner: _______

The Task Environment

1. How did you select the topic/book? ____

   ____

2. Are you interested in it?
   very interested _______ somewhat interested _______ not at all interested _______
3. What did the teacher do when giving out the assignment? ____________________________

	Yes	No	Notes
Probes: • give oral guidelines	_______	_______	
• give written guidelines	_______	_______	
• select the topic/book	_______	_______	
• provide structure	_______	_______	
• increase your interest	_______	_______	
• specify length	_______	_______	

4. Who are you expecting to read the essay? ____________________________________

Previous Knowledge

5. Have you previously been taught to write essays/projects/reports?
   Yes _______ No _______ What were you taught? ____________________________

   ____

6. What did you know about the toic before you started? ____________________________

   ____

7. What do you think are the expectations of your reader/teacher? ____________________

Planning

8. Did you have a plan for writing the essay/project/report: Yes _______ No _______
   What was it? ____
9. When did you begin thinking about the topic? ____________________________________
10. Did you do any research? Yes _______ No _______ What resources did you use?

    ____

11. How much time did you have for writing (i.e., between date assignment was given and assignment due)? __
    days. How did you use that time? ____
12. Did you make an outline? Yes _______ No _______ What kind of thinking did you do first? _______

    ____

    What was your organizational plan (outline)? ____________________________________

    ____

Translating/Reviewing

13. How many drafts did you write? one _______ two _______ three _______
14. How long did it take to write each one?
    1. _______ hrs/mins 2. _______ hrs/mins 3. _______ hrs/mins
15. Did you write your first draft with pencil? _______ Pen? _______ typewriter? _______
    word processor? _______
16. Did you double space your first draft: yes _______ No _______
17. Did you read your first draft over? Yes _______ No _______ What kind of changes did you make?

    ____

18. Did you ask a friend or family member to read the first draft and make suggestions? Yes _______ No __
    What kind of suggestions did they have? ____________________________________

    ____

19. Did you proof read the final draft? Yes _______ No _______

Evaluating

20. How did you feel about the essay/project/report in the end? ____________________________

    ____

21. What grade did you think you would get? _______ Why? ____________________________

    ____

22. What was the teacher's evaluation? ____

    ____

Figure 8.9

Interview questions on essay/project/report writing.

Source: From "Interview Questions on Essay/Project/Report Writing." In: "Alternatives in the Assessment of the Learning Disabled Adolescent: A Learning Strategies Approach" by J. Wiener, 1986, *Learning Disabilities Focus, 1,* p. 100. Copyright 1986 by Council for Exceptional Children. Reprinted by permission.

6. *Sentence verification.* The teacher selects the sentences for the assessment and, for each sentence, writes three other sentences. The student must select the sentence that has the same meaning as the original sentence.

7. *Vocabulary.* Sentences are written with synonyms provided for specific words. The student selects the word, from three choices, with the same meaning. Variations of the approach are shown in Figure 8.11.

A study by Fuchs and Fuchs (1992) found that the cloze and story retelling methods were not technically adequate and sensitive enough to measure the reading progress of students over time. The maze method, however, was determined to be useful for monitoring student growth. This seems to suggest that the story retelling and the cloze methods may be best used for diagnostic information or as instructional strategies rather than as a means to monitor progress within a curriculum.

Student Name: _______ Date: _______ Examiner: _______________

Type of Test:
Multiple Choice _______ Short Answer _______ Essay _______ Standardized _______
Class Test _______ % of Grade _______
Subject: _______________

Test Preparation

Interview the student by asking the open-ended question first, followed by the probe question as required. Tell me how you study: _______________

____

____

____

Probes:

1. Do you usually study in a special place? Yes _______ No _______ Where? _______
2. Do you have a special time for study? Yes _______ No _______ When? _______
3. How long can you study before you take a break? _______ hours _______ minutes
4. When you know you have a test coming up a week away, when do you start studying for it? _______
5. Do you usually find yourself having to cram the night before? Yes _______ No _______ For how long can you cram before you can't concentrate any longer: _______ hours _______ minutes
6. Do you prefer to study in a quiet place, with music playing or in front of the television set? _______ What do you normally do? _______
7. Do you sit at a desk, in an easy chair or lie on the bed or the floor when you study? _______
8. Do you study from your notebook? _______ textbook? _______ both? _______ Which do you like best? _______
9. Tell me what goes through your head as you study. _______

   ____
10. When you study, do you try to figure out what information is most important? Yes _______ No _______ or to predict what questions will be on the test? Yes _______ No _______ How do you do that? _______
11. Which subjects do you find the easiest to study? _______

    ____

    Why? _______
12. Which subjects do you find hardest to study? _______

    ____

    Why? _______

Test-Taking Behavior

Evaluate the student's performance in each area by marking a √ in the appropriate column:

	Excellent	Adequate	Inadequate	Notes
• Punctuality • Equipped (e.g., pen, pencil) • Motivation • Planning of time • Checking of work • Accuracy of prediction of grade				
	High	Moderate	Low	
• Anxiety Level				

Test Product

Analyze a recent examination or test by examining the areas listed below and questioning the student when clarification is needed. Evaluate the student's performance in each area by marking a √ in the appropriate column:

	Excellent	Adequate	Inadequate	Not Applicable	Notes
• Handwriting:					
• Accuracy of Reading of Questions					
• Comprehension of Subtleties of Questions					
• Spelling					
• Grammar					
• Punctuation					
• Appropriateness of Vocabulary to Discipline					
• Sequencing & Organization of Thoughts					
• Relevance of Answers					
• Conceptualization of Answers					
• Elaboration of Answers					

Comments: ______________________________

Figure 8.10
Checklist for assessing students' examinations.
Source: From "Checklist for Assessing Students' Examinations." In: "Alternatives in the Assessment of the Learning Disabled Adolescent: A Learning Strategies Approach" by J. Wiener, 1986, *Learning Disabilities Focus, 1,* p. 101. Copyright 1986 by Council for Exceptional Children. Reprinted by permission.

Barnes (1986) suggested using an error analysis approach when listening to students read passages aloud. With this approach, the teacher notes the errors made as the student reads and analyzes the errors to determine if they change the meaning of the passage. The teacher then notes whether the substituted words look or sound like the original words.

Decoding skills used in reading can also be assessed informally. The teacher may design tests to measure the student's ability to:

Orally read isolated letters, blends, syllables, and real words.

Orally read nonsense words that contain various combinations of vowel sounds and patterns, consonant blends, and digraphs.

Orally read sentences that contain new words.

The teacher may sample the reader used by the student to develop a list of words to decode if one has not been provided by the publisher. A sample may be obtained by selecting every 10th word, every 25th word or, for higher level readers, randomly selecting stories from which random words will be taken. Proper nouns and words already mastered by the student may be excluded (e.g., *a, the, me, I,* etc.).

Fluency is an area assessed to determine the reading rate and accuracy of a student using a particular reading selection. Reading fluency will be affected by the student's ability to decode new words and by the student's ability to read phrase by phrase rather than word by word. The teacher may assess oral reading fluency of new material and previously read material. Howell and Morehead

FORMAT A

Target word: *drill*

Synonyms: A. practice B. tool

Directions: "Match the synonym to the correct sentence."

1. Hand me the *drill.*
2. We need *drill* on our skills.

Answer(s): Sentence 1—synonym B. Sentence 2—synonym A.

FORMAT B

Target word: *drill*

Directions: "Select the words which make sentence 2 most like sentence 1."

Sentence 1. We need *drill* on our skills.
Sentence 2. If we want to get better at our skills, we should
. . . study them.
. . . put a hole in them.
. . . do them a lot.

FORMAT C

Target word: *drill*

Directions: "Write a synonym for the target word which can be used in each of the following sentences."

Sentence 1. Hand me the *drill.*
Sentence 2. We need *drill* on our skills.

Synonym 1: ______________________________
Synonym 2: ______________________________

FORMAT D

Target word: *drill*

Directions: "Read this sentence—"We need *drill* on our skills." In this sentence, does the *drill* mean to:

a. make a hole in something?
b. work on something over and over again?

Figure 8.11
Methods of informally assessing vocabulary.
Source: From *Curriculum-Based Evaluation for Special and Remedial Education* (p. 185) by K. W. Howell and M. K. Morehead, 1987, Columbus, OH: Merrill. Copyright 1987 by Macmillan Publishing Company. Reprinted by permission.

(1987) suggested that the teacher listen to the student read a passage, mark the location reached at the end of 1 minute, and then ask the student to read again as quickly as possible. The teacher may note the difference between the two rates as well as errors.

Another assessment device used by teachers to measure reading skills is informal reading inventories, which assess a variety of reading skills. These may be teacher-made instruments that use the actual curriculum used in instruction or commercially prepared devices. Commercially prepared instruments contain passages and word lists and diagnostic information that enables the teacher to analyze errors. One such instrument has been designed by Burns and Roe (1989).

Informal Reading Inventory, Third Edition. The Informal Reading Inventory, Third Edition (Burns & Roe, 1989) contains reading word-placement lists that enable the teacher to determine the level at which to begin passage testing. This instrument contains four equivalent forms of passages, which the student reads aloud. The teacher marks mistakes or miscues. The student is asked to answer comprehension questions as well. Comprehension is analyzed for main idea, detail, inference, vocabulary, sequence, and cause and effect. Figure 8.12 contains a summary of the errors analyzed in reading decoding skills on this instrument.

The Burns and Roe Informal Reading Inventory is contained in a spiral bound book, allowing the teacher to reproduce necessary pages and to laminate the student reading passages. Teachers should study the directions for administration before using the instrument. The scoring system provides percentages of errors, types of miscues, and percentages of comprehension. Such information can be used in planning interventions but may need to be verified by the teacher using the classroom curriculum. Grade levels provided are suggestions of placement and are not to be considered as grade-level equivalents as in norm-referenced testing.

Considerations When Using Informal Reading Inventories. The cautions about grade levels and curriculum verification stated in the previous section should be considered when using any commercially prepared informal reading inventory. Gillis and Olson (1987) advised teachers and diagnosticians to consider the following guidelines when selecting commercially prepared informal reading inventories:

1. If possible, select inventories which have mostly narrative selections for placing elementary students in basal materials and inventories which have mostly expository selections for placing students.

2. If possible, select inventories in which most of the selections are well organized.

3. When a passage on the form you are using is poorly organized or not of the appropriate text type for your purpose, use a passage at the same level from an

SUMMARY OF QUALITATIVE ANALYSIS

Miscue Analysis of Phonic and Structural Analysis Skills

(Tally total miscues on appropriate lines.)

Miscue	For Words in Isolation	For Words in Context		For Words in Isolation	For Words in Context
Single consonants	______	______	Word beginnings	______	______
Consonant blends	______	______	Word middles	______	______
Single vowels	______	______	Word endings	______	______
Vowel digraphs	______	______	Compound words	______	______
Consonant digraphs	______	______	Inflectional endings	______	______
Diphthongs	______	______	Syllabication	______	______
Prefixes	______	______	Accent	______	______
Suffixes	______	______			

Oral Reading Skills

(Place a [+] by areas that are strong and a [−] by areas that are weak.)

Reads in phrases (not word-by-word)	______
Uses expression	______
Attends to punctuation	______
Pronounces words correctly	______

Comments:

(Note: In order to fill out the analysis for words in context, it is helpful to make a list of expected reader responses and unexpected responses for easy comparison as to graphic similarity, syntactic acceptability, and semantic acceptability. See page 168 for a good way to record this information.)

Summary of Strengths and Weaknesses in Word Recognition (Include all of the important data that have been collected on word recognition skills):

Summary of Strengths and Weaknesses in Comprehension (Include all of the important data that have been collected about comprehension):

Figure 8.12
Analysis summary of the Burns and Roe Informal Reading Inventory.

Source: From *Informal Reading Inventory* (3rd ed., p. 166) by P. C. Burns and B. D. Roe, 1989, Boston, MA: Houghton Mifflin Company.

alternate form. If an appropriate passage is not available, rewrite a passage from the inventory or write an appropriate passage.

4. When a student's comprehension scores are erratic from level to level, examine the passages to see if the variability could be due to shifts between types of text or between well and poorly organized passages.

5. Finally, remember that the instructional level you find is just an estimate. Confirm it by observing the student's performance with classroom materials. Adjust placement if necessary. (pp. 36–44)

☐ CHECK YOUR UNDERSTANDING

Complete Activity 8.6.

Activity 8.6

Use the following passage to design brief informal assessment instruments in the spaces provided.

> Elaine sat on the balcony overlooking the mountains. The mountains were very high and appeared blue in color. The trees swayed in the breeze. The valley below was covered by a patch of fog. It was a cool, beautiful fall day.

1. Write an informal test using the cloze method. Remember to leave the first and last sentences intact.

____

____

____

____

____

____

2. Write an informal test using the maze method. Remember to leave three word choices beneath each blank provided for the missing words.

____

____

____

____

____

____

3. Select a sentence from the passage, and write an informal test using the sentence verification method. Write three sentences, one of which has the same meaning as the original sentence.

____

____

____

____

____

____

____

Informal Assessment of Mathematics

The teacher may use curriculum-based assessment to measure all areas of mathematics. The assessment should be combined with both task analysis and error analysis to determine specific problem areas. These problem areas should be further assessed by using probes to determine the specific difficulty. In addition to using these methods, Liedtke (1988) suggested using an interview technique to locate deficits in accuracy and strategies. Liedtke included techniques such as asking the student to create a word problem to illustrate a computation; redirection of the original computation to obtain additional math concept information, such as asking the student to compare two of her answers to see which is greater; and asking the student to solve a problem and explain the steps used in the process.

Howell and Morehead (1987) suggested several methods for assessing specific math skills. Their techniques provide assessment of accuracy and fluency of basic facts, recall, basic concepts, operations, problem-solving concepts, content knowledge, tool and unit knowledge, and skill integration. The procedure for checking the recall and handwriting necessary for a basic facts math test is illustrated in Figure 8.13.

Informal Assessment of Spelling

A common type of informal spelling assessment is a spelling test of standard format. The teacher states the word, uses the word in a sentence, and repeats the word. Most elementary spelling texts provide this type of direct curriculum-based assessment. The teacher may wish to assign different words or may be teaching at the secondary-level, where typical spelling texts are not used. The teacher may also need to assess the spelling of content-related words in areas such as science or social studies. Or, the teacher may use written samples by the student to analyze spelling errors.

One method of analyzing spelling errors, proposed by Guerin and Maier (1983), is shown in Table 8.1.

Informal Assessment of Written Language

A student's written language ability may be assessed informally by collecting and analyzing written work samples. Written samples may be analyzed for spelling, punctuation, correct grammar and usage, vocabulary, creative ability, story theme, sequence, and plot. If the objective of instruction is to promote creativity, actual spelling, punctuation, and other mechanical errors should not be scored against the student on the written sample. These errors, however, should be noted by the teacher and used in educational planning for English and spelling lessons.

Specific-Level Procedure 2: Checking Recall and Handwriting. We use a two-part procedure to determine if writing slowly or inadequate recall of facts is the cause of the rate failure on the basic facts survey-level test.

DIRECTIONS 2.1

1. Administer a basic facts test for each area of concern (+, −, ×, ÷). Have the student say the answers rather than write. (Flashcards or a fact sheet are appropriate stimuli.)
2. Say, "Tell me the answer to each problem."
3. Note corrects and errors. Compare the student's performance to your CAP* or the one we list in Appendix C. One hundred percent accuracy is an appropriate criterion for facts.

DIRECTIONS 2.2

1. Administer a writing-digits or a copying-digits test.
2. Say, "Write/copy numbers from 1 to 100 as quickly and carefully as you can. Please, begin."
3. Time the student for 60 seconds. Say, "Stop."
4. Score the sample and use the procedure for comparing basic movement cycle—writing digits to the skill of math facts.

Interpretation Guidelines

Question. Are the student's oral responses accurate?

If yes, answer the next question and use Teaching Recommendation 2.

If no, teach basic facts and use Teaching Recommendation 1, or employ Specific-Level Procedure 3.

Question. Can the student write fast enough to demonstrate math fact fluency?

If yes, teach fact fluency (Teaching Recommendation 2.2).

If no, teach the student to write digits (Teaching Recommendation 2.1).

Question. Is the student having trouble with both accuracy on facts and writing digits?

If yes, teach accuracy on facts (Recommendation 1) and writing digits (Recommendation 2.1). Also use Specific-Level Procedure 3.

Figure 8.13

Procedure for checking recall and handwriting necessary for a basic facts math test.

Source: From *Curriculum-Based Evaluation for Special and Remedial Education* (p. 260) by K. W. Howell and M. K. Morehead, 1987, Columbus, OH: Merrill. Copyright 1987 by Macmillan Publishing Company. Reprinted by permission.

*CAP = criterion for acceptable performance.

Table 8.1
Analysis of spelling errors used in informal assessment

	Definitions	**Example**	
		Heard	**Written**
Phonetic Ablilty			
PS	Substitutions: placing another sound or sylla-able in place of the sound in the word	match nation	mach nashun
PO	Omissions: leaving out a sound or syllable from the word	grateful tempera-ture	graful tempature
PA	Additions: adding a sound or syllable to the original	purchase importance	purchasing importantance
PSe	Sequencing: putting sounds or syllables in the wrong order	animal elephant	aminal efelant
Visualization			
VS	Substitutions: substitu-tion of a vowel or con-sonant for those in the given word	him chapel	hin chaple
VO	Omissions: leaving out a vowel, or consonant, or syllable from those in the given word	allow beginning	alow begining

Source: From *Informal Assessment in Education* (pp. 218–219) by G. R. Guerin and A. S. Maier, 1983, Palo Alto, CA: Mayfield Publishing. Copyright 1983 by Mayfield Publishing. Reprinted by permission.

	Definitions	Example	
		Heard	Written
Phonetic Ability			
VA	Additions: adding a vowel, consonant, or syllable to those in the given word	welcome fragrant	wellcome fragerant
VSe	Sequencing: putting letters or syllables in the wrong order	guardian pilot	guardain pliot
Linguistic Performance			
LS	Substitution: substitution of a word for another having somewhat the same meaning	ring house	bell home
	Substitution: substituting another word due to different language structure (teacher judgment)	came ate	come et
	Substitution: substitution of a completely different word	pear polish	pair collage
LO	Omissions: omitting word endings or prefixes, suffixes	pushed unhelpful	pusht helpful
LA	Additions: adding endings, prefixes, suffixes	cry forget	crys forgetting
LSe	Sequencing: reversing syllables	discussed disappoint	discusted dispapoint

One informal assessment technique for written language skills proposed by Shapiro (1989) includes the following steps:

1. A series of "story starters" should be constructed that can be used to give initial ideas for students to write about. These starters should contain items that most children will find of sufficient interest to generate a written story.

2. The evaluator should give the child a copy of the story starter and read the starter to him or her. The evaluator then tells the student that he will be asked to write a story using the starter as the first sentence. The student should be given a minute to think about a story before he or she is asked to begin writing.

3. After 1 minute, the evaluator should tell the child to begin writing, start the stopwatch, and time for 3 minutes. If the child stops writing before the 3 minutes are up, he or she should be encouraged to keep writing until time is up.

4. The evaluator should count the number of words that are correctly written. "Correct" means that a word can be recognized (even if it is misspelled). Capitalization and punctuation are ignored. The rate of the correct and incorrect words per 3 minutes are calculated. If the child stops writing before the 3 minutes are up, the number of words correct should be multiplied by 180 for the number of words correct per 3 minutes. (pp. 107–108)

Shapiro (1989) also suggested creating local norms to compare students. The number of words correct may be used as a basis for writing short-term objectives. This informal method may be linked directly to classroom curricula and may be repeated frequently as a direct measure of student writing ability.

Writing samples may also be used to analyze handwriting. The teacher uses error analysis to evaluate the sample, write short-term objectives, and plan educational strategies. One such error analysis of handwriting skills is shown in Figure 8.14 (Guerin & Maier, 1983).

Portfolio Assessment

portfolio assessment Evaluating student progress, strengths, and weaknesses using a collection of different measurements and work samples.

One method of assessing a student's current level of academic functioning is through **portfolio assessment.** A portfolio is a collection of student work that provides a holistic view of the student's strengths and weaknesses. The portfolio collection contains various work samples, permanent products, and test results from a variety of instruments and methods. For example, a portfolio of reading might include a student's test scores on teacher-made tests including curriculum-based assessments, work samples from daily work and homework assignments, error analyses on work and test samples, and the results of an informal reading inventory with miscues noted and analyzed. The assessment of the student's progress would assess decoding skills, comprehension skills, fluency, and so on. These measures would be collected over a period of time. This type of assessment may be useful in describing the current progress of the student with parents (Taylor, 1993).

Tindal (1991) cautioned that portfolio assessment should be studied further before it can be recommended as an alternative assessment strategy. Questions regarding the portfolio's sensitivity to student growth, implications for intervention and planning, and reliability and validity of such measures need additional study.

Directions: Analysis of handwriting should be made on a sample of the student's written work, not from a carefully produced sample. Evaluate each task and mark in the appropriate column. Score each task "satisfactory" or (1) or "unsatisfactory" (2).

I. Letter formation

A. Capitals (score each letter 1 or 2)

A	______	G	______	M	______	S	______	Y	______
B	______	H	______	N	______	T	______	Z	______
C	______	I	______	O	______	U	______		
D	______	J	______	P	______	V	______		
E	______	K	______	Q	______	W	______		
F	______	L	______	R	______	X	______		
								Total	______

B. Lowercase (score by groups)	Score (1 or 2)
1. Round letters	
a. Counterclockwise	
a, c, d, g, o, q	______
b. Clockwise	
k, p	______
2. Looped letters	
a. Above line	
b, d, e, f, h, k, l	______
b. Below lin	
f, g, j, p, q, y	______
3. Retraced letters	
i, u, t, w, y	______
4. Humped letters	
h, m, n, v, x, z	______
5. Others	
r, s, b	______

Figure 8.14
One method of handwriting analysis.

Source: From *Informal Assessment in Education* (p. 228) by G. R. Guerin and A. S. Maier, 1983, Palo Alto, CA: Mayfield Publishing. Copyright 1983 by Mayfield Publishing. Reprinted by permission.

continued

C. Numerals (score each number 1 or 2)

1	________	4	________	7	________	10–20	________
2	________	5	________	8	________	21–99	________
3	________	6	________	9	________	100–1,000	________
						Total	________

II. Spatial relationships

	Score (1 or 2)
A. Alignment (letters on line)	________
B. Uniform slant	________
C. Size of letters	
1. To each other	________
2. To available space	________
D. Space between letters	________
E. Space between words	________
F. Anticipation of end of line (hyphenates, moves to next line)	________
Total	________

III. Rate of writing (letters per minute)

	Score (1 or 2)
Grade 1:20	
2:30	
3:35	
4:45	
5:55	
6:65	
7 and above: 75	________

Scoring

	Satisfactory	*Questionable*	*Poor*
I. *Letter formation*			
A. Capitals	26	39	40+
B. Lowercase	7	10	11+
C. Numerals	12	18	19+
II. *Spatial relationships*	7	10	11+
III. *Rate of writing*	1	2	6

Figure 8.14, *continued*

Issues of Academic Informal Assessment

Some of the problems that exist in some standardized norm-referenced testing, such as bias or inadequate curriculum validity, also exist in informal testing. Other problems, such as lack of technical quality and scoring inconsistencies, are associated with the more variable nature of informal assessment.

A potential risk of informal, teacher-made instruments is bias. Item bias and cultural bias may be incorporated during the construction of the test. McLoughlin and Lewis (1990) listed the following considerations for teachers who are constructing instruments:

> Is the standard of comparison appropriate for the student in terms of race, culture, and gender?
>
> Are test items free from cultural bias?
>
> Is the language appropriate for the student?
>
> Does the measure bypass the limitations imposed by the handicapping condition? (p. 128)

To avoid inadequate curriculum validity, the teacher must maintain an adequate representation of the current curriculum in the development of test items. For example, a student who completed a math unit that included various types of division problems (multiple digits with and without remainders) should not be assessed on the unit by using only division problems representing multiples of 5 with no remainders. The sample of items should be representative of the curriculum taught during the instructional period.

Informal assessment methods are more likely to suffer from a lack of technical quality. High quality norm-referenced assessment instruments are researched by psychometrics professionals and constructed to reflect the best possible techniques of assessment. By contrast, the development of informal instruments usually relies on the professional expertise of one person: the teacher. The following guidelines for the development of informal assessment methods were adapted from Bennett (1982):

1. Specify the purpose of assessment.
2. Construct or select procedures so that they are relevant to the purpose of assessment.
3. Precisely define the domains to be assessed or objectives to be evaluated.
4. Select assessment tasks so that they are representative of the domain tied to the objective of interest.
5. Specify dimensions on which performance will be judged and criteria for determining what will be considered a correct response.
6. Specify criteria for evaluating overall performance and the rationale for selecting those criteria.
7. Use as long an assessment as possible. (p. 338)

A final area of concern is the accuracy with which educators rate students on informal measures across various developmental ages. In a study by Kenny and Chekaluk (1993), teachers were more accurate in assessing student reading ability when students were at least in the second year of school. It seems that too many factors may influence student reading behavior in the early grades and these confound the teacher's ability to accurately determine reading achievement. This suggests that, in the early grades, reading assessment may require a combination of formal and informal assessment for accuracy in monitoring progress.

Exercises

Part I

Match the terms with the correct definitions.

A. criterion-related assessment
B. curriculum-based measurement
C. task analysis
D. error analysis
E. informal assessment
F. questionnaire
G. direct measurement
H. direct daily measurement
I. probes
J. checklist
K. portfolio
L. subskill

_______ **1.** Tests used for in-depth assessment of the mastery of a specific skill or subskill.
_______ **2.** Measuring progress by using the same instructional materials or tasks as are used in the classroom.
_______ **3.** The daily measurement of progress using instructional materials.
_______ **4.** A collection of student work that represents current level of educational functioning.
_______ **5.** Nonstandardized methods of measuring student progress.
_______ **6.** Analyzing a task by breaking it down to the smallest steps or skills.
_______ **7.** A list of academic or behavioral skills that must be mastered by the student.
_______ **8.** When items of an assessment instrument are related to meeting objectives or passing skill-mastery objectives.
_______ **9.** Measuring student progress by mastery of a standard, objective, or criterion.
_______ **10.** Small unit of a skill that must be learned in order to master the skill.
_______ **11.** Using content from the currently used curriculum to assess student progress.

Part II

Use the terms in Part I to select a method of informal assessment for the following situations. Write the reason for your selection.

1. Standardized test results you received on a new student indicate that she is performing two grade levels below expectancy. You want to determine which reading book to place her in.
   Method of assessment: ______
   Reason: ______
   ______
2. A student who understands division problems when presented in class failed a teacher made test. You want to determine the reason for the failure.
   Method of assessment: ______
   Reason: ______
   ______
3. Following a screening test of fifth-grade level spelling, you determine that a student performs inconsistently when spelling words with short vowel sounds:
   Method of assessment: ______
   Reason: ______
   ______
4. A student seems to be performing at a different level than indicated by norm-referenced math test data. You think you should meet with her parents and discuss actual progress in the classroom.
   Method of assessment: ______
   Reason: ______

References

Barnes, W. (1986). Informal assessment of reading. *Pointer, 30,* 42–46.

Bennett, R. (1982). Cautions for the use of informal measures in the educational assessment of exceptional children. *Journal of Learning Disabilities, 15,* 337–339.

Brigance, A. H. (1977). *Brigance Diagnostic Inventory of Basic Skills.* N. Billerica, MA: Curriculum Associates.

Brigance, A. H. (1981). *Brigance Diagnostic Inventory of Essential Skills.* N. Billerica, MA: Curriculum Associates.

Brigance, A. H. (1991). *Inventory of Early Development–Revised.* N. Billerica, MA: Curriculum Associates.

Burns, P. C., & Roe, B. D. (1989). *Informal Reading Inventory* (3rd ed). Boston: Houghton Mifflin.

Canter, A. (1991). Effective psychological services for all students: A data based model of service delivery. In G. Stoner, M. R. Shinn, & H. M. Walker (Eds.), *Interventions for* *achievement and behavioral problems* (pp. 49–78). Silver Spring, MD: National Association of School Psychologists.

Connolly, A. J. (1988). *KeyMath–Revised: A Diagnostic Inventory of Essential Mathematics.* Circle Pines, MN: American Guidance Service.

Evans, S., & Evans, W. (1986). A perspective on assessment for instruction. *Pointer, 30,* 9–12.

Fuchs, L., Butterworth, J., & Fuchs, D. (1989). Effects of ongoing curriculum-based measurement on student awareness of goals and progress. *Education and Treatment of Children, 12,* 41–47.

Fuchs, L., & Fuchs, D. (1992). Identifying a measure for monitoring student reading progress. *School Psychology Review, 21,* 1, 45–58.

Fuchs, L., Fuchs, D., & Hamlett, C. (1989). Effects of instrumental use of curriculum-based measurement to enhance instructional programs. *Remedial and Special Education, 10,* 43–52.

Fuchs, L., Fuchs, D., Hamlett, C. L., Phillips, N. B., & Bentz, J. (1994). Classwide curriculum-based measurement: Helping general educators meet the challenge of student diversity. *Exceptional Children, 60*(6), 518–537.

Fuchs, L., Tindal, G., & Deno, S. (1984). Methodological issues in curriculum-based assessment. *Diagnostique, 9,* 191–207.

Gillis, M., & Olson, M. (1987). Elementary IRI's: Do they reflect what we know about text/type structure and comprehension? *Reading Research and Instruction, 27,* 36–44.

Good, R., & Salvia, J. (1988). Curriculum bias in published, norm-referenced reading tests: Demonstrable effects. *School Psychology Review, 17,* 51–60.

Guerin, G. R., & Maier, A. S. (1983). *Informal assessment in education.* Palo Also, CA: Mayfield.

Howell, K. W., & Morehead, M. K. (1987). *Curriculum-based evaluation for special and remedial education.* Columbus, OH: Merrill.

Hultquist, A. M., & Metzke, L. K. (1993). Potential effects of curriculum bias in individual norm-referenced reading and spelling achievement tests. *Journal of Psychoeducational Assessment, 11,* 337–344.

Kaufman, A. S., & Kaufman, N. L. (1985). *Kaufman Test of Educational Achievement.* Circle Pines, MN: American Guidance Service.

Kenny, D. T., & Chekaluk, E. (1993). Early reading performance: A comparison of teacher-based and test-based assessments. *Journal of Learning Disabilities, 26*(4), 227–236.

Liedtke, W. (1988). Diagnosis in mathematics: The advantages of an interview. *Arithmetic Teacher, 36,* 26–29.

Marston, D., Fuchs, L., & Deno, S. (1986). Measuring pupil progress: A comparison of standardized achievement tests and curriculum related measures. *Diagnostique, 11,* 77–90.

Marston, D., Mirkin, P. K., & Deno, S. L. (1984). Curriculum-based measurement: An alternative to traditional screening, referral, and identification. *The Journal of Special Education, 18,* 109–118.

McLoughlin, J. A. & Lewis, R. B. (1990). *Assessing special students.* Columbus, OH: Merrill.

Reynolds, C. R. (1982). The problem of bias in psychological assessment. In C. R. Reynolds & T. B. Gutkin (Eds.), *The handbook of school psychology* (pp. 178–208). New York: Wiley.

Rosenfield, S., & Kurait, S. K. (1990). Best practices in curriculum-based assessment. In A. Thomas & J. Grimes (Eds.), *Best practices in school psychology–II.* Washington, DC: National Association of School Psychology.

Salvia, J., & Hughes, C. (1990). *Curriculum-based assessment: Testing what is taught.* New York: Macmillan.

Shapiro, E. S. (1989). *Academic skills problems: Direct assessment and intervention.* New York: Guilford.

Shinn, M. R., Habedank, L., Rodden-Nord, K., & Knutson, N. (1993). Using curriculum-based measurement to identify potential candidates for reintegration into general education. *The Journal of Special Education, 27*(2), 202–221.

Shinn, M. R., Nolet, V., & Knutson, N. (1990). Best practices in curriculum-based measurement. In A. Thomas & J. Grimes (Eds.), *Best practices in school psychology.* Washington, DC: National Association of School Psychologists.

Stoner, G., Carey, S. P., Ikeda, M. J., & Shinn, M. R. (1994). The utility of curriculum-based measurement for evaluating the effects of methylphenidate on academic performance. *Journal of Applied Behavior Analysis, 27,* 101–113.

Taylor, R. L. (1993). *Assessment of exceptional students: Educational and psychological procedures, 3rd ed.* Boston: Allyn & Bacon.

Tindal, G. (1991). Operationalizing learning portfolios: A good idea in search of a method. *Diagnostique, 2*(3), 127–133.

Wesson, C., King, R., & Deno, S. (1984). Direct and frequent measurement of student performance: If it's so good for us, why don't we do it? *Learning Disabilities Quarterly, 7,* 45–48.

Wiener, J. (1986). Alternatives in the assessment of the learning disabled adolescent: A learning strategies approach. *Learning Disabilities Focus, 1,* 97–107.

Woodcock, R. W. (1987). *Woodcock Reading Mastery Tests–Revised.* Circle Pines: American Guidance Service.

Chapter Nine

Assessment of Behavior

Key Terms

academic engaged time
behavioral observation
target behaviors
systematic observation
baseline
informal assessment
anecdotal recording
event recording
frequency counting
time sampling
interval recording
duration recording
latency recording
checklists
questionnaires
interviews
sociograms
ecological assessment
projective techniques
drawing tests
apperception
sentence completion tests

This chapter addresses the assessment of behavioral problems, such as externalizing (acting out) behaviors (including those attributed to attention deficit disorders), and the assessment of emotional and social problems of students. Assessment of behavior through informal measures is presented first, followed by a discussion of instruments used to measure behavioral and emotional problems. The newly developed computerized methods of assessing attention disorders are presented at the end of the chapter. The methods covered in this chapter were among those listed in one study as most frequently used by school psychologists (Clarizio & Higgins, 1989). Members of the multidisciplinary team should be familiar with these techniques because they will be discussed during team meetings.

Informal Assessment of Behavior

Teachers will encounter students who have behavioral problems. These behavioral problems, if left unattended, will disrupt the individual student's academic progress and probably decrease the amount of **academic engaged time** of all students in the class. The teacher must intervene to maintain an atmosphere conducive to educational achievement.

academic engaged time The time when the student is actively involved in the learning process.

The teacher may observe behaviors that are problematic for the student in the classroom. Often, **behavioral observation** may be casual or unsystematic. Unsystematic observations may yield less than accurate results. Salvia and Hughes (1990) noted the following problems with unsystematic observations:

behavioral observation Observations of student behavior.

1. They are often inaccurate because unrepresentative behavior may be observed.
2. They may be inaccurate because the personal definitions of behavior used by the observer may not be precise or stable.
3. As unsystematic observations become more subjective, they become more susceptible to bias. (pp. 6–7)

target behaviors Specific behaviors that require intervention by the teacher to promote optimal academic or social learning.

The first step in the intervention of behavioral problems is the identification of **target behaviors**. Once the exact behavior or behaviors have been identified,

systematic observation Planned observations less subject to bias and inaccurate information about a student's behavior.

baseline The frequency, duration, or latency of a behavior determined before behavioral intervention.

systematic observation can begin. Systematic observation enables the teacher to note how often a behavior occurs and to establish a **baseline,** which will be used to monitor the students progress following intervention. Eventually, the student may be trained to self-monitor his behavior.

Behavioral Observations

informal assessment Nonstandardized methods of measuring student progress.

One of the most frequently used behavioral assessment methods is direct behavioral observation. Behavioral observations can be completed by the teacher or by another objective professional or trained paraprofessional, such as a teacher's aide. Behaviors may be observed for frequency, duration, and/or intensity. The observer should remember two important guidelines for effective behavioral observation: Be objective and specific. The observer should be fair, nonjudgmental, and should precisely pinpoint or identify problem behaviors. The identified behaviors should be stated exactly so that two observers would be able to agree about whether the behavior is or is not occurring. Behavioral observations may be completed as an **informal assessment** of behavior and are also important in the assessment of behavior using more structured instruments (McConaughy, Achenbach, & Gent, 1988).

Anecdotal Recording

anecdotal recording Observations of behavior in which the teacher notes all behaviors and interactions that occur during a given period of time.

Behavioral intervention strategies are based on a clear understanding of why a behavior occurs. Behavioristic principle is founded in the theory that behaviors are maintained or increased by the reinforcing events that follow the event or behavior. The teacher may recognize when a behavior occurs but not be able to identify the reinforcing event or the antecedent event, which occurs before the behavior. One behavioral observation technique that will enable the teacher to identify the exact behavior, antecedent event, and reinforcing event, or consequence, is called **anecdotal recording**.

In the anecdotal recording method, the teacher observes the student and writes down everything that occurs in the situation. The teacher observes the student for a specific time period, usually when the behavior seems to occur most frequently. The teacher may wish to observe during a particular academic subject time, such as math class, or during a nonacademic time when the behavior occurs, such as lunch or recess.

An anecdotal recording might look like this:

Name Mary

Observation Time

9:30 AM Language Arts—Mary enters resource room and walks around the room twice, then sits in her chair. Mary looks out of the window.

9:32 AM Mary speaks out: Teacher can I go to the office?
Response: Mary, get your workbook out and turn to page 56.

9:33 AM Mary gets workbook out and begins to look at the pictures on several of the pages. Continues for quite some time.

9:45 AM Mary speaks out: What page teacher?
Teacher responds: Page 56.

9:47 AM Mary speaks out: Teacher can I use a pencil?
Response: Here is a pencil Mary.

Using the anecdotal format for observation provides a basis for analyzing the antecedent, behavior, and consequences. The antecedent is the event that precedes the behavior, and the consequence is the event that follows the behavior. The antecedent may actually trigger the behavior, whereas the consequence is thought to maintain or reinforce the behavior. In the preceding example, the antecedent, behavior, and consequence analysis, or A-B-C, might look like this:

A	*B*	*C*
Mary enters room	walks around	allowed to walk freely
sits in chair and looks at the teacher	talks out	teacher responds
looks at pages in workbook, then looks at teacher	talks out	teacher responds
looks at teacher	talks out	teacher responds

This analysis provides information that will help the teacher plan a behavioral intervention strategy. It appears that the reinforcing event for Mary's talking out is the teacher responding to Mary. It also seems that the teacher has not provided an organizational intervention plan that will convey to Mary the behaviors expected of her when beginning academic work or instruction. Through this observation, two behaviors have been targeted for intervention: organizational behavior (ready for work) and talking out. The organizational behaviors expected can be broken down into specific behaviors for intervention: student in chair, pencils ready, books out, paper ready.

☐ **CHECK YOUR UNDERSTANDING**

Complete Activity 9.1.

Activity 9.1

Read the following anecdotal recording, which covers 2 days of class, and then answer the questions.

Name John

Monday

John enters classroom.

Teacher (*T*): Let's get ready for math class.

John (*J*): Can we go on the field trip Thursday?

T: Yes, John. We will go on Thursday.

J: I can't find my math book.
T: Look in your desk, John. Now, let's work problems 1 to 10 on page 284.
J: [Throws pencil on the floor. Picks pencil up.]
T: John, let's get to work.
J: [Crumbles paper up, throws on floor. Throws book on floor.]
T: That's it John! Go to the office.
J: [Smiles. Leaves the room.]

Tuesday

John enters classroom.

T: Now class, let's get our math books out.
J: [Out of seat. Goes to pencil sharpener.]
T: John, when do we sharpen our pencils?
J: [No response.]
T: Pencil time is after lunch. Now, get your math book out. Turn to page 286. Let's check our homework.
J: [Slams book on desk. Groans.]
T: Today we will continue the division problems—John, get your book open—
J: [Throws book on floor.]
T: Okay! To the office!
J: [Smiles, leaves the room.]

1. Analyze the observations of John's behavior for antecedent, behavior, and consequence.

A	B	C
______	______	______
______	______	______
______	______	______
______	______	______
______	______	______
______	______	______

2. Based on your analysis of the antecedents, behaviors, and consequences, what would you recommend for an intervention plan? ______________________

____

____

____

____

____

____

Event Recording

event recording Recording the frequency of a target behavior; also called frequency counting.

Event recording assesses the frequency with which behaviors occur. The teacher marks or tallies the number of times specific behaviors occur. This information, the initial recording of data, creates a baseline for the teacher to use as a comparison following intervention. This type of recording is useful for observing easily detectable behaviors for short periods of time. Examples of these types of behavior include time on task, talking out, hitting, and so on. One illustration of **frequency counting,** another name for event recording, is shown in Figure 9.1.

Observations using event recording are typically completed for an entire class period or continuously for a specified time period. Other methods for observing behaviors intermittently or for short periods of time are **time sampling** and **interval recording**.

frequency counting Counting the occurrence of a specific behavior; same as event recording.

time sampling When the behavioral observation samples behavior through the day or class period.

interval recording Sampling a behavior intermittenly for very brief periods of time; used to observe frequently occurring behaviors.

Time Sampling

Time sampling uses frequency counting or event recording techniques for various times throughout the day or class period. The teacher identifies the target behaviors and records student activity for a time period, such as 2 or 5 minutes, throughout the period or day. The teacher is sampling the behavior for an idea of how often the behavior occurs, without observing continuously. This enables the teacher to observe more than one student or more than one behavior throughout the day. An example of a time sampling observation is shown in Figure 9.2.

Interval Recording

Interval recording is used when the teacher wants to observe several students or behaviors at one time, record intermittently throughout the day or class period, and record behaviors that occur too frequently to record each event, such as stereotypical behaviors (Kerr & Nelson, 1989). During interval recording, the teacher notes if the behavior is occurring or not occurring. The time intervals may be very short throughout the day. The observation might be for a very brief period of time, such as 2 minutes, during which the teacher notes every 30 seconds whether or not the behavior is occurring. An example of interval recording is shown in Figure 9.3.

Name: Joe

Target behavior: Out of seat

	Mon.	Tues.	Wed.
9:00 – 10:00	卌 卌	卌 卌 II	卌 卌 I
10:00 – 11:00	II	I	III
11:00 – 12:00	I	III	II

Figure 9.1
An example of event recording (frequency counting).

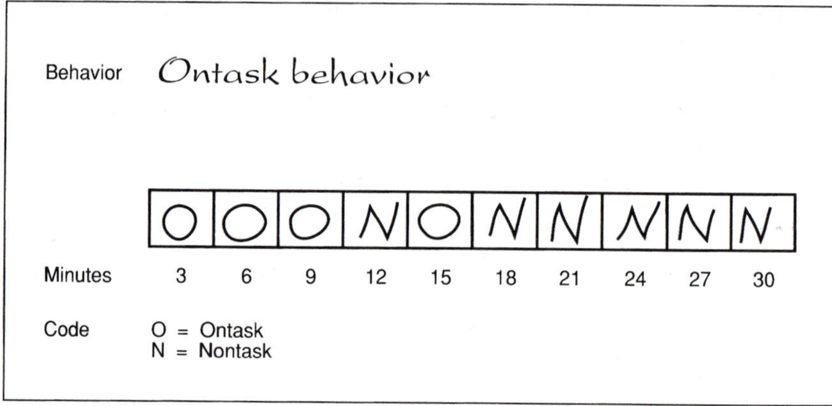

Figure 9.2
Sample chart for time sampling of on task and nontask behaviors.
Source:: From *Teaching Strategies for Children in Conflict* (2nd ed., p. 84) by H. L. Swanson and H. R. Reinert, 1984, New York: Times Mirror/Mosby College Publishing. Copyright 1984 by Times Mirror/Mosby College Publishing. Reprinted by permission.

Duration Recording

duration recording
Observations that involve the length of time a behavior occurs.

The **duration recording** technique is used when the length of the behavior is the target variable of the behavior. For example, a student may need to increase the amount of time spent on task. The teacher will record how long the student remains on task following the directive to do so. The duration recording might look like this:

Name Ralph
Task writing assignment

On Task	***Off Task***
2 min	60 s
60 s	2 min
60 s	60 s

Task/off task ratio is 4:8 min = 50% on task

This brief duration recording revealed that Ralph is on task only 50% of the expected time. Following intervention by the teacher, such as a prompting signal or behavioral contract or other strategy, it is hoped that the student's time on task would increase while time off task would decrease. Reinforcement for time on task would increase the probability that Ralph would remain on task longer. A duration recording of time on task during the intervention or treatment should be compared with the baseline data of 50% to note the effectiveness of the intervention strategies.

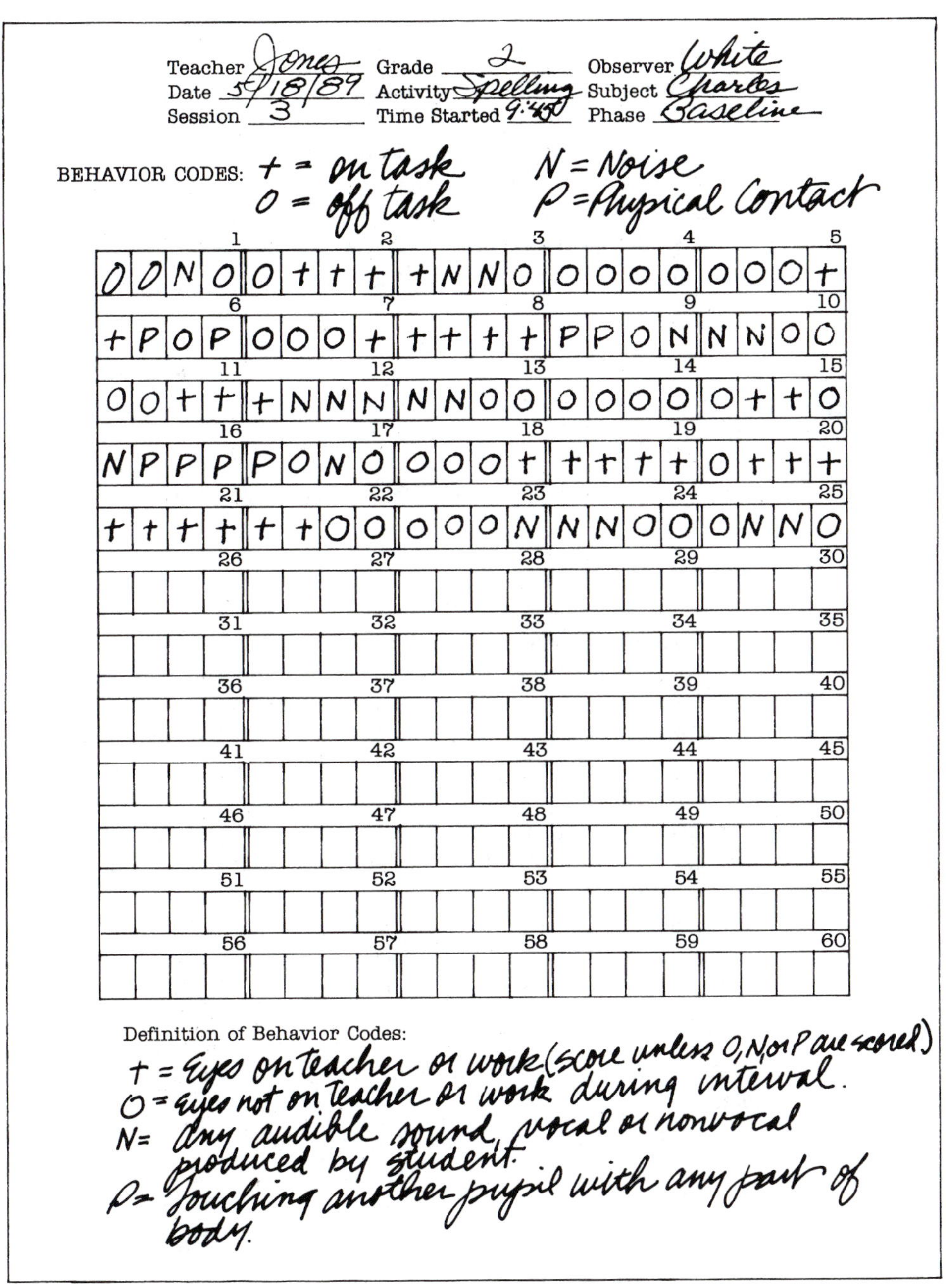

Teacher Jones Grade 2 Observer White
Date 5/18/89 Activity Spelling Subject Charles
Session 3 Time Started 9:40 Phase Baseline

BEHAVIOR CODES: + = on task N = Noise
O = off task P = Physical Contact

1	2	3	4	5
O O N O	O + + +	+ N N O	O O O O	O O O +

6	7	8	9	10
+ P O P	O O O +	+ + + +	P P O N	N N O O

11	12	13	14	15
O O + +	+ N N N	N N O O	O O O O	O + + O

16	17	18	19	20
N P P P	P O N O	O O O +	+ + + +	O + + +

21	22	23	24	25
+ + + +	+ + O O	O O O N	N N O O	O N N O

26	27	28	29	30

31	32	33	34	35

36	37	38	39	40

41	42	43	44	45

46	47	48	49	50

51	52	53	54	55

56	57	58	59	60

Definition of Behavior Codes:
+ = Eyes on teacher or work (score unless O, N, or P are scored)
O = Eyes not on teacher or work during interval.
N = Any audible sound, vocal or nonvocal produced by student.
P = Touching another pupil with any part of body.

Figure 9.3
Sample interval recording form.
Source: From *Strategies for Managing Behavior Problems in the Classroom* (2nd ed., p. 82) by M. M. Kerr and C. M. Nelson, 1989, Columbus, OH: Merrill. Copyright 1989 by Macmillan Publishing Company. Reprinted by permission.

Latency Recording

latency recording
Observations that involve the amount of time that elapses from the presentation of a stimulus until the response occurs.

The **latency recording** method of observation also involves the element of time. This is an observation in which the time is recorded from the moment a stimulus (such as a command) is given until the response occurs. The element of elapsed time is recorded. For example, the time is recorded from the moment the teacher gives spelling instructions until the student begins the assignment. If the student must be prompted several times during the completion of the task, the latency is recorded each time the student is prompted (Evans, Evans, & Schmid, 1989).

☐ **CHECK YOUR UNDERSTANDING**

Complete Activity 9.2.

Activity 9.2

Use the following information to analyze the behavior of a fifth-grade student named Amber.

Day 1

Anecdotal recording:

Amber was presented with her arithmetic worksheet following the direct instruction lesson with her group. After several minutes, she began to work on the first problem. During the time period of receiving the work and beginning the work, she was observed looking through her desk to find the necessary materials. When she located her pencil and paper, she dropped the assignment page on the floor. She picked the paper up and placed it on her desk. She sharpened her pencil and began to work. During the period that she was seated at her desk working, approximately 10 minutes, she was observed looking around the room and watching other students. When a sound occurred outside the room, she would look in the hallway or out the window. When papers were collected, she had completed the first 2 of 15 problems. One problem was correct, but the second problem was not calculated correctly due to a careless error.

Day 2

Latency recording: Time elapsed from assignment to working behavior = 5 minutes.

Interval recording: Observations during work time:

+ = On task   0 = Off task

	+	0	0	0	0	+	+	0	0	+
Minutes:	1	2	3	4	5	6	7	8	9	10

1. Analyze the anecdotal recording. What are the antecedents, behaviors, and consequences?

A	B	C
______	______	______
______	______	______

2. Analyze the latency recording information. ______

3. Analyze the interval recording data. How often is the student on task? Off task? ______

4. Based on the information provided, what recommendations would you suggest for Amber? What behavioral objectives would be included to begin the intervention? ______

Structured Classroom Observations

Observation methods discussed so far in this chapter may be teacher-made, informal instruments and may be used for prereferral, assessment, and intervention of behavioral problems. A structured classroom observation form called the Direct Observation Form (Achenbach, 1986) is one part of the Child Behavior Checklist (CBCL) system, a multiaxial system for assessment of behavioral and emotional problems. Other forms in this system are described throughout the chapter in the appropriate topical sections.

Child Behavior Checklist: Direct Observation Form, Revised Edition

The Direct Observation Form (Achenbach, 1986) is four pages in length, including general instructions and guidelines. The first page consists of the student's identifying information (name, date of birth, observation settings, and so on) and the general administration instructions. The inside pages of the form are comprised of three parts: an observation rating scale on which to mark observed behaviors and rate their intensity or severity, a space for anecdotal recording of all events during the observation period, and an interval recording form. The observer makes several observations of the target student across several different settings. The observer compares the target student with two grade and gender peers. When comparing the target student, the observer ascertains if the student is significantly different from the two control students in ontask behavior. This method is often used to assess behavioral disorders such as attention deficit disorder. Often, the criterion for indicating possible attention problems is that the target student's offtask behavior score be 1½ or 2 standard deviations above the control student's scores.

The observer marks the items on the rating scale if the target child exhibits the behaviors during the observation. Figure 9.4 illustrates the types of items represented on the Direct Observation Form. These items are then scored, as are the other rating scales and interviews of the multiaxial CBCL system, for significant behavior problems. The behaviors are defined on two broad bands: (a) externalizing (acting out) and (b) internalizing (turning inward), which includes problems such as anxiety or withdrawal. In addition, the system notes the occurrence of several clinical behavioral syndromes, such as social problems, somatic complaints, aggressive behavior, and attention problems. The other components of the CBCL are scored along the same broad and narrow bands of behavior and emotional functioning.

0 If the item was not observed

1 If there was very slight or ambiguous occurrence

2 If there was a definite occurrence with mild to moderate intensity and less than three minutes duration

3 If there was a definite occurrence with severe intensity or greater than three minutes duration

0 1 2 3 Doesn't sit still, restless or hyperactive
0 1 2 3 Shy or timid behavior
0 1 2 3 Explosive and unpredictable behavior
0 1 2 3 Sulks
0 1 2 3 Steals
0 1 2 3 Easily led by peers
0 1 2 3 Fidgets, including with objects

Figure 9.4
Selected items from Achenbach's Child Behavior Checklist.
Source: From *Child Behavior Checklist—Direct Observation Form, Revised Edition* by T. M. Achenbach, 1986, Burlington: University of Vermont Center for Children, Youth, and Families. Copyright 1986 by T. M. Achenbach. Reprinted with permission.

Other Techniques for Assessing Behavior

Some techniques of assessing behavior do not involve direct observation of behavior. These techniques include **checklists, questionnaires, interviews, sociograms,** and **ecological assessment**. These methods rely on input from others, such as parents, teachers, or peers, rather than on direct observation of behavior. When these indirect methods are used with direct observation, the teacher can plan effective behavioral intervention strategies.

checklists Lists of academic or behavioral skills that must be mastered by the student.

questionnaires Questions about a student's behavior or academic concerns, which may be answered by the student or by the parent or teacher; also called interviews.

interviews Formal or informal questions asked orally by the examiner.

sociograms Graphic representation of the social dynamics within a group.

ecological assessment Analysis of the student's total learning environment.

Checklists and Rating Scales

A checklist is a list of questions that the respondent completes by checking the appropriate responses. The respondent may answer yes or no or may check off the statements that apply to the student. The teacher and/or parents may complete the checklist. An example of a behavioral checklist is given in Figure 9.5.

A rating questionnaire may be similar in content to a checklist; however, the respondent rates the answer. For example, the format of the preceding checklist would change so that the respondent would rate student behaviors as never, almost never, sometimes, somewhat often, frequently, or almost always. This format allows for the interpretation of the extremes. The student behavior might be rated as almost never completing assignments but frequently being verbally

	Yes	No
1. Student is prepared for work each period.	______	______
2. Student begins assignment on request.	______	______
3. Student stays on task with no distractions.	______	______
4. Student completes tasks.	______	______
5. Student stays on task but is sometimes distracted.	______	______
6. Student complies with teacher requests.	______	______
7. Student raises hand to speak.	______	______
8. Student talks out inappropriately.	______	______
9. Student completes homework.	______	______
10. Student is aggressive toward peers.	______	______
11. Student is disruptive during class.	______	______
12. Student talks out of turn.	______	______
13. Student is verbally aggressive.	______	______
14. Student has damaged property belonging to others.	______	______

Figure 9.5
Behavioral checklist.

aggressive and sometimes damaging property. This information helps the teacher pinpoint areas that need observation and further evaluation.

Elliot, Busse, and Gresham (1993) suggested that the following issues be considered when using rating scales:

1. Ratings are summaries of observations of the relative frequency of specific behaviors.
2. Ratings of social behavior are judgements affected by one's environment and rater's standards for behavior.
3. The social validity of the behaviors one assesses and eventually treats should be understood.
4. Multiple assessors of the same child's behavior may agree only moderately.
5. Many characteristics of a student may influence social behavior; however, the student's sex is a particularly salient variable.

Several rating forms are commonly used in the assessment of behavior problems. Many of these include forms for teachers and parents. Common examples include the Teacher Report Form (Achenbach, 1991b) and the Child Behavior Checklist (Achenbach, 1991a), the Behavior Rating Profile–2 (Brown & Hammill, 1990), and the Conners Teacher Rating Scales and Conners Parent Rating Scales (1989, 1990). These forms and scoring systems ask a variety of questions about the student, and the parent or teacher rates the student on each item.

Child Behavior Checklist: Parent, Teacher, and Youth Report Forms. The CBCL system is built upon the Child Behavior Checklist (Achenbach, 1991a), which is the parent report form, and companion forms such as the Teacher Report Form (Achenbach, 1991b) and the Youth Self-Report (Achenbach, 1991c). (The system's Direct Observation Form and interview form are discussed in other sections of this chapter.)

The Achenbach system allows for the student to be rated on both positive, or adaptive, behaviors and behavioral syndromes. In 1991, the author revised the system to allow the profiles to be scored consistently across the parent, teacher, and youth scales (McConaughy, 1993). In addition to the rating scales, the parent form includes some open-ended questions, such as "What concerns you most about your child?"

Two CBCL forms are available for parents: one for children aged 2–3 years and another for students aged 4–18 years. The Teacher Report Form is for students aged 5–18. Items on these instruments are closely related so that both parents and teachers are rating the student on similar dimensions. An example of a Teacher Report Form profile is shown in Figure 9.6.

In addition to the teacher and parent forms, a self-rating form is available for students aged 11–18. The Youth Self-Report (Achenbach, 1991c) covers many of the same topics as the teacher and parent forms. This instrument can be evaluated qualitatively to determine the student's perceptions of himself. The student also answers items concerning current academic achievement and rates himself on social dimensions such as getting along with family members.

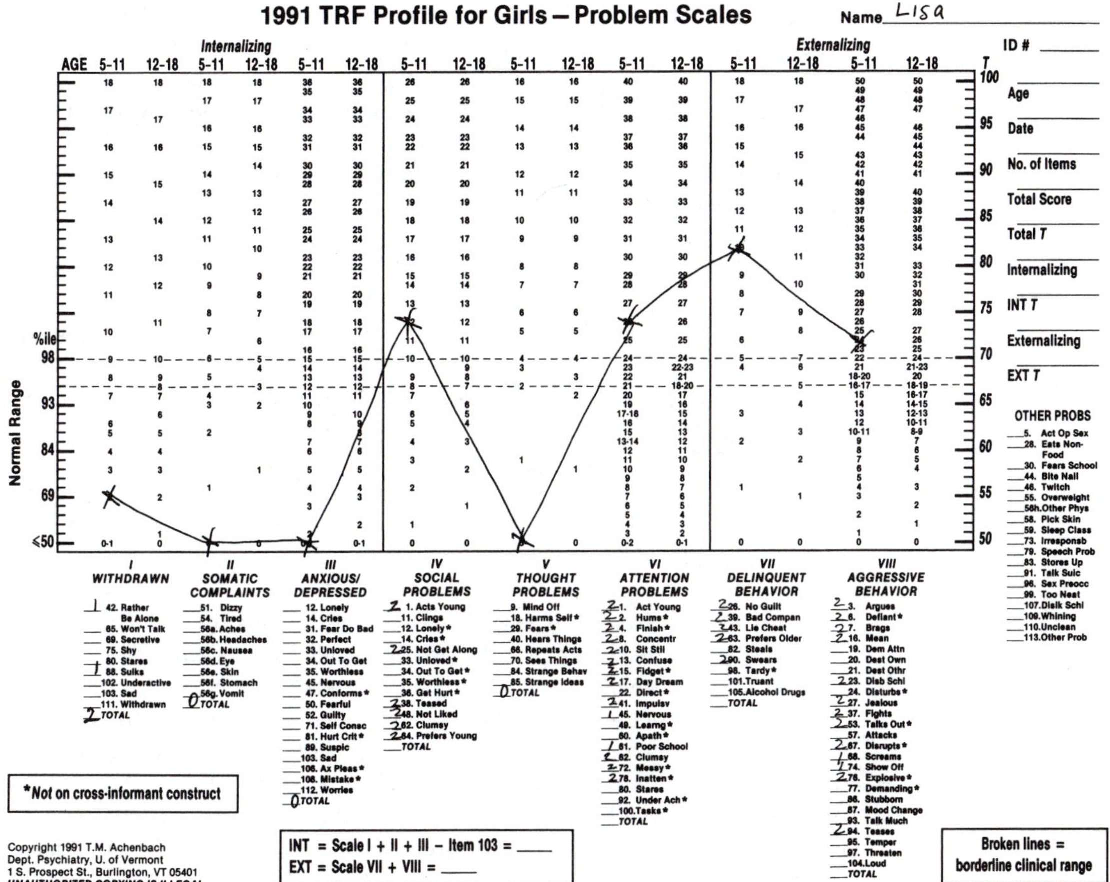

Figure 9.6

CBCL Teacher Report Form showing sample profile for female student.

Source: From *Manual for the Teacher Report Form and 1991 Profile* by T. M. Achenbach, 1991, Burlington: University of Vermont Department of Psychiatry. Copyright 1991 by T. M. Achenbach. Reprinted by permission.

Examiner manuals address the issues of validity and reliability for each of the individual parts of the multiaxial CBCL system by Achenbach (1991a, 1991b, 1991c). The examiner is provided with detailed information about content and criterion-related validity and the discriminant validity of using cutoff scores to identify students with specific behavioral problems. Test-retest, testing across time, and reliability of raters is presented, and technical quality of the systems appears to be adequate or above on all measures.

Behavior Rating Profile–2. The Behavior Rating Profile–2 (Brown & Hammill, 1990) includes forms for the student, parent, and teacher. The student completes the rating by marking that items are true or false about himself. The teacher and parents rate the student by marking that the items are very much like the student, not like the student, like the student, or not at all like the student. This system allows the examiner to compare how the student, teacher, and parent perceive the student. It also categorizes the student's perceptions into the various environments of the student's life: school, home, and peer relationships. This enables the examiner to determine if the student has more positive feelings about school, relationships with peers, or relationships with parents. The instrument is scored using a standard score with a mean of 10 and a standard deviation of 3. The examiner can plot a profile that presents a view of how the student, parent, and teacher perceive the student.

The manual provides reliability and validity information that includes studies conducted with relatively small samples. The internal consistency and test-retest coefficients seem to be adequate, with many reported to be in the .80s. Validity studies include criterion-related research with reported coefficients ranging from below acceptable levels to adequate. The authors provide discussion of content and construct validity.

Conners Rating Scales. The Conners system (Conners, 1990) includes a rating scale of 93 items for parents, another scale of 48 items for parents, a teacher rating scale of 39 items, and a shorter teacher rating scale of 28 items. The dimensions of the Conners Rating Scales include conduct disorders, learning problems, somatic disorders, hyperactivity, attention problems, and anxiety. The rating scales' special "Quick Score" paper enables the teacher or other member of the multidisciplinary team to score the form in minutes. The scoring is based on *T* scores, and students who score above 70 are considered to have behaviors clinically more significant than typical age and gender peers.

Conners presents a review of literature of reliability and validity studies in the examiner's manual. Reliability across time has been studied, and coefficients are listed in the manual for both teacher and parent rating forms. Coefficients range from below acceptable levels to adequate—from .33 to .91. Interrater reliability ranges from .39 to .94 on teacher ratings and from .46 to .85 between parents on the parent rating forms. Interrater reliability between teachers and parents ranges from .23 to .49 and is generally below acceptable levels. A study of internal consistency indicated coefficients ranging from .61 to .94 on individual clinical scales.

Validity studies in the Conners examiner's manual address predictive validity, discriminant validity, concurrent validity, and construct validity. Information concerning this research is brief and seems to range from below acceptable levels to adequate. Many of the studies included small samples, and it appears that additional research may enhance the information provided in the examiner's manual.

Questionnaires and Interviews

The questions found on questionnaires are similar to the items on checklists, but the respondent is encouraged to describe the behaviors or situations where the behavior occurs. The respondent answers with narrative statements. For example, the questions might appear as follows:

1. How is the student prepared for class each day?
2. Describe how the student begins assignments during class.
3. How does the student perform during distractions?
4. How often does the student complete homework assignments?
5. How does the student respond during class discussions?

The respondent should be encouraged to provide objective responses that describe as many variables of the behavior as possible.

Interviews are completed using questions similar to those used on questionnaires. The evaluator verbally asks the respondent the questions and encourages objective, detailed information. The interview format may also be used with the student to obtain information about the student's feelings and perceptions about the target behaviors. Figure 9.7 illustrates how an interview could be adapted so that both parents and the student could provide answers.

Child Behavior Checklist: Semistructured Clinical Interview. Interviews may be conducted by different members of the multidisciplinary team. Often, these interviews are unstructured and informal. Achenbach and McConaughy (1989, 1990) developed a semistructured interview and observation form to be used with students aged 5–11. This interview assesses the student's feelings about school, family, and peers as well as affect or emotional functioning. In addition to the interview, the examiner is provided

Parent Interview

1. How do you think your child feels about school this year?
2. Tell me how your child completes homework assignments.
3. Describe the responsibilities your child has at home.

Student Interview

1. Tell me how you feel about school this year.
2. Describe how you go about finishing your homework.
3. What type of things are you expected to do at home? Do you think you complete those things most of the time?

Figure 9.7
Interview questions adapted for both parent and student.

with an observation form to rate behaviors of and comments by the student observed during the interview. The student is asked open-ended questions and guided through the interview process. This interview can be useful in determining the current social and emotional issues concerning the student.

Sociograms

The sociogram method enables the teacher to obtain information about the group dynamics and structure within the classroom. This information can be interpreted to determine which students are well liked by their peers, which students are considered to be the leaders in the group, and which students are believed to be successful in school.

A sociogram is constructed by designing questions that all members of the class will be asked to answer. The questions might include: "Who would you select to be in your group for the science project?" or "Who would you invite to the movies?" The answers are then collected and interpreted by the teacher. The diagram in Figure 9.8a illustrates a sociogram; Figure 9.8b lists questions asked of a class of fourth-grade students.

The data are analyzed to determine who the class members perceive as being the class stars, the social isolates, and so on. The teacher also can determine where mutual choices exist (where two students share the same feelings about one another) and can identify cliques and persons who are neglected. The teacher can then use this information to intervene and structure social and academic situations that would promote fair social skills development. Role-plays, class projects, and school social activities could be used to increase the interpersonal interaction opportunities for social isolates and neglectees.

☐ CHECK YOUR UNDERSTANDING

Complete Activity 9.3.

Activity 9.3

Use Figure 9.8a to analyze the social dynamics of this classroom.

1. Which students have made mutual choices? ______________________

2. Which students are social isolates? ______________________

3. Which students appear to be in cliques? ______________________

4. Who are the class stars in social popularity? ______________________

5. Who are the academic stars? ______________________

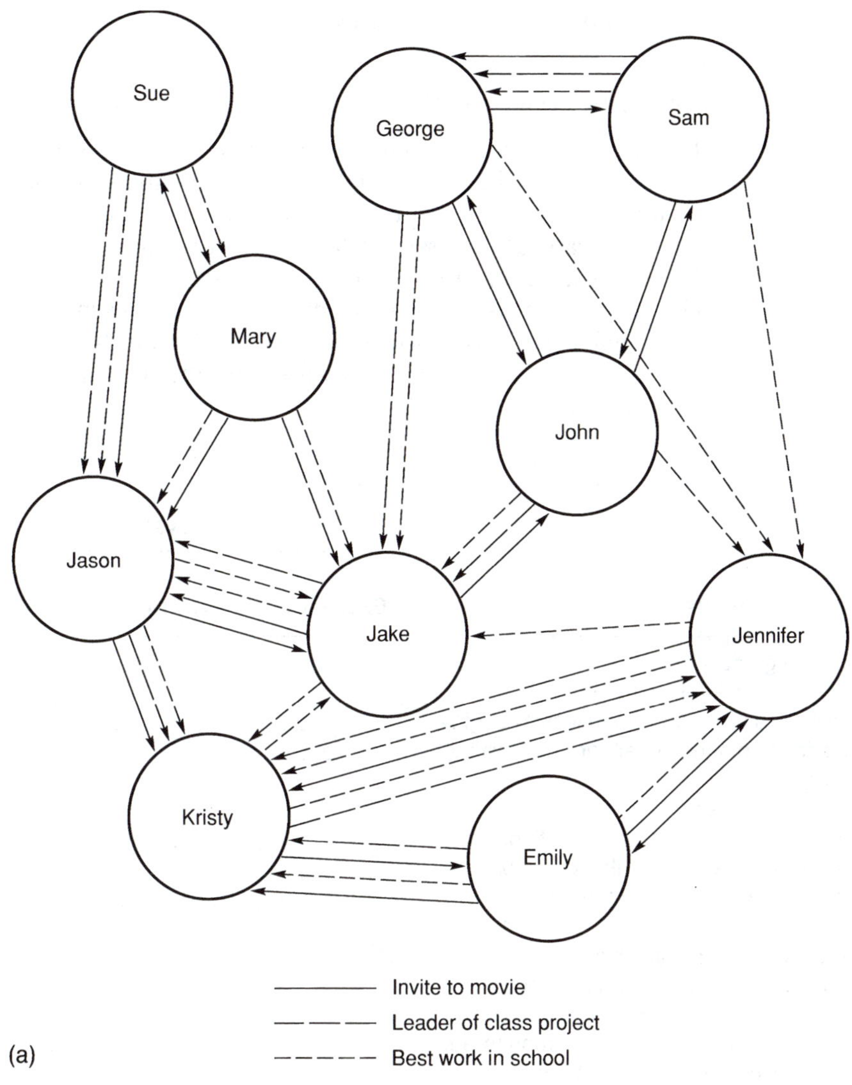

Sociogram questions.

1. Name two students in our class whom you would most like to invite to a movie (or other activity).

a. _______________

b. _______________

2. In our class, whom would you like to be the leader of our class project? _______________

3. Name two students in our class who do the best work in school.

a. _______________

b. _______________

(b)

Figure 9.8
Sociogram (a) and sociogram questions (b).

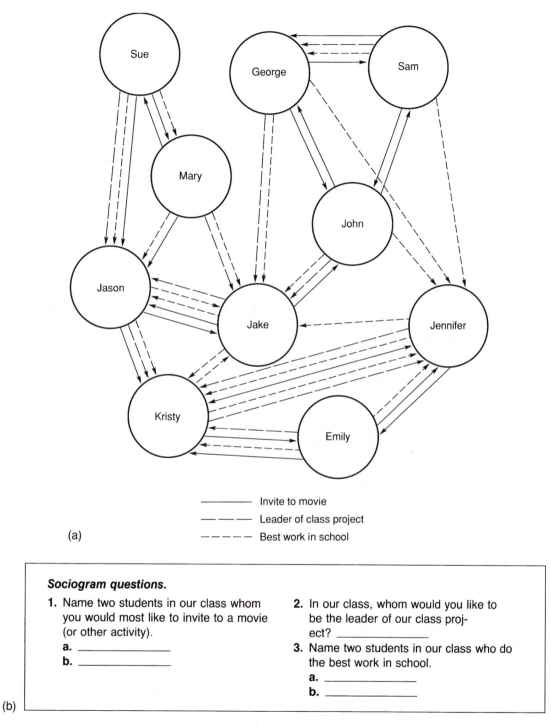

Ecological Assessment

Ecological assessment analyzes the student's total learning environment. This analysis includes the student's interactions with others (peers, teachers, paraprofessionals, parents, and other persons who are directly involved with the student's learning process); the teacher's interactions with other students in the classroom; the methods of presentation of materials; materials used in the classroom; the physical environment; and the student's interactions with others in different settings, such as the playground or lunchroom. All of the informal behavioral assessment methods presented thus far may be used as a part of ecological assessment.

Competencies	Evaluation		
	Excellent	Average	Improvement Comments
1. Classroom organization			
a. Instructional strategies are varied.	______	______	______
b. All materials are ready when lesson begins.	______	______	______
c. Lessons are planned in accordance with curriculum goals.	______	______	______
2. Instructional objectives			
a. Instructional objectives are identified.	______	______	______
b. Objectives are age- and ability-appropriate.	______	______	______
c. Objectives are in measurable terms.	______	______	______
3. Instruction			
a. Direct instruction is maximized.	______	______	______
b. Assignments are geared so that they meet needs of different abilities.	______	______	______
c. Individualized instruction is well monitored.	______	______	______
d. Instruction involves different student learning modalities.	______	______	______
e. Aides effectively managed.	______	______	______
4. Skill development			
a. Ideas are sequentially developed from simple to complex.	______	______	______
b. Steps in growth are monitored.	______	______	______
c. Teacher's language is clear and appropriate.	______	______	______
d. Questions and activities are appropriate.	______	______	______

Figure 9.9
Survey to evaluate teaching competency.
Source: From *Informal Assessment in Education* (pp. 341–344) by G. R. Guerin and A. S. Maier, 1983, Palo Alto, CA: Mayfield Publishing. Copyright 1983 by Mayfield Publishing. Reprinted by permission.

Competencies	Evaluation		
	Excellent	Average	Improvement Comments
5. Assessment and evaluation			
a. Group tests used to monitor program effectiveness.	________	________	________
b. Individual assessment used to measure pupil growth.	________	________	________
c. Informal assessment of program and pupil movement.	________	________	________
d. Group and individual records maintained in understandable form.	________	________	________
6. Reporting			
a. Parent conferences are preplanned and well organized.	________	________	________
b. Relationship with parents is supportive, cooperative, and informative.	________	________	________
7. Materials			
a. Audiovisual material is used effectively.	________	________	________
b. Aides are used to assist students understand concepts and develop skills.	________	________	________
c. Seat work is appropriate and can be successfully completed.	________	________	________
d. Blackboard is used to present material, illustrate lessons, organize activities, etc.	________	________	________
8. Interaction			
a. Communicates clearly and respectfully with students.	________	________	________
b. Maintains classroom order and discipline.	________	________	________
c. Listens to students and attempt to understand what they say.	________	________	________
d. Is positive and supportive of student accomplishments.	________	________	________

Figure 9.9 *continued*

The teacher variable is one area that may be assessed by direct observation and other techniques, such as questionnaires and self-assessment. One method of observing the teacher interaction variable, suggested by Guerin and Maier (1983), is a survey form to evaluate teaching competency (Figure 9.9). This type of survey can be completed by the teacher or by an objective observer. This information may also be obtained by using student evaluations that ask similar questions.

The student's educational materials should be evaluated for their appropriateness for the individual student. The level of difficulty, format, and mode of presentation and response are important considerations. The following variables should be evaluated when assessing materials:

Analyzing Instructional Materials

1. Are the objectives of the materials appropriate for the student?
2. Do the ability/readability levels match the current instructional level of the student?
3. Is the interest level appropriate for the student?
4. Does the method of presentation match the student's strongest modality for learning?
5. Are prerequisite steps needed before the student can attempt the task?
6. Does the format of the material contain extraneous stimuli that can confuse or distract the student?
7. Does the material contain information not necessary for task completion?
8. Are too many tasks contained on one page?
9. Is the student capable of completing the task in the amount of time allowed?
10. Does the task need to be broken down into smaller tasks?
11. Is the student capable of responding with relative ease, in the manner required by the materials?
12. Can the criterion level for success be reduced?
13. Does the material allow the student to self-check or self-correct?
14. Does the material allow the student to observe progress? (Overton, 1987, pp. 111–115)

Projective Assessment Techniques

projective techniques Techniques used to analyze a student's feelings by what the student projects into the story card or other stimulus.

sentence completion tests Stems of sentences that the student completes; analyzed for themes.

drawing tests Tests in which student draws figures, houses, trees, or families; scored developmentally and projectively.

apperception Student's feelings about what he perceives to be happening in a picture or other stimulus; influenced by personal experiences.

The measures presented in this section are measures that are scored more subjectively and are often referred to as **projective techniques**. These measures include **sentence completion instruments, drawing tests** by students, and **apperception** tests, which are tests that require the student to tell a story about picture cards. These instruments are most likely administered by the school psychologist, counselor, or other professional, such as a clinical psychologist, who has the training and experience required to administer such instruments. Teachers and other members of the multidisciplinary team may be required to make eligibility and planning decisions based on the results of these instruments. It is beneficial to teachers, therefore, to understand the nature of the instruments and how they might be used in the assessment process.

Sentence Completion Tests

Sentence completion tests provide stems or beginnings of sentences that the student is required to finish. The stems have been selected to elicit comments from the student on such topics as relationships with parents and friends and feelings about oneself. The examiner analyzes the comments written by the student for themes rather than analyzing each sentence independently. The Rotter Incomplete Sentence Blank (Rotter & Rafferty, 1950) is an example of this type of instrument. Figure 9.10 presents stems similar to those on sentence completion blanks.

Drawing Tests

Drawing tests attempt to screen the student's feelings about self, home, and family. Each of these instruments follow a simple format. The student is presented with a form or a piece of plain paper and is asked to draw a picture of himself; of a house, a tree, and a person; or of his family doing something together. These tests are commonly known as the Draw-a-Person, Human-Figure Drawing, House-Tree-Person, and Kinetic Family Drawings. The drawings may be scored subjectively by an examiner who has had training and experience in this type of assessment. More empirically based scoring systems are also available: the Kinetic Family Drawing System for Family and School (Knoff & Prout, 1985), the Draw-a-Person: Screening Procedure for Emotional Disturbance (Naglieri, McNeish, & Bardos, 1991), and the Human Figure Drawing Test (Koppitz, 1968). The Draw-a-Person can be scored developmentally using a system like those by Naglieri (1985) or Harris (1963); these systems are presented in chapter 11.

The newer versions of scoring systems include standardization information and developmental information. The Kinetic Family Drawing System for Family and School (Knoff & Prout, 1985) includes questions that the examiner asks the student about the drawings. For example, one question is "What does this person need most?" (Knoff & Prout, 1985, p. 5). The scoring booklet provides various characteristics that the student may have included in the drawings. The examiner checks to see if a characteristic, such as the omission of body parts, is present in the student's drawing. Guidelines for interpreting these characteristics are provided in the manual through a listing of relevant research on drawing analysis. The examiner analyzes themes that exist within the drawing on such dimensions as figure characteristics and actions between figures. Several case studies are provided for the examiner to use as guidelines for learning how to interpret the drawings.

1. Sometimes I wish ______________________.
2. I wish my mother would ______________________.
3. I feel sad when ______________________.
4. My friends always ______________________.
5. My father ______________________.

Figure 9.10
Sample items from a sentence completion test.

The scoring system of the Draw-a-Person: Screening Procedure for Emotional Disturbance (1991) uses scoring templates and a norm-referenced method of scoring the drawings. The instrument is to be used as a screening device to determine if the student needs further emotional or behavioral assessment. The manual provides examples of using the templates and scoring exercises using case studies for learning the system. Derived scores include *T* scores with a mean of 50 and a standard deviation of 10 and percentile ranks. The scores are interpreted as follows (Naglieri et al., 1991):

Less than 55	Further evaluation is not indicated
55 to 64	Further evaluation is indicated
65 and above	Further evaluation is strongly indicated (p. 63)

An example of the template scoring system from the manual is presented in Figure 9.11.

The standardization information and technical data provided in the Naglieri et al. (1991) manual is fairly extensive and impressive for a projective drawing instrument. The sample included 2,260 students, ages 6 to 17 years. Approximately 200 students were represented in each age group. Consideration was

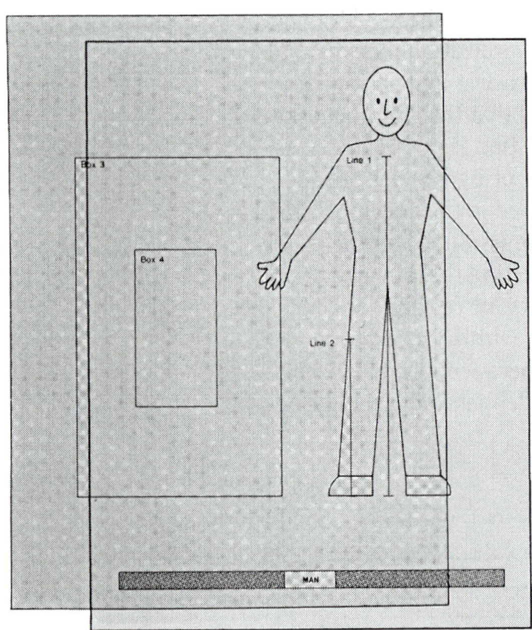

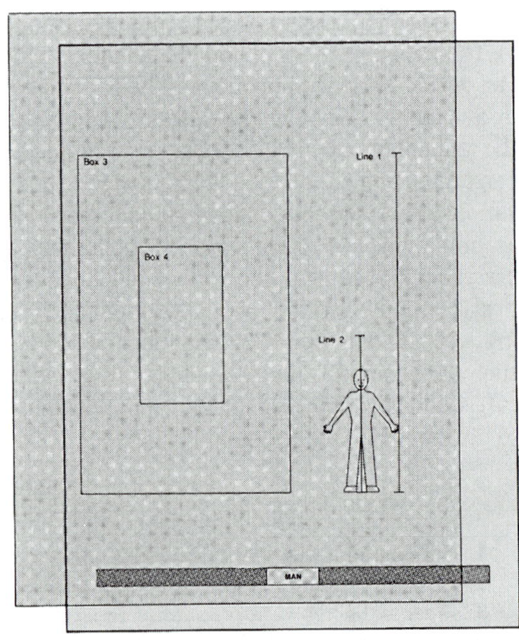

Figure 9.11

Example of Naglieri et al.'s template scoring system for the Draw-a-Person test.

Source: From *Draw a Person: Screening Procedure for Emotional Disturbance, Examiner's Manual* (p. 23) by J. A. Naglieri, T. J. McNeish, and A. N. Bardos, 1991, Austin, TX: Pro-Ed. Copyright 1991 by Pro-Ed, Inc. Reprinted by permission.

given for age, sex, geographic region, population of community, ethnicity, race, parent occupation, and socioeconomic status.

Internal consistency was researched using the coefficient alpha, and coefficients were adequate, ranging from .67 to .78. The standard error of measurement is approximately 5 for all ages. The test-retest information gives a coefficient of .67; however, the sample for this study was fairly small ($n = 67$). Both intrarater and interrater agreement was studied and resulted in coefficients of .83 and .84, respectively. This study was also small, using 54 cases and 2 raters.

Descriptive statistics are included for validity studies that used the scoring system to compare students who had been clinically diagnosed with emotional or behavioral problems to students without such problems. The scoring system did discriminate between the groups at least at the .05 significance level. Construct validity is supported by discriminant validity studies of intelligence testing and Naglieri et al.'s Draw-a-Person scoring system. The research presented indicates that two separate areas are assessed by the Draw-a-Person and intelligence tests.

Apperception Tests

Apperception tests consist of a set of picture or story cards that have been designed to elicit responses about emotional issues. These instruments may be administered and interpreted only by professionals with the training and experience required by the test developers. Most of these projective techniques require that the examiner possess advanced graduate-level training in psychological assessment. Because apperception tests may contribute information used by the multidisciplinary team to determine educational and behavioral interventions, teachers should understand what these instruments attempt to measure and how they are interpreted. Two commonly used instruments are the Children's Apperception Test (Bellak & Bellak, 1949, 1952; Bellak & Hurvich, 1965) and the Roberts Apperception Test for Children (Roberts, 1982).

Children's Apperception Test (CAT). Two tests and a supplement for special situations comprise the CAT (Bellak & Bellak, 1949, 1952; Bellak & Hurvich, 1965). The original test (animal figures) consists of 10 picture cards that depict animals engaged in human situations. The authors developed the instrument as an apperception method, which they define as "a method of investigating personality by studying the dynamic meaningfulness of the individual differences in perception of standard stimuli" (Bellak & Bellak, 1949, p. 1). The examiner evaluates a student's verbal responses to the picture cards in an effort to better understand how the student feels about himself and his relationships with family members.

The authors originally believed younger children would identify more readily with animal figures and that these figures were more cultural and gender free. They later developed the CAT human figures as an answer to research studies that indicated the value of human figure picture cards (Bellak & Hurvich, 1965). These picture story cards maintain many of the same story themes and emotionally charged situations as in the animal figures, but the figures are now human, with some remaining fairly gender neutral.

The supplement to the CAT (Bellak & Bellak, 1952) contains various pictures depicting unusual situations using animal figures. Examples include a picture of a pregnant "mother" type animal, an animal in a doctor's office, and an animal walking with crutches. Any of these specific cards may be selected by the examiner and used with the animal or human figures.

The CAT is scored subjectively along psychoanalytic themes such as regression, fear, anxiety, and denial; the manuals provide guidelines for scoring the instrument. Technical data provided in the manuals do not meet the standards set forth by many test developers in terms of reliability and validity. Figure 9.12 presents a picture story card from the animal figures of the CAT.

Roberts Apperception Test for Children. The Roberts Apperception Test for Children (McArthur & Roberts, 1982) presents story picture cards of human figures engaged in situations with family members and peers. The test was de-

Figure 9.12
Picture card 8 of the Children's Apperception Test.

Source: From *Children's Apperception Test (Animal Figures)* by L. Bellak and S. S. Bellak, 1949, Larchmont, NY: C.P.S. Copyright 1991 by C.P.S., Inc. Reprinted by permission of C.P.S., Inc., Box 83, Larchmont, NY 10538.

veloped for use with students aged 6 through 15 years. Of 27 stimulus cards, the student responds to 11 cards that are specific to the student's gender and to five gender-neutral cards. The cards were designed to elicit comments about the student's feelings about fear, parental relationships, dependency, peer and racial interaction, and so on. The examiner instructs the student to tell a story about what happened before, during, and after each scene pictured and to tell what the characters are doing, saying, and thinking.

The examiner scores responses according to guidelines set forth in the manual, which gives information on adaptive indicators, clinical problems such as aggression or anxiety, and supplemental measures, such as ego functioning. An interpersonal matrix allows the examiner to compute the child's responses about specific individuals, such as siblings, mother, father, school personnel, and so on.

The manual includes information about the standardization of the instrument as well as studies comparing students within the normal range of emotional functioning with several different clinical samples. Reliability information includes interrater reliability and split-half reliability studies. Coefficients ranged from .44 to .86 on split-half measures. The validity information included in the manual presents several studies of the factors measured as well as the instrument's ability to discriminate clinical from nonclinical groups. Generally, the information presented appears to be adequate for this type of projective instrument.

Computerized Assessment of Attention Disorders

Instruments have been developed for the assessment of sustained focused attention and impulsive responding patterns. Difficulty with these behaviors is believed to be characteristic of students with attention deficit disorders. These types of difficulties may be manifested as distractibility, impulsivity, and overactivity in classroom situations. These instruments should not be used as a single measure of attention problems, but rather should be used in combination with other measures, particularly classroom observations. Two such computerized systems currently used in clinical practice and research are the Continuous Performance Test (Gordon, 1983) and the Conners' Continuous Performance Test (Conners, 1993). All tests of this general type are known as CPTs.

Continuous Performance Test

In Gordon's (1983) Continuous Performance Test, the student must discriminate between visual stimuli presented for a period of 9 minutes. The stimuli are numbers that appear at the rate of 1 per second. Scores are computed for the number of correct responses, omissions, and commissions. This instrument has been widely researched, and the author reports reliability coefficients ranging from .66 to .80.

Conners' Continuous Performance Test

Conners (1993) Continuous Performance Test is presented in much the same manner as Gordon's (1983) version. This CPT, however, lasts for 14 minutes, and the visual stimuli, letters, appear at varying rates throughout the administration. The student must maintain focused sustained attention, and the number of targets hit is calculated to determine impulsivity and loss of attention. Interpretive, computer-generated reports give derived scores for hit rate, reaction time, pattern for standard error or variability, omissions, commissions, attentiveness, and response tendencies such as risk taking. Data included in the manual and from computer reports compare the student with age and gender peers in a clinical group of students with attention deficit disorders.

Research and Issues

The assessment of emotional and behavioral problems is by nature more ambiguous than other types of assessment, such as assessment of intellectual or academic achievement ability. The techniques range from systematic observations and computer assessment to projective techniques, such as telling stories about picture cards. The research on each of these methods has existed in volumes in the literature for many years. The research summarized in the following list represents some of the most recent studies using the instruments often employed in settings that serve children and youth. Other measures, such as the Rorschach Inkblot Test (Rorschach, 1921, 1942), are more often used in clinical settings and therefore were not included in this text.

1. In a study using school-referred males comparing the Teacher Report Form and the Child Behavior Checklist to the Youth Self-Report, it was found that the youth and the teacher and parent forms did not have high agreement, especially when the students rated themselves on externalizing behaviors (Lee, Elliott, & Barbour, 1994). The study found a somewhat higher agreement between parents and teachers in rating students. These findings seem to suggest that youth tend to underrate themselves on problem behaviors, which emphasizes the need for multimethod and multi-informant assessment.

2. Stanford and Hynd (1994) studied the difference in students with attention deficit disorder with and without hyperactivity and students with learning disabilities. Parents and teachers of students with hyperactivity endorsed more externalizing types of items on the Child Behavior Checklist. Parents and teachers of students who had attention deficit without hyperactivity and students with learning disabilities endorsed fewer externalizing items.

3. A study in a public school setting focused on interrater reliability among teachers using the Conners Teacher Rating Scale. Both certified teachers of students with emotional problems and their teacher aides were consistent in their ratings (Mattison, Bagnato, Mayes, & Felix, 1990). The strongest interrater correlations were on the scale's hyperactivity and conduct disorders factors. This seems to suggest that the Conners Teacher Rating Scale has adequate interrater reliability and may be an appropriate instrument, in conjunction with other assessment techniques, for screening for acting out or externalizing behaviors.

4. Research of family drawings by students with divorced parents and those without divorced parents indicated differences around themes of interpersonal relationships (Spigelman, Spigelman, & Englesson, 1992). Students from homes with divorce seemed to have more omissions of family members and indications of conflict within relationships with siblings.

5. A study of human figure drawings with 5-year-old students resulted in finding no significant differences between the drawings of aggressive and nonaggressive students (Norford & Barakat, 1990). It appears that this type of technique is not developmentally appropriate for use with students younger than 6.

6. Research using chronically ill children found that the Roberts Apperception Test for Children was able to differentiate children with adaptive coping styles and children with maladaptive coping styles (Palomares, Crowley, Worchel, Olson, & Rae, 1991).

7. A study of students with and those without attention deficit disorder identified both false positives and false negatives during use of a Continuous Performance Test (Trommer, Hoeppner, Lorber, & Armstrong, 1988). In addition, differences in these groups on other measures suggest that CPTs may involve some higher level cognitive tasks rather than pure attentive ability. Thus, CPTs should be interpreted with caution and always should be analyzed with data from multiple sources.

8. Research comparing CPT performance of students with learning disabilities and a matched control group indicated that students with learning disabilities made more omission errors but did not differ on the number of commission errors (Eliason & Richman, 1987). The authors suggest that the constructs of attention and memory are highly interrelated and may result in students with learning disabilities making more omission errors on this type of measure.

9. Research using a CPT determined favorable decreases in the number of errors made in a sample of students with attention deficit disorder following treatment with methylphenidate (Ritalin) (Forness, Swanson, Cantwell, Guthrie, & Sena, 1992). This suggests that CPTs may be sensitive to measurement of the treatment of students with stimulant medication.

10. On a CPT, students with attention deficit disorder with hyperactivity made almost twice the number of errors of commission as students with attention deficit disorder without hyperactivity (Barkley, DuPaul, & McMurray, 1990). In this same study, it was determined that students with attention deficit disorder and hyperactivity scored significantly worse on the CBCL aggressive and delinquent scales than did students with attention deficit disorder without hyperactivity, students with learning disabilities, and the control sample of students.

It is evident from the small sample of research reviewed in this chapter that many factors are to be considered in the assessment of students exhibiting behavioral and emotional problems. It is important that multiple measures and multiple informants be used and that the individual student's environment be assessed as well (Clarizio & Higgins, 1989). In a review of relevant research on assessment of attention and behavioral disorders, Schaughency and Rothlind (1991) stressed the need for the use of a variety of methods such as interviews, teacher ratings, observations, and peer nominations. These techniques may aid in the assessment of the student to determine if the difficulties are reactions to the environment or to current stress within the student's world. As with all assessment, a holistic view of the complete student and his environment is necessary.

Exercises

Part I

Match the following terms with the correct definitions.

A. checklist
B. behavioral observations
C. permanent product recording
D. academic engaged time
E. questionnaire
F. duration recording
G. interval recording
H. target behavior
I. systematic observation
J. projective techniques
K. apperception
L. work samples
M. CPT
N. anecdotal recording
O. event recording
P. latency recording
Q. time sampling
R. baseline
S. sentence completion tests
T. drawing tests

_______ **1.** Planned observations less subject to bias and inaccurate information about a student's behavior.
_______ **2.** Observations that involve the length of time a behavior occurs.
_______ **3.** Observations that involve the amount of time that elapses from the presentation of a stimulus until the response occurs.
_______ **4.** Recording the frequency of the target behavior.
_______ **5.** The time when the student is actively involved in the learning process.
_______ **6.** Observations of student behavior.
_______ **7.** Observations of behavior in which the teacher notes all the behaviors and interactions that occur during a given period of time.
_______ **8.** Samples of a student's work.
_______ **9.** The frequency, duration, or latency of a behavior determined before behavioral intervention.
_______ **10.** A specific behavior that requires intervention by the teacher to promote optimal academic or social learning.

_________ **11.** When the behavioral observation samples behavior through the day or class period.
_________ **12.** Sampling a behavior intermittently for very brief periods of time; used to observe frequently occurring behaviors.
_________ **13.** Stems of sentences that the student completes; analyzed for themes.
_________ **14.** Recording any products made by the student.
_________ **15.** A list of academic or behavioral skills that must be mastered by the student.
_________ **16.** Techniques used to analyze a student's feelings by what the student projects into the story card or other stimulus.
_________ **17.** Questions about a student's behavior or academic concerns, which may be answered by the student or by the parent or teacher.
_________ **18.** Student's feelings about what he perceives in a picture or other stimulus; used in projective assessment.
_________ **19.** Tests in which a student draws figures, houses, trees, or families; scored developmentally and projectively.

Part II

Use the terms in Part I to select a method of informal assessment for the following situations. Write the reason for your selection.

1. A student takes a very long time to complete assignments. You notice that he does not seem to begin his assignments immediately.
Method of assessment: ____
____
Reason: ____
____

2. A student turns homework in inconsistently. You want to know how often the student turns in the assignments.
Method of assessment: ____
____
Reason: ____
____

Part III

Select the correct assessment method to match the following descriptions.

A. Child Behavior Checklist (parent report form)
B. Child Behavior Checklist: Teacher Report Form
C. Child Behavior Checklist: Semistructured Clinical Interview
D. Child Behavior Checklist: Youth Self-Report
E. Child Behavior Checklist: Direct Observation Form

F. Conners' Continuous Performance Test
G. Behavior Rating Profile–2
H. Roberts Apperception Test for Children
I. Children's Apperception Test
J. Conners Teacher Rating Scale
K. Draw-a-Person: Screening Procedure for Emotional Disturbance

_________ **1.** This technique allows the examiner to determine if the child has more positive responses toward parents, school, or peers.

_________ **2.** This technique is completed by parents and is part of a multiaxial system that includes observation and teacher report forms.

_________ **3.** This computerized assessment method is a part of the assessment for attention deficit disorders.

_________ **4.** This observation form is used to compare the student with two grade and gender class peers.

_________ **5.** This projective assessment technique contains a version with animal figures.

_________ **6.** This self-rating system is part of a multiaxial system of assessing behavior for students 11–18 years.

_________ **7.** This projective drawing technique is scored as a screening instrument to determine if the student needs additional behavioral/emotional assessment.

_________ **8.** This projective technique can be scored for the student's ability to cope.

References

Achenbach, T. M. (1986). *Child Behavior Checklist—Direct Observation Form, Revised Edition.* Burlington: University of Vermont Center for Children, Youth, and Families.

Achenbach, T. M. (1991a). *Manual for the Child Behavior Checklist/4-18 and 1991 Profile.* Burlington: University of Vermont Department of Psychiatry.

Achenbach, T. M. (1991b). *Manual for the Teacher Report Form and 1991 Profile.* Burlington: University of Vermont Department of Psychiatry.

Achenbach, T. M. (1991c). *Manual for the Youth Self-Report and 1991 Profile.* Burlington: University of Vermont Department of Psychiatry.

Achenbach, T. M. (1992). *Manual for the Child Behavior Checklist/2-3 and the 1992 Profile.* Burlington: University of Vermont Department of Psychiatry.

Achenbach, T. M., & McConaughy, S. H. (1989, 1990). *Semistructured Clinical Interview—Observation Form.* Burlington: University of Vermont Center for Children, Youth, and Families.

Barkley, R. A., DuPaul, G. J., & McMurray, M. B. (1990). Comprehensive evaluation of attention deficit disorder with and without hyperactivity as defined by research criteria. *Journal of Consulting and Clinical Psychology. 58*(6), 775–789.

Bellak, L, & Bellak, S. S. (1949). *Children's Apperception Test (animal figures).* Larchmont, NY: C.P.S.

Bellak, L., & Bellak, S. S. (1952). *Manual for the supplement for the Children's Apperception Test.* Larchmont, NY: C.P.S.

Bellak, L., & Hurvich, M. S. (1965). *Children's Apperception Test (human figures) manual.* Larchment, NY: C.P.S.

Brown, L., & Hammill, D. (1990). *Behavior Rating Profile* (2nd ed.). Austin, TX: Pro-Ed.

Clarizio, H. F., & Higgins, M. M. (1989). Assessment of severe emotional impairment: Practices and problems. *Psychology in the Schools, 26,* 154–162.

Conners, C. K. (1993). *Conners' Continuous Performance Test.* North Tonawanda, NY: Multi-Health Systems.

Conners, C. K. (1989). *Conners Teacher Rating Scales.* North Tonawanda, NY: Multi-Health Systems.

Conners, C. K. (1990). *Conners Rating Scales manual—Conners Teacher Rating Scales, Conners Parent Rating Scales, Instruments for use with children and adolescents.* North Tonawanda, NY: Multi-Health Systems.

Eliason, M. J., & Richman, L. C. (1987). The Continuous Performance Test in learning disabled and nondisabled children. *Journal of Learning Disabilities, 20*(10), 614–619.

Elliot, S. N., Busse, R. T., & Gresham, F. M. (1993). Behavior rating scales: Issues of use and development. *School Psychology Review, 22*(2), 313–321.

Evans, W. H., Evans, S. S., & Schmid, R. E. (1989). *Behavioral and instructional management: An ecological approach.* Boston: Allyn & Bacon.

Forness, S. R., Swanson, J. M., Cantwell, D. P., Guthrie, D., & Sena, R. (1992). Responses to stimulant medication across six measures of school related performance in children with ADHD and disruptive behavior. *Behavioral Disorders, 18*(1), 42–53.

Gordon, M. (1983). *Gordon Diagnostic System.* DeWitt, NY: Gordon Diagnostic Systems.

Guerin, G. R., & Maier, A. S. (1983). *Informal assessment in education.* Palo Alto, CA: Mayfield.

Harris, D. B. (1963). *Goodenough-Harris Drawing Test.* New York: Harcourt Brace Jovanovich.

Kerr, M. M., & Nelson, C. M. (1989). *Strategies for managing behavioral problems in the classroom* (2nd ed.). Columbus, OH: Merrill.

Knoff, H. M., & Prout, H. T. (1985). *Kinetic Family Drawing System for Family and School: A Handbook.* Los Angeles: Western Psychological Services.

Koppitz, E. (1968). *Human Figure Drawing Test.* New York: Grune & Stratton.

Lee, S. W., Elliott, J., & Barbour, J. D. (1994). A comparison of cross-informant behavior ratings in school-based diagnosis. *Behavioral Disorders, 192,* 87–97.

Mattison, R. E., Bagnato, S. J., Mayes, S. D., & Felix, B. C. (1990). Reliability and validity of teacher diagnostic ratings for children with behavioral and emotional disorders. *Journal of Psychoeducational Assessment, 8,* 509–517.

McArthur, D. S., & Roberts, G. E. (1982). *Roberts Apperception Test for Children: Manual.* Los Angeles: Western Psychological Services.

McConaughy, S. H. (1993). Advances in empirically based assessment of children's behavioral and emotional problems. *School Psychology Review, 22*(2), 285–307.

McConaughy, S. H., Achenbach, T. M., & Gent, C. L. (1988). Multiaxial empirically based assessment: Parent, teacher, observational, cognitive, and personality correlates of Child Behavior Profiles for 6–11 year old boys. *Journal of Abnormal Child Psychology, 16,*485–509.

Naglieri, J. A. (1988). *Draw-a-Person: A quantitative scoring system.* New York: Psychological Corporation.

Naglieri, J. A., McNeish, T. J., & Bardos, A. N. (1991). *Draw-a-Person: Screening Procedure for Emotional Disturbance.* Austin, TX: Pro-Ed.

Norford, B. C., & Barakat, L. P. (1990). The relationship of human figure drawings to aggressive behavior in preschool children. *Psychology in the Schools, 27,* 318–325.

Overton, T. (1987). Analyzing instructional material as a prerequisite for teacher effectiveness. *Techniques: A Journal for Remedial Education and Counseling, 3,* 111–115.

Palomares, R. S., Crowley, S. L., Worchel, F. F., Olson, T. K., & Rae, W. A. (1991). The factor analytic structure of the Roberts Apperception Test for Children: A comparison of the standardization sample with a sample of chronically ill children. *Journal of Personality Assessment, 53*(3), 414–425.

Roberts, G. E. (1982). *Roberts Apperception Test for Children: Test pictures.* Los Angeles: Western Psychological Services.

Rorschach, H. (1921, 1942). *Psycho-Diagnostics: A diagnostic test based on perception* (P. Lemkau & B. Kroenburg, Trans.). Berne: Heber. (First German Edition: 1921. Distributed in the United States by Grune & Stratton.)

Rotter, J., & Rafferty, J. (1950). *The Rotter Incomplete Sentence Test.* New York: Psychological Corporation.

Salvia, J., & Hughes, C. (1990). *Curriculum-based assessment: Testing what is taught.* New York: Macmillan.

Schaughency, E. A., & Rothlind, J. (1991). Assessment and classification of attention deficit hyperactive disorders. *School Psychology Review, 20*(2), 187–202.

Spigelman, G., Spigelman, A., & Englesson, I. L. (1992). Analysis of family drawings: A comparison between children from divorce and nondivorce families. *Journal of Divorce & Remarriage, 18,* 31–51.

Stanford, L. D., & Hynd, G. W. (1994). Congruence of behavioral symptomology in children with ADD/H, ADD/WO, and learning disabilities. *Journal of Learning Disabilities, 27*(4), 243–253.

Trommer, B. L., Hoeppner, J. B., Lorber, R., & Armstrong, K. (1988). Pitfalls in the use of a Continuous Performance Test as a diagnostic tool in attention deficit disorder. *Developmental and Behavioral Pediatrics, 9*(6), 339–345.

Chapter Ten

Measures of Intelligence and Adaptive Behavior

Key Terms

intelligence
adaptive behavior
IQ
innate potential
environmental influence
acculturation
Verbal tests
Performance tests
scaled scores
factor analysis
culture fair

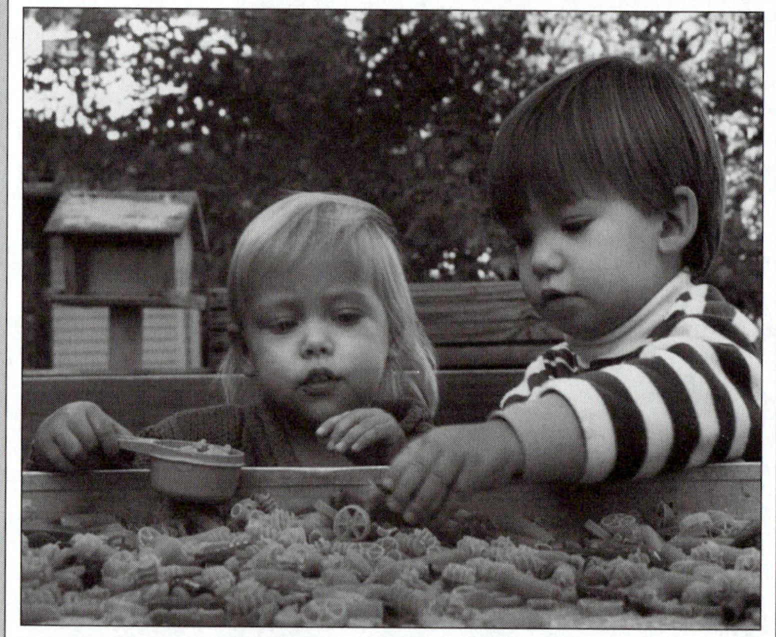

The measurement of **intelligence** has been a controversial issue in educational and psychological assessment for the past several years. Even though professionals in the field disagree to some extent about the definition of intelligence and about the fairness and importance of intelligence testing, the assessment of intellectual ability is mandated by IDEA for the diagnosis of many disabilities. This federal law also requires the assessment of **adaptive behavior,** or how a student functions within her environment, for the diagnosis of mental retardation.

intelligence A general concept of an individual's ability to function effectively within various settings; usually assessed by intelligence tests.

adaptive behavior One's ability to function in various environments.

This chapter presents a review of individual measures of intelligence and adaptive behavior that commonly are used in schools to diagnose students with learning or emotional disabilities. Group intelligence tests may be administered in school systems to students in the regular education curriculum; for special education diagnostic purposes, however, group IQ tests are not appropriate. Tests constructed to be administered in an individual setting are commonly used to measure cognitive abilities. Although teachers in most cases will not be responsible for administering intelligence tests, special education teachers should possess an understanding of the interpretation of intelligence test results and their possible implications for educational planning. A general discussion of intelligence testing and the court cases that have influenced current practice are presented before the review of intelligence tests.

The Meaning of Intelligence Testing

The results of intelligence tests are usually reported in the form of a standardized **IQ** (intelligence quotient) score. It is important for the special education professional to understand what an IQ score is and is not. To possess a basic understanding of IQ scores, the professional educator should consider what is measured by IQ tests, that is, the content and presentation of the items on an IQ test and what the items represent. It is a commonly held myth that IQ scores are measurements of potential that is innate in a person. The following state-

IQ Intelligence quotient; expressed as a standard score, usually with a mean of 100.

ments illustrate some of the current views about intelligence and intelligence testing expressed in the literature:

> The IQ does not reflect a global summation of the brain's capabilities and is certainly not an index of genetic potential, but it does predict school achievement effectively. (Kaufman, 1979, p. 9)
>
> Ultimately, intelligence is not a kind of ability at all, certainly not in the same sense that reasoning, memory, verbal fluency, etc., are so regarded. Rather it is something that is inferred from the way these abilities are manifested under different conditions and circumstances. (Wechsler, 1974, p. 5)
>
> Intelligence—unlike height and weight, but like all psychological constructs—must be measured indirectly; it must be inferred from intelligent behavior, past and present. (Hopkins, Stanley, & Hopkins, 1990, p. 374)
>
> Measurement of current intellectual performance has become confused with measurement of innate potential. Intelligence tests do not assess potential; they sample behaviors already learned in an attempt to predict future learning. (McLoughlin & Lewis, 1990, p. 187)
>
> Child-standardized intelligence performance provides a quantitative index of developmental status, but does not provide information on those functions that have not developed nor on the route by which the child arrived at his or her current developmental state. (Swanson & Watson, 1989, p. 93)
>
> Historically, intelligence has been an enigmatic concept. It is a much valued construct or quality that is extremely difficult to define. Is intelligence the same as verbal ability? Analytical thinking? Academic aptitude? Strategic thinking? The ability to cope? Different theorists might argue for each, or a combination of these abilities. Similarly, they might ask whether intelligence is, or should be, defined in the same way for individuals of different cultural, ethnic, or social backgrounds. (Taylor, 1989, pp. 185–186)

Even more controversial than the meaning of intelligence is the apparent bias that may occur by using individual IQ tests to classify and place students in special education (Reschly, 1981). Taylor (1989) questioned using the same definition of intelligence for individuals of all cultures, which reflects the concern that minority students are overrepresented in special education classrooms (Heller, Holtzman, & Messick, 1982). Specifically, black students have been overrepresented in classrooms for students with mental retardation (Heller et al., 1982; Tucker, 1980), and Hispanic students have been increasingly found in classrooms for the learning disabled (Mick, 1985; Tucker, 1980).

Salvia and Ysseldyke (1988) underscored the importance that culture and background have on intellectual assessment:

> Acculturation is the single most important characteristic in evaluating a child's performance on intelligence tests . . . The culture in which a child lives and the length of time that the child has lived in that culture effectively determine the psychological demands a test item presents. (p. 149)

Taylor and Richards (1991) noted that persons obtaining similar scores on IQ tests manifest differences in their pattern of responding. These authors found that while white students scored higher on the Wechsler Scales than black and

Hispanic students, different patterns were evident, with black students showing verbal strength and Hispanic students showing strength in perceptual ability.

The issues of **innate potential,** learned behaviors, **environmental influence,** and **acculturation,** and their influence on intelligence testing, have fueled the fire of many professional debates (Herrnstein & Murray, 1994). Intelligence testing, however, like all testing in education, is simply the way in which a student responds to a set of stimuli at a specific point in time. Reynolds (1982) reviewed and summarized the general problems with bias in assessment; these are presented, as adapted, in Figure 10.1. Some of the problems of intelligence testing stem from content validity, construct validity, predictive validity (Messick, 1980), the mean differences obtained by groups of different cultural or

innate potential Thought to be one's ability from birth.

environmental influence The impact of the environment on the student's learning ability.

acculturation The influence of one culture on another culture.

1. *Inappropriate content.* Black or other minority children have not been exposed to the material involved in the test questions or other stimulus materials. The tests are geared primarily toward white middle-class homes and values.
2. *Inappropriate standardization samples.* Ethnic minorities are underrepresented in the collection of normative reference group data.
3. *Examiner language bias.* Since most psychologists are white and speak primarily only standard English, they intimidate black and other ethnic minorities. They are also unable to accurately communicate with minority children. Lower test scores for minorities then are said to reflect only this intimidation and difficulty in the communication process and not lowered ability levels.
4. *Inequitable social consequences.* As a result of bias in educational and psychological tests, minority group members, who are already at a disadvantage in the educational and vocational markets because of past discrimination, are disproportionately relegated to dead-end educational tracts and thought unable to learn. Labeling effects also fall under this category.
5. *Measurement of different constructs.* Related to (1) above, this position asserts that the tests are measuring significantly different attributes when used with children from other than the white middle-class culture.
6. *Differential predictive validity.* While tests may accurately predict a variety of outcomes for white middle-class children, they fail to predict at an acceptable level any relevant criteria for minority group members. Corollary to this objection is a variety of competing positions regarding the selection of an appropriate, common criterion against which to validate tests across cultural groupings. Scholastic or academic attainment levels are considered by a variety of black psychologists to be biased as criteria.

Figure 10.1
Indicators of possible bias in assessment.

Source: From "The Problem of Bias in Psychological Assessment" by C. R. Reynolds in C. R. Reynolds and T. B. Gutkin (Eds.), *The Handbook of School Psychology,* 1982 (pp. 179–180), New York: John Wiley & Sons. Copyright 1982 by John Wiley & Sons. Adapted by permission.

ethnic backgrounds (Reschly, 1981), as well as problems that affect all types of standardized testing, such as examiner familiarity (Fuchs & Fuchs, 1989).

Litigation and Intelligence Testing

The issues of intelligence testing and the overrepresentation of minorities in special education classrooms led to litigation that has affected current practice in the field, including the decreased use of intelligence tests by some state and local education agencies for the diagnosis of disabling conditions (Bersoff, 1981). The major court cases that have involved the assessment of intellectual ability are *Larry P. v. Riles* (1984) and *PASE v. Hannon* (1980). Other cases have involved assessment and placement procedures: *Diana v. New York City Board of Education* and *Lora v. State Board of Education.* These cases are summarized in Figure 10.2.

Larry P. v. Riles (1984). This case resulted in the court finding that schools could no longer use standardized but unvalidated IQ tests for the purpose of identifying and placing black children into segregated special education classes for children designated as educable mentally retarded (EMR) (Turnbull, 1990, p. 92).

PASE v. Hannon (1980). Although PASE (Parents in Action on Special Education) found that some of the items in the tests were discriminatory, the court upheld the tests were generally nondiscriminatory. More important, it found that the tests were not the sole basis for classification and that the school district therefore was complying with the Education of the Handicapped Act, EHA, which requires multifaceted testing (Turnbull, 1990, p. 95).

Lora v. New York City Board of Education (1984). This case required that the school system use objective and improved referral and assessment methods and multidisciplinary evaluations to reach decisions for diagnosis of students with emotional disturbance. The court found that the method previously in use was racially discriminatory and ruled that the school system could no longer consider school monetary problems or availability of services as reasons to place or not to place students in special education (Wood, Johnson, & Jenkins, 1990).

Diana v. State Board of Education (1970). In this case, the state board of education of California agreed to test students in their native language, to omit unfair test items of a verbal nature, to construct tests that would reflect the culture of Mexican American students, and that tests would be standardized on Mexican Americans (Ysseldyke & Algozzine, 1982).

Figure 10.2
Summary of court cases involving IQ assessment.

As a result of the recent litigation involving the testing of intelligence as well as the information included in the assessment sections of IDEA, a movement toward more objective testing practices is currently under way in the assessment field. In addition, professionals are reminded to follow the *Code of Fair Testing Practices in Education* (see appendix) by the Joint Committee on Testing Practices and the standards set forth by the APA (1985).

Activity 10.1

Match the following terms to the descriptions.

A. *PASE v. Hannon*
B. *Diana v. State Board of Education*
C. inappropriate content
D. inequitable social consequences
E. inappropriate standardization sample
F. differential predictive validity
G. *Lora v. New York City Board of Education*
H. *Larry P. v. Riles*
I. examiner language bias
J. measurement of different constructs
K. IQ score
L. intelligence testing

________ **1.** Case involving administering tests in a language other than the child's native language.

________ **2.** Case concerning students who were placed in a school for the emotionally disturbed without the benefit of nondiscriminatory assessment.

________ **3.** Standardized norm-referenced assessment of cognitive abilities; the indirect measurement of the construct of intelligence.

________ **4.** When, as the result of discriminatory assessment, minority students are placed in dead-end educational or vocational tracts.

________ **5.** When a test measures different constructs for people of different groups.

________ **6.** A test may predict accurately for one group of students but not as accurately for another group which results in

________ **7.** A numerical representation of intellectual ability.

________ **8.** When the examiner does not possess skill in communicating in the student's native language it may result in

________ **9.** Case finding that the use of IQ tests to place black students in classes for the educable mentally retarded was discriminatory practice.

________ **10.** Case finding the same IQ tests to be nondiscriminatory even though a few items were found to be biased.

☐ **CHECK YOUR UNDERSTANDING**

Complete Activity 10.1.

Use of Intelligence Tests

The use of intelligence tests remains controversial in part because of inappropriate use in the past. Revised instruments, alternative testing practices, and understanding of the ethnic or cultural differences that may occur are promising improvements in the assessment of intelligence. Intelligence testing is likely to remain a substantial part of the assessment process due to the known correlation between performance on IQ tests and school achievement (Reschly & Grimes, 1990). Given the fact that IQ tests will continue to be used, educators must promote fair and appropriate use of intelligence measures. Reschly and Grimes (1990) set forth the following guidelines for appropriate use of IQ tests:

1. Appropriate use requires a context that emphasizes prevention and early intervention rather than eligibility determination as the initial phase in services to students with learning and behavior problems.
2. Intellectual assessment should be used when the results are directly relevant to well-defined referral questions, and other available information does not address those questions.
3. Mandatory use of intellectual measures for all referrals, multifactored evaluations, or reevaluations is not consistent with best practices.
4. Intellectual assessment must be part of a multifactored approach, individualized to a child's characteristics and the referral problems.
5. Intellectual assessment procedures must be carefully matched to characteristics of children and youth.
6. Score reporting and interpretation must reflect known limitations of tests, including technical adequacy, inherent error in measurement, and general categories of performance.
7. Interpretation of performance and decisions concerning classification must reflect consideration of overall strengths and weaknesses in intellectual performance, performance on other relevant dimensions of behavior, age, family characteristics, and cultural background.
8. Users should implement assertive procedures to protect students from misconceptions and misuses of intellectual test results. (pp. 436–437)

Special education professionals can obtain meaningful information from IQ test results if they understand the types of behavior that are assessed by individual subtests and items. Readers should take notice of the possible areas of testing bias as well as previous court case decisions as they study the tests reviewed in this chapter.

The Review of Intelligence Tests

This chapter reviews some of the tests most commonly used by schools to measure cognitive ability or intelligence.

Perhaps the best-known intelligence measures are the Wechsler Scales, three separate tests designed to assess intellectual functioning at different age levels. The Wechsler Preschool and Primary Scale of Intelligence–Revised (WPPSI–R) was developed for use with children aged 4 to 6½; it is reviewed in chapter 12, "Early Childhood Assessment." The Wechsler Adult Intelligence Scale–Revised (WAIS–R) is used with youth 16 years of age through adulthood. The Wechsler Intelligence Scale for Children–Third Edition assesses school-aged children ranging in age from 6 through 16-11. Called "the most popular and widely used individual intelligence test" (Taylor, 1989, p. 189), this particular test of the Wechsler Scales is covered in depth in this chapter.

Other measures of intelligence are commonly used with school-aged children. The following are reviewed briefly in this chapter: the Woodcock-Johnson–Revised Tests of Cognitive Ability, Stanford-Binet Intelligence Scale–Fourth Edition, Kaufman Assessment Battery for Children, Detroit Tests of Learning Aptitude–3, Cognitive Levels Test, Kaufman Adolescent and Adult Intelligence Test, and Kaufman Brief Intelligence Test. As with the Wechsler Scales, these tests may not be administered by the teacher; however, test results provided by the psychologist or diagnostician may be useful to the teacher.

Wechsler Intelligence Scale for Children–Third Edition (WISC–III)

The WISC–III (Wechsler, 1991) is composed of two separate tests, the **Verbal tests** and **Performance tests,** which yield three IQ scores; Verbal IQ, Performance IQ, and Full Scale IQ. These scores along with additional information provided by a multidisciplinary team evaluation, may be useful in determining a diagnosis. This edition of the WISC also provides scores, called indexes, that are based on the factor structure of the test. These scores are Verbal Comprehension Index, Perceptual Organization Index, Freedom From Distractibility Index, and a Processing Speed Index. Even more useful to the teacher may be information provided by individual subtest **scaled scores** when the influences on test performance and behaviors assessed are known.

Verbal tests A group of subtests on the Wechsler scales thought to measure verbal conceptual ability.

Performance tests A group of subtests on the Wechsler Scales thought to measure nonverbal ability.

scaled scores Derived scores on the Wechsler Scales for subtests; each has a mean of 10.

Verbal Subtests. The Verbal subtests are presented in the following paragraphs along with factors that may influence individual student performance.

Information. Questions in this subtest, presented to the student orally, assess general information and knowledge believed to be common to most school-aged youngsters. This subtest is designed to survey the knowledge of everyday events that the student gains from the world around her. A student's performance is highly influenced by school-related learning (Kaufman, 1993b).

Similarities. The examiner orally presents pairs of words, and the student must say how the two things (such as a wheel and a ball) are alike (Wechsler, 1991). This type of subtest is believed to measure verbal comprehension and conceptualization, cognition, degree of abstract thinking, distinguishing essential from nonessential details, verbal reasoning, and verbal expression; a student's performance may be influenced by interests or outside reading (Kaufman, 1979, p. 103).

Arithmetic. This subtest is basically composed of questions that the examiner presents orally, with some questions presented in written form at the higher end of the test. The questions are story-type math problems that the student must answer within a time limit. In addition to measuring some math abilities and familiarity with math processes, this type of subtest is believed to measure freedom from distractibility, verbal comprehension, sequencing, acquired knowledge, cognition, memory, facility with numbers, mental alertness, long-term memory, computational skill, and reasoning. A student's performance on this subtest is thought to be influenced by attention span, anxiety, concentration, distractibility, or working under time pressure (Kaufman, 1979, pp. 103–104), and general school-related learning (Kaufman, 1993b).

Vocabulary. The student is asked to define words presented orally. This type of subtest is thought to measure verbal comprehension and conceptualization, acquired knowledge, cognition, degree of abstract thinking, fund of information, learning ability, long-term memory, verbal concept formation, and verbal expression. A student's performance may be influenced by cultural opportunities at home, interests, outside reading, richness of early environment, or school-related learning (Kaufman, 1979, p. 104).

Comprehension. This subtest contains questions of a general nature, which the examiner asks orally. This type of subtest assesses verbal comprehension and conceptualization, evaluation, common sense of cause-effect relationships, verbal reasoning, social judgment, verbal expression, demonstration of practical information, and evaluation and use of past experience. A student's ability to perform on this subtest may be influenced by cultural opportunities in the home and development of conscience or moral sense (Kaufman, 1979, pp. 104–105). This subtest is heavily weighted by cultural factors (Kaufman, 1993b).

Digit Span. This supplementary Verbal subtest, which may be chosen in place of another subtest, may help the psychologist document specific types of memory or attentional deficits when used with other information obtained during assessment. The items consist of series of numbers, which the examiner orally presents and which the student must repeat, in the given order first and in reverse order on the second part of the test. This type of subtest is believed to assess freedom from distractibility, sequencing, memory, facility with numbers, mental alertness, and auditory short-term memory; performance may be influenced by attention span, distractibility, or anxiety (Kaufman, 1979, p. 105).

Performance Subtests. The Performance subtests of the WISC–III contain many timed manipulative tasks. The subtests and the variables that may influence a student's performance are described in the following paragraphs.

Picture Completion. This subtest is visually presented to the student, who is asked to tell the examiner what important part of the picture stimulus is missing. This type of subtest is thought to assess perceptual organization, verbal comprehension, spatial ability, cognition, evaluation, distinguishing essential from nonessential details, holistic processing, visual organization without essential motor activity, visual perception of meaningful stimuli, visual alertness, and visual recognition and identification. A student's performance on this subtest may be influenced by ability to respond when uncertain, cognitive style, concentration, or working under time pressure (Kaufman, 1979, pp. 105–106).

Coding. This test requires that the student copy symbols to match those presented as they are paired with other symbols, such as numbers, within a specific time period. This type of subtest assesses freedom from distractibility, sequencing, convergent production, evaluation, facility with numbers (on Coding B), integrated brain functioning, learning ability, paper and pencil skill, reproduction of models, visual-motor coordination, visual perception of abstract stimuli, ability to follow directions, clerical speed and accuracy, psychomotor speed, and visual short-term memory. Anxiety, distractibility, or working under time pressure may influence a student's performance (Kaufman, 1979, p. 108).

Picture Arrangement. The student must sequence sets of pictures in the correct order to complete a story sequence. This type of subtest is thought to measure perceptual organization, verbal comprehension, sequencing ability, convergent production, evaluation, common sense of cause-effect relationships, distinguishing essential from nonessential details, integrated brain functioning, planning ability, reasoning, social judgment, synthesis, visual perception of meaningful stimuli, visual organization without essential motor activity, anticipation of consequences, and temporal sequencing of time events. Creativity, cultural opportunities in the home, exposure to comic strips, or working under time pressure may influence a student's performance (Kaufman, 1979, p. 106).

Block Design. The student arranges three-dimensional blocks with red and white color patterns to match a specific pattern within a given period of time. The initial patterns require two blocks for young students and four blocks for older students, and the most difficult items require nine blocks. This type of subtest measures perceptual organization, spatial ability, cognition, evaluation, integrated brain functioning, reproduction of models, synthesis, visual-motor coordination, visual perception of abstract stimuli, analysis of whole into component parts, nonverbal concept formation, and spatial visualization. A student's ability to perform on this subtest may be influenced by cognitive style or working under time pressure (Kaufman, 1979, pp. 106–107).

Object Assembly. This subtest is also known as the puzzle subtest. The student is presented with sets of puzzle pieces, which must be put together correctly within a given period of time. The amount of time allowed increases for the more difficult items. This type of subtest assesses perceptual organization, spatial ability, cognition, evaluation, holistic processing, synthesis, visual-motor coordination, visual perception of meaningful stimuli, ability to benefit from sensory-motor feedback, anticipation of relationships among parts, and flexibility. A student's ability to perform on this subtest may be influenced by the ability to respond when uncertain, cognitive style, experience with puzzles, or working under time pressure (Kaufman, 1979, p. 107).

Symbol Search. This is a new fine-motor subtest. Presented with a series of pairs of symbols in a test booklet, the student must scan quickly and discriminate if the symbol exists in a given row of symbols. The student then marks a yes or no response. This is a timed subtest and is optional.

Mazes. This supplementary Performance subtest consists of several mazes that the student must solve within a specific time period. This type of subtest is believed to measure perceptual organization, spatial ability, cognition, integrated brain function, paper and pencil skill, planning ability, reasoning, visual-motor coordination, following a visual pattern, and foresight. The student's ability to respond when uncertain, experience in solving mazes, or working under time pressure may influence performance on this subtest (Kaufman, 1979, pp. 108–109).

☐ **CHECK YOUR UNDERSTANDING**

Complete Activity 10.2.

Activity 10.2

Match the following terms with the correct descriptions.

A. WAIS–R
B. WPPSI–R
C. WISC–III
D. Verbal tests
E. Performance tests
F. full-scale IQ
G. Digit Span
H. Coding
I. Object Assembly
J. Similarities
K. Block Design
L. Picture Arrangement
M. Picture Completion
N. Vocabulary
O. Mazes
P. Processing Speed Index
Q. Comprehension
R. Information
S. Arithmetic

_________ **1.** The Wechsler Intelligence Scale for Children–Third Edition.

_________ **2.** This Wechsler test is designed to be used through adulthood.

_________ **3.** This subtest presents math story problems, and performance may be influenced by attention span and concentration.

_________ **4.** Performance on this subtest may be influenced by interests and outside reading; the examiner asks the student how two things are alike.

_________ **5.** Performance on this Verbal subtest may be influenced by early environment, cultural opportunities in the home, or school learning; the examiner presents words for the student to define.

_________ **6.** Students are presented with visual stimuli to determine what important part is missing. Performance on this subtest may be influenced by working under time pressure or cognitive style.

_________ **7.** Performance on these puzzles may be influenced by the ability to respond when uncertain, cognitive style, or previous puzzle experiences.

_________ **8.** Many of the subtests on this portion of the WISC–R are timed, and thus the student's performance may be influenced by the ability to work under time pressure.

_________ **9.** This subtest contains red and white cubes and measures perceptual organization, spatial ability, synthesis, and reproduction of models.

_________ **10.** The items of these tests are presented, for the most part, orally, and the student responds orally.

_________ **11.** This subtest, which assesses verbal comprehension and acquired knowledge, contains general information questions.

_________ **12.** Performance on this Verbal test may be influenced by the student's conscience or moral sense.

_________ **13.** This subtest is divided into two parts, forward and backward, and measures auditory short-term memory and freedom from distractibility.

_________ **14.** Performance on this subtest may be influenced by the student's previous experience with comic strips.

_________ **15.** This paper and pencil performance subtest measures visual-motor coordination, psychomotor speed, and visual short-term memory.

_________ **16.** Performance on this supplementary subtest may be influenced by the student's previous experience with mazes.

_________ **17.** This IQ score reflects the performance of the student on both Verbal and Performance tests.

_________ **18.** This Wechsler test was designed to be used with children from the ages of 4 to 6½.

Technical Data

Norming Process. The standardization sample of the WISC–III reflected the total U.S. population statistics as obtained from 1988 census data. The following variables were addressed: gender, age, geographic region, parent(s) occupation, community size, and race/ethnicity.

Reliability. The reliability studies employed included split-half coefficients and test-retest reliability. Stability coefficients appear adequate for most subtests at most ages; however, the WISC–III seems to have somewhat lower stability on individual subtests when compared with the WISC–R (Kaufman, 1993b).

Validity. The examiner's manual provides extended information on validity studies and factor structure of the WISC–III. Information is presented for several studies with special populations, including students with giftedness, learning disabilities, mental retardation, attention deficit disorders, severe conduct disorders, epilepsy, hearing impairments, and speech or language delay. A table in the manual gives means and standard deviations for IQ and index scores for persons with learning disabilities, reading disorders, and attention deficit hyperactivity disorder.

Interpreting Scores of the WISC–III. The mean score for subtest scaled scores is 10 with a standard deviation of 3. The average IQ score for the Wechsler Scales is 100 with a standard deviation of 15. The classifications given in the manual are as follows (Wechsler, 1991, p. 32):

IQ	*Intelligence Classification*	*Percent Included in Theoretical Normal Curve*
130 and above	Very superior	2.2
120–129	Superior	6.7
110–119	High average	16.1
90–109	Average	50.0
80–89	Low average	16.1
70–79	Borderline	6.7
69 and below	Intellectually deficient	2.2

Much information can be gained by carefully studying the results a teacher may receive about a student's performance on the WISC–III. Each of the subtests on the WISC–III measures many behaviors and skills, and many factors may influence a student's performance. It is quite common for average students with no disabilities to perform inconsistently on the various subtests on the WISC–III. Because the standard deviation on the scaled scores is 3, students' scores may differ greatly between several subtests.

Students who perform with severe discrepancies between subtests and/or the three IQ scores may do so because of processing or learning difficulties. Psychologists often use this information, along with other test results, classroom observations, informal data, permanent products, and diagnostic academic tests to document the existence of a learning disability or deficiency. Typically, discrepancies between the three IQ scores must be significantly different and should be interpreted with caution due to other factors that may influence these differences (Kaufman, 1979).

The protocol for the WISC–III is shown in Figure 10.3. This protocol allows the examiner to calculate raw scores for the factors or indexes and then obtain the derived standard scores from the manual. This model, based on **factor analysis** research of the Wechsler, allows the examiner to compare the student's own strengths and weaknesses in addition to comparing the student with the norm group.

factor analysis A statistical method of reducing the variables of a test to lower the number of factors thought to influence test performance.

The individual discrepancies between subtest scores and the three obtained IQ scores are often used to diagnose specific learning disabilities. A student who exhibits academic problems, scores within the average IQ range, and exhibits

Name ______ Sex ______

School ______ Grade ______

Examiner ______ Handedness ______

WISC-III®

Wechsler Intelligence Scale for Children®–Third Edition

Subtests	Raw Scores	Scaled Scores					
Picture Completion							
Information							
Coding							
Similarities							
Picture Arrangement							
Arithmetic							
Block Design							
Vocabulary							
Object Assembly							
Comprehension							
(Symbol Search)			( )				
(Digit Span)		( )					
(Mazes)			( )				
Sum of Scaled Scores		Verbal	Perfor.	VC	PO	FD	PS
		Full Scale Score		OPTIONAL			

	Year	Month	Day
Date Tested			
Date of Birth			
Age			

	Score	IQ/ Index	%ile	___% Confidence Interval
Verbal				–
Performance				–
Full Scale				–
VC				–
PO				–
FD				–
PS				–

Subtest Scores

Verbal: Inf Sim Ari Voc Com DS — Performance: PC Cd PA BD OA SS Mz

(Scale 19 to 1)

IQ Scores: VIQ PIQ FSIQ — Index Scores (Optional): VCI POI FDI PSI

(Scale 160 to 40: 160, 150, 140, 130, 120, 110, 100, 90, 80, 70, 60, 50, 40)

THE PSYCHOLOGICAL CORPORATION®
HARCOURT BRACE JOVANOVICH, INC.

9 10 11 12 A B C D E

09-980004

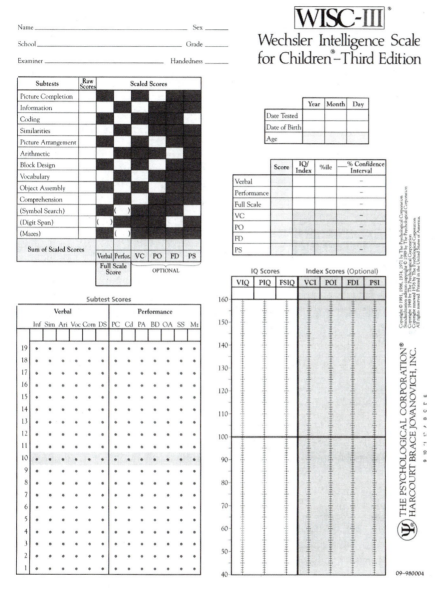

Figure 10.3
First page of the WISC–III protocol.

Source: From *Wechsler Intelligence Scale for Children–Third Edition: Manual* by D. Wechsler, 1991, San Antonio, TX: The Psychological Corporation. Copyright © 1991 by The Psychological Corporation. Reproduced by permission. All rights reserved.

significant discrepancies between factors or between performance and verbal abilities may be diagnosed as learning disabled. For example, a student may have significant difficulties according to the obtained scores on the WISC–III in verbal comprehension, have significant deficits on measures of academic achievement, and be average in intellectual ability. This student may very likely be diagnosed as having a learning disability.

Woodcock-Johnson–Revised (WJ–R) Tests of Cognitive Ability

The WJ–R Tests of Cognitive Ability (Woodcock & Mather, 1989) are an easel test with 7 subtests in the Standard Battery and 14 subtests in the Supplemental Battery. The subtests may also be grouped into the categories of cognitive abilities and differential aptitudes. Figure 10.4 illustrates the complete cognitive battery.

The Tests of Cognitive Ability were designed to be used with persons from the ages of 2 years to 90+. The resulting scores are like those obtained from the WJ–R Tests of Achievement (see chapter 6): age equivalents, grade equivalents, percentile ranks, *W* scores, relative mastery index standard scores, and expected standard scores. The authors of this test battery designed it so that comparisons can be made with academic achievement. Such comparisons may enable the psychologist to more accurately diagnose discrepancies between aptitude and achievement to document the possible existence of a specific learning disability. Instructions for calculating discrepancies are presented in the examiner's manual.

Technical Data

Norming Process. The WJ–R Tests of Cognitive Ability were standardized on 6,359 subjects in more than 100 different communities (Woodcock & Mather, 1989). During the norming process, the test developers considered these variables: community size, sex, race (white, black, Native American, Asian Pacific, Hispanic, or other), occupational status of adults, educational level of adults, and household income.

Reliability. Reliability studies included split-half procedures, except for the timed subtests, and coefficients ranged from .62 to .97, with most coefficients in the .80s to .90s. Reliability coefficients are also provided for the clusters contained in the battery.

Validity. Content validity is presented in the manual as a discussion of item validity. Concurrent validity studies presented in the manual include studies comparing the Tests of Cognitive Ability with the Boehm Test of Basic Concepts, Bracken Basic Concepts Scale, Kaufman Assessment Battery for Children, McCarthy General Cognitive Index, Peabody Picture Vocabulary Test–Revised, and Stanford-Binet IV Composite for early ages; the Kaufman Assessment Battery for Children, Stanford-Binet IV Composite, and WISC–R Full Scale for 9-year-olds; and the Stanford-Binet IV Composite and WAIS–R for

TESTS OF COGNITIVE ABILITY	COGNITIVE ABILITIES: Broad Ability			Cognitive Factors								DIFFERENTIAL APTITUDES: Scholastic Aptitudes					
	Early Development Scale	Standard Scale	Extended Scale	Long-Term Retrieval (Glr)	Short-Term Memory (Gsm)	Processing Speed (Gs)	Auditory Processing (Ga)	Visual Processing (Gv)	Comprehension-Knowledge (Gc)	Fluid Reasoning (Gf)	Oral Language	Reading	Mathematics	Written Language	Knowledge	Intra-Cognitive Discrepancies	Oral Language
STANDARD BATTERY																	
1. Memory for Names	●	●	●	●												●	
2. Memory for Sentences	●	●	●		●						●	●			●	●	
3. Visual Matching		●	●			●						●	●	●		●	
4. Incomplete Words	●	●	●				●								●	●	
5. Visual Closure	●	●	●					●								●	
6. Picture Vocabulary	●	●	●						●		●					●	
7. Analysis-Synthesis		●	●							●			●			●	
SUPPLEMENTAL BATTERY																	
8. Visual-Auditory Learning	○		●	●										●		●	
9. Memory for Words	○		●		●											●	
10. Cross Out			●			●										●	
11. Sound Blending	○		●				●					●		●	●	●	
12. Picture Recognition	○		●					●								●	●
13. Oral Vocabulary			●						●		●	●	●	●		●	
14. Concept Formation			●							●			●		●	●	●
15. Delayed Recall—Memory for Names				○													
16. Delayed Recall—Visual-Auditory Learning				○													
17. Numbers Reversed					○												●
18. Sound Patterns							○										●
19. Spatial Relations								○		○							
20. Listening Comprehension									○		●						
21. Verbal Analogies									○	○	●						

● = Tests to administer for a cluster score

○ = Tests which can supply additional information

Figure 10.4

The complete cognitive battery of the WJ–R Tests of Cognitive Ability.

Source: From *Woodcock-Johnson Psycho-Educational Battery–Revised: Tests of Cognitive Ability: Standard and Supplementary Batteries Manual* (p. 12) by R. W. Woodcock and N. Mather, 1989, Allen, TX: DLM Teaching Resources. Copyright 1989 by DLM Teaching Resources. Reprinted by permission.

adult ages. Concurrent validity coefficients ranged from .46 to .72. The construct validity information presented reports that a factor analysis of the Tests of Cognitive Ability revealed seven factors responsible for 79.6% of the total variance in scores (Woodcock & Mather, 1989).

Stanford-Binet Intelligence Scale–Fourth Edition (Stanford-Binet IV)

The Stanford-Binet IV (Thorndike, Hagen, & Sattler, 1986) was significantly revised in 1986, and the revisions made the test much more like the Wechsler Scales in number of scores. The earlier versions of this test yielded a single IQ score heavily weighted on verbal ability. The newer version contains 15 subtests grouped into four areas. The test manual describes a three-level hierarchial model, shown in Figure 10.5, that underlies this instrument. The three levels are defined by Thorndike et al. (1986) in the following manner:

1. *First level.* Measures general ability, or *g*. The term *g* is defined as ". . . what an individual uses when faced with a problem that he or she has not been taught to solve" (Thorndike et al., 1986, p. 3).

2. *Second level.* Composed of three factors: (Figure 10.5) crystalized abilities, fluid-analytic abilities, and short-term auditory memory. Crystalized abilities include the cognitive skills needed to learn and use information about verbal and quantitative concepts to solve problems. Fluid-analytic abilities include the skills needed to solve problems of figural or other nonverbal stimuli. Short-term

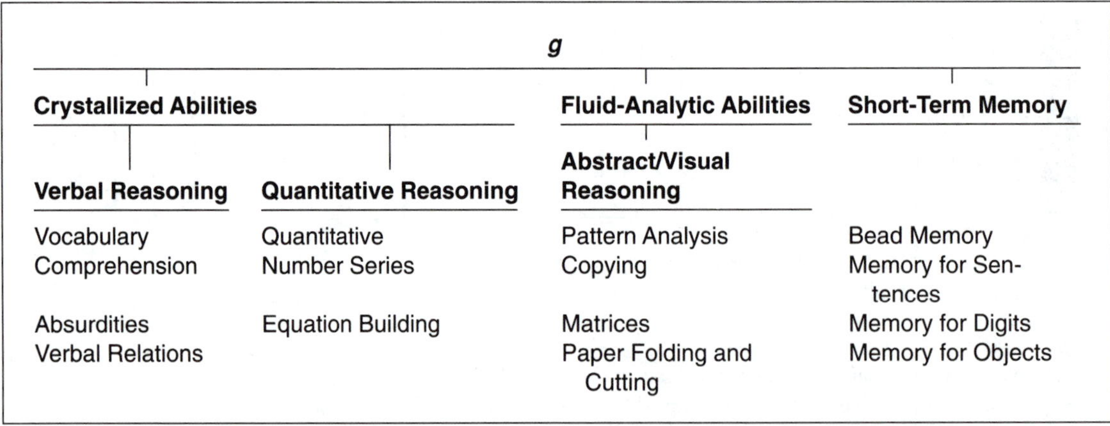

Figure 10.5
Cognitive abilities factors appraised in the Stanford-Binet IV.
Source: From *Technical Manual, Stanford-Binet Intelligence Scale, Fourth Edition* (p. 4), by R. L. Thorndike, E. P. Hagen, and J. M. Sattler, 1986, Chicago: Riverside. Copyright 1986 by The Riverside Publishing Company. Reproduced with permission of The Riverside Publishing Company, Chicago, Illinois.

memory includes the skills needed to retain new information for a short period of time until it is processed into long-term memory and the ability needed to hold information from long-term memory as it is used to solve problems.

3. *Third level.* Includes content-specific areas such as verbal reasoning, quantitative reasoning, and abstract/visual reasoning. This level is thought to be useful for diagnosticians and educators as they plan interventions for students.

Because subtest and area scores can now be determined, examiners will find that comparing individual abilities is easier with the Stanford-Binet IV than it was with earlier versions of this test. Area and total test scores have a mean of 100 with a standard deviation of 16. The age-normed standardized subtest scores are presented with a mean of 50 and a standard deviation of 8.

The Stanford-Binet IV was designed for use with students ages 2-0 to 23. This instrument seems to provide an adequate alternative measure for students of preschool age.

☐ **CHECK YOUR UNDERSTANDING**

Complete Activity 10.3.

Activity 10.3

Answer the following questions.

1. According to the information in the Wechsler classification system, what percentage of the population should be classified as gifted? _________
2. According to the information in the Wechsler classification system, what percentage of the population would have an IQ score of 69 or below? _________
3. The WJ–R Tests of Cognitive Ability were designed to be used for persons between the ages of _________ and _________ .
4. Unlike the Wechsler Scales and the Stanford-Binet IV, the WJ–R Tests of Cognitive Ability are a(n) _____________ test rather than a test kit with manipulatives.
5. The older Stanford-Binet test yielded a single IQ score; however, test results for the Stanford-Binet IV include _____________ scores and _____________ scores.
6. What are the three levels of the Stanford-Binet IV?

____

____

____

____

Technical Data

Norming Process. The Stanford-Binet IV was standardized using more than 5,000 persons from 47 states and the District of Columbia (Thorndike et al., 1986). The variables considered were geographic region, sex, community size, occupational and educational levels, and race/ethnic group. The standardization sample was representative of the 1980 census data.

Reliability. Reliability information provided includes test-retest reliability and internal reliability using the split-half method.

Validity. Concurrent validity studies were conducted using the 1973 Stanford-Binet, the WISC–R, WPPSI, WAIS–R, and Kaufman Assessment Battery for Children. The coefficients ranged from .73 to .91. Factor analysis information is provided in the technical manual.

Kaufman Assessment Battery for Children (K-ABC)

The K-ABC contains both achievement and intelligence measures for children from the ages of 2½ to 12½ (Kaufman & Kaufman, 1983a). This instrument was designed with heavy emphasis on neuropsychological and cognitive theory and is organized to reflect this theoretical basis. This test will not be administered by special education teachers but by psychologists or educational diagnosticians. The test authors list the goals for the K-ABC as:

1. Measure intelligence from a strong theoretical and research base.
2. Separate acquired factual knowledge from the ability to solve unfamiliar problems.
3. Yield scores that translate to educational intervention.
4. Include novel tasks.
5. Be easy to administer and objective to score.
6. Be sensitive to the diverse needs of preschool, minority group, and exceptional children. (Kaufman & Kaufman, 1983b)

The K-ABC is organized to yield four global scores: Sequential Processing, Simultaneous Processing, Mental Processing Composite (a combination of both the Simultaneous and Sequential areas), and Achievement. The scores are reported as standard scores with a mean of 100 and a standard deviation of 15. The protocol, shown in Figure 10.6, illustrates the various scores that may be obtained from this instrument.

Because it contains both mental and achievement measures, the K-ABC may aid in the diagnosis of learning disabilities when using a discrepancy criterion. The test also contains supplementary sociocultural norms that may be applied when testing students from culturally different backgrounds (Kaufman & Kaufman, 1983b).

The test kit includes three easels, additional manipulative materials, protocols, and two manuals: one for test administration and scoring and one for test interpretation. The administration manual contains Spanish instructions and correct responses for the Mental Processing and Achievement portions of the test. The Spanish instructions are for use with students who understand some English. Spanish-speaking students who do not know English should be administered the complete Spanish version of the K-ABC. Some of the subtests of the K-ABC are grouped in a Nonverbal Scale and can also be used for students with receptive language problems.

K·ABC Kaufman Assessment Battery for Children

by Alan S. Kaufman and Nadeen L. Kaufman

INDIVIDUAL TEST RECORD

Name ______________________ Sex ________

Parent's names ______________________

____

Home address ______________________

Home phone ______________________

Grade ________ School ______________________

Examiner ______________________

SOCIOCULTURAL INFORMATION (IF PERTINENT)

Race ______________________

Socioeconomic background ______________________

____

____

	YEAR	MONTH	DAY
Test date			
Birth date			
Chronological age			

Mental Processing Subtests $\overline{X} = 10$; $SD = 3$	Scaled Score: Sequen-tial	Scaled Score: Simul-taneous	Scaled Score: Non-verbal	Nat's. %ile rank Table 4	S or W Table 11	Other data
1. Magic Window						
2. Face Recognition						
3. Hand Movements						
4. Gestalt Closure						
5. Number Recall						
6. Triangles						
7. Word Order						
8. Matrix Analogies						
9. Spatial Memory						
10. Photo Series						

Sum of subtest scores ◯ ◯ ◯ Transfer sums to Global Scales, Sum of subtest scores column.

Achievement Subtests $\overline{X} = 100$; $SD = 15$	Standard score ± band or error ___% confidence	Nat's. %ile rank Table 4	Socio-cultural %ile rank Table 5	S or W Table 11	Other data
11. Expressive Vocabulary	±				
12. Faces & Places	±				
13. Arithmetic	±				
14. Riddles	±				
15. Reading/ Decoding	±				
16. Reading/ Understanding	±				

Sum of subtest scores ◯ Transfer sums to Global Scales, Sum of subtest scores column.

Global Scales $\overline{X} = 100$; $SD = 15$	Sum of subtest scores	Standard score ± band or error ___% confidence Table 2	Nat's. %ile rank Table 4	Socio-cultural %ile rank Table 5	Other data
Sequential Processing					
Simultaneous Processing					
Mental Processing Composite	◯				
Achievement					
Nonverbal					

Global Scale Comparisons

	Indicate >, <, or ≈		Circle the significance level		
Sequential	______	Simultaneous (Table 10)	NS	.05	.01
Sequential	______	Achievement (Table 10)	NS	.05	.01
Simultaneous	______	Achievement (Table 10)	NS	.05	.01
M P C	______	Achievement (Table 10)	NS	.05	.01

Figure 10.6
The protocol of the K-ABC provides a format for scoring mental processing, achievement, and other global scales.

Source: From *Kaufman Assessment Battery for Children: Protocol* (p. 1) by A. S. Kaufman and N. L. Kaufman, 1983, Circle Pines, MN: American Guidance Service. Copyright 1983 by American Guidance Service. Reprinted by permission.

Technical Data

Norming Process. The standardization of the K-ABC involved 2,000 students from various geographic regions in the United States. Demographic information reflects the national demographic information of the 1980 census, with the following variables considered: race or ethnic group, sex, geographic region, parental education, community size, and educational placement of students. The category of educational placement included students who were currently served in regular education, special education, and talented and gifted programs.

Reliability. The test interpretation manual provides in-depth information on reliability studies, including split-half reliability, test-retest, alternate levels reliability, and standard error of measurement. These reliability studies yield a psychometrically "tight" instrument (Wiebe, 1986), with reliability coefficients ranging from .71 to .97 for total group reliability.

Validity. The information provided on validity includes construct validity, predictive validity research, and concurrent criterion-related validity. The test interpretation manual also contains supportive validity information concerning factor analysis research founded in neuropsychological and cognitive theory.

Detroit Tests of Learning Aptitude–3 (DLTA–3)

The DLTA–3 contains 11 subtests, which are grouped into four domains: Linguistic Domain, Cognitive Domain, Attentional Domain, and Motoric Domain (Hammill, 1991). The structure of the DTLA–3 is shown in Figure 10.7.

In addition to the composites shown in Figure 10.7, there is a General Mental Ability composite score made up of all subtests in the instrument. An additional score, the Optimal composite score, may be derived from the four highest subtest scores. The DTLA–3 provides the examiner with the ability to use selected subtest scores to obtain scores that are somewhat more traditional when assessing intelligence, such as the theoretical fluid-crystallized constructs and the verbal-performance indexes that have been established by other instruments. The examiner's manual presents theoretical arguments for the association with these constructs; however, the test author presents no substantial research documenting that these factors are in fact measured by this instrument.

As suggested by the subtest and composite titles, some of the subtests are verbal in nature, some are presented visually and require fine motor responses such as reproducing line drawings, and still others require short-term auditory memory and the ability to follow oral directions. This instrument may be used, along with other measures, to document the possibility of distractibility or visual-motor difficulties. This instrument may provide insight into a student's

- I. Linguistic Domain
  - A. Verbal Composite Subtests
    1. Word Opposites
    2. Sentence Imitation
    3. Reversed Letters
    4. Story Construction
    5. Basic Information
    6. Word Sequences
    7. Picture Fragments
  - B. Nonverbal Composite Subtests
    1. Design Sequences
    2. Design Reproduction
    3. Symbolic Relations
    4. Story Sequences
- II. Attentional Domain
  - A. Attention-Enhanced Composite Subtests
    1. Design Sequences
    2. Sentence Imitation
    3. Reversed Letters
    4. Design Reproduction
    5. Word Sequences
    6. Story Sequences
  - B. Attention-Reduced Composite Subtests
    1. Word Opposites
    2. Story Construction
    3. Basic Information
    4. Symbolic Relations
    5. Picture Fragments
- III. Motoric Domain
  - A. Motor-Enhanced Composite Subtests
    1. Design Sequences
    2. Reversed Letters
    3. Design Reproduction
    4. Story Sequences
  - B. Motor-Reduced Composite Subtests
    1. Word Opposites
    2. Sentence Imitation
    3. Story Construction
    4. Basic Information
    6. Symbolic Relations
    7. Word Sequences
    8. Picture Fragments

Figure 10.7
Structure of the Detroit Tests of Learning Aptitude–3.

abilities in some areas; however, it seems to lack adequate research to stand alone as a measure of intelligence for the purposes of placement and intervention decisions.

Technical Data

Norming Process. The DTLA–3 was standardized using a sample of 2,587 students in 36 states (Hammill, 1991). This sample size includes the data retained from the 1985 sample of 1,532 students used to standardize the DTLA–2. Demographic data appear to represent that of the nation as presented in the manual. Demographic variables considered were sex, rural or urban community, race (white, nonwhite), ethnicity (African American, Hispanic, Native American, Oriental/Pacific Islander, or all others), and geographic region.

Reliability. Internal consistency coefficients were calculated using coefficient alpha and ranged from .77 for the Picture Fragments subtest to .96 for General Mental Ability composite score. Test-retest reliability yielded coefficients ranging from .75 on the Story Sequences subtest to composite scores in the .90s and .80s.

Validity. Content validity, criterion-related validity, and construct validity information are presented in the manual. Content validity is discussed theoretically and in terms of the tasks required by each subtest. A discussion of item analysis is presented as a form of content validity. The criterion-related studies include correlational information with the K-ABC, the Woodcock-Johnson Psycho-Educational Battery–Revised, and various achievement tests. The coefficients are reported as not significant (NS) for many subtests and range from NS to modestly adequate for others.

Cognitive Levels Test (CLT)

The CLT (Algozzine, Eaves, Mann, & Vance, 1988) is designed to be used as a supplement with other more extensive measures, such as the WISC–III or the Stanford-Binet IV. According to the test authors, the test was developed to be quickly and easily administered to determine cognitive functioning. Although administration of this instrument does not require extensive training, the examiner should thoroughly understand instructions for administration and scoring before testing.

The organization of the CLT is illustrated in Table 10.1. This instrument has the advantage of requiring only one basal and ceiling for the entire test. It does not contain timed items. These features aid in the administration of the test.

Available scores for the CLT are the Cognitive Index, Rapid Cognitive Index, Best g Index (BgI), and Abstract Quantitative Reasoning.

Technical Data

Norming Process. The CLT standardization sample included 1,509 students ages 5-0 to 21-11. Variables considered were sex, race/ethnic group (white,

Table 10.1
Organization of the cognitive levels test

Subtest	Description
Verbal Reasoning	Based on vocabulary, similarities, differences, comprehension, analogies, absurdities, and proverbs.
Abstract Reasoning	Based on figure analogies, figure relations, visual closure, missing elements, paper folding, and abstract visualization.
Quantitative Reasoning	Based on counting, numerical problem solving, equation building, number series, and numerical vocabulary.
Memory	Based on long-term and short-term memory items.

black, Hispanic, Asian/Pacific Islander, Native American, or other), parental education level, parental occupation, region, community size (large city, city, small town, or rural). Variables reported in the manual reflect U.S. census data, with the exception of overrepresentations of college-educated parents and students from the southern region and some differences in parental occupation.

Reliability. The technical manual reports internal consistency reliability and test-retest. The internal consistency study employed the K-R 20 method, which yielded coefficients in the .90s range for more than 75% of the scores studied. A single test-retest study for a sample of 14 students revealed a correlation of .94 for the Cognitive Index. The technical manual presents no other reliability information.

Validity. Criterion-related validity studies for cognitive instruments included three instruments in four separate studies. Two studies correlated the CLT Cognitive Index and the WISC–R Full Scale IQ, with coefficients of .84 and .83 reported for a total of 50 students. An independent criterion-related validity study with the Peabody Picture Vocabulary Test–Revised and the CLT Cognitive Index for a college sample of 30 students resulted in a coefficient of .57 (Overton & Mardoyan-Apperson, 1988). The final cognitive study correlated the CLT with the Index of Learning Potential of the Analysis of Learning Potential and resulted in a correlation of .72 for a sample of 33 grade school students. The manual includes additional criterion-related validity information concerning studies with these academic instruments: the Analysis of Learning Potential, Woodcock Reading Mastery Tests (Total Reading cluster scores), KeyMath, and California Achievement Test. Coefficients ranged from .62 to .83.

☐ **CHECK YOUR UNDERSTANDING**

Complete Activity 10.4.

Activity 10.4

Answer the following questions.

1. The K-ABC is administered to children aged ________ to ________ .
2. The K-ABC has a strong ________________ base, which applies the ____ ____________ - ________________ model of processing.
3. The K-ABC has the advantage of containing measures of both __________ ______ and ________________ , which is useful in calculating discrepancies.
4. The K-ABC has a complete ________________ version, which is used for Spanish-speaking children who do not know English.
5. The DTLA–3 has attention-enhanced and attention-reduced scoring to help document the possibility of ________________

Kaufman Adolescent and Adult Intelligence Test (KAIT)

The KAIT (Kaufman & Kaufman, 1993) was designed to measure the general intellectual ability of persons aged 11 to 85+. The theoretical construction includes measurement of fluid and crystallized scales. The manual states that the crystallized scales are thought to measure acquired concepts that may be influenced by one's previous educational and cultural experiences. The fluid scales are thought to measure the abilities one needs to solve new problems. The test may be administered as a whole battery or may be administered as a core battery comprised of six subtests. The standard scores are based on only the six core subtests: Definitions, Rebus Learning, Logical Steps, Auditory Comprehension, Mystery Codes, and Double Meanings.

Available scores include subtest percentile ranks, scaled scores for crystallized and fluid scales, crystallized IQ, fluid IQ, and standard IQ score (composite intelligence scale) derived from the core battery. The KAIT manual includes research that is relevant for professionals working with special adult populations, such as persons with clinical depression, persons with Alzheimer's type dementia, and so on.

Technical Data

Norming Process. The standardization of the KAIT included a sample of more than 2,600 persons aged 11 to 94 years. Twenty-seven states participated in the standardization process. The 1988 U.S. census data served as the framework for addressing the diversity of the sample. Geographic region, age, parental education, and race and ethnicity (white, black, Hispanic, or other) were considered in the selection of the sample.

Reliability. The reliability studies include split-half internal reliability and test-retest reliability studies. The average split-half reliability coefficients ranged from .71 to .97. Total sample average test-retest coefficients ranged from .63 to .95.

Validity. Research presented in the KAIT manual includes construct validity, criterion-related validity, and factor analysis. Data from concurrent validity studies vary by age, with the most acceptable correlations occurring with the WAIS for persons in the 16–19 age range. Correlations with the K-ABC ranged from not acceptable to modestly adequate for students ages 11–12. Concurrent validity research with the Stanford-Binet IV yielded coefficients that are modestly adequate.

The Kaufman Brief Intelligence Test (KBIT)

Designed to be used as a screening instrument, the KBIT (Kaufman & Kaufman, 1990) should not be used as part of a comprehensive evaluation to determine eligibility or placement. According to the manual, the test serves to screen students who may be at risk for developing educational problems and who then should receive a comprehensive evaluation. The test takes about 15–30 minutes to administer and consists of two subtests: Vocabulary and Matrices. The Vocabulary subtest has two parts: Expressive and Definitions. These two subtests are designed to measure crystallized intelligence (Vocabulary) and fluid intelligence (Matrices).

Technical Data

Norming Process. The standardization sample of the KBIT included 2,022 persons ranging in age from 4 to 90 years. Consideration was given to gender, educational level of parents, geographic region, and race and ethnicity. The sample selection was based on U.S. census data for 1985.

Reliability. Reliability information presented in the manual consists of split-half reliability and test-retest reliability. The split-half reliability coefficients are acceptable, with most reported to be in the .80s and .90s. Test-retest coefficients are all reported to be within the .80s and .90s.

Validity. The manual reports on item validity, construct validity, and criterion-related validity. Criterion-related validity studies were conducted with the WISC–R, K-ABC, and the WAIS–R. The criterion-related validity coefficients were modestly adequate for the K-ABC achievement scores and for the full-scale IQ scores of the Wechsler Scales.

Research on Intelligence Measures

Many of the most popular intelligence measures have recently been reviewed, and research continues to emerge in the literature. Some of the current research studies and test reviews are summarized here.

1. In a review of the WJ–R Tests of Cognitive Ability, Schrank (1993) stated that this instrument measures eight factors of cognitive functioning as defined in the theoretical construct of crystallized intelligence. Schrank further suggested that this allows the evaluator to describe the individual student's pattern of cognitive strengths and weaknesses.

2. Prewett (1992) found that the K-BIT's correlation with the WISC–III supports its use as a screening instrument. Prewett and McCaffery (1993) found that the K-BIT should be interpreted as only a rough estimate of the IQ that can be obtained on the Stanford-Binet. Kaufman and Wang (1992) found that the differences in means obtained by blacks, Hispanics, and whites on the K-BIT are in agreement with mean differences found on the WISC–R.

3. For students aged 11 to 12½ years of age, the KAIT was found to be a more accurate measure of general intelligence than the K-ABC (Kaufman, 1993a). This may be partly the result of the ages specified for each test: the KAIT for ages 11–85 and the K-ABC for ages 2½ to 12½.

4. Olivarez, Palmer, and Guillemard (1992) found that the WISC–R and the K-ABC demonstrated biased results when used with referred and nonreferred minority and nonminority students. Using a discrepancy model for identifying learning disabilities, examiners overpredicted the academic achievement of blacks and Hispanics based on cognitive scores from the K-ABC and the WISC–R (Palmer, Olivarez, Willson, & Fordyce, 1989). The discrepancy between achievement and IQ scores may be inaccurate and could lead to the overidentification of students with learning disabilities.

5. In one study using the Stanford-Binet IV, students in a general education classroom were found to have more variability in their scores than students already receiving special education services. This may be due in part to the greater degree of homogeneity of the group of students receiving services (Kline, Synder, Guilmette, & Castellanos, 1993). Gridley and McIntosh (1991) found that the scores of children aged 2–6 years and 7–11 years did not support the factor theory purported by the test authors.

6. Use of the WISC–III as a replacement for the earlier edition, the WISC–R, is supported although differences in subtest and IQ scores have been found (Smith, Stovall, & Geraghty, 1994). In a study by Smith, Smith, and Mohlke (1994), the differences were greater for the Verbal IQ score than stated in the manual, somewhat less for the Performance IQ score, and similar for the Full Scale IQ score.

Assessing Adaptive Behavior

Adaptive behavior is a term used to describe how well a student adapts to her environment. The importance of this concept was underscored by the passage of PL 94–142, which contained the requirement of nondiscriminatory assessment—specifically, the mandate to use more than one instrument yielding a single IQ score for diagnosis (*Federal Register,* 1977). The measurement of adaptive behavior must be considered before a person meets the criteria for mental retardation. A student who functions within the subaverage range of intelligence as measured on an IQ test but who exhibits age-appropriate behaviors outside of the classroom should not be placed in a setting designed for students with mental retardation.

Adaptive behavior measurement is also emphasized as one possible method of promoting nonbiased assessment of culturally different students (Mercer, 1979; Reschly, 1982). Use of adaptive behavior scales in the assessment of students with learning problems can add another perspective that may be useful in planning educational interventions (Bruininks, Thurlow, & Gilman, 1987; Horn & Fuchs, 1987). Other researchers have found the assessment of adaptive behavior useful in educational interventions for learning disabled students (Bender & Golden, 1988; Weller, Strawser, & Buchanan, 1985). Adaptive behavior scales are instruments that usually are designed to be answered by a parent or teacher or some other person familiar with the student's functioning in the everyday world. The questions are constructed to obtain information about the student's independent functioning level in and out of school. Many of the items measure self-reliance and daily living skills at home and in the community.

Reschly (1982) reviewed literature of adaptive behavior and determined that several common features were presented. The measuring of adaptive behavior had the common concepts of (a) developmental appropriateness, (b) cultural context, (c) situational or generalized, and (d) domains. Reschly found that definitions of adaptive behavior and the measurement of that behavior were based on expectations of a particular age, within the person's culture, in given or general situations, and that the behaviors measured were classified into domains.

Harrison (1987) reviewed research on adaptive behavior and drew the following conclusions:

1. There is a moderate relationship between adaptive behavior and intelligence.
2. Correlational studies indicate that adaptive behavior has a low relationship with school achievement, but the effect of adaptive behavior on achievement may be greater than the correlations indicate and adaptive behavior/in school may have a greater relationship with achievement than adaptive behavior/outside school.
3. There is typically a moderate to a moderately high relationship between different measures of adaptive behavior.
4. Adaptive behavior is predictive of certain aspects of future vocational performance.
5. There is a possibility that the use of adaptive behavior scales could result in the declassification of mentally retarded individuals, but no evidence was located to indicate that this is actually happening.
6. There are few race and ethnic group differences on adaptive behavior scales.
7. There are differences between parents' and teachers' ratings on adaptive behavior scales.
8. Adaptive behavior scales differentiate among different classification groups such as normal, mentally retarded, slow learner, learning disabled, and emotionally disturbed.
9. Adaptive behavior scales differentiate among mentally retarded people in different residential and vocational settings.
10. Adaptive behavior is multidimensional.
11. Adaptive behavior can be increased through placement in settings which focus on training adaptive behavior skills.
12. Adaptive behavior scales exhibit adequate stability and interrater reliability.

Source: From "Research with Adaptive Behavior Scales" by P. Harrison, 1987, *The Journal of Special Education, 21,* pp. 60–61. Copyright 1987 by Pro-Ed, Inc. Reprinted by permission.

Although earlier research found that there were differences between parent and teacher ratings on adaptive behavior. Foster-Gaitskell and Pratt (1989), found that when the method of administration and familiarity with the adaptive behavior instrument were controlled, differences between parent and teacher ratings were not significant.

The formal measurement of adaptive behavior began with the development of the Vineland Social Maturity Scale (Doll, 1935). The assessment of adaptive behavior as a common practice in the diagnosis of students, however, did not occur until litigation found fault with school systems for the placement of minority students based only on IQ results (Witt & Martens, 1984). Some researchers feel that the assessment of adaptive behavior in students being evaluated for special education eligibility should not be mandated until further research on adaptive behavior instruments has occurred (Kamphaus, 1987; Witt & Martens, 1984). After reviewing several of the newer adaptive behavior scales, Evans and Bradley-Johnson (1988) cautioned examiners to select instruments carefully due to the low reliability and validity of the instruments. These authors issued the following considerations for professionals using adaptive behavior instruments:

(a) Scales must be selected that were standardized using the type of informant to be employed in the assessment (e.g., ABI [Adaptive Behavior Inventory] with teachers and Vineland Survey Form or SIB [Scales of Independent Behavior] with caregivers).
(b) If valid information is to be obtained, the response format of the scale must be readily understood by the informant, i.e., not be confusing.
(c) In some cases it will be helpful to select a scale with both normative data on both a nonretarded and a retarded group.
(d) If information on maladaptive behavior is desired, only ABS:SE [Adaptive Behavior Scale, School Edition], the SIB, and the Vineland Survey Form address this area.
(e) The number of items on subtests of interest should be considered in interpretation to insure that an adequate sample of behavior has been obtained.
(f) For eligibility decisions, total test results, rather than subtest scores, should be used. Total test results are based upon a larger sample of behavior and are much more reliable and valid.
(g) If different scales are used for the same student, quite different results may be obtained due to many factors, including different response formats, content, and technical adequacy.
(h) Different informant (teacher vs. parent) may perceive a student's performance differently due to personal biases and the different demands of the settings.
(i) Validity of results must be evaluated in each case based upon problems inherent to rating scales (e.g., informant bias, avoidance of extreme choices).

Source: From "A Review of Recently Developed Measures of Adaptive Behavior" by L. Evans and S. Bradley-Johnson, 1988, *Psychology in the Schools, 25,* p. 286. Copyright 1988 by Psychology in the Schools. Reprinted by permission.

The examiner should remember these considerations when selecting an adaptive behavior scale and choose the instrument that best suits the needs of the student.

☐ **CHECK YOUR UNDERSTANDING**

Complete Activity 10.5.

Activity 10.5

Complete the sentences and answer the questions that follow.

1. Adaptive behavior is the ability one has to ______
2. Assessments of adaptive behavior may be used to ______
3. According to Reschly (1982), what are the four common concepts in the assessment of adaptive behavior? ______
4. What are some of the findings summarized by Harrison (1987) about research of adaptive behavior? ______

The Review of Adaptive Behavior Scales

The adaptive behavior scales reviewed in this chapter are the Vineland Adaptive Behavior Scales (Survey Form, Expanded Form, and Classroom Edition), the AAMR Adaptive Behavior Scale–School, Second Edition, the Adaptive Behavior Inventory (ABI and ABI Short Form), and the Adaptive Behavior Inventory for Children. As stated previously, examiners should be cautious in selecting the scale appropriate for the student's needs. Some scales have been normed using special populations only, some scales have been normed using both special and normal populations, and some scales contain items for assessing maladaptive behavior as well as adaptive behavior. The size of the samples used during standardization and the reliability and validity information should be considered.

Vineland Adaptive Behavior Scales

A revision of the original Vineland Social Maturity Scale (Doll, 1935), the Vineland Adaptive Behavior Scales (Sparrow, Balla, & Cicchetti, 1984), contain revisions so extreme that the battery can be considered new. The scales have three forms: Interview Edition, Survey Form; Interview Edition, Expanded

Form; and Classroom Edition. The differences between the three instruments are number of items, method of administration, and areas assessed (the Classroom Edition does not contain items to assess maladaptive behavior). Table 10.2 illustrates the number of items for each version of the scale. Materials used for each of the three scales are different.

Interview Edition Survey Form. The Interview Edition Survey Form (Sparrow, Balla, & Cicchetti, 1984) was designed to replace the original Vineland Social Maturity Scale. The 297 items, administered in an interview fashion to a parent or caregiver, are used to assess the adaptive behavior of individuals from birth through 18-11 years of age. The areas assessed include communication, daily living skills, socialization, motor skills, and maladaptive behavior. The maladaptive portion is an optional section that may be administered if worrisome behavior is of concern for a particular student. The scores that may be obtained include standard scores (mean, 100; standard deviation, 15), percentile ranks, stanines, adaptive levels, and age equivalents. The "Score Summary"

Table 10.2
Number of items in each version of the Vineland by domain and subdomain.

Domain and Subdomain	Survey Form	Expanded Form	Classroom Edition
Communication	67	133	66
Receptive	13	23	10
Expressive	31	76	29
Written	23	34	24
Daily Living Skills	92	201	99
Personal	39	90	36
Domestic	21	45	21
Community	32	66	42
Socialization	66	134	53
Interpersonal Relationships	28	50	17
Play and Leisure Time	20	48	18
Coping Skills	18	36	18
Motor Skills	36	72	29
Gross	20	42	16
Fine	16	31	13
ADAPTIVE BEHAVIOR COMPOSITE	261	541	244
Maladaptive Behavior	36	36	0

Source: From *Vineland Adaptive Behavior Scales* (p. 3) by S. S. Sparrow, D. A. Balla, and D. V. Cicchetti, 1984, Circle Pines, MN: American Guidance Service. Copyright 1984 by American Guidance Service. Reprinted by permission.

portion of the protocol is shown in Figure 10.8. The Survey Form includes supplementary norms that enable the examiner to compare student with disabilities to other students with the same disabling conditions. The supplementary norms included students with mental retardation, emotional disturbance, visual impairments, and hearing impairments.

Technical Data for the Survey Form

Norming Process. The standardization sample for the Vineland included 3,000 persons ranging in age from birth to 18-11 years. Variables considered in the sample were sex, geographic region, parental educational level, race or ethnic group, community size, and age. Variables considered for the supplementary norm group were disabling condition, ambulatory and nonambulatory persons with mental retardation, and age. The Vineland was administered to 723 persons from six states in a national tryout before the actual norming and standardization process. This tryout enabled the authors to refine items and scoring procedures in the developmental version of the interview format.

Reliability. Three types of reliability studies are included in the manual: split-half, test-retest, and interrater reliability. The split-half reliability coefficients ranged from .83 to .94 for median coefficients reported for domains and adaptive behavior composites. Test-retest coefficients ranged from the low .80s to the high .90s for a sample of 484 persons. The interrater reliability coefficients ranged from .62 to .78.

Validity. Validity information included construct validity, content validity, and criterion-related validity studies. Construct validity was based on developmental progression and factor analysis of domains and subdomains. Content validity is presented as a discussion of item development and the national tryout of items in a developmental version of the Interview Edition. In criterion-related validity studies, the new version was compared with the original Vineland, the K-ABC, and the Peabody Picture Vocabulary Test–Revised. The domain of communication had the highest correlation with the K-ABC achievement scale and the Peabody Picture Vocabulary Test–Revised. As would be expected when comparing an adaptive behavior scale with academic or intellectual measures, other areas compared yielded low correlations. This is due to the different domains or constructs measured by these different types of instruments.

Interview Edition Expanded Form. Like the Survey Form, this scale is administered in an interview format. The Expanded Form contains 577 items and can be used to design IEP objectives for adaptive behavior (Sparrow, Balla, & Cicchetti, 1984). Of the 577 items, 297 are contained in the Survey Form. Adaptive behavior for persons ranging in age from birth through 18-11 may be assessed using the Expanded Form. This form requires from 60 to 90 minutes to administer and provides a detailed assessment of adaptive behavior functioning of the student. It also includes normative data for both nondisabled and disabled populations. Figure 10.9 illustrates the Expanded Form program planning report.

Vineland Adaptive Behavior Scales: INTERVIEW EDITION Survey Form

Individual's name ______________________ Chronological age ____________

Date of interview ____________ Supplementary norm group (if applicable) ____________

Before beginning the score summary, read Chapter 5 in the manual.

SCORE SUMMARY

SUBDOMAIN		Raw Score	Standard Score $\bar{X}$ = 100, *SD* = 15 Tables B.1 and B.2	Band of Error ___% Confidence Tables B.3	National %ile Rank Tables B.4	Stanine Tables B.4	Supplementary Norm Group %ile Rank Tables B.5	Adaptive Level TableB.6 and B.8	Supplementary Norm Group Adaptive Level TableB.7 and B.9	Age Equivalent TableB.10 and B.11
	Receptive									
	Expressive									
	Written									
COMMUNICATION DOMAIN	SUM			±						
	Personal									
	Domestic									
	Community									
DAILY LIVING SKILLS DOMAIN	SUM			±						
	Interpersonal Relationships									
	Play and Leisure Time									
	Coping Skills									
SOCIALIZATION DOMAIN	SUM			±						
(For ages to 5-11-30)	Gross									
	Fine									
MOTOR SKILLS DOMAIN	SUM			±						
	SUM OF DOMAIN STANDARD SCORES									
ADAPTIVE BEHAVIOR COMPOSITE				±						

(See Chapter 5 in the manual to graph scores.)

SCORE PROFILE

	Standard Score ± Band of Error	20	30	40	50	60	70	80	90	100	110	120	130	140	150	160
COMMUNICATION DOMAIN	±															
DAILY LIVING SKILLS DOMAIN	±															
SOCIALIZATION DOMAIN	±															
MOTOR SKILLS DOMAIN	±															
ADAPTIVE BEHAVIOR COMPOSITE	±															

percentile rank: 1 2 5 9 16 25 37 50 63 75 84 91 95 98 99

−5*SD* −4*SD* −3*SD* −2*SD* −1*SD* MEAN +1*SD* +2*SD* +3*SD* +4*SD*

OPTIONAL MALADAPTIVE BEHAVIOR DOMAIN (Administer for ages 5-0-0 and older)		Raw Score	Maladaptive Level: Table B.12	Supplementary Norm Group Maladaptive Level: Table b.13
	Part 1			
	Parts 1 and 2			

Additional interpretive information (see Chapters 5 and 6 in the manual) ____________________

Recommendations ____________________

AGS®

Figure 10.8
Score summary portion of the protocol for the Vineland Adaptive Behavior Scales.
Source: From *Vineland Adaptive Behavior Scales, Protocol* by S. S. Sparrow, D. A. Balla, and D. V. Cicchetti, 1984, Circle Pines, MN: American Guidance Service. Copyright 1984 by American Guidance Service. Reprinted by permission.

COMMUNICATION DOMAIN

GENERAL OBJECTIVES: **Improvement will be exhibited in the following areas of *Receptive* communication (check all that apply):**

_____ A. Beginning to understand
_____ B. Beginning to listen
_____ C. Pointing to body parts
_____ D. Following instructions
_____ E. Listening and attending

Short-term Objective	Program Beginning Date	Method of Implementation	Method of Evaluation	Mastery Criterion	Program Ending Date

GENERAL OBJECTIVES: **Improvement will be exhibited in the following areas of *Expressive* communication (check all that apply):**

_____ A. Beginning affective expression
_____ B. Pre-speech sounds
_____ C. Pre-speech nonverbal expression
_____ D. Beginning to talk
_____ E. Vocabulary
_____ F. Talking in sentences
_____ G. Using names
_____ H. Asking questions
_____ I. Using abstract concepts
_____ J. Relating experiences
_____ K. Using prepositions
_____ L. Using function words
_____ M. Articulating
_____ N. Reciting
_____ O. Using plural nouns and verb tense
_____ P. Giving information about self
_____ Q. Expressing complex ideas

Short-term Objective	Program Beginning Date	Method of Implementation	Method of Evaluation	Mastery Criterion	Program Ending Date

Figure 10.9
Expanded Form program planning report of the Vineland Adaptive Behavior Scales.
Source: From *Vineland Adaptive Behavior Scales, Program Planning Report* (p. 2) by S. S. Sparrow, D. A. Balla, and D. V. Cicchetti, 1984, Circle Pines, MN: American Guidance Service. Copyright 1984 by American Guidance Service. Reprinted by permission.

Technical Data for the Expanded Form

Norming Process. The standardization and norming process was the same for both the Expanded and Survey Forms of the Interview Edition.

Reliability. The manual reports on reliability studies using split-half, test-retest, and interrater reliability measures. Split-half reliability coefficients were in the .80s for the standardization sample and in the .80s and .90s for supplementary norms. Information for the test-retest and interrater reliability is based on the Survey Form information. The manual also gives information regarding intercorrelations and standard error of measurement.

Validity. Information given includes construct validity, content validity, and criterion-related validity. Studies were based on the Survey Form, and discussion of estimating coefficients for the Expanded Form is included.

Classroom Edition. The Classroom Edition of the Vineland contains 244 items designed to assess the adaptive behavior functioning of students in the classroom (Sparrow et al., 1984). Students from the age of 3 to 12-11 may be assessed using this version. Figure 10.10 illustrates the type of items and the format used on the Classroom Edition. The areas assessed include communication, daily living skills, socialization, and motor skills.

Technical Data for the Classroom Edition

Norming Process. Although the norming process was representative of the U.S. population for the other editions of this instrument, the Classroom Edition sample was underrepresented by students from rural areas, and other differences in norming have been noted (McLoughlin & Lewis, 1990).

Reliability. Test developers studied internal consistency using coefficient alpha, with coefficients for specific domains ranging from .77 to .96 and .96 to .98 for composites.

Validity. Validity studies included construct, content, and criterion-related studies. The manual presents construct validity through a discussion of developmental progression and factor analysis. Selection and development of test items are given as evidence of content validity. The Classroom Edition was compared with the K-ABC, the Peabody Picture Vocabulary Test–Revised, and the WISC–R. Additional studies compared the Classroom Edition with the Stanford-Binet and the Woodcock-Johnson Preschool Scale. Correlation coefficients ranged from low (.20s) to fair (.50s to .60s).

AAMR Adaptive Behavior Scale–School, Second Edition (ABS–S2)

Test developers constructed the ABS–S2 (Lambert, Nihira, & Leland, 1993) as one method to determine if persons meet the criteria for the diagnosis of mental retardation. The ABS–S2 is divided into two parts based on (a) independent

	Observed Performance	Estimated Performance
40. Demonstrates understanding of $\frac{1}{2}$, $\frac{1}{3}$, and $\frac{1}{4}$. (If the child demonstrates understanding of only one or two of the symbols, score 1.)	2 1 0	2 1 0
41. Demonstrates understanding of the following symbols: $, =, %, and [decimal point]. (If the child demonstrates understanding of only two or three of the symbols, score 1.)	2 1 0	2 1 0
42. Demonstrates knowledge of the multiplication tables through 9. (If the child demonstrates knowledge of the multiplication tables through some number between 1 and 9, score 1.)	2 1 0	2 1 0

FOR PERSON SCORING AND INTERPRETING ONLY:

Sum of 2s, 1s, 0s		
COMMUNITY RAW SCORE (Total observed and estimated sums)		

COMMENTS AND OBSERVATIONS ________

ITEM SCORES
2—Yes, usually
1—Sometimes or partially
0—No, never

SOCIALIZATION DOMAIN
INTERPERSONAL RELATIONSHIPS SUBDOMAIN

	Observed Performance	Estimated Performance
1. Shows desire to please parent or caregiver or other familiar person (for example, gives a gift or performs a helpful task).	2 1 0	2 1 0
2. Labels happiness, sadness, fear, and anger in self (for example, says, "I'm sad").	2 1 0	2 1 0
3. Imitates simple adult movements, such as clapping hands or waving good-bye, in response to a model.	2 1 0	2 1 0
4. Imitates a relatively complex task several hours after it was performed by another. (For example, the child imitates sweeping, hammering nails, or drying dishes. Any object required to do the actual task need not be present.)	2 1 0	2 1 0
5. Imitates adult phrases heard on previous occasions. (For example, the child has one doll call to another, "Honey, I'm home.")	2 1 0	2 1 0
6. Addresses at least two familiar people by name (for example, "Mommy," "Daddy," a first name, or a nickname).	2 1 0	2 1 0
7. Identifies people by characteristics other than name, when asked (for example, says, "That's Tony's sister").	2 1 0	2 1 0
8. Laughs or smiles appropriately in response to positive statements. (The child must understand what is being said, not simply respond to the tone of voice, to score 2.)	2 1 0	2 1 0
9. Responds verbally and positively to good fortune of others. (For example, the child congratulates a friend who receives an award.)	2 1 0	2 1 0
10. Initiates conversations on topics of particular interest to others. (If the child does so only when the topic is also of interest to the child, score 0.)	2 1 0	2 1 0

The next item is on the following page. Before going on, please determine that you recorded a score for every item on this page.

Figure 10.10
A portion of the protocol for the classroom edition of the Vineland Adaptive Behavior Scales, showing the type of items and the format.

Source: From *Vineland Adaptive Behavior Scales, Classroom Edition, Protocol* (p. 11) by S. S. Sparrow, D. A. Balla, and D. V. Cicchetti, 1984, Circle Pines, MN: American Guidance Service. Reprinted by permission.

living skills and (b) social behavior. The domains assessed in each are listed in Figure 10.11.

The person most familiar with the student may administer the scale by completing the items, or a professional who is familiar with the child may complete the items. The information is plotted on a profile sheet to represent the student's adaptive behavior functioning. Standard scores, percentile ranks, and age equivalents are provided in the manual.

Technical Data

Norming Process. The ABS–S2 was normed on a sample of 2,074 persons with mental retardation and 1,254 persons who were nondisabled. The variables of race, gender, ethnicity, urban and rural residence, geographic region, and age (3–18) were considered in the sample.

Reliability. Information on interrater reliability, internal consistency, and test-retest reliability is presented in the manual. All coefficients presented range from adequate to high.

Validity. The examiner's manual addresses construct and item validity for students with and without mental retardation.

Adaptive Behavior Inventory (ABI)

The ABI (Brown & Leigh, 1986) was constructed for use with students with mental retardation and students with developmental delay ranging in age from 6-0 to 18-11; it may also be used for nondisabled students aged 5-0 to 18-11. The ABI contains five scales: Self-Care, Communication, Social Skills, Academic Skills,

Part I: Independent Living Domains	***Part II: Social Behavior Domains***
Independent Functioning	Social Behavior
Physical Development	Conformity
Economic Activity	Trustworthiness
Language Development	Stereotyped and Hyperactive Behavior
Numbers and Time	Self-Abusive Behavior
Prevocational/Vocational Activity	Social Engagement
Self-Direction	Disturbing Interpersonal Behavior
Responsibility	
Socialization	

Figure 10.11
Areas assessed by the AAMR Adaptive Behavior Scale–School, Second Edition.

and Occupational Skills. Each of the scales contains approximately 30 items that are rated by a teacher or professional who is familiar with the student.

Also available is the ABI Short Form, an abbreviated form of the ABI that may be used as a screening or research instrument. Items were selected from all five scales to make up this 50-item instrument.

The scoring of both the ABI and the ABI Short Form is the same. This instrument uses a basal level of 5 consecutive items scored perfectly (3-point response) and a ceiling level of 5 consecutive failures (scored as 0 points: Student does not perform skill). The scoring system is located on the protocol as well as explained in the manual. The derived scores available include scaled scores (mean, 10; standard deviation, 3), Adaptive Behavior Quotient (mean, 100; standard deviation, 15), and percentile ranks. The protocol for the full ABI is shown in Figure 10.12.

Technical Data

Norming Process. The ABI has two norm-reference groups: 1,296 students age 5-0 to 18-11 in the nondisabled sample population and 1,076 students aged 6-0 to 18-11 in the sample population with the mental retardation. The variables considered in the nondisabled population were sex, age, race, ethnicity, language spoken in the home, geographic region, community size, parental occupation, and parental educational level. In the sample of persons with mental retardation, the variables were sex, measured intelligence, etiology of retardation, instructional arrangement, presence of other disabling conditions, and the parental variables of educational and occupational level, community size, and geographic region. The manual also contains the following information regarding the teachers who responded in the norming process: sex, years of experience, and highest degree completed. In most cases, variables appeared to represent total U.S. population percentages reported in the manual.

Reliability. Internal consistency reliability using the coefficient alpha method was studied for sample populations with and without mental retardation. Coefficients were in the .80s and .90s for both groups for both the full scale and the ABI Short Form. Test-retest reliability studies on both sample populations and for the full scale and Short Form yielded coefficients in the .90s.

Validity. The manual includes information on content and criterion-related validity. Item discrimination coefficients are briefly discussed and reported as high. Criterion-related validity studies, for both the full scale and Short Form, were conducted with the Vineland Social Maturity Scale, the Vineland Adaptive Behavior Scales, and the AAMD Adaptive Behavior Scales (a previous edition of the ABS–S2). Coefficients ranged from .35 on Part II of the AAMD scales (maladaptive behavior) to .89 on the AAMD scales' Cognitive domain. Construct validity studies included developmental progression and correlation with measures of intellectual ability, including the WISC–R, Cognitive Abilities Test, Stanford-Binet, Slosson Intelligence Test, Otis-Lennon School Ability Test, the K-ABC, Peabody Picture Vocabulary Test–Revised, and the Arthur Adaptation of

ABI

Adaptive Behavior Inventory

ABI Profile
Response Sheet

Linda Brown & James E. Leigh

Student's Name ____
Address ____

School ____ Grade ____
Examiner's Name ____
Examiner's Title ____
Date of ABI Rating ____ year ____ year
Student's Date of Birth ____ year ____ year
Student's Age ____ year ____ year

SECTION I. ABI PROFILE

ABI SCALES STANDARD SCORES						ABQ-FS	OTHER MEASURES OF INTELLIGENCE, ACHIEVEMENT, OR ADAPTIVE BEHAVIOR					
M = 10 SD = 3	Self-Care	Communication	Social	Academic	Occupational	M = 100 SD = 15	Test Used	Test Used	Test Used	Test Used	Test Used	Test Used
						160						
						155						
20						150						
19						145						
18						140						
17						135						
16						130						
15						125						
14						120						
13						115						
12	•	•	•	•	•	110 •	•	•	•	•	•	•
11	•	•	•	•	•	105 •	•	•	•	•	•	•
10	—	—	—	—	—	100 —	—	—	—	—	—	—
9	•	•	•	•	•	95 •	•	•	•	•	•	•
8	•	•	•	•	•	90 •	•	•	•	•	•	•
7						85						
6						80						
5						75						
4						70						
3						65						
2						60						
1						55						
						50						
						45						
						40						

X = Normal Intelligence Sample **O = MR Sample**

SECTION II. SCORE SUMMARY

ABI SCALES

	Self-Care Skills	Communication Skills	Social Skills	Academic Skills	Occupational Skills
Raw Score =	____	____	____	____	____
Performance Based on the Normal Intelligence Normative Sample					
Standard Score (SS) (Table A) =	____	____	____	____	____
Standard Error of Measurement (SEM) (Tables 8 & 9) =	____	____	____	____	____
Percentile Rank (PR) (Table A) =	____	____	____	____	____
Performance Descriptor (Table 1) =	____	____	____	____	____
Performance Based on the Mentally Retarded Normative Sample					
Standard Score (SS) (Table B) =	____	____	____	____	____
Standard Error of Measurement (SEM) (Tables 8 & 9) =	____	____	____	____	____
Percentile Rank (PR) (Table B) =	____	____	____	____	____
Performance Descriptor (Table 1) =	____	____	____	____	____

ABI COMPOSITE QUOTIENT

	Performance Based on the Normal Sample	MR Sample
Sum of 4 or 5 Standard Scores (SS) =	____	____
ABQ-FS (Table C) =	____	____
Standard Error of Measurement (SEM) (Tables 8 & 9) =	____	____
Percentile Rank (PR) (Table C) =	____	____
Performance Descriptor (Table 1) =	____	____

SECTION III. ADMINISTRATION CONDITIONS

How long has the examiner known the subject being rated?

If the examiner employed information that was obtained from secondary sources (subjects themselves, parents, other professionals), please specify the source(s), the items to which the source(s) contributed, and the degree of reliability which the examiner attributes to the information:

Source	Items	Reliability + Avg. -

How often has the examiner used the ABI?

____ less than 5 times ____ 5 times or more

SECTION IV. INTERPRETATION/RECOMMENDATIONS

Figure 10.12

Protocol for the Adaptive Behavior Inventory.

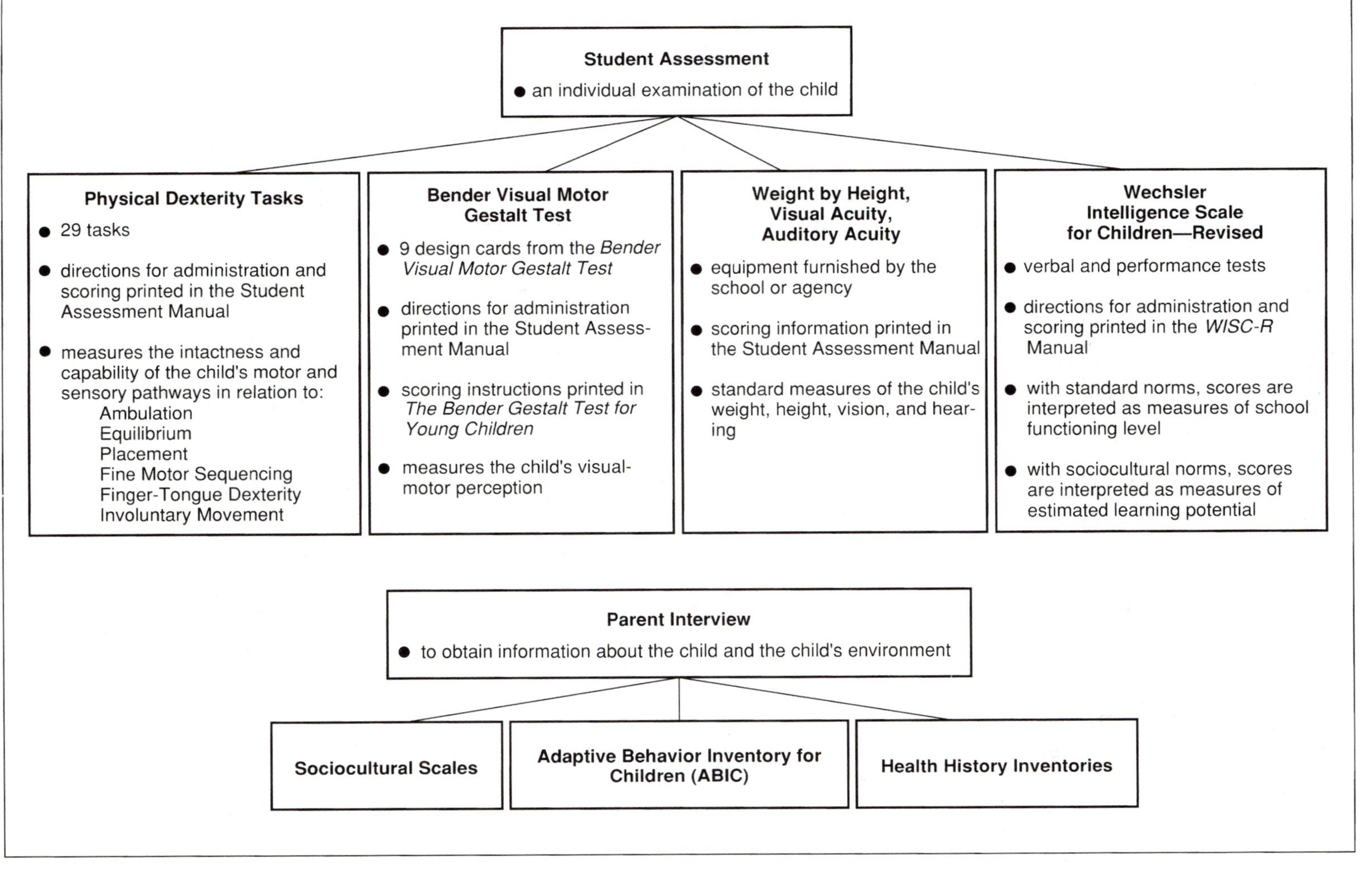

Figure 10.13
Outline of the System of Multicultural Pluralistic Assessment.

Source: From *System of Multicultural Pluralistic Assessment: Student Assessment Manual* (p. 4) by J. R. Mercer and J. F. Lewis, 1978, New York: The Psychological Corporation. Copyright 1978 by The Psychological Corporation.

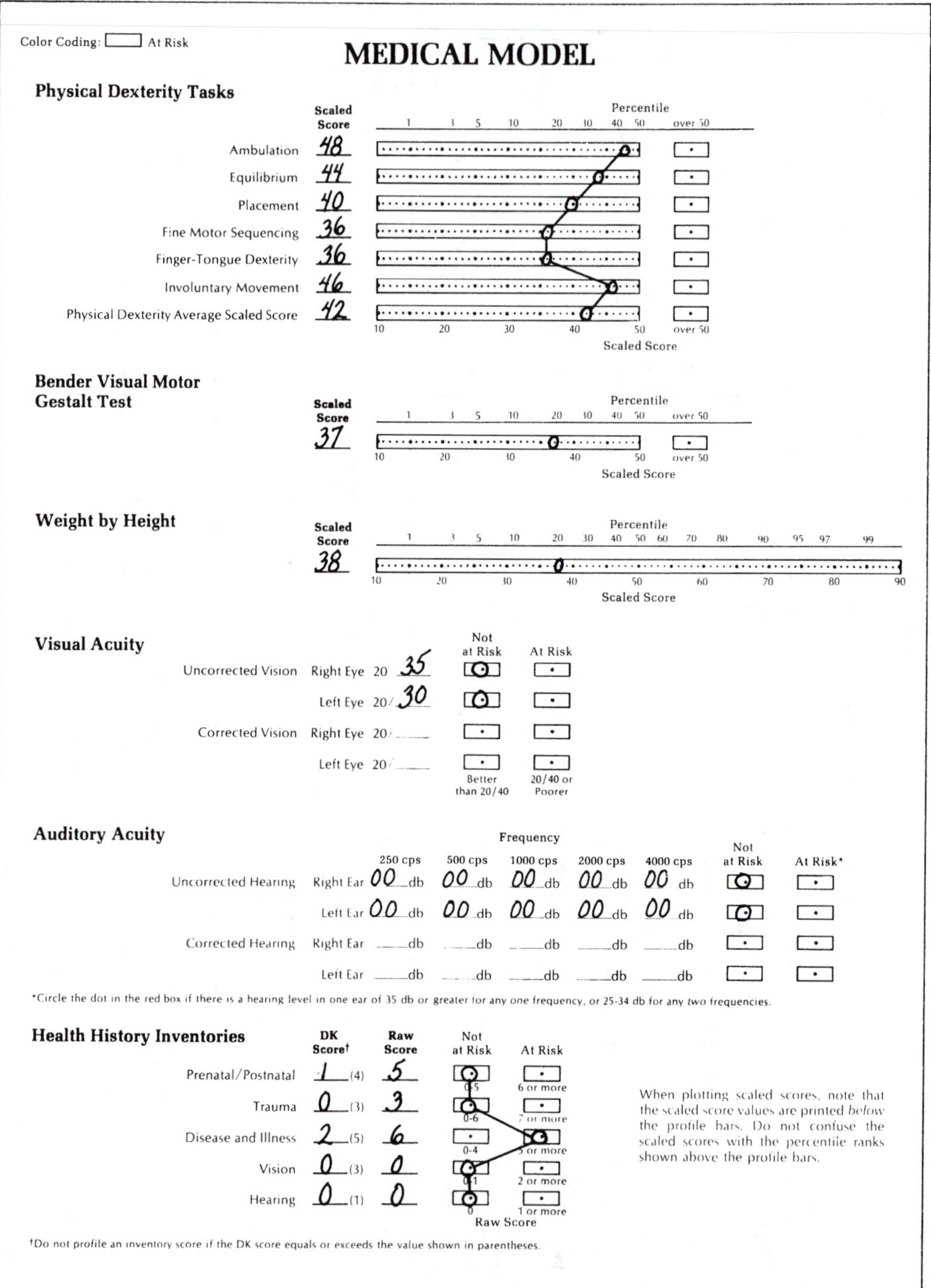

Color Coding: [ ] At Risk

MEDICAL MODEL

Physical Dexterity Tasks

Percentile: 1, 3, 5, 10, 20, 30, 40, 50, over 50
Scaled Score: 10, 20, 30, 40, 50, over 50

	Scaled Score
Ambulation	48
Equilibrium	44
Placement	40
Fine Motor Sequencing	36
Finger-Tongue Dexterity	36
Involuntary Movement	46
Physical Dexterity Average Scaled Score	42

Bender Visual Motor Gestalt Test

Percentile: 1, 3, 5, 10, 20, 30, 40, 50, over 50
Scaled Score: 10, 20, 30, 40, 50, over 50

Scaled Score: 37

Weight by Height

Percentile: 1, 3, 5, 10, 20, 30, 40, 50, 60, 70, 80, 90, 95, 97, 99
Scaled Score: 10, 20, 30, 40, 50, 60, 70, 80, 90

Scaled Score: 38

Visual Acuity

			Not at Risk (Better than 20/40)	At Risk (20/40 or Poorer)
Uncorrected Vision	Right Eye	20/35	⊙	•
	Left Eye	20/30	⊙	•
Corrected Vision	Right Eye	20/___	•	•
	Left Eye	20/___	•	•

Auditory Acuity

		250 cps	500 cps	1000 cps	2000 cps	4000 cps	Not at Risk	At Risk*
Uncorrected Hearing	Right Ear	00 db	00 db	00 db	00 db	00 db	⊙	•
	Left Ear	00 db	00 db	00 db	00 db	00 db	⊙	•
Corrected Hearing	Right Ear	___db	___db	___db	___db	___db	•	•
	Left Ear	___db	___db	___db	___db	___db	•	•

*Circle the dot in the red box if there is a hearing level in one ear of 35 db or greater for any one frequency, or 25-34 db for any two frequencies.

Health History Inventories

	DK Score†	Raw Score	Not at Risk	At Risk
Prenatal/Postnatal	1 (4)	5	0-5	6 or more
Trauma	0 (3)	3	0-6	7 or more
Disease and Illness	2 (5)	6	0-4	5 or more
Vision	0 (3)	0	0-1	2 or more
Hearing	0 (1)	0	0	1 or more

Raw Score

When plotting scaled scores, note that the scaled score values are printed *below* the profile bars. Do not confuse the scaled scores with the percentile ranks shown above the profile bars.

†Do not profile an inventory score if the DK score equals or exceeds the value shown in parentheses.

Figure 10.14
An illustrative SOMPA profile.

Source: From *System of Multicultural Pluralistic Assessment: Student Assessment Manual* (pp. 56 & 57) by J. R. Mercer and J. F. Lewis, 1978, New York: The Psychological Corporation. Copyright 1978 by The Psychological Corporation.

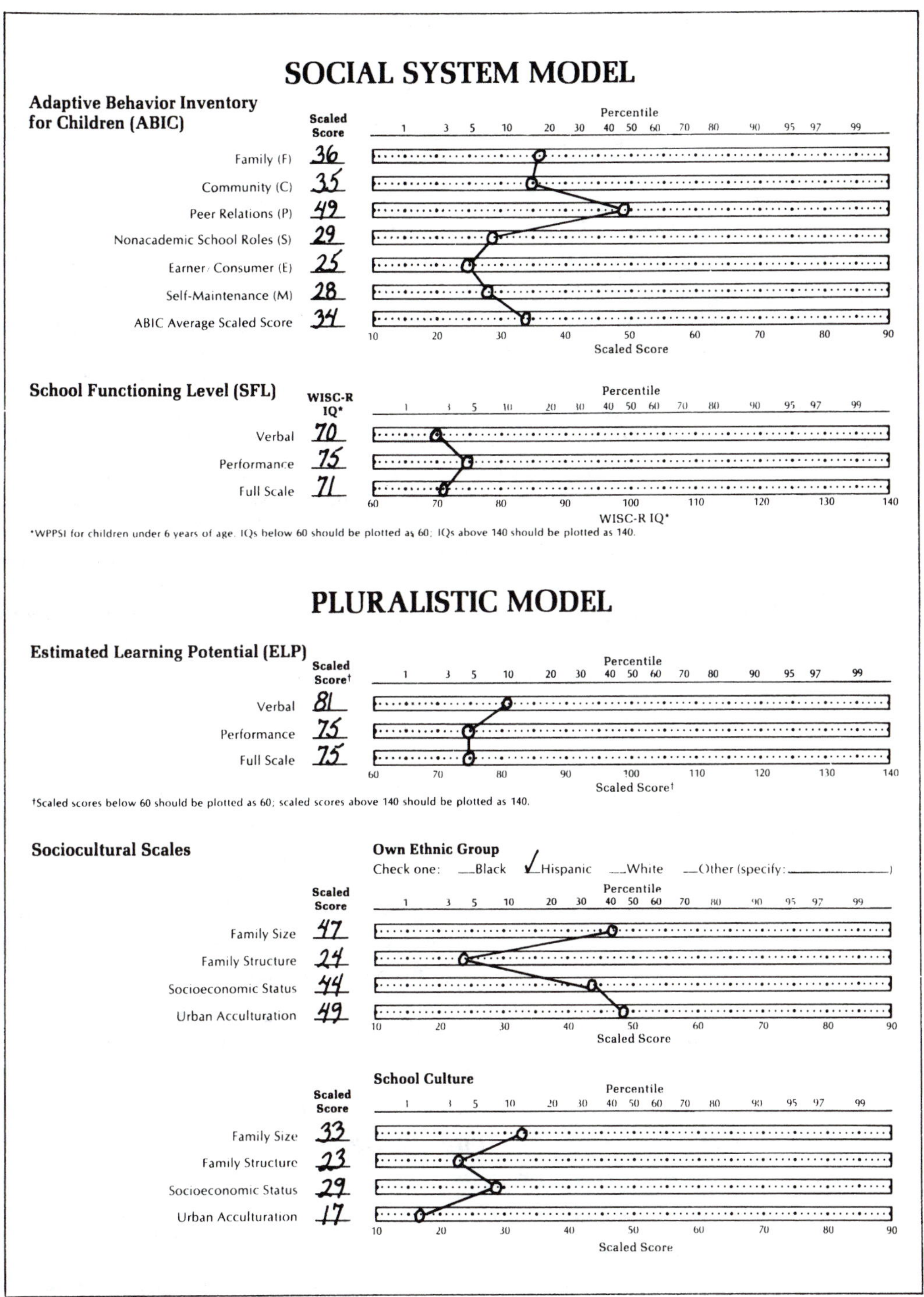

SOCIAL SYSTEM MODEL

Adaptive Behavior Inventory for Children (ABIC)

	Scaled Score
Family (F)	36
Community (C)	35
Peer Relations (P)	49
Nonacademic School Roles (S)	29
Earner/Consumer (E)	25
Self-Maintenance (M)	28
ABIC Average Scaled Score	34

School Functioning Level (SFL)

	WISC-R IQ*
Verbal	70
Performance	75
Full Scale	71

*WPPSI for children under 6 years of age. IQs below 60 should be plotted as 60; IQs above 140 should be plotted as 140.

PLURALISTIC MODEL

Estimated Learning Potential (ELP)

	Scaled Score†
Verbal	81
Performance	75
Full Scale	75

†Scaled scores below 60 should be plotted as 60; scaled scores above 140 should be plotted as 140.

Sociocultural Scales

Own Ethnic Group

Check one: __Black ✓Hispanic __White __Other (specify: ________)

	Scaled Score
Family Size	47
Family Structure	24
Socioeconomic Status	44
Urban Acculturation	49

School Culture

	Scaled Score
Family Size	33
Family Structure	23
Socioeconomic Status	29
Urban Acculturation	17

Figure 10.14, continued

the Leiter International Performance Scale. Most coefficients were in the .30s to .60s range, with the highest coefficients of .86 for the Slosson and the Cognitive Abilities Test.

Adaptive Behavior Inventory for Children (ABIC)

The ABIC is actually a small part of a larger assessment system, the System of Multicultural Pluralistic Assessment (SOMPA) (Mercer, 1979). Jane Mercer designed the system in an attempt to provide nondiscriminatory assessment for children from different cultural or linguistic backgrounds. SOMPA is used by psychologists and other professionals to obtain a more **culture fair** representation of a student's educational potential. Much of Mercer's work reflects an effort to eliminate the overrepresentation of minority populations in special education classes. The SOMPA design is illustrated in Figure 10.13.

culture fair Describes testing that is thought to be fair for minority cultures.

The ABIC is the second part of a comprehensive parent interview that can be completed by a teacher or other professional. The ABIC contains six scales reflecting the various environments to which a student must adapt: family, community, peer relations, nonacademic school roles, earner/consumer, and self-maintenance (Mercer & Lewis, 1977). Responses are scored as 0, 1, or 2 by the interviewer. Derived scores available include scaled scores and percentile ranks. A profile of percentile scores may be plotted as shown in Figure 10.14.

Technical Data

Norming Process. The ABIC was standardized on 2,085 children aged 5 years to 11 years, 11 months. Students included in the sample were described as black, Hispanic, and white. Socioeconomic levels were considered, and normative data exist for comparison by ethnic group. The technical manual describes the development of the instrument and how items were selected.

Reliability. The technical manual includes information on reliability coefficients and standard error of measurement of the scaled scores by age and ethnic group. Coefficients ranged from the .70s to the high .90s.

Validity. The technical manual discusses predictive validity but provides little statistical information to support the ABIC's ability to predict future performance.

Intelligence and Adaptive Behavior: Concluding Remarks

The use of intelligence tests for diagnosis of learning problems should be applied with caution. Tables 10.3 and 10.4 summarize the strengths and weaknesses of the intelligence and adaptive behavior scales presented in this chapter. In addition to the many problems and issues surrounding the use of intelligence tests, the interpretation of test results is largely dependent on

Table 10.3
Summary of intelligence measures.

Instrument	Strengths	Weaknesses
Wechsler Scales	Available for various ages Good technical quality Yield several scaled scores to be used for intra-individual interpretation Computer-assisted scoring available	Time-consuming to administer and score Have been found to be biased culturally Have mean differences for minority populations
Woodcock-Johnson–Revised Tests of Cognitive Ability	Can be compared with achievement tests (WJ–R Tests of Achievement) for determining discrepancies Good technical quality Computer-assisted scoring available Yield several scores for intra-individual interpretation	Time-consuming to administer and score
Stanford-Binet Intelligence Scale–Fourth Edition	Yields subtest and area scores Can be used for intra-individual interpretation Adequate technical quality	Some researchers reported difficulty with initial norm tables and scoring procedures Requires significant amount of training to administer and interpret Time-consuming to administer and score
Kaufman Assessment Battery for Children	Strong theoretical base Yields information for achievement and cognitive functioning Good technical quality Allows for cultural differences in interpretation	Yields nontraditional scores due to theoretical basis but may be difficult to use for traditional interpretation Time-consuming to administer and score Limited age range
Detroit Test of Learning Aptitude–3	Yield scores for support in diagnosis of motor-enhanced and attention-enhanced skills Fair technical quality	To be used with other cognitive measures: not to be used alone for eligibility decisions Time-consuming to administer and score
Cognitive Levels Test	Quick to administer Yields scores for intra-individual interpretation Adequate technical quality	Needs further research To be used as a quick cognitive screening instrument only; not to be used alone for eligibility decisions

the training of the individual examiner. Some professionals believe that appropriate diagnosis can occur only after numerous formal and informal assessments and observations. Others rely on only quantitative test data. Some professionals may use a factor analysis approach to diagnose learning disabilities, while others use informal and curriculum-based achievement measures.

The diagnosis of mild mental retardation or educational disability is complicated by many social and legal issues. In a review of the problems and practices in the field for the last 20 years, Reschly (1988) advocated the need for a change of focus in the diagnosis and classification of students with mental retardation.

Table 10.4
Summary of adaptive behavior measures.

Instrument	Strengths	Weaknesses
Vineland Adaptive Behavior Scales	Three versions available Interview Edition contains a measureof maladaptive behavior Classroom Edition was designed for use by educational professionals Contain norms for students with mental retardation, visual and hearing disabilities, and emotional disturbance Good technical quality	Time-consuming to administer
AAMR Adaptive Behavior Scale–School, Second Edition	To be used with students who have mental retardation Coincides with AAMR criteria for adaptive behavior	Does not have as many items in areas as other scales
Adaptive Behavior Inventory (full scale Short Form)	Has norms for both nondisabled and mentally retarded populations Adequate technical quality Short Form may be used for screening	Designed for use with mentally retarded or developmentally delayed students Short Form not to be used for diagnosis but for screening only
Adaptive Behavior Inventory for Children	A part of the SOMPA but may be used to measure adaptive behavior Good technical quality Designed to promote culture fair assessment	Limited age range Some research indicates limited predictive validity of the SOMPA

The classification system reforms advocated would place more emphasis on three dimensions: 1) Severe, chronic achievement deficits; 2) Significantly deficient achievement across most if not all achievement areas; and 3) Learning problems largely resistant to regular interventions. The students meeting these criteria will be virtually the same as the current population with MMR; however, their classification will not carry the stigma of comprehensive incompetence based on biological anomaly that is permanent. (Reschly, 1988, p. 298)

Exercises

Part I

Match the following terms with the correct definitions.

A. intelligence
B. adaptive behavior
C. IQ
D. achievement
E. innate potential
F. environmental influence
G. acculturation
H. Verbal tests
I. Performance tests
J. scaled scores
K. factor analysis
L. culture fair

_________ **1.** Intelligence quotient; expressed as a standard score, usually with a mean of 100.
_________ **2.** A general concept of an individual's ability to function effectively within various situations; usually assessed by intelligence tests.
_________ **3.** Derived scores for subtests on the Wechsler Scales.
_________ **4.** A statistical method of reducing the variables of a test to lower the number of factors thought to influence test performance.
_________ **5.** A group of subtests on the Wechsler Scales thought to measure verbal conceptual ability.
_________ **6.** The impact of the environment on the student's learning ability.
_________ **7.** The influence of one culture on another culture.
_________ **8.** A group of subtests on the Wechsler Scales thought to measure nonverbal ability.
_________ **9.** One's ability to function in various environments.
_________ **10.** Thought to be one's ability level from birth.
_________ **11.** Describes testing that is thought to be fair for minority cultures.

Part II

Answer the following questions.

1. What are the general problems of bias according to Reynolds (1982)? List your answers in the spaces provided.

a. ______

b. ______

c. ______

d. ______

e. ______

f. ______

2. Why is it important for an educator to understand what is measured by intelligence tests? ______

3. What is the underlying basis of the K-ABC? ______

4. How is the WISC–III used for intra-individual assessment? ______

Part III

Summarize the conclusions or problems of adaptive behavior scales according to Harrison (1987) and Evans and Bradley-Johnson (1988).

______

References

Algozzine, B., Eaves, R. C., Mann, L., & Vance, H. R. (1988). *Cognitive Levels Test.* Norristown, PA: Arete.

American Psychological Association (1985). *Standards for educational and psychological testing.* Washington, DC: Author.

Anastasi, A. (1988). *Psychological testing* (6th ed.). (pp. 237–370). New York: Macmillan.

Bender, W., & Golden L. (1988). Adaptive behavior of learning disabled and non–learning disabled children. *Learning Disability Quarterly, 11,* 55–61.

Bersoff, D. N. (1981). Testing and the law. *American Psychologist, 36,* 1047–1056.

Brown, L., & Leigh, J. E. (1986). *Adaptive Behavior Inventory.* Austin, TX: Pro-Ed.

Bruininks, R., Thurlow, M., & Gilman, C. (1987). Adaptive behavior and mental retardation. *The Journal of Special Education, 21,* 69–88.

Code of Fair Testing Practices in Education. (1988). Washington, DC: Joint Committee on Testing Practices.

Diana v. State Board of Education, Civil Act. No. C-70-37 (N.D. Cal. 1970, further order, 1973).

Doll, E. A. (1935). A genetic scale of social maturity. *The American Journal of Orthopsychiatry, 5,* 180–188.

Elliot, R. (1987). *Litigating intelligence: IQ tests, special education, and social science in the courtroom.* Dover, DE: Auburn House.

Evans, L., & Bradley-Johnson, S. (1988). A review of recently developed measures of adaptive behavior. *Psychology in the Schools, 25,* 276–287.

Federal Register. (1977). Washington, DC: U.S. Government Printing Office. August 23, 1977.

Foster-Gaitskell, D., & Pratt, C. (1989). Comparison of parent and teacher ratings of adaptive behavior of children with mental retardation. *American Journal of Mental Retardation, 94,* 177–181.

Fuchs, D., & Fuchs, L. (1989). Effects of examiner familiarity on Black, Caucasian, and Hispanic children: A meta-analysis. *Exceptional Children, 55,* 303–308.

Gridley, B. E., & McIntosh, D. E. (1991). Confirmatory factor analysis of the Stanford-Binet: Fourth Edition for a normal sample. *Journal of School Psychology, 29,* 237–248.

Grossman, H. J. (Ed.). (1983). *Classification in mental retardation.* Washington, DC: American Association on Mental Deficiency.

Hammill, D. D. (1991). *Detroit Tests of Learning Aptitude–3.* Austin, TX: Pro-Ed.

Harrison, P. (1987). Research with adaptive behavior scales. The *Journal of Special Education, 21,* 37–61.

Heller, K., Holtzman, W., & Messick, S. (Eds.). (1982). *Placing children in special education: A strategy for equity.* Washington, DC: National Academy Press.

Herrnstein, R. J., & Murray, C. (1994). *The bell curve: Intelligence and class structure in American life.* New York: The Free Press.

Hopkins, K. D., Stanley, J. C., & Hopkins, B. R. (1990). *Educational and psychological measurement and evaluation* (7th ed., pp. 339–388). Englewood Cliffs, NJ: Prentice-Hall.

Horn, E., & Fuchs, D. (1987). Using adaptive behavior in assessment and intervention. *The Journal of Special Education, 21,* 11–26.

Kamphaus, R. (1987). Conceptual and psychometric issues in the assessment of adaptive behavior. *The Journal of Special Education, 21,* 27–35.

Kaufman, A. S. (1979). *Intelligent testing with the WISC–R.* New York: Wiley.

Kaufman, A. S. (1993a). Joint exploratory factor analysis of the Kaufman Assessment Battery for Children and the Kaufman Adolescent and Adult Intelligence Test for 11 and 12 year olds. *Journal of Clinical Child Psychology, 22*(3), 355–364.

Kaufman, A. S. (1993b). King WISC the third assumes the throne. *Journal of School Psychology, 31,* 345–354.

Kaufman, A. S., & Kaufman, N. L. (1983a). *Kaufman Assessment Battery for Children: Administration and scoring manual.* Circle Pines, MN: American Guidance Service.

Kaufman, A. S., & Kaufman, N. L. (1983b). *Kaufman Assessment Battery for Children: Interpretive manual.* Circle Pines, MN: American Guidance Service.

Kaufman, A. S., & Kaufman, N. L. (1990). Kaufman Brief Intelligence Test. Circle Pines, MN: American Guidance Service.

Kaufman, A. S., & Kaufman, N. L. (1993). *Kaufman Adolescent and Adult Intelligence Test.* Circle Pines, MN: American Guidance Service.

Kaufman, A. S., & Wang, J. (1992). Gender, race, and education differences on the K-BIT at ages 4 to 90 years. *Journal of Psychoeducational Assessment, 10,* 219–229.

Kline, R. B., Synder, J., Guilmette, S., & Castellanos, M. (1993). External validity of the profile variability index for the K-ABC, Stanford-Binet, and the WISC–R: Another cul-de-sac. *Journal of Learning Disabilities, 26*(8), 557–567.

Lambert, N., Nihira, K., & Leland, H. (1993). *AAMR Adaptive Behavior Scale–School, Second Edition.* Austin, TX: Pro-Ed.

Larry P. v. Riles, 343 F. Supp. 1306, aff'd., 502 F.2d 963, further proceedings, 495F. Supp. 926, aff'd., 502 F.2d 693 (9th Cir. 1984).

Lora v. New York City Board of Education, 1984: Final order, August 2, 1984, 587F. Supp. 1572 (E.D.N.Y. 1984).

McLoughlin, J. A., & Lewis, R. B. (1990). *Assessing special students* (3rd ed., 184–221). Columbus, OH: Merrill.

Mercer, J. (1979). *System of Multicultural Pluralistic Assessment: Technical manual.* New York: Psychological Corporation.

Mercer, J., & Lewis, J. F. (1977). *System of Multicultural Pluralistic Assessment: Parent interview manual.* New York: Psychological Corporation.

Mercer, J., & Lewis, J. F. (1978). *System of Multicultural Pluralistic Assessment: Student assessment manual.* New York: Psychological Corporation.

Messick, S. (1980). Test validity and the ethics of assessment. *American Psychologist, 35,* 1012–1027.

Mick, L. (1985). Assessment procedures as related to enrollment patterns of Hispanic students in special education. *Educational Research Quarterly, 9,* 27–35.

Nihira, K., Foster, R., Shellhaas, M., & Leland, H. (1974). *AAMD Adaptive Behavior Scale.* Washington, DC: American Association on Mental Deficiency.

Olivarez, A., Palmer, D. J., & Guillemard, L. (1992). Predictive bias with referred and nonreferred black, Hispanic, and white pupils. *Learning Disabilities Quarterly, 15,* 175–186.

Overton, T., & Mardoyan-Apperson, J. (1988). The relationship between the CLT and the PPVT–R in a college freshman sample: Part 2. *CLT Technical Reports.* Norristown, PA: Arete.

Palmer, D. J., Olivarez, A., Willson, V., & Fordyce, T. (1989). Ethnicity and language dominance-influence on the prediction of achievement test scores in referred and non-referred samples. *Learning Disabilities Quarterly, 12,* 261–274.

PASE (Parents in Action in Special Education) v. Hannon, 506 F. Supp. 831 (N.D. Ill. 1980).

Prewett, P. N. (1992). The relationship between the Kaufman Brief Intelligence Test (K-BIT) and the WISC–R with referred students. *Psychology in the Schools, 29,* 25–27.

Prewett, P. N., & McCaffery, L. K. (1993). A comparison of the Kaufman Brief Intelligence Test (K-BIT) with the Stanford-Binet, a two-subtest short form, and the Kaufman Test of Educational Achievement (K-TEA) Brief Form. *Psychology in the Schools, 30,* 299–304.

Reschly, D. (1981). Psychological testing in educational classification and placement. *American Psychologist, 36,* 1094–1102.

Reschly, D. (1982). Assessing mild mental retardation: The influence of adaptive behavior, sociocultural status, and prospects for nonbiased assessment. In C. R. Reynolds & T. B. Gutkin (Eds.), *The handbook of school psychology* (pp. 209–242). New York: Wiley.

Reschly, D. (1988). Assessment issues, placement litigation, and the future of mild mental retardation classification and programming. *Education and Training in Mental Retardation, 23,* 285–301.

Reschly, D. J., & Grimes, J. P. (1990). Best practices in intellectual assessment. In A. Thomas & J. Grimes (Eds.), *Best practices in school psychology–II.* Washington, DC: National Association of School Psychologists.

Reynolds, C. R. (1982). The problem of bias in psychological assessment. In C. R. Reynolds & T. B. Gutkin (Eds.), *The handbook of school psychology* (pp. 178–208). New York: Wiley.

Salvia, J., & Ysseldyke, J. E. (1988). *Assessment in special and remedial education* (4th ed.). Boston: Houghton Mifflin.

Schrank, F. A. (1993). Unique contributions of the Woodcock-Johnson Psychoeducational Battery–Revised to psychoeducational assessment. *Journal of Psychoeducational Assessment Monograph Series: Advances in Psychoeducational Assessment: Woodcock-Johnson Psychoeducational Battery–Revised,* 71–79.

Smith, B. L., Smith, T., & Mohlke, L. (1994). *Use of the WISC–III in reevaluations of learning disabled students.* Paper presented at the meeting of the National Association of School Psychologists, Seattle, WA.

Smith, D. K., Stovall, D. L., & Geraghty, B. L. (1994). *WISC–III/WISC–R relationships in special education re-evaluations.* Paper presented at the meeting of the National Association of School Psychologists, Seattle, WA.

Sparrow, S. S., Balla, D. A., & Cicchetti, D. V. (1984). *Vineland Adaptive Behavior Scales.* Circle Pines, MN: American Guidance Service.

Swason, H. L., & Watson, B. L. (1989). *Educational and psychological assessment of exceptional children* (2nd ed., pp. 87–134). Columbus, OH: Merrill.

Taylor, R. T. (1989). *Assessment of exceptional students: Educational and psychological procedures* (2nd ed.). Englewood Cliffs, NJ: Prentice-Hall.

Taylor, R. L., & Richards, S. B. (1991). Patterns of intellectual differences of black, Hispanic, and white children. *Psychology in the Schools, 28,* 5–9.

Thorndike, R. L., Hagen, E. P., & Sattler, J. M. (1986). *Technical manual, Stanford-Binet Intelligence Scale, Fourth Edition.* Chicago: Riverside.

Tucker, J. (1980). Ethnic proportions in classes for the learning disabled: Issues in nonbiased assessment. *The Journal of Special Education, 14,* 93–105.

Turnbull, H. R. (1990). *Free and appropriate public education: The law and children with disabilities* (3rd ed.). Denver: Love.

Wechsler, D. (1974). *Manual for the Wechsler Intelligence Scale for Children–Revised.* San Antonio, TX: Psychological Corporation.

Wechsler, D. (1991). *Wechsler Intelligence Scale for Children-Third Edition: Manual.* San Antonio, TX: Psychological Corporation.

Weller, C., Strawser, S., & Buchanan, M. (1985). Adaptive behavior: Designator of a continuum of severity of learning disabled individuals. *Journal of Learning Disabilities, 18,* 200–203.

Wiebe, M. J. (1986). Test review: The Kaufman Assessment Battery for Children. *Education and Training of the Mentally Retarded, 21,* 76–79.

Witt, J. C., Elliot, S. N., Gresham, F. M., & Kramer, J. J. (1988). *Assessment of special children: Tests and the problem-solving process.* Glenview, IL: Scott, Foresman.

Witt, J., & Martens, B. (1984). Adaptive behavior: Tests and assessment issues. *School Psychology Review, 13,* 478–484.

Wood, F., Johnson, J., & Jenkins, J. (1990). The *Lora* case: Nonbiased referral, assessment, and placement procedures. *Exceptional Children, 52,* 323–331.

Woodcock, R. W., & Mather, N. (1989). *Woodcock-Johnson Tests of Cognitive Ability: Standard and Supplemental Batteries manual.* Allen, TX: DLM Teaching Resources.

Ysseldyke, J., & Algozzine, B. (1982). *Critical issues in special and remedial education.* Boston: Houghton Mifflin.

Chapter Eleven

Other Diagnostic Instruments

Key Terms

visual-motor ability
sensory-motor ability
perceptual ability
developmental levels
language assessment
receptive language
expressive language
written language
visual perception
visual retention
visual memory
motor-free test
auditory memory
auditory discrimination

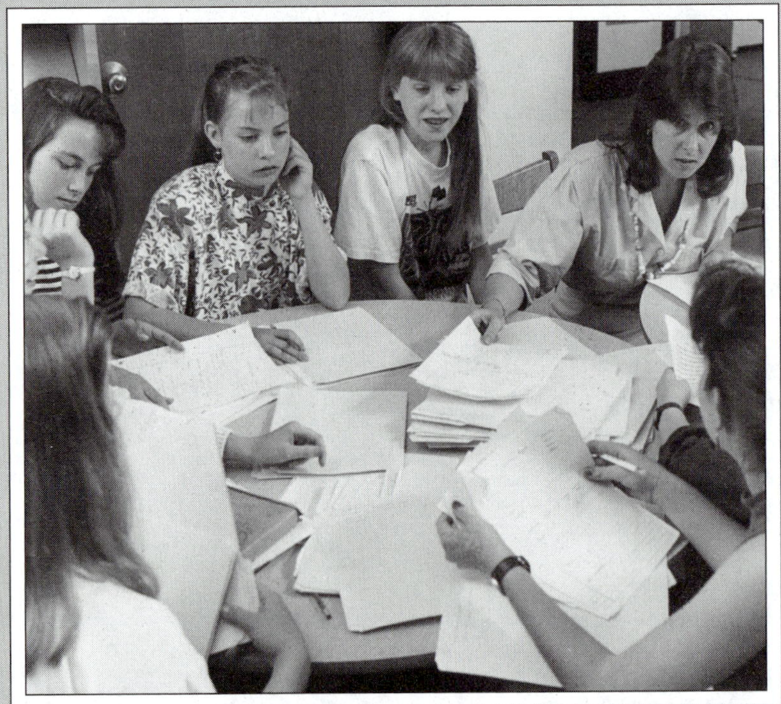

A thorough psychoeducational evaluation includes tests that may assess abilities other than achievement, intelligence, or adaptive behavior. Members of the multidisciplinary team may wish to determine language skills, **visual-motor ability** or **sensory-motor ability, perceptual ability,** or **developmental levels.** Teachers may administer tests to measure specific abilities or receive test results of student abilities and be required to use such results in educational planning. The tests presented in this chapter are typical examples of those used in assessing language, sensory-motor, or other ability areas. The usefulness of these test results and how they can be incorporated into educational planning is the focus of this chapter.

visual-motor ability Responding motorically to visual input.

sensory-motor ability Responding to sensory input with motor responses.

perceptual ability Ability to receive and understand perceptual stimuli.

developmental levels Levels of expected maturation and/or achievement.

Assessing Language

The ability to understand and express ideas using correct language is fundamental for school achievement. **Language assessment,** through tests that measure a student's understanding and use of language, is presented in this section. Tests administered by speech clinicians in an effort to diagnose and remediate speech disorders (articulation, voice, or fluency disorders) are beyond the scope of this text. Effective remediation of language disorders is considered a shared responsibility of the clinician, teacher, and parent, who each must be familiar with the tests to diagnose and monitor these skills. These tests assess a student's **receptive language** vocabulary, oral **expressive language,** and **written language** skills.

language assessment Measuring verbal concepts and verbal understanding.

receptive language Inner language concepts applied to what is heard.

expressive language Language skills used in speaking or writing.

written language Understanding language concepts and using those in writing.

Peabody Picture Vocabulary Test–Revised (PPVT–R)

The PPVT–R (Dunn & Dunn, 1981) measures the student's verbal comprehension skills by presenting a series of four visual stimuli and requesting the student to discriminate the stimulus that best represents the orally stated word. An example of this format is illustrated in Figure 11.1. Two equivalent forms of this individually administered language test allow retesting to monitor

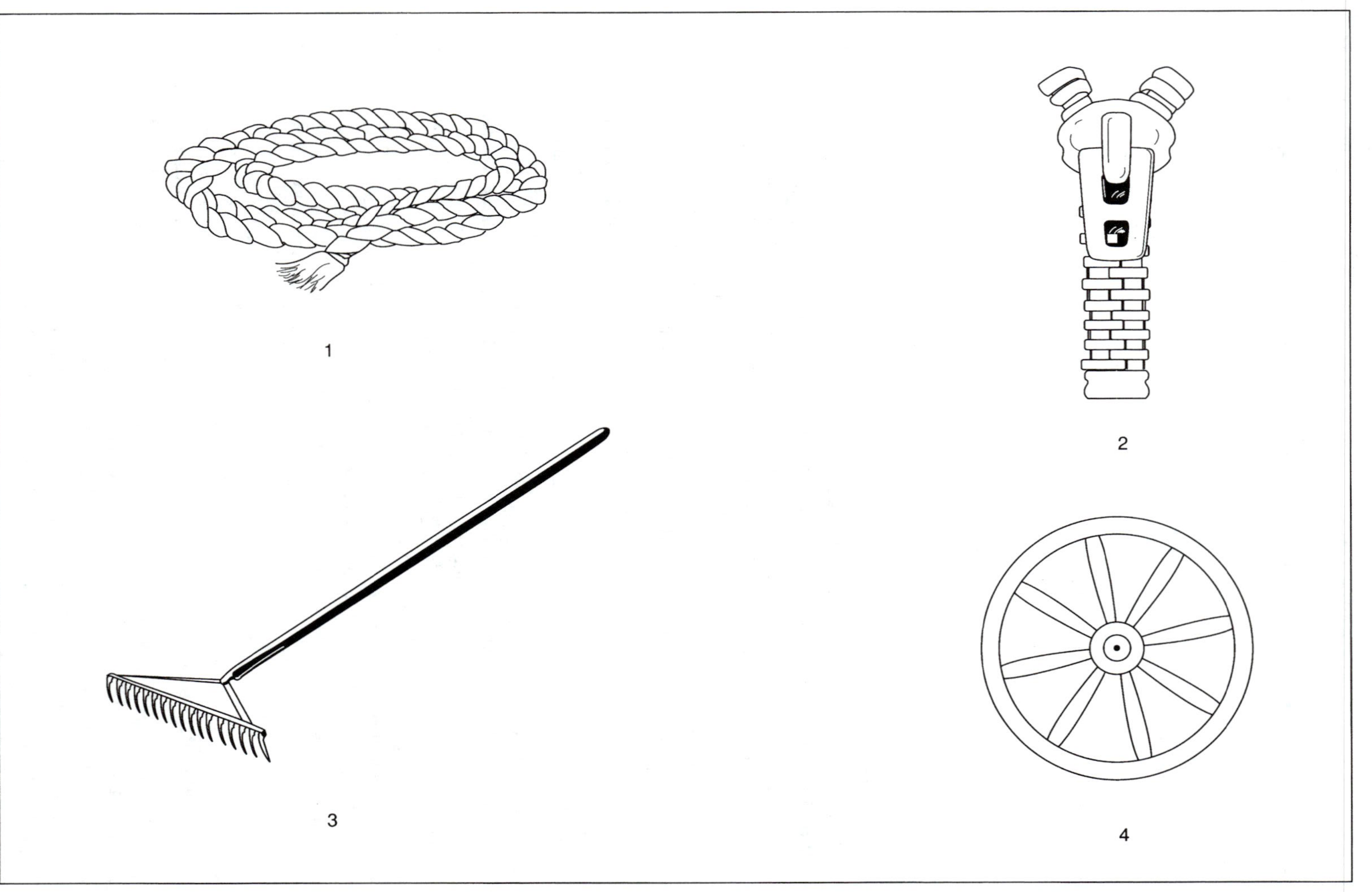

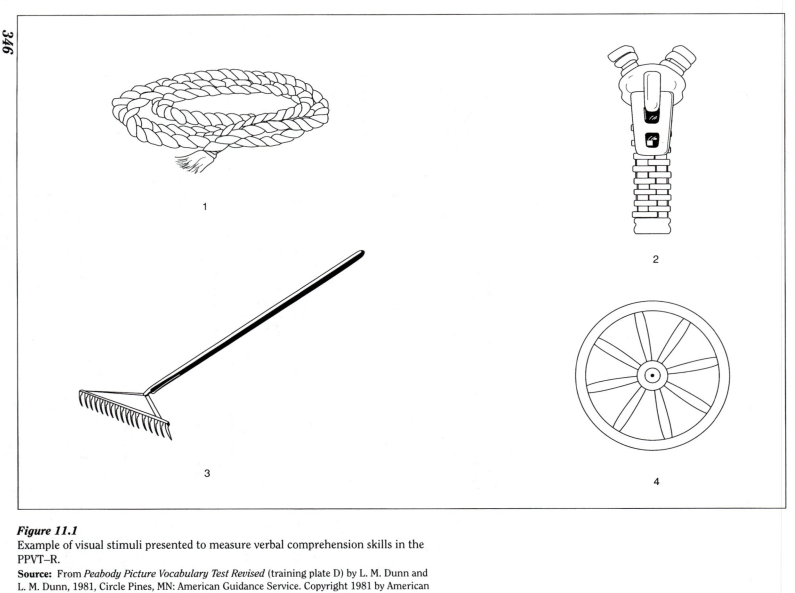

Figure 11.1
Example of visual stimuli presented to measure verbal comprehension skills in the PPVT–R.

Source: From *Peabody Picture Vocabulary Test Revised* (training plate D) by L. M. Dunn and L. M. Dunn, 1981, Circle Pines, MN: American Guidance Service. Copyright 1981 by American Guidance Service. Reprinted by permission.

progress. The test includes an easel test, examiner's manual, and protocol. Derived scores include standard scores, percentile ranks, stanines, and age equivalents. Band of confidence information provided for both raw scores and standard scores is based on 68% confidence, and scores should be interpreted with caution (Naglieri & Bardos, 1987; Robertson & Eisenberg, 1981). Naglieri and Bardos (1987) have provided additional confidence intervals, at the 80% to 95% levels, which the teacher may wish to consult when interpreting PPVT–R test scores.

Research on the PPVT–R indicates several interesting results. Much research has focused on the use of the PPVT–R as an estimate of intellectual ability using verbal comprehension (Altepeter & Johnson, 1989; Overton & Mardoyan-Apperson, 1988) and prediction of school achievement (D'Amato, Gray, & Dean, 1987; Naglieri & Pfeiffer, 1983). Research indicates that this instrument measures specific traits that involve the understanding of words rather than measuring global intelligence (Overton & Mardoyan-Apperson, 1988). The test was constructed to measure vocabulary comprehension, or receptive language as measured by the understanding of single words, and not intelligence. Therefore, it should not be used to screen for intellectual ability but rather to diagnose vocabulary comprehension deficits.

The teacher should interpret the derived score with caution if the student has learning difficulties. Groshong (1987) found that students with learning disabilities may perform better on picture vocabulary tests than on tests with orally presented items. The teacher who has only the results of the PPVT–R on which to base language skill ability may be using a score that is higher than the student's true ability of understanding words. The instrument's forced-choice format may also result in slightly higher scores. The scores obtained on this instrument are thought to represent a large domain with a single score rather than several subtest scores across multiple subdomains. The student's skill in understanding words can be subdivided by word types or usage and may not be accurately assessed by a single test. The teacher should follow PPVT–R assessment of language skills with additional instruments or by informal assessment using curriculum-based assessment or teacher-made tests.

Technical Data

Norming Process. The PPVT–R standardization sample included 4,200 students for Forms L and M, ranging in age from 2–6 through 18–11. The variables considered were age, sex, geographic location, community size, occupation, and ethnic group (white, black, Hispanic, or other). Data provided appear to be representative of the U.S. population from the census data available at the time of the instrument's development (Dunn & Dunn, 1981).

Reliability. Reliability information includes reliability studies with the PPVT and the PPVT–R. Additional research includes internal consistency and alternate forms reliability. Internal consistency was studied using split-half reliability, which resulted in coefficients ranging from .67 to .88 on Form L (ages 2–6 to 40–11) and .61 to .86 on Form M (ages 2–6 to 18–11). Both immediate and delayed alternate forms reliability was studied and yielded coefficients ranging from .54 to .90 (delayed retest) and .71 to .89 (immediate retest).

Validity. The content validity is presented in the context of the validity of the construction of the original PPVT. Construct validity for the PPVT–R is presented as a discussion of the importance of the ability to define words, or a hearing vocabulary, and how this relates to the constructs measured by intelligence tests. Item selection is presented, and the reader is referred to the technical manual for further statistical data (Dunn & Dunn, 1981).

Test of Word Finding (TWF)

The TWF (German, 1986) measures the expressive language skill of word finding. Used with students aged 6–6 to 12–11, the TWF is an easel format test divided into the following subtests: (1) Picture Naming: Nouns, Sentence Completion Naming, Description Naming, (2) Picture Naming: Verbs, and (3) Picture Naming: Categories. These subtests allow for the formal measurement of word-finding skills on "two dimensions: accuracy of naming and speed of naming" (German, 1986, p. 2).

The TWF manual includes suggestions for programming following the diagnosis of a word-finding problem. The diagnostic model for this instrument is shown in Figure 11.2. Information is provided in the manual to help the teacher analyze errors and secondary characteristics of students who have word-finding problems.

The TWF derived scores include standard scores based on age and grade level and percentile ranks based on age and grade level. The protocol provides space for the inclusion of the standard error of measurement by age and grade level and the range of confidence (at 68%) for both age and grade-level scores.

Technical Data

Norming Process. The standardization sample for the TWF included 1,200 students aged 6–6 through 12–11 from four geographic regions in the United States. The variables considered in the sample were age, sex, geographic region, grade, parent education level, and ethnicity or race (white, black, Hispanic, or other). Also represented in the sample were persons with linguistic disabilities.

Reliability. Reliability information includes test-retest studies, internal consistency of the K-R 20, and intercorrelation coefficients. Test-retest reliability coefficients ranged from .82 to .90 on raw and standard scores. Internal consistency using the K-R 20 resulted in coefficients that ranged from .69 to .83. The K-R 20 was also studied with the students who were identified as having word-finding problems and yielded coefficients in the .80s. Intercorrelations on timed items and total response time resulted in coefficients that ranged from .61 to .80 for nondisabled students.

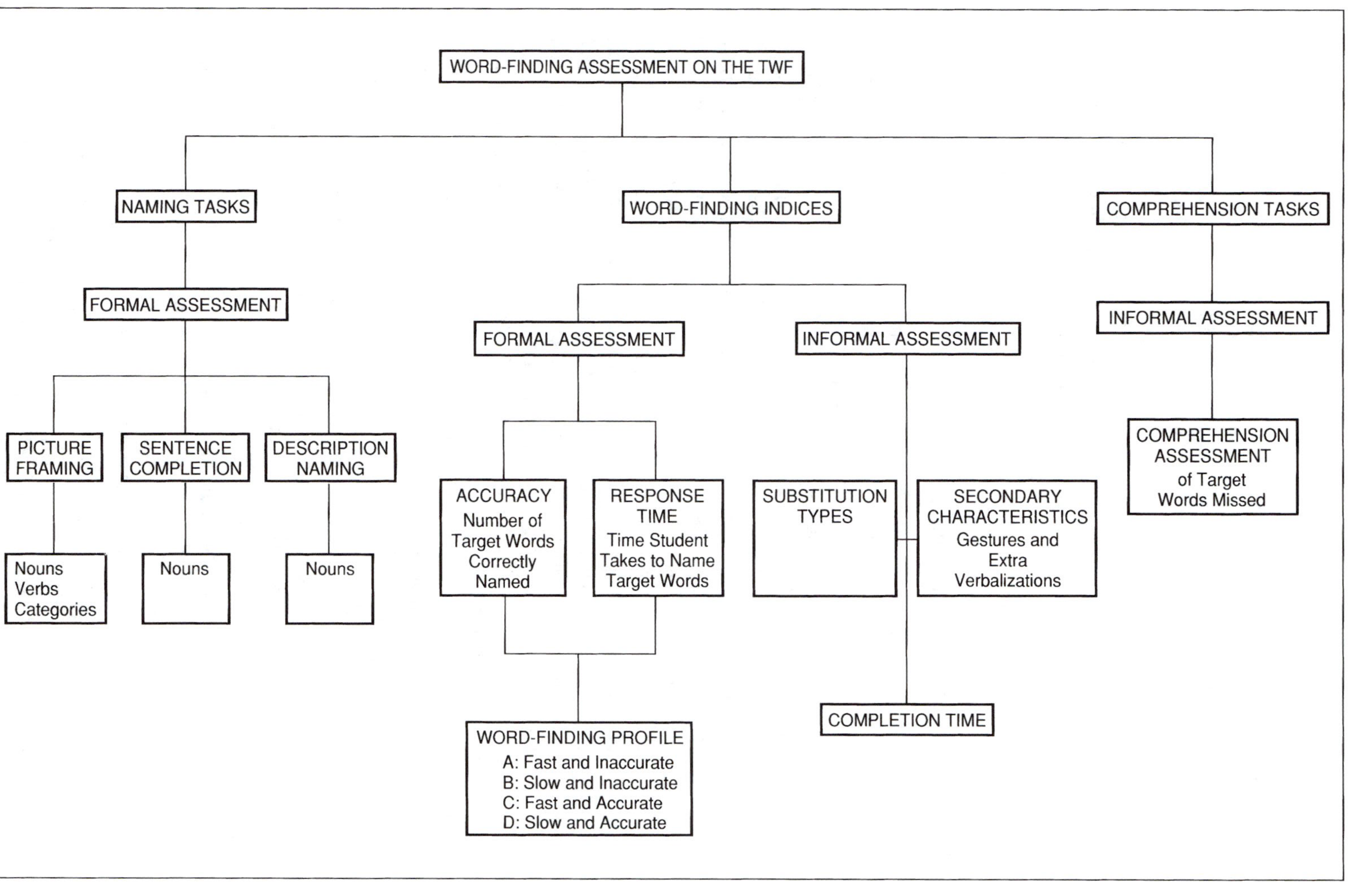

Figure 11.2
Diagnostic model for comprehensive assessment of word-finding skills in children using the National College of Education TWF.

Source: From *Test of Word Finding: TWF. Administration, Scoring and Interpretation Manual* (p. 6) by D. J. German, 1986, Circle Pines, MN: American Guidance Service. Copyright 1986 by American Guidance Service. Reprinted by permission.

Validity. The technical manual presents content validity, criterion-related validity, and construct validity in detail. Content validity includes the selection of items and assessment procedures employed. Criterion-related validity studies include studies with the Boston Naming Test, Expressive One-Word Picture Vocabulary Test, Word Test (antonyms and synonyms), and Rapid Automatized Naming Test for nondisabled subjects. The coefficients ranged from −.56 to .75. Additional studies of the TWF and subjects with word-finding problems are included. Construct validity is presented through developmental progression information, factor analysis studies, intercorrelations between word-finding indices, discrimination between groups, and additional field research.

Test of Language Development–2: Primary (TOLD–P:2)

The Primary edition of the TOLD–2 (Newcomer & Hammill, 1988b) was designed for use with students ranging in age from 4–0 to 8–11. The theoretical structure is based on a two-dimensional language model, described in the manual. TOLD–P:2 contains the following subtests: Picture Vocabulary, Oral Vocabulary, Grammatic Understanding, Sentence Imitation, Grammatic Completion, Word Discrimination, and Word Articulation. The standard scores on these subtests may be used to obtain quotients for the following composites: spoken language, listening, speaking, semantics, syntax, and phonology. Derived scores include standard scores (mean = 10), quotients (mean = 100), and percentile ranks. The format of response includes both forced-choice and open-ended responses. The student is also asked to repeat sentences on the Sentence Imitation subtest and fill in missing words for the Grammatic Completion subtest. In the Word Discrimination subtest, the student must discriminate between same and different items, which the examiner states orally. The student must name pictured items and pronounce the names correctly in the Word Articulation subtest. Table 11.1 lists the skills measured by the subtests; understanding the skills enables the teacher to interpret results and use the interpretations to develop educational plans.

Technical Data

Norming Process. The norming process for the TOLD–P:2 included 2,436 students ranging in age from 4–0 to 8–11. The variables considered were sex, community size, race (white, black, or other), ethnicity (American Indian, Hispanic, Asian, or everyone else), geographic area, and parental occupation.

Reliability. Reliability studies included internal consistency and test-retest studies. Internal consistency was studied using coefficient alpha and resulted in coefficients from .75 to .95 on subtests and from .88 to .97 on the composite and overall scores. The average test-retest coefficients ranged from .84 to .96.

Validity. The manual presents information regarding content validity, criterion-related validity, and construct validity. Criterion-related validity studies were conducted with the PPVT, WISC–R, Northwestern Syntax Screening Test,

Table 11.1
Content of subtests of the TOLD–P:2.

Subtest	Description
Picture Vocabulary	Measures the ability to understand the meaning of individual words when spoken in isolation
Oral Vocabulary	Measures the ability to define individual stimulus words precisely
Grammatic Understanding	Measures the ability to comprehend sentences having differing syntactic structures
Sentence Imitation	Measures the ability to repeat complex sentences accurately
Grammatic Completion	Measures the ability to complete a partially formed sentence by supplying a final word that has a proper morphological form
Word Discrimination	Measures the ability to discern subtle phonological differences between two words spoken in isolation
Word Articulation	Measures the ability to say (i.e., articulate) a series of single words properly

Source: From *Test of Language Development 2: Primary* (p. 31) by P. L. Newcomer and D. D. Hammill, 1988. Austin, TX: Pro-Ed. Copyright 1988 by Pro-Ed. Reprinted by permission.

DTLA, Illinois Test of Psycholinguistic Abilities, Auditory Discrimination Test, Templin-Darley Tests of Articulation, and Test for Auditory Comprehension of Language. Validity coefficients ranged from .69 to .84. The discussion of construct validity in the manual includes developmental progression and age differentiation, subtest interrelationships, and the relationship of the TOLD–P:2 to intelligence tests.

Test of Language Development–2: Intermediate (TOLD–I:2)

The Intermediate edition of the TOLD–2 (Hammill & Newcomer, 1988) was constructed to aid in the diagnosis of students with language problems. The theoretical structure of the TOLD–I:2 is similar to the two-dimensional model of the TOLD–P:2. The following subtests are used to assess language skills for students aged 8–6 through 12–11: Sentence Combining, Vocabulary, Word Ordering, Generals, Grammatic Comprehension, and Malapropisms. The examiner presents all subtests orally; items include forced-choice and open-ended questions. Derived scores of the TOLD–I:2 are standard scores (mean = 10), quotients (mean = 100), and percentile ranks by age norms.

Technical Data

Norming Process. The norms for the TOLD–I:2 were based on the test scores of 1,214 children. A portion of the test results were from previous norming studies. Variables considered were age, sex, community size, race (white, black, or other), ethnicity (American Indian, Hispanic, Asian, or everyone else), geographic area, and parental occupation.

Reliability. Internal reliability studies resulted in coefficients from .86 to .96 on subtests and .91 to .97 on composite and overall scores. Test-retest reliability coefficients ranged from .77 to .96 on subtests and were in the .90s on composites and overall scores.

Validity. In discussing content validity, the manual presents the rationales for item selection and subtest content. Criterion-related validity coefficients are given for the TOLD–I:2 and the Test of Adolescent Language. This information is somewhat limited. Construct validity includes age differentiation and interrelationships of subtests. Factor analysis and item validity are presented.

Test of Adolescent and Adult Language–Third Edition (TOAL–3)

The TOAL–3 (Hammill, Brown, Larsen, & Wiederholt, 1994) assesses students aged 12-0 to 24-11 for language problems. The test was constructed on the three-dimensional test model illustrated in Figure 11.3. The test composites include listening, speaking, reading, writing, spoken language, written language, vocabulary, grammar, receptive language, and expressive language.

The third revision of the Test of Adolescent Language, the newly named Test of Adolescent and Adult Language, has an extended age range that allows it to

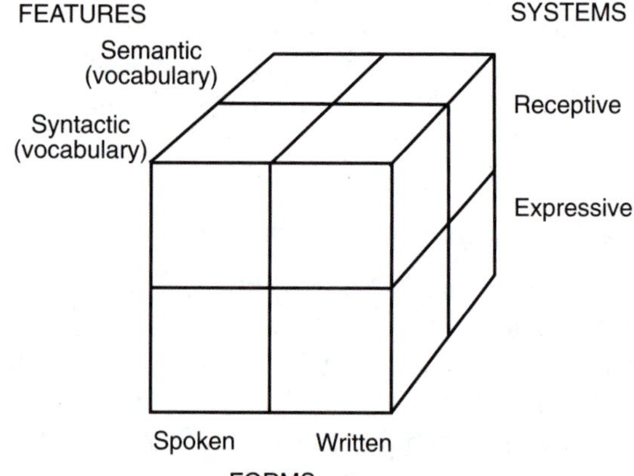

Figure 11.3
The three-dimensional TOAL–3 test model.
Source: From *Test of Adolescent and Adult Language, Third Edition* (p. 4) by D. D. Hammill, V. L. Brown, S. C. Larsen, and J. L. Wiederholt, 1994, Austin, TX: Pro-Ed. Copyright 1994 by Pro-Ed, Inc. Reprinted by permission.

be used in postsecondary settings. The administration procedures have also been improved in this revision.

The test authors caution the examiner to interpret scores on the TOAL–3 carefully because it is an ability test that assesses only specific areas of language (Hammill et al., 1994). The manual provides guidelines for interpreting significant composite differences and for testing the limits of student ability.

Technical Data

Norming Process. TOAL–3 developers used a normative sample of more than 3,000 persons in 22 states and 3 provinces in Canada. The sample representation was based on 1990 U.S. census data.

Reliability. Internal consistency, test-retest, and interscorer reliability coefficients were reported to be above .80.

Validity. Validity studies are reported for content, criterion-related, and construct validity. The manual discusses correlations between the TOAL–3 and other language tests (the TOLD–I:2 PPVT, DTLA–3, and Test of Written Language–2). The discussion of construct validity includes age differentiation, the relationship of the TOAL–3 to intelligence testing, and group differentiation.

Reliability. Internal consistency reliability was studied using coefficient alpha, yielding coefficients from .80 to .96 on subtests and in the .90s on composite and overall scores. Interscorer reliability studies produced coefficients from .70 to .99 for three subtests.

Validity. Content validity is covered briefly in the manual. Criterion-related validity studies included the PPVT, the DTLA Memory for Related Syllables, Reading and Language from the Comprehensive Test of Basic Skills, and total scores from the Test of Written Language. Coefficients ranged from not significant to .79. Additional research for studies of the TOAL and the TOLD–I yielded coefficients from not significant to .83. Discussion of construct validity focused on age differentiation, subtest interrelationships, relationship of the TOAL–2 to intelligence testing, and group differentiation. The manual includes a table that contains mean standard scores for groups of learning disabled students, students with mental retardation, students with emotional problems, judicated youth, poor readers, and nondisabled students.

□ **CHECK YOUR UNDERSTANDING**

Complete Activity 11.1.

Activity 11.1

Use the following terms to answer the questions.

PPVT–R	TOAL–2
TWF	TOLD–P:2
TOLD–I:2	receptive language
expressive language	vocabulary

1. Which test was constructed for use with students ages 12-0 to 18-5?

   ____

2. Which test measures very early skills of communication and includes a subtest of articulation? ________________
3. The test that has only a forced-choice format is the ________________ .
4. Which test was constructed to assess skills of communication in students of the ages 8-6 through 12-11? ________________
5. Which tests were founded on a two-dimensional language model? ________________ and ________________
6. The ________________ measures a student's skills using timed and untimed items.
7. The ________________ measures comprehension of single words and not global intellectual ability.
8. The ________________ measures a student's ability to find different types of words for different uses.
9. ________________ refers to the knowledge or understanding of single words.
10. The understanding of language that is heard is known as

    ________________ .

11. The skills involved in using language to convey thoughts or ideas in speaking or writing are known as ________________ .

Testing Sensory-Motor and Perceptual Abilities

Researchers have examined the usefulness of sensory-motor and perceptual assessment in the planning and delivery of educational services with mixed results (Hupp, Able, & Conroy-Gunter, 1984; Kavale & Forness, 1987; Locher, 1988; Locher & Worms, 1981; Mather & Kirk, 1985). In sensory-motor and perceptual assessment, the examiner is concerned with the way a student perceives information best and the way the student responds. This includes concern for visual perception, visual memory and discrimination, auditory memory and discrimination, and visual-motor responses. In psychoeducational assessment, the determination of a student's strengths and weaknesses in information and sensory processing has been useful in providing the teacher with a better picture of how the child learns (Locher, 1988). According to Mather and Kirk (1985), the reason for the lack of substantial evidence to support the perceptual processing model is that there are very few students who have perceptual problems of severe significance that will affect learning:

> Clinical experience indicates that modality preference is an important teaching consideration for only a very small percentage of children. There is a continuum of per-

> ceptual abilities; those with the most severe visual or perceptual or auditory perceptual deficits, perhaps 1% of the population, will benefit from instruction geared toward a specific learning modality. The other 99% of children will have the minimal amount of visual or auditory perception necessary for learning to read. . . . In considering modality instruction . . . [how] severe must a visual or auditory modality deficit be before it interferes with school learning? (Mather & Kirk, 1985, p. 61)

Locher (1988) believes that perception and strategies for using perceptual input should be assessed before other psychometric assessment is conducted. According to Locher, preassessment screening of these abilities is necessary because they may affect higher functioning skills. Kavale and Forness (1987) analyzed research of modality assessment and instruction and did not find support for widespread use of such concepts. Mather and Kirk (1985) believe the lack of evidence may be due to asking the wrong questions in research or due to the very small percentage of students who have perceptual impairments.

Regardless of the small amount of support for this type of assessment and planning, it remains a part of the psychoeducational assessment batteries for students with moderate to mild disabilities. Teachers often use the results obtained from perceptual-motor and sensory-motor tests to plan interventions that capitalize on individual student strengths. Determining the student's strengths for receiving input or information (e.g., through auditory or visual channels, etc.) may aid the teacher in planning the mode of presentation for new material. Similarly, determining the student's preferred mode of response (e.g., written, oral, etc.) may help the teacher to maximize the student's performance.

Teachers and psychologists use test results of perceptual-motor and sensory-motor assessment to support and better understand diagnoses of some learning problems. For example, students who have been determined to have weaknesses in the auditory discrimination area may have difficulty in related academic tasks such as phonics and discriminating new words. In a like manner, students who have been found to exhibit visual-motor difficulties may have problems with handwriting and written expression. Visual memory may be linked to difficulty in retaining what is read. Examples of types of perceptual-motor assessment are presented in the following sections.

Tests of Visual Perception

When a visual problem is suspected due to a student's behavior in class (e.g., squinting eyes, difficulty copying from board, etc.), the student's visual acuity should first be assessed. The parents should be notified and the student referred to the school nurse or appropriate medical personnel before conducting any visual perceptual assessment. After determining that the student's visual acuity is normal or has been corrected, the teacher may wish to obtain additional information about how the student perceives and retains visual stimuli. Tests constructed to measure **visual perception** may assess visual-motor skills (such as

visual perception Ability to receive and understand visual stimuli.

visual retention Ability to retain visual stimuli.

visual memory Ability to remember what is seen.

motor-free Refers to test responses that are made without using motor ability.

drawing), **visual retention** or **visual memory** (by reproducing a figure from memory), or may be **motor-free** visual perceptual or memory tests. Tests with subtests that measure these abilities have been included throughout this text: for example, the WJ–R Tests of Cognitive Ability, the DTLA–3, and the K-ABC. The following tests were designed to measure a visual-perceptual area only rather than being larger tests with visual-perceptual subtests.

Developmental Test of Visual-Motor Integration (VMI), Third Revision

In the VMI (Beery, 1989), the examiner presents 24 geometric shapes for the student to copy. Children aged 4–0 through 17–11 may be administered this instrument. The examiner's manual provides tables for obtaining the derived scores, including standard scores (mean = 100), percentile ranks, and age equivalents. According to the author, the purpose of this instrument is to "help prevent learning and behavioral problems through early screening and identification" (Beery, 1989, p. 8). The VMI can be administered individually or in groups. The author reports that this instrument is virtually free of cultural bias.

The manual provides illustrations to help examiners score the drawings. Criteria for assigning points are provided as well as descriptions of drawing characteristics by age. Supplemental information also assists the examiner in determining how to score items. Figure 11.4 illustrates the developmental trends presented in the manual for scoring purposes.

Technical Data

Norming Process. The VMI manual presents information regarding the norming and standardization process. The sample selected for the 1989 edition included 2,734 children from various states. The performance on these items was not determined to be significantly different from the earlier samples on previous versions. The norm tables, therefore, are based on a total of 5,824 children ranging in age from 2–6 to 19–0. The variables considered in sample selection were gender, income, ethnicity (black, white, Hispanic, or other), and community residence (rural, suburban, or urban).

Reliability. Information on interrater, test-retest, and split-half reliability is reported in the manual. All coefficients presented in the manual appear to be within the adequate to above adequate range.

Validity. Concurrent validity and predictive validity are presented. The coefficients for like tasks are, for the most part, within the adequate range.

Bender Visual Motor Gestalt Test: The Watkins Bender-Gestalt Scoring System

The original version of the Bender Visual Motor Gestalt Test was published in a research monograph in 1938 (Bender, 1946). The intended use was to determine visual-motor gestalt functioning in children "to explore retardation, re-

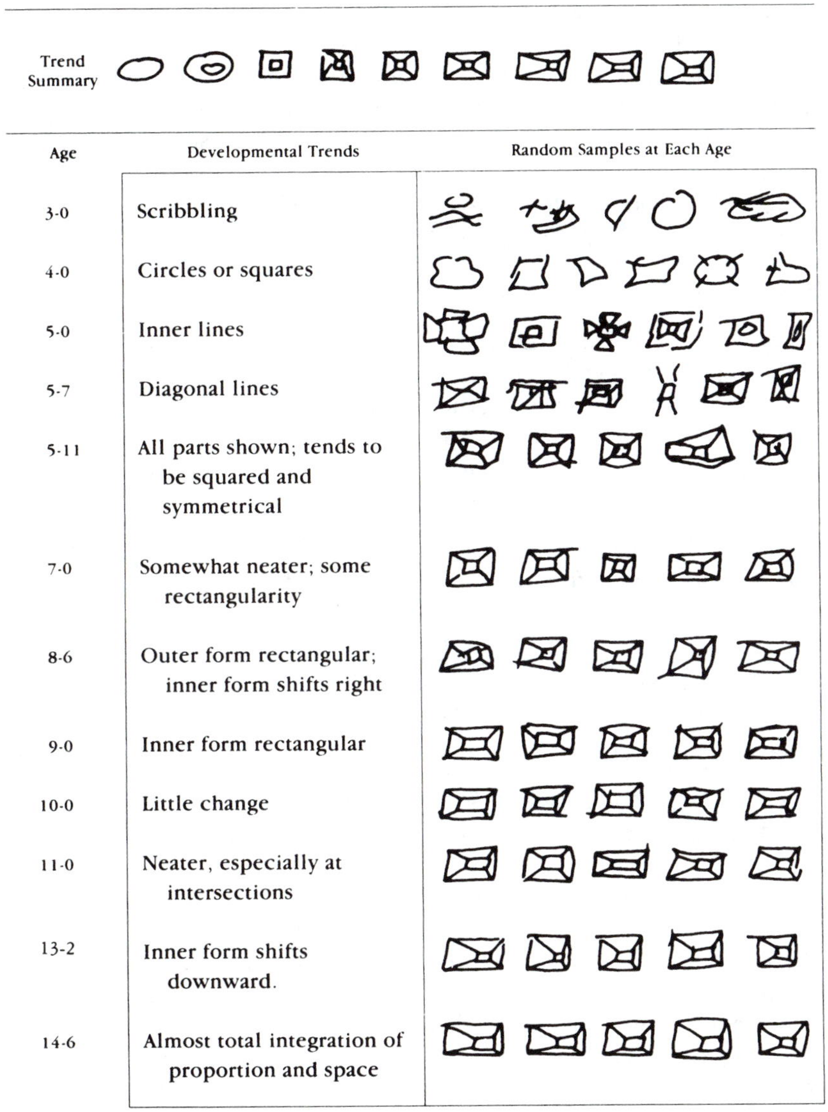

Trend Summary

Age	Developmental Trends	Random Samples at Each Age
3-0	Scribbling	
4-0	Circles or squares	
5-0	Inner lines	
5-7	Diagonal lines	
5-11	All parts shown; tends to be squared and symmetrical	
7-0	Somewhat neater; some rectangularity	
8-6	Outer form rectangular; inner form shifts right	
9-0	Inner form rectangular	
10-0	Little change	
11-0	Neater, especially at intersections	
13-2	Inner form shifts downward.	
14-6	Almost total integration of proportion and space	

Figure 11.4
Drawing characteristics evident at particular ages.
Source: From *The VMI: Developmental Test of Visual-Motor Integration: Administration, Scoring, and Teaching Manual (Revision)* (p. 71) by K. E. Beery, 1989, Cleveland, OH: Modern Curriculum Press. Copyright 1989 by Modern Curriculum Press. Reprinted by permission.

gression, loss of function and organic brain defects in both adults and children, and to explore personality deviations" (Bender, 1946, p. 3). The test consists of a set of stimulus cards, which the student is required to reproduce. Koppitz (1964) and many others have researched the Bender Visual Motor Gestalt Test as a measure of discriminating children with brain injury.

There are different methods of scoring the Bender Visual Motor Gestalt Test. The Watkins (1976) scoring system focuses on visual-perceptual deficits rather than brain injury or emotional indications. The Watkins scoring manual includes normative data for the number of errors necessary to indicate the presence of mild, moderate, or severe visual-perceptual problems. The errors scored are specified on the scoring form for each figure copied. The errors for the first four figures are listed in Figure 11.5. Explanations of each scoring criterion and examples of errors are presented in the manual.

Technical Data

Norming Process. The Watkins scoring system was developed by administering the items of the Bender Visual Motor Gestalt Test to 3,355 nondisabled students and 1,046 students with learning disabilities. The test administration included both group and individual administrations. Variables considered in the sample were sex, age, socioeconomic status of sample schools, and race or ethnic classification.

Reliability. Test-retest reliability coefficients ranged from .72 to .95, and interscorer reliability coefficients for three scorers of 166 test responses ranged from .80 to .97.

Validity. Limited information is presented on scoring and item selection.

Developmental Test of Visual Perception, Second Edition (DTVP–2)

The DTVP–2 (Hammill, Pearson, & Voress, 1993) consists of eight subtests that measure different visual-perceptual and visual-motor abilities for children aged 4 through 10. This instrument may be used to obtain scores for motor-reduced and motor-enhanced abilities. The visual-motor and visual-perceptual tasks require the child to use visual discrimination and short-term visual memory to determine form constancy, discrimination to determine figure-ground relationships, copying skills, visual understanding of spatial relations, and visual-motor ability to perform on timed fine motor tasks. Figure 11.6 presents a page from the picture book for the Positions in Space subtest. Derived standard scores (mean = 10) and percentile ranks may be obtained from tables provided in the manual. Quotients for composites and age equivalents are also provided.

Technical Data

Norming Process. The sample used in the norming procedures of the DTVP–2 included 1,972 children from various states. The sample was representative of the 1990 U.S. census, according to the authors. The characteristics considered were race (white, black, or other), ethnicity (Native American, Hispanic, Oriental/Pacific Islander, African-American, or other), gender, residence (rural or urban), geographic area, handedness, and age.

SCORING FORM

for the Watkins Bender-Gestalt Scoring System

Name: ______________________ Date Tested: ____________

Chronological Age: ________ Mental Age: ________ Total Error Score: ________

(Circle One)

Number of Errors Compared to Chronological Age: ______ Normal Mild Moderate Severe

Number of Errors Compared to Mental Age: ________ Normal Mild Moderate Severe

Figures and Item Number — *Description of Items*

________ 1. Total time ______ minutes ______ seconds (score if less than 4 or more than 9 minutes) (age 5).

Items Scored on Each Figure

Figure A

________ 2. Rotation (age 6).
________ 3. Fail to touch or overlap by one-eigth inch or more (age 6).
________ 4. Missing and/or extra angle(s) in diamond (age 5).
________ 5. Disproportion of parts, one approximately one-third larger or more, than other (age 6).

Figure 1

________ 6. Substitution of five or more circles for dots (age 7).
________ 7. Rotation (age 5).
________ 8. Dashes and commas for dots, three or more (age 7).
________ 9. Perseveration of two or more dots (age 6).
________ 10. Truncation of two or more dots (aage 5).

Figure 2

________ 11. Dashes and commas for circles (age 7).
________ 12. Truncation of one or more columns of circles (age 6).
________ 13. Perseveration of one or more circles in the rows (age 7).
________ 14. One or two rows of circles omitted (age 5).
________ 15. Truncation of one or more circles in the rows (age 7).
________ 16. Perseveration of one or more columns of circles (age 7).
________ 17. Rotation (age 9).

Figure 3

________ 18. Substitution of five or more circles for dots (age 6).
________ 19. Substitution of lines for dots (age 5).
________ 20. Dashes and commas for dots, three or more (age 7).
________ 21. Shape of design lost (age 7).
________ 22. Rotation (age 6).

Figure 11.5

Errors noted on the Watkins Bender-Gestalt scoring form.

Source: From *The Watkins Bender-Gestalt Scoring System, Protocol* by E. O. Watkins, 1976, Novato, CA: Academic Therapy Publications. Copyright 1976 by Academic Therapy Publications. Reprinted by permission.

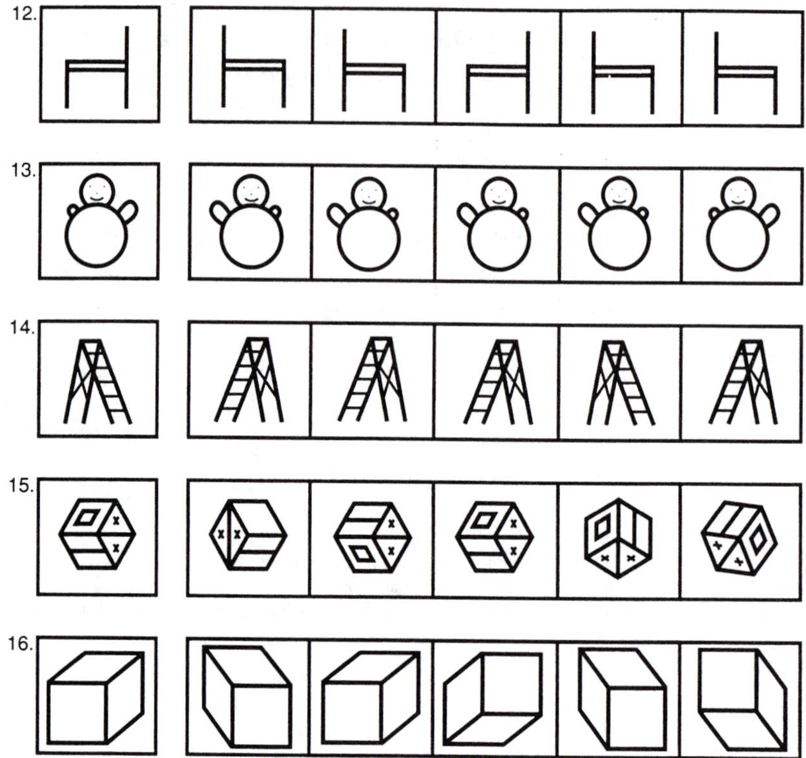

Figure 11.6
Portion of Positions in Space subtest from DTVP–2.
Source: From *Developmental Test of Visual Perception, Second Edition* by D. D. Hammill, N. A. Pearson, and J. K. Voress, 1993, Austin, TX: Pro-Ed. Copyright 1993 by Pro-Ed, Inc. Reprinted by permission.

Reliability. The manual presents research of internal consistency, test-retest, and interscorer reliability. All coefficients presented are within the adequate to high range.

Validity. The types of validity studied include content, item, criterion-related, and construct validity. Criterion-related research presented is limited, includes a sample size clinical sample, and resulted in low to adequate coefficients.

Motor-Free Visual Perception Test (MVPT)

The MVPT (Colarusso & Hammill, 1972) assesses visual-perceptual abilities without the involvement of fine motor tasks, such as copying designs or writing. The test consists of a test item book with design plates, a manual, and a scoring protocol. The examiner asks the student to point to like shapes or designs (visual matching/discrimination), to locate a shape like the one previously shown (visual memory and discrimination), to find a shape that would resemble the unfinished shape if finished (visual gestalt), and to distinguish which shape is different or the same (visual matching or discrimination). The student responds by pointing to the correct response.

Technical Data

Norming Process. The MVPT was standardized using a sample of 881 children, ages 4 to 8. The variables considered were race, age, sex, economic level, and community size. Specific data regarding these variables are limited. Derived scores include perceptual age and a standardized perceptual quotient.

Reliability. Test-retest reliability coefficients ranged from .77 to .83. Coefficients for split-half reliabilities were all in the .80s range. K-R 20 reliability coefficients ranged from .71 to .82.

Validity. Criterion-related validity coefficients for several tests and subtests are presented in the manual. The tests include both motor-free and nonmotor-free visual-perceptual measures. The validity coefficients ranged from .31 to .73.

☐ **CHECK YOUR UNDERSTANDING**

Complete Activity 11.2.

Activity 11.2

Match the following terms to the correct descriptions.

A. sensory-motor perception
B. sensory-motor assessment
C. visual-motor ability
D. motor-free visual perception
E. Developmental Test of Visual Perception
F. Watkins Bender-Gestalt Scoring System
G. visual memory
H. visual discrimination
I. visual matching
J. Developmental Test of Visual-Motor Integration
K. Motor-Free Visual Perception Test

_________ **1.** Tasks that require the student to remember a visual stimulus and reproduce it or locate a like shape.
_________ **2.** Tasks that require the student to find a shape among several others or to be able to tell the difference between shapes.
_________ **3.** Measures visual perception without using motor abilities.
_________ **4.** A scoring system of a copying test that is used to measure visual-perceptual problems.
_________ **5.** Measurement of sensory-motor abilities.
_________ **6.** The ability to complete visual-motor tasks.
_________ **7.** Measures visual-motor integration using developmental expectations and norms.
_________ **8.** The ability to perceive through the senses and react motorically.
_________ **9.** Provides scoring for motor-enhanced and motor-reduced tasks.
_________ **10.** The ability to remember visual stimuli.

Tests of Auditory Ability

A student who is suspected of having auditory difficulty should first be referred for auditory acuity assessment. As with visual acuity assessment, the student's parents should be notified before the referral. The student may be tested by an audiologist or other medical personnel, who may determine if a hearing loss exists. Once auditory acuity has been found to be within the normal range, the teacher may wish to investigate the possibility of an auditory-perceptual problem. Determining how well a student is able to discriminate and remember sounds may be important when the student seems to have difficulty with remembering oral directions or discriminating sounds associated with written symbols. Several assessment instruments contain subtests that measure short-term **auditory memory,** such as the DTLA–3, WISC–III, CLT, and K-ABC. The subtests require the student to repeat numbers or words sequentially or in reverse order. Some subtests require the student to repeat entire sentences. Other subtests indirectly measure a student's auditory memory by assessing verbal comprehension and receptive vocabulary skills. Some measures, such as the Test of Auditory Discrimination, assess **auditory discrimination.** This test and the Test of Auditory-Perceptual Skills are discussed next.

auditory memory Remembering what is heard.

auditory discrimination Ability to differentiate between auditory stimuli.

Test of Auditory Discrimination

The Test of Auditory Discrimination (Goldman, Fristoe, & Woodcock, 1970) assesses a student's ability to discriminate between similar-sounding one-syllable words when the background environment is either quiet or noisy. The test contains an easel kit of picture plates, a test presentation tape with the discrimination tasks, a manual, and protocols. The student first completes a training exercise in which the examiner presents unlike-sounding words. The student discriminates and responds by pointing to the corresponding picture on the training exercise. For example, the pictures may be of a girl, chair, mail, and coal. The examiner says, "Put your finger on chair" (Goldman, Fristoe, & Woodcock, 1970, Plate 1). The first subtest, which contains like-sounding words, is presented in a quiet environment, and the second is presented against a noisy background. The information obtained may provide the speech-language clinician or audiologist with data about how the student best discriminates between like-sounding words. Error analyses for both the Quiet and Noise subtests are calculated on the protocol.

Technical Data

Norming Process. The standardization sample consisted of 745 subjects from 3 to 84 years in age. The data of 505 of the subjects were analyzed to determine if there were differences in performances due to age, sex, and type of test (Goldman et al., 1970). Data in the manual indicate that auditory discrimination appears to be a developmental skill that continues to improve through about the age of 30 and then begins a gradual decline (Goldman et al.,

1970). Detailed information regarding error analysis information is provided in the manual.

Reliability. Internal consistency reliability studies for both Quiet and Noise subtests were calculated and yielded correlations of .53 to .83 for the Quiet subtest and .52 to .68 for the Noise subtest. Test-retest reliability correlations ranged from .87 on the Quiet subtest and .81 on the Noise subtest.

Validity. Content validity is presented as related to item selection. Concurrent validity information is presented as a study of correlation between the subtests and clinical judgments; coefficients were in the .60s and .70s. Intercorrelations ranged from .32 to .62, and construct validity is presented through studies with clinical populations and other special groups.

Test of Auditory-Perceptual Skills (TAPS)

The TAPS (Gardner, 1985) assesses the auditory-perceptual skills that affect the language of children 4 to 12 years old. The six areas of auditory skills measured by this instrument include:

1. auditory number memory
2. auditory sentence memory
3. auditory word memory
4. auditory interpretation of directions
5. auditory word discrimination
6. auditory processing (thinking and reasoning) (Gardner, 1985, p. 7)

The manual provides tables for determining the derived scores for percentile ranks, language ages, scaled scores (mean = 10), stanines, and auditory quotient (mean = 100).

Technical Data

Norming Process. The norm sample included 808 children, ages 4 to 12. The children were all from the San Francisco Bay area. Gender and age were the only characteristics described of the sample. Gender was not equally distributed across all ages but was equal for total sample.

Reliability. The manual presents internal consistency information that appears adequate for the total test across all ages. Reliability information is very limited.

Validity. The types of validity addressed in the manual include content validity, item validity, diagnostic validity, and criterion-related validity. The coefficients presented for diagnostic validity ranged from low to adequate. The criterion-related coefficients were low and may represent discriminant validity as the instruments used appear to be assessing other types of abilities rather than auditory processing.

Assessing Developmental Levels with Drawing Tests

Psychoeducational assessment batteries have often included the task of drawing as a measure of general ability or maturity of children (Naglieri, 1988). Examiners often present students with the task of drawing a human figure. The task can then be scored using various scoring systems. Two scoring systems are presented here: the Goodenough-Harris Drawing Test and its revision, Draw-a-Person: A Quantitative Scoring System.

Goodenough-Harris Drawing Test

The Goodenough-Harris Drawing Test (Harris, 1963) consists of a manual, scoring plates, and response sheets for the students. The student is asked to draw a picture of a man, a woman, and of him/herself. The scoring system lists and illustrates several examples of how to interpret the drawings. The scoring includes items such as clothing (sleeves, neckline, etc.) and inclusion, placement, and proportion of body parts. Scores are thought to indicate overall general ability and maturity levels or developmental levels of children. Derived scores include standard scores and percentile ranks.

The manual provides limited technical data for this scoring system.

Draw-a-Person: A Quantitative Scoring System

Draw-a-Person: A Quantitative Scoring System (Naglieri, 1988) is a refined and revised system for scoring the figure drawing tasks of the Goodenough-Harris Drawing Test. Naglieri (1988) lists the following goals for the Draw-a-Person:

> To provide a nonverbal measure of ability which can be administered in a relatively short time and may be used as either part of a test battery or as a screening device.
>
> To provide a scoring system using modern scoring criteria and reducing the influence of current styles of dress, hair, and other characteristics.
>
> To provide a scoring system normed on a large representative sample of students stratified according to recent U.S. Census data.
>
> To increase the precision of standard scores by providing norms for half- and quarter-year age intervals.
>
> To provide a scoring system that is as objective and efficient as possible in order to reduce subjectivity and thereby increase interrater reliability.
>
> To provide norms for the Self drawing.
>
> To provide a composite standard score composed of the scores of all three drawings, for greater reliability. (p. 2)

The derived scores for this scoring system include standard scores (mean = 100) and percentile ranks. This scoring system may be used to determine a general estimate of intelligence, to supplement other measures, or as a screening instrument (Naglieri, 1988).

The Draw-a-Person system provides a chapter of training exercises for learning the scoring system. The manual also presents information for comparing the three drawings.

Technical Data

Norming Process. The Draw-a-Person standardization sample included 2,622 students ranging in age from 5 to 17 years. Variables considered in the standardization were age, sex, geographic region, socioeconomic status, occupation, race, and Spanish origin.

Reliability. Internal consistency studies produced coefficients in the .80s using coefficient alpha. Test-retest reliability coefficients ranged from .58 to .74 for individual drawings. Interrater reliability coefficients ranged from .86 to .95.

Validity. Construct validity is addressed through a discussion of developmental progression. Criterion-related validity studies researched correlations with the Matrix Analogies Test and the Multilevel Academic Survey Test, with coefficients ranging from .17 to .31.

Using Results from Diagnostic Tests

Although diagnostic tests have been used historically in the assessment of special education students, their predictive and content validity have been questioned. When a teacher is concerned with the manner in which a student learns, processes, and responds to information, the teacher may benefit from informal assessment using actual curriculum (see chapter 8). Testing a student's ability to process and respond to specific academic tasks may prove to be more useful for planning than relying on results from perceptual-motor tests. When test results are included in the student's records, the teacher may wish to investigate further through informal curriculum-based assessment.

Table 11.2 summarizes the strengths and weaknesses of the instruments reviewed in this chapter.

Table 11.2
Summary of diagnostic instruments that assess language, visual-motor ability, sensory-motor ability, perceptual ability, and developmental level.

Instrument	Strengths	Weaknesses
Peabody Picture Vocabulary Test–Revised	Quick measure of verbal comprehension and receptive language Adequate technical validity Well-researched instrument	Yields a single score rather than multiple measures of language ability

continued

Table 11.2 continued

Instrument	Strengths	Weaknesses
Test of Word Finding	Yields several scores for ability to recall various types of words Comprehensive Adequate technical quality	Time-consuming to administer
Test of Language Development–2 (Primary and Intermediate), Test of Adolescent and Adult Language–Third Edition	Good measures of written language skills Adequate technical quality	Time-consuming to administer Subjective scoring
Developmental Test of Visual-Motor Integration, Third Revision	Developmentally based Extensive scoring criteria	Scoring takes clinical practice and can be influenced by subjectivity or lack of experience
Bender Visual Motor Gestalt Test: Watkins Bender-Gestalt Scoring System	Quick measure of visual-perceptual deficits Adequate technical quality	Somewhat subjective scoring system
Developmental Test of Visual Perception, Second Edition	Improved norms Assesses across a variety of visual-motor areas Provides motor-enhanced and motor-reduced scores	Limited to ages 4–10
Motor-Free Visual Perception Test	Quick measure of visual perception without requiring motoric responses Fair technical quality	Forced-choice format
Test of Auditory Discrimination	Easy to administer Provides sample of auditory discrimination skills for both quiet and noisy environments	Provides limited scores Only fair technical quality
Test of Auditory-Perceptual Skills	Easy to administer Measures a variety of auditory-perceptual abilities	Small standardization sample Limited reliability and validity information
Goodenough-Harris Drawing Test	Easy to administer	Subjective scoring Limited technical data provided
Draw-a-Person: A Quantitative Scoring System	Easy to administer Good technical quality More objective scoring	Some training required for interpretation

Exercises

Part I

Match the following terms with the correct definitions.

A. visual-motor ability
B. sensory-motor ability
C. perceptual ability
D. language assessment
E. receptive language
F. expressive language
G. developmental levels
H. written language
I. visual perception
J. visual retention
K. visual memory
L. motor-free
M. auditory memory
N. auditory discrimination

_______ **1.** Ability to retain visual stimuli.
_______ **2.** Refers to test responses that are made without using motoric ability.
_______ **3.** Measuring verbal concepts and verbal understanding.
_______ **4.** Inner language concepts applied to what is heard.
_______ **5.** Ability to receive and understand perceptual stimuli.
_______ **6.** Responding motorically to visual input.
_______ **7.** Ability to remember what is heard.
_______ **8.** Ability to remember what is seen.
_______ **9.** Understanding language concepts and using those in writing.
_______ **10.** Language skills used in speaking or writing.
_______ **11.** Responding to sensory input by motor responses.
_______ **12.** Ability to receive and understand visual stimuli.
_______ **13.** Ability to differentiate between auditory stimuli.

Part II

Answer the questions and complete the problems that follow.

1. List the areas of language assessed by diagnostic language tests in this chapter. _______________

2. Referring to the research presented in this chapter, discuss the usefulness of testing sensory-motor and perceptual abilities. _______________

3. In addition to assessing sensory-motor and perceptual-motor abilities, what procedures should the teacher complete to determine how a student processes information and responds to an academic task? ______________
____
____
____

4. Match the following deficit areas with the academic skills areas that may be affected.

auditory memory	visual-motor ability
auditory discrimination	receptive language
visual memory	written language
visual discrimination	expressive language
	fine motor ability

Academic Skill	*Deficit Area*
Phonics	a. ______________
Handwriting	b. ______________
Speaking	c. ______________
Oral reading	d. ______________
Math calculation	e. ______________
Math story problems	f. ______________
Reading comprehension	g. ______________
Spelling	h. ______________
Written math work	i. ______________
Content areas	j. ______________

References

Altepeter, T., & Johnson, K. (1989). Use of the PPVT–R for intellectual screening of adults: A caution. *Journal of Psychoeducational Assessment, 7,* 39–45.

Beery, K. E. (1989). *The VMI: Developmental Test of Visual-Motor Integration: Administration, scoring, and teaching manual (third revision),* Cleveland, OH: Modern Curriculum Press.

Bender, L. (1946). *Instructions for the use of Visual Motor Gestalt Test.* New York-American Orthopsychiatric Association.

Colarusso, R. P., & Hammill, D. D. (1972). *Motor-free Visual Perception Test.* Novato, CA: Academic Therapy.

D'Amato, R., Gray, J., & Dean, R. (1987). Concurrent validity of the PPVT–R with the K-ABC for learning problem children. *Psychology in the Schools, 24,* 35–38.

Dunn, L. M., & Dunn, L. M. (1981). *Peabody Picture Vocabulary Test–revised.* Circle Pines, MN: American Guidance Service.

Gardner, M. F. (1985). *Test of Auditory-Perceptual Skills.* San Francisco: Children's Hospital of San Francisco.

German, D. J. (1986). *Test of Word Finding: TWF,* Circle Pines, MN: American Guidance Service.

Goldman, R., Fristoe, M., & Woodcock, R. (1970). *Test of Auditory Discrimination.* Circle Pines, MN: American Guidance Service.

Groshong, C. (1987). Assessing oral language comprehension: Are picture-vocabulary tests enough? *Learning Disabilities Focus, 2,* 108–115.

Hammill, D. D., Brown, V. L., Larsen, S. C., & Wiederholt, J. L. (1994). *Test of Adolescent and Adult Language, Third Edition.* Austin, TX: Pro-Ed.

Hammill, D. D., & Newcomer, P. L. (1988a). *Test of Language Development–2: Intermediate.* Austin, TX: Pro-Ed.

Hammill, D. D., & Newcomer, P. L. (1988b). Test of Language Development–2: Primary. Austin, TX: Pro-Ed.

Hammill, D. D., Pearson, N. A., & Voress, J. K. (1993). *Developmental Test of Visual Perception, Second Edition.* Austin, TX: Pro-Ed.

Harris, D. B. (1963). *Goodenough-Harris Drawing Test.* New York: Harcourt Brace Jovanovich.

Hupp, S., Able, H., & Conroy-Gunter. (1984). Assessment of sensorimotor abilities of severely retarded children and adolescents. *Diagnostique, 9,* 208–217.

Kavale, K., & Forness, S. (1987). Substance over style: Assessing the efficacy of modality testing and teaching. *Exceptional Children, 54,* 228–239.

Koppitz, E. M. (1964). *The Bender Gestalt Test for young children,* New York: Grune & Stratton.

Locher, P. (1988). The usefulness for psychoeducational evaluation of preassessment screening for sensory-motor and perceptual encoding deficits. *Psychology in the Schools, 25,* 244–251.

Locher, P., & Worms, P. (1981). Visual scanning strategies of perceptually impaired and normal children viewing the Motor-Free Visual Perception Test. *Journal of Learning Disabilities, 14,* 416–419.

Mather, N., & Kirk, S. (1985). The type III error and other concerns in learning disability research. *Learning Disabilities Research, 1,* 56–64.

Naglieri, J. (1988). *Draw-a-Person: A Quantitative Scoring System.* New York: Psychological Corporation.

Naglieri, J., & Bardos, A. (1987). Confidence intervals for the PPVT–R. *Diagnostique, 12,* 103–108.

Naglieri, J., & Pfeiffer, S. (1983). Stability, concurrent and predictive validity of the PPVT–R. *Journal of Clinical Psychology, 39,* 965–967.

Newcomer, P. L., & Hammill, D. D. (1988). *Test of Language Development–2: Primary,* Austin, TX: Pro-Ed.

Overton, T., & Mardoyan-Apperson, J. (1988). The relationship between the CLT and the PPVT–R in a college freshman sample: Part 2, *CLT Technical Reports,* Norristown, PA: Arete.

Robertson, G. J., & Eisenberg, J. L. (1981). *Peabody Picture Vocabulary Test–Revised technical supplement.* Circle Pines, MN: American Guidance Service.

Watkins, E. O. (1976), *The Watkins Bender-Gestalt Scoring System.* Navota, CA: Academic Therapy Publications.

Chapter Twelve

Early Childhood Assessment

Key Terms

Public Law 99–457
developmental delay
at risk for developmental delay
biological risk factors
environmental risk factors
Individual Family Service Plan
family-centered program
family-focused program
arena assessment
interactive strategies
situational questionnaires
ecobehavioral interviews

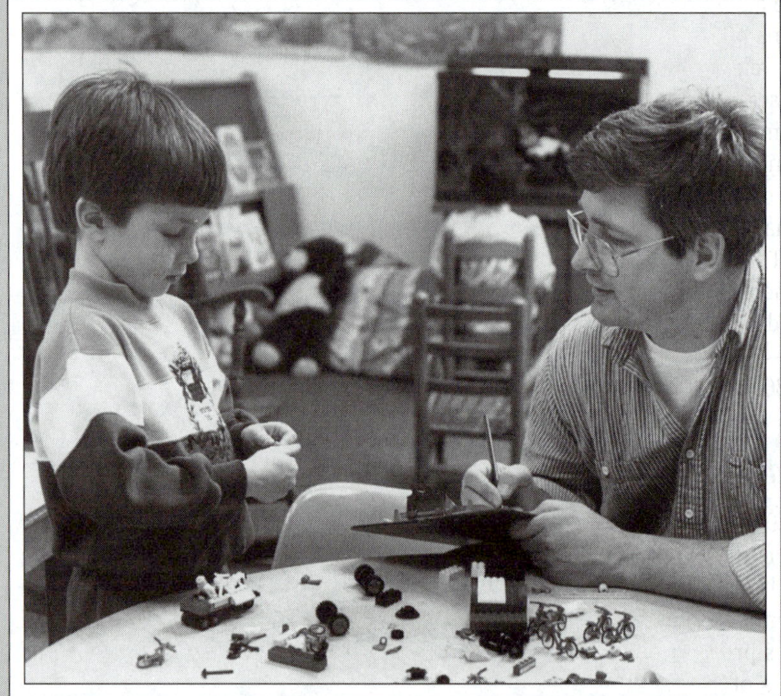

The assessment of infants and young children presents several issues and concerns not found in the assessment of school-age children. Many of these issues are related to the young age of the child. For example, these young children present unique challenges in assessment because they must be evaluated in domains and areas that are not based on school-related competencies such as academic achievement. These children are evaluated in other areas such as physical challenges, developmental motor skills, functional communication skills, behaviors in specific situations, and developmental competence.

The assessment of young children and infants also includes the unique component of family needs and a family plan for appropriate intervention. The guidelines for assessing young children and infants are specified in **Public Law 99–457,** the Education of the Handicapped Amendments. PL 99–457, passed in 1986, supplements the regulations put forth in IDEA (see chapter 2).

Public Law 99–457 IDEA amendments that extend services for special needs children through infancy and preschool years; mandates services for children ages 3–5 with disabilities.

Public Law 99–457 and Assessment

PL 99–457 mandates that children aged 3 to 5 be served through early childhood intervention and provides incentives for states to serve children aged birth to 2 years. The law defines the population of children eligible to be served, defines the methods of assessment, provides procedural safeguards, and outlines procedures to be used for intervention based on the family's needs. Sections of PL 99–457 that are relevant to the assessment of infants and young children are included throughout this chapter. The definition of infants and toddlers with disabilities can be found in PL 99–457, and the definition of children aged 3 to 5 with disabilities can be found defined in IDEA.

Eligibility for Infants and Young Children

Infants and toddlers aged birth to 2 who are experiencing developmental delays in one or more of the following areas are eligible for services: cognitive development, physical development (includes vision and hearing), communication development, social or emotional development, or adaptive development. Infants and toddlers may also be eligible for services if they have a diagnosed physical or mental condition that is likely to result in **developmental delay.** PL 99–457 leaves to the individual state's discretion whether services will be provided for infants and toddlers who are **at risk for developmental delay** if intervention is not provided (*Federal Register,* 1993).

developmental delay When an infant or child experiences delay in physical, cognitive, communicative, social, emotional, or adaptive development.

at risk for developmental delay When a child is believed to be at risk for delay in one or more areas if interventions are not provided.

IDEA leaves to the states' discretion the eligibility of children aged 3 to 5 with developmental delays. Children eligible for early childhood services are those with the same disabilities defined for school-aged children: autism, deaf-blindness, deafness, hearing impairment, mental retardation, multiple disabilities, orthopedic impairment, other health impairment, serious emotional disturbance, specific learning disability, speech or language impairment, traumatic brain injury, and visual impairment (*Federal Register,* 1993).

Although not all states choose to serve infants and toddlers who are at risk for developmental delays, many states have responded to this category of infants and toddlers and provide intervention services. Katz (1989) lists as **biological risk factors** "prematurity associated with low birthweight, evidence of central nervous system involvement (intraventricular hemorrhage, neonatal seizures), prolonged respiratory difficulties, prenatal maternal substance use or abuse" (p. 100). These risk factors may not always result in an early diagnosed physical condition but may prove problematic as the child develops.

biological risk factors Health factors, such as birth trauma, that place a child at risk for developmental disabilities.

In addition to biological risk factors, **environmental risk factors** often exist. The most often cited environmental risk factors found by Graham and Scott (1988) are poor infant/child interaction patterns, low maternal educational level, young maternal age, disorganization or dysfunction of the family, and few family support networks. Suggestions for assessing infants at risk are given later in this chapter.

environmental risk factors Environmental influences, such as the mother's young age, that place a child at risk for developmental disabilities.

Evaluation and Assessment Procedures

PL 99–457 defines evaluation as the ongoing procedures used by qualified personnel to determine the child's eligibility and continued eligibility while the child is served under this law. Assessment procedures focus on the identification of:

> **(i)** the child's unique strengths and needs and the services to meet those needs
> **(ii)** the resources, priorities, concerns of the family and the supports and services needed to help the family meet the developmental needs of their infant or toddler with the disability. (§ 303.322, *Federal Register,* 1993, p. 40971)

The procedures during the assessment process must meet specific criteria established by PL 99–457. Included in the criteria are the requirements that assessment be conducted by trained professionals who will use appropriate methods, including clinical opinion. The assessment must include reviewing the child's medical records and health and evaluating the child's current physical, cognitive, language, social, and adaptive development.

PL 99–457 also mandates assessment of the child's family for the purpose of determining their resources, priorities, and concerns related to enhancing the development of the infant or young child. Any assessment of the family must (a) be voluntary on the part of the family, (b) be conducted by trained personnel, (c) use appropriate measures, and (d) be based on information provided by the family through a personal interview. This assessment must also incorporate the family's description of their resources, priorities, and concerns. The evaluation must be completed within a 45-day time period unless special circumstances prevent its completion. The law includes procedures for documentation if the timeline cannot be met.

The assessment of infants and young children must also follow IDEA's regulations concerning nondiscriminatory assessment, parental consent, confidentiality, and due process procedural safeguards. The law requires annual evaluation of progress but notes that due to the rapid development during this period of a child's life, some evaluation procedures may need to be repeated before the annual review (*Federal Register,* 1993).

☐ **CHECK YOUR UNDERSTANDING**

Complete Activity 12.1.

Activity 12.1

Complete the sentences using the following terms.

developmental delay	birth to 2 years
at risk for developmental delay	vision and hearing
45 days	family assessment
PL 99–457	voluntary
clinical opinion	procedural safeguards
family resources	health records

1. Family assessment includes determining the ________________ priorities, and concerns related to enhancing the development of the child.
2. The assessment of the family is ________________ on the part of the family.
3. A child with ________________ may be measured by the appropriate instruments and found in one or more of the following areas: cognitive development, physical development, communication development, social or emotional development, adaptive development.
4. The term *physical development* includes ________________ .
5. ________________ must incorporate the family's description of its resources, priorities, and concerns related to the development of the child.
6. The evaluation of an infant or young child must include a review of current and previous ________________ and must be based on formed ________________ .
7. ________________ includes incentives for states that choose to serve children aged ________________ .

8. The time set for completion of assessment of infants and young children is _________________ .
9. PL 99–457 includes _________________ like those found in IDEA.
10. The decision to serve children who are _________________ is left to the discretion of individual states.

Individual Family Service Plans

Individual Family Service Plan (IFSP) Plan required by PL 99–457 that includes the related needs of the family of the child with disabilities.

Within 45 days following the initial evaluation of the child, the **Individual Family Service Plan (IFSP)** must be written. According to PL 99–457, the IFSP must contain information about the child's current levels of functioning in physical development (including vision and hearing), cognitive development, communication development, social or emotional development, and adaptive development and about the family's resources, priorities, and concerns as related to the child's development. The plan must state expected outcomes, degree of progress made toward reaching those expectations, and whether modifications are necessary to meet those outcomes. A statement specifying the early intervention services required to meet the needs of the child and family is also a part of the IFSP, as is the frequency, intensity, and method of service delivery. The location of the interventions, which are to be in a natural environment for the child, must be included and any additional services listed. These additional services may not be paid for by the school system or agency, but the IFSP may indicate the source of finances where appropriate.

Issues and Questions About PL 99–457

A goal of PL 99–457 was to incorporate family members as partners in the assessment of and planning for the infant or child with developmental disabilities. Since the law's passage in 1986, many concerns have been raised by clinical practitioners working with these regulations. Of chief concern is the role of the parents in the assessment and planning process (Dunst, Johanson, Trivette, & Hamby, 1991; Goodman & Hover, 1992; Katz, 1989; Minke & Scott, 1993).

The issues raised by Goodman and Hover (1992) include the confusion with the interpretation and implementation of the family assessment component. The regulations may be misunderstood as requiring mandatory assessment of family members rather than voluntary participation on the part of the parents. The family's strengths and needs as they relate to the child, not the parents themselves, are the objects of the assessment. Furthermore, these authors contended that a relationship based on equal standing between parents and professionals may not result in a greater degree of cooperation and respect than the traditional client-professional relationship. When the parents and professionals are viewed as equal partners, the professional surrenders the role of expert. Goodman and Hover suggested that the relationship be viewed as reciprocal rather than egalitarian. An assessment process directed by the parents may not be in the child's best interest because the parents retain the right to restrict professional inquiry.

Katz (1989) observed that the family's view of the child's most important needs takes precedence over the priorities perceived by the professional team members. In some instances, parents and professionals must negotiate in order to agree on the goals for the child. The family will be more motivated to achieve the goals that they believe are important.

The law clearly states that the IFSP be developed with parent participation. This is true whether or not the family participates in the assessment process. In practice, parent participation varies, according to a study of the development of IFSPs in three early childhood intervention programs (Minke & Scott, 1993). This study found that parents do not always participate in goal setting for their children, play a listening role without soliciting input from professionals, appear to need better explanations by professionals, and may become better child advocates with early participation. These issues are similar to issues associated with parent participation during eligibility meetings for school-aged children (see chapter 2).

Differences in the implementation of PL 99–457 may be the result of state-determined policies and procedures. One area of difference seems to be in the interpretation of how families should be involved in the early intervention process. Dunst et al. (1991) described the **family-centered program** and the **family-focused program** as paradigms representing two such interpretations. In the family-centered program paradigm, family concerns and needs drive the assessment, anything written on the IFSP must have the family's permission, and the family's needs determine the actual roles played by case managers. The family-focused program paradigm restricts assessment to the family's needs only as they relate to the child's development, the goals are agreed on mutually by professionals and parents, and the role of the case manager is to encourage and promote the family's use of professional services. It seems clear that the interpretation and implementation of PL 99–457 differs from state to state and may yet be problematic.

family-centered program Program in which the assessment and goals are driven by the family's needs and priorities.

family-focused program Program in which the family's needs are considered but goals and plans are reached through mutual agreement between the family and education professionals.

Activity 12.2

Answer the questions and complete the sentences.

1. What five areas of child development must the IFSP address?
   ____
   ____
   ____
   ____
   ____
2. The IFSP must include the expected ____________ of the interventions and the degree to which ____________ toward achieving those outcomes is being made.

☐ **CHECK YOUR UNDERSTANDING**

Complete Activity 12.2.

3. In which of the program paradigms does the parent play a more active role in the assessment and planning process? ______________________________

____

4. According to Minke and Scott (1993), parents may need better __________ from professionals.
5. Katz (1989) stated that in some instances, parents and professionals must __________ to agree on goals for the child.
6. According to Goodman and Hover (1992), when assessment is directed by the parents, what problems may occur? ______________________________

____

Methods of Early Childhood Assessment

As previously noted, many states serve children who are considered at risk for developmental disabilities. The discussion of assessment methods presented in this text applies to children with existing developmental disabilities as well as to those who may be at risk for developmental disabilities if they do not receive early childhood intervention.

PL 99–457 mandates that qualified personnel assess children in many developmental areas—for example, assessments of vision, hearing, speech, and medical status are part of a multifactored evaluation. Assessment in these areas is beyond the scope of this text. Measures presented include behavior questionnaires, observations, interviews, checklists, and measures of cognitive and language functioning. Techniques used in the assessment process are also presented.

Assessment of Infants

Documenting developmental milestones and health history is primarily the responsibility of health professionals. Infants may be suspected of having developmental delays or of being at risk for developmental delays if there are clinical indications for concern. Mayes (1991) cited the following indications as need for an infant assessment:

1. Regulatory disturbances—Sleep disturbances, excessive crying or irritability, eating difficulties, low frustration tolerance, self-stimulatory or unusual movements.
2. Social/environmental disturbances—Failure to discriminate mother, apathetic, withdrawn, no expression of affect or interest in social interaction, excessive negativism, no interest in objects or play, abuse, neglect, or multiple placements, repeated or prolonged separations.
3. Psychophysiological disturbances—Nonorganic failure to thrive, recurrent vomiting or chronic diarrhea, recurrent dermatitis, recurrent wheezing.

4. Developmental delays—Specific delays (gross motor, speech delays). General delays or arrested development. (p. 445)

The prenatal, birth, and early neonatal health history is an important component of the evaluation of infants and is required by PL 99–457. Following the careful history taking of the infant's health factors, Greenspan (1992) organizes the infant/toddler/young child assessment using the following factors:

1. Prenatal and perinatal variables.
2. Parent, family, and environmental variables.
3. Primary caregiver and caregiver/infant-child relationship.
4. Infant variables: Physical, neurologic, physiologic, and cognitive.
5. Infant variables: Formation and elaboration of emotional patterns and human relationships. (pp. 316–317)

Of particular concern in assessing the infant are regulatory patterns, or how the infant reacts to stimuli in the environment and processes sensory information (Greenspan, 1992; Mayes, 1991). This includes how the infant interacts with and reacts to caregivers, sleeping habits, irritability, and so on. This type of assessment relies on observations using checklists and parent interviews or questionnaires. One commonly used observation assessment instrument used for newborn infants is the Neonatal Behavioral Assessment Scale (Brazelton, 1984). This scale includes both reflex items and behavioral observation items. Use of this scale to determine control states (such as sleeping, alert, etc.) underscores the importance of this aspect of infant behavior to more complex functions, such as attention (Mayes, 1991). This scale can be used with infants up to 1 month of age.

The Uzgiris-Hunt Ordinal Scales of Psychological Development (Uzgiris & Hunt, 1975) present a Piagetian developmental perspective for assessment during the first 2 years of the infant's life. These six scales include assessment for such skills as visual pursuit, object permanence, manipulation of and interaction with factors in the environment, development of vocal and gestural imitation, and development of schemes for relating to the environment. This instrument requires the use of several objects and solicitation of reactions and responses of the infant. This system presents a comprehensive assessment based on the Piagetian model; however, it has been criticized for being developed using primarily infants from middle-class families (Mayes, 1991).

Another instrument used to assess young children and toddlers (ages 1–42 months) is the Bayley Scales of Infant Development–II (Bayley, 1993). This recently revised formal instrument now includes improved statistical research regarding reliability and validity in the manual. Like most infant/toddler instruments, the Bayley requires the examiner to manipulate objects and observe the reactions and behavior of the infant. The scale assesses mental functions such as memory, problem solving, and verbal ability and motor functions such as coordination and control; it also includes a behavioral rating scale. In addition to the standardization sample, clinical samples were included in the development of this revision. The clinical samples included infants and young children who were premature, HIV positive, exposed prenatally to drugs, or asphyxiated at birth and those who had Down's syndrome, autism, developmental delays, or otitis media.

☐ **CHECK YOUR UNDERSTANDING**

Complete Activity 12.3.

Activity 12.3

Match the following terms with the correct descriptions.

A. Uzgiris-Hunt Ordinal Scales of Psychological Development
B. Bayley Scales of Infant Development–II
C. Neonatal Behavioral Assessment Scale
D. regulatory disturbances
E. infant variables
F. developmental delays

_________ **1.** This measure of infant assessment is used to determine the possible risk of developmental disabilities of infants from birth to 1 month of age.

_________ **2.** These include physical, neurological, and emotional factors that influence the child's development.

_________ **3.** This instrument is based on Piagetian developmental theory and is used for infants through 2 years of age.

_________ **4.** These include sleep disturbances, irritability, and unusual movements.

_________ **5.** This revised instrument includes research on several clinical samples and is used for children aged 1 to 42 months.

Assessment of Toddlers and Young Children

Many of the instruments discussed in earlier chapters contain basal-level items for toddlers and young children; these include the K-ABC, WJ–R Tests of Achievement, Vineland Adaptive Behavior Scales, Achenbach's Child Behavior Checklist, and Stanford-Binet IV. Following is a brief survey of some of the most commonly used and newest instruments that are specifically designed to assess the development and behavior of young children.

Wechsler Preschool and Primary Scale of Intelligence–Revised (WPPSI–R)

The WPPSI–R (Wechsler, 1989), like the Wechsler Intelligence Scale for Children, is composed of several subtests. Assessment of a young child using these subtests is believed to reflect the different aspects of intelligence (Wechsler, 1989) and provide standardized scores to indicate intellectual functioning. The WPPSI–R was normed for use with children ranging in age from 3–0 to 7–3 years. It is designed primarily to assess the cognitive functioning of young children.

Subtests.

Object Assembly. Like the Object Assembly subtests on the other Wechsler Scales, this subtest is comprised of puzzles that the child assembles. Unlike the other subtests, this subtest on the WPPSI–R is presented in full color.

Information. This subtest presents items that concern environmental objects or events. Initial lower level items are presented as questions with visual stimuli. Upper level items are presented verbally.

Geometric Designs. This subtest assesses two different skills: visual matching of geometric shapes and the visual-motor task of copying geometric shapes.

Comprehension. The examiner asks the child to answer questions concerning concepts learned in everyday environmental and educational experiences. Items are presented orally.

Block Design. The blocks included in this scale are flat, two-colored blocks. The child must use the blocks to reproduce patterns in the stimulus booklet. These items must be completed within specified time limits.

Arithmetic. Lower level items present counting tasks to measure early concepts of math, and higher level items include simple mental operations. These items range in presentation format from concrete blocks and pictures for counting to verbal items for mental math.

Mazes. This subtest presents increasingly difficult mazes that the child must solve using a pencil and the maze booklet.

Vocabulary. This subtest is now composed of two parts. The easiest level of the subtest includes pictures that the child must name. The higher level items are orally presented items in which the child is asked to explain the meaning of common words.

Picture Completion. In this subtest, the child must determine the missing parts of the pictures.

Similarities. Three separate tasks assess the child's ability to determine how things are similar. In the first task, the child views visual stimuli and indicates which of the objects pictured are similar to the group presented. In the second task, the child completes sentences that contain analogies. The third tasks requires the child to explain how two objects or events are similar.

Animal Pegs. The child places pegs of the correct color beneath a series of animal pictures. The colors must match the test stimuli of animals and colored pegs at the top of the pegboard. The score is based on both speed and accuracy of response. This subtest is optional.

Sentences. Designed to measure short-term auditory memory, this optional subtest presents verbal stimuli in the form of sentences which the child must repeat verbatim.

Technical Data

Norming Process. The manual includes much information about the revision of the WPPSI, discussing the developmental versions and national trials and reviewing old and new items. The standardization version of the WPPSI–R was administered to more than 2,100 children. Of this number, 1,700 were included in the standardization sample and 400 were minority children who were given the instrument to assess item bias. Variables considered in the representativeness of the standardization sample were age, gender, geographic location, ethnicity, educational level of parents, and parental occupation.

Reliability. The manual presents information on internal reliability, interrater reliability, and test-retest reliability. Reliability coefficients are adequate on most subtests, especially when the instability of the age group is considered. The reliability coefficients are most stable for the Verbal, Performance, and Full Scale IQs—higher than individual subtest reliability coefficients.

Validity. Research on validity included concurrent criterion-related validity research with well-known cognitive measures for young children and predictive validity studies. Most coefficients presented are adequate; however, some are below acceptable levels when compared to like measures. This is not surprising considering the greater variability of skills and abilities at such young ages.

AGS Early Screening Profiles

The AGS Early Screening Profiles (Harrison, Kaufman, Kaufman, Bruininks, Rynders, Ilmer, Sparrow, & Cicchetti, 1990) present a comprehensive screening for children aged 2 to 6–11 years. The battery contains items that are administered directly to the child and surveys that are completed by parents and/or teachers. The components, shown in Figure 12.1, are described in the following paragraphs.

Components

Cognitive/Language Profile. The child demonstrates verbal abilities by pointing to objects named or described by the examiner, discriminates pictures and selects ones that are the same as the stimulus, solves visual analogies by pointing to the correct picture, and demonstrates basic school skills such as number and quantity concepts and the recognition of numbers, letters, and words. Items are presented in an easel format, and sample items are included to teach the tasks.

Motor Profile. These items assess both gross motor and fine motor developmental skills. Gross motor skills measured include imitating movements, walking on a line, standing on one foot, walking heel to toe, and performing a standing broad jump. Fine motor tasks include stringing beads, drawing lines and shapes, and completing mazes.

PROFIILES

Cognitive/Language Profile

Source: direct testing of child
Time: 5 to 15 minutes

Cognitive Subscale
Visual Discrimination Subtest (14 items)

Logical Relations Subtest (14 items)
Language Subscale
Verbal Concepts Subtest (25 items)
Basic School Skills Subtest (25 items)

Motor Profile

Source: direct testing of child
Time: 5 to 15 minutes

Gross Motor Subtest (5 items)
Fine Motor Subtest (3 items)

Self-Help/Social Profile

Source: parent, teacher questionnaires
Time: 5 to 10 minutes

Communication Domain (15 items)
Daily Living Skills Domain (15 items)
Socialization Domain (15 items)
Motor Skills Domain (15 items)

SURVEYS

Articulation Survey

Source: direct testing of child
Time: 2 to 3 minutes

Articulation of Single Words (20 items)
Intelligibility During Continuous Speech (1 rating)

Home Survey

Source: parent questionnaire
Time: 5 minutes

(12 items)

Health History Survey

Source: parent questionnaire
Time: 5 minutes

(12 items)

Behavior Survey

Source: examiner questionnaire
Time: 2 to 3 minutes

Cognitive/Language Observations (9 items)
Motor Observations (13 items)

Figure 12.1
Components of the AGS Early Screening Profiles.

Source: From *Early Screening Profile* by Patti Harrison, Alan Kaufman, Nadeen Kaufman, Robert Bruininks, John Rynders, Steven Ilmer, Sara Sparrow, & Domenic Cicchetti.

Self-Help/Social Profile. Questionnaires completed by teachers and parents measure the child's understanding of oral and written language, daily self-care skills such as dressing and eating, ability to do chores, and community skills like telephone manners. Social skills that assess how well the child gets along with others and questions measuring the child's fine and gross motor skills are included in this section of the instrument.

Articulation Survey. In this easel-format task, the examiner asks the child to say words that sample the child's ability to articulate sounds in the initial, medial, and final position.

Home Survey and Health History Survey. These questionnaires completed by the parents assess parent-child interactions; types of play; frequency of parent reading to the child; health problems of the mother's pregnancy, labor, and delivery; and health history of the child, such as immunization schedule.

Behavior Survey. An observation form is used to rate the child's behavior in several categories such as attention, independence, activity level, and cooperativeness.

Technical Data

Norming Process. The test manual provides detailed descriptions of the development of test items and questions included on parent and teacher questionnaires. The following variables were considered in the national standardization sample: age, gender, geographic region, parental educational level, and race or ethnic group. These were representative of the 1986 U.S. census data.

Reliability. Reliability research presented in the manual includes coefficient alpha for internal consistency, and immediate test-retest and delayed test-retest research. Coefficients are adequate to moderately high for all measures.

Validity. Validity studies presented in the manual include content validity, construct validity, part-total correlations, and concurrent validity research with cognitive measures used with early childhood students. Many of the validity coefficients are low to adequate.

Kaufman Survey of Early Academic and Language Skills (K-SEALS)

The K-SEALS (Kaufman & Kaufman, 1993) was developed as an expanded version of the language measure of the AGS Early Screening Profiles. Normed for children aged 3–0 to 6–11, the instrument includes three subtests: Vocabulary; Numbers, Letters, and Words; and Articulation Survey. Scores for expressive and receptive language skills may be obtained from the administration of the Vocabulary and Numbers, Letters, and Words subtests. Scores for early academic skills, such as number skills and letter and word skills, may be computed for children aged 5–0 to 6–11. Items are presented in an easel format with visual and verbal stimuli and are similar to the items on the AGS Early Screening

Profiles. Half of the items from the Vocabulary and Numbers, Letters, and Words subtests are identical to those on the AGS Early Screening Profiles. The Articulation Survey from the AGS test is repeated in its entirety on the K-SEALS, but the error analysis is expanded on the K-SEALS.

Technical Data

The K-SEALS was standardized as part of the standardization of the AGS Early Screening Profiles. The same variables were considered to promote representativeness in the sample. Reliability and validity information for the K-SEALS includes split-half reliability, test-retest reliability, intercorrelations, construct validity, content validity, concurrent validity, and predictive validity. Individual subtest coefficients for reliability and validity studies ranged from low to adequate, but total test coefficients appear adequate for most studies cited.

☐ **CHECK YOUR UNDERSTANDING**

Complete Activity 12.4.

Activity 12.4

Answer the following questions about the assessment instruments used with young children.

1. Which instrument includes many of the same subtests as the WISC–III, for younger ages?
 ____
2. Which instrument was standardized at the same time as the AGS Early Screening Profiles?
 ____
3. What instrument provides scores for expressive and receptive language skills as well as early academic skills for children aged 5 and 6 years?
 ____
4. Which instrument includes an articulation survey but does not have the expanded error analysis included in the K-SEALS?
 ____
5. Which instrument includes both direct assessment and questionnaires to be completed by caretakers?
 ____

Techniques and Trends in Infant and Early Childhood Assessment

The assessment methods presented in this chapter are formal methods of assessment. Current literature suggests that alternative methods of assessment be used with or in place of traditional assessment of infants and young children (Cohen & Spenciner, 1994; Fewell, 1991; Paget, 1990; Sinclair, Del'Homme, & Gonzalez, 1993). Among the alternative methods sug-

interactive strategies
Strategies used by the examiner that encourage the child to use communication to solve problems.

arena assessment
Technique that places the child and facilitator in center of the multidisciplinary team members during the evaluation.

situational questionnaires
Questionnaires that assess the child's behavior in various situations.

ecobehavioral interviews
Interviews of parents and teachers that assess behavior in different settings and routines.

gested by various studies are play evaluations, **interactive strategies,** observations, **arena assessment, situational questionnaires,** and **ecobehavioral interviews.**

Play evaluations can yield useful information about how the child interacts with people and objects and can be completed in a naturalistic environment. Play evaluations can be useful in determining the child's activity level, reaction to novel stimuli, and affect. The characteristics of play listed by Bailey and Wolery (1989) are presented in Table 12.1. Using these characteristics as guidelines, the examiner can assess many behaviors of the child in a naturalistic environment. These behaviors can be analyzed for developmental progress in social skills, activity level, motor skills, frustration tolerance, communication skills with the examiner or caretaker while playing, and so on.

Table 12.1
Characteristics of play.

Characteristic	Description
Intrinsic motivation	Play is not motivated by biological drives (e.g., hunger) but comes from within the child and not from the stimulus properties of the play objects.
Spontaneous and voluntary	Play involves free choice; children engage in play because they want to, not because someone assigns it to them.
Self-generated	Play involves the child actively generating the activities.
Active engagement	Play involves active attention to the activities of play.
Positive affect	Play involves pleasurable or enjoyable activities or results in pleasurable and enjoyable consequences.
Nonliterality	Play involves activities that are carried out in a pretend or "as-if" nature—less serious or real.
Flexibility	Play involves variability in form or context and can be done in a variety of ways or situations.
Means more than ends	Play involves emphasis on the activity itself rather than on the goal of the activity.

Source: From *Assessing Infants and Preschoolers with Handicaps* (p. 432) by D. B. Bailey and M. Wolery, 1989, Englewood Cliffs, NJ:. Merrill/Prentice Hall. Reprinted by permission.

Interactive strategies may be useful in the assessment of young children. These strategies assess the child's abilities to solve problems through interpersonal interactions with the examiner (Paget, 1990). The examiner may alter the problems presented to observe the child's responses to frustration, humor, or different types or objects of play. The strategies are aimed at encouraging the child to communicate with the examiner to solve the problem.

Observations may be used in a variety of settings and across a variety of tasks. The child may be observed in the home or preschool classroom environment, with peers, siblings, and caretakers. All areas of assessment in early childhood can be enhanced through observations. The child's behavior, social skills, communication, cognitive level, speech, motor skills, motor planning, adaptive behaviors, activity level, frustration tolerance, attention span, and self-help skills can be assessed through multiple observations. When combined with information from parent questionnaires and more formal assessment measures, the examiner can gain a holistic view of the child's developmental progress.

Arena assessment can be arranged for any method of assessment defined in this chapter, except perhaps for formal cognitive assessment on standardized instruments. Arena assessment is a technique in which all members of the multidisciplinary team surround the child and examiner or facilitator and observe as they interact in multiple situations. Play evaluations, formal play or preacademic tasks, communication items, and so on may all be presented in this format. All members of the team record the child's responses throughout the evaluation session. This may be a more effective method of assessment of infants and young children because it may reduce the number of assessment sessions (Cohen & Spenciner, 1994). Figure 12.2 illustrates the arena assessment model.

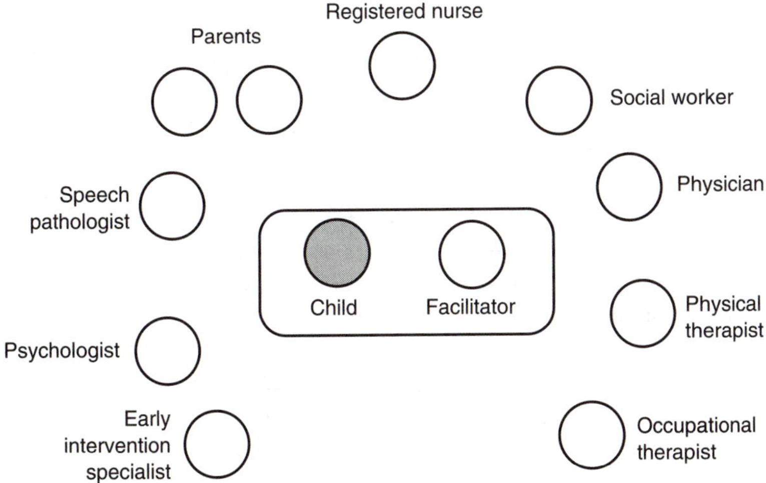

Figure 12.2
Team member conducting an arena assessment.

Source: From *Assessment of Young Children* by Libby G. Cohen and Loraine Spenciner. Copyright © 1992 by Longman Publishers. Reprinted with permission.

Situational questionnaires are useful when comparing the child's behavior in specific situations. Examples of these are the Home Situations Questionnaire and the School Situations Questionnaire (Barkley, 1990). The parents and teachers rate the child's behavior, activity level, and attention in a variety of situations, such as when the parents talk on the telephone, when visitors are in the home, and when interacting with peers. These questionnaires allow for more direct analysis and intervention for problematic behaviors.

In ecobehavioral interviews, parents and teachers describe a child's behaviors in everyday situations such as during daily routines, bedtimes, class activities, transitions from one activity to the next, and so on (Barnett, Macmann, & Carey, 1992). These responses are analyzed to determine problem behaviors that occur across settings or situations. Behavioral interventions are then targeted to remediate the behaviors in the situations described by the parents and teachers.

Other Considerations in Assessing Very Young Children

The best practice of assessment across all ages of children involves multiple measures, multiple examiners, and multiple situations or environments. This is especially important for infants, toddlers, and young children due to the influence that temperament, physical health, and current physical state (alertness or sleepiness) may play during an evaluation period. A holistic view of the child's developmental level can be gained by observing the child in many different settings, using both formal and informal assessment, and analyzing the observed behaviors.

Due to the very rapid pace of development of young children, assessment and monitoring of progress should be ongoing as stated in PL 99–457 (*Federal Register,* 1993). This rapid progress contributes to the instability of scores obtained at very young ages. The variability of the educational and home environments may also contribute to the instability of scores.

Analysis of formal early childhood assessment instruments indicates that the reliability and validity of the subtests are moderately adequate to below acceptable levels. The coefficients tend to be more acceptable for total test or total instrument scores. Barnett et al. (1992) cautioned against using profile analysis of individual subtests at young ages and suggested that only global scores be used. Katz (1989) warned of the dangers that may occur when very young children are falsely identified through assessment. That is, the child's scores may indicate developmental difficulties, but in reality, the child is not disabled. This false identification may result in changes in parent-child interactions and diminished expectations held for the child.

At the other end of the identification process are the children who need services but remain unidentified. In a study by Sinclair et al. (1993), students who were previously undiagnosed were referred for assessment of behavioral disor-

Table 12.2
Summary of instruments for early childhood assessment.

Instrument	Strengths	Weaknesses
Neonatal Behavioral Assessment Scale	Useful for infants through 1 month of age Assesses behavior and reflex actions	Not typically used in educational setting Requires specific training for use
Uzgiris-Hunt Ordinal Scales of Psychological Development	For children up to 2 years of age Good theoretical basis	Lengthy administration time Norm sample not representative
Bayley Scales of Infant Development–II	Manual has improved statistical data Standardization included clinical samples Assess many areas of development	Lengthy administration time Specific training necessary
Wechsler Preschool and Primary Scales of Intelligence	Subtests are like those in other Wechsler Scales Appropriate for ages 3–0 to 7–3	Lengthy administration time Have lower reliability and validity coefficients than other Wechsler Scales
AGS Early Screening Profiles	Include both direct and indirect assessment across multiple situations and skills	Low to adequate reliability and validity coefficients
Kaufman Survey of Early Academic and Language Skills	Expands the language sections of the AGS Early Screening Profiles Offers expanded analysis of articulation errors	Subtest coefficients low to adequate

ders. This study involved a three-stage, multiple-gating system that was used to screen preschool children for behavioral disorders. In this study, 5% of the sample who had not previously been identified as having behavioral difficulties were referred for a comprehensive evaluation.

Review of the literature on the assessment of infants and young children indicates that new trends are emerging. It is hoped that these trends will remedy some of the difficulties of assessing children at very young ages.

Table 12.2 summarizes the strengths and weaknesses of the instruments presented in this chapter.

Exercises

Part I

Match the following terms with the correct definitions and descriptions.

A. PL 99–457
B. developmental delay
C. at risk for developmental delay
D. biological risk factors

E. environmental risk factors
F. IFSP
G. family-centered program
H. family-focused program
I. arena assessment
J. interactional strategies
K. situational questionnaire
L. ecobehavioral interview
M. play evaluations

_____ 1. This technique used in the assessment of infants and toddlers may decrease the time spent in assessment.
_____ 2. This is required by PL 99–457 and considers the family's priorities and concerns.
_____ 3. Factors that fall in this category might include low birth weight or prolonged respiratory problems.
_____ 4. This technique encourages the child to use communication to solve problems presented by the examiner.
_____ 5. In this type of program, the assessment and needs are driven by the family's expressed needs and priorities.
_____ 6. Questions on this instrument focus on the behaviors in different situations.
_____ 7. Without interventions in early childhood, some children may be identified in this category.
_____ 8. This type of program included goals that are mutually agreed on by the parents and team members.
_____ 9. This term describes a delay in cognitive, physical, communicative, social, emotional, or adaptive development.
_____ 10. Factors in this category might include low educational level of the mother.
_____ 11. This mandate services for children aged 3–5 with disabilities.
_____ 12. This interview technique includes questions that target behaviors in different settings, routines, and times.

Part II

Answer the following questions.

1. What are some of the criticisms and issues of family involvement as specified in PL 99–457? _____

2. What are the clinical indications that an infant may need a full evaluation according to Mayes (1991)? _____

3. What areas are assessed when infants are evaluated? Describe these areas in your answer. ____________________

4. What are some of the general considerations and problems of assessing infants, toddlers, and young children? ____________________

References

Bailey, D. B., & Wolery, M. (1989). *Assessing infants and preschoolers with handicaps,* Columbus, OH: Merrill.

Barkley, R. A. (1990). *Attention deficit hyperactivity disorder: A handbook for diagnosis and treatment.* New York: Guilford.

Barnett, D. W., Macmann, G. M., & Carey, K. T. (1992). Early intervention and the assessment of developmental skills: Challenges and directions. *Topics in Early Childhood Special Education, 12*(1), 21–43.

Bayley, N. (1993). *Bayley Scales of Infant Development–II.* San Antonio, TX: Psychological Corporation.

Brazelton, T. (1984). *Neonatal Behavioral Assessment Scale Second Edition.* Philadelphia: Lippincott.

Cohen, L. G., & Spenciner, L. J. (1994). *Assessment of young children.* NY: Longman.

Dunst, C. J., Johanson, C., Trivette, C. M., & Hamby, D. (1991). Family-oriented early intervention policies and practices: Family-centered or not? *Exceptional Children, 58*(2), 115–126.

Federal Register (1993). Washington, DC: U.S. Government Printing Office, July 30, 1993.

Fewell, R. R. (1991). Trends in the assessment of infants and toddlers with disabilities. *Exceptional Children, 58*(2), 166–173.

Goodman, J. F., & Hover, S. A. (1992). The Individual Family Service Plan: Unresolved problems. *Psychology in the Schools, 29,* 140–151.

Graham, M., & Scott, K. (1988). The impact of definitions of high risk on services of infants and toddlers. *Topics in Early Childhood Special Education, 8*(3), 23–28.

Greenspan, S. I. (1992). *Infancy and early childhood: The practice of clinical assessment and intervention with emotional and developmental challenges.* Madison, CT: International University Press.

Harrison, P. L., Kaufman, A. S., Kaufman, N. L., Bruininks, R. H., Rynders, J., Ilmer, S., Sparrow, S. S., & Cicchetti, D. V. (1990). *AGS Early Screening Profiles.* Circle Pines, MN: American Guidance Service.

Katz, K. S. (1989). Strategies for infant assessment: Implications of P.L. 99–457. *Topics in Early Childhood Special Education, 9*(3), 99–109.

Kaufman, A. S., & Kaufman, N. L. (1993). *K-SEALS: Kaufman Survey of Early Academic and Language Skills.* Circle Pines, MN: American Guidance Service.

Mayes, L. C. (1991). Infant assessment. In M. Lewis (Ed.), *Child and adolescent psychiatry: A comprehensive textbook* (pp 437–447). Baltimore: Williams & Wilkins.

Minke, K. M., & Scott, M. M. (1993). The development of Individualized Family Service Plans: Roles for parents and staff. *The Journal of Special Education, 27*(1), 82–106.

Paget, K. D. (1990). Best practices in the assessment of competence in preschool-age children. In A. Thomas & J. Grimes (Eds), *Best practices in school psychology–II* (pp. 107–119). Washington, DC: National Association of School Psychologists.

Sinclair, E., Del'Homme, & M. Gonzalez, (1993). Systematic screening for preschool assessment of behavioral disorders. *Behavioral Disorders, 18*(3), 177–188.

Uzgiris, I. C., & Hunt, J. McV. (1975). *Assessment in infancy: Ordinal Scales of Psychological Development.* Urbana: University of Illinois Press.

Wechsler, D. (1989). *Wechsler Preschool and Primary Scale of Intelligence–Revised.* San Antonio, TX: Psychological Corporation.

Part Four

Interpreting Assessment for Educational Intervention

Chapter Thirteen
Interpreting Test Results

Chapter Fourteen
Case Studies

Chapter Thirteen

Interpreting Test Results

Key Terms

educational planning
eligibility decision
behaviorally stated objectives
projective tests
interindividual interpretation
intra-individual interpretation

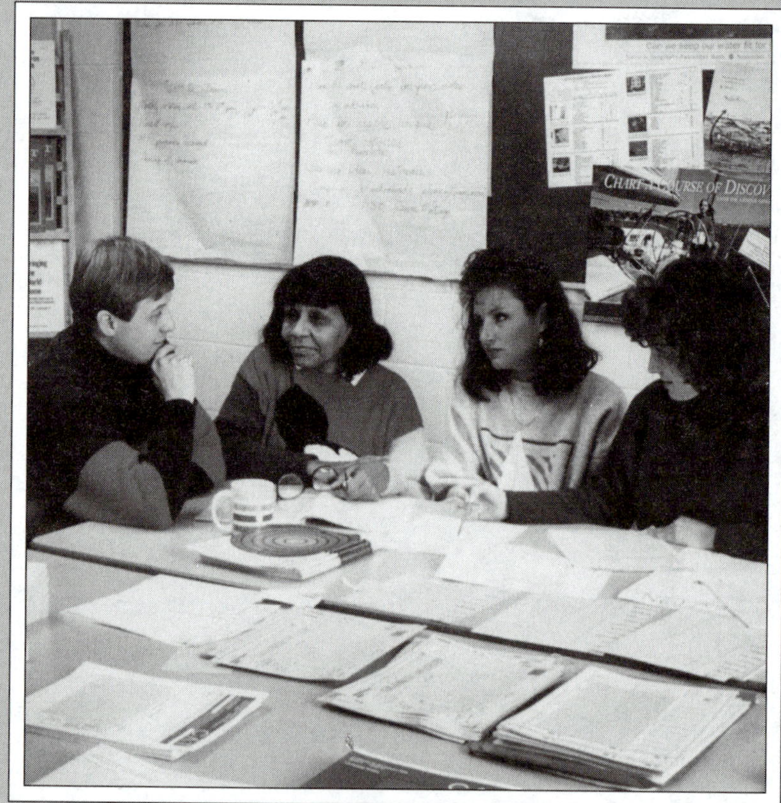

Test results help educators make decisions about educational interventions, planning, and eligibility for special education services. After the professional interprets a student's test results from norm-referenced tests, classroom observations, and informal assessment, the multidisciplinary team uses the results as part of the data to make a decision concerning eligibility. The teacher then uses curriculum-based assessment, teacher-made tests, and direct measurement techniques to monitor progress and adapt instruction.

Test results are most useful when interpreted and presented in a clear format with specific information relating to educational and behavioral strategies. Hoy and Retish (1984) determined that test reports generally lacked the characteristics necessary for ease of **educational planning.** In this chapter, a model of interpreting test results to support an **eligibility decision** and plan program interventions is presented. The second part of the chapter illustrates how to use test results to write effective **behaviorally stated objectives** and how to continue to monitor student progress through direct assessment.

educational planning Interventions and strategies used to promote educational success.

eligibility decision The determination of whether a student will receive special education services.

behaviorally stated objectives Observable and measurable objectives.

When interpreting the results of formal tests, classroom observations, student interviews, parent interviews, questionnaires, surveys, and other methods of evaluation, it is important to remember the holistic view of the child or adolescent as well as the environment from which the child comes. Tharinger and Lambert (1990) offered the following guidelines for the assessment and interpretive process:

1. A child is dependent on the environment to fulfill basic physiological and psychological needs.
2. A child's family is the most active shaper of her or his environment.
3. A child is also an active participant in shaping her or his environment.
4. A child's functioning is multiply and transactionally determined.
5. A child strives to adapt to her or his environment regardless of the health of the environment.
6. A child's motivations for her or his behavior may not be conscious.

7. A child's attachment, separations, and losses are very significant factors in her or his psychological development.
8. A child's current functioning must be evaluated in light of her or his past functioning.
9. A child's behavior can only be understood in relation to current context and the influence of past contexts.
10. As a child develops, conflicts, tensions, and problems are inevitable and necessary. The important factor for assessment is how the child and significant others respond to these conflicts.
11. If the child's thoughts, behaviors, or feelings appear atypical, it is important to consider where, under what circumstances, and at what developmental level this thought pattern, behavior, or emotional expression would make sense.
12. Both the child and her significant environments (i.e., school and home) need to be assessed. (Tharinger & Lambert, 1990, p. 95)

Interpreting Test Results for Eligibility Decisions

Eligibility is determined by using set criteria stated in IDEA. These criteria may vary from state to state for the different types of disabilities but must remain within the IDEA guidelines. This means that the definitions and criteria may be written by the state; however, students who would be found eligible according to the federal law must not be excluded by the state criteria.

The scope of this text focuses on mild to moderate disabilities. The most common types of mild to moderate disabilities are learning disabilities, mental retardation, speech/language impairment, and emotional or behavioral disturbances. Students with attention disorders are also often served by educators who teach students with mild to moderate disabilities. These students may be served in the general education environment under the provisions of section 504 of the Rehabilitation Act of 1973 (see chapter 2) or, since attention disorder is not a separate category under IDEA, under the IDEA category of "other health impaired" if the attention problem does not coexist with another disability, such as a learning disability.

The criteria for the diagnosis and eligibility for special education services as stated in IDEA are used as a basis for interpreting test results. Table 13.1 lists the criteria for mild to moderate disabilities as well as the common characteristics of students with attention deficit disorders.

projective tests Subjective instruments thought to indicate a student's personality or behavioral characteristics.

Table 13.1
Key diagnostic criteria of IDEA.

Disability	Key Criteria	Assessment Devices
Mental retardation	Subaverage intellectual, academic, and adaptive behavior (2 or more standard deviations below expectancy for age and according to generally accepted guidelines).	Standardized IQ tests, academic achievement and diagnostic tests, adaptive behavior scales, parent interviews, classroom observations.
Learning disability	Average or above in intelligence; specific deficits in academics, cognitive language, or perceptual processing (1 to 2 or more standard deviations between ability and academic performance and according to generally accepted guidelines).	Standardized IQ test, academic achievement and diagnostic tests, classroom observations, permanent products, informal measures, parent interviews, perceptual-motor tests.
Emotional disturbance	Behavioral and/or emotional difficulties that interfere with academic and/or developmental progress: unexplained physical problems, pervasive unhappiness, withdrawal, and so on.	Standardized IQ tests, academic achievement and diagnostic tests, clinical interviews, parent interviews, classroom observations, **projective tests,** personality or behavioral inventories.
Speech/language impairment	Communication difficulty that interferes with academic progress, ability to speak, and/or normal developmental progress.	Speech or language diagnostic tests, classroom observations, parent interviews, academic achievement tests.
Attention deficit disorders		
1. With hyperactivity	Externalizing behaviors, talking out, talking too much, impulsive actions, activity level beyond developmental expectations, poor school work, incomplete and/or missing assignments.	DSM–IV evaluation, behavioral ratings by different persons and in different environments, Continuous Performance Tests, cognitive and achievement tests, multiple direct classroom observations.
2. Inattentive type	Poor school work, incomplete or missing assignments, confusion, excessive daydreaming, self-distracting behavior, difficulty following directions and following through.	Same as for hyperactive type.
3. Combined (hyperactivity and inattention)	Combination of characteristics found in hyperactive and inattentive ADD.	Same as for hyperactive type.

☐ **CHECK YOUR UNDERSTANDING**

Complete Activity 13.1.

Activity 13.1

Answer the following questions.

1. What are the general criteria used in diagnosing mental retardation? ________
2. Which of the disabilities listed in Table 13.1 is diagnosed if the student has communication problems affecting developmental progress? ________
3. Which of the disabilities in Table 13.1 is diagnosed if the student has discrepancies between ability and academic performance? ________
4. For the diagnosis of ________, behavioral observations, clinical interviews, and projective tests may be used.
5. Which tests are typically administered to diagnose learning disabilities? ________
6. For what disabilities are classroom observations recommended? ________
7. How are the characteristics of students with attention disorders with hyperactivity and the characteristics of students with attention disorders, inattentive type, similar? How are they different? ________

The Art of Interpreting Test Results

A majority of this text has focused on quantitative measurement of student abilities. A teacher or diagnostician may know how to effectively administer test items and score tests; however, the art of interpreting meaning from quantitative data must also be mastered.

interindividual interpretations Comparing a student to a peer norm group.

intra-individual interpretations Comparing a student with his or her own performance.

Accurate interpretation involves both **interindividual** and **intra-individual interpretation** of test results. Interindividual interpretation involves comparing the student with other students in the norm group to determine how different the student is from that group. Intra-individual interpretation may be even more important than interindividual interpretation. For intra-individual interpretation, the teacher uses the test results to compare the student's own performances to determine strengths and weaknesses. These strengths and weaknesses are then in effective educational planning.

Generally, all possible areas of suspected disability are assessed according to the recommended tests and evaluation measures given in Table 13.1. The following procedures are suggested for evaluating the student and interpreting test results:

1. ***Parental permission.*** The professional must secure parental permission before conducting an individual assessment or making a referral.

2. ***Screening for sensory impairments or physical problems.*** Before a psychoeducational evaluation is recommended, the student's vision, hearing, and general physical health should be screened. When these areas are found to be normal, or corrections for vision/hearing impairments made, the evaluation procedure can continue.

3. ***Parent interview.*** The professional should question the parent regarding progress, development, developmental history, structure of family, relationships with family and peers, and independent adaptive behavior functioning.

4. ***Intellectual and academic assessment.*** The professional should administer an intelligence measure and academic achievement and/or diagnostic instruments, conduct classroom observations, and complete an informal evaluation.

5. ***Behavioral assessment.*** If the assessment and the information from the parents and teacher indicate behavioral, emotional, or attention problems, the student should be assessed by a school or clinical psychologist to obtain behavioral, emotional, and personality information.

6. ***Test interpretation.*** Several members of the evaluation team may interpret test results. The team members may write separate or combined reports. In interpreting results, the assessment team should accomplish the following:

a. Rule out any sensory acuity problems and refer or consult with medical personnel if physical problems are suspected.

b. Determine if any home conflicts are present and refer to school psychologist or school counselor if these are suspected or indicated.

c. Determine if learning or school problems are exhibited in a particular school environment (unstructured play or lunchroom) or if the problems are associated with one subject area or a particular teacher, peer, or adult.

d. Compare ability on intellectual, academic, and/or adaptive behavior measures. Are there apparent discrepancies in functioning? Do perceptual or motor deficits appear to influence ability in specific academic areas? Is the student functioning higher in one area than in others? Is the student functioning significantly below expectancy in one or more areas?

e. Determine if emotional/behavioral problems exist. Does the student appear to be progressing slowly due to behavioral or emotional problems? Does the student adapt well in various situations? Does the student have good relationships with peers and adults? Is attention or activity level interfering with academic and social progress?

f. Determine if speech/language problems are present. Is the student having difficulty understanding language or following oral lectures or directions? Does the student make articulation errors that are not age appropriate?

As these questions are answered, the diagnostician or special education teacher begins to form a picture of how the student processes information and how the strengths and weaknesses noted during test performance may affect learning and behavior. From these interpretations, the teacher can make recommendations that will provide educational intervention and support to benefit the student and promote academic progress. The psychoeducational report is then written to facilitate appropriate intervention strategies.

☐ CHECK YOUR UNDERSTANDING

Complete Activity 13.2.

Activity 13.2

Complete the following sentences.

1. Before a diagnosis is made which involves educational or intellectual ability, screening for ________________ should be completed.
2. If there appears to be a conflict in the home or emotional or behavioral problems are suspected, the student should be referred for ________________ .
3. If a student has average or above intellectual functioning, average emotional/behavioral functioning, and average adaptive behavior skills but has difficulty in academic areas and specific fine-motor ability, he may be found to have ________________ .
4. A student who is below expectancy in all academic areas, is subaverage in intellectual ability, and has subaverage adaptive behavior skills may have ________________ .
5. A student who has a communication problem that is affecting his relationships with peers and his ability to progress in school may have a ________________ .
6. A student who is impulsive, acts out, has poor school work, exhibits too much activity when observed, and whose parents and teachers rate the student as having these types of behavioral problems may be found to have ________________ .

Intelligence and Adaptive Behavior Test Results

Cognitive or intellectual measures are generally administered by school psychologists or educational diagnosticians. The results from these tests should be interpreted and used to plan educational interventions. Interindividual interpretations may indicate mental retardation, learning disability, emotional disturbance, developmental immaturity, or average or above-average intellectual functioning. Intra-individual interpretations should be provided by the person who administered the tests. These interpretations may pinpoint problems with distractibility, attention deficits, auditory short-term memory, visual retention, verbal comprehension, and so on.

The interpretation of the cognitive measures may refer to patterns of functioning noticed. Patterns of functioning may be explained as significant differences between verbal areas of functioning and visual-motor abilities, spatial reasoning or functioning, or perceptual-organization abilities. These patterns may be indicated by significant deficits in particular areas or by more global scores, such as significant differences between verbal and performance IQ scores (e.g., a verbal IQ of 108 and a performance IQ of 71). These deficits or discrepancies may be linked to particular learning difficulties. The examiner's descriptions of the student's performance may help the teacher plan effective educational strategies.

Educational Achievement and Diagnostic Test Results

The educator may be responsible for administering both educational achievement and other diagnostic tests. Scoring these instruments may be somewhat mechanical; however, great care should be taken when scoring tests and interpreting the results. The first method of interpretation involves interindividual interpretation: Compare the student with age/grade expectations. Data provided on norm tables will enable the examiner to determine how a student compares with age/grade peers. Is the student significantly above expectations (in the 90th percentile, for example)? Is the student average (in the 50th percentile range) on some measures but significantly below peers (below the 10th percentile) on other measures? The examiner must plot a profile of how the student performs when compared to expectations.

Intra-individual interpretation means that the examiner will identify specific strengths and weaknesses in academic achievement, other abilities, and behavioral areas. Because the areas of strength and weakness should be defined as specifically as possible, tests that provide error analysis are most helpful. This analysis can be broken down further by task and used to develop teacher-made tests or informal probes if more information is needed.

Writing Test Results

Interpreting and writing test results so that meaningful information is available for the persons responsible for the delivery of educational service is the most important concern when preparing reports. Bagnato (1980) suggested the following guidelines for making psychoeducational reports easy to use in the development of IEPs:

1. Be organized by multiple developmental or functional domains rather than only by tests given.

2. Describe specific areas of strength and skill deficits in clear behavioral terms.

3. Emphasize process variables and qualitative features regarding the child's learning strategies.

4. Highlight lists of developmental ceilings, functional levels, skill sequences, and instructional needs upon which assessment/curriculum linkages can be constructed to form the IEP.

5. Detail efficient suggestions regarding behavioral and instructional management strategies. (p. 555)

Although psychoeducational reports may differ in format, they include the same general content. Typically, the identifying information is presented first: student name, date of birth, parents' names, address, grade placement, date(s) of evaluation, methods of evaluation, and the name of the examiner. Presented next is the background and referral information, which may include sociological information such as the size of family, student's relationship with family members, other schools attended, and any previous academic, behavioral, or health problems.

Following the preliminary information are the test results. An interpretation is presented, and recommendations for interventions, further evaluations, or changes in placement are then suggested. The following is an outline of a psychoeducational report.

I. Identifying Data
II. Background and Referral Information
  A. Background
  B. Referral
  C. Classroom Observation
  D. Parent Information
III. Test Results
IV. Test Interpretations
V. Summary and Recommendations
  A. Summary
  B. Recommendations for Educational Interventions
  C. Recommendations for Further Assessment

The following case study presents test results and interpretations. Read the results and interpretations and how they are implemented in the educational recommendations. For instructional purposes, the reasons for the recommendations are given with each recommendation.

☐ CASE STUDY

Name: Sue Smith
Date of Birth: 6-8-84
Dates of Evaluation: 11-20-94, 11-28-94
Age: 10-6
Current Grade Placement: 3.3

Examiner: Hazel Competent
Instruments: Wechsler Intelligence Scale for Children, Third Edition
Woodcock-Johnson–Revised Tests of Achievement:
Standard Battery
Woodcock Reading Mastery Test–Revised, Form G
Test of Auditory Perceptual Skills
Teacher Report Form (Achenbach)
Work Sample Analysis
Classroom Observation

BACKGROUND INFORMATION AND REFERRAL

Sue was referred for testing by her parents for the possible consideration of special education services. Sociological information reported normal developmental progress and a warm, caring home environment. Sue's parents reported that they felt education was important and wanted Sue's progress to improve. Sue appears to have good relationships with both parents and her two older brothers.

Sue repeated kindergarten and received low grades during her first- and second-grade years. Sue is currently enrolled in third grade, and the teacher reported that Sue has difficulty with phonics and reading words that "she should know." Sue attended a special summer program in an attempt to improve her reading skills.

Sue has normal vision and hearing and no apparent physical problems. Peer relationships are as expected for her age.

Classroom Observation

Sue was observed on two separate occasions before the testing sessions. Sue seemed to stay on task and attempted all assigned work. Her teacher reported that more than half of Sue's assignments were incomplete. It appeared that the pace of the class might be too rapid, especially in reading and language arts. Sue did not exhibit any inappropriate behaviors for her age and seemed to have friends within the classroom. Sue's teacher used peer tutors for some of the reading and language arts assignments, which she reports helped Sue to finish some of her work.

TEST RESULTS

Wechsler Intelligence Scale for Children–III

Verbal Subtests		*Performance Subtests*	
Information	2	Picture Completion	10
Similarities	7	Coding	9
Arithmetic	5	Picture Arrangement	9

Verbal Subtests		*Performance Subtests*	
Vocabulary	7	Block Design	7
Comprehension	7	Object Assembly	7
Digit Span	4		

Verbal IQ	73
Performance IQ	88
Full Scale IQ	79

Woodcock-Johnson–Revised Tests of Achievement, Standard Battery

Subtest	*Grade Equivalent*	*Standard Score*	*Percentile Rank*
Letter-Word Identification	2.6	80	9
Passage Comprehension	2.0	74	4
Calculation	2.5	63	1
Applied Problems	2.3	78	7
Dictation	2.3	77	7
Writing Samples	2.0	75	5
Science	1.9	79	8
Social Studies	1.9	78	7
Humanities	1.3	77	6

Standard Battery Clusters	*Standard Score*	*Percentile Rank*
Broad Reading	79	8
Broad Mathematics	66	1
Broad Written Language	37	3

Woodcock Reading Mastery Tests–Revised, Form G

Subtest	*Grade Equivalent*	*Standard Score*	*Percentile Rank*
Visual-Auditory Learning	1.2	75	5
Letter Identification	2.7	60	.4
Word Identification	2.3	66	1
Word Attack	1.7	71	3
Word Comprehension	2.9	79	8
Passage Comprehension	1.7	57	.2
Readiness Cluster	2.5	63	1
Basic Skills Cluster	2.2	68	2
Reading Comprehension	2.2	65	1
Total Reading Cluster	2.3	64	1

Test of Auditory-Perceptual Skills

	Scaled Score	*Percentile Rank*
Auditory Number Memory		
Forward	6	9
Reversed	5	5
Auditory Sentence Memory	8	25
Auditory Word Memory	5	5
Auditory Interpretation of Directions		
Total Correct Sentences	7	16
Auditory Word Discrimination	3	1
Auditory Processing		
(thinking and reasoning)	7	16

Auditory Quotient 70

TEST INTERPRETATIONS

On measures of intellectual ability, Sue performed within the low average range of ability. A discrepancy exists between her verbal and performance IQ scores and individual subtest scores. Overall, Sue exhibited strength in the performance areas. Significant strength was noted in the area of visual memory and nonverbal ability. Sue's performance revealed significant weaknesses in verbal areas, with severe deficits in auditory memory and attention.

On overall achievement measures, Sue performed below expectancy in all areas. The Woodcock Reading Mastery Tests–Revised revealed severe deficits in visual-auditory learning, phonics, and passage comprehension. The deficits result in the inability to decode new words and comprehend content that is read. Sue's performance on the analogies portion of the reading vocabulary (Word Comprehension) subtest was very high when compared to other areas of reading. Her performance on the analogies portion of the subtest may be more indicative of her true potential.

An error analysis of word attack skills revealed weaknesses in decoding single consonants, digraphs, consonant blends, vowels, and multisyllable words.

Sue demonstrated weakness in most areas assessed by the Test of Auditory-Perceptual Skills. She seems to have relative weaknesses on subtests that measure memory for isolated words and numbers. She appears to have slightly higher ability to remember meaningful auditory stimuli, such as sentences or directions.

Responses provided by Sue's teacher on the Teacher Report Form of the Child Behavior Checklist indicated that Sue is unable to complete most of her schoolwork as expected of students her age. The teacher endorsed items that indicate Sue may be having some emerging problems with anxiety. This may be related to her current performance in school. None of the scores were within a clinical range for behavior problems.

Work sample analysis indicated that Sue has a relative strength in the ability to compute simple math operations, although her ability was below the level expected for her current grade placement. Her samples for spelling, writing, and reading comprehension were within the failure range.

Three separate classroom observations indicated that Sue was cooperative and remained quiet during all of the observation periods. She attempted to begin her work when instructed to do so but was unable to complete language arts assignments as instructed.

SUMMARY

Sue is currently functioning within the low average range of intellectual ability, with severe deficits in short-term auditory memory. This deficit influences Sue's ability to decode words and comprehend new material. The deficit will also decrease the efficiency with which Sue can obtain new information through a standard teaching (lecture) format. Sue is functioning as a student with a specific learning disability in reading and language arts due to her inability to process information presented auditorily and an inability to form sound-symbol relationships.

Recommendations

1. Sue will benefit from instruction in a resource room setting where she can receive individualized instruction. (Reasons: Student has not been successful in the regular classroom environment; low auditory memory, verbal skills, and attention would support decision that she may benefit from resource room placement.)

2. New material should be presented through both visual and auditory formats. (Reasons: Weakness appears to be auditory memory; pairing all auditory material with visual cues may help student to focus attention.)

3. Sue will benefit from direct instruction techniques that require her to actively respond to new material. (Reasons: Student may increase academic engaged time; active responding may help student to focus attention and receive positive feedback from teacher.)

4. Sue may benefit from advanced organizers in content areas, introduction of new vocabulary terms before reading them in new chapters, outlines of class lectures or presentations, and note-taking training. (Reasons: Student may increase ability to focus on relevant material, increase attention to task.)

5. Additional diagnostic testing is recommended for mathematics to determine specific skill weaknesses. (Reasons: overall math scores were low; specific disability may exist.)

Hazel Competent

Hazel Competent, M.Ed.
Educational Diagnostician

Activity 13.3

☐ **CHECK YOUR UNDERSTANDING**

Complete Activity 13.3.

Answer the following questions about the case study.

1. Why was Sue referred for testing? ____________________
2. How was Sue functioning intellectually? ____________________
3. What were the discrepancies in Sue's functioning according to the test results? ____________________
4. What were Sue's strengths as indicated through the assessment process? ____________________
5. What were Sue's weaknesses, and how do these weaknesses appear to influence Sue's academic functioning? ____________________
6. What additional assessment was recommended for Sue? ____________________
7. According to these results, what are Sue's specific academic skill deficits? ____________________
8. What types of educational interventions and strategies were recommended? ____________________

Writing Educational Objectives

The multidisciplinary team members present the results and recommendations of the psychoeducational report to parents at the eligibility meeting and, if the student is eligible for special education services, write the specific educational objectives that will comprise the student's IEP. Let's continue with the example of Sue Smith to see how the team would use their results to write Sue's educational objectives.

During the eligibility meeting, the team members determined that Sue would be placed in the resource room for instruction in language arts. It was also determined that the special education teacher would administer the Key-Math–Revised test to determine any significant deficits in math. These plans were written on page 1 of Sue's IEP. The teacher wrote beginning objectives for reading/language arts instruction on the second page of the IEP. These behaviorally stated short-term objectives would be monitored through direct daily measurement and curriculum-based assessment. The short-term objectives from Sue's IEP are listed in Table 13.2.

Table 13.2
Best School System individual education plan: short-term objectives.

Objective	Materials	Evaluation
1. When presented with consonent-vowel-consonent (cvc) flashcards, Sue will be able to pronounce cvc words with 95% accuracy by Jan. 15.	Flashcards Words on tape Taped stories	Direct daily measurement Teacher-made tests
2. When presented with short vowel sounds, Sue will be able to match short vowel sounds for *a, e, i,* with the written letter with 95% accuracy by Feb. 15.	Flashcards Teacher-made materials Taped vowel sounds	Direct daily measurement Curriculum-based assessment Teacher-made tests
3. When presented with visual and auditory cues, Sue will be able to dictate a short story using specific cvc words with 95% accuracy by Jan. 15.	Picture file Flashcards Teacher-made materials Student journal	Direct daily measurement

As seen in Table 13.2, Sue's teacher followed a standard format for writing short-term objectives. Because they are behaviorally stated, and performance can be easily observed and measured, these objectives are easily adapted to lesson planning, and progress can be monitored with ease. The format for the objectives is:

When presented with ________ ,
Sue will be able to ________
with ____ % accuracy by ________ .

☐ **CHECK YOUR UNDERSTANDING**

Complete Activity 13.4.

Activity 13.4

Assessment with the KeyMath–R revealed that Sue Smith had difficulty with the following skills:

1. Understanding fractions (terms *half, divided equally, 2 halves = 1).*
2. Adding two-digit numbers with renaming (i.e., 46 + 37).
3. Subtracting two-digit numbers without borrowing (i.e., 35 – 23).
4. Measurement and comparisons (greater than, heavier, inch, yard, etc.).

Using this information, write a behaviorally stated short-term objective for each of the following skills: fractions, addition, subtraction, measurement, and comparison.

1. When presented with ______________________
   Sue will be able to ______________________
   with ____ % accuracy by ______________________
   ____
2. ______________________
3. ______________________
4. ______________________

Exercises

Part I

Match the following terms with the correct definitions.

A. educational planning
B. eligibility decisions
C. behaviorally stated objectives
D. section 504
E. interindividual interpretation
F. intra-individual interpretation
G. projective tests

_______ **1.** Comparing a student to a peer norm group.
_______ **2.** Comparing a student with his or her own performance.
_______ **3.** Observable and measurable objectives.
_______ **4.** Interventions and strategies used to promote educational success.
_______ **5.** The determination of whether a student will receive special education services.
_______ **6.** Subjective instruments thought to indicate a student's personality or behavioral characteristics.

Part II

Identify the correctly written behavioral objectives by writing a plus sign (+) in front of the objective.

_______ **1.** When given four addition problems, Mary will be able to find the sums with 100% accuracy by Friday.

_________ **2.** To correctly solve multiplication facts by next year.

_________ **3.** To read a passage with 90% accuracy and within a 2-minute time limit.

_________ **4.** When presented with 10 cvc words, Joan will be able to spell the words with 90% accuracy by Feb. 15th.

_________ **5.** To identify the 50 states with 100% accuracy on a map by November.

References

Bagnato, S. (1980). The efficacy of diagnostic reports as individualized guides to prescriptive goal planning. *Exceptional Children, 46,* 554–557.

Federal Register, (1977). Washington, DC: U.S. Government Printing Office, August 23, 1977.

Hoy, M., & Retish, P. (1984). A comparison of two types of assessment reports. *Exceptional Children, 51,* 225–229.

Tharinger, D. J., & Lambert, N. M. (1990). The contributions of developmental psychology to school psychology. In T. Gutkin & C. R. Reynolds (Eds.), *The handbook of school psychology,* (2nd ed, pp. 74–103). NY: Wiley.

Chapter Fourteen

Case Studies

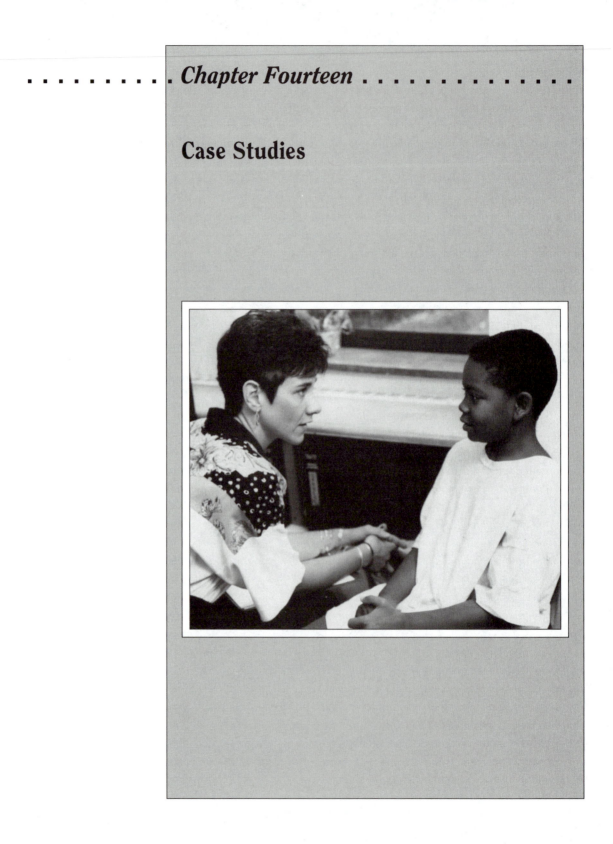

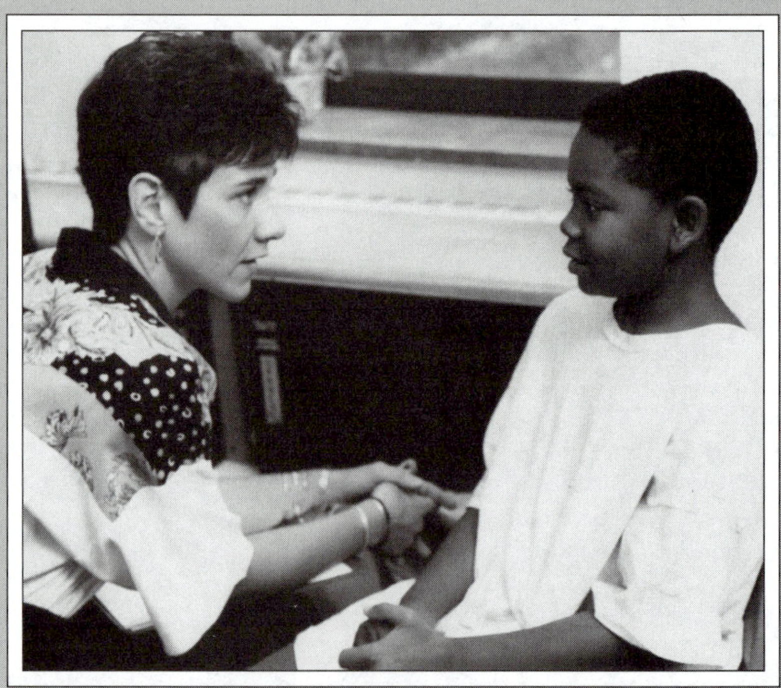

This chapter contains partially completed case studies. Each case is different and requires different input to complete. Use information provided in chapter 13 to interpret the case study test results and to write short-term behaviorally stated objectives. In the first case, you are asked to answer questions about the interpretation and write behaviorally stated objectives for specific skill deficits. The second case study presents test results and interpretations. You will be required to write recommendations for interventions and behaviorally states short-term objectives. Two cases include test results and partial interpretations. You will be asked to interpret the educational test results, make recommendations, and write behaviorally stated short-term objectives. You will interpret the test results for three of the cases. Space is allowed for you to support the recommendations you make.

□ CASE 1: JOE

Name: Joe Brown
Date of Birth: 5–8–86
Date of Evaluation: 10–28–94
Age: 8–6
Current Grade Placement: 2.3
Examiner: James Perfection
Instruments: Wechsler Intelligence Scale for Children–III
Woodcock-Johnson–Revised Tests of Achievement, Standard Batteries
Test of Word Finding
Classroom observations
Teacher Report Form of the Child Behavior Checklist (Achenbach)

BACKGROUND AND REFERRAL INFORMATION

Joe was referred because of academic problems. Review of school records indicated that Joe's grades are within the low to failing range. Joe had been retained in kindergarten. He is currently in the second grade and is experiencing academic difficulty.

The information available from the sociological report revealed that Joe lives in a single-parent household and that his mother works the night shift. Joe is responsible for his two younger siblings. Joe's responsibilities include preparing the evening meal for the children and helping the two younger girls complete homework and go to bed. Joe's aunt occasionally stays with the family to help; however, she lives in another town, so the visits are infrequent.

Health reports indicate that Joe has a mild hearing loss, and speech-language assessment revealed errors in the /th/ sound in *bathroom* and the /o/ in *window*. Joe makes other misarticulations that are not age appropriate.

Classroom Observation and Teacher Ratings

During the classroom observation sessions, Joe worked quietly in his chair. Twice during a direct-instruction session, the teacher had to call his attention to the questions by calling his name. He did not volunteer to respond but did answer when requested by his teacher. As the students put away their materials to prepare for lunch, many students quietly talked with each other. Joe was not observed to have any interactions with his peers during transition periods. At a later observation period, Joe did interact during a group project. His comments were simple, and he did not initiate conversation but only responded to other students' comments.

Responses by Joe's teacher on the Teacher Report Form of the Child Behavior Checklist indicate some concern for anxiety and withdrawal; however, the extent of these behaviors did not within the clinical range. The teacher did not indicate any other areas of concern except academic progress.

TEST RESULTS

Wechsler Intelligence Scale for Children–III

Verbal Subtests		*Performance Subtests*	
Information	8	Picture Completion	6
Similarities	3	Picture Arrangement	6
Arithmetic	3	Block Design	4
Vocabulary	4	Object Assembly	8
Comprehension	8	Coding	10
Digit Span	5		

Verbal IQ	70
Performance IQ	78
Full Scale IQ	72

Woodcock-Johnson–Revised Tests of Achievement, Standard and Supplemental Batteries

	Grade Equivalent	*Standard Score*	*Percentile Rank*
Standard Battery Subtest			
Letter-Word Identification	1.7	82	12
Passage Comprehension	1.6	83	12
Calculation	1.3	68	2
Applied Problems	1.4	77	6
Dictation	1.4	76	5
Writing Samples	1.4	61	.5
Science	1.2	84	14
Social Studies	K.5	81	10
Humanities	K.9	85	16
Cluster			
Broad Reading	—	81	10
Broad Mathematics	—	69	2
Broad Written Language	—	68	2
Broad Knowledge	—	81	10
Supplemental Battery Subtest			
Word Attack	1.1	77	6
Reading Vocabulary	1.7	86	17
Quantitative Concepts	1.7	84	14
Cluster			
Basic Reading Skills	—	78	7
Reading Comprehension	—	84	14
Basic Mathematics	—	72	3

Test of Word Finding

Standard score based on age 75 Standard score based on grade 75

TEST INTERPRETATIONS

Joe was very cooperative throughout the testing session and attempted most items presented with the encouragement of the examiner. Joe eventually seemed at ease during the testing session; however, his timidity may have influenced the testing results. Joe did not respond to a few items until prompted by the examiner.

On measures of intellectual ability, Joe performed within the low average range of ability. The examiner noted no significant discrepancies between IQ scores; however, he noted some differences between subtests. Analysis of performance on individual subtests revealed that Joe has significant strength in visual memory and relative strength in the area of long-term memory and nonverbal ability.

Joe's performance on academic measures revealed that he is currently functioning below grade level in all areas tested. Joe's greatest areas of weakness are in the skill areas of mathematics and word attack and the content areas of science and social studies.

The areas of weakness, which were determined by both academic and intellectual assessment, may have been influenced by Joe's mild hearing loss. Joe seems to lack the skills in basic phonics (sound-symbol relationships), basic reading skills, general vocabulary development, written language and spelling skills, and knowledge of content subjects. Joe was found to be a slow and inaccurate namer according to his performance on the Test of Word Finding. Joe's strengths of visual memory, long-term memory, and nonverbal ability are less likely to be influenced to the same degree by a mild hearing loss.

SUMMARY AND RECOMMENDATIONS

Joe is currently functioning within the borderline range of ability according to his performance on the WISC–III. The performance on the WISC–III and other measures may have been influenced by his timidity and mild hearing loss. Joe's strengths appear to be in the areas of visual memory, long-term memory, and nonverbal ability. Academic achievement is significantly below expectancy in most areas.

Recommendations

1. Joe may benefit from instructions provided in a small group setting. He may be able to make better progress in a setting with a lower student/teacher ratio.
2. When instructions are presented orally by teachers, visual instructions or cues should be provided as well.
3. Joe would probably benefit from training that emphasizes how to attend to and use auditorily presented material.
4. Academic remediation for all areas is recommended: Beginning reading skills (decoding short vowel words, recognizing sight words), spelling skills, written language skills, math calculation (addition and subtraction) and reasoning, science and social studies content.
5. Social Services has been notified of this case.
6. Joe may benefit from school counseling services and support.

James Perfection

James Perfection, MA
School Psychologist

Answer the questions and complete the activities for Case 1.

1. According to the report in Case 1, what are Joe's strengths and weaknesses? ____________________

2. Why was Joe not referred for placement as a student with mental retardation? ____________________

3. Why was Joe not diagnosed as a student with a specific learning disability? ____________________

4. Why was school counseling suggested? ____________________

Based on the information in the psychoeducational report on Joe, write a behaviorally stated short-term objective for each of the following skills.

1. Decoding short vowel consonent-vowel-consonent (cvc) words.
2. Writing short sentences about experiences when words are spelled for him.
3. Calculation of simple addition and subtraction problems.
4. A science or social studies unit.

Short-Term Objectives

1. ____________________
2. ____________________
3. ____________________
4. ____________________

☐ CASE 2: BETTY

Name: Betty Jones
Date of Birth: 11–12–82
Date of Evaluation: 9–8–95
Age: 12–10
Current Grade Placement: 6.1
Examiner: Mary Psyche
Instruments: Wechsler Intelligence Scale for Children–III
Woodcock-Johnson–Revised Tests of Achievement, Standard Battery
Vineland Adaptive Behavior Scales, Survey Form (data reported from previous assessment)
classroom observation

BACKGROUND AND REFERRAL INFORMATION

Betty was referred for a psychoeducational evaluation to assist in her placement to receive educational services. Betty was living in a residential facility for youths with behavioral/emotional problems.

Information provided through the city juvenile court system revealed that Betty was born 2 months premature and the pregnancy was reported to be complicated by toxemia and possibly high blood pressure. Current family structure consists of a mother and a sister and brother. Each child has a different father; however, there is no father figure currently in the home. Previous reports described the family as dysfunctional, and appropriate role models do not seem to be available for Betty. The mother's emotional stability and mental competence are reported to be questionable.

Betty was suspended from school last year because of disciplinary problems that included destruction of school property. In the initial evaluation, Betty was diagnosed as a student with behavioral problems. School staff in the current residential facility question this diagnosis and referred Betty for a possible change in diagnosis to mental retardation.

Classroom Observation and Work Sample Analysis

Classroom observations were made on four different dates. Betty was observed to exhibit behaviors indicating confusion and a general inability to keep up with her peers on class assignments. On one occasion, Betty became very frustrated when unable to complete a math computation, and she subsequently tore her paper and placed it in the trash. She did not demonstrate any difficulties with her peers when observed in both structured and unstructured situations.

Work samples were analyzed for language arts and math. All written work was well below the skill level demonstrated by her peers. Of the 10 pieces of work analyzed, none was complete, and very little of the work analyzed was correct.

TEST RESULTS

Wechsler Intelligence Scale for Children–III

Verbal Subtests		*Performance Subtests*	
Information	2	Picture Completion	7
Similarities	7	Picture Arrangement	4
Arithmetic	2	Block Design	6
Vocabulary	6	Object Assembly	4
Comprehension	9	Coding	2
Digit Span	2		

Verbal IQ	70
Performance IQ	69
Full Scale IQ	66

Woodcock-Johnson–Revised Tests of Achievement, Standard Battery

	Grade Equivalent	*Standard Score*	*Percentile Rank*
Subtest			
Letter-Word Identification	1.6	63	1
Passage Comprehension	K.5	57	.4
Calculation	1.0	53	.1
Applied Problems	K.2	34	.1
Dictation	K.5	57	.2
Writing Samples	K.1	56	.2
Science	1.0	62	1
Social Studies	K.6	61	.5
Humanities	K.4	57	.2
Cluster			
Broad Reading	—	66	1
Broad Mathematics	—	57	.2
Broad Written Language	—	64	1
Broad Knowledge	—	58	.2

Vineland Adaptive Behavior Scales, Survey Form

Previous data from an interview with the classroom teacher revealed Betty's overall adaptive behavior functioning to be within the moderately low to low range. Betty's communication and motor skills domain scores were within the moderately low range, but daily living skills and socialization were considered to be low and inappropriate for Betty's age.

TEST INTERPRETATIONS

On measures of overall intellectual, academic, and adaptive behavior, Betty appears to be functioning within the subaverage to borderline range. All academic areas measured were within the kindergarten to first-grade level. Although Betty may have exhibited behavioral problems in her previous setting, she does not appear to be eligible for the diagnosis of emotional disturbance. Betty's adaptive functioning is like that of a 5- or 6-year-old, and her understanding of coping with conflict situations may be equally as deficient. A setting in which Betty can have social skills training designed for students within the subaverage range of intellectual ability may be a more appropriate setting.

SUMMARY AND RECOMMENDATIONS

Betty is currently functioning within the subaverage range of ability according to intellectual, academic, and adaptive behavioral measures. Her inappropriate behavior in a previous classroom setting is likely the result of inappropriate learning and the lack of appropriate role models. Betty continues to need special services in a structured environment; however, a setting for persons with mental retardation is more suitable to meet her needs.

Answer the questions and complete the activities for Case 2.

Recommendations

What recommendations would you make for Betty?

1. ______________________________

____

____

Reasons: ______________________________

____

2. ______________________________

____

____

Reasons: ______________________________

____

3. ______________________________

____

____

Reasons: ______________________________

____

4. ______________________________

____

____

Reasons: ______________________________

____

Write short-term behaviorally stated objectives for Betty. Remember that her academic, social, and intellectual skills are more like those of a first-grade student or a 5- to 6-year-old child. Her interests, however, may be more similar to those of her age peers (i.e., preteen level for clothes, music, recreation, etc.).

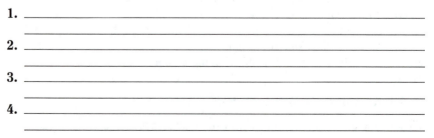

1. ______________________________

____

2. ______________________________

____

3. ______________________________

____

4. ______________________________

____

Answer the following questions.

1. Why was the diagnosis changed for Betty? ______________________________

____

____

2. Within a school environment, what types of behavior management and observational techniques would you use? ______________________________

____

☐ CASE 3: SAM

Name: Sam White
Date of Birth: 3–25–80
Date of Evaluation: 11–16–95
Age: 15–8
Current Grade Placement: 8.3
Examiner: Steve Smart
Instruments: Wechsler Intelligence Scale for Children–III
Woodcock-Johnson–Revised Tests of Achievement Standard Battery
classroom observation
teacher interview

BACKGROUND AND REFERRAL INFORMATION

Sam was referred for assessment because of academic problems. Review of school records indicated that Sam's grades have been declining since sixth grade. Sam reported that his favorite subject was math and that science was the most difficult. Sam's mother agreed to the testing because she was concerned about Sam's low grades on report cards.

Sociological information revealed that Sam has a warm relationship with both parents, who live in the home. Sam has two older brothers and a younger sister. He reported having fun with his siblings.

Classroom Observation and Teacher Interview

Sam's teacher has been concerned about Sam's lack of progress this year. The teacher reported trying several types of prereferral intervention strategies before making a formal referral.

The classroom observations were made on three separate occasions, and Sam was observed working well with his peers. The classroom environment seemed to be one that would promote academic achievement. The examiner analyzed Sam's work samples and noted many spelling and calculation errors. Generally, the work level seemed to be difficult for Sam.

TEST RESULTS

Wechsler Intelligence Scale for Children–III

Verbal Subtests		*Performance Subtests*	
Information	4	Picture Completion	7
Similarities	5	Picture Arrangement	7
Arithmetic	4	Block Design	4
Vocabulary	6	Object Assembly	7
Comprehension	9	Coding	6
Digit Span	9		

Verbal IQ	73
Performance IQ	74
Full Scale IQ	72

Woodcock-Johnson–Revised Tests of Achievement, Standard Battery

	Grade Equivalent	*Standard Score*	*Percentile Rank*
Subtest			
Letter-Word Identification	6.2	87	19
Passage Comprehension	5.6	87	19
Calculation	7.3	91	27
Applied Problems	3.3	74	4
Dictation	4.3	72	3
Writing Samples	4.4	83	14
Science	4.5	83	13
Social Studies	5.4	81	10
Humanities	2.8	74	4
Cluster			
Broad Reading	—	86	18
Broad Mathematics	—	80	9
Broad Written Language	—	78	7
Broad Knowledge	—	80	9

Test Interpretations

Sam was friendly during the test session, and rapport was easily established. Sam attempted all items presented to him, and the obtained results appear to be representative of Sam's current functioning.

On the WISC–III, Sam obtained scores in the borderline range. Analysis of individual subtests revealed that Sam seems to have relative strength in the areas of auditory memory and attention. Sam's relative weakness seems to be in the area of long-term memory, which may influence overall intellectual functioning.

How would you analyze Sam's academic functioning according to the test results? What other tests might you suggest to help with diagnosis?
Academic functioning: ______

Answer the questions and complete the activities for Case 3.

Other tests or evaluation procedures: ______

Write short-term behavioral objectives based on the following information, which was obtained through an error analysis of Sam's test performance.

1. Sam has difficulty with applied math problems in which he is required to select the appropriate operation to solve a problem (e.g., the phrase "how many more" means to find a difference).
2. Sam needs development of vocabulary terms associated with content areas such as science or social studies.
3. Sam has weakness in using context to understand what is read. Overall reading comprehension is weak.
4. General written language skills (spelling, grammar, etc.) are weak.

Short-Term Objectives

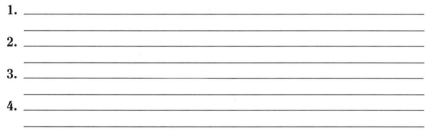

1. ______
2. ______
3. ______
4. ______

☐ CASE 4: SHARON

Name: Sharon Williams
Date of Birth: 6–5–87
Date of Evaluation: 10–6–95
Age: 8–4
Current Grade Placement: 1.2
Examiner: Ruby Bright

Instruments: Wechsler Intelligence Scale for Children–III
Kaufman Test of Educational Achievement, Comprehensive Form
informal curriculum-based measurement
Vineland Adaptive Behavior Scales: Interview Edition (Expanded Form)
Peabody Picture Vocabulary Test–Revised
classroom observation

BACKGROUND AND REFERRAL INFORMATION

Sharon was referred for psychoeducational assessment by her teacher. Sharon repeated kindergarten and is currently in her second year in the first grade. Previous consideration for assessment was delayed at the parents' request. Sharon's parents felt that she was developing slower than her siblings and requested that she be allowed to repeat kindergarten and, subsequently, first grade. Sharon's parents provide a warm home environment for Sharon and her five older siblings. Sharon's father works an evening shift and is consequently away from the home when Sharon attempts to complete her homework. Both parents completed the eighth grade in school.

Classroom Observation and Teacher Interview

Although this is Sharon's second year in the first grade, she was placed with a different teacher this year. Sharon's teacher reported that Sharon has difficulty with all schoolwork, although spelling short three- and four-letter words seems to be less difficult for her. Sharon does not interact much with her peers and has had some difficulty adjusting to the classroom environment. When observed, Sharon remained in her seat the entire period and did not attempt to participate in a classroom discussion. When asked questions by her teacher, she responded "I don't know" or gave inappropriate answers (i.e., Question: "What do policemen do for us?" Answer: "My daddy and I seen one").

TEST RESULTS

Wechsler Intelligence Scale for Children–III

Verbal Subtests		*Performance Subtests*	
Information	5	Picture Completion	5
Similarities	4	Picture Arrangement	4
Arithmetic	3	Block Design	5
Vocabulary	4	Object Assembly	3
Comprehension	5	Coding	4
Digit Span	5		

Verbal Subtests	*Performance Subtests*
Verbal IQ	65
Performance IQ	63
Full Scale IQ	60

Kaufman Test of Educational Achievement

	Grade Equivalent	*Standard Score*	*Percentile Rank*
Subtest			
Math Applications	<1.0	66	1
Reading Decoding	<1.0	65	1
Spelling	<1.0	73	4
Reading Comprehension	<1.0	<74	<4
Math Computation	<1.0	<68	<2
Composite			
Reading Composite	<1.0	67	1
Math Composite	<1.0	64	1
Battery Composite	<1.0	65	1

Vineland Adaptive Behavior Scales: Interview Edition (Expanded Form)

Communication	
Receptive	Adequate
Expressive	Moderately low
Written	Moderately low
Daily Living Skills	
Personal	Moderately low
Domestic	Moderately low
Community	Low
Socialization	
Interpersonal Relationships	Low
Play and Leisure Time	Moderately low
Coping Skills	Low

Peabody Picture Vocabulary Test–Revised

Standard score 65

Informal Curriculum-Based Assessment

On measures derived from the first-grade basal reader series, Sharon was not able to complete more than 50% of the items correctly for a set of three reading stories. The items included both written and oral questions and both written and oral responses. Sharon's teacher has adapted a parallel math series at the kindergarten level for Sharon. In the adapted math curriculum, Sharon is currently functioning with approximately 65% to 70% accuracy. No content area curriculum-based measurement results were obtained for science or social studies because Sharon continues with her reading, spelling, and math work during science and social studies class time.

Answer the questions and complete the activities for Case 4.

What is your evaluation of this case?

SUMMARY AND RECOMMENDATIONS

Write your summary and recommendations in the space provided.

Recommendations

1.

Reasons:

2. ____

Reasons: ____

3. ____

Reasons: ____

4. ____

Reasons: ____

5. ____

Reasons: ____

Sharon is basically functioning at the kindergarten level in all areas and has below average adaptive behavior skills. Write behaviorally stated short-term objectives for her.

1. ____

2. ____

3. ____

4. ____

☐ CASE 5: STEVE

Name: Steve Jones
Date of Birth: 10–6–84
Date of Evaluation: 11–15–95
Age: 11–1
Current Grade Placement: 5.3

Examiner: Tom Knowall
Instruments: Wechsler Intelligence Scale for Children–III
Woodcock Reading Mastery Tests–Revised, Form G
Test of Written Spelling–II
Test of Written Language
KeyMath–Revised, Form B
Watkins Bender-Gestalt Scoring System
Conner's Continuous Performance Test
Achenbach's Teacher Report Form, Direct Observation Form, Child Behavior Checklist (parent)

BACKGROUND AND REFERRAL INFORMATION

Steve was referred for evaluation by his parents, who were concerned about Steve's academic progress. Steve was reported as always having difficulty in school, especially with reading and math. Steve appears to get along well with his peers and has not had behavioral problems in school or at home. Steve's family is supportive of taking whatever steps are necessary to improve Steve's academic performance. Steve's father reported that he too had difficulty learning to read and did not make good grades in school. Both parents completed a high school education, and the mother completed practical nurse's training. Steve's younger brother is not experiencing any learning difficulties, according to the parents.

Classroom Observation and Teacher Ratings

Steve's teacher reported that he often has difficulty decoding new words and copying material correctly from the board. Steve has been able to construct simple sentences and seems to be more able to write during independent seat work than when copying from the board. Steve's teacher reported that Steve has been unable to keep up with the class during oral math lessons but responds better to one-to-one instruction using concrete objects or pictorial representations. Responses provided by the teacher on Achenbach's Teacher Report Form were within the clinical range for attention problems and slightly elevated for social problems.

During a classroom observation of math period, Steve looked out of the window for long periods of time and did not always seem to be attending to class or to be on task. Recordings taken on the Direct Observation Form indicated that when Steve was compared with his peers across multiple settings and times, he was off task 65% of the time, nearly 2 standard deviations more than his peers.

TEST RESULTS

Wechsler Intelligence Scale for Children–III

Verbal Subtests		*Performance Subtests*	
Information	10	Picture Completion	9
Similarities	9	Picture Arrangement	7
Arithmetic	7	Block Design	6
Vocabulary	9	Object Assembly	7
Comprehension	10	Coding	6
Digit Span	6		

Verbal IQ	94
Performance IQ	80
Full Scale IQ	85

Woodcock Reading Mastery Tests–Revised, Form G

	Grade Equivalent	*Standard Score*	*Percentile Rank*
Subtest			
Visual Auditory Learning	16.4	113	80
Letter Identification	3.5	73	4
Word Identification	4.1	88	22
Word Attack	2.9	89	23
Word Comprehension	4.8	96	40
Passage Comprehension	3.5	88	22
Cluster			
Readiness Cluster	3.7	85	15
Basic Skills Cluster	3.9	88	21
Reading Comprehension	4.1	92	30
Total Reading Cluster	3.8	89	23

Test of Written Spelling–II

	Standard Score	*Percentile Rank*
Subtest		
Predictable Words	90	26
Unpredictable Words	86	17
Total	90	26

Test of Written Language

	Standard Score	*Percentile Rank*
Vocabulary	9	37
Thematic Maturity	10	50
Word Usage	9	37
Style	10	50

Written Language Quotient 97

KeyMath–Revised, Form B

	Grade Equivalent	*Percentile Rank*	*Standard Score*
Subtest			
Numeration	—	9	6
Rational Numbers	—	5	5
Geometry	—	37	9
Addition	—	2	4
Subtraction	—	5	5
Multiplication	—	16	7
Division	—	2	4
Mental Computation	—	9	6
Measurement	—	25	8
Time and Money	—	16	7
Estimation	—	50	10
Interpreting Data	—	37	9
Problem Solving	—	16	7
Area			
Basic Concepts	3.3	80	9
Operations	3.4	68	2
Applications	4.1	87	19
Total Test	3.7	78	7

Watkins Bender-Gestalt Scoring System

Steve's scores indicate that he has a moderate to severe visual-perceptual deficit. Errors included rotations, overlapping, shape of design lost, and disproportion of shapes.

Conner's Continuous Performance Test

Steve's omission and commission errors were within the clinical range when compared to the sample of same-age males with attention disorders. The rate of hits was like that of the clinical sample. Sustained attention decreased across time.

What is your evaluation of this case?

__Answer the questions and complete the activities for Case 5.__

SUMMARY AND RECOMMENDATIONS

Write your summary and recommendations in the space provided.

Recommendations

1.

   Reasons:

2.

   Reasons:

3.

   Reasons:

4. ____

____

____

Reasons: ____

____

____

5. ____

____

____

Reasons: ____

____

____

Write behaviorally stated short-term objectives in the following space.

1. ____

____

2. ____

____

3. ____

____

4. ____

____

5. ____

____

☐ CASE 6: ALICIA

Name: Alicia Young
Date of Birth: 2–7–92
Date of Evaluation: 4–7–95
Age: 3–2
Current Grade Placement: None
Examiner: Beth Child
Evaluation Methods: AGS Early Screening Profiles
Play evaluation
Observations
Home visit

BACKGROUND AND REFERRAL INFORMATION

Alicia was referred by her maternal grandmother, who is her legal guardian. Sociological information indicates that Alicia's grandmother does not know her daughter's residence at this time. Health information provided by the grandmother on the Health History Survey indicates that Alicia was born prematurely and that Alicia's mother has a long history of substance abuse. At the time of Alicia's birth, her mother was 17 years of age. Alicia has one older sibling, a 6-year-old brother who is currently receiving special education support services. Alicia's grandmother believes that Alicia is not developing at the expected paces and requested a screening evaluation to determine if Alicia might be considered for the early childhood at risk program.

TEST RESULTS

AGS Early Screening Profiles

	Standard Score	***Percentile Rank***	***Age Equivalent***
Cognitive/Language	60	<1	<2–0
Motor	75	5	2–1
Self-Help/Parent	68	2	<2–0

Survey Scores	
Articulation	Below average/poor
Home behavior	Average
Cognitive/Language	Below average
Motor	Below average

Play Evaluation and Home Visit

Alicia sat quietly on the carpet during the play evaluation. Alicia's grandmother was present during the first part of the evaluation. When her grandmother left the room to complete a survey, Alicia sat motionless and did not exhibit any change in her behavior as a result of the separation. Alicia did not initiate any spontaneous use of language or communication, such as gesturing. She did not interact with the examiner when encouraged to do so and played with only one object, a stuffed toy. Her play can be best described as mechanistic and without any noticeable motive or affect exhibited. Alicia did not react to her grandmother when she returned but joined her grandmother on the sofa when requested.

A home visit was made 2 days following the evaluation. The home environment was clean, and several educational toys and materials were available. All interactions between the grandmother and Alicia were initiated by the grandmother. Alicia displayed very flat affect during both the home visit and the evaluation. Alicia's grandmother stated that the only reaction she sees from Alicia is when it is time to eat. She described her appetite as fair because Alicia likes only a few types of food. When she is given something new to taste, she usually spits it out after she tries it.

Parent Interview

When Alicia's grandmother was asked to list her priorities and concerns for Alicia, she expressed the need for some support to help her toilet train Alicia, improve Alicia's speech development, and improve Alicia's self-help skills, such as dressing and washing her face. Alicia's grandmother believes that Alicia's motor skills are different than her grandson's. She believes that Alicia is somewhat clumsy and too dependent on her for routine activities that other 3-year-olds are learning to do, such as self-feed with a spoon.

Answer the questions and complete the activities for Case 6.

What is your evaluation of the case?

SUMMARY AND RECOMMENDATIONS

Recommendations

1.

   Reasons:

2.

   Reasons:

3.

Reasons: ____

____

____

____

4. ____

____

Reasons: ____

____

____

____

Write behaviorally stated short-term objectives in the space provided.

1. ____

____

2. ____

____

3. ____

____

4. ____

____

5. ____

____

6. ____

____

____

Appendix

Code of Fair Testing Practices in Education

Joint Committee on Testing Practices

The *Code of Fair Testing Practices in Education* (1988) is not copyrighted material, and its dissemination is encouraged.

A. *Developing and Selecting Appropriate Tests*

Test developers should provide the information that test users need to select appropriate tests.

Test Developers Should:

1. Define what each test measures and what the test should be used for. Describe the population(s) for which the test is appropriate.
2. Accurately represent the characteristics, usefulness, and limitations of tests for their intended purposes.
3. Explain relevant measurement concepts as necessary for clarity at the level of detail that is appropriate for the intended audience(s).
4. Describe the process of test development. Explain how the content and skills to be tested were selected.
5. Provide evidence that the test meets its intended purpose(s).
6. Provide either representative samples or complete copies of test questions, directions, answer sheets, manuals, and score reports to qualified users.
7. Indicate the nature of the evidence obtained concerning the appropriateness of each test for groups of different racial, ethnic, or linguistic backgrounds who are likely to be tested.
8. Identify and publish any specialized skills needed to administer each test and to interpret scores correctly.

Source: *Code of Fair Testing Practices in Education.* (1988). Washington, DC: Joint Committee on Testing Practices. Reprinted in its entirety.

Test users should select tests that meet the purpose for which they are to be used and that are appropriate for the intended test-taking populations.

Test Users Should:

1. First define the purpose for testing and the population to be tested. Then, select a test for that purpose and that population based on a thorough review of the available information.
2. Investigate potentially useful sources of information in addition to test scores, to corroborate the information provided by tests.
3. Read the materials provided by test developers and avoid using tests for which unclear or incomplete information is provided.
4. Become familiar with how and when the test was developed and tried out.
5. Read independent evaluations of a test and of possible alternative measures. Look for evidence required to support the claims of test developers.
6. Examine specimen sets, disclosed tests or samples of questions, directions, answer sheets, manuals, and score reports before selecting a test.
7. Ascertain whether the test content and norm group(s) or comparison group(s) are appropriate for the intended test takers.
8. Select and use only those tests for which the skills needed to administer the test and interpret scores correctly are available.

B. Interpreting Scores

Test developers should help users interpret scores correctly.

Test Developers Should:

9. Provide timely and easily understood score reports that describe test performance clearly and accurately. Also explain the meaning and limitations of reported scores.
10. Describe the population(s) represented by any norms or comparison group(s), the dates the data were gathered, and the process used to select the samples of test takers.
11. Warn users to avoid specific, reasonably anticipated misuses of test scores.
12. Provide information that will help users follow reasonable procedures for setting passing scores when it is appropriate to use such scores with the test.
13. Provide information that will help users gather evidence to show that the test is meeting its intended purpose(s).

Test users should interpret scores correctly.

Test Users Should:

9. Obtain information about the scale used for reporting scores, the characteristics of any norms or comparison group(s), and the limitations of scores.
10. Interpret scores taking into account any major differences between the norms or comparison groups and the actual test takers. Also take into ac-

count any differences in test administration practices or familiarity with the specific questions in the test.

11. Avoid using tests for purposes not specifically recommended by the test developer unless evidence is obtained to support the intended use.
12. Explain how any passing scores were set and gather evidence to support the appropriateness of the scores.
13. Obtain evidence to help show that the test is meeting its intended purpose(s).

C. *Striving for Fairness*

Developers should strive to make tests that are as fair as possible for test takers of different races, gender, ethnic backgrounds, or handicapping conditions.

Test Developers Should:

14. Review and revise test questions and related materials to avoid potentially insensitive content or language.
15. Investigate the performance of test takers of different races, gender, and ethnic backgrounds when samples of sufficient size are available. Enact procedures that help to ensure that differences in performance are related primarily to the skills under assessment rather than to irrelevant factors.
16. When feasible, make appropriately modified forms of tests or administration procedures available for test takers with handicapping conditions. Warn test users of potential problems in using standard norms with modified tests or administration procedures that result in noncomparable scores.

Test users should select tests that have been developed in ways that attempt to make them as fair as possible for test takers of different races, gender, ethnic backgrounds, or handicapping conditions.

Test Users Should:

14. Evaluate the procedures used by test developers to avoid potentially insensitive content or language.
15. Review the performance of test takers of different races, gender, and ethnic backgrounds when samples of sufficient size are available. Evaluate the extent to which performance differences may have been caused by inappropriate characteristics of the test.
16. When necessary and feasible, use appropriately modified forms of tests or administration procedures for test takers with handicapping conditions. Interpret standard norms with care in the light of the modifications that were made.

D. Informing Test Takers

Under some circumstances, test developers have direct communication with test takers. Under other circumstances, test users communicate directly with test takers. Whichever group communicates directly with test takers should provide the information described below.

Test Developers or Test Users Should:

17. When a test is optional, provide test takers or their parents/guardians with information to help them judge whether the test should be taken, or if an available alternative to the test should be used.

18. Provide test takers the information they need to be familiar with the coverage of the test, the types of question formats, the directions, and appropriate test-taking strategies. Strive to make such information equally available to all test takers.

Under some circumstances, test developers have direct control of tests and test scores. Under other circumstances, test users have such control. Whichever group has direct control of tests and test scores should take the steps described below.

Test Developers or Test Users Should:

19. Provide test takers or their parents/guardians with information about rights test takers may have to obtain copies of tests and completed answer sheets, retake tests, have tests rescored, and cancel scores.

20. Tell test takers or their parents/guardians how long scores will be kept on file and indicate to whom and under what circumstances test scores will or will not be released.

21. Describe the procedures that test takers or their parents/guardians may use to register complaints and have problems resolved.

Reference

American Educational Research Association, American Psychological Association, & National Council on Measurement in Education. (1985). *Standards for educational and psychological testing.* Washington, DC: American Psychological Association.

Author Index

Able, H., 354
Achenbach, T. M., 260, 267, 268, 270, 271, 273
Alff, M., 15
Algozzine, B., 6, 17, 51, 52, 67, 296, 314
Allinder, R. M., 183
Altepeter, T., 347
American Psychological Association (APA), 28, 31, 32, 34, 36, 51, 52, 68, 116, 127, 140, 297
Anastasi, A., 116, 125, 147
Armstrong, K., 285
Artiles, A. J., 51

Bagnato, S., 401
Bagnato, S. J., 284
Bailey, D. B., 386
Balla, D. A., 321–325, 327
Barakat, L. P., 285
Barbour, J. D., 284
Bardos, A., 182, 347
Bardos, A. N., 182, 183, 279, 280
Barkley, R. A., 285, 388
Barnes, W., 241
Barnett, D., 47, 48, 53
Barnett, D. W., 14, 388
Barringer, K., 51
Bayley, N., 379
Beery, K. E., 356, 357
Bellak, L., 281, 282
Bellak, S. S., 281, 282
Bender, L., 356, 357
Bender, W., 318
Bennett, R., 52, 68, 223, 253
Benowitz, S., 51
Bentz, J., 234
Bersoff, D. N., 296
Betz, N., 103
Bonstrom, O., 11
Borg, W., 68
Bos, C., 47
Boyer-Stephens, A., 15
Bradley-Johnson, S., 320
Brantlinger, E., 47
Braswell, L. A., 183
Brazelton, T., 379
Brigance, A. H., 225, 226, 228, 230
Brown, L., 270, 271, 328, 330
Brown, V. L., 202, 203, 214, 352
Bruininks, R., 318
Bruininks, R. H., 382, 383
Bryant, B. R., 214
Buchanan, M., 318
Budoff, M., 55
Burns, P. C., 243, 244
Busse, R. T., 270
Butterworth, J., 234

Cahan, S., 113
Calhoun, M., 17
Callaway, B., 215
Canter, A., 234
Cantwell, D. P., 285
Carey, K. T., 388
Carey, S. P., 234
Carter, J., 6
Casey, A., 8, 11
Castellanos, M., 318
Chalfant, J., 49
Chalfant, J. C., 12
Chekaluk, E., 254
Chissom, B., 52
Christenson, S., 6, 8
Cicchetti, D. V., 321–325, 327, 382, 383
Clarizio, H. F., 7, 259, 286
Clark, H. T., 54
Clark, T., 48, 49
Cohen, L. G., 385, 387
Colarusso, R. P., 360
Cole, J., 140
Cole, N., 117
Connelly, J., 149
Conners, C. K., 272, 283, 284
Connolly, A. J., 105, 110, 111, 141, 192, 193, 195–202, 224
Conroy-Gunter, 354
Cooter, R., 215
Cronin, M. E., 202, 203
Crowley, S. L., 285
Crumbacker, M., 149
Curry, L., 47

D'Alonzo, B., 140
D'Amato, R., 347
Darch, C., 215
Davis, W., 51, 67
Dean, R., 347
Del'Homme, 385
Deno, S., 224
Deno, S. L., 234
Derr, T., 182
Dodd, J. M., 6
Doll, E. A., 320, 321
Doll, E. J., 182
Duffy, J. B., 51

Dunn, L. M., 345–348
Dunst, C. J., 376, 377
DuPaul, G. J., 285

Eaves, R., 67, 215
Eaves, R. C., 314
Education, U. S. Department of, 37, 38, 49
Eisenberg, J. L., 347
Eliason, M. J., 285
Elliot, S. N., 270
Elliott, J., 284
Englesson, I. L., 285
Erickson, D., 215
Evans, L., 320
Evans, S., 229
Evans, S. S., 266
Evans, W., 229
Evans, W. H., 266

Federal Register, 14, 27–31, 33, 35, 37, 41, 44, 318, 374, 375, 388
Feldt, L., 110, 113
Felix, B. C., 284
Fewell, R. R., 385
Flaugher, R., 50
Fordyce, T., 318
Forness, S., 354, 355
Forness, S. R., 285
Foster-Gaitskell, D., 319
Fowler, D. B., 182
Fradd, S., 51
Fristoe, M., 362
Fuchs, D., 7, 51, 52, 138, 233, 234, 240, 296, 318
Fuchs, L., 51, 52, 138, 224, 233, 234, 240, 296
Fuchs, L. S., 183

Gallegos, A., 140
Gardner, M. F., 363
Gent, C. L., 260
Geraghty, B. L., 318
German, D., 149
German, D. J., 348, 349
Giannuli, M. M., 181, 182
Gillis, M., 243
Gilman, C., 318
Giordano, G., 140
Golden, L., 318
Goldman, R., 362
Goldstein, S., 47, 48, 53
Gonzalez, M., 385
Good, J. F., 224
Goodman, J. F., 376
Gordon, M., 283
Graden, J., 7, 8, 11, 17, 67
Graham, M., 374
Gray, J., 347
Greenspan, S. I., 379
Greenstein, J., 215
Gresham, F. M., 270
Gridley, B. E., 318
Grimes, J., 233
Grimes, J. P., 297
Groshong, C., 347
Guerin, G. R., 246, 248, 250, 251, 276, 277
Guillemard, L., 318
Guilmette, S., 318
Guthrie, D., 285
Gutkin, T. B., 295

Habedank, L., 234
Hagen, E. P., 308
Halgren, D. W., 7
Hallman, C., 51
Hamby, D., 376
Hamlett, C., 233
Hamlett, C. L., 234
Hammill, D., 270, 271
Hammill, D. D., 210–212, 214, 312, 313, 350–353, 358, 360
Harrell, J., 47
Harris, D. B., 279, 364
Harrison, P., 319
Harrison, P. L., 382, 383
Harvey, V., 6
Hasazi, S. B., 54
Heller, K., 49, 51, 117, 294
Herrnstein, R. J., 295
Hewett, B., 149
Higgins, M. M., 259, 286
Hoeppner, J. B., 285
Holtzman, W., 49, 117, 294
Hopkins, B. R., 294
Hopkins, K. D., 294
Horn, E., 318
Horton, W., 52
Hover, S. A., 376
Howell, K. W., 234, 238, 241, 242, 246, 247
Hoy, M., 395
Huebner, E. S., 54, 67, 142
Hughes, C., 223, 259
Hultquist, A. M., 182, 224
Hunt, J. McV., 379
Hupp, S., 354
Hurvich, M. S., 281, 282
Hynd, G. W., 284

Ikeda, M. J., 234
Ilmer, S., 382, 383

Jackson, G. D., 52
Jaeger, R., 215
Jenkins, J., 296
Johanson, C., 376
Johnson, B., 149
Johnson, J., 296
Johnson, K., 347
Johnson, M. B., 150, 154–159
Johnston, A. P., 54

Kamphaus, R., 320
Katz, K. S., 374, 376, 377, 388
Kaufman, A. S., 127, 128, 162, 163, 164, 166, 167, 169, 171, 173, 224, 294, 299–304, 310, 311, 316, 317, 382, 383, 384
Kaufman, N. L., 127, 128, 162–164, 166, 167, 169, 171, 173, 224, 310, 311, 316, 382–384
Kavale, K., 354, 355
Kenny, D. T., 254
Kerr, M. M., 263, 265
Kirk, S., 354, 355
Kline, R. B., 318
Knoff, H. M., 279
Knutson, N., 232, 234
Koppitz, E., 279
Koppitz, E. M., 357
Kubicek, F. C., 54
Kurait, S. K., 231

LaGrow, S., 51–52, 149
Lambert, N., 326
Lambert, N. M., 395, 396
Larsen, S. C., 210–212, 352
Lasky, B., 47
Lee, S. W., 284
Lehmann, I., 103
Leigh, J. E., 328, 330
Leland, H., 326
Lenk, L. L., 54
Lewis, J. F., 331, 332, 334
Lewis, R., 87, 90, 129, 130, 140, 253, 294, 326
Liedtke, W., 246

Liggett, A. M., 54
Lillis, W. T., 183
Locher, P., 354, 355
Lorber, R., 285

Macmann, G. M., 14, 388
Macready, T., 54
Maheady, L., 51
Maier, A. S., 246, 248, 250, 251, 276, 277
Mandelbuam, L., 52
Mann, L., 215, 314
Mardoyan-Apperson, J., 315, 347
Markwardt, F. C., 139, 160–163
Marston, D., 224, 234
Martens, B., 320
Mather, N., 149–151, 182, 306–308, 354, 355
Mattison, R. E., 284
Maxam, S., 15
Maxwell, L., 52
Mayes, L. C., 378, 379
Mayes, S. D., 284
McArthur, D. S., 282
McCaffery, L. K., 317
McConaughy, S. H., 260, 270, 273
McEntire, E., 202, 203
McGrew, K. S., 182
McIntosh, D. E., 318
McIntyre, L., 6
McLaughlin, M. J., 50
McLoughlin, J., 52, 68, 87, 90, 129, 130, 140, 253, 294, 326
McMurray, M. B., 285
McNeish, T. J., 279, 280
McNutt, G., 52
Mehrens, W., 103
Mercer, J., 51, 318, 331, 332, 334
Messick, S., 8, 11, 49, 117, 294, 295
Metzke, L. K., 182, 224
Mick, L., 50
Minke, K. M., 376, 377
Mirkin, P. K., 234
Mohlke, L., 318
Moore, D., 215
Morehead, M. K., 234, 238, 241, 242, 246, 247
Morsink, C. V., 54
Murray, C., 295

Naglieri, J., 347
Naglieri, J. A., 279–281, 364, 365
Nelson, C. M., 263, 265
Nelson, J. R., 6, 12
Newcomer, P. L., 350, 351
Nihira, K., 326
Nolet, V., 232
Norford, B. C., 285
Noyce, R., 215
Nunnally, J., 112

Olivarez, A., 318
Olson, M., 243
Olson, T. K., 285
Orenstein, A., 55
Overton, T., 48, 315, 347
Owings, M. F., 50

Paget, K. D., 385, 387
Palmer, D. J., 318
Palomares, R. S., 285
Pearson, N. A., 358, 360
Pfeiffer, S., 347
Pfohl, W., 47
Phillips, N. B., 234
Pianta, B., 6
Podell, D. M., 6
Ponti, C., 7
Potter, M., 52, 67
Powell, G., 215
Pratt, C., 319
Prewett, P., 182, 183
Prewett, P. N., 181–183, 317
Prochnow-LaGrow, J., 149
Prochow-LaGrow, J., 51–52
Prout, H. T., 279
Psychological Corporation, 174, 176
Psyh, M., 12

Rae, W. A., 285
Rafferty, J., 279
Reavis, K., 6
Regan, R., 51, 52, 67
Reinert, H. R., 264
Reschly, D., 6, 8, 49, 51, 110, 113, 149, 294, 295, 318, 319, 336, 337
Reschly, D. J., 51, 52, 297
Retish, P., 395
Reynolds, C. R., 50, 224, 295, 296
Reynolds, M. C., 51

Richards, S. B., 294
Richey, L., 17, 67
Richman, L. C., 285
Roberts, G. E., 281, 282
Robertson, G. J., 347
Rodden-Nord, K., 234
Roe, B. D., 243, 244
Roit, M., 47
Rorschach, H., 284
Rosenfield, S., 231
Rothlind, J., 286
Rotter, J., 279
Rynders, J., 382, 383

Sabers, D., 110, 113
Salend, S. J., 48
Salvia, J., 3, 6, 51, 106, 112, 113, 215, 223, 224, 259, 294
Sapp, G., 52
Sattler, J. M., 308
Schacht, R., 48, 53
Schattman, R. A., 54
Schaughency, E. A., 286
Schmid, R. E., 266
Schneider, M., 149
Schrank, F. A., 317
Scott, K., 374
Scott, M. M., 376, 377
Sena, R., 285
Shapiro, E., 182
Shapiro, E. S., 223, 224, 227, 229, 234, 249, 250
Shepard, L., 51, 67
Shepherd, M., 52, 68
Shinn, M., 6, 52
Shinn, M. R., 232, 234
Shriner, J., 215
Silver, S., 27
Sinclair, E., 385, 388
Smith, B. L., 318
Smith, D. J., 6
Smith, D. K., 318
Smith, T., 318
Sontag, J. C., 48, 53
Soodak, L. C., 6
Sparrow, S. S., 321–327, 382, 383
Spenciner, L. J., 385, 387
Spigelman, A., 285
Spigelman, G., 285
Spira, D., 6
Spodak, R. B., 182
Stanford, L. D., 284
Stanley, J. C., 294

Stile, S., 140
Stoneman, Z., 47, 53
Stoner, G., 234
Stovall, D. L., 318
Strain, P., 215
Strawser, S., 318
Strickland, B., 47, 55
Sugai, G., 6
Swanson, H. L., 264, 294
Swanson, J. M., 285
Synder, J., 318

Taylor, L., 6, 48
Taylor, R. L., 51, 250, 294
Taylor, R. T., 294, 299
Tharinger, D. J., 395, 396
Thomas, A., 233
Thorndike, R. L., 308, 309
Thurlow, M., 5–8, 20, 52, 53, 149, 318
Tindal, G., 6, 224, 250
Towne, R., 51
Trent, S. C., 51
Trivette, C. M., 376
Trommer, B. L., 285
Tucker, J., 50, 51, 294
Turnbull, A., 47, 48
Turnbull, A. P., 55
Turnbull, H. R., 42, 55, 296

Uzgiris, I. C., 379

Valcarce, R., 68
Vance, H. R., 314
Vance, R., 215
Vaughn, S., 47, 53
Vogel, S., 182
Voress, J. K., 358, 360

Walsh, B., 103
Wang, J., 317
Wang, M. C., 51
Ward, S. B., 54
Ward, T. J., 54
Watkins, E. O., 358, 359
Watson, B. L., 294
Weber, J., 47, 53
Webster, R., 149, 183
Webster, R. E., 183
Wechsler, D., 294, 299, 304, 305, 380
Weller, C., 318
White, R., 17
Wiebe, M. J., 312
Wiederholt, J. L., 212, 214, 352
Wiener, J., 238, 239, 241
Wilkinson, G. S., 115, 149, 177, 179–181
Williams, R., 110
Williams, V., 48
Willson, V., 318
Wilson, V., 142
Wise, L., 47
Witt, J., 320
Wolery, M., 386
Woodcock, R., 362
Woodcock, R. W., 150, 151, 154–159, 203, 206, 207, 224, 306–308
Wood, F., 296
Worchel, F. F., 285
Worms, P., 354
Worthen, B., 68
Worthington, C., 149

Ysseldyke, J., 3, 5–8, 17, 20, 51–53, 67, 106, 112, 113, 149, 294, 296
Ysseldyke, J. E., 51

Zern, D., 138
Zetlin, A. G., 51
Zimmerman, D., 110
Zins, J., 7, 47

Subject Index

AAMD (American Association on Mental Deficiency) Adaptive Behavior Scales, 329
AAMR (American Association on Mental Retardation), 84
AAMR (American Association on Mental Retardation) Adaptive Behavior Scale-School, Second Edition (ABS-S2), 321, 326, 328, 336
ABI (Adaptive Behavior Inventory), 320, 321, 328–330, 334, 336
ABIC (Adaptive Behavior Inventory for Children), 321, 334, 336
Ability tests. *See* Diagnostic tests
ABI Short Form (Adaptive Behavior Inventory), 321, 329, 336
ABS:SE (Adaptive Behavior Scale, School Edition), 320
ABS-S2 (AAMR Adaptive Behavior Scale-School, Second Edition), 321, 326, 328, 336
Academic engaged time, 259
Acculturation, 295
Achievement tests. *See also* Diagnostic tests; Norm-referenced tests; *specific tests*
  age and, 155, 401
  in case studies, 404, 415, 419, 422, 425
  definition of, 147
  equivalent forms of, 102
  group vs. individual, 148
  interpretation of, 401
  learning disabilities and, 182, 183
  norm-referenced tests vs. curriculum-based assessment, 148–149
  review of, 149–181
  selection of, 183–184
Adaptive behavior. *See also specific scales*
  adaptive behavior scales, 148, 321–334, 336
  assessment of, 318–320
  in case studies, 419, 425
  definition of, 293
  individualized education program and, 323
  intelligence tests and, 334–337
  mental retardation and, 318–319, 326, 328
  test interpretation, 400–401
Adaptive Behavior Inventory (ABI), 320, 321, 328–330, 334, 336
Adaptive Behavior Inventory (ABI Short Form), 321, 329, 336
Adaptive Behavior Inventory for Children (ABIC), 321, 334, 336
Adaptive Behavior Scale, School Edition (ABS:SE), 320
Advocate, 43
Age. *See also* Early childhood assessment
  achievement tests and, 155, 401
  chronological, 126, 129–132, 141
  informal assessment and, 254
  norm-referenced tests and, 124, 137, 223
  reliability and, 104, 105, 110, 111, 113
AGS Early Screening Profiles, 382–384, 389, 433
Alternate forms reliability, 101
Alternative planning, 21
American Association on Mental Deficiency (AAMD) Adaptive Behavior Scales, 329
American Association on Mental Retardation (AAMR), 84
American Association on Mental Retardation (AAMR) Adaptive Behavior Scale-School, Second Edition (ABS-S2), 321, 326, 328, 336

American Educational Research Association, 17
American Psychological Association Standards. *See* APA *Standards*
Analysis of Learning Potential, 315
Anecdotal recording, 260–261
Annual goals, 44
APA *Standards*
  definition of, 17
  disabilities and, 34
  nondiscriminatory assessment guidelines, 32, 116
  professional expertise and, 52, 68test administration and, 32–33, 127, 140
  testing purpose and, 35–36, 51–52
Apperception, 278
Apperception tests, 281–283
Aptitude tests, 148
Arena assessment, 386, 387
Arthur Adaptation of the Leiter International Scale, 329, 334
Assessment. *See also* Evaluation; Tests and testing; *specific tests and types of assessment*
  arena assessment, 386, 387
  assessment plan design, 14–17
  bias in, 31, 50–51, 295
  in case studies, 15–16
  comprehensive evaluation and, 20–22
  as continuous process, 3–5, 17, 20, 21, 388
  definition of, 3
  ecological, 8, 11, 269, 276–278
  Individuals With Disabilities Education Act and, 17, 28
  P.L. 99–457 and, 373–377
  prereferral intervention strategies and, 5–12
At risk for developmental delay, 374
Attention deficit disorders, 37–38, 234, 283–284, 285, 396–397
Auditory abilities, 362–364
Auditory discrimination, 362
Auditory Discrimination Test, 351
Auditory memory, 362
Autism, 18, 43
Average performance, 71–78

Basals, 132–136, 139
Baseline, 260
Basic Achievement Skills Individual Screener, 177
Bayley Scales of Infant Development-II, 379–380, 389
Behavior. *See also* Adaptive behavior; Behaviorally stated objectives
  in case studies, 418
  checklists and, 269–272
  ecological assessment of, 276–278
  informal assessment of, 3, 259–266
  interviews and, 273–274
  projective assessment techniques, 278–283
  questionnaires and, 273–274
  rating scales and, 269–272
  research on, 284–286
  sociograms and, 274–275
  structured classroom observations, 267–268
  test interpretation and, 399
Behaviorally stated objectives
  in case studies, 413, 420, 423, 427
  definition of, 395
  test interpretation and, 407–408
Behavioral observations, 3, 259–266
Behavioral problems, 6
Behavior Rating Profile-2, 270, 271–272
Bell curve, 71
Bender Visual Motor Gestalt Test: The Watkins Bender-Gestalt Scoring System, 356–358, 359, 366, 430
Bias. *See also* Diversity issues; Nondiscriminatory assessment
  in adaptive behavior assessment, 318
  in assessment process, 31, 50–51, 295
  in curriculum-based assessment, 234
  in informal assessment, 253
  in intelligence tests, 318
  item bias, 117, 253
  minority overrepresentation and, 50, 294–295
  norm-referenced tests and, 224
  predictive validity and, 117
  in tests, 50–51, 117, 224, 253
Bimodal distribution, 73
Biological risk factors, 374
Blindness, 18, 20, 43
Boehm Test of Basic Concepts, 159, 306
Bracken Basic Concepts Scale, 159, 306
Brigance Diagnostic Inventory of Basic Skills, 225–226, 228
Brigance Diagnostic Inventory of Early Development-Revised, 225
Brigance Diagnostic Inventory of Essential Skills, 226
Brigance inventories, 225–227, 228

California Achievement Test (CAT), 181, 212, 213, 315
California Test of Basic Skills (CTBS), 181
Case manager, 48
Case studies, 15–16, 45, 402–407, 413–435
CAT (California Achievement Test), 181, 212, 213, 315
CAT (Children's Apperception Test), 281–282
CBCL (Child Behavior Checklist), 267–268, 270–271, 273–274, 380, 414, 428
Ceilings, 132–136, 139
Central tendency, 71, 76, 78, 79

Checklists
for behavior assessment, 267–268, 269–272, 273–274, 380, 414, 428
definition of, 4, 237, 238
prereferral, 9–11
Child Behavior Checklist (CBCL), 267–268, 270–271, 273–274, 380, 414, 428
Child Behavior Checklist: Direct Observation Form, Revised Edition, 267–268, 428
Child Behavior Checklist: Parent, Teacher, and Youth Report Forms, 270–271, 284, 414, 428
Child Behavior Checklist: Semistructured Clinical Interview, 273–274
Children's Apperception Test (CAT), 281–282
Chronological age, 126, 129–131, 133, 141
CLT (Cognitive Levels Test), 215, 299, 314–315, 335
Code of Fair Testing Practices in Education, 17, 297, 436–439
Coefficient alpha, 102, 103
Cognitive Abilities Test, 329
Cognitive Levels Test (CLT), 215, 299, 314–315, 335
Communication, mode of, 29, 31
Compliance, 27
Comprehensive educational evaluation, 20–22, 28
Comprehensive Test of Basic Skills, 202, 213, 353
Computerized assessment, of attention deficit disorders, 283–284
Concurrent validity, 114–115
Confidence interval, 107
Conners' Continuous Performance Test, 284, 430–431
Conners Parent Rating Scales, 270
Conners Rating Scales, 272
Conners Teacher Rating Scale, 270, 284–285
Consent, informed, 28–29, 46, 47, 375
Consent forms, 29
Construct validity, 116–117, 295
Consultation services, 7, 11
Consulting model for parent participation, 48, 49
Content validity, 115–116, 295
Continuous assessment, 3–5, 17, 20, 21, 388
Continuous Performance Test, 25, 283–284, 285
Correlation, 93–99, 117
Correlation coefficient, 94
CPT (Continuous Performance Test), 25, 283–284, 285
Criterion-referenced tests, 4, 224, 227, 229–231
Criterion-related assessment
Brigance inventories as, 225–227, 228
definition of, 4, 224
as informal assessment technique, 224–231, 237
teacher-made, 227, 229–231
Criterion-related validity, 114–115, 116
CTBS (California Test of Basic Skills), 181
Cultural bias. *See* Bias; Diversity issues; Nondiscriminatory assessment
Culture fair, 334
Curriculum-based assessment
bias in, 234
in case studies, 425–426
definition of, 3–4, 149, 227
as informal assessment technique, 231–234, 237, 246, 364, 425
nondiscriminatory assessment and, 52
norm-referenced tests and, 148–149

Deaf-blindness, 18, 43
Deafness, 18, 43
Derived scores, 70, 140, 142
Descriptive statistics
average performance and, 71–78
central tendency and, 71, 76, 78, 79
definition of, 71
dispersion and, 78–84
importance of, 67–68
mean differences, 84
meaning of, 68–69
numerical scales, 69–70
percentile ranks and, 86–87
skewed distributions, 85–86
z scores and, 86–87
Detroit Tests of Learning Aptitude (DTLA), 351
Detroit Tests of Learning Aptitude-3 (DTLA-3), 299, 312–314, 335, 353
Developmental delays, 374, 379
Developmental differences, 6
Developmental drawing tests, 364–365
Developmental Test of Visual-Motor Integration (VMI), Third Revision, 356, 366
Developmental Test of Visual Perception, Second Edition (DTVP-2), 358, 360, 366
Developmental version, 123
Development levels, 117, 345, 364–365
Diagnostic tests. *See also* Achievement tests; Norm- referenced tests; *specific tests*
for auditory abilities, 362–364
in case studies, 404–405, 415, 425, 429–430
definition of, 148, 191
of development levels, 364–365
equivalent forms of, 102
interpretation of, 401
for language, 345–353
learning disabilities and, 230
for mathematics, 192–203
for perceptual abilities, 354–355

for reading, 203–210, 212–215
research on, 215
results from, 365–366
review of, 192–210
selection of, 215–217
for sensory-motor abilities, 354–355
uses of, 191
for visual perception, 355–361
for written language, 210–212, 215
Diana v. State Board of Education, 296
Differential Ability Scales, 177
Direct daily measurements, 231, 234
Direct measurement, 191, 227, 231–234, 237
Disabilities, 18–20, 33–34, 43. *See also* Individuals With Disabilities Education Act (IDEA); Learning disabilities; *specific disabilities*
Dispersion, 78–84
Diversity issues. *See also* Bias; Nondiscriminatory assessment
adaptive behavior assessment and, 318–319
culture fair, 334
intelligence tests and, 294–295, 320
language accessibility, 29, 31, 48, 310
mean differences and, 84, 295
minority overrepresentation, 48–50, 294–295
norm groups and, 123–124
norm-referenced tests and, 123
of parents, 48
prereferral intervention and, 8
reliability and, 104
test bias and, 50–51, 117, 224, 253
Domains, 123, 192, 199
Draw-a-Person: A Quantitative Scoring System, 364–365, 366
Draw-a-Person: Screening Procedure for Emotional Disturbance, 279–281
Drawing tests, 278, 279–281, 285, 364–365, 366
DTLA (Detroit Tests of Learning Aptitude), 351
DTLA-3 (Detroit Tests of Learning Aptitude-3), 299, 312–314, 335, 353
DTVP-2 (Developmental Test of Visual Perception, Second Edition), 358, 360, 366
Due process
definition of, 28
early childhood assessment and, 375
individual education plan process and, 55
Individuals With Disabilities Education Act and, 45–46
informed consent and, 29
Duration recording, 264
Durrell Analysis of Reading, 212

Early childhood assessment. *See also specific tests*
in case studies, 433
considerations in, 388–389
evaluation and, 374–375
infant assessment, 378–380
methods of, 378
P.L. 99–457 and, 27, 373–377
summary of tests, 389
toddler/young child assessment, 373–374, 380–385
trends in, 385–388
Early intervention, 27
Ecobehavioral interviews, 386
Ecological assessment, 8, 11, 269, 276–278
Educational objectives. *See* Behaviorally stated objectives
Educational planning, 364–365, 395
Educational tests. *See* Achievement tests
Education for All Handicapped Children Act. *See* Individuals With Disabilities Education Act (IDEA); P.L. 94–142
Education of the Handicapped Amendments. *See* P.L. 99–457
Eligibility decisions, 395, 396–397
Eligibility determination, 43–44, 234, 373–375, 396, 407
Eligibility meeting, 21, 43–44, 53, 407
Emotional disturbance, 19, 43, 396–397, 418
Environmental influence, 295. *See also* Ecological assessment
Environmental risk factors, 374
Equivalent forms reliability, 101–102
Error analysis, 4, 235–236, 237, 246
Estimated true scores, 112–113
Evaluation. *See also* Assessment; Tests and testing; *specific tests*
comprehensive educational evaluation, 20–22, 28
independent educational evaluation, 46
Individuals With Disabilities Education Act procedures for, 31
of learning disabilities, 37
by multidisciplinary team, 38–40
P.L. 99–457 and, 374–375
play evaluation, 386, 433
preplacement evaluation, 28
Event recording, 262–263
Expressive language, 345, 348–350. *See also* Language assessment

Factor analysis, 117, 304
Family-centered program, 377
Family-focused program, 377

Field test, 123
Formal Reading Inventory, 212–214, 217
Frequency counting, 263
Frequency distribution, 72–73
Frequency polygon, 73–74

Gender issues, 6, 234. *See also* Bias
General education classroom
  attention deficit disorders and, 38, 396
  consultation services in, 7, 11
  curriculum-based assessment in, 234
  Individuals With Disabilities Education Act and, 54
  multiple gating system and, 14
  Rehabilitation Act of 1973 and, 396
Global skill comparisons, 165
Goodenough-Harris Drawing Test, 364, 366
GORT-3 (Gray Oral Reading Tests-Third Edition), 214, 217
Grade equivalents, 44, 142
Grade level
  achievement tests and, 155, 401
  norm-referenced tests and, 124, 137, 140, 223
  reliability and, 105, 110, 113
Graduate Record Exam (GRE), 115
Gray Oral Reading Tests-Third Edition (GORT-3), 214, 217
GRE (Graduate Record Exam), 115
Group achievement tests, 147, 148

Handicapping conditions. *See* Disabilities; Diversity issues; *specific conditions*
Handwriting. *See* Written language
Health impairments, 19
Hearing impairments, 18, 43, 414
Hearing officer, 46
Home Situations Questionnaire, 388
House-Tree-Person, 279
Human Figure Drawing Test, 279
Humanities, 152

IDEA. *See* Individuals With Disabilities Education Act (IDEA)
IEP. *See* Individualized education program (IEP)
IFSP (Individual Family Service Plan), 22, 42, 376–377
Illinois Test of Psycholinguistic Abilities, 351
Independent educational evaluation, 46
Individual achievement tests, 148, 162
Individual assessment plan, 15, 17
Individual Family Service Plan (IFSP), 22, 42, 376–377
Individualized education program (IEP). *See also* Behaviorally stated objectives
  adaptive behavior and, 323
  Brigance inventories and, 225
  development of, 44–45
  due process and, 55
  eligibility meeting and, 21
  parents and, 47–49
  prereferral intervention and, 8
  written language test interpretation and, 401–402
Individuals With Disabilities Education Act (IDEA)
  assessment and, 17, 28
  in case studies, 45
  definition of, 27
  diagnostic criteria of, 18–20, 43, 396–397
  due process and, 45–46
  early childhood assessment and, 373, 374
  eligibility determination, 43–44, 396
  intelligence tests and, 293, 297
  least restrictive environment and, 44, 54
  multidisciplinary team and, 34–35, 38–40
  nondiscriminatory assessment and, 30–36, 48–52, 116, 117, 375
  parent guidelines, 41–42
  preplacement evaluation and, 28
  professional expertise and, 31–32, 38, 52
  research and issues concerning, 47–55
  special education services and, 18–20
  test administration and, 31–32, 127, 140
Infants, 27, 373–374, 378–380. *See also* Early childhood assessment
Informal assessment
  behavioral observations, 259–266
  criterion-related assessment, 224–231, 237
  curriculum-based assessment, 231–234, 237, 246, 364, 425
  definition of, 5, 260
  direct measurement, 231–234
  issues in, 253–254
  of mathematics, 246
  methods of, 237
  norm-referenced tests, 223–224
  portfolio assessment, 250
  of reading, 238–245
  task and error analysis, 235–236
  of written language, 246–250, 251–252
Informal instruments, 191
Informal Reading Inventory, Third Edition, 243–244
Informed consent, 28–29, 46, 47, 375
Innate potential, 295
Instructional level, 191
Instructional materials, 278

Instructional planning, 233–234
Intelligence, 293
Intelligence Quotient (IQ), 33, 52, 84, 293
Intelligence tests. *See also specific tests*
  adaptive behavior and, 334–337
  in case studies, 403–404, 414, 418, 422, 424–425, 429
  diversity issues, 294–295, 320
  interpretation of, 400–401
  litigation and, 296–297, 320
  for mathematics, 299–300
  meaning of, 293–296
  nondiscriminatory assessment and, 33, 52, 294–296, 318
  protocol of, 304–305, 311
  for reading, 300
  research on, 317–318
  review of, 298–317
  summary of, 335
  use of, 297–298
Interactive strategies, 386, 387
Interindividual interpretations, 398, 400–401
Internal consistency, 100
Internal consistency measures, 102–103
Interpolation, 125
Interpretation of test results. *See* Test interpretation
Interrater reliability, 103
Interval recording, 263, 265
Interval scale, 69
Interviews, 269, 273–274, 386. *See also* Questionnaires
Intra-individual interpretations, 398, 401
Iowa Test of Basic Skills, 202
IQ. *See* Intelligence Quotient (IQ)
Item bias, 117, 253
Item pool, 123

K-ABC. *See* Kaufman Assessment Battery for Children (K-ABC)
Kaufman Adolescent and Adult Intelligence Test (KAIT), 299, 316, 317
Kaufman Assessment Battery for Children (K-ABC)
  early childhood assessment and, 380
  research on, 317, 318
  review of, 299, 310–312
  summary of, 335
  in validity studies, 159, 169, 172, 174, 306, 310, 314, 316, 317, 323, 326, 329
Kaufman Brief Intelligence Test (KBIT), 299, 316–317
Kaufman Survey of Early Academic and Language Skills (K-SEALS), 384–385, 389
Kaufman Test of Educational Achievement (K-TEA)
  brief form, 169–174, 182–183
  in case studies, 425
  comprehensive form of, 163–169, 170, 171, 182–183
  criterion-related assessment and, 224
  as individual achievement test, 162
  protocol of, 127–128, 173
  research on, 181–183
  scoring of, 164–168, 169, 171, 173
  summary of, 184
  technical data on, 168–169, 172, 174
  uses of, 149
  in validity studies, 159, 177
KBIT (Kaufman Brief Intelligence Test), 299, 316–317
KeyMath, 202, 203, 315
KeyMath-Revised
  in case studies, 430
  chronological age and, 141
  content specifications of, 192–193
  criterion-related assessment and, 224
  protocol of, 195, 201
  research on, 215
  scoring of, 194, 196–201
  standard errors of measurement for, 110–111
  summary of, 216
  technical data on, 202
Kinetic Family Drawings, 279
Kinetic Family Drawing System for Family and School, 279
K-R 20 (Kuder-Richardson 20), 102, 103
K-SEALS (Kaufman Survey of Early Academic and Language Skills), 384–385, 389
K-TEA. *See* Kaufman Test of Educational Achievement (K-TEA)
Kuder-Richardson (K-R) 20, 102, 103

Language accessibility, 29, 31, 48, 51, 310
Language assessment. *See also* Expressive language; Reading; Written language; *specific tests*
  definition of, 345
  diagnostic tests for, 345–353
  Peabody Picture Vocabulary Test-Revised (PPVT-R) review, 345–348
  Test of Adolescent and Adult Language-Third Edition (TOAL-3), 352–353, 366
  Test of Language Development-2: Intermediate (TOLD-I:2), 351–352, 353, 366
  Test of Language Development-2: Primary (TOLD-P:2), 350–351, 366
  Test of Word Finding (TWF), 348–350, 366, 415
Larry P. v. Riles, 33, 296
Latency recording, 266

Laws and litigation, 14–15, 27, 296–297, 320. *See also* Individuals With Disabilities Education Act (IDEA); P.L. 94–142; P.L. 99–457
Learning disabilities
achievement tests and, 182, 183
adaptive behavior assessment and, 318
Continuous Performance Test and, 25
curriculum-based assessment and, 234
diagnostic tests and, 230
evaluation of, 37
Individuals With Disabilities Education Act criteria of, 19, 43, 396–397
P.L. 94–142 and, 49–50
Least restrictive environment, 44, 54
Linear scores. *See* Standard scores
Local education agencies, 27
Lora v. New York City Board of Education, 296

Mainstreaming, 44
MAT6, 182
Mathematics
achievement tests for, 152, 153, 160, 163–164, 169, 174, 178
curriculum based assessment of, 233
diagnostic tests for, 192–203
informal assessment of, 246
intelligence tests for, 299–300
Matrix Analogies Test, 365
McCarthy General Cognitive Index, 306
Mean, 77–79, 81
Mean differences, 84, 295
Measurement. *See* Descriptive statistics
Measures of central tendency, 71, 76, 78, 79
Measures of dispersion, 78–84
Median, 75–76
Mediation, 55
Mental retardation
adaptive behavior and, 318–319, 326, 328
diagnosis of, 326, 336
Individuals With Disabilities Education Act criteria of, 18, 43, 396–397
intelligence quotient and, 52, 84
intelligence tests and, 293, 294
minority overrepresentation, 49–50
Minority overrepresentation, 48–50, 294–295. *See also* Diversity issues
Mode, 73, 75, 76
Motor-free, 356
Motor-Free Visual Perception Test (MVPT), 360–361, 366
Multidisciplinary team
decision-making process and, 53–54
definition of, 5
eligibility determination and, 43, 407
evaluation by, 38–40
Individuals With Disabilities Education Act guidelines for, 34–35, 38–40
nondiscriminatory assessment and, 38
professional expertise and, 38
screening by, 14
Multihandicap, 18, 43
Multilevel Academic Survey Test, 365
Multimodal distribution, 73
Multiple gating, 14
MVPT (Motor-Free Visual Perception Test), 360–361, 366

National Council on Measurement in Education, 17
Native language, 29, 31, 48, 51, 310. *See also* Diversity issues; Language assessment
Negative correlation, 96–98
Negatively skewed, 85
Neonatal Behavioral Assessment Scale, 379, 389
No correlation, 98–99
Nominal scale, 69
Nondiscriminatory assessment. *See also* Bias; Diversity issues
APA *Standards* and, 32, 116
curriculum-based assessment and, 52
Individuals With Disabilities Education Act and, 30–36, 48–52, 116, 117, 375
intelligence tests and, 33, 52, 294–296, 318
multidisciplinary team and, 38
P.L. 94–142 and, 318
Normal distribution
definition of, 71
median and, 75
percentile ranks and, 87
standard deviation and, 78, 84
standard error of measurement and, 107
Norm group, 123–124. *See also specific tests*
Norming process
for achievement tests, 159, 161, 168, 172, 175–177, 180
for adaptive behavior scales, 323, 326, 328, 329, 334
for auditory ability tests, 362–363
for drawing tests, 365
for early childhood assessment, 382, 384
for intelligence tests, 303, 306, 312–317
for language assessment, 347, 348, 350, 352, 353
for mathematics tests, 202, 203
for reading tests, 209, 213, 214
for visual perception tests, 356, 358, 361
for written language tests, 211, 212

Norm-referenced tests. *See also* Achievement tests; Diagnostic tests; *specific tests*
  administration of, 127–142
  construction of, 123–127
  curriculum-based assessment and, 148–149
  definition of, 20, 123, 148
  grade level and, 124, 137, 140, 223
  interpretation of, 69
  problems of, 223–224
  selection of, 86
  use of, 51
Northwestern Syntax Screening Test, 350
Numerical scales, 69–70

Objectives
  behaviorally stated objectives, 395, 407–408, 413, 420, 423, 427
  short-term objectives, 44, 407, 408, 423
Obtained score, 106–107, 113
Ordinal scale, 69
Orthopedical impairment, 18, 43
Otis-Lennon School Ability Test, 329
Overidentification, 7

Parents
  adaptive behavior assessment and, 319–320
  behavioral assessment and, 270, 272, 273
  consulting model, 48, 49
  due process rights of, 28, 29, 45–46, 55, 375
  early childhood assessment and, 376–377
  ecological assessment and, 276
  eligibility meeting with, 21, 43–44, 407
  Individual Family Service Plan and, 22, 42, 376–377
  individualized education program and, 47–49
  Individuals With Disabilities Education Act guidelines for, 41–42
  informed consent and, 28–29, 46, 47, 375
  passivity of, 47–48, 53
  percentile ranks and, 142
  surrogate parents, 29
  test interpretation and, 399
Parents' rights booklet, 29
PASE v. Hannon, 296
Peabody Individual Achievement Test (PIAT), 203, 348, 350, 353
Peabody Individual Achievement Test-Revised (PIAT-R)
  basal and ceiling rules for, 139
  in case studies, 425
  protocol of, 162
  research on, 181–183
  scoring of, 160–162, 163
  summary of, 184
  technical data on, 161
  uses of, 149
  in validity studies, 159, 161, 169
Peabody Picture Vocabulary Test (PPVT), 172
Peabody Picture Vocabulary Test-Revised (PPVT-R)
  review of, 345–348
  summary of, 365
  in validity studies, 159, 169, 174, 177, 306, 315, 323, 326, 329
Pearson's *r,* 100
Percentile ranks, 86–87, 140, 142
Perceptual abilities, 345, 354–355
Performance tests, 299
Permanent products, 237, 238
PIAT (Peabody Individual Achievement Test), 203, 348, 350, 353
PIAT-R. *See* Peabody Individual Achievement Test-Revised (PIAT-R)
Picture Story Language Test, 182
P.L. 94–142. *See also* Individuals With Disabilities Education Act (IDEA)
  attention deficit disorders and, 37–38
  definition of, 27
  learning disabilities and, 49–50
  nondiscriminatory assessment and, 318
P.L. 99–457
  assessment and, 373–377
  continuous assessment, 388
  definition of, 27, 373
  Individual Family Service Plan (IFSP) and, 42, 376
  issues concerning, 376–377
  parent involvement and, 42
  professional expertise and, 378
Play evaluation, 386, 433
Portfolio assessment, 250
Positive correlation, 94–96, 97
Positively skewed, 85
PPVT (Peabody Picture Vocabulary Test), 172
PPVT-R. *See* Peabody Picture Vocabulary Test-Revised (PPVT- R)
Practice effect, 101, 102
Predictive validity, 115, 117, 295
Preplacement evaluation, 28
Prereferral checklist, 9–11
Prereferral intervention strategies, 5–12
Preschool children, 27, 373–374, 380–385. *See also* Early childhood assessment
Presentation format, 116
Probes, 191, 224, 237
Procedural safeguards, 46
Professional expertise
  Individuals With Disabilities Education Act and, 31–32, 38, 52
  P.L. 99–457 and, 378
  test results and, 67–68, 138, 140

Projective assessment techniques
apperception tests, 281–283
drawing tests, 279–281
sentence completion tests, 278–279
Projective techniques, 278
Projective tests, 396, 397
Protocol
of achievement tests, 154, 162, 166, 170, 173, 179
of adaptive behavior scales, 324, 327, 330
definition of, 127–128
of diagnostic tests, 195, 201, 209
of intelligence tests, 304–305, 311
use of, 136–138
Psychoeducational report, 402, 407
Psychophysiological disturbances, 378

Questionnaires
for behavioral assessment, 273–274
definition of, 237, 238, 269
situational, 386, 388

Range, 79
Rating scales, 269–272
Ratio scale, 70
Raw score, 69, 132, 136, 137, 140
Reading. *See also specific tests*
achievement tests for, 151, 152–153, 160, 164, 169, 174, 177–178
curriculum-based assessment of, 232
diagnostic tests for, 203–210, 212–215
informal assessment of, 238–245
intelligence tests for, 300
in norm-referenced tests, 224
Receptive language, 345
Regulatory disturbances, 378
Rehabilitation Act of 1973, 38, 396
Related services, 44
Reliability. *See also specific tests*
age and, 104, 105, 110, 111, 113
correlation and, 94–99
definition of, 93
for different groups, 104–105
early childhood assessment and, 388
grade level and, 105, 110, 113
measurement methods, 100–103
standard error of measurement and, 106–111, 113
types of, 103–105
understanding of, 68
validity and, 114, 118
Research. *See also specific tests*
on achievement tests, 181–183
on behavior, 284–286
on diagnostic tests, 182, 215
on Individuals With Disabilities Education Act, 47–55
on intelligence tests, 317–318
Response mode, 116
Roberts Apperception Test for Children, 281, 282–283, 285
Rorschach Inkblot Test, 284
Rotter Incomplete Sentence Blank, 279

Sample, 123
SAT (Scholastic Aptitude Test), 115
SAT (Stanford Achievement Test), 181
Scaled scores, 299
Scales of Independent Behavior (SIB), 320
Scattergrams, 95, 97–99
Scholastic Aptitude Test (SAT), 115
School Situations Questionnaire, 388
Science, 152
Scientific Research Associates (SRA) Achievement Series, 203, 211, 212
Scores and scoring. *See also* Descriptive statistics
of achievement tests, 154–159, 160–162, 163, 164–168, 169, 171, 173, 175, 178
average performance and, 71–78
basals and, 132–136, 139
ceilings and, 132–136, 139
central tendency and, 71
Code of Fair Testing Practices in Education and, 437–438
derived scores, 70, 140, 142
of diagnostic tests, 194, 198–199, 205–208, 356–358, 359, 366, 430
dispersion and, 78–84
of drawing tests, 279–281, 364–365
extremes in, 85–86
in informal assessment, 253
of intelligence tests, 155, 304–306
mistakes in, 68
obtained score, 106–107, 113
percentiles and, 86–87
raw score, 69, 132, 136, 137, 140
scaled scores, 299
skewed distributions, 85–86
standard error of measurement and, 106–111, 113
standard scores, 44, 70, 140, 198
w scores, 150, 205
z scores and, 86–87, 140
Screening, 14, 17, 33, 234
Screening tests, 147, 148, 399
SEM (Standard error of measurement), 106–111, 113
Sensory-motor abilities, 345, 354–355
Sentence completion tests, 278–279
Short-term objectives, 44, 407, 408, 417, 423
SIB (Scales of Independent Behavior), 320

Single IQ score, 33, 52
Situational questionnaires, 386, 388
Skewed, 85
Skewed distribution, 85–86
Slosson Intelligence Test, 203, 329
Social/environmental disturbances, 378
Social studies, 152
Sociograms, 269, 274–275
SOMPA (System of Multicultural Pluralistic Assessment), 331–333, 334, 336
Special education services
  definition of, 44
  eligibility decisions, 395, 396–397
  eligibility determination, 43–44, 234, 373–375, 396, 407
  eligibility meeting, 21, 43–44, 53, 407
  Individuals With Disabilities Education Act guidelines for, 18–20
  reform in, 6, 17, 51
Specific skill comparisons, 165
Speech/language impairment, 20, 43, 396–397, 414. *See also* Language assessment
Spelling. *See* Written language
Split-half reliability, 102–103, 105
SRA (Scientific Research Associates) Achievement Series, 203, 211, 212
Standard deviation, 78, 79, 81–82, 84
Standard error of measurement (SEM), 106–111, 113
Standardized tests, 20. *See also* Achievement tests; Descriptive statistics; Norm-referenced tests; *specific tests*
Standard scores, 44, 70, 140, 198
Standards for Educational and Psychological Testing. See APA *Standards*
Stanford Achievement Test (SAT), 181
Stanford-Binet Intelligence Scale (1973), 310
Stanford-Binet Intelligence Scale-Fourth Edition (Stanford-Binet IV)
  in early childhood assessment, 380
  research on, 182, 317, 318
  review of, 299, 308–310
  summary of, 335
  in validity studies, 306, 316, 326, 329
State educational agencies, 27
Statistics. *See* Descriptive statistics
Structured classroom observations, 267–268
Subskill, 226
Subtasks, 235
Subtests, 148
Surrogate parents, 29
Systematic observation, 260
System of Multicultural Pluralistic Assessment (SOMPA), 331–333, 334, 336

TAPS (Test of Auditory-Perceptual Skills), 363, 366, 405
Target behaviors, 259
Task analysis, 235–237, 246
Teacher-made criterion-referenced tests, 227, 229–231
Templin-Darley Tests of Articulation, 351
Test administration
  APA *Standards* and, 32–33, 127, 140
  basals and, 132–136, 139
  beginning testing, 128–129
  ceilings and, 132–136, 139
  chronological age and, 129–131
  derived scores and, 140, 142
  guidelines for, 130–131, 138, 140
  Individuals With Disabilities Education Act and, 31–32
  protocols and, 127–128, 136–138, 140
  raw scores and, 132
  rules for, 68
Test for Auditory Comprehension of Language, 351
Test interpretation
  of achievement tests, 401
  of adaptive behavior, 400–401
  behaviorally stated objectives and, 407–408
  in case studies, 402–407, 413–435
  of diagnostic tests, 401
  eligibility decisions and, 396–397
  guidelines for, 395–396
  of intelligence tests, 400–401
  interindividual and intraindividual, 398, 400–401
  of norm-referenced tests, 69
  procedures for, 399–400
  of written language tests, 401–402
Test manual, 127, 134
Test of Adolescent and Adult Language-Third Edition (TOAL-3), 352–353, 366
Test of Adolescent Language, 352
Test of Auditory Discrimination, 362–363, 366
Test of Auditory-Perceptual Skills (TAPS), 363, 366, 405
Test of Language Development-2: Intermediate (TOLD-I:2), 351–352, 353, 366
Test of Language Development-2: Primary (TOLD-P:2), 350–351, 366
Test of Mathematical Abilities-2 (TOMA-2), 202–203, 216
Test of Reading Comprehension-Revised Edition (TORC-R), 214–215, 217

Test of Word Finding (TWF), 348–350, 366, 415
Test of Written Language-2 (TOWL-2), 182, 210–211, 216, 353, 430
Test of Written Spelling-2 (TWS-2), 215, 429
Test of Written Spelling-3 (TWS-3), 211–212, 216
Test-retest reliability, 100–101
Tests and testing. *See also* Reliability; Test administration; Test interpretation; Validity; *specific tests and types of tests*
  APA *Standards* and, 35–36, 51–52
  bias in, 50–51, 117, 224, 253
  Code of Fair Testing Practices in Education and, 436–437
  definition of, 3
  purpose of, 31, 33, 35–36, 51–52, 67, 110
  selection of, 51
  standard error of measurement and, 110–111
  standardized tests, 20
  test results and, 67–68, 138, 140
  time variables, 101
Third-party hearing, 46–47, 55
Time sampling, 263
Time variables, 101
TNS, 215
TNS-2, 215
TOAL-3 (Test of Adolescent and Adult Language-Third Edition), 352–353, 366
Toddler/young child assessment, 373–374, 380–385. *See also* Early childhood assessment
TOLD-I:2 (Test of Language Development-2: Intermediate), 351–352, 353, 366
TOLD-P:2 (Test of Language Development-2: Primary), 350–351, 366
TOMA-2 (Test of Mathematical Abilities-2), 202–203, 216
TORC-R (Test of Reading Comprehension-Revised Edition), 214–215, 217
TOWL-2 (Test of Written Language-2), 182, 210–211, 216, 353, 430
Transition services, 42
Traumatic brain injury, 19, 43
True scores, 106–108, 112–113
TWF (Test of Word Finding), 348–350, 366, 415
TWS-2 (Test of Written Spelling-2), 215, 429
TWS-3 (Test of Written Spelling-3), 211–212, 216

Uzgiris-Hunt Ordinal Scales of Psychological Development, 379, 389

Validity. *See also specific tests*
  definition of, 114
  early childhood assessment and, 388
  measurement of, 68
  nondiscriminatory assessment and, 295
  reliability and, 114, 118
  test purpose and, 51, 67, 110
  types of, 114–117
Validity coefficient, 114
Validity of test use, 117
Variability, 78, 79. *See also* Dispersion
Variance, 79, 80, 82
Verbal tests, 299
Vineland Adaptive Behavior Scales
  in case studies, 419
  early childhood assessment and, 380
  protocol of, 327
  review of, 321–326
  summary of, 336
  in validity studies, 323, 329
Vineland Adaptive Behavior Scales, Classroom Edition, 326
Vineland Adaptive Behavior Scales, Interview Edition Expanded Form, 323, 425
Vineland Adaptive Behavior Scales, Interview Edition Survey Form, 322–323
Vineland Social Maturity Scale, 320, 329
Vineland Survey Form, 320
Visual impairment, 20, 43
Visual memory, 356
Visual-motor ability, 345
Visual perception
  Bender Visual Motor Gestalt Test: The Watkins Bender-Gestalt Scoring System, 356–359, 366, 430
  definition of, 355
  Developmental Test of Visual-Motor Integration (VMI), Third Revision, 356, 366
  Developmental Test of Visual Perception, Second Edition (DTVP-2), 358, 360, 366
  diagnostic tests for, 355–361
  Motor-Free Visual Perception Test (MVPT), 360–361, 366
Visual retention, 356
VMI (Developmental Test of Visual-Motor Integration), 356, 366
Vocabulary. *See* Reading

WAIS-R (Wechsler Adult Intelligence Scale-Revised), 299, 306, 310, 317
Watkins Bender-Gestalt Scoring System, 356–359, 366, 430
Wechsler Adult Intelligence Scale-Revised (WAIS-R), 299, 306, 310, 317
Wechsler Individual Achievement Test (WIAT), 174–177, 184
Wechsler Intelligence Scale for Children-Revised (WISC-R)

research on, 182, 318
in validity studies, 306, 310, 315, 317, 326, 329, 350
Wechsler Intelligence Scale for Children-Third Edition (WISC-III)
in case studies, 403–404, 414, 418, 422, 424–425, 429
performance subtests, 300–302
research on, 317, 318
scoring of, 304–306
technical data on, 303–304
verbal subtests, 299–300
Wechsler Intelligence Scales, 203, 294, 298, 335. *See also specific scales*
Wechsler Preschool and Primary Scale of Intelligence (WPPSI), 310
Wechsler Preschool and Primary Scale of Intelligence-Revised (WPPSI-R), 298–299, 380–382, 389
WIAT (Wechsler Individual Achievement Test), 174–177, 184
Wide Range Achievement Test (WRAT), 172, 203
Wide Range Achievement Test-Revised (WRAT-R), 177, 182, 212
Wide Range Achievement Test-Revision 3 (WRAT3)
content validity of, 115
research on, 182–183
scoring of, 178
subtests of, 177–178
summary of, 184
technical data on, 180–181
uses of, 149
in validity studies, 159, 169
WISC-R. *See* Wechsler Intelligence Scale for Children-Revised (WISC-R)
WISC-III. *See* Wechsler Intelligence Scale for Children-Third Edition (WISC-III)
WJ-R Tests of Achievement. *See* Woodcock-Johnson Psycho-Educational Battery-Revised (WJ-R) Tests of Achievement
WJ-R Tests of Cognitive Ability. *See* Woodcock-Johnson Psycho-Educational Battery-Revised (WJ-R) Tests of Cognitive Ability
Woodcock-Johnson Preschool Scale, 326
Woodcock-Johnson Psycho-Educational Battery-Revised (WJ-R) Tests of Achievement
in case studies, 404, 415, 419, 422
early childhood assessment and, 380
features of, 150
organization of, 150–151
research on, 181–183
scoring of, 154–159
standard battery, 151–152
summary of, 184
supplemental battery, 152–153
technical data on, 159
uses of, 149
in validity studies, 159, 177
Woodcock-Johnson Psycho-Educational Battery-Revised (WJ-R) Tests of Cognitive Ability
research on, 317
review of, 299, 306–308
scoring of, 155
summary of, 335
in validity studies, 314
Woodcock Reading Mastery Tests (WRMT), 215, 315
Woodcock Reading Mastery Tests-Revised (WRMT-R)
in case studies, 404
criterion-related assessment and, 224
research on, 182, 215
review of, 203–210
scoring of, 205–208
subtests of, 204–205
summary of, 216
technical data on, 209–210
in validity studies, 210
Word attack. *See* Reading
Work samples, 237, 238
WPPSI (Wechsler Preschool and Primary Scale of Intelligence), 310
WPPSI-R (Wechsler Preschool and Primary Scale of Intelligence-Revised), 298–299, 380–382, 389
WRAT (Wide Range Achievement Test), 172, 203
WRAT-R (Wide Range Achievement Test-Revised), 177, 182, 212
WRAT 3. *See* Wide Range Achievement Test-Revision 3 (WRAT3)
Written language. *See also* Reading
achievement tests for, 152, 153, 160, 164, 169, 174–175, 178, 182
curriculum-based assessment of, 232–233
definition of, 345
diagnostic tests for, 210–212, 215
informal assessment of, 246–250, 251–252
test interpretation of, 401–402
WRMT (Woodcock Reading Mastery Tests), 215, 315
WRMT-R. *See* Woodcock Reading Mastery Tests-Revised (WRMT-R)
W scores, 150, 205

Young children. *See* Early childhood assessment; Preschool children

Z scores, 86–87, 140